LIBRARY OF RELIGIOUS BIOGRAPHY

Edited by Mark A. Noll, Nathan O. Hatch, and Allen C. Guelzo

THE LIBRARY OF RELIGIOUS BIOGRAPHY is a series of original biographies on important religious figures throughout American and British history.

The authors are well-known historians, each a recognized authority in the period of religious history in which his or her subject lived and worked. Grounded in solid research of both published and archival sources, these volumes link the lives of their subjects — not always thought of as "religious" persons — to the broader cultural contexts and religious issues that surrounded them.

Marked by careful scholarship yet free of academic jargon, the books in this series are well-written narratives meant to be *read* and *enjoyed* as well as studied.

D1454043

LIBRARY OF RELIGIOUS BIOGRAPHY

Abraham Kuyper

*Modern Calvinist,
Christian Democrat*

James D. Bratt

WILLIAM B. EERDMANS PUBLISHING COMPANY

GRAND RAPIDS, MICHIGAN / CAMBRIDGE, U.K.

Published 2013 by
Wm. B. Eerdmans Publishing Co.
2140 Oak Industrial Drive N.E., Grand Rapids, Michigan 49505 /
P.O. Box 163, Cambridge CB3 9PU U.K.

Printed in the United States of America

19 18 17 16 15 14 13   7 6 5 4 3 2

Library of Congress Cataloging-in-Publication Data

Bratt, James D., 1949-
Abraham Kuyper: modern Calvinist, Christian democrat / James D. Bratt.
p.   cm.   — (Library of religious biography)
Includes bibliographical references (p.   ) and index.
ISBN 978-0-8028-6906-7 (pbk.: alk. paper)
1. Kuyper, Abraham, 1837-1920.   I. Title.

BX9479.K8B73   2012
284′.2092 — dc23
[B]

2012036355

www.eerdmans.com

To
George Marsden and Ronald Wells:
mentors, colleagues, friends

Contents

Contents

Foreword

The interwoven questions that this splendid biography answers are, "Who was Abraham Kuyper, and why should we care?" Answering the first question is not easy, since Kuyper's career was as filled with noteworthy achievement as that of any single individual in modern Western history. From his birth in 1837 in the Dutch seaport of Maassluis to his death in The Hague in 1920, Kuyper's life encompassed an extraordinary range of enterprises. As only a partial list, he was a minister of the Dutch Reformed Church, the driving force behind a major schism in that church, a professor of theology, the longtime editor of a daily newspaper, the founder of the Netherlands' first mass-based political party, an effective advocate for public funding of religious schools, the founder of a university, a much celebrated traveler in Britain and America, a member of the Dutch Parliament (and later Senate), from 1901 to 1905 the prime minister of the Netherlands, and throughout his adult life an absolutely indefatigable author on topics political, theological, cultural, and devotional. Somehow he also managed to fit time for several long collapses from nervous exhaustion that seemed only to bring him back with larger ambitions for longer agendas.

If Kuyper's ideas had been entirely humdrum, his list of achievements alone would make him worthy of sustained attention. But since his ideas were well articulated beliefs that propelled his many activities, trying to answer "who was Kuyper?" requires full attention to his thought. He was first a convinced Protestant who held the image of Reformation guided by the word of God as the highest ideal. Almost as intensely he believed that the French Revolution had unleashed the most destructive forms of rationalism, individualism, and atheism imaginable. He inherited the instincts of European Christendom (and the assumption that all aspects of life needed to be held organically together), but was also committed to heartfelt personal piety (and so could write movingly about the work of the Holy Spirit). He believed that the creation in its fullest extent was a gift of God beyond imagining and that Christ's redemption extended to the uttermost reaches of that creation. He matched his confidence in the New Testament's message of redemption in Christ with an equally firm belief that the Old Testament showed God's intimate concern for family life, agriculture, politics, economic structure, warfare, international relations, and more. He was deeply committed to "sphere sovereignty," the belief that God had organized the creation into discrete theaters of activity (family, business, art, education, church, state) with each one given specific purposes by the Creator and each possessing its own integrity. He held a positive conception of government, not as an all-purpose solution to every problem, but as the God-given "sphere" ordained to adjudicate disputes among other spheres, to defend the weak against the strong, and to maintain the state's natural duties for developing infrastructure and promoting the general welfare. At the highest level, he held both that God had gifted all humanity with the ability to contribute meaningfully to the common good ("common grace") and that regeneration in Christ created a community, a mind, a predisposition, and a sensitivity utterly opposed to everything of the world ("the antithesis").

The vigor of Kuyper's convictions, along with his strenuous efforts at putting them into practice for religious, educational, and political purposes in the Netherlands — and with the significant numbers around the world who have found his ideas inspiring — makes him a figure of world historical significance. It also means that a biography like this one must be done with care, so that readers come to understand Kuyper in his own life context as well as the influence his ideas have had. The range of that influence is noteworthy — as a contributor to European Christian Democracy, a beacon for Dutch immigrants in many parts of the world, a figure used to justify South African apartheid, a guide for many leaders of evangelical higher education in America, a special inspiration for modern Christian philosophers, and a stimulus with his concept of "worldview" to active culture warriors in our own day.

James Bratt's great success in meeting that challenge comes from a subtle blend of well-researched facts and carefully considered judgments. Both are important. Given the range of Kuyper's activities, the life was extraordinarily complicated, but the clarity of the narrative that follows never flags. Given the lofty range of Kuyper's thought as well as the rare mix of his personal qualities (humble Christian, arrogant steamroller, sensitive theologian, populist stem-winder, wily politician, principled statesman), the demands on an interpreter are extreme, but Bratt's judgments are throughout as convincing as they are empathetic.

There is, in addition, that other question: "Why should we care?" The chance to reflect on the life opened in this book offers much to ponder for those with eyes to see. More than any Protestant of the modern era, Kuyper succeeded at bringing together theology (especially creation and redemption) and life in the world (especially through the practice of sphere sovereignty). But how convincing, a Protestant must inquire, was Kuyper's scriptural basis for his notion of sphere sovereignty? Along with only a few other statesmen of the modern era (perhaps Konrad Adenauer and the almost-Christian Vaclav Havel), Kuyper carried out a political strategy that kept faith with both transcendent spiritual realities and the gritty realities of practical power. But does Kuyper's approach to Christian politics require a nation as small as the Netherlands was in his day (a population just over five million) or as relatively monocultural as the Dutch were back then? Kuyper's vision of thoroughly Christian reflection bravely fathoming Christ's claim on "every square inch" of human life has been one of the key background factors behind the best of modern Christian higher education. But what should observers make of Kuyper's own great project, the Free University of Amsterdam, which secularized quite rapidly a half-century after his passing? And not least, to whom in the contemporary maelstrom of American politics does Kuyper belong? To the Right with his strong advocacy of traditional values and his ardent defense of family rights? Or to the Left with his relatively large role for government and his suspicions of the rich and powerful?

Attentive readers of this landmark biography will come away learning a great deal about a noteworthy individual. They should also be in much better position to reflect on vital questions of Christianity and education, church and state, Christian universalism and Chris-

tian particularism, and many more that remain of first-order importance still today, nearly a century after Kuyper passed away.

Mark A. Noll

Introduction

E ven if he were only a historical curiosity, Abraham Kuyper would
still be remarkable. The catalogue of what Kuyper achieved in his
homeland of the Netherlands in the period between 1870 and 1920 is
astonishing. He authored over twenty thousand newspaper articles,
scores of pamphlets, and numerous multivolume treatises. He edited
two newspapers, one published weekly and one daily. He co-founded
a new university, where he also served as professor. He co-founded a
new religious denomination. If all that were not enough, he led a major political party in the Netherlands for four decades — and served as
the nation's prime minister for four years.

But perhaps Kuyper's greatest significance for our own religiously
and culturally fractured world is the way he proposed for religious believers to bring the full weight of their convictions into public life
while fully respecting the rights of others in a pluralistic society under
a constitutional government. His was no right-wing crusade: he
wanted to align religious conviction behind the progressive, liberat-
ing wave of modern development while securing his followers in a
conservative commitment to their own tradition. He taught them how
to use that tradition to counter their secularizing opponents — but
also to promote self-criticism and reconstruction. He asked them to
reassess their accommodations to contemporary life and to rethink
what justice and freedom meant under the reign of a transcendent
God. In short, he was a religious reformer and something of a religious crusader, even as he defied our own stereotypes of what religiously driven public life looks like.

This may be particularly surprising because of where references to Kuyper show up in contemporary life, especially in the United States. A much-watered-down understanding of some of his seminal concepts is sometimes heard from the Christian Right in invocations of a "Christian worldview" and the putative Christian foundations of the United States. But Kuyper can and should be invoked in other settings. More moderate evangelicals have found help from Kuyper for reconceiving education, scholarship, and political action. Going further left, analogies to Kuyper's project are present in the American liberal heritage of Woodrow Wilson and Martin Luther King Jr. More broadly, observers throughout the world might consider the ways Kuyper's life teaches how devotees of any faith — Islam and Hinduism as well as Christianity, but also any secular "replacement religion" — can carry on a responsible public life in contention, and concert, with people of other convictions.

Fragmentary reports about Kuyper's life have been published in English before now, and some of them are unusually helpful. But there has never been in English a full-scale, well-rounded account of his entire life. It was a life, as this book tries to show, that repays close attention in order to understand its many triumphs, but also to reveal that this quintessential man of God was also very much a person of ordinary flesh and blood.

A Tradition for Modernity

As the father of Dutch Neo-Calvinism, Kuyper cultivated a small but potent religious strand in a small nation of outsized historical influence. He made something big of that combination by claiming a relevance for religion across the whole spectrum of public life — not "church and state" narrowly defined, but religion and politics, religion and culture, religion and society. For Kuyper, Calvinism was a world religion, indeed a world-formative one, and his titanic energies, deployed across many fields over a very long career, were devoted to fashioning fresh, authentic ways of making religion work in the modern world.

Three adjectives in that last sentence were key to Kuyper's work. His was first of all a *modern* project. Born (1837) at a low point in Dutch national fortunes, Kuyper began his career in the 1860s as modernization in the Netherlands gained real momentum: rapid, integrated transportation and communications systems, urbanization and the rudiments of industrialization, religious disestablishment, mandatory elementary education, increased prestige for the sciences and secular outlooks in higher education, and the rise of elected assemblies over hereditary monarchy in politics. Kuyper's genius was to affirm the salience of traditional faith in this modernizing context by remarkably innovative means. He founded one of the Netherlands' first mass circulation newspapers, its first popular political party, and a distinctively Christian university. He provided the ideas and the political support for an alternative Christian public school system and encouraged the emergence of a Christian labor union, soon the nation's largest. Most controversially, he split the traditional national church, the Nederlandse Hervormde Kerk, for the sake of recovering the integrity of doctrine, governance, and life that — in his view — had been compromised by its establishment status.

These were all *fresh* ventures for a new age, articulated against secularist naysayers and religious opponents. The latter came in three types: traditionalists, who pined for the old days and old ways; modernists, who wanted to reduce Christianity to terms dictated by the new order; and moderates, who wished to avoid both of those unpleasant scenarios by making faith a matter of the inner self with little public corporate weight. All of these options — and secularism too, Kuyper argued — violated the *authenticity* of the Christian faith or the equity of the modern public order, or both. Historic Christianity, he repeated, was based on enduring biblical foundations and expressed in definitive creeds or confessions that needed to be retained, reclaimed, and reaffirmed over against secularist denials and modernist dilutions. At the same time, he understood that historic Christianity, like every other product of human culture, was deeply historical — that is, evolving over the course of time and thus to some extent relative to particular stages along the way. Kuyper recognized, in other words, that the Calvinist or Reformed tradition in Christianity *was* a tradition. Over against literalists and in parallel with modernist critics, he said that it needed to be upgraded according to the needs of the age. Let us "go back to the living root" of the tradition, he said, "to clean and to water it, and so to cause it to bud and to blossom once more, now fully in accordance with our actual life in these modern times, and with the demands of the times to come." Just where "accordance" became "conformity," or what in a given situation was the perennial "principle" and what a relative "expression" thereof, could become issues of pointed dispute. Many of his epic battles in a life full of conflict were devoted to settling that question; some of Kuyper's key conceptual break-throughs occurred as he worked his way through the process of finding an answer.

Just as controversial was Kuyper's insistence that religious activism be authentic to the modern — that is, pluralistic — socio-political order. For him pluralism came in two forms. The first was ontological. Human society in his view was comprised of autonomous "spheres," and a society's health could be measured by the relative independence with which those spheres operated according to their God-given principle of development. His own crusades under this rubric were to purify the church from the residue of state control and to free higher education from the control of both church and state. The other pluralism was religious, and it stemmed from God's work of redemption just as ontological pluralism came from creation. People in modern Europe, as in various traditional Asian societies, lived in a common polity but out of different fundamental convictions — historically called religions but also understandable as first principles, core values, or ultimate loyalties. The modern distinctive in such situations was to prevent any one of these "world and life views" from gaining official preference or privilege. This lack of preference was a good thing, Kuyper said; in fact, it was the authentic Calvinist thing. The latter assertion embroiled him in polemics with secularists, while the former outraged some Dutch traditionalists who yearned for the days of Reformed establishment.

Kuyper's most creative move was to unmask the emerging modern regime of putative religious "neutrality" as in fact a scheme of secularist hegemony and to devise a system whereby those loyal to each of the Netherlands' salient belief-blocs — Reformed or Anabaptist, Roman Catholic or Jewish, liberal Protestant or labor-socialist — could assert their claims in public affairs without apology, but also without aiming to take over the whole and subordinate the rest. After all, Kuyper thought, the two types of pluralism were made for each other: a society of vigorous autonomous development would thrive best in a polity of maximal religious assertion under rules of mutual regard.

In short, Kuyper taught that in a modern society religious pluralism had to be respected, but the individualization and privatization of faith had to be avoided. Each confessional community (including secularists) must be granted its legitimate proportion of access to and participation in all sectors of public life, especially political representation, educational funding, and media access. Let a dozen flowers bloom, Kuyper said on his happy days; let their relative beauty compete for attention, and let the Lord at the last day take care of the tares sown among the wheat. This is a different way of adjudicating the church-state issue from those we more often hear about today. It is a model of no little relevance to nations around the globe that are engaged with similar tensions: from Ghana and Nigeria to Turkey and Israel, India and Pakistan, Indonesia and Korea, and perhaps most portentously, China.

Principle and Paradox

Kuyper was a rare combination of first-rate intellectual and first-rate organizer. The ideas he espoused made up a powerful abstract theory; the institutions he created made them something more than just theory. This combination injected a pragmatic note into any given statement of his ideas. With some justice, Kuyper could insist that he was a consistent and systematic thinker, proceeding from fixed principles to their logical conclusions. His architectonic approach excelled at disclosing hidden connections linking disparate domains, even as it aspired to capture the divine coherence in all things. It was an approach that could challenge the conventional wisdom, especially the sociopolitical applications that people might draw from theological dogma. Not least it gave him and his followers confidence in holding to their positions against protests that they were defying common sense.

At the same time Kuyper was instinctive and creative; his logical deduction from principle could be remarkably adaptive — "convenient," his critics said. Any innovator is susceptible to inconsistency, especially an innovator who claims to be steering by tradition and orthodoxy, and most especially one who is trying to be a popular leader besides. Where paradox gives over to self-contradiction or outright duplicity is each observer's right to judge. Kuyper in his lifetime was often accused of both. In my opinion he was neither entirely consistent nor abjectly pragmatic; instead, he operated in a third mode, moving through a force-field suspended between opposite poles, the very opposition making for creative tension.

Paradox characterized him nonetheless, in substance as well as style. Thus the generous Kuyper who could espouse a beauty contest among a dozen ideological flowers in the garden of public life was more often the movement builder mobilizing his forces in tones of alarm: the tares of error and unbelief were threatening to take over all of God's Dutch acres, and the Calvinist faithful were a righteous remnant called to win back as much as they could. Other of his seeming paradoxes lie in our preconceptions, however, and call them to account. For instance, present-day right-wingers who cheer Kuyper's aspersions against the encroaching state will be nonplussed to read on the next page his warnings about the inequities of free markets. It is the same for his insistence on both social justice and small government. In the intellectual sphere, Kuyper would have been fully — and instantly — conversant with recent postmodernist controversies; he articulated his own intermediate position in that debate at the dawn of high modernism over a hundred years ago. He believed that a — *the* — real world did exist, created and upheld by God's providence; but he also held that people's cognitive grids (owing in part to their relative social power) so sorted and shaped their perceptions that human beings are, in a real and proper sense, framers of their own worlds. Here the seeming paradoxes piled up. Christians were no exception to the rule of human framing, he taught, yet Christian truth was final and the only firm ground for human morality, even though that truth was still developing and even though other believers often outdid Christians in ethical as in cultural achievement.

Further, Kuyper taught that Europeans and their North American kin stood at the apex of world civilization. Accordingly, he felt that the West's global empires (the peak of Kuyper's career, 1885-1905, coincided with theirs) were natural; yet he also pictured them as besmirched by depredations and injustice that cried to heaven — and that would be heard. Again, the traditionalist Dutch Calvinist Kuyper deplored the theory of popular sovereignty as a denial of God's authority; yet he was also an enthusiastic supporter of democracy — indeed, fashioned an early, and the principal Protestant, entry in the Christian Democratic movement that spread across Europe in the next generation. Without any political training, he rose to become prime minister of the Netherlands. Educated in theology, he formulated a political theory on the basis of independent reading and then compiled a practical agenda that spoke to every issue of the day. He called his followers to rise above the secular left-right political spectrum of the day and build an independent platform on consistently Christian premises — an appeal that might serve as an example for Christians, or people of any faith, amid the deadlocks of our own day.

The most striking tension in his thought probably lay between the twin themes of liberation and order. This, being an inherent trait in Calvinism, can be ascribed to the tradition to which Kuyper was a loyal devotee, but as the pages below will detail, it lay deep in Kuyper's personality as well. It was also a leading issue of his times. Marxism, modern conservatism, and the pioneering works of sociology as a discipline all arose alongside of Kuyper, and over the same question: how was society to cohere and freedom survive under the conditions of modernity? The question has never gone away, more recently under the conditions of decolonization, globalization, and postmodernity. In that light it is revealing to think about Kuyper as a type of liberation theologian, galvanizing faithful followers of the Lord to throw off the belittling consciousness imposed by their oppressors and build a new order with justice for all. Yet an *order* this would be: Calvinism, Kuyper's personality, and the social location of his following guaranteed that. Calvinist freedom is freedom to do the right thing, and in a pinch it can translate into the duty to obey. Kuyper's God was first of all a sovereign, a lawgiver; hence his social theory, political program, and theology all opened by trying to identify, understand, and fix due authority.

Much of Kuyper's legacy has divided along these two lines. His "conservative" heirs have amplified the themes of order, ontological fixedness, suspicions of secularism, and aspersions toward the Left. His "progressive" progeny have followed his call for fresh thinking, epistemological openness, social justice, and aspersions toward the rich. Which of these is the "real" Kuyper? Both, and more in between. This very diversity testifies to perhaps Kuyper's greatest value. He asked a set of astute questions, and he creatively parlayed answers both theoretical and practical to the most pressing issues of the day.

A Comprehensive Calvinist

Progressive and conservative, principled and adaptive, modern and traditional: Kuyper would recognize all these terms in himself but would rate them all below his first allegiance, to Calvinism — better, to apostolic Christianity, of which Calvinism was the purest distillation. (Kuyper was never modest on that line, but then neither were the champions of every other Christian tradition, especially in his era.) Even better yet: to the God of Abraham, Isaac, and Jacob, revealed ultimately in Jesus Christ as recorded in Scripture and evident throughout creation. Kuyper's self-description as Calvinist is insufficient, however, since the several strains of that faith tradition have often mounted titanic quarrels among themselves as to which holds true title to the heritage. So which sort of Calvinist was Kuyper?

In terms of British and American history, Kuyper stood consciously and proudly in the extroverted, Puritan, New-School tradition of political activism and cultural engagement. He is most interesting, however, because he did not trim or deny the hard predestinarian dogma of Calvinism, as this side of the heritage tended to do in the nineteenth century. Instead, he amplified it. It was precisely the doctrine of election, he insisted, that both mandated and empowered Christians' public engagement, and that warranted democracy as the political order of modern life. Kuyper tended the boundaries of Reformed orthodoxy with as much passion as did the other, more introverted strain of Calvinism characteristic of various Old-School Presbyterian and pietist circles. He was just as devoted as they to a pure church, closely regulated sacraments, and by-the-book governance. The problem with this more introverted kind of Calvinism, he said, was that it sold God short. Public engagement, too, was part of Calvinist orthodoxy, a direct consequence of that heartiest of Calvinist perennials, the sovereignty of God. To quote his most famous saying: "There is not a square inch in the whole domain of our human existence over which Christ, who is Sovereign over *all*, does not cry, '*Mine!*'" Thus, in terms of the great quarrel in nineteenth-century American Calvinism, Kuyper combined the organization skill of Lyman Beecher, the platform presence of Charles Finney, and the public activism of both with the theological convictions — and no less the theological acumen — of Charles Hodge.

Yet if Calvinism opens up the question of public life, it no less leads into the inner heart, where one wrestles with the most intense of personal questions. Kuyper stood at the front of that line too. He passed through tumults of conversion as keen as Beecher or Finney — or Edwards, Whitefield, and Spurgeon — might have wished. His most characteristic literary production, in a career marked by fifty years of daily journalism and over 200 books and pamphlets, was the Sunday devotional meditation. Here the individual believer encountered a God she could not help but disappoint but who still held her up, called her on, and gave her ample cause for joy and thanksgiving. Kuyper worked this old vein with rare discernment, but also drew heavily on Romantic ideals absorbed from his voluminous reading as an undergraduate literature major. He experienced Romanticism's titanic struggles of heart, understood them in the categories of Reformed practical theology, and refracted the whole in a compelling way to ordinary readers. That was his margin of excellence as a pastoral counselor. His distinctive contribution as a public theologian was to call Christians to attend to the structural, institutional, and philosophical dimensions of their witness, both for the health of the faith and the fulfillment of their public duty. Kuyper's excellence in both lines of work at once was, and remains, exceedingly rare.

Kuyper as a Subject

This book is a biography. It does not aim to systematically treat any one piece of Kuyper's thought or action, as many valuable studies have done. Such systematizations are reflections after the fact, after the whole life is finished and all the utterances compiled. A biography instead watches as the various pieces of the whole emerge, as now one and now another waxes, then wanes, only to come out again at a later date, perhaps reshaped and relocated. Good biography is contextual, and I will provide as much context as I feasibly can. After all, Kuyper was not the virgin recipient of pure principle revealed above the contingencies of time; no one is. I will explore the parallels between Kuyper's work and comparable projects on the contemporary scene, between Kuyper's experiences and those of notable contemporaries such as William James and Friedrich Nietzsche, between the ambience in which he worked and those in other nations at the time. This is not to explain Kuyper's project away by ascribing it to forces of the age, but rather to determine just where he was distinctive, how he combined his era and his insights into a creative new whole.

"Nations" above is intentionally plural. The treasure of Dutch scholarship upon which I have drawn, and here most gratefully acknowledge, tends to stay within that country's perimeters, its complex institutions, its rich and variegated past. As an outsider I have taken the opportunity, and risk, of drawing some international comparisons and of (silently) drawing on more theoretical literature than Dutch historians are wont to do. I hope as a consequence to have enriched a Dutch audience's self-understanding and to have translated some of their fascinating history, and this one fascinating man, into terms that an international audience can more readily appreciate.

A biography also invites the reader (as it demands of the author) to come to terms with the *person* at the center of the story. Readers are free to draw their own conclusions about Kuyper as they move along through this volume; I only hope to have supplied ample, nuanced evidence to make theirs a balanced judgment. Here is mine: Abraham Kuyper was a great man but not a nice one. He was immensely talented, energetic, and driven to great exploits. He appeared always confident, partly to quiet his own insecurities. He was an ambitious person who sought power, and often felt uneasy over that quest. He could be congenial and polemical, sometimes to the same person in fairly quick succession. He loved radical options and was typically more generous to opponents than to spiritual kin who differed with him on details. He loved having collaborators and disciples but drove them away when they stepped up as equals. In public he often showed a better understanding of God than of himself. He majored in ideas — Big Ideas above all — with some impatience over the intricacies of mid-range policy or scholarly discourse as it evolved in its own deliberate way.

This description, however, applies to any number of people who have ascended to power over time, and especially to such in Kuyper's age of an emerging mass society, where the stakes seemed so high, the alternatives so starkly opposed, the guidance of the past so attenuated. The late nineteenth century was filled with not-so-nice men — and some women — who were building ideologies and organizations to sustain society, protect their followers, and save the world. "Nice" has long since become a cliché, like "interesting." It is an easy choice. Most British and American evangelicals, for example, would much rather spend time in a fishing boat with Benjamin Franklin than with his contemporary Jonathan Edwards, however contradictory that preference might be to their own theology. By this measure Kuyper belongs with Edwards — in his own time, with William Ewart Gladstone,

William Jennings Bryan, and Eugene Victor Debs, for all of whom truth and justice were objects of an urgent, unyielding quest.

I will thus paint Kuyper warts and all — both the real ones and the ones that might seem like blemishes only to us. As a real Calvinist he would understand such a portrait, even though he might not like it. My critical observations are not meant to disparage his motives, his goals, or his achievements; indeed, these are remarkable enough to survive any record of his personal foibles. Just as Kuyper would own that he was in part a child of his times, formed by the providential circumstances in which God placed him, so he would, ultimately, appreciate the citation I make, as a fellow Calvinist, from the apostle Paul, that the treasure of the gospel comes to us in earthen vessels to show that its transcendent power belongs to God (2 Cor. 4:7).

Technical Notes and Acknowledgements

This book is intended primarily for native English readers but, unlike most Kuyper studies rendered in that language, draws off voluminous Dutch sources, primary and secondary. For ease of reading I decided to keep original Dutch terms and quotations to a minimum in the text. The Netherlands' States-General I often refer to as (the Dutch) Parliament, composed of an Upper and a Lower House or Chamber, rather than the Eerste and Tweede Kamer. Kuyper's Vrije Universiteit is rendered as the Free University; the Nederlandse Hervormde Kerk as the national or Dutch Reformed Church. All translations from Dutch sources are my own, and all italics in quotations are in the original, unless otherwise indicated. Readers knowledgeable of Kuyper will note that I cite his 1898 Stone Lectures at Princeton minimally. I do so because these *Lectures on Calvinism* are readily available to English readers and might be the only Kuyper text they have read, because the *Lectures* are digests of themes he treated at greater length and with greater nuance in other places, and because the *Lectures* themselves have been treated in detail in Peter Heslam's *Creating a Christian Worldview: Abraham Kuyper's* Lectures on Calvinism.

This project has taken many years to complete, and I have accumulated many obligations along the way. I was awarded a Fulbright research grant in 1985 for what I thought would be a short, stand-alone project involving Kuyper. I received another, as Roosevelt-Dow Distinguished Research Chair at the Roosevelt Study Center in Middelburg, to close off the research process on this book in 2010. I am grateful to the Council for the International Exchange of Scholars and the Netherlands America Commission for Educational Exchange for their support in this regard; likewise to Dow Benelux, the Royal Netherlands Academy of Arts and Sciences, and the Fulbright Scholar Program. Special thanks to Hans Krabbendam, Giles Scott-Smith, Kees van Minnen, and Leontien Joosse at the RSC for the encouragement and hospitality that made my time there as pleasant as it was productive.

Dick Kuiper of the Free University of Amsterdam was my academic host for that first Fulbright. Not only did he perform ably in that role, he provided exceptional hospitality for my family in our residence abroad and has ever since remained a faithful and discerning reader of my Kuyper work. As a resource for information and interpretation on Kuyper, his legacy, and the dynamics that surrounded him, Dick has proven an invaluable aid to whatever merit this book may have. Likewise, I have gleaned much benefit from the knowledge, wisdom, and friendship extended to me by Kees and Margriet van der Kooi, Jasper Vree, and George Harinck together with the excellent staff at the Historisch Documentatiecentrum at the Free University of Amsterdam. Professors van der Kooi, Harinck, and Vree all read significant portions of the manuscript with helpful comments and critique. If I have not adopted all of their suggestions, I was certainly stimulated by them to try to formulate my own conclusions with better warrant and clarity. The Rev. Tjitze Kuipers provided bibliographical help in the process of compiling his definitive record of Kuyper's writings, and along the way extended me personal kindnesses as well — not least my first tour of Flevoland. Very early in my research Kuyper-master George Puchinger offered some sage advice: "First you'll love the man, then you'll detest him, finally you'll understand him. Then you're ready to write." Truth, perhaps, for all biographers; I hope I have attained the third stage, encouraged by his counsel.

Over the course of this project I also received very generous aid from my home institution of Calvin College: two sabbatical leaves, a Calvin Research Fellowship, two stipends from the Calvin Alumni Association, as well as the grant from the Calvin Center for Christian Scholarship that supported the production of my earlier Kuyper book, *Abraham Kuyper: A Centennial Reader.* More than that, Calvin has provided the environment of splendid colleagues dedicated to the better part of Kuyper's project, reappropriating the Christian tradition for fresh ventures into an unknown future. It is a rare privilege to have the concerns of one's scholarly work enacted in their own way by so many able people on an everyday basis.

Particular assistance came from Richard Harms and Lugene Schemper at Hekman Library; from David Diephouse, Doug Howard, and Bert de Vries in their timely readings of several chapters; from the History Department's collective critique of the Introduction (thanks to Will Katerberg for a terse title); and from my student assistants, Grace Hardy and Jake Zwart, in title-, translation-, and source-checking. It was my pleasure to assign Suzanne Bratt the task of compiling the index in the sure and certain knowledge that it was in much better hands than her father's. My gratitude also goes to three friends at Eerdmans Publishing Company: David Bratt, who ably steered the manuscript through production; Jon Pott, who favored me with the wry humor which means, finally, that all is well; and Bill Eerdmans Jr., who extended me trust and patience beyond any reasonable measure. So did Mark Noll, editor of the series in which this title appears, to whom I offer these pages in explanation, and expiation, of my Dutch completeness hunger.

My Calvin colleague and treasured friend Bill Romanowski read the entire manuscript with the best writing advice this historian has ever received: think like a screenwriter. The reader will readily detect which chapters profited most from that counsel. George Marsden also read all the pages that follow, right off his own experience of writing a biography of Jonathan Edwards that deserved all the prizes it won. I have tried to follow many of his suggestions, and where I have not it is because Kuyper was not Edwards and so deserves some sterner measures. More importantly, as one of my first teachers and prime mentors in the field George endowed me with confidence that I could find my way as a historian. That that way was indeed shaped by him, and likewise by his partner in this endeavor, Ronald Wells, has been one of the great good fortunes of my life, and so it is a pleasure to dedicate this book to them as a token of my gratitude and of their legacy.

Brief Time-Line

1837   born October 29 in the manse at Maassluis (South Holland). Father is an ecumenical conservative in the national Reformed church. Family moves to Middelburg (capital of Zeeland), later to Leiden for young Bram's educational advantage.

1858   finishes undergraduate studies

1860   wins medal in national scholarship competition

1861   suffers first nervous breakdown

1862   completes doctorate at Leiden, experiences earnest evangelical conversion.

1863   marries Johanna Schaay; installed as pastor in rural parish of Beesd (province of Gelderland, near Utrecht). Moves toward strict Calvinist orthodoxy. Publishes his first pamphlet, mixing theological and political concerns and aimed against reigning liberalism and stolid bureaucracy in church affairs.

1867   vaults to pulpit in Utrecht, capital of national "God & Country" conservatism. Soon alienates other leaders there by advocating a religiously pluralistic public school system.

1870   takes pulpit in Amsterdam. A radical conservative (or conservative radical), popular with orthodox working-class audience, and a skilled agitator in local ecclesiastical councils.

1872   assumes editorship of *De Standaard,* a daily newspaper (with its Sunday supplement, *De Heraut*) that would be his perennial pulpit and power base. By this means he shapes an audience and a cause, both of which would ever be identified with him as a person.

1874   resigns active ministry to take seat in Parliament; remains in the city-wide consistory of Amsterdam.

Through 1875   scandalizes Parliament with his rhetorical vehemence; attends Robert Pearsall Smith's Holiness meetings in Brighton, England; proselytizes for same in the Netherlands.

1876-77   suffers second breakdown; long recuperation in Italy, Switzerland, and south of France; resigns parliamentary seat.

1877-80   reaffirms strict Calvinist (as opposed to evangelical-holiness) orthodoxy and crystallizes the three national networks that lastingly define the Neo-Calvinist movement: the Antirevolutionary Party (ARP), the Christian school association, and the Free University (VU) society.

1880   opens the VU with his famous "Sphere Sovereignty" address; professor there through 1901.

1883-86   agitates church reform question on the basis of confessional orthodoxy and anti-bureaucratic polity. This campaign culminates in the Doleantie: the splitting off of 10% of Hervormde Kerk membership. In 1892 these congregations

xxvii

merge with most of the churches descended from the Secession of 1834; together they form the Gereformeerde Kerken in Nederland (GKN).

1891   with educational and church questions settled and the ARP a force to be reckoned with, he revives his earlier concern with the "social question." Gives famous address on "Christianity & the Social Question," with democratic-radical tones. Encourages Patrimonium, a Christian labor union.

1893-95   split in the ARP over his socio-political radicalism. Conservatives form the Christian-Historical Union (CHU); Kuyper consolidates control over ARP. Suffers his third breakdown.

1893-99   his high tide as a scholar, symbolized by honorary degree from and Stone Lectures at Princeton on trip to USA (in 1898). Begins writing *Common Grace,* stressing ongoing divine sustenance of creation and social order, legitimating Christian participation with people of other convictions in public life.

1901-5   prime minister of the Netherlands.

1905-6   electoral defeat propels him on an extended trip around Mediterranean. Keen observations of the European periphery in *Om de Oude Wererldzee.*

1907-15   intra-party maneuvering leaves him frustrated. Writes *Pro Rege,* with renewed emphasis upon Christian cultural (as opposed to political) mission in conditions of advanced modernity.

1911-20   the much honored chief on the sidelines. Continues party chair and editorial functions; member of (semi-honorific) upper house of Parliament; harsh polemics vs. his successors in ARP. Takes German side in World War I; writes of the second coming of Christ and the hollow core of Western civilization; calls ARP to renewed commitment to the social question.

Dies, 8 November 1920

PART ONE

Foundations, 1837-77

CHAPTER ONE

Heritage and Youth

A braham Kuyper was born on Sunday, October 29, 1837, in the parsonage of the Reformed Church at Maassluis, in the Netherlands province of South Holland. Little "Bram" was the third child, and first son, of Dominie Jan Frederik Kuyper and his wife, Henriëtte Huber. In keeping with custom, he was named after his paternal grandfather, an Amsterdam shopkeeper. His earliest biographers, looking for portents of his remarkable life to come, rehearsed bits of family lore about his birth. Supposedly, an old neighbor woman prophesied greatness at seeing the caul that clung to the newborn's head, and a visiting "wonderdokter" (a "quack," perhaps a phrenologist) expressed astonishment at the sight of the lad's prodigiously large head. Others saw in his big dreamy eyes the token of a Romantic visionary.

Kuyper's head *was* big by any measure. Far too big, according to his enemies. Capacious enough, his supporters noted, to produce in the hundreds of titles he wrote a body of commentary on the entire religious, political, and cultural landscape of his times, as well as the blueprints, rationale, and operating instructions for a network of institutions that put his proposals into practice. Various of these labors were, perhaps, foreshadowed at his birth. The cries that echoed through the parsonage that Sunday morning, keeping the older Kuyper from his pulpit duties, were faint anticipations of the uproar that his son would raise in the Dutch Reformed Church — that would, in fact, cause its largest rupture in 250 years. That turmoil the younger Kuyper intended as a new reformation in the line of John Calvin; his father registered his infant son at the Maassluis town hall on October 31, the 320th anniversary of Martin Luther's manifesto at Wittenberg.

Kuyper's hometown stood near the mouth of the Maas (Meuse) River, downstream from Rotterdam and right next to the Waal (Rhine), thus athwart the arteries of continental trade that would make Rotterdam the great port of Europe in the twentieth century. For now the drowsy pace of trade gave only faint echoes of Holland's seventeenth-century "golden age" at the head of global commerce. Kuyper would argue that the Calvinist Reformation had something to do with that prosperity, and that his own crusade would help renew Holland's glory. It could hardly do worse: in his birth-year the Netherlands stood near the bottom of a long century of decline.

Kuyper's vision also had an international scope that was mirrored in his remarkably cosmopolitan set of ancestors. Six, perhaps seven, of his eight great-grandparents were born outside the Netherlands. The source of his patronym, Dirk Kuyper, came to Holland from Latvia via the Baltic trade in grain and lumber that provided the foundations of Dutch golden-age commerce. In 1739 Dirk married the widow Anna van Duyn van Dort and duly enrolled as a burgher of the city of Amsterdam, employed with his new father-in-law as a carpenter, at the other end of the lumber business. Of Dirk and Anna's ten children, Abraham the grandfather was eighth born, in 1750. Like his mother he married twice, the second time at fifty years of age to Anna Bauer, a native of Neukirchen bei Kassel, probably in Switzerland though possibly in Germany.* This Abraham ran a brush-making shop between two of Amsterdam's canal rings. On that modest base and amid economic hard times, he and Anna had seven children, beginning with Jan Frederik in 1801.

On his mother's side Abraham the grandson could trace his lineage back four generations to the 1680s in the Winterthur district of Switzerland, north of Zurich. With an occasional officer post in the local watch or Swiss Guard adorning their history, the Hubers held a little higher status than the Kuypers. Like Anna Bauer, Kuyper's grandfather Jean Jacques Huber arrived fairly late in Amsterdam, marrying there as a twenty-eight-year-old in 1790, but he seems to have brought along enough capital to open his own business. His bride, Christina Andressen, was of half-Dutch, half-Hessian ancestry, with links, according to family tradition, to Liege in Wallonia. The dry-goods store

---

*The Swiss town by that name is less than ten kilometers from the site where Kuyper and his wife, Jo, were vacationing when she died suddenly in 1899.

that Jean Jacques, now Jan Jacob, operated on Leidsestraat suffered along with grandfather Abraham's shop and much other Dutch trade and industry during the French occupation of the Netherlands (1795-1813), especially when Napoleon's Continental System shut down sea-borne commerce. That the Hubers's only son was conscripted into the Grand Army that Napoleon led into Russia in 1812 redoubled the family's animosity toward French rule. Young Samuel deserted — and survived.

The Hubers, and the Kuypers too, thus entered the nineteenth century seared by some epochal events of history. Though their particular trial might appear to modern eyes to have arisen from political and economic forces, they along with thousands of their countrymen understood it in religious terms. More broadly, the nineteenth century in Europe was *the* age of history, in which personal, national, even metaphysical destiny was defined by an understanding of the past. We need to review some of the main lines of Dutch historical development, then, to identify the furnishings of Kuyper's mind — its heroes and villains, its lessons and warnings — the better to understand which items he would keep, which ones he would discard, and which ones he would rearrange over the course of his long career.

Golden Age and Trying Times

It was common in Kuyper's circles to blame Holland's early nineteenth-century malaise on the French occupation and French ideas. In fact it was rooted much earlier, in some grand, home-grown aspirations. Dutch hegemony in European commerce arose in the 1590s in the wake of the successful revolt against Spanish rule, and it crested in the mid-seventeenth century under the leadership of Johan de Witt and the Amsterdam commercial regency. But the French invasion in 1672, besides triggering De Witt's assassination by a Dutch mob, put the Netherlands at the forefront of a long campaign led by William of Orange to repel the aggressions of Louis XIV. To Dutch Protestants this was as much a religious as a strategic or economic cause; their land was to be the bulwark for the true faith against Catholic ("papist") tyranny. In the process William, along with his wife, Mary Stuart, eventually took the crown of England in the Glorious Revolution of 1688-89, cementing an Anglo-Dutch alliance that launched a virtual twenty-five-year war against

France. In these campaigns (1689-97 and 1702-13) the Netherlands supplied the bulk of the land forces and the British focused on their navy. The resulting burden on Dutch finances and manpower left them with a substantial and growing debt, while Britain gained lasting supremacy at sea. Dutch trade held its own until 1740 (the year after Dirk Kuyper settled in Amsterdam) but then entered a long decline that hit its trough just about the time Kuyper was born.

The nation hardly became impoverished overnight, since its seventeenth-century boom set marks — in levels of urbanization, the scale of its manufacturing sector, and per capita standard of living — that England would not match until the 1820s. Thus even in the decades of decline the Netherlands continued to attract immigrants of modest means, especially from Germany — people like Kuyper's grandmother Bauer and his Hessian great-grandfather Nicolaas Andressen, who showed up on the Delft city register in the lowly status of lamplighter, gravedigger, and night-watchman. Yet, as contemporary critics sensed and later historians have confirmed, the expansive commerce and spirit of the Dutch seventeenth century, its unsurpassed art and architecture, its world-class science and universities, and its shipbuilding and finishing industries, gave way in the eighteenth to the imitative, decorative, and depressed. Income inequality widened well before the "French time," as regressive tax policies transferred wealth from the poorer, rural, and eastern provinces to the regents in the big maritime cities. These became less merchants than rentiers, living off the interest on their government bonds and shares in the East India Company, targeting new investments abroad rather than at home.

These economic developments were mirrored in politics. The Dutch Republic ran under multiple, discrete, yet overlapping shares of sovereignty parceled out among the States-General, the States (parliaments) of particular provinces, the cities and towns, and the stadtholder (the prince of Orange). These assorted "spheres" of authority loomed large in the political thinking of the time as they would later, transformed, in Kuyper's own thought. Within this complexity, however, a persistent political division prevailed over the Republic's two-hundred-year existence. On the one side were the urban regents, centered in the States of Holland. Not nobles in the traditional sense, they were nonetheless patricians of the purest water, claiming the right to rule by virtue of their wealth, education, and public spirit —

not to mention the importance of their commercial and industrial interests to the general prosperity. Their political philosophy, inscribed by Hugo Grotius, glorified republics, placed sovereignty in the provinces, and elevated civil power over the ecclesiastical. That is, it gave town and provincial councils the right to control religious policy on the understanding that the church existed for the purposes of social morality and order as much as for ends eternal.

At the opposite pole, and high in the esteem of Kuyper's forebears, stood the prince of Orange, around whom clustered groups that shared little more than a common antagonism to the regents: notables from the interior provinces, artisans and workers from the larger cities, members of town militias, agricultural laborers, and anyone especially devoted to the faith or interests of the national Reformed church. The House of Orange itself sometimes emitted the tones of absolute monarchy, but its supporters more often endorsed the constitutional type. They elevated central over local authority and had a strong sense of "natural" hierarchy, two elements with which Kuyper would sharply disagree. He was one with them, however, in prizing national unity and dignity as much as wealth, and in tying public virtue to the ministrations of the Reformed church. Some Orangists sincerely, others for political reasons, wished to make the church more independent of the state, to shore up orthodoxy within its halls, to augment its controls over public morals and education, and to enforce more uniformly its rights as the only legitimate public religious body.

This last provision meant that, during the Republic, while non-Reformed believers were not punished for their personal convictions, they were also not allowed to advertise their assemblies or educate their children by their own lights. Understandably, religious outgroups — especially Roman Catholics, Anabaptists, and Lutherans (although not Amsterdam's Jews) — sided with the Holland regents, while Reformed orthodoxy typically went with Orangist politics. These correlations were not without contradictions, however. The regent party could tolerate anything but orthodox intolerance, and for all their talk about the rights of different spheres they would subordinate the church to larger civic purposes. For their part, the orthodox Reformed could support Orange more consistently as a concept than as a person, for two of the most notable stadtholders, Maurice and William II, cut a swath of dissolute womanizing around The Hague that hardly fit Calvinist norms of sexual morality. Populist as well as Calvinist taste had to swallow hard at the lavish style the stadtholders started cultivating in the mid-eighteenth century, particularly since the princes' pretensions were rising just as their character and abilities were falling. Indeed, in the riots by which they enforced their will in emergencies (as when they dismembered De Witt) but also in their assertiveness vis à vis town councils during ordinary times, Orange populists showed a rebellious streak quite beyond what the regents or the stadtholders would countenance. Kuyper had that rebellious streak in quantity.

The Divided Heart of Dutch Protestantism

The country's political division ran parallel to a theological divide dating back to the time of the original revolt against Spain. On the one hand, that revolt was inextricably entwined with the rise of Protestantism. It was the explosion of iconoclasm — the wholesale sacking of churches, cathedrals, and monasteries — in the 1560s that sealed Philip II's decision to suppress Protestantism in the Low Countries by military force. And at every low point in the subsequent war it was Calvinist conviction, organization, and inspiration that proved to be the irreducible nugget of resistance. On the other hand, the iconoclasm of the south (present-day Belgium) was little seen in the north (the future Netherlands), where the Catholic establishment melted away under apathy more than by Protestant zeal. In fact, when Calvinist preachers started filtering up from the south, they discerned an alarming religious vacuum. In the United Provinces that finally did gain their independence, hard-core, positive Protestants amounted to about ten percent of the population. Those numbers were certainly augmented by a flood of Calvinist refugees from the south (the Spanish reconquest of Antwerp, for instance, sent 38,000 — half the city's population — into exile), but the intense zeal the newcomers brought with them hardly altered the milder convictions of many old families in the north.

From the start, then, the United Provinces harbored two founding myths: one of true freedom, the other of true religion. The home of the first was the old families and civic elites; of the second, the overlapping sets of refugees, guild-members, small proprietors, and skilled

8

workers that included families like the Kuypers and Hubers. Each side acknowledged the other in a secondary role, though that tolerance tended to get squeezed out under duress. Both dwelt in the Reformed church but had different expectations for its teachings. The party of freedom identified with a native northern spirit of Erasmus and Thomas à Kempis, a Christian humanism of personal religion, an undogmatic Bible, and the ethics of Jesus. The party of true religion favored Calvin's disciplined system of theological reflection, moral discipline, and church organization. The most famous clash between the two erupted early in the seventeenth century over the teachings of Leiden theologian Jacobus Arminius, whose accommodation of Calvinism to human free will resonated with the heritage of Erasmus. The opposition sided with Franciscus Gomarus, an exile from the south, in his forceful reassertion of divine sovereignty. The dispute was resolved at the Synod of Dort (1618-19), which found against the Arminian "Remonstrant" position. While the Synod represented the last and worthy gathering of the Calvinist International, its edicts coincided with a coup d'etat by Maurice, Prince of Orange, against the regent regime headed by Johan van Oldenbarnevelt and Hugo Grotius. Both of these took the Remonstrant side. Oldenbarnevelt paid with his life, Grotius was smuggled out of town in a trunk, and the alliance of Orange and orthodoxy was sealed for all time.

The underlying antagonism lived on, however. It cropped up in the next generation in a clash between Johannes Cocceius, another Leiden theologian, and Gijsbert Voetius of Utrecht. Aligned with the new critical philosophy of Descartes, Cocceius proposed a more figurative reading of Scripture and a looser authority for the documents that Dort had established as binding standards. The Voetians, who stood fast by Bible, Aristotle, and the confessions, took the battle to the plain of practical conduct via an alliance with the forces of the Netherlands' "later (also "further") Reformation." This was a pietist movement inspired by English Puritanism for the purpose of deepening personal devotion and tightening the moral regulation of everyday life. It frowned on theater, dancing, card playing, and popular festivals like the fabled Sinterklaas day — also upon the use in worship of the equally famous Dutch pipe organs. It tried to get city and provincial councils to enforce Sabbath-observance and moral education, and church councils to suppress Cocceian and Socinian (Unitarian) teachings. No conclusive resolution was forthcoming this time, however. William III established a model of alternating pulpit and university appointments between the two parties, while educational and behavioral matters were left to local option.

Accordingly, robust theological argument gave way to other concerns over the eighteenth century. Humanist circles started attending to the various schools of Enlightenment thought that were coursing over from France and Scotland. In the Dutch case these translated into close empirical studies more than grand theories of human nature or society, while concern for virtue and order made the Dutch Enlightenment more moderate, averse to any shades of atheism or political radicalism. For their part, the orthodox gave up on purifying the Reformed church as a whole and concentrated on cultivating true religion in smaller circles. Sometimes as study and discussion groups and sometimes as well-defined conventicles, sometimes supplementing official church services and occasionally replacing them, the pious gathered to read classics of confessional and devotional orthodoxy by "old writers" *(oude schrijvers)* like Voetius, Willem à Brakel, and Bernardus Smytegelt. Both sets of Kuyper's grandparents frequented such meetings. Besides yielding personal edification, these sessions cultivated hopes and prayers that a reformation of public morals, a return to confessional rigor, or simply a more heartfelt repentance on their own part might restore the Reformed church, the Netherlands, the House of Orange — any or all of these — to their former glory.

In vain. In the second half of the eighteenth century the Republic, by now "inherently hollow and precarious," became a pawn on the chessboard of international politics. The most concerted protest against this devolution came from the Patriot movement of the 1780s, inspired by the American Revolution. Appalled by William V's toadying before Britain and Prussia and vindicated when he brought Holland to utter humiliation in the fourth and final Anglo-Dutch War (1780-84), the Patriots called for a new republic invigorated by a renewed civic virtue. Alas, their citizen militias melted away before the Prussian invasion of 1787. The restored stadtholders did no better when the armies of revolutionary France invaded eight years later; William fled to England and the Patriots rose up to greet the invader. For the moment the French behaved themselves, especially compared to a British relief force that pillaged the countryside, but their attempt at reform stumbled from one experiment to another until they cleared the board in 1806 and deposited the Republic in the dustbin of history. The regime they put in its place instituted a uniform law code, centralized administration, more equitable taxation, and freedom of religion, along with plans for more robust, state-supervised primary education. These elements remained in place when Napoleon erased the nation itself by absorbing the Netherlands into his empire in 1810. To this the Dutch submitted, one historian puts it, "without resistance and without enthusiasm." In the collective memory under which Kuyper was reared, the French reforms were all suspect by association and usually condemned in substance. They amounted to a legacy of bad faith and humiliation. Kuyper's task would be to sort through them, spying out some that lived on, also under the guise of orthodox religion, while trying to redeem others from their revolutionary taint.

Toward 1848

Napoleon's defeat at Leipzig in 1813 opened the way for a new beginning and laid out the landscape on which Kuyper grew up. The next prince of Orange was installed as "King" (not just stadtholder) William I and ruled over a country that had been doubled in size by amalgamation with present-day Belgium. In exchange William ceded to Britain most remaining Dutch colonies — that is, he traded distant potential for immediate gains. To his credit, he invested much of his personal fortune in economic development projects in both the north and the south. At the same time he exuded absolutist airs that contradicted Dutch sensibilities, not to mention the limited monarchy inscribed in the country's new constitution. He kept in place the French system of centralized administration. He thus resembled at once a latter-day enlightened despot and the prototype of the nineteenth-century businessman-king. William's investments helped launch Belgian industrialization, but his attempt to replace parochial education there with secular secondary schools alienated Roman Catholics, who joined a petition drive in 1830 for general civil liberties that netted 350,000 signatures. William took it as an anti-Dutch rebellion and mounted an invasion to suppress it, only to see his army flee before a French counter-assault. For a decade he refused to negotiate terms, embittered that Britain had deserted his cause. He finally abdicated in 1840, also to avoid a crisis over his second marriage, to a Roman Catholic.

The Belgian troubles worsened the north's economic woes. The French period had not only crippled Dutch commerce but, through revaluations, had cost the financial classes some forty percent of their capital. William I had inherited a colossal national debt from the eighteenth-century wars, redoubled it by assuming the arrears of the bankrupted East India Company, deepened it further through his investments in infrastructure, then lost the Belgian revenue while insisting on maintaining a costly military presence along their contested border. By 1837, the year of Kuyper's birth, the nation was facing an acute fiscal crisis on top of a deep depression in agriculture, which worsened with extensive crop failures in the 1840s. Thus, if the Netherlands in 1850 might still claim the third highest per capita GDP in Europe, its productivity was falling along with real wages and nutrition. The only curves going up tracked food prices and mortality rates.

The government survived the crisis by three measures: it refinanced its debt, rationalized its accounting procedures, and returned to exploiting the colonies. The "Cultivation System" introduced under William I required the inhabitants of the East Indies to devote twenty percent of their land or labor to growing crops exclusively for export to the Netherlands. This generated huge revenues for the government (some forty percent of the total by 1857, enough to balance the budget already by 1847) and boosted the Dutch carrying trade and domestic manufactures. It created a safe harbor for investment and eventually paid for the infrastructure that would carry future economic development. It even supplied the compensation that owners received when slavery was abolished in the Dutch empire in 1863. All in all, the 1850s marked a turning point in the Dutch economy; old investment and new revenues generated real economic growth that would boom for a quarter century. This was the matrix of Kuyper's education and early career.

At the same time a new chapter was opening in Dutch political history. Soon after assuming the throne in 1840, King William II agreed to submit biennial budgets (rather than one a decade!) and make his ministers partially responsible to the States General (rather than to himself alone). More radical changes were spurred by the revolutionary upheavals that swept Europe in 1848. Even though these did not wash over into the Netherlands, they prompted an anxious

William II to commission the leading Liberal politician of the time, Johan Rudolph Thorbecke, to draft an entirely new constitution. A Leiden historian of German ancestry and English sympathies, Thorbecke crafted a pick-and-choose document from different models without any fixed ideology. Nonetheless, it was made for classic Liberal constituencies: the well-educated, well-heeled professional and business classes who personified the mantra of "careers open to talent and merit" by which the rising bourgeoisie justified its status. The new regime was still a constitutional monarchy, but the cabinet was now fully responsible to the States General instead of to the king. It genuinely nationalized politics by having the lower house of Parliament elected directly by the voters rather than by provincial assemblies. It made education a concern of national rather than of local government. At the same time it kept politics an elite preserve. Voting rights were determined by such a high property qualification that the percentage of eligible voters actually declined under the new system, from 3 to 2.5 percent of the population. By 1870 that percentage had increased only to 2.9, placing the Netherlands — third or fourth in Europe in prosperity — close to the bottom in democracy, lagging behind not only France, Britain, and the Scandinavian countries, but also Greece, Portugal, Serbia, and the Austro-Hungarian Empire.

The new constitution also separated church and state, a step of fundamental import for Kuyper's future. For now, Reformed traditionalists were dismayed by the restoration of self-rule to the Roman Catholic Church, then horrified (along with some progressives) when, in March 1853, the papacy reinstituted the old archbishopric at Utrecht, the city of Voetius, and appointed bishops for five dioceses across the land. A wave of anti-Catholic protest exploded the next month (hence called the "April Movement") in mass demonstrations and a massive petition campaign. The plaintiffs included royalists, who disapproved of constitutions and parliamentary rule in general; conservatives, who disliked the new constitution in particular; and a wide swath of Protestants — orthodox and liberal alike — who took their religion to be synonymous with political liberty and true Dutch character. In the short term the protest toppled the Thorbecke government; over the longer run it put religious questions at the center of political discussion. In between, the Conservative cabinet bungled its opportunity by showing little vision for policy or readiness to rule.

Some Reformed traditionalists were less enthusiastic for the April movement, for they had no love for the older order. The General Regulation *(Algemeen Reglement)* instituted for the Dutch Reformed Church in 1816 displayed William I's full centralizing bent. Protestant and Catholic "Departments of Worship" were made cabinet ministries. All public functions of the church — including properties, professorial appointments, and regulatory control — became matters of the national state. All internal functions were consigned to a small synod appointed by and reporting to the king that passed its edicts down a chain of command to local congregations. The system reflected Enlightenment values of order and efficiency, and Protestants who were worried about being swamped by Belgian Catholics in the expanded Kingdom of the Netherlands saw enough merit in its consolidation of forces to accept it. But it reversed the church's presbyterian order of delegated rule from the bottom up and destroyed its old measure of autonomy. Moreover, the new administrators came from the old Patriot bourgeoisie who valued toleration above doctrinal tradition. Thus, even the belated amendment of the Regulation to make the Synod responsible for the "maintenance of doctrine" had little prospect of effectiveness, especially since no procedures of enforcement were specified.

To its critics, the church's new name *(Hervormde,* no longer *Gereformeerde)* was sadly appropriate; it was more "re-shaped" than truly "reformed." Scores of local congregations began to secede from the national church in 1834 to "return to the standpoint of the fathers." King William I responded with a ham-handed suppression that imposed fines, prison terms, and police disruption of Seceder worship services under old Napoleonic restrictions on public assemblies.

The Question of Church Reform

The Seceders prospered despite (or because of) these sanctions. By 1870 they were a denomination of over 100,000 members and had seeded a significant emigration to the United States besides. But most Dutch Protestants disagreed with the step of secession, regardless of how much they faulted the king's severity. Its most faithful devotees regarded the Reformed church as the providentially appointed instrument of God's kingdom in the Dutch nation. Even the less ardent esteemed it as "the visible order of a moral society." From this generic point of view, to disrupt the national church was to threaten the unity of the nation, and to do so in the name of doctrinal precision or grievances about church government was to miss the essential purpose of religion, which was to provide the general population with moral discipline and consolation across the ups and downs of everyday life.

The national church included two parties of "reformers" (in contrast to the Seceder "rebels") who hoped to revitalize it from within, and renew the nation in the process. The first, known as the "Groningen school" by virtue of being centered at the university there, proposed to tap the native resources of Erasmus and the medieval mysticism on which he drew as the basis of an ecumenical Dutch Protestantism on which national renewal could go forward. If tired of the tepid spirit and compromised posture of the current church, they were just as averse to the dogma and logic-chopping of strict Calvinists — and to the foreign (French!) style that they alleged Calvin had interposed on tolerant Dutch soil. The Groningers were thus ready to ride easy on traditional theological points or to translate them freely into what they regarded to be the more advanced understanding of their day. Their approach proved particularly attractive in the educational sphere. By mid-century the Groningen school not only dominated in the preparation of Dutch clergy but was also effectively promoting literacy and ethical formation in elementary and secondary schools.

The other reformers were more traditional in theology and of fervent evangelical spirit. They comprised the Dutch wing of the Réveil, the wave of Protestant renewal that arose across Western Europe after Waterloo in hopes of filling the void left by the failed revolution with the message of the gospel. The Dutch Réveilers tended to be young, educated, and elite, aspiring leaders who wanted solid ideals but wanted them personally warmed in the Romantic spirit of the day. Thus, the head notions of Calvinism, which they generally affirmed, had to be grounded in heart experience, translated into the reformation of life, and promoted far and near. This led on to significant campaigns for the relief of social suffering, particularly in the domains of temperance, the abolition of slavery, and the improvement of working conditions in farms and factories. That required organization, which raised the question of institutions, also of the institutional church. These were precisely the animating questions of Kuyper's career, and the children of the Réveil were the audience to whom he first appealed.

Two figures in whom he found lasting inspiration personified the choice at hand. Isaac da Costa, a Réveil convert from Sephardic Judaism, defined the evangelical option. Like his mentor, the fierce Romantic reactionary William Bilderdijk, Da Costa published extensive poetry and conducted private seminars in literature and history to counter the perceived liberal disposition of the universities. To these he added biblical studies of an increasing millenarian bent. Eventually he came to a more benign reading of the times than Bilderdijk had been able to muster. He likewise moved toward a more progressive view of revelation, trusting that readers who loved Christ and were led by his Spirit would get from Scripture greater light than had their predecessors. For that reason, and for fear that doctrinal precision would prove divisive, Da Costa was reluctant to invest binding authority in the church's confessional standards. None of this made him remotely like a theological liberal or lessened his dismay over conditions in the Reformed church, but he viewed these "medically" — as illnesses to be cured by the free and faithful preaching of the Word, through which the Spirit would breed conviction in the needy heart. In twentieth-century terms, Da Costa became a parachurch evangelical of irenic disposition.

The alternative churchly and confessional path was personified by Guillaume Groen van Prinsterer. Educated as a classicist and jurist, archivist of the House of Orange and eventually a member of Parliament, Groen was steeped in texts and law. Further, his conversion came under the influence of Jean-Henri Merle d'Aubigné, William I's court preacher and a giant in the Réveil by virtue of his magisterial, if polemical, history of the Reformation. Merle thus reinforced Groen's appreciation of history and institutions and helped engender his "juridical" approach to ecclesiastical affairs. That is, Groen thought the church not to be ill but in error, thought the error to be theological, and thought the corrective to be enforcement of confessional standards by church judicatories. Accordingly, he brought formal charges against the Groningen theologians for deviating from Dortian orthodoxy, only to have the Synod declare itself procedurally unable to pass judgment. The impasse moved William II to institute some church reforms in 1842, alongside his first political modifications. It prompted the Synod to mandate that pastors and officials show agreement with "the essence and chief themes of the Reformed Church." Defining those themes would be the work of the next generation of Dutch theologians. That enterprise that would leave behind both the Groningers and the Réveil and help launch Kuyper's own efforts.

Theology and Politics at Home

Kuyper's father shared little of these worries. On the contrary, Jan Frederik valued the church as it was, not only for its moral and spiritual resources but also for his own career aspirations. Rejecting family plans that he take over the brush-making shop, he joined a commercial firm in Amsterdam whose considerable English trade could make use of his gift for languages. That talent in conjunction with his pious upbringing brought him to the attention of Algernon Sydney Thelwall, an Anglican missionary to the city's Jewish quarter and a member of the Dutch Religious Tract Society. Soon busy translating English tracts into Dutch, Jan Frederik showed theological acumen as well. The Society's general secretary, Amsterdam pastor D. M. Kaakebeen, arranged a scholarship for him at the Amsterdam Athenaeum, where Jan Frederik started prep school in 1823, a twenty-two-year-old among teenagers. In two years he was ready for theological studies at Leiden, and in 1828 he was ordained to the ministry of the Reformed church. That same year he married Henriëtte Huber, an accomplished French-language teacher at a girls' boarding school. Having been nurtured in the same sort of piety, when the two met at a soiree where card-playing was on order, they turned away from worldliness and fell to elevated conversation with each other, he in English, she in French.

Meanwhile, a dispute at the Tract Society confronted Jan Frederik with a revealing choice. Thelwall wanted the Society's literature to bring out Calvinist distinctives; Kaakebeen favored more generic flavors. Notably, it was Kaakebeen who installed Dominie Kuyper in his first church, in the village of Hoogmade, near Leiden, and eventually arranged for him to be called to Middelburg, the provincial capital of Zeeland. In between those pastorates Kuyper served one other village post and then his first city pulpit, in Maassluis, where he was installed in 1834, the year of the Secession. Nothing of the strife or dogmatism in that protest would come near him. From Kaakebeen he had learned to abhor "extremes"; from Thelwall, a friend of Da Costa, he had absorbed an earnest evangelical spirit exhorting unto "joy, humility, simplicity, and seriousness." From the record of Jan Frederik's extant sermons, he favored two themes: that at the Cross, atonement was rendered for the sins of all the world, and that under benign Providence the faithful could move forward in simple trust. He was most emphatic in urging household devotions, careful nurture of the young, and daily Bible study. That is, Jan Frederik aspired to conventicle qualities in the household, unity of spirit in the congregation, and respect for his professional standing in the world.

In family ways Jan Frederik was nearly as prolific as his father. Bram's two older sisters (Anna Christina and Henriëtta Johanna) were also born in Maassluis; a third, Sophia, arrived in 1839, only to die soon after the birth of a fourth daughter, Anna Cornelia, in autumn 1840. The move to Middelburg came a year later; there Bram's only brother, Herman, was born in 1843, and his youngest sister, Jeanette Jacqueline, in 1847. Mother Henriëtte did not seem fazed by all these labors, joining her husband in home-schooling the children. Dominie Kuyper fared worse, losing a year to illness and (his son Abraham would recall late in life) losing more and more of his audience to rival preachers in town.

Meanwhile, little Bram snapped out of a dreamy early childhood and began to explore the world. He liked to visit a neighboring gardener, a pious Seceder, who would let him pick some fruit and take him home for lunch. He undoubtedly absorbed the grand memorials in Middelburg's venerable Abdijkerk to the thirteenth-century Count William II of Holland, who had perished in battle just before being crowned Holy Roman Emperor, and to the Evertsen brothers, who died leading Zeeland's fleet against England in 1666. Late in life Kuyper testified to a yearning for the seaman's life kindled in him by the wharves of this old hub of the West Indies Company. Family lore added that Bram already now showed a tactical knack by lifting cigars from his father's desk and dispensing them to the sailors in exchange for their attention to his little sermons. He also rebuked their cursing.

Additional family lore held that Dominie Kuyper accepted a call to Leiden, his fifth and final pastorate, because of his daughters' demands to reside in a more fashionable city; in the process, supposedly, young Bram renounced his hopes for the sea for the toils of formal education. The latter was likely the real priority in the matter, for

Kuyper enrolled at the Leiden gymnasium right after the family moved there in the summer of 1849. Equally to the point was Dominie Kuyper's move from a difficult to a more favorable post — a site with more prestige, greater family opportunity, and the prospect (not fulfilled, it turned out) of less theological strife. As Abraham would put it late in his own life, his father, never having been strictly Reformed, had run into difficulty in Middelburg in the face of orthodox competition. By contrast, he recalled, "in Leiden at that time it was so utterly impossible to call a genuine Calvinist preacher that one had to be content with the appearance of a supernaturalist, in the spirit of my father." In any case, Jan Frederik stayed there for twenty years.

The Leiden gymnasium was propitious for Bram. It was, like him, just eleven years old, having been founded amid the national renewal campaign of the 1830s. It followed the traditional classical curriculum of immersing students in the humanities and languages so as to mold them into wise and virtuous leaders, able to discern the transient and permanent in human affairs. Thus Kuyper began Latin in his first year, Greek in the second, and French, German, and English thereafter, all intermixed with history, philosophy, and Dutch literature. Because he had plans for the ministry he was allowed to start Hebrew his last year, as a seventeen-year old. The rising star on staff was the historian Robert Fruin, who would one day at the university become the founder of modern Dutch historiography. For now he drilled his schoolboys in a liberal narrative of true freedom. At the same time, Fruin gave credit to Calvinism for sustaining the war for independence. Kuyper would one day extend that lesson to the present, as his rationalist teacher did not.

For the moment, however, Kuyper's historical interest tracked the era's fascination with all things medieval. Kuyper chose for his graduation oration the figure of the bishop Ulfilas (Wulfila, c. 310-83), whose translation of the Bible into Gothic is the oldest document in Germanic literature. The speech was pure hagiography, but the linguistic command Kuyper showed in his research, not to mention the quality of his high-German text, was an accomplishment worthy of class salutatorian. (Only a rival who had taken on more summer homework outdid him.) As to its convictions, Kuyper's essay blended Romantic hero-worship with patriotic verve. That by the standards of Reformed theology the Arian Ulfilas was a rank heretic Kuyper mentioned not at all. This comports with his own later confession that he had been no Calvinist as a youth. Rather, he traveled "in half-believing conservative circles that honored the old tradition and took Rome to be the arch-enemy of the nation's honor," that felt "bitter disappointment" at the innovations of Thorbecke, and that exacted their revenge in the April Movement. He had been unequalled in his fiery anti-papist stance as a gymnasium student, Kuyper recalled, and seen few happier days than when he burst into his father's study in 1853 shouting, "Father, father, Thorbecke has fallen!"

But in fact, Kuyper owed Thorbecke a lot. His new constitution had nationalized politics; Kuyper would found the state's first nationally organized political party. The Reformed church as well as the Roman Catholics had new possibilities for self-rule, and if it took the former longer than the latter to seize the opportunity, Kuyper would be among the upstarts to lead the way. By the mid-1850s a new economic vitality was clearly evident, as Thorbecke's free-trade policies converged with William I's infrastructure investments to sustain rapid growth. On the religious front, the council of "Christian Friends" that tried to coordinate the two wings of the Réveil held its last meeting in 1854. The next year Kuyper began university by enrolling, just like his father, in the theological faculty at Leiden, where a new tough-minded movement was rising to challenge the Groningen theology from the Left. All in all it turned out to be a propitious moment for an ambitious young man to start his course.

CHAPTER TWO

Education

During Abraham Kuyper's eight years at Leiden University, where he earned his baccalaureate in 1858 and a doctorate in 1863, he lived at his parents' home but roamed far afield in his mind. Unlike his father, he became acutely interested in intellectual matters. He showed a volatile spirit, developed bold ambitions, and rode the radical edge in his chosen field of theology. He traveled the world via history and literature; he won special distinction as a promising young scholar; he fell in love with a girl to whom he could play Pygmalion; and at the end of it all, he wound up just where his father had been at a comparable stage — in a village pastorate with a new wife and an uncertain future. Small wonder that in the middle of the process he suffered a complete breakdown, or that at the end he underwent a religious conversion triggered by the agonies of ambition and pride.

Romance Academic and Domestic

Although fallen some from its glory days in the seventeenth century, the university that Kuyper entered in September 1855 was still the Netherlands' largest and best. Leiden's law faculty was especially renowned, attracting half the student body, especially those from upper-class families. These were the students who controlled campus life and put on the university's famous masquerades, public spectacles on the order of later American intercollegiate athletics.

Leiden was at heart an institution devoted to perpetuating the Dutch governing elite. But its theology students, like Kuyper, were predominantly middle class in background and faced uncertain employment. Almost half of them were pastors' sons, and the rest often had an uncle or grandfather in the profession. Their numbers at Leiden were down 25 percent from the 1830s, when theology students had received special government subsidies, and would drop 50 percent again by the 1880s. Kuyper's entry in the late 1850s came amid a temporary boom in their ranks, which forecast competition for good posts in the future. Compared to the Golden Age, fewer students in any field were coming to Leiden from abroad or even from outlying Dutch provinces, so that the students who lived at home as Kuyper did were the provincials among the provincial. Hallway gossip doubtless communicated his tight circumstances as well. With his father supporting a family of seven on an annual salary of 1850 guilders ($740 US), Kuyper depended on a government stipend for tuition and expenses. Spending money was scarce.

Kuyper naturally chafed at these arrangements. He resisted his father's pressure to interrupt study time for tea and small talk with the family. He heard all the usual warnings about women and drink and cringed on the occasion when, unable to find his house key upon returning from a late night with friends, he had to rouse "the old man in his sleeping cap" to open the door. Such occasions were infrequent, though, since Kuyper devoted himself ceaselessly to work — seven days and six nights a week. After morning lectures he gave afternoon tutorials to earn spending money, then returned home to study until midnight or even 2:00 a.m. In one nine-month period, the barely-twenty-two-year-old wrote a 320-page manuscript entirely in Latin, using sources so rare that he had to requisition them from French and German libraries. His time was as constrained as his budget, for his state subsidy would run out in six years. Then, presumably with doctorate in hand, he could look forward to competing in a glutted market for a parish with an average starting salary of 800 guilders ($320 US).

Kuyper was spiritually discontent as well. As his work schedule implies, he did not attend church regularly, despite his pastor father, nor, after his profession of faith, did he take Communion with any relish. His most famous public reflection on the situation came later, in 1873. It should be read cautiously in light of his polemical purposes at the time, but there is little in his letters, in his reported behavior, or in the model of his professors to cast doubt on the substance of his recollections:

In the years of my youth the church aroused my aversion more than my affection . . . particularly through the way that church life manifested itself in Leiden. . . . [There] a most pitiful situation prevailed, and the deceit, the hypocrisy, the unspiritual routine that sap the lifeblood of our whole ecclesiastical fellowship were most lamentably prevalent. . . . The spirit was absent, and my heart could feel no sympathy either for a church that so blatantly dishonored itself or for a religion that was represented by such a church.

Kuyper remembered, incorrectly, that he had therefore "postponed my profession of faith until the last possible moment" before his ministerial candidate's examination; in fact, he took that step in 1857, not at the 1859 deadline. But it was true enough that "upon entering the academic world, I stood without defense or weapon against the powers of negation." He put some of the blame on his father's theology, but the real problem lay within: "My faith was not deeply rooted in my unconverted, self-centered soul and was bound to wither once exposed to the scorching heat of the spirit of doubt."

With such an attitude it was not surprising that in his undergraduate work Kuyper was far more taken with history and literature than with theology. For extra credit he participated in Professor C. G. Cobet's select "disputations" — debates over particular passages in classical texts. Cobet, one of Europe's outstanding Greek philologists, used these exercises as research assistance; undergraduates sought them out as a bracing excursion into the world of advanced analysis and scholarly debate. The nineteen-year-old Kuyper thus found himself in the dock of an afternoon defending, in Latin, two dozen propositions about Lysias, or nineteen on Livy and four about Demosthenes, or — in his last year — eight on Tacitus, eight on Homer, and eight on Plato's *Symposium*. Besides acquainting him deeply with classical literature, the exercises afforded excellent training in close argumentation.

Kuyper's favorite teacher was Matthias de Vries, professor of Dutch literature. Indeed, De Vries was the favorite of many. One of them, the future eminent Dutch historian P. J. Blok, located the lure of "our beloved Thijs" in the "enthusiasm" he exuded amid a faculty of cold fish. Greatly learned himself, De Vries kindled in students love for study as such, whatever their field. His specialty in medieval Dutch literature was immediately attractive to the young Kuyper, but Bram followed him across the whole range of Dutch letters and attended the master's private home seminars even while working on his doctorate. Kuyper would do some research for the definitive new dictionary of the Dutch language that De Vries was compiling, and admired the respect for Dutch culture that the work raised beyond the Netherlands' borders. De Vries was equally important in introducing the historical method at Leiden, superseding traditional static approaches with a passion to trace a language's "organic development" from its roots through its many branches and literary fruit. At the same time he took language to be the key to understanding history — "language as it dwells and blooms in the heart of the people, free and unencumbered, loose and living, and thus pure and true." In short, De Vries exemplified the Romantic linguistics pioneered in the previous century by Johann Gottfried Herder. That Kuyper absorbed these concepts at the bedrock of his thinking is evident from their many allusions, invocations, and operations across his writings.

Another romance bloomed closer at hand. In the summer of 1858, twenty years old and newly graduated from college, Kuyper met Johanna Schaay, a sixteen-year-old Rotterdam girl who happened to be visiting her aunt at Leiden. Whether because his professional future needed some permanent commitment in his personal life, or because he yearned for something beyond his parents' house, or simply because he was madly in love, Kuyper that summer entered upon an all-consuming courtship of Jo. Neither set of parents was enthused. Jo first struck Kuyper's parents and sisters as a fashion-plate daughter of a stockbroker father; Jan Frederik advised his son to wait for better prospects. With the young lovers exchanging pledges anyway (on September 14, three months into their relationship), the Schaays insisted that they exchange two and not Kuyper's preferred four letters a week. They refused entreaties that the betrothal be publicly announced already that Christmas; the next Easter, 1859, seemed soon enough. There followed a classic Victorian engagement of long delay between the declaration and consummation of marital desire.

In this case it entailed five years of Bram's assertiveness and Jo's patience. Some friends had joined his father in advising against their match, Kuyper wrote Jo, "but I've always thought to myself: I'd rather shape a girl, teach her to think, raise her more and more up to the level where I stand." Specifically, Jo had to be refitted to become "a Dominie's wife, a cultured woman, a mother . . . who might have to educate her own children." The chief obstacle to that end came from her social location, Bram discovered: "Never have I so fully recognized as since our engagement what a gulf exists between the business class and learned folks"; "we" are classically educated and "you" are not. Don't blame yourself, Bram reassured her; it's your family's fault: "by the nature of things, in circles such as yours more work is often done with the *body* than with the *mind.*" His solution was to prescribe a daily reading program to get Jo up to speed on French, English, and German literature. Pope, Shakespeare, and Schiller set the standard for style, but he thought she should begin with *Paradise Lost* for its elevated substance. Jo acquiesced and wrote back that she had acquired the books. "Not *books!*" Bram scolded. "Use their *names.* Byron and Racine — so they are called." He was exasperated that she could not extract more time from her household duties (she was the third surviving daughter in a family by now grown to ten), and dismayed that she preferred Dickens to Shakespeare. He ignored her requests for some Dutch titles; he urged her to spend less on clothes and more on building a library. He chided her for filling her letters with chit-chat when his bore higher concerns. The future they were forming together was "a matter of such weight that it must be well compensated."

Theological Discontent

Bram pressed Jo on the religious front as well. The first months of their engagement coincided with her preparations for public profession of faith, and the graduate student treated the teenager to a seminar in theological method and modern doubt. To his questions about various doctrines she replied with answers drawn variously from the catechism, natural theology, evangelical sentiment, or biblical quotations. None of it was good enough. "Tell me *why* you believe as you do," Kuyper demanded, or your belief is not real religion. Perhaps they should debate the Canons of the Synod of Dort for practice. Your most recent reply is more promising but no better grounded than a Catholic's belief in the Virgin Mary. Finally having had enough, Jo snapped back: Write down some of *your* convictions and let me ask you "the 'why' question"; we'll see how you do. They finally agreed to let her minister do the catechizing, but all the while Bram let her in on how far from the traditional answers he himself had traveled.

From their correspondence Kuyper's theology during his doctoral studies can best be described as Unitarian with pronounced Calvinist and moralist accents. It was Unitarian in that he denied the eternal divinity of Christ: "You don't believe that anyone can doubt that Jesus did not exist before he appeared on earth," he answered a protest from Jo. "You're wrong — I deny it and hundreds with me. . . . He is not God to me, for my religious sense teaches me to know but one God. To me he is a man and nothing but a man." Yet his denial had Calvinist reasons: ". . . most people put Jesus too much in the foreground and thereby so often forget God. Truly, Jo! That may not be; that is not Religion. Jesus himself would be the first to come out against it. He too did everything for God's honor. We want to follow his example. So give God alone the glory." Then ethics took over. God's glory was besmirched at every drop into sin, but disgusted as Kuyper was with gross carnality, he turned his most searching judgment inward. "The rational and religious feeling in us is God, who reveals Himself overall and thus also in man." Therefore, if the "moral religious consciousness within us . . . is not as it should be, then *sin* rules in us — in other words, there is sin in us so long as the godly spirit is not all in all within us." Predictably, it was at this point that the founder of Christianity "becomes so important to me, for the man Jesus became so great, so perfect, as I too am commanded to become."

The young theologian doubted other doctrines that Jo was memorizing as well. On immortality, "I feel that I need" such a belief, he wrote her, "but I cannot make it clear and comprehensible. And does needing it make it true?" On the atonement: "To me forgiveness through the blood of Christ is completely unintelligible." As to revelation, "how do you know that Jesus indeed said such and such? And is what Jesus said still unconditionally true? Wasn't Jesus also a man?" Church trappings fared worst of all. "Religion does not consist in forms — going to church, celebrating the Lord's Supper, baptism, confession, and what have you," he fumed. "Were we perfect, I'd have nothing to do with any of them — indeed, would renounce them." *All* material expressions of the divine were suspect. Seeing God's majesty in the starry sky, as Jo wrote she was wont to do, "is not yet Religion. That is nothing more than a taste for religion, religious feeling, and the momentary upwelling of that feeling." The beautiful and lovely might be foremost in the human imagination of God, "but that's a side issue, a form, a change of clothes — not the essence. The chief matter is and remains: holy, holy, holy is the Lord. That is, for whatever is sinful and impure, for whatever does not fully concur with the highest ideal of virtue, there is no place with God. The moral element, the holiness of God we must feel above all else." He urged her to leave behind everything material and "feel God in your inmost parts, feel his breath run through your limbs, and then fervently thank him as you know that you are human, that God has passed down something of his spirit also in you."

Kuyper's discontent rode the cutting edge of Dutch theology, which by now had moved beyond conventional forms of piety but also the two forms of Romantic religion that had proposed to replace them. The conventional pieties included, first, the rote repetition of Reformed standards that Kuyper suspected in Jo's catechism classes, and secondly the "rational supernaturalism" that had once held sway among the learned and still survived in people like his father. Arising in the late eighteenth century, rational supernaturalism attempted to reassert traditional Christian doctrines against Enlightenment criticism by appeal to the latter's standards of reason rather than first of all to its own faith or revelation. The result, the visiting Scottish theologian James Mackay later observed, was a system that affirmed miracles while trying to explain them by nature; that accepted biblical authority without specifying its grounds or particular claims; that acknowledged biblical revelation, though remaining vague as to what exactly Scripture was revealing; that followed Jesus without deciding the question of his two natures. Theological minimalists felt the system worked well enough, but to orthodox Reformed circles like the Seceders, this was the old humanist program restyled for rationalist taste. To others, of more Romantic inclination, the approach was arid and outmoded.

The Réveil, where Kuyper would one day find his first audience, belonged in the Romantic camp in appealing to a young generation dissatisfied with the skeptical spirit of their parents. Their yearnings ran in traditional channels, enwrapped in love of Jesus and the bonds of evangelical fellowship. Those priorities put limits on theological pursuits as such, lest intellectual demands cool heart religion or doctrinal particulars disrupt group unity. The more constructive theology that Kuyper encountered as a student thus came from the more liberal Groningen school. It was Romantic in reaching out to such German luminaries as Friedrich Schleiermacher and Johann Herder. Philosophically it borrowed from German Idealism, even more from Plato. Substantively, it was Christocentric, vesting ultimate authority for doctrine and life in the "Spirit of Christ as revealed in the New Testament." Yet the Groningers were susceptible to charges that they taught more an Arian than a Trinitarian Christ. In their view, Jesus, preexistent but not divine, brought down to earth the perfection attained by virtue of his unity with the Father and thus served as the ultimate inspiration for all who would follow him. On this account the spiritual life became less a struggle with compulsive depravity than a progressive movement toward fellowship with God; to attain that was to realize true humanity. And the Groningers saw that destiny to be promised for more than individuals. Just as the risen Lord was further revealed in the historical development of the society he founded — the church — so the progress of world history would yield perfection for whole nations, the entire race. The Groningers' crusade for national betterment, especially in public schooling, was as good as its word.

The New Realism

The only problem — so thought the rising theologians of the 1850s — was that the Romantic premises no less than the biblical claims of these schools were outmoded. A new realism was ascendant at Leiden along with the hard-nosed liberalism of Thorbecke, who was expected back on the faculty once his political diversion was over. If the natural sciences still lagged in enrollment at mid-century, the positivism and empiricism represented by the country's foremost philosopher, Cornelis W. Opzoomer of Utrecht, made a compelling case to refute — or to emulate. In Kuyper's case the answer came from Joannes Henricus Scholten, the pioneer of Modernist theology in the Netherlands and Kuyper's graduate-school mentor. The most important Dutch theologian of his generation, Scholten sounded a tough-minded naturalism that discarded dreamy Romantic wishes. "Nature" no longer spoke in beatific harmonies but in a long struggle in which spirit sought to triumph over flesh, the moral over the willful. All religion at bottom was a function of this process, Scholten taught, a school of sublime morality for the less tutored that would give way as the progress of reason advanced. As for Christianity in particular, Scholten and his Leiden colleagues adopted the astringent biblical hermeneutics of the German Higher Criticism, demoting Scripture and especially the Groningers' beloved New Testament as a reliable historical record. What remained of rational supernaturalism was exposed as a bundle of inconsistencies, while the Groningen theology seemed quite sentimental. The Modernist agenda was to forthrightly naturalize Christian theology as an allegory — the best available allegory — of human development toward full responsible freedom, which was God's ultimate purpose in history.

The vision was bracing in its honesty, freshness, and courage, and in Scholten's heyday students flocked to his lecture hall to hear it. They came not just from theology, like Kuyper, but from across the university to witness, as Scholten's successor remembered it, "one great, fully fledged world and life view [being] built up before their eyes." This was "an all-inclusive monism . . . wherein all questions had an answer, wherein no divisions remained for human thought, but wherein everything flowed out from God 'as the power of all powers, the life of all life.'" The vision retained "a fascinating charm" upon the audience, wherever they came to rest intellectually or vocationally.

Kuyper was a case in point. However much he eventually came to disagree with Scholten in substance, he retained much of the master's style and spirit. Abraham Kuenen, Scholten's foremost contemporary, remembered him as "a picture of strength," "a character of granite." K. H. Roessingh, Scholten's successor, described him as "a prophet in the podium." All these images Kuyper assiduously cultivated. Scholten never espoused a position, Kuenen observed, without first retreating into private meditation, testing the notion at the bar of his own spiritual life, there also entertaining every reason against it, until at last he could come before his students and speak with all doubts resolved. The procedure describes Kuyper's lifelong practice to a T. As would Kuyper, Scholten became interested in classic Reformed theology at his first village parish, where its tough lineaments looked attractive compared to other options. Both men then set out to "develop" Reformed theology from its outdated language until it came into rapport with the needs of the day. *Comprehend, think,* and *know* were both the teacher's and the student's favorite imperatives, and system and consistency were the hallmarks of their finished products. Kuyper would remember Scholten when he championed theology as a science with its own rights, from Scholten bear the conviction that Calvinism was the purest form of Christianity, and with

Scholten take the supralapsarian track within Reformed theology. As in some understandings of classic Calvinism, Scholten's predestination verged on determinism, with the sovereign will of God moving ineluctably toward the consummation of the world-order. Kuyper would de-naturalize (or re-supernaturalize) that conception, but when one day he roiled the waters of the national church by insisting on the doctrine of divine election, he could claim accurately enough to be transmitting a lesson learned at Scholten's feet.

Scholten's project bore a twofold direction. In one respect it obeyed the Modernist injunction that theology be a "free science," set loose to study "the religious life of humanity in its historical and psychological variety." Yet in Scholten's eyes the Reformed tradition stood supreme amid that variety. Although it is possible to infer that, if theology simply reflects human values, then the best theology reflects the best people, Scholten saved his praise for Reformed "principles" operating within Reformed churches, especially for those figures who followed those principles consistently over the flux of time. Kuyper learned nothing so fundamentally as this point: as to method, Reformed theology had grown by extrapolation from certain fixed "principles"; as to substance, first among these principles was the absolute sovereignty of God. One other lesson reverberated as well. Just as the sovereignty of God was (in the parlance of the trade) the "material" principle of the Reformed tradition, so Scripture constituted its "formal" rule. But with Scripture's textual credibility being undermined as he wrote (even by what he wrote), Scholten returned to the old Reformed emphasis upon the testimony of the Holy Spirit — namely, that the Bible remains inert until the Spirit quickens the believer's heart to accept its truth. For Scholten this inner witness in effect became the ultimate authority in the church as well as in the individual soul. Christ as the sinless one alone revealed God as author of the moral order, but only the pure in heart could see him as such. In Scholten's Modernist translation, the testimony of the Holy Spirit was "the witness of reason in its moral purity."

German Philosophy

This was the language of Immanuel Kant, indicating that from Scholten Kuyper was acquiring philosophical along with theological habits. The philosophy proved to be just as lasting as the theology, and of much greater consequence for Kuyper's long-term influence as a thinker. His key proposal would come in the area of epistemology, the theory of how humans acquire knowledge or certify truth. Here, in contrast to other contemporary Protestants of orthodox hue, Kuyper would combine Reformed Christian and German Idealist sources. Scholten again showed how. Though he advertised Modernism as a response to the rising tide of science, in fact an Idealist set of presuppositions controlled all of Scholten's thinking, including his empiricist claims. The course of human history to him remained more Hegelian than Darwinian, not an evolutionary struggle in which a materialist nature selected among random variations, but a saga of Mind asserting ever more control over matter, of Will becoming ever more infused with Right so as to infuse Mind with a yearning for the Good. Reason within — especially what Kant had called "practical reason," anchored in the moral will — still shaped the world without, and could have, must have, increasing effect over time, as all the heirs of Hegel knew.

That Kuyper swam in these waters at Leiden is particularly evident from the way he treated Modernist theology in a major public address he delivered a decade later, after he had converted to orthodoxy. Again, extrapolation backwards from that text requires caution, but the leading question in the speech is unmistakably the epistemological question of "appearance" vs. "reality." How he and the others packing Scholten's lectures had grasped at the parade of German philosophers which there passed in review, Kuyper recalled: "People turned their gaze on the hieroglyphics of Kant's oracular language, bathed in Jacobi's streams of feeling, raved a while about Fichte's Idealism of the Ego and Non-Ego, hoped for a moment to find firmer ground in Schelling's gnosticism, and at last gaped at the dizzying mental gymnastics whereby Hegel won admiration as an athlete." None of it had worked, the now orthodox Kuyper of 1871 concluded, but that did not lead him to dismiss it all as a bad dream or to celebrate the succeeding Realist turn instead. Rather, the latter represented a deeper sinking still, "back to the lowest level of spiritual existence . . . fashioning an idol out of gross empiricism." The new "realism threatens us with a real danger," Kuyper continued. "The distance from its base to the fatal abyss of materialism is easily measured, and we are well on our way to it."

We will return to how Kuyper resolved the appearance-reality issue later, but we need to pause first to register how deep and permanent was the impact of German Idealism on his thinking. For both theological and political reasons, Kuyper would always denounce Hegel's nomination of the State as the true incarnation of the divine; yet Kuyper literally could not think outside the Hegelian method by which Mind(s) developing down through time constituted the essence of history. In 1892, thirty years out of university and defending Christian orthodoxy from its latest and most fearsome scorner, he scolded that "not a single element surfaces in Nietzsche that does not stem, by legitimate descent, from the premises of Schelling and Hegel." On the other hand, the theological summa he was writing at the same moment took its method from Fichte, and his final word on epistemology warned that "whoever neglects to maintain the autonomy of the spiritual over against the material in his point of departure will eventually come to the idolization of matter via the adoration of man." On this score he gave tribute where it was due: "Whatever bloody lashings Kant brought us, he was nevertheless the one who released orthodoxy" from the "cookie-cutter" superficialities of rational supernaturalism. Kant had endowed the far better project of framing "a Christian worldview" in which reason put together the world on Christian premises. This was Kuyper's own signal endeavor, and he confessed that it "owe[d] to the powerful command with which the Athlete of Koningsberg dared to direct his operations from the subject" — that is, from the convictions of the thinker instead of the world thought about.

Vocationally, too, the Germans cast their spell. As he sent off his finished dissertation, Kuyper penned an Idealist rhapsody to Jo about the study where he had just expended so much effort — and where he would like to spend the rest of his life. Gazing at the flowers in his window, the pictures of his friends all around, and "above all the busts of great men . . . and the products of learning and good taste on my table and bookcase," he rhapsodized: "Oh then I feel so infinitely much richer, more blessed and happy" than in contemplating a career of practical routine. "Here I have faith and hope for the future, for here I see what man can be; here I create my world around me, for [now quoting in German] here my heart is my world!"

The orthodox Kuyper who spoke in critique of Modernism in 1871 would fault it at just this point. Modernism was but a human projection, he concluded, a beautiful fantasy spun out of the imagination, doomed to shatter against the hard rocks of fact. All the more surprising, then, to see how much of the method he retained — that is, to see what constituted "reality" for Kuyper and to which "facts" he appealed. His speech presented no "positive" case from evidence, even the evidence of Scripture or dogmatic theology. It invoked not the prestige of science but the dangers of scientism. The real issues of life were being fought out on a supernatural level invisible to the human eye, Kuyper averred, and to comprehend that scene he conducted his listeners through the channels of inward experience, calling upon poets to mark the way. He turned to "Hamlet" for the test of adjudicating between appearance and reality, and he illustrated the perils of imagination by comparing the word and real-life deeds of poets famous — Dante, Goethe, Schiller — and now obscure — Gottfried Bürger and Friedrich von Matthison.

German Literature

This particular list of poets is telling for Kuyper's philosophical questions and life issues alike. It is a canon of the German *Sturm und Drang* ("Storm and Stress"), an explosion of literary creativity in the 1770s that founded the modern era of German literature and reverberated across the Continent. The movement's godfather was J. G. Hamann, the Lutheran "magus of the North" and foremost opponent of the Enlightenment. Hamann's student Johann Herder was its leading theoretician, Shakespeare its icon, Goethe its greatest poet, Schiller its channel to later Romantics, Bürger its bestseller and the coiner of its name. Tired of the dry rationalism and neo-classical aesthetics on offer from the Enlightenment, the poets of *Sturm und Drang* yearned for the intense experience of an authentic self. Life as prescribed by court, church, and school was so dreadful as to demand resistance, and so became a heroic theater of conflict and passion. Appropriately, Goethe's *Faust* was *Sturm und Drang's* greatest creation, and Prometheus its favorite hero from antiquity. At the end of these struggles beckoned perfect unity: unity within the integrated self, unity of the self with nature, unity of all separate domains — occupation and imagination, personal and public, the routine and the transcendent — into a single whole consistent with one's tested, triumphant soul.

This profile closely matches that of the mature Kuyper. Certainly it resonated with his youthful disquiet over the penny-pinching compromises of his father, the snobbery of the chosen in Law, the prospect of a life spent observing ecclesiastical rote. The movement spoke to his spirit too. His 1871 address on "Modernism" begins by invoking conflicts of "volcanic" force and cosmic sweep: "Look around: from all directions the battle of the spirits rushes in upon you. Underneath and around you everything is seething and in ferment." Twenty years later, in his speech of 1892, he was still joining with the protesters of the 1770s in reproaching theirs as "an age of cold Deism, of a spirit-deadening Rationalism, of omnipresent artifice and conventionality. Its society resembled the waiting room of a morgue, uninspired and devoid of idealism." Kuyper disavowed the pantheism that, with some justice, he saw the *Sturm und Drang* generating in opposition to the Enlightenment, but he added: "I would not be classified with those who have nothing good to say about pantheism in any form." *Sturm und Drang* and its Romantic child had done well to infuse the nineteenth century with "enthusiasm and resilience." Therefore, he concluded, "if I had to choose between an icy Deism . . . and a melting pantheism . . . I could not possibly hesitate. In India I would have been a Buddhist and probably praised the Vedanta. In China I would have preferred the system of Lao-tse over that of Confucius. And in Japan I would have turned from the official Shintoism in order to share the suffering of the oppressed Buddhist priests."

Finally, *Sturm und Drang* fit Kuyper's prevailing philosophical question. Proto-Romantics though they were, its writers were too taken with the concrete detail of the world to share their descendants' penchant for mysticism, ghosts, and fantasy. They were Realists in their confidence that nature was meaningful and that imagination marked the high road into rather than away from things "as they actually are." They sired the vibrant realist fiction of Kuyper's mature years as much as the Romantic poetry of his youth. But their program left them with exactly the problem that Kuyper explored in "Modernism": how to determine where subjectivity ended and reality began; more broadly, how to harness vaulting spiritual yearnings to concrete earthly forms, how to reconcile the demand for personal autonomy with the goal of universal harmony. Kuyper even pinpointed the spot where the contradictions in fact often came to tragedy, in the poets' consuming idealization of simple country girls. Schiller's Laura,

Matthison's Adelaide, Bürger's Lenore — all were either illusions from the start or finally immolated in the poet's love. To the list Kuyper could have added Faust's Gretchen in the second category. Perhaps Jo fit in the first.

Glory and Trial

Heady as these thoughts may have seemed, Kuyper could get down to earth in the most expeditious way. Such was the case in April 1859 — i.e., in the spring of his first year in graduate school, in the middle of his twenty-second year, and in the immediate wake of his public betrothal — when the theology faculty at Groningen announced a national student research competition. The gold medal would be worthwhile in itself, but Matthias de Vries, who passed along the announcement to Kuyper, had launched his own academic career in just such a contest and knew what an opportunity it offered. The essay, which was to compare John Calvin's and Johannes à Lasco's (Jan Laski) views of the church, involved the church-history track that Kuyper had pursued from his gymnasium oration on Ulfilas to a major research paper on the medieval Pope Nicholas I, finished just the previous January.

The agenda behind the contest was more complicated. The Groningers aimed to use à Lasco against Scholten's critique of their theology. For Scholten the Reformed tradition centered on dogma in general and on the doctrine of election in particular, and was international in character, all of which warranted Calvin as a father of the Dutch Reformed Church. The Groningers' interest in a distinctively Dutch church found à Lasco much more promising. His theology, like theirs, centered on the person of Christ and the doctrine of the church. Moreover, though of Polish origin himself, à Lasco had led Dutch-language churches in exile during the Spanish persecution, and his 1554 catechism and the 1571 Synod at Emden, where he pastored, were the earliest in Dutch Reformed history. They thus had precedence over their counterparts among the French-oriented southerners who, the Groningers complained, had introduced the alien Calvin into the Netherlands. In a way, then, the contest invited Kuyper to reject his Leiden master.

Career-wise, it gave him a chance at an unexpected future, beyond the toils of his father, toward the influence and intellectual fulfillment of an academic career. The ambitions that Kuyper invested in this project are manifest in his correspondence of the time and from the pride of place he would give the "à Lasco" episode in his 1873 memoir. The two sources do not tell the same story, however. In his memoir, a scouring of all the library catalogues in the country, in all of Europe, found them bereft of à Lasco titles, tempting him to despair of the project. At this point Professor de Vries recommended a visit to his father, a book collector (indeed, one of the country's foremost) in Haarlem. But De Vries Senior, Kuyper recalled, did not know whether he had anything relevant on the topic. Kuyper was to come back in a week. When he did, he saw "a collection of Lasciana more complete than was — and is — to be found in any library in all of Europe." The moral was clear: ". . . you must personally experience such a surprise in your own life-struggle to know what it is to encounter a miracle of God on life's journey." In fact, the record shows that his search did not last six months but three weeks; proceeded via Utrecht, where nearly half of à Lasco's corpus was available; and involved a return the next day (not the next week) to the senior De Vries who knew that, but not exactly where, the pertinent titles were in his collection. De Vries did own one crucial volume that Utrecht lacked; in that regard, he did offer up, as Kuyper recalled, the "treasure" that constituted "the 'to be or not to be' of the contest."

Whatever the role "the finger of God" played in setting his work in motion, Kuyper relied on his outstanding preparation in Latin and the staggering labors of his own right hand to bring it to completion. By September he had written 130 pages; by the end of October, his twenty-second birthday, he was complaining of headaches (happily, not caused by the cholera epidemic then afflicting Leiden). The next month his international queries brought in more à Lasco rarities along with ten dissertations on Calvin from Strasbourg. In January 1860 he could send the completed manuscript of 320 pages to a copyist. In March he had a nightmare of having received the gold medal, only to have it crumble to dust in his hands. In April he submitted the manuscript "that contains all my hopes and wishes for the future, and that perhaps will determine my lot forever." He need not have worried. Kuyper's was the only entry, but even so, the Groningen faculty awarded him the prize with "exceptionally flattering praise." Kuyper took the occasion of the award ceremony in October 1860 to make a side trip to the à Lasco archives at Emden, with a view to writing a full biography of the reformer for his doctoral dissertation. His plans would become grander yet: to compile a definitive collection of primary sources and write a history of the Dutch churches in exile. The reward, surely, would be a professorship.

But old pressures awaited him back home. His stipend would run out the next summer, so he had to send out applications for other scholarships. He was scheduled to take his doctoral qualifying exams the next March and was determined not only to meet that deadline but to add another summa cum laude to his record. Redoubling his labors after an exhausting year had predictable consequences. By Christmas 1860 his headaches were back, and his frustrations with Jo were acute. He could put up with her going through "the forms" of profession of faith but not when she lagged in proper self-formation. "A girl that can frankly admit that she doesn't care for Shakespeare, that she wants to drop her French, and yet reads nine volumes of [Eugene] Sue — and that while engaged to someone whose position requires precisely that the development of the mind must provide for his career and bread for his wife and children . . . !" What must be said about your taste? Your neglect of duty? Your preference of poor taste over duty? "Turn back from this smooth way, my dear, dearest Johanna! I pray, I abjure you! Shake yourself awake and become what you must be." If he seemed wrathful, he assured her, "it is the *wrath of love.*" In any case, someday "you will thank me for my efforts to make you happy." Jo could well recall that, earlier, she had echoed his father's warnings: "Oh, Bram, I think it would have been infinitely better for you had you chosen a girl that had been reared like you and your sisters. Classically, as you call it. Then perhaps everything you wished for you would be fulfilled." Under so much strain, Kuyper appeared to be close to a complete breakdown. In February 1861 a medical doctor thought Kuyper looked so bad that he took him to his house north of Amsterdam for a two-week rest. He returned home to the good news that his fellowship had been extended, went back to work — and immediately relapsed. Now he sat for hours in his room, listless and dreaming. He could not write more than a letter or read more than two pages at a time. His recovery would take five months, during which the Schaays turned out to have the right qualities after all. They took him into their home in Rotterdam, then on a seven-week cruise through the Rhineland where they had relatives — and where Kuyper could visit à Lasco scholars in Frankfurt, Heidelberg, and Strasbourg.

First Conversion

Kuyper's return to work in autumn 1861 held good, but it resurrected more starkly than ever the question of his occupational future. He had lost some of the extension on his fellowship to illness, and his exhaustion from research cast his fitness for a scholarly career into doubt. He passed his exams summa cum laude as intended, but he had to revise his dissertation plans radically to fit his foreshortened schedule. With the permission of Groningen he worked on revising his prize essay to satisfy the degree requirements. Thus, he was awarded the doctorate in divinity in September 1862 for a dissertation that encompassed but a large third of the original work. It still found for à Lasco, rather than for Scholten's Calvin, in judging who had the better conception of the church. Cobet offered him an assistantship in Greek, but its stipend was not enough to support a spouse.

Accordingly, Kuyper shifted his gaze toward the parish ministry, with much apprehension. The prospects of a long tenure in a mean village had revolted him from the start, at the same time that it drove some of his imperatives towards Jo's self-cultivation. Upon entering active candidacy, however, he found even such a post unlikely, since only orthodox candidates seemed in demand. For six months, from October 1862 through March 1863, he peddled his wares around the provinces. The "sure death" spelled by one village in Friesland was redeemed only by the research trip he took on the side to the archives in Emden. The authorities there let him take back troves of original records to review in Leiden. Old papers paid no bills, however, and again in February, gloom and anxiety threatened to overtake him.

This time the cure came from a book that Jo sent *him* — not high classic literature, but the bestselling British novel of 1853, *The Heir of Redclyffe* by Charlotte Yonge. The book had been especially popular among earnest young men — Crimean War officers, Oxford undergraduates, young aesthetes like Dante Gabriel Rossetti and Henry James. Yonge herself had intended it as an object lesson for the Anglican Tractarian movement, one of whose leaders, John Keble, was her parish priest and had vetted the work in production. In his 1873 memoir Kuyper would pick up "the church question" that the Tractarians had in view, but for the moment the story line involved more riveting existential issues. First and foremost, the male co-lead of Yonge's drama, Philip de Morville, is pride and ambition incarnate. An honors classics student at Oxford, Philip seemed destined for a career of rare distinction, only to lose his chance — as Kuyper had with Cobet and his à Lasco plans — for want of money. In revenge he takes to building his own reputation by dominating others. Kuyper recognized the part. "I was fascinated by Philip's character," he recalled. "Philip was my hero, Philip I admired." But the melodrama turns when Philip falls sick in Italy. He is saved by his cousin Guy, whom he has been manipulating and censuring by now for 400 pages, only to see Guy contract and then die from the same fever. Philip is plunged into the throes of Victorian remorse, and Kuyper went down with him. When Philip "recognize[d] his own limitations and Guy's moral superiority," Kuyper was stricken at two key points of self-image. "Oh, at that moment it seemed as if in the crushed Philip my own heart was devastated, as if each of his words of self-condemnation cut through my soul as a judgment on my own ambitions and character."

At this point in his 1873 memoir Kuyper would make much of the Anglican burial liturgy in *Redclyffe* but also disclosed a ritual dimension of his own breakthrough ten years before. "I read how Philip knelt, and before I knew it" this proud sovereign of mind, this disdainer of "forms," was "kneeling in front of my chair with folded hands. Oh, what my soul experienced at that moment I fully understood only later. Yet, from that moment on I despised what I used to admire and sought what I had dared to despise."

Put simply, Kuyper had experienced a religious conversion. He was not yet a Calvinist, nor for the moment a theologian; it was enough to be a Christian with an engaged heart. He started going to church again and looked forward to taking the Lord's Supper. Small wonder that he came to rank *Redclyffe* "next to the Bible in its meaning for my life."

The pride and unbelief of his recent past Kuyper would publicly confess. In a letter to Jo he added "lascivious thoughts" to the list, understandably enough for a man in his mid-twenties coming up to the five-year mark of a celibate engagement. Other letters, and other threads in *Redclyffe,* point to further offenses that had amplified his crisis. The learned Philip pulled tightly on the reins of his (secret) fiancée in the book, urging her on to a program of self-cultivation, while assigning the fledging collegian Guy a reading list to correct his woeful taste. From the very start of their engagement, Kuyper realized, he had sinned against the humble Jo as well as against the Lord, and he now painfully confessed that in the form of a prayer: "When I think that you could have been taken away, and how hopeless my soul would have cried then to get you back, then I feel . . . how much you possess me. God, spare her long yet, let me keep her as an Angel on my life's way. Let me be a child with her and have for You a child's heart."

Besides having been converted, Kuyper was in love again. He copied Jo a Robert Burns epigram from one of Yonge's chapters: "She is a winsome wee thing,/. . . a bonnie wee thing,/This sweet wee wife of mine." He identified Guy as a model of the childlike faith he had lost. But the Guy in the text reflected far more of Kuyper than that. Accommodating and self-sacrificial as he is, Guy appears in the novel as the very picture of a Byronic hero, all deep feeling, honor, daring, and ardent poetry against a backdrop of wild scenery. Yet through arduous practice he disciplines Romantic passion with proper form and noblesse oblige into perfect love. Where Goethe missed, Yonge succeeded; Guy brought the *Sturm und Drang* to quiet harbor. Tellingly, when Kuyper once again thanked Jo for sending him *Redclyffe,* it was for "giving me Guy. Oh! That was so dear of you! One of the best deeds of your life."

Yet Kuyper's vocational question remained. Earlier in February, just before he started reading *Redclyffe,* a "little jewel" of a parish had come to his attention at the town of Beesd in south Gelderland. It was half Catholic, lacked a railroad link, but offered a salary of 2400 guilders — three times the norm, more than his father's, more than enough to hire an assistant so that he could proceed with his à Lasco project. He wrote Jo: "Never have I been in such fateful tension over a place as with this one. I'd move heaven and earth for it." It is not fair to conclude, as has one critic, that Kuyper's conversion was simply his way of "moving heaven" to secure the post. But money and scholarly ambition were certainly on his mind as he read the early chapters of *Redclyffe.* "O wealth, wealth!" he quoted from the lips of Philip's fiancée, "What cruel differences it makes! . . . for want of hateful money," Philip's dreams were "spurned." Kuyper later seconded Philip's renunciation of this self-pity, and took Jo's admonition not to hire an assistant. A week after his conversion he told her, "I am calm and resigned, also over Beesd."

But heaven, or earth, did move for him. Kuyper was invited to give a candidate's sermon on Good Friday 1863; he received the call Easter Monday. It was exactly four years since his official betrothal to Jo;

their banns could now be posted. The only spot on the horizon was the declining health of Jo's father. Bram's father presided at their wedding on 1 July 1863; her father died five days later. The couple moved into the parsonage at Beesd, and Kuyper was officially installed in the pulpit on August 9, his father again presiding. Kuyper featured sweetness and light for the day. Church unity was his theme; 1 Corinthians 13 the preparatory reading; Psalm 133:1 the song before the sermon: "How good and pleasant is the sight/When brethren make it their delight/To dwell in blest accord." He preached on 1 John 1:7: "If we walk in the light as He is in the light, we have fellowship, one with another." Time would tell.

CHAPTER THREE

The Young Pastor

T he young pastor who somewhat anxiously entered his first charge that summer of 1863 need not have feared for his future. Kuyper quickly established himself at Beesd as a dynamo of social and spiritual ministry. He completed the next part of his à Lasco project, then opened a new career path by publishing a pamphlet on a hot issue in church politics. That helped win him a call to the university city of Utrecht, where he got involved in civil politics as well. By 1870, just seven years after entering the pastorate, he had moved to Amsterdam where he soon became a nationally recognized leader in religion and politics alike: the editor of two newspapers, a scholar of international repute, an orator in high demand, a cultural commentator of some promise, and a partisan with as strong an aptitude for organization as for polemics. Behind these moves and energizing all his action was the final step in his religious odyssey: he turned to orthodox Calvinism as a firm rock in a stormy world.

These changes were as unexpected as they were dramatic. His sudden prominence was so opposite his nightmare of dying in a dusty parish, his political involvements so far from the quiet study he idealized, Calvinist dogma such a backwater compared to the fresh Modernist tide — one can see how Kuyper associated these years with the qualities of miracle. Just as remarkably, all the themes of his mature career crystallized quickly between his moves to Calvinism in 1865 and to Amsterdam in 1870. By the end of that process his conceptual kit was largely set. It would prove to be sturdy, as it needed to be: it would have to upgrade Calvinism from an old dogma to an active life, to put Modernist methods to orthodox ends, and to redefine the church to make it fit, and challenge, the contemporary world.

The Apprentice Pastor

Kuyper arrived at Beesd still buoyed by his *Redclyffe* conversion, and his inaugural sermon breathed its air of spiritual intimacy. Fellowship with God was "the highest aspiration of the human heart"; fellowship with each other — and with the pastor — came a close second. Hear my prayer, Kuyper asked his new parishioners, "that you will all be my friends, and that you will fill the empty place in my heart" vacated by his having just left the only home he had ever known. Their fellowship would go forward in a common search for truth at which Kuyper confessed himself to be only a little more advanced than they. The "struggle to comprehend the infinite in the finite" was especially taxing because all earthly "forms" were so inadequate to the task. Strife over theological formulas was particularly to be avoided, as it "lovelessly puts off the brother . . . and builds endless evil." Kuyper rounded off the point with a sentiment that he would never retract: "Religion is always a matter of the heart, and in that heart God the Holy Spirit speaks according to his divine good pleasure." But there followed another phrase, this one utterly contrary to his mature practice: "Thus, I carry no one's banner and shall battle for no single slogan." He concluded on a social-gospel note. The only favoritism he would show, he pledged, would be in passing by those who were rich by the standards of the world for the sake of the one "who has to struggle for his daily bread." A telling political afterword followed. The tide of democracy stood at the church's door, Kuyper declared to the trustees, sitting in the front row; "Shall this awaken you, too, to give an ear to the cry of the age?"

His social consciousness showed up immediately in Kuyper's parish activities. He worked with the local chapter of the national Society for the General Welfare to open a bank for small savers. He galvanized the parish deacons to visit the poor more regularly and to modernize church accounts. But inevitably he came up against two powerful leaders in town. The local noble, O. W. A. Count van Bylandt, Lord of Mariënweerd, Enspijk, Ooy, and Persingen, was forty-year chair of the church trustees; his estate manager had been mayor for thirty-five.

Kuyper had privately chafed at Van Bylandt's power over his own appointment, and his resentment built up to an explosion in the summer of 1866, when a cholera epidemic swept through the village, followed shortly by a devastating outbreak of cow typhus. Kuyper proposed to hold special prayer services; the count replied that, as such were not covered in the church budget, the pastor would have to cover the additional expense himself. Kuyper's retort challenged the count's integrity; the deacons' sloppy bookkeeping gave rise to rumors about financial malfeasance that some in the village laid at Kuyper's door. The old money problem from *Redclyffe* and his father's house was flaring up again.

Kuyper's spiritual labors were just as intense. He prepared and delivered two sermons a week, on top of thirteen hours of catechism lessons for children and an evening book discussion with interested laymen. He led visitation teams in an annual sweep of all the homes in the parish. By contrast, during his four years at Beesd he attended only one of the annual meetings of classis, the church's regional unit where denominational business was reviewed. Although he would always disdain ecclesiastical routine, this was a rare neglect of the centers of power.

His visitations with Jo were more consistent. Their first child, Herman Huber, named after Kuyper's brother and mother, arrived in July 1864, one year after the wedding. Jan Hendrik Frederik, named for both their fathers, came nineteen months later, in February 1866. Thereafter, with only two breaks, Jo would be pregnant every two years through 1882. Citified the Kuypers might have been, but they had not made the bourgeois turn to limiting family size.

Amid all his duties Kuyper still had his eye on an academic post and pushed forward with his à Lasco project. He signed a contract to publish a complete edition of the reformer's works, to which end he sent queries to libraries and book-dealer networks from Dublin to St. Petersburg to Rome. As copies of à Lasco's publications and correspondence began to arrive at the parsonage, Kuyper kept his study lamp burning well past midnight. When necessary, he moved heaven and earth again. The Dutch minister of foreign affairs intervened for him at the Vatican library. In a three-year chase he had Professor De Vries write Europe's foremost historian, Leopold von Ranke, who got Prussian chancellor Otto von Bismarck to pry a manuscript out of a private archive in Köningsberg. Between times he composed a 120-

page introductory essay, and in late 1865 sent the manuscript to press. The next spring the work appeared in two volumes, to solid acclaim from church historians.

Kuyper immediately proceeded to phase two, a biography of à Lasco himself. He intended to spend his summer vacation in 1866 on a research sortie to Frankfurt, only to be thwarted by the outbreak of Prussia's war with Austria. The next summer he was in London, working in the stuffy archives of the Dutch exile churches. But there he also decided to accept the call he had received from the church at Utrecht, in part because of the grumblings he had heard about his research trips. Yet when he left Beesd Kuyper also left off the à Lasco book, as well as the history of the exile churches that was to follow it. As one biographer has put it, Kuyper decided not to write church history but to shape it. Eventually he would use the model of à Lasco's churches in exile to lead a church exodus himself.

Conversion to Calvinism

Behind this turn lay a decisive religious shift. Kuyper did not label it a conversion and talked about it only some time after the fact, and then in different ways to different audiences. On the one solid trail left from the time, however — his sermons — a new theological tone and urgency can be detected around late 1865, the same moment when he sent off his book. Up to that point his preaching tended to alternate between the plaintive, the inspirational, and the reassuring. His morning messages focused on the figure of Jesus; his (afternoon) catechism sermons used Christian doctrine as tropes for the stages of life; the two came together in ethical mandates. The "knowledge of God is, on the Christian terrain, a moral question," Kuyper put it. To move his parishioners to answer that challenge aright, he tried to melt their hearts with pictures of Jesus' sacrifice, pointed to the moral world order affixed within the Father's creation, and called them to ever-higher reaches of self-sacrificing love, all of which operations were mediated by the Holy Spirit. Kuyper thus fit the pattern of the emerging Ethical school in Dutch Reformed theology, which tried to pose a moderate alternative between Scholten's Modernist reductions and strict Confessionalism of the Seceders' sort. The "Ethical" label reflected their centering of the Christian message in the existential decisions of the believer's conscience and the leavening effect that was to radiate out from there into culture and society. Without surrendering to Modernist "neology," the Ethicals gave Christian experience priority over Christian doctrine, put less stock in institutions than in individuals, and vested their hopes for church and nation in the free play of the gospel from person to person. Theirs was in a significant sense an extension of the "medical" side of the fading Réveil in the spirit of Isaac da Costa.

Kuyper remembered reading Ethical theology at Beesd to good effect; it provided "substance for my soul and pulled it out of its cocoon." Yet, "inspiring, fascinating, captivating" as it was, it seemed "too relative, too uncertain of definition." Likewise the Ethicals' international kin, the doyens of the Mediating theology in Denmark, Germany, and Switzerland. What he longed for instead was a "shelter in the rocks which, being founded on the rock and being hewn from the rock of thought, laughs at every storm." That turned up in an old place. "It was Calvin himself . . . who first disclosed to me those solid, unwavering lines that only need to be traced to inspire full confidence." In Calvin's system were laid "the foundations which, banning all doubt, permitted the edifice of faith to be constructed in a completely logical style — and with the surprising result that the most consistent ethic ruled in its inner chambers." Kuyper's old psychology was coming back as his *Redclyffe* experience wore off. The old demanding "why" of the "logical, consistent thinker" was on the hunt and could come to rest only in *"the power of the absolute."*

Kuyper never said what prompted him to re-connect to Calvin just now, but his new sense of urgency followed closely upon two signal events. In 1864 his old mentor J. H. Scholten published a study of the Gospel of John in which he reversed the judgment he had made just a few years earlier about the text's authorship; where once he had held to the traditional view, now he repudiated it. Such variability in the master was unsettling in itself. The challenge to the warrant of a text that stood central in Kuyper's preaching was even worse. Then in 1865 Allard Pierson, scion of an illustrious Réveil family and one of the Dutch Reformed Church's leading lights, became the second prominent disciple of Scholten to quit the ministry in fidelity to Modernist principles. If Christianity was to be superseded by Culture and had been all along simply the expression of human moral evolution (and an erratic one at that), Pierson asked, then why not devote oneself straight out to science and education? Pierson's defection stalled the confident march of Modernism; some of Scholten's students started to leave to the Right as well.

Kuyper announced his move in a series of three sermons delivered in November and December 1865. Pierson's logic was correct, he began; the church confronted a definite choice between "Humanism and Christianity." The options allowed of no compromise or middle ground and involved the highest stakes. Not only was the church as a body at issue, but the very existence of the soul itself, or of any reality beyond the material realm. The specter of blank materialism would represent, from now on, the deepest horror of Kuyper's imagination, the ultimate in a remorseless, meaningless world.

For the moment he responded with extreme measures. He chose Reformation Sunday 1865 to voice approval of the spirit of the Syllabus of Errors that the papacy had issued the year before. Though the Vatican went too far in its prohibitions, Kuyper said to a congregation not used to hearing anything positive about Catholicism from the pulpit, it recognized the theological and ethical issues at stake and had taken its stand with the true Christian tradition. Kuyper also gave a lecture that season to the town's self-styled progressives' club in which he appealed to Mesmerism and other psychic phenomena to prove the reality of the spiritual plane.

For the longer run his preaching settled into a new pattern, featuring biblical episodes of stark conflict, counterpoising opposite persons or traits. He put more emphasis on the suffering and adversity that come before consolation and reward, on Jesus' confrontation with death and evil, on the exclusive character of Christ. God became more active in direct relation to persons and less a sum of abstract qualities helpful to humanity in general. For Easter 1867 Kuyper emphasized Jesus' resurrection as a literal event and not just a metaphor. It alone constituted the necessary "proof of the validity of a Christian world- and life-view" over against the fatal logic of materialism, as well as the only sufficient bridge over the hard passages of life.

In making his change Kuyper struck a chord that he would repeat for the rest of his life: the mandate to make a "definite choice" between stark opposites rooted logically in differing first principles. The method was clearly reminiscent of Scholten's seminar. But the substance of his new faith was the opposite.

Both the embrace of his mentor's approach and the rejection of his theology were on display in a remarkable speech on Modernism that Kuyper delivered at Amsterdam a few years later — an event that put him on the national map as a cultural commentator and that might have been the first occasion in any country on which "modernism" was used in what would become the common sense of the term. The subtitle of the speech was meant to impress his upscale audience: "Modernism," Kuyper said, was a "Fata Morgana on the Christian Scene." Kuyper drew the metaphor from Arthurian legend (Morgan le Fey) as refracted through Sicilian folklore about optical illusions at sea. Modernism was an enticing picture that arose on a barren scene "by a fixed law" of optics, refracting an actual — and beautiful — reality, but bound to disappear on the morning air. Translation: Modernist theology reflected real faith amid the pallid offerings of compromised Christianity, and did so all the more persuasively for promising to meet the scientific temper of the age; yet its proposals finally amounted to human self-projection within a naturalistic frame. It failed the tests of its truthclaims by calling real what its language treated as metaphor. Even more, it disappointed the yearnings of true piety. It was bound to evaporate in the mists of time, but not before damaging many of the faithful and feeding the company of scoffers.

Beneath the accumulating weight of his long critique, Kuyper's listeners might forget the compliments with which the speech began, but compliments they were. Compared to the "theological dwarves" of the previous hundred years, whose attempts to accommodate faith to Enlightenment reason had produced "rootless little fungi," Modernists thought rigorously and delved deeply. They were not the theological "dealers in varnish and plaster" of the sort Kuyper had learned to detect at university. Dialectically, by its "bold negations" Modernism called the forgotten convictions of genuine Christianity back "from their grave," forced the church to find a real "connection with our age," and brought to light "all the passages of the mind and . . . [the] countless bypaths and side roads" of the world "that the church had not yet imbued with its Christian spirit." Notably, these three points — recovery, relevance, and comprehensive program — would constitute Kuyper's long-term agenda.

So also his attitude. In a sense, "Modernism has saved orthodoxy in the church of Jesus Christ," Kuyper argued, since without its challenges "we would still be groaning under the leaden weight of an all-killing Conservatism." Nor were historical dialectics the end of the matter. In contrast to its closest analogue on the American Calvinist side, J. Gresham Machen's *Christianity and Liberalism,* written fifty years later, Kuyper's speech did not argue by close textual analysis to show Modernism's propositional divergence from Scripture. Nor on this occasion did he posit a philosophical-theological defense of the supernatural as such. Rather, his history lesson led on to a phenomenological critique of the movement's claims and achievements. In short, Kuyper met Modernism on its own grounds of human religious experience.

It was appropriate, then, that Kuyper closed his speech with a summons to the gospel framed in personal memories. The firm footing of reality, he told his audience, lay in the incarnation of the Logos as stated in John 1: "The Word became flesh and dwelt among us." This was the realization that had awakened him, too, who had "once dreamed the dream of Modernism . . . [until] a gentle breeze from higher realms caused the horizon of my life to quiver and the truth appeared to me in the glory of my Lord and King." This sweet and gentle language, however, gave way in the next sentence to images of horror, tapping a different memory — and a continuing threat. There is "a poisonous snake which seeks to enter the hearts of us all," Kuyper warned, where it "sucks the last drop of lifeblood from our veins." Indeed, "that monster has wrapped itself around our age and crept into its breast." This beast was not the Morgana of Modernism but "Addiction to Doubt," not illusion but disillusion, and Kuyper shuddered at the toll it was taking: "I have seen its victims, have seen the enervated souls, the weak of heart who float along with the crowd, powerless to resist the tide, people who know only the momentary flush of excitement but are inwardly dying so that only a dissembling life can, for the moment, conceal their spiritual death."

This insight would be repeated a thousand times, in every mode of dress, from every point of view — national, philosophical, literary, of high taste and low — in European and American writing over the next seventy years. Kuyper in 1871 was indeed a pioneer modernist critic, even if his antidote remained manly combat of a late Victorian type: "As soon as principles that are contrary to your deepest convictions gain ground, then resistance is your duty and acquiescence a sin." But that tack did not always work. One historian attributes Kuyper's phobia toward doubt not only to his own struggles but also to his brother Herman's loss of faith in just these years. Try as he might, the older brother could not win back the younger by logical arguments. Masculine pose did not avail, either: Herman joined the real army — the Dutch military, soon to be at war in the East Indies.

The Birth of Politics

If Calvin provided the foundations that "banned all doubt," the new Kuyper insisted that the "edifice of faith" had to be remodeled in contemporary style. His reading to that end brought him in touch with a bracing new voice of Reformed orthodoxy, Herman Friedrich Kohlbrügge, pastor of an independent church across the German border. Kohlbrügge's radical message of all-sufficient grace, drawn straight from Calvin's pages and one day to be saluted by Karl Barth, cut through the cult of religious experience favored by Ethicals and conservative pietists alike. The correspondence the two began at this time makes Kohlbrügge's influence on Kuyper's development undeniable. Yet Kuyper talked little about that and much more about confrontations he had with certain parish "malcontents" who refused to attend his preaching, then turned his monitory visits into debating sessions. These were devotees of the later Reformation and its conventicle system, conversant with the "old writers" if with no one else and uncompromising in their predestinarian convictions. In one of his memoirs, Kuyper remembered becoming increasingly drawn to their model. Though uttered in the "coarse dialect [of] simple peasants," he said, their theology was "the same thing that Calvin gave me to read in his precise Latin." Even more, they evinced such "a well-ordered worldview, be it of the old Reformed type . . . [that] it seemed as if I were back in the classroom hearing my talented professor Scholten lecture about the 'doctrine of the Reformed church,' though with reversed sympathies."

Much later, fifty years after the fact, Kuyper identified a young woman, Pietje Baltus, as having been the most relentless interlocuter of them all and the key to his final conversion. He did not record Pietje by name at the time, however, and his gesture of 1914 might be ascribed to Kuyper's wish to curry favor with common folk at a stage in his political career when he was waxing especially anti-elitist. By the same token, however, the Kuyper of the 1860s had reason not to publicize the impact that an uneducated woman might have had on him as a newly minted doctor of divinity. He certainly knew the Baltus family at Beesd; Pietje's brother Herman would be a supporter of his on the church council. Perhaps the church-political connection, like the civil-political situation half a century later, was the real point. It crystallized what proved to be Kuyper's enduring dream. What if old-fashioned Calvinism, without being diluted in substance, were to "advance exegetically, psychologically, and historically" in form so as to become as current a program as the one offered by Modernism? And what might happen if the "simple peasants" loyal to the old faith won the right to vote?

The Dutch Reformed Church was poised at just that possibility in 1867, and Kuyper determined to make the most of it. The church reforms of 1842 had given twenty-five year notice that each local congregation was to decide for itself whether to assume more power in appointing elders and deacons (hence also pastors) or to leave that to the self-perpetuating councils that had long been in charge of parish affairs. If accepted, this augured a new autonomy for Protestants analogous to that attained by the Roman Catholics in 1853, and it galvanized some of the same controversy. Kuyper's passion for the democratic option led him to a step that would change his career as sharply as the recent crisis had his convictions. He published his first pamphlet for a national audience: "What Must We Do?"

The brochure supported popular rule with several layers of argumentation. First, Kuyper cast the issue under his newfound contest of ultimate principles. The decision about polity entailed support for either "the modern or the anti-modern life-conception," he said — either "the Judeo-Christian, divine-human, ethical world- and life-view" or one that was at bottom "heathen, humanistic, [and] aesthetic." He added a practical calculus of voting patterns that bore out this seeming abstraction. Modernists, appealing to the prosperous and educated, needed the protections of elite rule; orthodoxy was much more popular; thus, the politics of the Left would give pulpits over to the theology of the Right. With greater difficulty Kuyper's brochure had to make what would in fact be a startling change seem moderate and historically rooted. His church-historical skills helped some, but his conservative invocation of rights and precedents could not hide a stereotypically "revolutionary" appeal to abstract ideals. Since the priesthood of all believers was the starting point of the Reformed "church idea," Kuyper argued, a "democratic church form flows forth from it . . . wholly logically and consistently" — even though such had never been practiced in the Netherlands.

In another foretaste of polemics to come, Kuyper poured out contempt upon the current system. It was an "arbitrary caesaropapism," "oligarchical in marrow and bone," governed by "nepotism, hypocrisy, small-mindedness, and clerical pride." Count van Bylandt responded in turn, trying to obstruct the election at Beesd. When the vote was finally held, the congregation chose for popular rule and put four of Kuyper's strongest supporters onto the church council — including the "malcontent" Herman Baltus. Nationally, parishes started to freeze out Modernist ministers just as Kuyper had foreseen.

He did not tarry at Beesd to enjoy the fruits of victory, however. His brochure on top of his à Lasco book gained him favorable attention at Utrecht. He was installed there on November 10, 1867, at the venerable Domkerk, where the Netherlands' leading bishop had reigned in the Middle Ages, where the future Pope Adrian VI had worshipped as a child, and where Reformed traditionalists had since fashioned their citadel.

He and his hosts soon had reason to rue their decision — his hosts most of all. They were a well-placed, well-educated circle used to running their own show; they wanted Kuyper for his energy, not his own initiatives. Their national agenda called for the maintenance of solid morals, proper tone, and a unitary culture under the custodianship of the Reformed church. The most eminent of them, Nicolaas Beets, had conveyed these values in the poetry that made him famous earlier in the century, and now preached them from the pulpit that he invited the new arrival to share. Theologically, the Utrecht powers were Calvinists of congenial temperament, tending toward either the Ethical wing of the church or an "apologetic" school that tried to defend the essentials of Christian conviction by rational argument with opposing parties. They did not know about Kuyper's turn away from such approaches, nor fathom how ready he was to shake up their arrangements. He did not wait long to let them find out.

A High Churchman at Utrecht

Kuyper focused his inaugural sermon on the incarnation of Christ as "the life-principle of the church." That in itself did nothing to trouble the crowd, for the Ethicals liked the theme too. His second point was common enough as well: the church as the body of Christ continued the incarnation to the present, representing a whole new life that one day, as the Kingdom of God, would become all in all. The shoe began to pinch at the third step: a fully faithful and effective church had to be arrayed in and keep a close watch over its visible, institutional forms. This was a revolution for Kuyper, long a critic of "forms" as such. The "malcontents" at Beesd, the Ethicals at Utrecht, and the Modern Idealists at Leiden could all agree that it was the "invisible church" (whether that be the truly elect, the best of the human spirit, or the sacrality of conscience) that counted, just as the institutional church could be discounted. Kuyper now put forward the opposite claim as a clarion call to a new work. "An external church as a continuation of Christ's historical appearance has been absolutely needed for Christianity in every age." It was needed again, here and now.

In turning back toward the importance of the visible church, or a "high-church" position, Kuyper was part of a much larger company in nineteenth-century Europe, from neo-confessionalists in German Lutheranism to Anglican Tractarians to Protestant converts to Rome, with variations on all these themes playing out in the United States. In some cases the high-church impulse proceeded from the dynamics of personal salvation, in others from disgust with state interference with the church. Sometimes, as in Kuyper's case, the two went together. Whatever the source, the consequence was to elevate the rights and dignity of the church, its world-historical significance as the continuing body of Christ, and its authority over questions of truth and justice, as well as the need to purify its usages, fortify its leaders, and call its members to truer holiness. The ultimate statement of the case had appeared just as Kuyper made his turn to Calvin, in John Cardinal Newman's *Apologia pro Vita Sua* (1864). It was not Newman who sparked Kuyper's fire, however, but Charlotte Yonge in *The Heir of Redclyffe* and her pastor John Keble, who took leadership in the Tractarian movement after Newman went over to Rome.

With Kuyper, the Tractarian arrow hit its mark. We last saw him in tears of repentance prompted by the death of the noble Guy. Describing the ensuing burial service, Yonge wrote: "The word of peace rustled over the graves with the melodious sounds of the English Liturgy as his remains were laid to rest below the foliage of a beautiful chestnut tree, rendered a home by those words of his Mother church

— the mother who had guided each of his steps in his orphaned life." The passage struck Kuyper to the core: "That was what I wanted. Such a church I never saw or knew. . . . That was my homesickness, the thirst of my whole being." More specifically, "Guy had been touched by what we seem to have lost, by the lofty significance of the Sacrament, by the prescribed forms of private and public worship, by the impressive liturgy and the blessed 'Prayer-book.'" Kuyper might have been reading too far backward in claiming that *Redclyffe* "rooted" his yearnings for churchly forms "for all time." But he concluded this section of his memoir with a high-church declaration worthy of Newman himself: "From then on I have longed with all my soul for a sanctified Church wherein my soul and those of my loved ones can enjoy the quiet refreshment of peace, far from all confusion, under its firm, lasting, and authoritative guidance."

Kuyper's passion at this point was as acute as his anxiety over doubt, and it is worth exploring the connections between the two. Kuyper did not enjoy it when, apropos of his arguments with brother Herman over religion, their father observed that the older brother had always felt compelled to dominate his siblings. The alternative, to Kuyper's mind, was his father's typical waffling and the spiritual costs it had exacted from his sons. One of Bram's letters to Jo after reading *Redclyffe* explicitly associated her "gift of Guy" with childlike faith, and his farewell sermon at Beesd confessed that at his arrival there he had not completely recovered the lost faith of "my childhood days." His *Redclyffe* reflections attributed that loss to his lack of "such a church" as Guy's — "the mother who had guided each of his steps in his orphaned life" but now also, after his latest conversion, the "mother" that Calvin "had so beautifully [described] in the fourth book of his *Institutes*." That was the "church I never saw or knew," Kuyper rued. What he remembered instead was "the deceit, the hypocrisy, the unspiritual routine" of the church at Leiden where his father presided for twenty years.

The compliments Kuyper could accord Modernism he never lent to the Dutch Reformed hierarchy or the time-servers in the pulpit that he saw abetting its negligence. It is worth wondering, then, whether the acid in Kuyper's forthcoming critique of the Dutch Reformed Church was distilled from the passion to redeem that suborned "mother" from his father, who had slid into her arms for personal advantage. Such speculation can note that, over a lifetime of writing,

Kuyper cited Shakespeare more often than any other author, and *Hamlet* first among his plays. The vacillating son's "To be or not to be" Kuyper quoted in his conversion memoir; and exactly Hamlet's plea for the ghost of his true father to speak, Kuyper used as the litmus test of reality in his speech on "Modernism." Both sons indeed heard the ghost's command; in Kuyper's case it was the inner witness of the Holy Spirit. Both took action, with explosive results.

The particular measures that Kuyper proposed locate him more precisely on the high-church spectrum of his time. His liturgical reform was not the multi-sensory ceremony beloved of Anglo-Catholics but literal adherence to prescribed formularies, especially at baptism — this both to create a common, familiar order and to enforce Trinitarian language against Modernist deviation. In polity he protested less against the state (the Tractarians' foe) than against the church's own "yoke of synodical hierarchy," so his solution was to amplify the power of local congregations. At his initiative the Utrecht church council sent a petition up the denominational chain of command, urging strict enforcement of the baptismal formulary. They got back a compromise that Kuyper found typically empty: the Synod requested pastors to keep "arbitrary departures" to a minimum for the sake of conscience and good order.

His next move raised a "great commotion in the land." When the Synod sent its annual questionnaire to the Utrecht consistory, Kuyper persuaded them not to answer on the grounds that "these questions are put by a Synod with whose current dignitaries the Council has no fellowship of belief or confession." He followed up with two new pamphlets putting his case to a national audience. By not enforcing confessional discipline, he argued, the Synod had exposed itself as either incompetent or illegitimate — and the twists and turns by which that body tried to reply gave some warrant to the charge. It first temporized by deciding to put the question of orthodoxy to church councils only on the triennial visit made by its personal representatives; then, in successive years, it heard, rejected, heard again and accepted, only to subsequently reject again, then entertain again, motions to drop the question entirely.

Yet when Kuyper pushed for still further defiance, none of the other Utrecht clergy supported him. Part of their reason was that by this time Kuyper had also become involved in civil politics and in its most divisive question, public education. The details of that controversy must wait for the next chapter; for now it is enough to say that he espoused there the same voluntarist position as in his ecclesiastical policy. Church and school alike, he insisted, needed to be freed from the dead hand of establishment, be it synod or state. If rendered responsible to their local constituents, they would become more vibrant, honest, and effective, delivering at once the safety that conservatives wanted and the progress dear to liberals. The Utrecht powers recognized that voluntarism also spelled pluralism, however, and they were not ready to take that step. Some, Kuyper's strongest foes, were opposed on principle. Their heart still lay with the ideal of a unitary culture upheld by a common church and school, and if the official Reformed character of the first and Christian character of the second had to be stretched to cover increasing diversity in society, that was an accommodation they were prepared to make. Kuyper was not; in fact, he called it a formula for atrophy. Thus, when he received a call to Amsterdam in 1870, both parties were glad that he accepted it.

Preparing for the Capital

He did not leave quietly. His farewell sermon at Utrecht, along with his first two he gave at Amsterdam, delivered Kuyper's full and final answer to the "church question," a bold portrait of a Reformed church that was to be at once progressive and orthodox, confessional and activist, democratic and disestablished. By the standards of the day — and of much subsequent history — the first two pairs were each contradictory, and the three together an unlikely mélange. It took all of Kuyper's visionary capacity to make them cohere. Calvin would marry à Lasco.

Kuyper's Utrecht farewell, delivered on July 31, made the case for progressive orthodoxy; more precisely, it disrupted the equation that his audience assumed between the two terms in his title, "Conservatism and Orthodoxy." Christianity did have a preservative nature, Kuyper granted, and Dutch patriots were properly allergic to the destruction wreaked by "revolution." Still, conservatism was wrong theologically, precisely by virtue of the reality of sin, for the heritage of the past bore the fruits of depravity as well as the wisdom of the ages. Moreover, conservatism bred bad strategy. Three errors were particularly rife at Utrecht, Kuyper observed. The ultra-Calvinists insisted on re-instituting literal formulas from the past, dooming themselves to irrelevance in the present. The heirs of the Réveil were content with souvenirs, invoking a religious spirit that made for a pious "circle of friends" but lacking the clear theological definition required to make a "church." As for the Apologists, they were content with whatever their opponents left them. Having sacrificed the initiative to their hungry opponents, they necessarily sacrificed more and more of the heritage they meant to maintain.

Back of all these schools, and back of Kuyper's counterproposal, lay the question of "spirit" and "form" that had preoccupied him since his university days. His answer sounded German in its ontology and its remarkable confidence in historical development. The "principle" at the "core" of a spirit naturally produces an appropriate form for its "expression in life," he declared, but for a body to stay vital its forms had to evolve with the age. Neglecting forms, Ethicals and Apologists doomed themselves to impotence; neglecting development, the "repristinators" did the same. That the Reformed confessional heritage, firmly asserted, was the necessary form of a vibrant church, his own work among them had demonstrated, he ventured. That the confessional "principle" must be reborn in the "life-form" which history bequeathed to their own times was the meaning of the incarnational theme on which his Utrecht ministry had begun. That Christ's incarnation had its fulfillment in his resurrection spelled out the dynamic promise, the lure of God's future, toward which their own share in the energies of the age ought to be dedicated. "Christ posits an all-embracing and absolute *principle* [*beginsel*]," he punned; "from him a whole new life derives its *beginning*." That "germ of life . . . can regenerate the world, and you are the ones called to bring that life to the world."

Kuyper's debut at Amsterdam the next Sunday advanced this analysis with a new metaphor: the church was a body both "rooted" as an organism and "grounded" as a human institution. It could engage the future safely under the doctrinal supervision of the church "institute," where the weekly rounds of worship, instruction, and administrative routine were conducted. But all that was to serve the "church organic" — believers engaged in the work of the world, collectively witnessing to Christ on weekdays as well as Sundays.

This became so characteristic a Kuyperian theme that it is important to register its provenance. Kuyper had been playing with the idea already at Beesd, disturbed by Allard Pierson's complaint that Christianity was irrelevant to modern life. He had sounded it more boldly in his Utrecht inaugural: "No area of life remains alien to the Christian!" It was full blown by the time of his departure: "Christ does not tolerate our living a double life: our lives must be one, controlled by one principle." His Amsterdam inaugural outlined the ecclesiology to sustain this insight. It also added a fourth party to the conservative schools faulted on his Utrecht list. This was the capital's Evangelical band, which had long been proselytizing Jews, sending missionaries abroad, and trying to evangelize the urban wilderness around them. Noble enterprises, Kuyper assured them, but too fixed on individual conversion. Vital as that was, the quality of the whole — of the church as a body, and of that body in the world — was the ultimate point.

That said, it is also true that Kuyper did not flesh out his theology of Christian action or his ecclesiology of "institute" and "organism" for another twenty-five years, in the 1890s. He was busy in the meantime with the practicalities of movement-building. The church organic turned out to need a greenhouse to grow in, and Kuyper devoted his next two decades to its construction and operation. Meanwhile, his Amsterdam inaugural sermon was so novel and complex as to leave his audience confused. He returned to familiar ground the next week by serving up his supporters a rousing sermon on divine election. Why had this doctrine, once deemed "the heart of the church," fallen into such neglect? Because of its adherents as well as its foes, he answered. The latter caricatured the tenet as cruel; the former made it seem fatalistic. True orthodoxy needed instead to recall the teaching's original purpose of providing comfort to the faithful, assuring them that their salvation lay not in their own fallible hands but in those of a gracious Sovereign. The tensions that necessarily marked the church — institute and organism, orthodox and activist, progressive and confessional — likewise could be harmonized so long as the common root of all these elements in divine election was remembered. Most of all, he concluded, the modern descendants of John Calvin would find at just this point the vital power needed to motivate their ceaseless service for the glory of God. Thirty years later the German sociologist Max Weber would make the same point to a larger world.

With these three sermons, Kuyper's conceptual set was virtually complete. Principial analysis, principial antithesis, principle extrapolating into world- and life-view, the church growing out of the incarnation of Christ and, bearing its dual character of institute and organism, radiating into "every terrain of life" empowered by the mandate of election — the salient themes of Kuyper's life work emerged in one creative outburst between 1865 and 1870. By any measure it was a remarkable achievement.

It also left him with a daunting personal agenda. Where should he begin? What should he *not* do? The questions were amplified by his relocation to Amsterdam, where the theological strains were greater than at Utrecht and the establishment well apprised of Kuyper's means and ends. The leading pastor in town wrote him a letter of warning to that effect. A more sympathetic observer thought that the greater diversity, and the city's greater need, afforded greater room to maneuver.

A Pastor in Politics

Certainly Amsterdam was religiously under-served. The Dutch Reformed Church there had ten buildings, twenty-eight clergy, a 140-member council, and virtually no parish work. Of its 130,000 nominal members, barely five percent attended weekly worship. Its finances were dropping even faster than attendance — down 50 percent just in the 1860s. The situation was likely to get worse: the city's population was finally beginning to grow again, but no new church had been constructed for almost 150 years.

The ten ministers called to the city over the previous twenty years were all Modernists; Kuyper was the first ardent Calvinist in memory, and the first called under the new democratic system. He was assigned to a district west of the canal-ringed center of town, but as relatively few of his followers resided there, they traveled across the city to attend his services, sometimes packing a lunch in order to hear both of his sermons. They chose his slot in the rotation to present their children for baptism; he might administer the rite to seventy or eighty at a time. Besides his pulpit duties, Kuyper hosted the usual catechism sessions for children and began Bible studies for adult women.

He had to attend to the general population as well. His district put some 7,000 souls under his care, many unschooled in the rudiments of the faith, most absent from services, and too many suffering from the early stages of Dutch industrialization. With another young pastor Kuyper created a new system of lay parish-care teams to attend to these needs. Two years later, when he moved near the docks on the east side, he brought some of these assistants along and turned them into an efficient machine to relieve his busy schedule.

As everyone expected, Kuyper also turned his skills to mobilizing the confessional cause. He focused on the consistory's lay elders, emphasizing their equality as officers with the clergy to whom they had typically deferred. He formed his sympathizers into a caucus to coordinate voices and votes ahead of time, much to the disgust of traditionalists.

In fact, these "moderates" — of orthodox hue but traditionalist disposition — proved to be his most consistent opposition, for on some issues Kuyper made common cause with the Modernists. Both he and they wanted to devolve more control over congregational activities to the parish level, away from the city-wide council and especially from the synodical boards. They sometimes maneuvered together on new pastoral appointments out of a common hostility to the powers in place. On liturgical reform Kuyper went forward on his own, pressing for baptismal uniformity (motion defeated) and for more solemn and frequent — even weekly — celebration of the Lord's Supper (issue tabled). After the council had been fully democratized in 1871, Kuyper could organize a bare majority without Modernist support. He then set out against their preaching, as it "undermines the very foundation of the church." After appealing in vain to the authorities to enforce confessional discipline, his caucus put forward a slate of seventeen elders who pledged henceforth to boycott any service at which a Modernist pastor participated.

The maneuvering wore on everybody, especially the moderates who yearned for the peaceful, pre-democratic days before 1867. When they circulated a mass petition against the new order, Kuyper replied with brochures repeating his church-historical arguments for democratization and local control. He then added a 100-page book that joined that case to a narrative of his own conversion. It was entitled *Confidentie* ("Confidentially") — and was published to a nationwide market. Finally, he produced a plan to end all the wrangling. It divided the city into five districts, assigning two to the orthodox, two to the Modernists, and one to the moderates. Each parish would be largely autonomous, responsible for its own religious, educational, and social services. Kuyper believed such a plan was the key to making them more vigorous and effective. Likewise, worship attendance would improve as laity developed stronger bonds with their local church. He defended the plan politically as an equitable division between different parties in the church, each of which had a right to exist but none of which could flourish if constrained by the others. Localist, pluralist, accountable, vital — Kuyper's motion fit all his ideals. It was telling, then, that the council turned him down flat. They argued unity and tradition; they also meant to keep control of appointments and properties.

All the while Kuyper had to meet the expectations for national leadership that came with his call to the capital. Journalism seemed the best avenue, for the States General had just cancelled a per-copy tax on newspapers and magazines, making a mass-circulation press viable for the first time. In October 1870 he assumed editorship of *De Heraut* ("The Herald"), an old Réveil magazine for Jewish evangelism which he turned into an organ devoted to "a free church and a free school in a free Netherlands." "Free school" meant speaking out on state as well as church affairs, and his taking on such subjects led to requests that he stand for Parliament. In May 1871, after much inner turmoil, Kuyper acceded. While he professed great relief when he lost, the experience made him wonder what might be done with effective organization. By April 1872 he had support in place for a separate daily newspaper to concentrate on politics. Its name, *De Standaard,* evoked the banner of the armies of the Lord, but Kuyper also meant it to define proper Reformed opinion nationwide. With *De Heraut* appearing as its Sunday supplement, Kuyper now had a public forum seven days a week. That did not keep him from publishing sermons, polemical brochures, and his first volume of Bible studies on the side.

It was no wonder, then, that illness became as common a feature as work at the Kuyper residence. The pattern began with their move to the city when Jo, seven months pregnant, was hospitalized for angina. She managed to give birth to Henriëtte Sophia Susanna, named after both their mothers, in October 1870, but was pregnant again in a year. She miscarried in January 1872, was soon pregnant again, and delivered Abraham Jr., their fourth child, that November. Kuyper himself seemed to get sick every winter and verged on collapse every time his work load was compounded by personal stress. He took the same cure as at university. In the wake of Jo's miscarriage, he was off to London.

When deciding whether to run for Parliament in 1871, he went to Switzerland for a month, visiting Kohlbrügge en route but also Allard Pierson, "Holland's Hamlet," with whom he discussed his "Modernism" address. In January 1873 he took a water cure for sore throat and rheumatism, but after baring his soul in *Confidentie* that summer, he needed two months of recuperation in the Alps. The stench of Amsterdam's canals contributed to the problem (Jo fled for sea breezes in her latest pregnancy), but the housemaids back in Beesd already had voiced alarm at the long hours Kuyper kept. There he had been trying to finish à Lasco while searching the Reformed fathers for footing on polity, liturgy, and doctrine. Now he faced questions of career besides.

It boiled down to pulpit vs. politics. His parliamentary candidacy in 1871 came at the insistence of Groen van Prinsterer, who we will see had emerged by this time as something of a surrogate father to Kuyper. But Kuyper was again having doubts about his clerical calling, just like ten years before. His frustration with the Amsterdam church council made him wonder whether "holding true to principles will be possible" in the ecclesiastical strife to come. "Don't forget," he needlessly reminded Jo, "I'm prickly. . . . As the battle proceeds and people turn bitter against me . . . might I not become bitter and misanthropic myself?" An opposite assessment came from a pastor-colleague in the Amsterdam church, a Modernist who wanted him to stay. I have never seen the insincerity others have alleged in you, he wrote Kuyper, but I wonder "whether you are completely honest *with yourself.* . . . Your special pleading and dialectics sometimes give me the impression that you might not be *serious* enough" in self-assessment to see that "the devil of ambition is sometimes too strong for you and that your genuine holy enthusiasm . . . sometimes makes you one-sided." Could you, then, really remain upright on "so slippery and dangerous a field as *political* life?"

While the voters mooted the question in 1871, it never went away. Kuyper gave himself a crash course in political theory and started tracking voting patterns in likely districts. Opportunity dawned again in December 1873 when, the day after submitting his plural-parish plan to the Amsterdam consistory, Kuyper agreed to run for an open seat in the lower house of the States General. He won — and promptly entered another crisis of conscience. Active clergy were prohibited from taking parliamentary posts, so accepting office as politician would entail emeritation as minister. Petitions from his parishioners asked him to stay. A letter from his closest friend at university, the liberal minister Isaac Hooykaas, told the truth: "In your whole ecclesiastical bearing and history lies *much* more the statesman than the churchman. . . . There would be something forced, against your nature, if you should decline." On February 10, 1874, Kuyper officially accepted his seat. He preached his farewell at Amsterdam on the ides of March and was installed in Parliament on March 20. One month later his brother Herman died in combat in the East Indies, as far away from the faith as he was from home.

CHAPTER FOUR

The Young Politician

Kuyper's political career would last so long and become so absorbing that it might seem to have been destined from the start. Already before friends told him that politics was his true métier, his talent as an organizer and orator was evident in his church work. These were not necessarily relevant in the Netherlands' pre-democratic situation of 1870, however, nor did his conservative Orangist heritage seem to offer much promise for a more progressive future. The Calvinist line he had recently joined featured some outright reactionary strains. Kuyper had no formal political education to speak of, nor any in economics or social theory. Theology, his passion to this point, seemed an unlikely portal into statecraft. His future lay in turning these very limitations to his advantage.

Kuyper's reason for turning to politics in the first place can be understood in the same light as his conversion to Calvinism at Beesd. If Europe stood at the edge of a precipice ending in rank materialism, and if that materialism, like its Christian alternative, was ultimately a matter of conviction, then the realm of ideas was decisive, and culture-forming institutions were the key sites of struggle. Kuyper had come to Utrecht focused on the church as the first of those institutions. But the school was just as important, and the explosion he set off in 1869 at an Utrecht convention on public education marked his entrée into an issue that would be the most decisive in Dutch national politics for the rest of the century. Nothing was more instrumental than Kuyper's agitation in making "the school question" so significant, nor any issue more instrumental in triggering the democratization of Dutch political life. In the process all sides of the man would be on full display: the organizational genius, which created the Netherlands' first mass-circulation newspaper and first popular political party; the quick mind, which acquired political theory with startling facility; the charisma by which, in observers' eyes and his own, his person became identical with the cause; and the nervous exhaustion which loomed as this phase of his crusade came to a crisis in 1875.

Liberal Capitalism, at Home and Abroad

Kuyper's politics would matter well beyond the exertions of a strong personality in a small country because the European — indeed, the global — stage was being reset precisely as he made his political debut. In the 1860s the Netherlands was seeing significant population growth for the first time in generations. It was also at the start of an economic boom triggered by a quarter-century of capital investment in infrastructure. The railroad reached obscure villages like Beesd during Kuyper's tenure there, and by the mid-1870s every decent-sized city was within a day's travel of any other. The Dutch telegraph network was completed at the same time, and postal rates fell as volume increased. In short, the political Kuyper was made possible by the country's first fully integrated communications and transportation system. The economy soared with the completion of signal projects like the North Sea Canal to Amsterdam in 1866 and with the linkup of Dutch transport with the German system; volumes in the Rhine trade would increase some 6,000 percent from 1870 to 1914.

The first signs of modern industrialism, already two generations old in neighboring Belgium, were finally appearing in the Netherlands, too, but these were not nearly as significant for the economy as was deregulation of the colonial trade. As the mercantilist "cultivation system" gave way to free markets, huge capital investment flowed to the East Indies, and huge private profits returned. The shift brought less benefit to the native peoples than promised, however, and Dutch free traders were soon demanding massive military intervention in Aceh province, where Dutch hegemony had never been sealed. The ensuing war, launched in 1873, would drag on for thirty years, putting colonial policy next to education on the national agenda.

Expanded markets at home and abroad were the fairest fruit of

Liberal hegemony in Dutch politics since 1848. This was classic, nineteenth-century Liberalism, of course, similar to much of what would pass as "conservatism" a century later in the era of Reagan and Thatcher. Its Dutch acolytes were called "doctrinaires" because of their appeal to such thinkers as John Stuart Mill, but in fact they were quite pragmatic and adaptive. They did hold consistently, even religiously, to the "sanctity" of private property and the policies of free markets and free trade. They cherished civil liberties and asserted parliamentary over against monarchical prerogatives. They pushed the extension of a simple, uniform set of laws to every corner of the kingdom, erasing local exceptions and special privileges. In short, they stood for the standardization and rationalization of society and economy that are hallmarks of "modernization."

Two additional Latinate labels came along in the process. Though not uniformly free-thinkers, Liberals in Kuyper's era promoted *secularization:* socially, because the church was the ultimate in privileged corporations; intellectually, because the rationality behind economics should also erase the superstition and obscurantism endemic to religion. From their position atop business and the professions, the Liberals also promoted the *centralization* that integrated the nation into a coherent whole, promoted the efficiency of uniform standards, and (not incidentally) extended their own authority. Thus, while Liberalism had been born out of resistance to state power, and while the mid-nineteenth-century version of Liberalism continued to voice that suspicion, Liberals on the ground were rarely — and the mid-century Dutch version least of all — averse to using government to promote their interests: to improve infrastructure (see railroads and canals), extend and integrate markets (see the East Indies), and otherwise accelerate economic growth. By 1870 investment in human capital — especially education — stood as the next frontier. That called forth a "Progressive" wing in Dutch Liberalism, dedicated to carrying out the secularist agenda as part of "improving" the school system.

All these were Dutch currents in a continent-wide tide that was now cresting. The third quarter of the nineteenth century was a golden age of industrial expansion across Europe, beginning in the north and radiating east and south. From the end of the revolutions of 1848 to the crash of 1873, the European economy experienced a rarely equaled boom signified by the same icons of steam, iron, telegraph, and rail that were spreading across the Netherlands. Dutch population increases were about average for the continent; their Liberal economic policy was par for the course; their increases in foreign trade, both next door and around the world, were typical of an era in which the global economy became truly integrated for the first time. Concludes historian E. J. Hobsbawm: "Never did Europeans dominate the world more completely and unquestionably than in the third quarter of the nineteenth century." The dominion was that of industrial capitalism, and its values were those of the "victorious bourgeois order": reason, science, technology, and progress. The engine, the dominion, and the value system would last a very long time. Kuyper's work commenced at the peak of its first triumphs.

He could also witness its political portents firsthand. His research sortie down the Rhine in 1866 was thwarted by the mobilization of German troops on their way to the Austrian front. He saw the same thing in 1870, during the Franco-Prussian War. This was national unification German-style, a model being duplicated simultaneously in Italy. In the United States it came not by foreign but by civil war; in Japan by an elite coup in the Meiji "restoration"; in Russia by tsarist fiat.

Typically, the political integration of the 1860s led on to coercive cultural integration in the 1870s, with a particularly hard edge in education. It did not surprise Kuyper's fellow Calvinists when the newly declared French republic took vengeance upon the church along with its other conservative opponents in an anticlerical offensive that would culminate in 1905, when the public schools were fully secularized. More complicated was the *kulturkampf* upon Roman Catholic institutions in the new German Empire launched by its "Iron," but also seemingly pious, Chancellor Otto von Bismarck. This was a "culture war" indeed, conducted by conservatives for purpose of unity and good order. It began with the expulsion of the Jesuits and the dissolution of most religious orders, and it hoped ultimately to usurp church authority over marriage and parish appointments. In between it attempted state censorship of sermons and church publications. The attack upon Catholic schools — or public schools as de facto Catholic institutions — was especially pointed and provoked the stoutest resistance, a resistance that eventually caused Bismarck to drop his offensive and come to an understanding with the Vatican. The Dutch school struggle unfolded at exactly the same time.

From Church to School

The Dutch case was a Liberal offensive that suffered from excess confidence and ideological contradictions; in the end it inadvertently created possibilities for a wholesale political realignment. Ever since the 1848 Constitution ordained religious equality, Dutch Catholics had allied with the document's Liberal authors, an alliance reinforced by Conservatives' support of the 1853 anti-papist April Movement. The alignment held so long as the Liberal regime stuck to its economic agenda. But when Pope Pius IX denounced all things Liberal in the 1864 *Syllabus of Errors,* and when Dutch Catholics turned out enthusiastically to defend the papal territories during the wars of Italian unification, the coalition started to dissolve. The school wars finished the job. The pope singled out secular education as a particular danger; the Progressive Liberals pressed secularization nonetheless, then added symbolic insult to substantive injury by dropping diplomatic recognition of the Vatican in 1870. Suddenly, Dutch Catholics were political free agents.

But again, as after the crisis of 1853, the Conservative opposition bungled the opportunity. Theirs had to be a normatively Protestant nation, so they could not appeal to the Catholics. Theirs was also a generic Protestantism, however, with no taste for confessional strictures, little clue about the knots of the school question, and an outright aversion to religious activism in politics. Like many of the name before and since, Dutch Conservatives could value religion less for themselves than for other people, particularly for the lesser sorts who needed its social discipline. Well-born, such Conservatives did not need to be born again, but they did need some warrant to remain in what they took to be their rightful place atop the social pyramid that nature (or God, or history) had ordained. Yet "progress," which the genuinely religious elements among them were supporting with mass literacy campaigns and moral education, was undoing "nature," and the new economy held little promise for their customary base of royal administrators, old rentiers, and big barons in the countryside. Thus, Conservatives had no interest in mass politics but also, absent some mass support, no way to challenge the Liberal elite of the new order. Kuyper's project was to organize just such a movement on the basis of religion instead of class and to make it the chief rival to Liberalism in Dutch politics.

It was into this matrix that Kuyper made his dramatic debut in civil politics. In May 1869 the Union for Christian National Education held its annual convention at Utrecht and assigned the keynote address to the new local star of pulpit and press. Since Kuyper was known by now for his polemics in church politics, there could not have been much surprise when he used the occasion to pry open the fault-line in the Union's vision and purpose.

In doing so he exposed a tension that went back to the mixed mandate for education set by the 1848 Constitution. That text had kept the standing provision that public schools train youth in all the "Christian and social virtues" but added that this be done without offense to the conscience of any pupil or parent. The Réveil political wing led by Groen van Prinsterer had argued from the start that the formula was not viable, waffling as it did between a watered-down moralism too weak for committed believers and an implicitly established religion that oppressed dissenters. His solution was to split the system along Protestant and Catholic lines, permitting each side to educate on the basis of their own convictions. Liberals wanted to continue secularizing education, however, while the Réveil's traditionalist wing did not want to give up the residual Protestant hegemony of the unitary public school. Over Groen's objections a compromise was proposed in 1857 for the state to fund a "neutral" system with subsidies for private religious schools. The States General passed the bill — but dropped the subsidies. Groen resigned from Parliament in disgust and turned instead to building a national network that might eventually force a change in the law and meanwhile would assist privately funded Christian schools. The Union attracted parties sympathetic to one or the other of these two purposes, but not necessarily both. Groen's intention to force the political agenda accounted for Kuyper's being awarded the opening speech at the 1869 convention.

He started by carefully working both sides of the room. Calvinism had sounded the "tonic note" of the chord of the nation in the wars of independence, he declared, and it had preserved ever since the ethic that lay at the bedrock of Dutch national character. But the Reformed now had to recognize, he continued, that "our old Holland" is no longer "the Netherlands of our day." The recent "flowering of Catholic life" and the emergence of a "mixed" population (meaning liberal Protestants and free-thinkers) required a frank acknowledgement that "we are a minority." How to resolve the tension? By recognizing that it was Calvinism that had stamped upon "our folk-character" the principle of "rights for all and freedom for each." That is, Calvinism was not an erstwhile establishment, but a philosophy of diversity. Accordingly, the Union ought to work for a full and fair pluralization of the public schools, even beyond Groen's proposal of 1857. Unfortunately, that would require the Reformed to demand state subsidies for their own schools and so appear to be driven by self-interest. All the more reason, then, that they keep God, country, and the poor foremost in their minds. God, because believers were obliged to educate their children in the faith. Country, because a withering of the "core of the nation" would erode the character upon which Holland's liberty and prosperity depended. The poor, because such could not afford private religious schools and so were forced to choose between their conscience and their children's education.

Two mixed pairs in this his maiden voyage into national politics would echo for the rest of Kuyper's career: a tension regarding whether Calvinism should be a privileged "core" or pluralistic part of society, and a double helix of conscience and social justice in his warrant for reform. For now, the speech set off two days of discussion that devolved into open rancor. Utrecht had been the capital of the anti-Catholic April Movement, and some ultra-Calvinists in the crowd, along with those for whom Protestantism and patriotism were synonymous, denounced the idea of subsidizing Catholic schools. Harsher yet was an exchange between Kuyper and Nicolaas Beets, dean of the Utrecht pulpit. Beets opined that a "neutral" school teaching traditional ethics from generally theistic principles could render a valuable service. Kuyper replied, in what would become a lasting slogan, that the supposedly "neutral" school was in fact a "sect school of Modernism," with a Christian veneer as dishonorable as it was thin. Even worse, its underlying premises — naturalism in the curriculum and state monopoly over children — made the whole system "satanic." If the state insisted on one school for all, he thundered, it would have to multiply its jails to accommodate all the parents who would be prisoners of conscience. Beets responded that such rhetoric was "demonic." For his part, Groen made his support of Kuyper clear. With that the Réveil really did come to an end, and the Ethicals and Confessionals parted ways.

By this time strong personal as well as policy bonds linked Kuyper and Groen. Despite their disparity in social class (Groen's inherited wealth allowed him to fund his own newspaper and buy a townhouse at the heart of The Hague, overlooking the prime minister's residence and the halls of Parliament), Kuyper struck Groen as the talent able to pick up his flagging cause and take it into an age of mass movements. Kuyper had originally written Groen from Beesd for help with his à Lasco research, but the relationship quickened in April 1867, when Groen sent him a note of thanks for his first pamphlet on church reform. Kuyper's neediness was manifest in the long letter he sent off the very next day detailing his conversion, theological development, and sense of spiritual isolation. A burst of correspondence ensued, including an exchange of portraits. Kuyper quickly brought things to an intimate emotional plane. "The warm interest in my person and lot in life" that your letter so "unexpectedly shared," he wrote Groen, "gives my heart promise enough of love . . . to make it feel quickened and refreshed." Your spiritual kinship "has fulfilled a wish that I had almost given up out of the many disappointments with which I had to struggle." Those disappointments included potential friends lost to his ecclesiastical polemics — also his father, with whom a parishioner remembers Kuyper arguing politics in the Beesd parlor.

If Groen was heartened by finding so promising an acolyte as Kuyper, Kuyper clearly found in Groen, who was born the same year as Jan Frederik, a paternal model he could admire. After all, Groen could show a career of conviction, not compromise; of reform, not routine; of full Calvinism, not vague piety. The fellowship he had never experienced at home Kuyper found in the frequent visits he made to Groen in The Hague and in a correspondence that would run to 500 letters in little over eight years.

In Praise of Diversity

Groen was also instrumental in Kuyper's education in political theory — instrumental but not, as sometimes argued, in control. Already a month before the tumultuous Union meeting in Utrecht, Kuyper had laid out the baseline of his sociopolitical thought in the first of what turned out to be a lifelong series of "state-of-the-culture" addresses. This one was titled "Uniformity: The Curse of Modern Life," and it sounded a full-throated cry against the culture of globalization, homogenization, and centralization that was emerging under the new political economy. Against that, it celebrated "multiform diversity . . . [as the] deepest principle of natural life." Rhetorically, the speech was a catalogue of Romantic values, celebrating the wild over the tamed, the free-forming over the calculated, the unique individual over the standardized type, and above all the organic over the mechanical. To witness the design of God, urged the new-born Calvinist, go to the "wild forest" and see

> the crooked trunks, the twisted branches, the mingling colors, the endless variety of shades, and note how it is precisely in the whimsical interplay of colors and lines that unity is revealed in its finest expression. But what is our age doing? On the model of [an] iron fence, it trims frolicsome shrubbery into a smooth hedge and prunes those wild trunks to the very top. . . . The *average* is the standard to which it artificially elevates the one and forcibly flattens others, which explains the mediocrity of modern life.

Kuyper could have been quoting the manifestos of the insurgent Impressionist painters gathering at the same time (1869) in Paris when he continued: as "the flourishing of the arts is the true measure of the vitality of an era," the age stands condemned for being "almost totally devoid of artistic talent of any kind, poverty-stricken in aesthetic vitality, and totally destitute of great artistic creations."

He applied the same critique to city architecture, bewailing Amsterdam's urban sprawl and Baron Haussman's modernization of Paris. He bemoaned the passing of folk costume to the cult of fashion, the standardization of manners across age and sex, the mongrelization of language brought by increased international contact. Even the heroism of war was blighted: "No longer an intrepid mind and a chivalrous heart but the reliability of a gun and the caliber of the weapon decide the battle." All this portends "the disappearance of the human personality. It is finally machines, not people, that you see in motion . . . machines all put together in the same way, operating by the same drill." Bourgeois society, though premised on liberty and the individual, was destroying both.

Kuyper prefaced these ruminations with ideological analysis he was learning from Groen. It was "the Revolution" that lay at the bottom of the blight, Kuyper proclaimed; it was the Revolutionary spirit that, by insinuating itself into the human heart, aimed to realize the age-old dream of world empire more effectively than had the crude old method of military conquest. Ironically, this part of his speech reads today as abstractly as the Revolutionary ideologues whom Groen faulted, and is redeemed only by Kuyper's color tour of the current scene. Yet the logic Kuyper saw at work is endorsed by the neo-Marxian Eric Hobsbawm's observation that by 1870, under the convergence of *two* Revolutions — French and Industrial — a Liberal capitalist system was beginning to standardize the world so that, for all the era's movements of national unification, there were diminishing prospects of genuine national distinctiveness.

That specter troubled Kuyper the most as he moved to the applicatory part of his oration. If the railroads of international commerce "do not facilitate the lively exchange of our own thoughts but have to serve the monotonous exchange of standardized ideas, then the soul of a people is lost." Prussia and France ("The uniformity of Caesarism . . . [and] the uniformity of Cosmopolitanism") continued to be the worst threats from outside, but spiritual lassitude posed the gravest problem within. Thus, the "national will" had to be "anchored" in God's will, and "godliness," not armaments, had to be the "primary weapon in the struggle for independence." To revitalize that godliness Kuyper invoked his two current initiatives. For the church question, "I know of no other solution than to accept — freely and candidly, without any reservations — a free multiformity" of religious organization in public life. As to schools, he called his audience "not to oppose the mixed [secular] form of education for those who want it, but to challenge the supremacy, the monopoly, of the mixed school and to demand alongside of it equal and generous legal space for every life-expression [worldview or fundamental conviction] that desires its own form of education." "Indeed," he continued, "our unremitting intent should be to demand justice for all, to do justice to every life-expression." Likewise, just as the Dutch themselves ought to guard against "Anglomania" in applying their own constitution, so they ought "to oppose with vigor the attempts to structure our colonies by [Dutch] standards" and seek rather to enable the "Javanese" to protect their own way of life.

Political Theory

To qualify as Groen's heir, Kuyper needed better command of anti-revolutionary theory proper; to take that theory into a democratic future, he had to redeem it from its reactionary strains. Back of both the tradition and the problem stood the ferociously counter-revolutionary poet, William Bilderdijk (1756-1831). During the Restoration, Bilderdijk had written Romantic paeans to Dutch heritage and the House of Orange, but before that, during the French occupation, he had inscribed odes to Louis Bonaparte and even to Napoleon for restoring law and order. Bilderdijk despised constitutions as such, squabbling parliaments, the solvents of rationalism, the specter of democracy, the tide of progress, the nightmare of technology — really, anything tied to the Enlightenment — and took shelter in history, nostalgia, fantasy, feeling, and faith. He endorsed Calvinism because it was old, Orangist, and authoritarian. This vision he had inculcated in a circle of young alienated aristocrats who gathered for his private seminars on the "history of the fatherland." Some of them produced tracts in the same vein, notably *Protest against the Spirit of the Age* (1823) by Isaac da Costa. Kuyper never tired of quoting Da Costa's poetry or celebrating Bilderdijk's scorched-earth spirit, as well as his contempt for compromise and his holistic vision of a radically different world. The challenge was to make these usable for progressive ends.

Da Costa had begun the adaptation after Bilderdijk's death, coincident with the humiliation of the Belgian Revolution. His biblical millenarianism led him to look for portents of the end times, which made the birth of the Evangelical Alliance in the early 1840s appear especially promising. He began to measure European developments in the Alliance's anti-Catholic light — England and Prussia were good, France and the papacy bad — and even welcomed the revolutionary spring of 1848 for discomfiting "papist" Paris and Vienna. Groen took a more skeptical path. Having been introduced by Merle d'Aubigné to Edmund Burke as well as to Reformation history, his policies were less progressive than Da Costa's, but his theoretical weight was more substantial and of greater salience for the long run. Thus, Groen was just as suspicious of "Protestant" Prussia's ambitions as of "papist" France's, and pondered not only the immediate goals but the logical trajectory of "democratic progress" as it unfolded (to cite 1848) from the springtime of the peoples to the summer of the radicals to the winter of reaction.

Kuyper got his reading list in political theory from Groen. In September 1869, five months after delivering "Uniformity," Kuyper wrote that he was digging into Burke. Groen recommended next the German Lutheran Friedrich Julius Stahl and French Protestant François Guizot. A few years later Kuyper wrote that he was absorbing the French liberal Alexis de Tocqueville and Catholic Félicité Lamennais. But these were all supplementary to Groen's own *Lectures on Unbelief and Revolution,* published in 1847. Like other signal works that had appeared at that outburst of revolutionary zeal — *The Communist Manifesto* and Thoreau's "Essay on Civil Disobedience," to cite the most famous — Groen's series attempted to set out a fundamental critique of the liberal order and a brief outline of its proper antidote. Along with Bilderdijk's spirit, Groen's method would endow Kuyper's approach to his own times.

Groen's argument was based on the premise that all political rule derives from divine right, which is delegated via revelation and history. The modern age sought to displace that authority with Reason, manifest politically in republicanism, social-contract theory, and notions of popular sovereignty. As the cult of Reason gathered momentum across the eighteenth century, its radical logic became evident: mild English deism gave way to Voltaire's radical sort, then to Diderot's atheism; Montesquieu's analysis of national character bred Rousseau's espousal of civil religion; all of it culminated in Helvetius and LaMettrie's bald philosophical materialism. The corrosion of French thought inevitably destabilized French politics, Groen continued, and the ensuing revolution followed *its* radical logic from the calling of the Estates General to the Reign of Terror, until a despairing reaction brought in the law-and-order regime of the Directory. But the latter were simply revolutionaries of the Right, lacking any basis in divine authority and thus giving way to further revolution from the Left. The cycle culminated finally in the tyranny of Napoleon Bonaparte, whose power, rooted in violence and conquest, was forced to pursue endless warfare to sustain its luster. Those wars at once spread the taint of revolution across Europe and proved to be its undoing. Yet the Restoration had not settled the matter, Groen concluded, for its monarchies proved to be variations of human devising. Only the firm foundations of God and history could dispel what threatened to become a chronic cycle of upheaval and repression.

To put it mildly, there was not much potential for democracy or any other modern notion here. All social-contract thinking was suspect, John Locke's as well as Jean Jacques Rousseau's. All republics were dubious and liable to degradation, including the American and those of classical antiquity. The pre-1795 Dutch Republic really had not been a republic at all but a monarchy — with a sometimes absent monarch! The state, Groen repeated after German Restoration theorist Ludwig von Haller, belonged to the monarch as his private property; notions of compacts, commonwealths, and written constitutions as well as republics and popular sovereignty were perforce illegitimate and in defiance of divine ordination.

The roots of Groen's "Revolution" extended very far back in time as well. If events in France post-1789 were its purest fruit, its "principles" went back behind the Enlightenment through the Renaissance and into the late Middle Ages. Just how (for so the theory implied) seventeenth- and eighteenth-century absolute monarchs qualified as "revolutionaries," and how the papacy and Counter-Reformation propounded "unbelief," was not transparently clear, nor did lumping all these together with nineteenth-century radicals and socialists yield much analytical help. The antirevolutionary habit of abstraction started with Groen, along with the elevation of ideas to the virtual exclusion of material forces in explaining historical causation.

Yet Groen was too good a historian and too practical a statesman to stay in pure ideology. Before he had learned about revolution from Burke, he had learned about the organic development of society from F. Karl von Savigny, founder of the German historical school of political thought. Savigny championed the importance of local variation for jurisprudence over against uniform prescriptions, which he blamed on abstract, deductive modes of thought. If Groen instinctively preferred standing institutions, no matter what violence had gone into their making, over insurgencies, no matter what grievances they bore, he was also sensitive to nuance and exceptions. The type of monarchy he championed was Holland's prior to 1795, "tempered" as it had been by the wide dispersal of privileges, rights, and powers among the nation's many layers. That arrangement amounted to a constitution he could defend for having evolved through history as a bulwark of the people's liberties. Groen further granted that culture and circumstance could (in historical fact, almost always did) restrain the outworking of pure revolutionary spirit. If history was God's agent, then current developments needed a discerning eye to tell true from false progress.

Groen was also willing to make use of changes he originally opposed. Once the 1848 Constitution had been ratified, he pushed in

Parliament for its fair and exact enforcement. He appreciated the spread of various humanitarian ideals as commensurate with the gospel, becoming a leader in the Dutch anti-slavery movement. Finally, if Dutch history made clear that the true people of God were more often commoners than patricians, then this patrician could serve as a "tribune" for "the people behind the voters" — the masses unrepresented under the Netherlands' exclusive franchise.

Groen had precedent for going even further down the progressive road. The French Catholic theorist Félicité Lamennais, who first taught him the link between unbelief and revolution, exemplified how a counter-revolutionary could turn into a democrat. Theocratic norms, seemingly so prone toward reaction, could actually loosen the spell of the status quo. Without breaking with the Dutch Reformed Church, Groen persistently criticized its operations. Disgusted with the pallid religion of the public schools, he demanded that they be secularized. Resolute for his own convictions in public life, he could more easily than many Conservatives countenance the same in Catholics. By the time he met Kuyper — in fact, already after the fiasco of the Education Act of 1857 — Groen had reluctantly concluded that the Netherlands was no longer a normatively Christian nation; its divine calling to be a beacon of pure religion and liberty to the nations had passed to its Calvinist remnant. At the same time, however, these constituted the nation's *saving* remnant and were bound to proclaim a Christian witness, even in a neutralized public space, by appealing to transcendent sources in hopes of bringing the nation back to its holy mission.

Calvinism as a Revolutionary Tradition

There was little of this that Kuyper did not espouse. He simply did so in bolder style, unhindered by the stately manners that bound a person of Groen's time and class. Kuyper started from, rather than coming to, a pluralist posture. He was more forthrightly and consistently democratic. When it came time to set forth his own principles, therefore, he chose a theme that Groen would endorse — his speech was entitled "Calvinism, the Source and Stronghold of Our Constitutional Liberties" — but argued it by precedents that the younger Groen would have found troubling at best.

In part, this was determined by the occasion. Kuyper gave the speech on the Dutch university lecture circuit in 1873, hoping to recruit leaders for the political party he had in mind. That required some fireworks. It being the twenty-fifth anniversary of the Dutch Constitution of 1848, however, he had to make something out of a moment his party did not relish. His solution was to virtually ignore the Constitution in pursuit of the source of constitutionalism, which he found in Reformed theology, and to bypass the Netherlands for the annals of international Calvinism. The result was an argument for stability and order from a narrative of resistance, rebellion, and revolution — good, *Christian* revolution.

The Calvinist particulars with which Kuyper began were the absolute sovereignty of God and the pervasiveness of human sin. Far from warranting monarchy, as Catholic and Lutheran Restoration theorists had argued, these tenets pointed toward a republic, Kuyper declared. On the first point, divine majesty brooked no human imitation; republicanism was the political counterpart of iconoclasm, both being rooted in the Calvinist horror of idolatry. On the second point, while depravity seemed to exert a special magnetic pull upon monarchs, as Kuyper cheekily argued after Calvin, "he [Calvin] also knows that the same sin pervades the masses and that, as a result, there will be no end to resistance and rebellion, mutiny and troubles, except for a just constitution that restrains abuse of authority, sets limits, and offers the people a natural protection against lust for power and arbitrariness." Quite contrary to Groen, who deemed Calvin a monarchist that had reluctantly accommodated to Geneva's republicanism, Kuyper insisted that, "given a free choice, Calvin certainly prefers the republic." He then took a quick two-step even further from his mentor. The doctrine of election, which Groen avoided for the wrangling it caused, Kuyper invoked as a charter for a "democratic form of church government." The implication for civil government was clear. With its leveling effect upon all human pretensions, election made democracy safe for Calvinism; with the selfless dedication it bred in the believer, it made Calvinists safe for democracy.

As Kuyper made historical narrative do most of the work in his speech, the case studies he chose were telling. One derived directly from Geneva: the Huguenot justification of armed resistance set forth by Calvin's successor, Théodore Béza, and amplified by François Hotman and Philippe du Plessis-Mornay. Theirs was a *constitutional* resistance to *tyrants,* Kuyper underscored, which required authorization by proper officials, the "lesser magistrates." Yet as deployed during the French wars of religion, it entailed a violent defiance that Groen could never endorse. Central though their work was to the development of modern political theory, he responded to Kuyper's request to say that he did not have these authors in his library to lend him. Huguenot resistance amounted to a rebellion persistent, systematic, bloody, and radicalizing enough to count as a revolution, save for its lack of success. The seventeenth-century English Puritan rising was not thus limited. It drew Kuyper's unmitigated praise, even though it involved violent insurrection, regicide, destruction of church properties, terror in the (Irish) countryside, instability eventuating in military dictatorship, and any number of other features resembling the French Revolution. This was a permissible, even commendable, revolution because it was a godly one, as manifested by its formal declarations of purpose and the good discipline of Cromwell's New Model army.

In both the French and English cases Kuyper gave most attention to church rather than to civil politics, reflecting the priority of religious freedom among the "constitutional liberties" in his title and also his current polemics on the consistory of Amsterdam. Kuyper traced the bane of synodical hierarchy back to the Huguenots' adaptation to military (not churchly) necessity. English Presbyterians had then tried to import these French ways on the assumption that "Calvinism was a petrifaction, bound to the form it had assumed, take it or leave it." Kuyper lauded the English Independents instead, who had properly adapted "the Calvinist principle" to their own time and place. In this they had the clearer claim on Calvin himself, who "unambiguously rejected the idea that one should be bound to an established form." Thus Kuyper's ideal of a "circle of free, autonomous congregations" bound in a "voluntary, not coerced, relationship with the synod" had the imprimatur of the Genevan reformer, whatever the actualities of Genevan practice. So also the "separation of church and state," which Puritans in old England and New saw following "necessarily" from "Calvinistic principle."

The bridge to New England allowed Kuyper to return to civil politics and make the rosiest case for his thesis. No one could deny that "modern liberties flourish in America without restriction," he began, or that "the people of the Union bear a clear-cut Christian stamp more than any other nation on earth." This was not a coincidental but a causal relationship, rooted in the nation's Puritan origins. Kuyper had plenty of sources for this casual conflation of "New England" and "America," since the standard histories of the time exercised the same assumption. His organic sociology was at work too. Whatever the cultural complexity and numbers on the ground in 1873, New England represented "the core of the nation"; and whatever the developments over the two-and-a-half centuries since Plymouth Rock, the original Puritan stamp still held on America's contemporary character. By this point Kuyper's definition of "Calvinism" had left behind any confessional particulars (the Wesleyans were included!) to become broadly cultural, connoting moral earnestness, healthy enterprise, middle-class discipline, and public respect for religion. So taken, he could hammer home his point: the best of modern liberties were not the fruit of the French Revolution but of Calvinism.

He put it to the students before him with a flourish:

> We are Antirevolutionaries not because we reject the fruits of the revolutionary era but because, history book in hand, we dare contest the paternity of these good things. With much evil the revolution also brought Europe much good, but this was stolen fruit, ripened on the stem of Calvinism under the nurturing warmth of our martyrs' faith, first in our own land, then in England, and [now dropping the French Huguenots] subsequently in America.

Kuyper had to acknowledge ruefully that in Europe "what had been refused from the hand of Calvinism was eagerly accepted from the hands of the French heroes of freedom." Yet it would not do to accept that surrogate, for along with "Calvinistic liberties . . . [the Revolution] introduced a system, a catechism, a doctrine; and this system, running counter to God and his righteousness, destroys the bonds of law and order, undermines the foundations of society, gives free play to passion, and gives the lower material realm rule over the spirit." Put positively, only Calvinism supplies "the moral element," "the heroic faith," and the mediating institutions which serve as the modern version of the "lesser magistrates." All of these, and only these, together gave order to liberty and so assured its perpetuation.

As history, Kuyper's lecture is open to critique at many points. To maintain the United States' "Calvinist" political foundation, he chose a strategic moment in the 1790s, venturing neither backward to 1776 nor ahead to the "revolutionary" Jefferson's triumph in 1800. To warrant his model of church and state, he had to ignore (arguably, he had the facts wrong) that his beloved New England Congregationalists maintained an established church longer than anyone else in the new nation, and that the group who did most closely approximate his churchly ideal — the Baptists — were Jefferson's most enthusiastic supporters. His segue from the Puritan to the Glorious Revolution in seventeenth-century England ignored the latter's fear of precisely the religious zeal Kuyper praised in the former. His critique of the French Reformation opens the interesting possibility that national character, not revolutionary principles, accounted for much that went wrong after 1789, for the Huguenots also come off as unitary, hierarchical, centralizing, and given to passion — that is, as quintessentially French. His acknowledgement but then steamrolling of material factors beneath the force of ideas shows some but not enough conceptual progress past the example of Groen, especially in light of the dramatic technological and economic transformations underway as he was writing. Most seriously, some of the hardest questions of political theory — as to forms of government or the criteria and means of legitimate resistance — got passed over quickly by appeal to first principles. "The question is not whether the people rule or a king but whether both, when they rule, do so in recognition of Him." By extension, violence or non-violence, rebellion or obedience, could be justified or reprobated depending on whether the actor called on the name of the Lord.

Still, Kuyper hit his main target. The Puritan stamp on the American ethos would be confirmed by a fleet of twentieth-century historians, atheists and theological liberals chief among them. The Calvinist contribution to modern constitutional freedom, both in theory and in practice, would be likewise upheld. Kuyper's insight that, in France, the Revolution became necessary owing to the stifling of the Reformation and effected many of its results, has been borne out as well. More broadly, the rediscovery of Calvinism as an activist, culture-forming faith, not in spite but exactly in consequence of its theological convictions, would proceed from Max Weber's work thirty years after Kuyper's speech to Michael Walzer's study of English Puritanism, *The Revolution of the Saints,* a century later. Kuyper's speech concluded on that note: "I hope . . . that at least the young people of the Netherlands will not echo the old libel . . . that we, Dutch Calvinists, are a party of reaction!"

Organizing

If Dutch Calvinists were to be political players in the future, they would need more than updated theory. They needed new methods, new organization, and a new operational identity. This was the burden of most of Kuyper's correspondence with Groen and of his day-to-day political labors. The antirevolutionary movement had to become a full-fledged party, independent of the Conservatives. It had to have a national network penetrating down to the local level, a comprehensive program of action, a parliamentary delegation held accountable to that program, and a mass-circulation newspaper to reach the rank and file. Opposition to such a plan arose from all over the map. Liberal opinion across Europe worshipped the rational autonomous individual in politics as in philosophy, and Dutch Liberal voices like Robert Fruin, Kuyper's old teacher at Leiden, thought political parties to be inherently wrong in a parliamentary system. Members of the Dutch States-General from all persuasions objected to any prior constraint upon their independent judgment. Leaders as well as many ordinary clergy in the Dutch Reformed Church feared too close a connection between church and politics; the Ethical descendants of the Réveil, with their goal of leavening society with general spiritual influence, were especially "politicophobic," in Kuyper's epithet. Remarkably, Kuyper's vision would prevail nonetheless, and within ten years. But in the near term, the painful reality was persistent conflict and false starts.

His initiative began in earnest immediately after the Utrecht school convention. He started compiling lists of likely leaders in regional capitals and publishing articles in *De Heraut*. He was deeply enmeshed in the parliamentary elections of 1871, well beyond his own candidacy. He consulted on candidates and tactics in other districts and gathered the editors of five friendly newspapers from around the country to coordinate publicity and mobilize voters. He insisted on a broader, more democratic platform than Groen wanted — including planks on church and franchise reform as well as school equity — even though Groen rejected the very idea of a comprehensive platform as "*unnecessary* and *dangerous.*" The first measures of party discipline appeared when Groen endorsed just three candidates in the campaign, dropping everyone — including some of his longstanding associates — who might deviate from the platform come voting time. The inclusion of his own name among the three discomfited Kuyper, but the results of the election, despite his own defeat, did not. The "unbelievable spike" in the independent Roman Catholic vote, he wrote Groen, spelled the dismantling of a "once-fixed" political structure and revealed "uncommonly serious" portents to anyone "with an eye on the future." For now, the 5,000 voters who had supported the independent "antirevolutionary" slate formed a hard core around which to build.

The most crucial instrument for that project had to be a newspaper. Groen had published an elite journal off and on over the years but saw the need for a regular, popular sheet and had adopted Kuyper not least for his potential in this vein. Kuyper wanted to get started already in 1869, but Groen cautioned him to slow down until adequate preparations were in place. While Groen assembled the necessary capital, Kuyper started promoting a new paper to antirevolutionary voter lists and at summer mission festivals, the favored holiday of pious folks. For the inaugural issue Kuyper chose April 1, 1872, the 300th anniversary of the insurgent "Sea Beggars'" raid on Brielle, which had marked the beginning of concerted hostilities in the Dutch war for independence. That momentous achievement, said Kuyper's opening editorial, could be matched today if people paused amid their patriotic hoopla to remember God and recommit themselves to the sacred mission for which their nation had been raised up. Happily, a band of the faithful, though small and scorned like the Beggars, was ready at hand; the new paper was designed to instruct and inspire them to their destiny.

For editor and reader alike, the April date in 1872 would have lasting significance. The *Standaard* editorship was the one post Kuyper would hold for the rest of his career, and the role where he could combine all the others through which he passed in the meantime — preacher, teacher, and politician. The paper was the only place where most of his followers ever heard him, but there they heard him to great effect. For many it provided a post-elementary school education, a sustained induction into politics, culture, and social affairs. In the process Kuyper not only promoted a party but organized a movement and shaped a people. The personal loyalties and the deep affection thus bred proved the power of mass journalism; on that Kuyper instructed the whole country.

Such loyalty required a sense of distinct identity, and in cultivating it Kuyper offered the counterpoint to the principled pluralism of his political theory. The issue came up already in selecting the paper's name. Kuyper wanted to call it *De Geus,* "The Beggar," after the motley heroes of 1572, and acceded only reluctantly to warnings of how grossly this would offend Catholics. In his early columns and in speeches on special occasions, he rallied his troops (and military terminology was his typical idiom) with the assurance that they were the "conscience" of the nation, guardians of its calling. "[T]here still remain people who, in keeping with the demand of history, carry this precious legacy in their heart," his *Standaard* inaugural declared.

> It is my prayer that they will not lose heart, though their number is small and their strength is little. 'Small, too, was the fleet of the Beggars!' . . . Their calling is so beautiful! To fight not just for themselves and their children but for their fellow citizens, for the peoples of Europe, for all of humanity, so that justice remain *justice,* that *freedom* of conscience not be smothered.

At a convention of Christian school teachers Kuyper likened them to the old "hedge-preachers" of the Dutch Reformation, the vanguard then, as the teachers ought to be now, of "the spiritual liberation of the nation." Of course, non-Calvinists might wonder what promise that "liberation" held for them.

As educational policy continued to roil national politics, Kuyper used the emerging Christian school movement to build a political organization. It featured a Central Committee (Kuyper as chair) that helped organize local chapters ("voter clubs"), usually out of the ranks of the local Christian school association. The Central Committee coordinated the locals via a direct communications hierarchy. A whole class of "new men" thus entered the political arena, people of modest middle-class background but empowered by the party apparatus to challenge or circumvent local elites. This generated some tension with another new network, the Anti-School-Law League (ASWV), which operated on a classic-liberal premise of local notables exerting their "influence" upon "intelligent" opinion. (In fact, the ASWV was modeled on the great success of British Liberalism, the Anti-Corn Law League.) For the next elections, in 1873, the two organizations coordinated their efforts, occasioning along the way some correspondence between Kuyper and P. C. Mondriaan, secretary of the ASWV's Amersfoort chapter and father of an infant son, Piet. The antirevolutionary slate more than doubled its support over 1871, to 12,000 votes, but the limits of dual organization became apparent over the next few years. In the 1875 elections Kuyper's voter clubs did better work than the ASWV chapters, but the returns were disappointing. Kuyper blamed those who had opposed his push for thorough organization: single-issue voters who did not want a comprehensive program, members of Parliament who did not want a binding program, Reformed church members who disliked his appeal to Christian Reformed seceders, and traditional leaders of anti-democratic hue.

Stress and Strain

The conflict took a toll on Kuyper, but he stoked it all the same. He baited the Ethicals with a speech at a church gathering in 1872. He kept up a running battle with Conservatives for command of anti-Liberal ground. He preferred to battle with Liberals, he repeated, because they held to principle; Conservatives' private talk was so at odds with their public votes that one had to wonder about their integrity. He even scolded Groen in *De Standaard* for endorsing a Liberal proposal to erect statues in the capital in honor of Johan van Oldenbarnevelt and Johan de Witt — this, within a month of his election to the States General and without advance word to his mentor.

Groen doubtless understood what was going on. Already in 1869 he had admonished Kuyper: "Don't try too much, dear friend! Your [latest] letter makes me uneasy." Now again, he repeated: "I worry about your health. You do *too much*." True enough; that Christmas Kuyper could not get out of bed, prostrated by "tic and rheumatism." "Tic" meant "tic douloureux" or trigeminal neuralgia — short, successive bursts of extremely intense facial pain. "Rheumatism" described painful inflammation of the joints, in Kuyper's case particularly of the neck and shoulders. Sometimes asthma was added to the mix. Kuyper was sick in the summer of 1870, again the following February, then again in January and August of 1873. Kuyper routinely ascribed it all to overwork, a sad necessity of his calling, curable by a week's rest here, a month abroad there. But gradually the light shone through. "My throat distemper," he wrote Groen in 1873, "seems to be nerve-related. A heated debate, and those come every day, does me harm." Perhaps that explains Kuyper's mood upon being elected to Parliament. He professed anxiety about the "unholy atmosphere" of politics, but the problem lay within as much as without. If conflict aggravated his "nerves," and if defense of the cause spurred him to "overwork," then politics posed a most unhealthy ambience for his soul.

The strain became acute when he had to move his family from their spacious home on the Amsterdam harbor to a flat in The Hague. There, somehow, Jo and the four children had to stay out of his way while he prepared for the next day's debates in the Second Chamber, composed copy for the next day's *Standaard,* wrote a meditation and Bible study for the next Sunday's *Heraut,* and kept up his correspondence with voter clubs, Christian school leaders, and church councils around the country. That left out of the question composing the next big lecture to follow up "Uniformity" or "Modernism." Yet "our people," God's people, needed leadership in times of such momentous change, and had been so grateful on previous occasions when he had risen to the challenge. Perhaps in his study in 1874 Kuyper detected beneath these lyrics a tune he had heard before — once when he had exhausted himself on the prize essay, once when he had despaired over his career prospects. He had just recounted these crises the previous year in *Confidentie.* Soon he would turn again toward the same solution he had found in *The Heir of Redclyffe,* a religious renewal back in England. This time it would come under the auspices of American evangelicals, who were burdened neither with Calvinism nor with any notion of "the Revolution."

CHAPTER FIVE

Brighton and Breakdown

For Kuyper, the year 1875 dawned in misery. "The tic torments me terribly," he wrote Groen. "I can't sleep at night and am incapacitated for any work. Literally worn out. And now I fear that our third child [four-year-old Henriëtte] has gone to bed with the measles." He did not have to add that the disease might spread to the other four children in the family. Nor that, for the first time in twelve years, he had not ascended the pulpit to give Old Year's and New Year's sermons, always a special occasion for him. Instead, aching though he was, he had to think about the hard issues in the upcoming summer elections and the ongoing strife on the Amsterdam consistory. Meanwhile, he added, would Groen be so good as to give his opinion about the enclosed invitation?

The invitation was to join an international gathering of Protestants at the English resort town of Brighton to learn about the "higher life" of Christian holiness. Groen replied positively, since one of the meeting's Dutch promoters was a friend and collaborator of his. Kuyper took his advice, made his plans, and for ten days in May enjoyed the raptures of consecrated fellowship, American evangelical style. He came back professing that, for him, "Brighton was a Bethel experience," a life-changing encounter with the immediate presence of God. Another conversion of English provenance, coming again amid the toils of conflict and ambition, seemed to be at hand. Yet Brighton and Anglo-American "holiness" turned out to be a great false start for Kuyper, leading to the most severe collapse of his life. Recuperating abroad for fifteen months, he had ample time to reflect on his past and his future, to trim his roles into a manageable career, and to seal himself once and for all upon the foundations of classic Reformed orthodoxy.

Polemics Political and Ecclesiastical

By the time the Brighton meetings opened, Kuyper needed some spiritual bliss. The election campaign was at full steam, and Kuyper's polemics were supplying and drawing no little of the fire that stoked it. With education policy again the central issue, Kuyper turned his daily column in *De Standaard* into a series of arguments for the "restitution" system that his political coalition had recently endorsed. Under that proposal, the taxes paid by parents with children in religious schools would be refunded to those institutions, eliminating the parents' burden of double payments and making parochial education affordable to the less affluent. These columns, collected into campaign brochures, showed a remarkable variety of voices and tactics. They asked sympathy for the poor, defended personal rights, and fired off statistics to prove that the pluralistic English system was superior to the Netherlands' for justice and success.

His principal target was the secular model being advocated with a bracing frankness by the Progressive Liberal leader Joannes Kappeyne van de Coppello. In response to Kuyper's warnings that poorer families would have their rights of conscience violated under his proposal, Kappeyne opined in one terse exchange in Parliament that "the needs of the minority must be suppressed lest they be the fly that makes the whole ointment smell." A warm demonstration of Liberal solicitude, Kuyper cried; perhaps the lion in the Dutch national seal should be replaced with an eagle tearing up an innocent lamb! Yet he appreciated the Liberal's candor, he continued, for precisely that virtue he found lacking among the Conservatives. Given that theirs was the cabinet in power, it was irresponsible for them to vacillate behind vague generalities, he chided their MPs. Unmanly too. As a proper standard for that virtue Kuyper then recited the chorus of the current American revivalist hit. "'Dare to be a Daniel,'" he intoned, "'Dare to stand alone!/Dare to have a purpose firm!/Dare to make it known!' Let me emphasize this last," he concluded. "Don't just have your war-plan but DARE TO MAKE IT KNOWN!"

Kuyper had the lyrics in mind because, it being mid-May, he was following British news reports of the Dwight Moody-Ira Sankey revival crusade in the country to which he would soon repair. But to his fellow MPs this was just more of the insufferable conduct he had been exhibiting since his entry into Parliament the year before. Kuyper had arrived as their second-youngest member, the first to have come out of the pulpit ministry. Both clergy and parliamentarians had observed strict separation of affairs since 1848. Thorbecke had instilled as secular an ambience in Parliament as possible, and all sides showed outright aversion to discussions of political theory. Thus Kuyper's insistence on bringing every issue back to fundamental questions, along with his quotations from Scripture, provoked criticism. One Conservative called him a "demagogue" with "the manner and allure of an enthusiast [fanatic]"; another espied the ghost of Oliver Cromwell plotting to replace monarchy with military despotism. While Kappeyne could slyly turn Scripture back on Kuyper ("fly in the ointment" alluded to Ecclesiastes 10:1), the Conservative leader Willem Wintgens lectured him on the bad taste of bringing religion into politics and the rank irresponsibility of invoking first principles when specific policy proposals were on the table. Doubtless Wintgens resented the skill with which Kuyper was shearing Calvinist voters from the Conservative column, and doubtless the silencing of theoretical issues was the ploy of a comfortable elite, whatever the party.

It was all the more perturbing then, when, amid a discussion of social legislation, Kuyper fired at the parliamentary gentlemen from the Epistle of James:

> Go to now, ye rich men, weep and howl for your miseries that shall come upon you. Your riches are corrupted, and your garments are moth-eaten. Your gold and silver is cankered; and the rust of them shall be a witness against you, and shall eat your flesh as it were fire. Ye have heaped treasure together for the last days. Behold, the hire of the labourers who have reaped down your fields, which is of you kept back by fraud, crieth: and the cries of them which have reaped are entered into the ears of the Lord of sabaoth. [James 5:1-4]

This alienated even potential allies. The most popular Roman Catholic leader predicted that the antirevolutionary cause would not attain "serious influence" until it got past "the great stumbling-block . . . [that is] Mr. Kuyper. . . . He is an orator, not a statesman. Writing or speaking, always an orator." Some Catholic delegates on the floor were terser, and knew how to use the Bible, too: Kuyper was a Pharisee, they charged, a "whitewashed sepulcher."

Church affairs were no happier. Although he had resigned from the pastorate upon election to Parliament, Kuyper returned to the Amsterdam church council as a lay elder and continued his close maneuvers there. The results were no better than in Parliament. The irenically-minded leadership blocked his proportionate parish plan, only to lose control of the consistory at the next election to a Calvinist coup. The Irenicals formed a caucus of their own, thus splitting the anti-Modernist forces and allowing that party to regain some of its power. Kuyper bewailed the factionalism and bitterness, not to mention the strategic folly, of the process. The "unbrotherly" divisions in the cause of Christ compounded the lethargy of the church at large, which ought to be the first concern. He was tired of the back-biting, tired of failure, tired of being tired. He voiced a theme overheard from the revival in England: the church and the weary soul needed the "unction of the Holy Spirit."

Consecration at the Sea-Shore

Onto this scene sailed Robert Pearsall Smith. A Pennsylvania glass manufacturer by trade, Smith was, in his son's words, "a magnificent salesman" at heart, capable "of persuasion and blandishment, almost of hypnotization." Smith had been converted in the great American prayer-meeting revival of 1857-58 and had subsequently experienced an ecstatic "second blessing" at a Methodist camp meeting, sealing his sanctification. This "Christian perfection" had Wesleyan Arminian roots but had found some Congregational and Presbyterian advocates such as William Boardman and Asa Mahan, an old associate of the consummate Yankee revivalist Charles Finney. After suffering a riding accident in 1871, Smith left his business to recuperate abroad only to become a promoter of the "Holiness" cause, beginning in London, then at Oxford, and soon across the northern half of Europe. Himself a descendant of James Logan, the Penn family's secretary in colonial days, Smith acquired a circle of prominent sponsors in Britain, most notably Lord and Lady Cowper Temple, the natural son and daughter-in-law of Lord Palmerston.

After successful conferences in the summer of 1874, Smith took to the Continent the following spring, where he moved in leading circles again. In Berlin he ministered to the empress and her daughter, to 150 scholars and statesmen assembled by the secretary of state, to crowds of over 4,000 at royally-sponsored services at the Garrison Church. At Basel he addressed 5,000 daily at outdoor rallies like the old camp meetings. Then he moved back through Germany on a five-city crusade that enlisted sixty ministers for the conference at Brighton, to which all these preliminaries were pointing. Before crossing the Channel, he stopped off at Utrecht and The Hague, rallying more clergy as well as introducing Queen Sophie, the crown prince, and his daughter to the promises of personal consecration.

Kuyper joined the forty Hollanders who followed Smith to England and was immediately impressed by what he saw. For one, Smith was a master of organization. The arrangements were perfectly efficient, and the meetings cycled nimbly from Bible study to exhortation to prayer meeting and testimony time, culminating in moments of tears and "decision." For the Dutch delegates, Kuyper not least, the change from their customary formal, head-oriented services to the public spontaneous melting of affections was novel and moving. They too broke down, and broke through: "My cup overfloweth," Kuyper shared in his circle.

It was an end as much as a means of the Brighton meetings to provide earnest Victorians some release from their constant dedication to duty. "Rest" and "trust" were particularly prominent in the discourses of Smith's wife, Hannah Whitall, a better speaker and more acute theologian than most of the men on the Brighton rostrum, though listed as something other than a preacher to spare ecclesiastical sensitivities. They struggled not because they were weak but because they felt themselves strong, she told her listeners; if they would but acknowledge their weakness and surrender to Jesus, they would find perfect peace. For Kuyper the words were gospel. He could be excused for sighing, even with tears, to a popular Brighton hymn: "Love of Jesus, all divine,/Fill this longing heart of mine:/Ceaseless struggling after life,/Weary with the endless strife." He was roused with the morning song, "Simply trusting ev'ry day/Trusting through a stormy way;/Even when my faith is small,/Trusting Jesus, that is all." He felt the eternal presence of God hovering over Brighton, he wrote in *De Standaard,* and he rested in it.

But no one, not Kuyper and not Hannah Whitall Smith, ended there. In weakness Christ's *power* was made perfect, she repeated after Paul, and power, strengthening, victory constituted the second part of the Holiness promise. "Yielding" to Jesus wrought "entire consecration," and entire consecration brought so complete a triumph over sin that, released from inner conflict and temptation, one was better fit for battle than ever. These redoubled energies would then be doubled again by the certainty of triumph in the coming fray. After first giving them rest, in short, Brighton called Victorian strivers back to work, endowed with fresh energies that would bear them forever above weariness. Kuyper could join in the conference's favorite song heartily, with an eye upon his return to the summer's campaign:

> I join the fight though not begun,
> I'll trust and shout, still marching on.
> Jesus saves me now.
> Why should I ask a sign from God?
> Can I not trust the precious blood?
> Jesus saves me now.
> Strong in his word, I meet the foe
> And, shouting, win without a blow.
> Jesus saves me now.

As its third promise, Brighton modeled unity. It discouraged theological debate as much as possible by calling participants to focus on the essentials they held in common. In the glow of the moment Kuyper was glad for the deliverance. He was especially struck by the communion service he was called upon to officiate at the Sunday evening service. A pair of recent antagonists in the Franco-Prussian War came forward, repeated the sacramental formulary in their respective languages, received the elements from Kuyper, and gave each other an embrace. If the higher life of the Spirit could heal such still-fresh wounds, Kuyper mused, what could it not overcome?

Indeed, the war and the challenges it posed were close to the center of Brighton's consciousness. Many of its leaders were veterans of the Evangelical Alliance, the international Protestant network Da Costa had hailed thirty years earlier. It was now fading, not least because the hierarchical social order it had assumed was eroding under the pressures of mass industrial society signaled by Germany's ascent. The religious enthusiasm of wartime had also faded, especially in Germany. Brighton thus aimed to teach a more flexible, personalized model of Protestant piety, frankly sacrificing the Alliance's old socio-political concerns.

Fatefully, Kuyper was not prepared to take that step. Instead, he returned to the Netherlands on a spiritual flight of Holiness rhetoric but with a political mission. He was suffused somehow with both power and peace, with energy and calm, entwined with God and entangled with the enemy. The Smiths had talked exclusively of internal spiritual warfare that was to eventuate in sober personal conduct. Kuyper wanted to translate that into a campaign in public culture, aiming for structural change, to be decided at the polls. If anyone could do it, he could. If he could not, something would fall apart.

Collapse

After his return home Kuyper promoted the Brighton message at a series of regional mission festivals, the Dutch equivalent of the British resort conference. At the same time, with elections drawing near, these became a "higher" form of campaign stop. He opened on a grand scale before a gathering in Zeeland, evoking epochal moments in church history and declaring that another such turning point was at hand. In the Reformation, the last previous watershed, people had been afflicted with guilt, so that the message of justification brought salvation. Now, people languished under pain, so sanctification with its peace and power was on call. The secret of Brighton's success, he explained, came in its "making all the promises of God real from *eternity* to *time,* in this moment." This could be the very place and time when God, bringing down his "tangible presence through the powerful working of the Holy Ghost," broke through the lethargy, hopelessness, and resignation that had for too long entombed the faithful in the Netherlands. If people of faith for once would truly believe the prayers they ritually uttered, they could end their wandering in the political wilderness and enter the promised land, bringing the Dutch nation as a prodigal son back to the Father's house. Empowered and confident for the strife that loomed, Zeeland could once again, as in the Reformation, lead in the redemption of the nation.

Contrary to evangelical custom, Kuyper's speech put this collective story first; only later did he get personal. He now had a third, if abbreviated, conversion narrative to add to those of *Redclyffe* and Beesd. If the liberal press derided it as sanctimonious, orthodox ears might have been troubled for a different reason. For Kuyper here pronounced the traditional Reformed paradigm to have been inadequate. At Brighton,

> I felt something in my soul that I had not known before. Before I had indeed professed the Lord but kept complaining about the barren circumstances in which believers found themselves; but there [at Brighton] my soul and my life received the conviction besides — indeed, saw it revealed in its full reality — that Jesus lives in my heart.

He called his listeners to join him in the second step of higher spirituality:

> An open acknowledgement . . . that a new revelation must come to the soul is necessary. . . . There must be and develop what the English express so crisply and aptly with the word *consecration,* a surrendering to the Lord, laying one's very self upon the altar with our dear wives and children and gold and goods.

The phraseology came directly from the mother of American Holiness, the forthrightly Wesleyan Arminian Phoebe Palmer, via her Brighton step-children the Smiths, Boardman, and Mahan. Kuyper therefore hastened to add that such a step had been taught by the devout in every age, particularly by the Reformed fathers, who had called it "sealing"; further, that it upheld the promises of the church's sacraments. But a critical eye might notice that a functionally new sacrament of "second blessing" had been added to the mix.

Accordingly, his efforts turned apologetical. He joined Dutch Brighton veterans at a reunion in early August. While they started up a new journal to promote the cause, he used his Sunday columns to lay good foundations. He lamented again the half-heartedness and hairsplitting to which Dutch churchgoers seemed addicted. He exhorted them to the deep self-examination needed to scale the heights of the life God had in store. To help in that effort, he launched a series on "sealing" and planned to follow it with others on vows and fasting as practiced in the Reformed tradition. He gave space to a lengthy extract from Hannah Whitall Smith's bestseller, *The Christian's Secret of a Happy Life* (1875) — albeit a section on plain living, not the chapter teaching "the baptism of the Holy Ghost." His own writing turned more and more toward the "fathers" of the Dutch Later Reformation, with their experiential piety. Yet his shaky hold on Holiness promises became apparent already in mid-summer when, at his third consecutive mission festival, he complained to his hostess of sleeplessness from overwork.

Unfortunately, Pearsall Smith's example again became apropos. Since Kuyper had extolled Smith's Herculean energies at Brighton (fifty-three speeches in ten days) as an example of the power wrought by consecration, the news from England that Smith had returned to Philadelphia prostrate from exhaustion had theological as well as personal implications. At the end of summer Kuyper heard from Smith himself in even more disquieting language: "I am deeply moved in the reading of ecclesiastical history," Smith wrote him, "in watching the vibrations between the carnal life in which so large a portion of the church is involved and the success of Satan in transforming himself into an angel of light before those more devoted souls who have escaped the grosser allurements of the world." Smith's embroilment in sexual scandal would not be revealed for some time yet, but Kuyper had to wonder. Yet Smith's overt malady was familiar enough from his own experience. Smith explained that his current exhaustion was the third in a series of "severe attacks of pressure on the brain," the two previous of which had each "last[ed] a year or more. . . . Even quite light occupation is too much" for me, Smith continued, "and I am consigned to a time — perhaps a year — of idleness and suffering." But then we can "hope for more and not less power in the movement from the withdrawal of one who perhaps was placed too prominently before the eyes of men. God may use us, but he does not *need* us."

On that note, Kuyper returned to his parliamentary combats. The summer elections had not been entirely disappointing; the antirevolutionary vote increased from 12,000 to 14,000, while the Conservatives were clearly eroding as the prime opposition party. The gains had not countermanded the losses, however, and the Liberals had emerged with an absolute majority of forty-three out of eighty seats.

The opening session made clear that education — including the

Dutch university system — would dominate the agenda. But Kuyper heard this secondhand, being laid up once again with rheumatism. Nor was his family yet in lodgings for the term, he wrote Groen. Still, his Brighton voice returned: "my inmost state of soul remains blessed and happy." It did not long remain so. Through November and December 1875 he engaged in hard debates about the future of Dutch higher education. He found company with Catholics or Liberals at one point or another, but beyond that lay pure polemics. He worried that he had offended Groen by something he said on church and school. He suffered a particular humiliation in late November upon asking that a discussion from the previous day be reopened. A Cabinet member sneered, "I am not surprised that the honorable member from Gouda [Kuyper] . . . cannot find anything more pleasant and more natural than that every discussion which calls him once again to fulfill his duty last as long as possible." The citations of call and duty, aimed directly at Kuyper's self-conception, amounted to an insult that the chair ruled out of order and that Kuyper deemed "highly unparliamentary and totally unwarranted." He ruined his effect, however, by rambling on about honor, the people, and parliamentary prerogatives before getting to the substance of the issue. Even after good days he prepared deep into the night, holding cold compresses to his head to relieve his own "brain pressures" and dousing his arms and shoulders with chilled water against the "rheumatism." He took up early-morning horse rides for relaxation.

With the new year he started up a new skein of writing on the spiritual disciplines. Consecration, the strengthening of faith, commitment to unpleasant duties — the language of Brighton and the Reformed fathers twined around each other. But then one of his principal funders and Brighton sponsors, Willem Hovy, wrote him the devastating news that Pearsall Smith had not been sent home from physical afflictions alone but had been dismissed for a "double delusion" in doctrine and life. The Holiness leaders who issued this edict contended that Smith had only given unfortunate appearances of acting on his error, but his own family would set the record straight. After research in his mother's papers, Smith's son explained that for some time, since his first "brain attack," his father had been under the care of a Christian therapist who associated the baptism of the Holy Ghost with the erotic thrill of intense prayer, and who therefore prescribed, for those sufficiently sanctified to understand, ritual gestures re-enacting the unity of the Bridegroom and His church. Smith served in the former role, comely maidens in the latter. Hannah Whitall Smith had warned Robert already in 1873 against his habit of "petting kind young deaconesses," but he did not desist, not even at Brighton, where he was discovered sharing the holy kiss with a devoted convert. Even his revival associates knew enough to send him packing. "My soul is shocked at this," Hovy wrote. "Why must these things happen?" To Kuyper, now gravely disappointed on top of being exhausted, the biblical citation with which Hovy closed carried little comfort: "Not many of you should presume to be teachers, my brothers, because you know that we who teach will be judged more strictly" (James 3:1).

January had been a sickly month for Kuyper ever since his move to Amsterdam, but this time his collapse was total. In early February 1876 his friends packed him off to the south of France; Jo followed later with the children. The day he telegrammed her with travel directions he also wrote Groen: "The situation with my head is still sad. . . . It's been almost a month now and I'm still far from my goal." Just the same, he passed along some strategy for the education bill. Groen returned some advice of his own. Enough of "goals" and strategizing; "Now, with your eye directed Above, with humility, and if it might be with glad submission, *take rest.*" The next week he added sentiments more familiar to Reformed piety than to Brighton cheer: "Bow beneath the mighty hand of the Lord so that he can raise you up in *his time.*" Remember too, he said, the "tender-hearted care of your wife, the assurance also of the heartfelt love of your children. . . ."

Exile

Reunited, the family moved to the Hotel Bellagio at Lake Como. By April Jo was pregnant again, a welcome sign of Kuyper's vitality, though anxious news for a mother with a history of difficult deliveries. She also had to face the sale of their beloved home on the Amsterdam harbor to cover the costs of their exile. The family moved to the Engadin valley in southern Switzerland for the summer, and friends back home started talking of his recuperation in terms of months, not weeks. Philip J. Hoedemaker and Alexander F. de Savornin Lohman — a theologian and jurist, respectively — took over the daily *Standaard;* Johannes Gunning, a longtime colleague in the clergy, covered Sundays.

Kuyper's temporary incapacity even to write letters makes it difficult to date the start of his recovery, but the story he later recounted tells much about his personality. He decided to pay a visit to an acquaintance across a mountain and took a dangerous path to get there, two hours up and two hours down. The exertion broke his nervous tension and sleeplessness, so he repeated the exercise — in fact, he developed a lifelong habit that would see him scale every mountain ridge from Norway to the Pyrenees. He later reflected in a statement of unalloyed Romanticism:

> Wandering in the great mass of people that flows through the streets of London and climbing the high peaks of Switzerland are the only things that bring rest to my nervous system. In London, amid the whirling sea of humanity, I feel myself a forgotten man. In the mountains I learn something different. In climbing you notice that the prospect becomes ever more beautiful and glorious. Hence the push to climb ever higher.

But then came a check upon Holiness aspirations: "Finally there comes a moment when you can't go any further. You see the peaks touching the heavens, but they are not to be reached. So you must enjoy the enchanting panorama of the overwhelming mountain scene." Kuyper's Romanticism would thus remain Calvinistic: "And so I come again to the realization that God did not create the world in the first place so that we mortals should enjoy it but so that He should delight in the works of His hands."

Another mountaintop experience came in the form of Reformed folk piety. On May 18, 1876, he remembered, he slept alone out on the Simplon and dreamt that Groen had died; in fact, the master passed away that very night. While the coincidence cannot be independently verified from the time (Kuyper told the story ten years later), one critic has noted another conjunction which, if it did not prompt Kuyper's recollection, certainly showed the lure of late-Romantic visions among the intellectuals of his generation. Friedrich Nietzsche, who precisely like Kuyper was stricken at Christmas 1875 and gave up his post in February 1876, sojourned in the same Swiss valley five years later and there, atop the Simplon, had the first vision of what would become *Also Sprach Zarathustra*.

What can definitely be said with respect to signs and portents in

Kuyper's case is that Groen's passing amounted to the death of a father and came laden with sorrow, guilt at his own absence from the scene, and questions about the succession. Responding to his widow's letter detailing Groen's last days, Kuyper begged for a blessing: what were Groen's last words? Were any for me? He barely spoke the last ten days, Betsy replied, and then whispered only of his trust in God. Are you sure, Kuyper persisted, and might I look over the books and papers in his library before it is dispersed? Quite sure, Betsy insisted; you may visit when you are well.

In fact, Groen had left no doubt that Kuyper was the indispensable man for the future of his cause. The closing words of his last letter to Kuyper pronounced as apt a benediction as possible. Evoking Question and Answer 1 of the Heidelberg Catechism, Groen reminded him: "Above all the one-sufficient comfort in life and death, which alone is fireproof against anything, for day-laborer and scholar, is sure!"

In October, the family moved to Nice, and Kuyper's pace began to pick up. A long letter from Lohman brought him up to date on the political scene. Gunning wrote that he was happy to hear that "my dear friend" was doing better. Sufficiently better, in fact, to make a trip to Florence, whither Jo forwarded the note. I'll send any others to Rome, she added — including cards for his thirty-ninth birthday, which Kuyper would celebrate there, alone. She was sleeping well despite the discomforts of her condition, Jo continued. Fortunately, Kuyper returned just before she went into premature labor, on November 30. His widowed sister Anna had arrived earlier to help deliver the Kuypers' third daughter, Catharina. Kuyper made a brief business trip to the Netherlands in February, including a stop at Groen's house that left him with his "nerves all in a tumble." In May 1877 Kuyper was back for good, needing to sort out the paths his life should take.

His February trip had coincided with the renewal of the higher education debate in the Second Chamber. Kuyper's final return only in May thus amounted to a decision to give up his seat. Brighton friends hoped he would return to their cause; Cowper Temple wrote to invite Kuyper to a select leadership conference at his private estate. A parish in Friesland, one of the richest livings in the church, called him to their pulpit with assurances that he could continue editing *De Standaard* there.

Faced with this crossroads, Kuyper took to his darkened chamber for a day of solitary prayer and fasting. He emerged to decline the church offer and turned toward the future with the tough comfort of Habakkuk 3:17-19: "Though the fig tree does not bud and there are no grapes on the vines, though the olive crop fails and the fields produce no food, though there are no sheep in the pen and no cattle in the stalls, yet I will rejoice in the LORD, I will be joyful in God my Savior. The Sovereign LORD is my strength; he makes my feet like the feet of a deer, he enables me to go on the heights."

Calvinist Repentance

Kuyper simply would not ascend to those heights by the Brighton path. Cutting back his activities to journalism and organizing, he set about to bolster the newspaper that had struggled in his absence. More important was clarifying his theological commitments, a task he undertook in a series on "Perfectionism" which ran in *De Heraut* over the spring and summer of 1878. During his Brighton phase Kuyper had downplayed the more sensational claims of the movement along with its Arminian roots, but neither could be denied. The Smiths and Mahan declared not just peace, power, and unity but even moral perfection, sinlessness, to be attainable — attainable in this lifetime, even at this moment, by an act of will; and if attainable, then compulsory, a matter of some moment in motivating that will. To this position Kuyper now responded with an assessment of both the psychology and the theology of Brighton Holiness. To some extent he was evaluating Anglo-American evangelicalism as a whole, since the Brighton conference led directly into the Keswick movement, which would give Holiness themes a central place in trans-Atlantic evangelicalism for a century to come.

It was a "mixture of truth and untruth [that] prompted groups of the most tender and God-fearing folks to join the spiritual feast in England," Kuyper began. In words echoing his critique of Modernism, the Holiness prospect too had been made compelling by artful depictions. "There was something bewitching in this mighty event, so glorious a contrast, it seemed, with the materialistic and ungodly driving forces of our age." The delusion began when Scripture gave way to personal experience as the touchstone of spiritual truth, and worsened as that experience was sculpted by the evangelical technique of sharing testimonies under emotional duress. Sensitive souls were urged "to push forward as quickly as possible" and conditioned to "the habit of boasting . . . of ever greater blessings, ever more powerful grace, still more marvelous overflowings of love, in ever more surprising and mounting doses."

Just as the urgency and promise of a "decision" for consecration were exaggerated, Kuyper continued, so the Brighton event as a whole required a sensational exaggeration of its news. The conference offered "a spiritual delicatessen to which all the fleet-footed among the devout will flock," whereas a genuine awakening "always starts with the quietly devout of God, is spontaneous in its expressions, and shuns human exhibitionism, external boisterousness, and artificiality in its organizations." The malign forces then converged in a cult of personality premised on charismatic authority. The pattern resembled the Catholic cult of the saints, Kuyper observed, only Rome at least retained "the significant guarantee that the saints did not canonize themselves" but were elevated only after their deaths and due investigation. But the "Enthusiasts" who checkered church history and were now spreading again on the current scene "are not declared but declare themselves to be saints or allow their friends to do so . . . in their own lifetime . . . upon most superficial impressions . . . despite certain well-known facts, on the image of their own good qualities which they have seen in the mirror of their own imagination." With Pearsall Smith clearly in mind, Kuyper warned that such leaders court "the deadly danger of spiritual self-elevation, pride, and arrogance"; their work, "separated from the certainties of conscience, so often begins in the spirit but ends up in the flesh."

Unwittingly, Kuyper had replicated a list of complaints that American churchmen had compiled against evangelical revivalism a generation earlier. He had also raised a caution against his own performance as a charismatic leader in years to come. But for now he focused on tracing the fault of perfectionism back to the root of bad theology. "Pelagius *always* lurks in the shadows of this heresy," he declared — not the Pelagius of arrogant rationalism but the one of "genuine desire for the holy." The lofty standards of God's righteousness, the prospect of laboring for a lifetime against inherent sin, the struggle with one's divided will, the relapses that occur precisely upon some exceptional achievement — all these were so discouraging that believers were tempted to accept the two false measures that perfectionists erect: "Of the holiness of God they have much too low, and of the corruption of sin much too light, a view." As to the first, especially in a moral desert like the present age, they content themselves with "an incredibly low" standard of righteousness and so take a person of objectively middling sanctity to be a giant of faith. As to the second, they number sins individually and try to erase them one by one, rather than plumbing the Sin that occupies the core of their whole person. Emerging as it did amid the nineteenth century's infatuation with its record of achievement, Christian perfectionism was at bottom an attempt "by the born-again sinner to re-erect a throne for humanity instead of casting them down with a crushed heart before the throne of almighty God."

More particularly, the Holiness voices at Brighton, on the teaching of Finney, Palmer, and Mahan, defined sinlessness as the perfect alignment of one's conscious actions with the will of God; but this premise Kuyper deemed to be "precisely the shallow and utterly unholy view of Pelagius that you find in all his intellectual children. . . . Sin is not what you but what God sees and knows and detests as sin." "Unconscious Sin is Also Sin!" Kuyper thundered, and if his long exposition of Scripture to the point was not enough to convince the doubter, he made his own appeal to Christian experience.

> [T]he rule prevails that allows for no exceptions and is regularly confirmed: precisely those who are most advanced in the killing, denial, and control of external evil have also entered most deeply into contrition and persevered most powerfully in calling out for the forgiveness of their guilt! They no longer cling to the external but have been taught by their God to press deeper. And just there, in the depth of their existence, they discovered the loathsome essence, the scandalous root of sin and became acquainted with the demon who stirs up these ungodly realities from the depths of Satan!

The worst danger of Christian perfectionism, he continued, lay in its acclimating people to moral lethargy once their supposed model saints had inevitably fallen into disgrace. Against that Kuyper called his readers to be a "solid, single-minded people" characterized by "spiritual energy and depth and sturdy cohesiveness." Such were less likely to develop under Brighton's parachurch auspices than by traditional Dutch Reformed measures of "quiet seclusion, . . . fasting and prayers . . . born out of need among close relatives or friends, emerg[ing] very gradually into the light of day, and then remain[ing] on the ecclesiastical tracks." To that cause Kuyper now rededicated himself, officially foreswearing his Brighton bypath. While at the time he had not said anything technically incorrect about the revival, he confessed to his readers, he did "not wish to conceal from friend or foe alike that, in retrospect, the Arminians were in control of the field at Brighton." He was guilty of very poor judgment: "Indeed, we wish to state openly, with deep sorrow before God and men, that our understanding of this entire revival was partly in error and, being in error, sinful!"

Kuyper rarely got this personal in public, so it is important to follow what he did and did not say in self-diagnosis. He sounded quite modern in an early passage when he noted that "our holiest high points are paired with the deepest abysses." But he then made the typical Victorian move of ascribing the soul's woe to the body, not vice versa. "Whether the nervous exhaustion which shortly thereafter broke out in such serious illness may help explain [my] misappraisal I leave to the judgment of the spiritually minded among God's children, above all to the judgment of Him who knows our bodies as well as our souls." He did suggest a new standard for pastoral education that he might well have applied to his own future work: "Perhaps I may add that the one-sidedness of our theological training, which makes us more at home in the byways of criticism than in the labyrinth of the spiritual life, leaves us open to such misappraisal."

The Work of the Holy Spirit

The "sealing" that Kuyper took away from the whole episode was in the theology of "the Reformed fathers" that he had learned in one way from Scholten, another way at Beesd, thirdly on the mountaintop, and that was now to be promulgated for the rest of his career. His central theological project of the 1880s would be *The Work of the Holy Spirit,* the divine Person traditionally associated with sanctification and newly emphasized in Keswick Holiness. To that main current of Anglo-American evangelicalism Kuyper's hard-nosed Calvinism would offer a clear alternative. He aimed the work against the mediating theology of his own country as well. These two, "the Ethicals" and "the Methodists," were the extensions of the Enlightenment and the evangelical awakening, respectively. For solutions to the problems of the nineteenth century, therefore, Kuyper leaped over the false starts of the eighteenth back to the "golden age" of the seventeenth.

That leap required first of all some changes in mental habit. However much they disagreed on theological substance, Kuyper argued, Ethicals and evangelicals both tended toward atomism, focusing on the discrete self, deed, or thought; toward sentimentalism, drifting with moods and feelings; toward subjectivism, orbiting around human experience; and hence toward superficiality, enchanted with appearances. Scripture and history supported the Reformed profile instead: a holistic approach that sought out the organic unity behind the individual parts; a probing in depth that got to roots and sources; a rigor willing to sacrifice any human need and hope to the judgment of revealed truth; and above all, a God-centeredness that put everyone and everything in proper perspective. The three parts and 650 pages of *The Work of the Holy Spirit* thus return relentlessly to the big picture and ultimate forces, and enthusiastically — perhaps even with a "subjective" relish — to the bar of divine decree. In many of its chapters the human is associated with a passivity and insufficiency far removed from the hyper-activism of Kuyper's own life. Yet, the august deity to whom mere humans are subject turns out to have love as his deepest motive. God's "entire counsel may be reduced to one thought," Kuyper put it, "that in the end of the ages he may have a Church which shall understand His love and return it."

Effecting that love, Kuyper said, was the chief office of the Holy Spirit, and that work was both cosmic and everlasting. Faith and hope would not be needed in heaven, but love would be, and so the Spirit would never cease its labor of conveying Christ's perfections to the saints. Such had been the Spirit's charge at creation and would have continued as its unbroken activity had not sin disrupted the world. Once that happened, the Spirit advanced its mission by bringing out of sin and chaos a new creation that would one day fulfill its original purpose of singing unending hymns of praise to God. The Spirit-work most visible to history was calling forth the Scriptures, the person of Christ ("conceived by the Holy Spirit"), and the church as instruments of re-creation. But since *all* human gifts and talents were required to that end, Kuyper continued, the Spirit also gives everyone, whether redeemed or not, a vocation, and gives each nation its characteristic genius. In fact, the "work of the Holy Spirit . . . touches every creature, animate and inanimate . . . quickening and sustaining life with reference to [that creature's] being and talents." The Spirit "bears the same character in creation and re-creation," Kuyper summarized. To limit the Spirit's work to the elect, as hyper-Calvinists did, or to matters of salvation, like evangelicals, was to suffer from "crude superficialities." The Reformed genius was to "unite organically the natural and spiritual life . . . the realm of nature and that of grace." Not the mere perfection of the person but of the cosmos was on order.

So ageless, so unfathomable a work could proceed only under the sovereign will of God, and Kuyper spent the second volume of *The Work of the Holy Spirit* and half of the third spelling out exactly what that entailed. Here his focus shifted dramatically to human individuals and the process of their salvation — that is, to the *ordo salutis* that had been anatomized by three centuries of Reformed theology. Now the Ethicals replaced the evangelicals as Kuyper's chief target, although both suffered from the self-inflation that he belabored. Personal redemption was not the point, Kuyper repeated, and any insistence that it was, much less the notion that one had somehow contributed to its accomplishment, probably indicated that it was yet to occur for the individual in question. The glory of God was the point and the cosmic hymn at the end of time its true fulfillment; the salvation of the self was the preparation of one note, one tiny player, in filling out that song. How necessary, how absolutely essential, then, that such salvation be the work of God, start to finish. Kuyper anchored his logic in a bracing supralapsarian understanding of divine election: God had chosen the elect before (supra), not after (infra), the human fall into sin. That dispelled any possibility threatening the security and certainty that remained the prime requisites for cosmic redemption and personal assurance. The "rock hewn from the rock" of his Beesd conversion still provided "shelter from every storm."

Theologically, Kuyper depicted the process this way. In all eternity, before the foundation of the world ("supra"), God implanted the elect in Christ. These elect were not virtual or notional but real persons, since all reality and every individual exists first in the mind of God. This implanting effected regeneration; as Kuyper put it, "in love's hour Eternal Love conceives in us the child of God." A sort of dual personhood thus grows in the self: the natural person, fallen in original sin and inclined to all manner of depravity; and a graft therein, the regenerated self, which is fed by the Holy Spirit from a new "root of life" in Christ. Somewhere in the course of a lifetime — perhaps in the cradle, perhaps very much later — the Holy Spirit effects the "calling" inherent in regeneration. That is, the Spirit makes the self inescapably conscious of the fact of regeneration accomplished for her by God in eternity. The "conversion" upon which evangelicals were so fixated is simply our compliance with this consciousness, Kuyper explained. In fact, borrowing language that Arminians had been using for ages, this conversion is work that we do: "The elect, born again [regenerated] and effectually called, *converts himself.*" Yet the Calvinist saint will need to repeat this conversion again and again, "as often as he discovers conflict between his will and that of the Holy Spirit." The perceived travails of sanctification that Brighton tried to exorcise in a second blessing Kuyper thus put on the "lower" level of human, as opposed to divine, activity, and made them part of a perpetual struggle. Real sanctification, just like real justification, was a finished act of God, "gradually wrought in the converted and manifested according to times and circumstances" in their lives.

Good as his word, Kuyper remained remorselessly "objective" in his analysis, seldom deigning to illustrate or prove a point experientially. He made Scripture and a logical progression from first principles rule, even when one of those first principles might suffer spotty scriptural standing. One wonders if Kuyper remembered at this point how ill-fit his scholastic training had left him for the "labyrinth of the spiritual life," and how compellingly Brighton had appealed to his starved affections. Hannah Whitall Smith's *The Christian's Secret to a Happy Life* has never gone out of print for a reason: it offers concrete discourse about inward struggles, something readers will rarely find in Kuyper's tome. Yet the moments Kuyper did link the divine to the human show how winsome his theocentricity could be. A memorable passage in *The Work of the Holy Spirit* discusses 1 Corinthians 13, Paul's "exquisite delineation of . . . [divine love] which shall not cease to command the admiration of the saints on earth as long as taste for heavenly melodies shall dwell in their hearts." This chapter was only secondarily painting an ideal to which the saints should aspire, Kuyper declared; it was first of all a portrait of the Spirit's own accomplished action.

With endless long-suffering and touching kindness He sought to win us. Of the love which we gave to the Father and the Son He was never envious, but rejoiced in it. . . . However much grieved, [the Spirit's love] was never provoked. It never misunderstood or suspected us, but ever stimulated us to new hope. . . . [W]hen we had strayed and done wrong, it covered the wrong, whispering in our ear that it still believed and hoped all good things of us. Wherefore it endured in us all evil, all unloveliness, all contradictions. . . . [Bearing us through all time] its perfect bliss shall appear only when, looking no more by means of the glass at the phenomenal, we shall behold the eternal verities.

God's Mountaintops

Kuyper wrote like this much more often in his meditations, which ran next to his theology column in *De Heraut* for nearly half a century. An apt example is the reflection on Psalm 42 that he published proximately with the book edition of *The Work of the Holy Spirit.* Here he brilliantly meshed his exalted view of God with the memories of his recuperation in the Alps and with his Calvinist sense of calling. To meet God, Kuyper began, one must leave "the plains and the valleys" — and the Brighton seaside — where the landscape is cluttered with human works, and ascend the mountains, where "God alone is the majestic master craftsman." One is there surrounded first in "a sacred silence," then gradually begins to hear "the roar of the waterfalls of the Almighty." To David, hiding in the mountains from the murderous Saul, the sound of these waterfalls came as "a revelation of His wrath" that echoed in the "abyss" of "his own soul." The abyss, the wrath, the exile — Kuyper had passed through them all. But now he had to press on further, into the dreadful memories of a mountain storm. The dark clouds descend thickly, provoking "deep anxiety and inner distress," and the rain-filled streams "double the power of their cataracts. Now," Kuyper wrote, "the thunder of God's waterfalls becomes truly gripping. In the plunging roar on every side it sounds as if God the Lord has turned up the volume of His majestic voice tenfold."

Kuyper had at last met his Romantic sublime. It was in biblical verse, and it delivered the peace and power that Brighton had fumbled: "the child of God, sitting amidst those dark clouds, does not col-

lapse but instead is comforted and again rises to his feet in God."
Strengthened, he could return, like David, "to the plain of the Jordan,"
there to testify to scoffers who earlier in the psalm had taunted him,
"Where is your God?" Further — Kuyper's eye falling upon the text of
Psalm 43, once one with 42 — he should there seek "vindication . . .
against an ungodly nation . . . [of] deceitful and wicked men." To that
task Kuyper would proceed, fixed and finished at last, with "the memory of his God as he received it in God's mountains . . . indelibly imprinted on his soul."

PART TWO

Constructions, 1877-97

CHAPTER SIX

Organizer

When Kuyper returned home for good in the spring of 1877, he had reason to feel anxious about the future. He was nearly forty years old, the father of six children, and unemployed: a former pastor, an about-to-be-former member of Parliament, a journalist on hiatus, and a once-promising scholar whose project lay ten years in the past. Moreover, the times seemed to be in the hands of forces that boded ill for the future, at least any future he wanted. Germany, the power to the east, was surging ahead on a military-industrialist model run by an authoritarian government, while France, to the south, was a new republican regime intent on pursuing an aggressive course of secularization. Britain, to the west, contemplated its next moves against the small Dutch-founded republics at the tip of Africa. At home, Dutch agriculture was about to fall into a twenty-year depression that would drive small farmers out of business and pose fundamental questions for the Dutch economy. Most immediately, the hour of reckoning on educational policy was at hand. The Higher Education bill that had so concerned Kuyper a year before as he was bundled off to recuperate had indeed been passed, effectively secularizing Dutch universities. That had happened at the hands of a moderate coalition cabinet. Now, the upcoming elections augured victory for the Liberals, who were promising a thorough modernization of elementary education. One of their prime targets was religious "obscurantism."

Given his recent trauma, Kuyper could understandably have chosen an altogether new course. Instead, he determined to pursue the old one, but in a different way. He turned down all the calls that prominent churches extended to him, including the old post in Amsterdam that Hovy urged upon him. Nor did he want to return to Parliament. Instead of formal offices he settled into journalism, where he took up his new vocation as a movement organizer. At this he showed real genius: within three years he founded a university, instituted a formal political party, and helped build a nationwide network of Christian elementary schools. The first two were not only the first of their type in the Netherlands — indeed, pioneering efforts in all of Europe — but represented something of a social revolution as well, steps toward a genuinely democratic social order. The king who pointedly refused to invite him to court, the leaders of the opposition who battled him at every turn, and the members of his own group who were discomfited by his innovations all recognized this. So did the many commoners who were galvanized by his vision — and his charisma.

Kuyper's initiatives were accompanied by two other rising movements on the Dutch scene. In 1879, the climactic year of his organizational drive, the Progressive Liberals added to educational reform a campaign for radical franchise extension to fully democratize the country. And in September of the same year, Lutheran pastor Ferdinand Domela Nieuwenhuis quit his post to begin a crusade (and he meant the term literally) on behalf of the growing ranks of industrial labor and the broadening masses of the rural poor. He founded the first major Dutch socialist organization, the Social-Democratic Union, served by his own newspaper with a Kuyper-like title: *Justice for All!*

The three movements obviously had sharply different goals and rationales, but they reflected a common condition. The quarter-century of economic expansion that began at mid-century had bred optimistic expectations but also eroded many customary social relations, creating a more aggressive, self-seeking public ambience. The economic downturn in the mid-1870s thus mixed together material woes, disappointed hopes, and aggravated uncertainty. The old order had died without a new one being fully born. The rising Calvinists, Progressive Liberals, and Socialists each offered a new model for that purpose and promoted it by sustained campaigns of persuasion, identity-building, and morale-boosting. In chronology and effectiveness, Kuyper's movement led the way.

Much of Kuyper's long-term influence came from the base that his new institutions gave his ideas; at the same time, he insisted that it was the ideas which made the institutions matter. The conjunction itself was his strongest suit. Visionaries of a new society were plentiful among European intellectuals of the day, and commanders of social movements were to be found in every country, but few combined the two roles as well as Kuyper. It helped that he faced a situation made for his temperament and his worldview. He returned from exile onto a scene of stark polarities, where the ungodly seemed ascendant over the baffled disciples of the Lord.

Renewed in courage and energy as he had been by God on the mountaintops, Kuyper was ready to fight. Yet the fight would also take some unexpected turns. His theological target shifted for good from Modernists to people much closer to his own beliefs, while in politics he was aided by a callow opposition that overplayed its hand. The lower-education bill galvanized a counterforce that would not lead just to the Liberals' defeat but to the creation of a whole new political system — one that was forged in significant part by Kuyper's own hand.

Founding a Party

He pursued reform in both church and state simultaneously. First up was politics, for he arrived back in The Hague during the 1877 election season, more determined than ever to create a complete party apparatus. In fact, he had broken his long silence from Nice already in February to enjoin formal organization as "an urgent *confessional* necessity." Other leaders in the group still demurred, but when the June elections gave the Liberal ticket a 60 percent majority in the Lower House of the States General, Kuyper's case seemed proven. He quickly circulated an eighteen-point party platform for comment, amended it per suggestions, and then sent it around again in the fall. Finally approved by a provisional coordinating committee, the document went out on New Year's Day 1878 to potential local chapters for discussion — until Kuyper published it in *De Standaard* a week later as the officially approved platform which local members were to endorse. To some committee members the announcement came as "a thunderclap out of a clear sky," leaving them permanently distrustful of Kuyper. It was their introduction to a modern political operator.

Kuyper's model for a political party had five requirements: that it be defined by a common set of principles and policy goals (the "program" or platform); that it be composed of formally organized chapters in as many localities as possible; that delegates from these chapters gather at national conventions to nominate candidates for Parliament; that endorsed candidates and sitting MPs, like the local chapters themselves, be bound by the party platform; and that party operations be coordinated by a central committee. These might seem to be the obvious building blocks of modern political organization, but until this moment they still waited to be discovered. As historian E. J. Hobsbawm notes, workers' movements across Europe had accumulated plenty of grievances in the previous decades of liberal capitalist hegemony but had failed to gain ground precisely because they lacked "organization, ideology, and leadership." Real potential for concerted opposition lay instead with the "little people" of the middling sort who had a national (not class) identity, yearned for respectability, sensed what a party mechanism offered them, and possessed the aptitude to exploit it. Kuyper was offering just that mechanism to just that audience, and for just that reason political incumbents — more accurately, the whole Dutch political class — objected, regardless of how they regarded his political philosophy. Dutch politics to this point had remained the preserve of elites who assumed deference from those of lower standing. Election campaigns and parliamentary sessions tended to be gentlemanly discussions in self-selected clubs, purged of frank questions of interest or fundamental philosophy. Politics was a game in which the quest for personal advantage was accepted, while ideology, divisiveness, and passion — especially popular passion — were not. Kuyper detested this system, and his proposals were well calculated to upset it.

At the same time Kuyper wanted passion to be disciplined by knowledge. Local elites were not to be replaced by "the people" themselves (as the socialists urged) but with a national leadership network defined by ideology and closely linked to the grassroots. Characteristically, Kuyper saw these two last elements as mutually dependent, so in March 1878 he began a yearlong series of commentary on the party platform in *De Standaard*. Upon completion, the seventy-three installments were published in book form as *Ons Program,* a two-volume, 1,300-page open-university course in applied Calvinistic political philosophy, meant to be kept close at hand by the party faithful. Not incidentally, the work put Kuyper's personal imprint on the party's creed, just as his editorship of *De Standaard,* which brought his voice directly to the rank and file, lent him enormous advantage in intra-party quarrels.

At the same moment that Kuyper began his commentary, the Liberal cabinet headed by Joannes Kappeyne van de Coppello introduced its lower-education reforms. The purpose of the bill was to make Dutch schools fit for the demands of modern times; its political significance was to bring a new generation of Liberals upon the national stage. Liberal legislation to date had focused on economic development by building communication and transportation infrastructure, enhancing material capital. Kappeyne's Progressive Liberals recognized that, having been integrated into a global economy premised upon technological innovation, the Netherlands now had to develop its human capital. To that task they brought a loud, dogmatic version of the earlier Liberals' quiet secularism. Religion, they insisted, especially religious education among young children, bred ignorance, superstition, and backwardness. It stunted the full development of the individual and of the nation.

Accordingly, it was with two barrels — philosophical and practical — that Kappeyne shot his education bill across the bow of the faithful. All schools would have to meet costly new mandates of smaller class sizes, healthier facilities, broader and more rigorous curriculum, higher teacher salaries, and stricter teacher qualifications. To help with the expense, the national government was ready to supplement local funding (heretofore the source of school budgets) up to thirty percent of the total bill, but not a penny would go to religious schools. This meant that if these schools survived, it would be as havens for the wealthy — but the wealthy were precisely the social class not interested in religious schooling. Regarding education, Kuyper did not have to invoke "mortal threat" as a mere figure of speech.

The School Petition

Kappeyne's bill galvanized the opposition as nothing else could, and Kuyper improvised to make the most of it. In scores of towns, villages, and city precincts across the country, committees sprang into action to petition their legislators against the measure. Usually these were not the new political clubs Kuyper had been planting, but entire church councils along with veterans of the old Anti-School-Law League, which to this point had variously contested and cooperated with Kuyper's budding organization.

Kuyper now organized a committee that would coordinate all these local efforts into one great national campaign, the "People's Petition." A surviving forty-seven-page register of local correspondence committees testifies to the detail with which he attended to recruitment and maintenance, while his daily columns in *De Standaard* comprise a model of movement-promotion. The entire effort culminated in a one-week drive in July 1878 to gather signatures. The results were unprecedented: 305,596 signed (including some illiterates who "made their mark") on the Protestant side, and over 164,000 more in a parallel Catholic campaign. The signatures were delivered to the king, who by this time had the duly-passed Kappeyne bill on his desk awaiting his signature. William indicated that among the delegation presenting the petition "that agitator" would not be welcome, but Kuyper knew how to handle the situation. When the king signed the bill, as he was constitutionally obliged to do, Kuyper mourned that "Orange has broken with the past" and forsaken the people. Meanwhile, he had a precious data base upon which to build a party. The *Standaard* and *Heraut* subscription rolls (about 5,000 each) constituted a likely list of leaders, and the petition listed the recruits. He also could see public sentiment finally coming around to his sense that history was nearing a crisis, demanding a choice between stark alternatives.

Some opponents would criticize Kuyper's as a single-issue party — that, despite the weekly commentary running in *De Standaard* before, during, and after the petition campaign, treating every facet of national politics from colonies to waterways. It is more accurate to see education as the party's catalyst and heart. So it was in many countries at the time, for secular and religious parties alike: thus the recently fought *kulturkampf* in the German Empire on the right, the pending campaign for *laïcité* in the French Republic on the left, the perennial endeavor in the United States to establish a "Christianity above creeds" (i.e., a generic Unitarianism) in public schools against Roman Catholicism. In the freshly consolidated nation-states of the 1870s, public education served as the first place to cultivate collective identity with the nation, and no regime countenanced dual loyalties. Kuyper did not exactly either; he thought a good Calvinist could be a good — in fact would be the best — Hollander. But as we will detail further in the next chapter, his political philosophy made freedom of conscience the heart of national culture, made education a function of conscience — that is, of religion — and of the family, and made the family the first counterpoise to the engrossing state. Simply put, Kuyper, with many others of all convictions on both sides of the Atlantic, thought the future rested on the education question.

Kuyper was blessed not only with a perfect issue but with an odd mirror-image in the person of Kappeyne. Both men came from outside the traditional Dutch political class and disdained its genteel clubbiness. Both thought the world was ruled by ideas and wanted parties to set theirs forth in comprehensive form. Both favored ideological polarization and radical innovations to build a democratic future. Kappeyne's party even pioneered a critical demolition of classic Liberal assumptions that Kuyper happily repeated for years to come. The "universal laws" that supposedly governed the operation of society and that were supposedly discovered by neutral reason amounted to an expression of group interests, the Progressives declared; witness the rather embarrassing prosperity that the Liberals' social base had enjoyed under their party's hegemony. Thus, shibboleths like free trade and the minimal state could only be defended prudentially, not from "eternal principle," and only if those policies demonstrated clear utilitarian advantage over other options.

At the same time Kappeyne posed the perfect opposite to Kuyper as a person. A witty lawyer and bohemian dandy, he seemed even to neutral observers to treat life as a game, and politics simply as the most interesting sport in town. In fact, the Progressive Liberals as a whole tended to see themselves as an intermediate generation called to clear out the old for the sake of the new without sharing any firm conviction as to what that new would, or should, entail. Actually, they held two convictions: that public life be purged of any residue of religion, the oldest and most seductive body of universalist illusions; and that law be understood as the register of competing social interests, aiming to keep a rough equilibrium as these interests evolved under no apparent guide but their own internal momentum. Thus combining the style of Oscar Wilde with the convictions of Oliver Wendell Holmes Jr., Kappeyne had to be the bête noire to one as absolutely earnest, and earnest for absolutes, as Kuyper. To top it all off, Kappeyne, reared in a Christian home, had not simply lost his faith but thrown it away. He raised the specter of a future civilization bereft not only of faith but of hope and love as well — cynical, remorseless, rudderless, and hollow.

Founding a University

Just as Kuyper's new career debuted in politics, the new cadre of leaders he called for emerged first in the church, and through an opening created by the very Higher Education law that the faithful had decried as the crack of doom. The 1876 Act was a modernizing measure on several fronts. By turning the theology faculties at state universities into departments for the "neutral" or "scientific" study of religion as a human phenomenon, the Dutch government pioneered the discipline of religious studies around the world. Simultaneously, it authorized the national Reformed church to fill (and fund) collateral chairs at the universities to train clergy. It upgraded the Amsterdam gymnasium to university status to expand access to higher education. Finally, it authorized any private party to found its own institution so long as it provided at least three faculties and an endowment of 100,000 guilders ($40,000 US). Thus, soon after the City University of Amsterdam opened in October 1877, Kuyper joined a small group at the home of William Hovy to strategize. They first mulled over the new theological chairs. Perhaps if they provided the funding, the group thought, the authorities would fill the positions with professors of orthodox sentiment. That possibility evaporated — to the outrage of the Calvinist rank and file around the country — when the nominations filed by the church appointments board included no such names. Why not exercise the other provision of 1876, Hovy ventured at the next meeting, and found a university of their own?

Kuyper welcomed the idea nearly as much as that of a political party. He had mused about the virtues of a "free university" — free from the controls of church or state — already as a pastor in 1870, and he had never forgotten his old dream of being a professor. But the notion was sure to trigger opposition among national-church loyalists, not least from the church's moderate wing. For a university to offer theological education on its own was to them not only a legal anomaly but a direct threat to the Dutch Reformed Church's normative position in the nation. A divided Protestantism, after all, could open the way to greater Catholic influence. That had been the objection ten years before to Kuyper's proposals for pluralizing public elementary and secondary education; now he was broaching the same for pastoral training. Kuyper recognized how deep this fear ran in all segments of the national church, including the orthodox, so his newspaper columns had to emphasize how forlorn were the circumstances in the church, and particularly how hopeless were the prospects for orthodox instruction in the revamped university system.

His university initiative therefore took the opposite strategy of the school campaign. That first campaign had been as ecumenically Christian as possible; the university would be as strictly Calvinistic as he could make it. First, he had to warrant a separate institution at all, and a university at that. Some Reformed moderates proposed renewed efforts to win orthodox slots in the new university system — alternatively, to fund private tutors whom orthodox students could seek out for supplementary instruction. This had been a common practice in Réveil days, but Kuyper declared it wholly inadequate for the new era. The "methodistic" and "evangelical" approach of the Réveil might suffice for "the care of souls and preaching, evangelism and missions, philanthropy and dilettantism," he allowed, but when it came to matters of "scholarship, politics, and law," then "Calvinism," with its formal institutions, comprehensive system, and tight organization, was required.

Moreover, the problem in the church's educational program had spread so deep and wide that the suggested palliatives were worse than useless. For six consecutive weeks Kuyper opened his column in *De Heraut* with the same plaint:

> Our future preachers shall henceforth be taught the core of theology, namely dogmatics . . . by men whose mindset for years already has deliberately sought to eradicate and ridicule the confession of the divine authority of Holy Scripture, of God's Triune Being, of the divinity of the Son, of the personality of the Holy Spirit, and of atonement through the blood of the Lamb. . . . May this be passively indulged?

But why a whole university if theological education was the problem? The question was put most tellingly by Groen's widow, whom Kuyper approached for a substantial donation. Why not join in with the seceded Christian Reformed Church's seminary at Kampen, she probed. Kuyper replied that the crisis in culture went well beyond the capabilities of a mere "pastor-factory" to redress.

Kuyper and his allies kept on the initiative until October 31, 1878, the symbolic anniversary of Luther's Reformation, when they convened a meeting at Utrecht to establish a "Union for Higher Education on a Reformed Basis." That basis was specified as the three doctrinal standards established by the Synod of Dort in 1618-19: the Belgic Confession, the Heidelberg Catechism, and the synod's own Canons against the Arminian Remonstrants. The announcement drew the fire of eminent pastors of conservative stripe, some of whom had just helped with the school campaign. The Rev. J. J. van Toorenenbergen, a longtime critic of Groen's confessionalist approach in Réveil circles, scotched the new university's constitution as educationally sterile and historically ill-informed. He argued that the formulas upon which Kuyper would build a university had been given a loose construction already in 1620, lest scholarship become mere catechesis; Kuyper was extrapolating his own perceived embattlement in the present back to a more tolerant age. Kuyper thundered back that if anyone had presumed a climate of conflict and danger, it had been the august assembly at Dort and the theologians it supervised. Then and now, "enemies from without . . . and enemies from within" assailed the church, necessitating the strictest confessional line in defense. Fueling Kuyper's enmity was Van Toorenenbergen's successful counsel to Elisabeth Groen van Prinsterer that she withhold her money from the cause. To Kuyper's chagrin, she donated not the quarter of the 100,000-guilder endowment he had hoped for, but a nominal 1,000 guilders.

Kuyper's second polemic went on against a onetime pastor acquaintance at Utrecht, Andries Bronsveld. Also an able journalist, Bronsveld personified the passion to maintain national-church unity against Roman Catholic incursions. He regarded Kuyper's proposed university as certain to ruin the first and facilitate the second. Since that combination spelled the worst possible calamity for the nation, he declaimed, there could be no moral right, just as there was little scholarly warrant, for such an institution. The only plausible end it might serve, he suspected, was to feed Kuyper's threefold ambition to be professor, politician, and pope. To such charges Kuyper replied at book-length, addressing the issues but also asking his readers to judge who in the situation was sounding like a demagogue. Neither combatant prevailed outside his own constituency, but that did not keep them from carrying on a war of words far into the future.

Beyond personal animosities, these quarrels were the Dutch version of a tension that flared everywhere the Christian-Democratic movement spread. For all the anti-clericalism that provoked the movement, the cause drew more opposition than support from national church leaders, especially at its formative stages. The ecclesiatics — typically Roman Catholic bishops, but in the Dutch case, Reformed synodical boards and their clerical apologists like Van Toorenenbergen and Bronsveld — worried about the lay initiative that Christian Democracy aroused. They were also concerned that its agenda would enmesh the faithful too deep in worldly affairs, but they worried most about control. As Kuyper was demonstrating, there could be no university or political party such as he envisioned without mass mobilization, and mass mobilization, according to the leading student of European Christian Democracy, "carried important costs that the church was a priori unwilling to undertake" — principally, "the weakening of hierarchical control." Here Bronsveld was prescient: within five years of the founding of the Free University, Kuyper would be inciting the faithful to "throw off the yoke of the synodical hierarchy" and reform — or leave — the national church.

Even some friends wondered about Kuyper's readiness to alienate potential allies. His closest collaborator was Alexander F. de Savornin Lohman, a jurist of significant pedigree, a future professor at the university, and Groen's successor in Parliament as Kuyper was in the press. Lohman liked straight lines in law but less so in theology. He worried that the Dortian formula afforded too narrow a base for academic research and proposed that the Apostles' Creed be used instead. Failing that, he suggested that anyone who could sign Dort's Three Forms in good faith, including the parties Kuyper had been battling, ought to be invited in. Kuyper replied with a formula at once mystical, historical, and dogmatic. Trust not what Ethical theologians professed with their pens, he wrote Lohman, but intuit what they mean in their hearts. Know that the stricter formula simply anticipated the inevitable future: "Protestantism in the Netherlands will eventually be Calvinist or nothing at all." Leave it to the future to remodel or refurbish the university, he advised; as a mistake in the foundations could never be fixed, it was best to cast them without the slightest ambiguity.

Support for his strategy came in telling rhetoric from his old professor, J. H. Scholten. Most of the people calling themselves orthodox in these quarrels were really liberal or half-baked in their theology, he wrote Kuyper at Christmas 1879. From "the historical standpoint" they were less Calvinist than the Modernists, while their ecclesiology was unworthy of the name of Reformed. They were semi-Arian in Christology, had "no genuine trinitarians" in their ranks, and were uniformly captive to "the dualism" and "mechanistic worldview of our time." Personally, said the old Modernist, he found Kuyper's attempt at theological "repristination" to be "scientifically impossible," but it was certainly better than the "half-Lutheran indeterminism and synergism" that characterized his opponents. Scholten signed off "with high regard and also with the wish that from your work something might grow for the Kingdom of God." The following year, a month before the Free University opened, he added a valedictory postcard. "If our paths from here on out diverge, the feelings from the past do not die." The reference "1 Cor[inthians] 13:13b" followed: the greatest of these is love.

Building a Movement

With the foundations set, the institutions themselves opened in quick succession. In January 1879 a national Union for the School with the Bible was formalized at a meeting in Utrecht. In April the first delegate assembly of the Antirevolutionary Party met in the same building and quickly ratified the proposed platform, central committee, and formal party structure. In August the Free University was announced with its requisite faculties and endowment. Kuyper would be professor of theology at the university, chairman of the central committee of the party, and perennial propagandist for the Christian schools in his newspapers. (He left formal involvement in school governance to Lohman.) His greatest contribution, however, was melding these ventures into *a cause,* building a movement that would take them from their exceedingly modest beginnings to long-term prosperity and shape the future of the country in the process. The elementary and secondary schools mattered most immediately to people, and they were the most readily built. The university and party were more novel and required more calculated support. Kuyper built that support with parallel populist structures.

The pomp and circumstance with which the Free University opened on October 20, 1880, could hardly hide the meagerness of its resources. Kuyper acknowledged as much near the end of his inaugural address: "And so our little School comes on the scene, blushing with embarrassment at the name *university*, poor in money, most frugally endowed with scholarly might, more lacking than receiving human favor." In hard fact, its three faculties numbered but five professors: three in theology, one in law, one in letters. They taught a grand total of eight students. They had no library to speak of, an annual budget of 50,000 guilders ($20,000 US), and met for the first two years in the Scottish Mission Church on the edge of Amsterdam's red-light district. Most of the students turned out to be interested in theology, just as Elisabeth Groen van Prinsterer had predicted. Even so, they had to take their qualifying exams twice, because the school's degrees were not recognized by the government. By 1885, however, the student body had grown to fifty, and by 1896 to over one hundred. If they still mostly enrolled in the theology department, they made it one of the largest in the Netherlands.

More novel in the Netherlands was the institution's success as a private undertaking, thanks to Kuyper's cultivation of a cross-class constituency. Half of the initial endowment came from two donors — Hovy and Amsterdam stockbroker T. Sanders, who contributed 25,000 guilders each. Another 10,000 came from Rotterdam businessman P. van Ordt; six more individuals put up 10,000 together. That left 30,000 guilders, not to mention annual gifts and future endowment growth, to come from a national rank-and-file of modest means. In short order the "VU busje," a tin box for spare change, became a staple item on Calvinist kitchen counters around the country. News of the Union became a staple genre in Kuyper's papers. Faculty pamphlets and study guides became staple materials for church discussion groups. Topping it off was the annual meeting of the Union membership, held mid-summer in quasi-holiday circumstances. After the dispatch of formal business, attendees would hear lectures by university worthies, followed by discussion sessions with the shopkeepers, clerks, grade-school teachers, and farmers who had come to view this as *their* school.

Among all the other institutions he built, Kuyper's choice of a university was notable. In part he was anticipating the massive expansion of higher education just underway around the North Atlantic world in 1880. Most of the new universities, public or private, aimed to promote national or technological "progress," however, not to supply leaders for a religious movement. In this respect Kuyper was copying a venerable design in both Western history and Christian missions, which saw the road of advance to be paved with books and study. He paid an enormous compliment to the value of higher learning: "To possess wisdom is a divine trait in our being," he intoned at the university's inaugural ceremonies, and to develop that wisdom ranked among the finest of human pursuits. Scholarship sought to plumb the very bounds of being, celestial and terrestrial: "Thinking after God what He has thought before and about and in us"; grasping "the being- and life-consciousness not of a single person but of humanity through all the ages!" Moreover, down on earth "scholarship often stands at the forefront . . . [of those] means that God has granted nobler peoples to defend their liberties," both civil and religious. Mindful "that every State power tends to look upon all liberty with a suspicious eye," a vital bulwark for freedom could be built only with a well-grounded and systematic knowledge of law and history that thorough study could provide. In religion it was notable that, of all New Testament authors, "the man of Tarsus was the [one who had been] academically trained, and it was from that Pauline treasure chest, not from the mystical John nor from the practical James, that Luther drew the freedom of the Reformation."

Thus engaged, ordinary people could enter into the process of redeeming higher learning even as they were elevated by it. Their participation might save learning from pedantry: "Is this not a practical solution to the problem of connecting learning to life? Must not scholars who are supported by the people's money grow closer to the people and more averse to all that is dry and abstract?" In turn, was it not inspiring in a flat and jaded land like the Netherlands to see (spitting back the elite's epithet for his followers) "the least respected of the 'non-thinking' part of the nation come running from the plow and the feed-trough to collect money to build a university"? It might be the Calvinists and not the Progressives who did the most to enhance the country's human capital. But this demanded even greater sacrifice from his followers:

> . . . is not *giving* itself a power and the ability to part with money a moral asset? Who then can assess the moral capital that will accrue to our people precisely through this costly institution? . . . For with us precisely the "struggle for life" [here invoking Kappeyne's Darwinian shibboleth] generates the power of glorious devotion. In the

money entrusted to us lies something more, something higher than the intrinsic worth of the metal. In the gold that flows into our coffers there is prayer, there is love, and the sweat of the brow.

It would take a cynic of Kappeyne's proportions to withstand that rhetoric.

Since political parties lacked the lustrous precedents of a university, Kuyper's initiatives there posed a greater challenge. For all the fervor roused by the People's Petition just the summer before, and for all his networking prior to the meeting, the inaugural convention of the Antirevolutionary Party in April 1879 attracted only twenty-eight delegates. Just four years later, however, the party numbered ninety-five chapters, and four years after that, 154. In short, it was not in forming but in deepening and broadening commitment that Kuyper's true success as a party organizer lay. His right arm in this effort was journalism. Projecting daily events on a screen of cosmic scale, he cast politics (just as his simultaneous publicity for the university did scholarship) as an arena where people faced basic choices over ultimate stakes. As the university traced the thoughts of God across nature and society, the party would try to get the "ordinances of the Lord" adopted by popular consent as the law of the land. Both would warn against the depredations sure to arise from the humanistic alternatives.

Kuyper's organizational left arm was more mundane but also more innovative: the creation of an entire political *culture* among his following. Politics was not to be just an election-eve affair, but a year-round interest, and it was not to involve only eligible voters but the unenfranchised — the whole community — who shared the party's concerns and for whom the voters had to speak. The party, like the university, would have its binding rituals, especially the delegates' convention every election season, where the assembled faithful could personally grasp the national scale of their movement and cheer the oratory of their leaders. Kuyper unfailingly rose to these occasions. For Kuyper, politics, like higher education, was for everyone, not least because it was — or could be — an elevated pursuit. That "could be" depended upon nothing so much as activating, educating, and sustaining enthusiasm among ordinary people. If traditionalists in his party deeply suspected democracy, Kuyper saw that here too a redemptive cycle might emerge, this time between people and politics.

His cultivation of a consciousness that sustained, even as it was sustained by, an activated community represented a breakthrough that other Dutch parties had to match, or face oblivion.

In effecting this structure, however, Kuyper the operator crossed Kuyper the theorist. On paper the Antirevolutionary Party was an affiliation of local chapters built from the bottom up to the national level. In fact, its Central Committee — especially with Kuyper as chairman — went out and planted, cultivated, directed, and disciplined those chapters. It encouraged affiliates in a region to start their own news sheets, linked those subscription lists to *De Standaard*'s, and prodded local chairmen for updated reports on past and potential voting patterns. Some leaders tired of the drill; it was one reason that Amersfoort chairman P. C. Mondriaan quit and moved to Winterswijk near the German border, where he started an arts school. His most famous pupil would be his son, Piet; the more immediate product was the stock of cartoons that Mondriaan Sr. continued to supply to the Antirevolutionary press. Kuyper's command in all these initiatives, along with his fixation upon national at the expense of provincial and local affairs, not only contradicted the party's credo but prompted suspicions that he aspired to dictatorial powers. The loudest charges came from the outside, but a number of insiders echoed them. Sometimes these were rival journalists, looking for more clout; sometimes they were members of Parliament or local leaders, resisting central control; sometimes they were national-church loyalists suspicious of Kuyper's ecclesiastical designs; sometimes they were "aristocratic" traditionalists wary of Kuyper's "democratic" reforms. Often enough, these circles overlapped. For now, the various elements in the party held together, but there was plenty of potential for splintering once it gained power.

Tribe and Family

Kuyper's initiatives built a thick sociology that — just as conservatives warned — replaced traditional local hierarchies with a national network as the locus of identity and social control. The arrangement worked by overlapping roles and interlocking directorates. A village baker, for instance, might be a member of the local church council, an officer in the Antirevolutionary local, brother to a member of the

Christian school board, and husband to an earnest volunteer for the provincial Bible and missions societies. The latest *Standaard* and *Heraut* would lie in the parlor behind the shop to keep the family informed about the latest developments in the struggle. If some of the children moved to the city for work, they would find the same organizations and reading there. In fact, their first jobs might well have been arranged along the movement network, and at the right church the newcomers could find a number of potential mates whose families had the same loyalties. The pattern even stretched across the oceans to Dutch immigrant communities in the United States and South Africa.

This network was still more pronounced at the elite level. The roster of the boards supervising the party, the university, and — eventually — the separate denomination that Kuyper would lead out of the national church featured the same family names for generations. The inner ring closest to Kuyper was especially prominent either in their own persons, their relatives, or their acolytes, three categories that tended to mesh in a thicket of intermarriages that is daunting to sort out. Thus Kuyper's oldest son, Herman, would marry the daughter of one of his chief Amsterdam backers (and neighbor) and follow him onto the theological faculty at the Free University. A son of Lohman would marry a daughter of Hovy and join his father on the law faculty. One of Lohman's daughters would marry Hovy's business partner; one of his aunts married Groen's brother-in-law; and his widowed sister-in-law married a powerful pastor and professor in the Christian Reformed Church, Lucas Lindeboom. Another of Hovy's daughters would marry the son of Frederik L. Rutgers, Kuyper's closest colleague on the university faculty, himself a graduate of Leiden just a year ahead of Kuyper — who in turn had had Rutgers's father for a professor. Hovy himself, after his first wife died, married into the Esser clan, descendants of an old Amsterdam regent family whose heir had become so immersed in Réveil spirituality as to forsake his considerable secular interests to become a street preacher in The Hague. This Isaak Esser, who chose Hovy's sister in *his* second marriage, produced one son who would marry a Rutgers daughter, another who would marry a Hovy sister, and third who would marry Herman Kuyper's sister-in-law. A daughter of Isaak's marriage to Hovy's sister would wed Anthony Brummelkamp Jr., who helped Kuyper on *De Standaard,* on the party Central Committee, in Parliament, on the university board, and in merging his own native Christian Reformed Church (of which his father was a founder) to the denomination that Kuyper founded.

If Brummelkamp exemplified the principle of interlocking directorates, Hovy perfected it. Between marriages, parenthood, and raising his brewery to the Netherlands' top echelon (where it successfully competed with the upstart Heineken firm), Hovy served as Kuyper's most faithful financier, as co-founder (in 1876) and perpetual board member of the Antirevolutionary labor association, Patrimonium, for seventeen years as president of the university's board of directors, for the same duration as Antirevolutionary representative on the Amsterdam city council, for ten years as a member of the provincial legislature, for fourteen as member of the national Upper House, for decades on the boards of the national Christian school union and the Amsterdam Christian nursing home, besides being in season and out a member of the Amsterdam church council on which he had helped engineer Kuyper's initial call to the city in 1870 and in whose orthodox caucus he thereafter collaborated to plot local and national church reforms. With a few other figures replicating one arc or another of this circle, and with the children of the founders extending the regime beyond the Netherlands into the administration of the East Indies early in the twentieth century, it can be said that Kuyper's movement fulfilled not only the dynamics of democratization but also Robert Michel's theory of the circulation of elites to which he believed democratization was prone. That is, while democracy might give "the people" some sense of power, it certainly afforded ambitious figures of the second rank a mechanism by which to move up.

The nodal point of the Calvinist network remained the home, and Kuyper proved equally methodical there. In June 1878, amidst the school-petition campaign, his family had expanded to seven children with the birth of Guillaume, named after Groen. When the Free University opened in 1880, he moved them back from The Hague to Amsterdam, into a townhouse at Prins Hendrikkade 173, one block away from their old place. The house was owned by Hovy, near his brewery and the accommodations he had built for his workers. It still looked out over the old East Dock of the Dutch West Indies Company, but it would also be within view of Amsterdam's Central Station when that was completed in 1889. Kuyper could view the old and the new in the Dutch economy from his upstairs window. In the home Kuyper supervised a regimen familiar to his followers. He kept close knowledge of each child's conduct and concerns. The main meal of the day featured Bible reading and prayer, kneeling, for the entire household including staff. In the same posture did the household observe New Year's Eve as a "watch night," shorn of revelry.

On the other hand, the Kuyper home showed a diversity at some odds with his movement's sociology. He tended to attract sons from the opposition as his students, probably because they found in him what he had loved in Scholten: cosmic sweep, logical system, and vital passion, unlike the compromises and technicalities of their fathers. Moreover, just as his own closest friend from university days was the Remonstrant pastor Isaac Hooykaas, Kuyper's children cultivated associates outside strict Calvinistic circles.

One of the most detailed, and respectful, accounts of Kuyper family life comes from a student of Ethical slant, Christian Hunnigher, who spent a lot of time at the house as a schoolmate of the oldest sons. To his testimony we owe the remarkable revelation that at some time in this period Kuyper stopped attending church on a regular basis. When he did go, there had to be a non-Calvinist in the pulpit, for "sermons from likeminded ministers would — in his [Kuyper's] words — 'thump his head like hammers.'" More often, he stayed at home Sundays, using the worship hour to write a meditation for the next issue of *De Heraut*. His desk had become his pulpit, a national readership his congregation, his study a populist version of the "sanctuary" where, in his graduate-school reveries, he dreamed of spending his days writing great thoughts in communion with great men. In the throes of the battles that lay ahead, Kuyper would invoke that dream now and then, professing to desire nothing more than to set aside all polemics, withdraw from public view, and devote himself to scholarship. That he had the talent to do so was never in doubt, but the genius he showed at organizing a movement kept that dream from ever coming to pass. Instead, Kuyper himself became a great man to his followers, and for the next forty years they would drink from the unending stream of prose that flowed from that study.

CHAPTER SEVEN

Political Theorist

The most memorable piece ever to come from Kuyper's study-sanctuary was "Sphere Sovereignty," the oration with which he formally opened the Free University. Virtually every thread of his thought makes an appearance in its pages, as do the countervailing forces whose tensions (to invoke the emerging science of the day) hold the whole together like a field of electromagnetic energy. As we have seen, the speech gives intellect regal standing, yet it also characterizes Christians as the foolish of the earth. It treats Calvinists as the core, then as the despised and rejected, of the nation.

As the charter of a university, "Sphere Sovereignty" memorably unveils the pluralistic epistemology that warrants a distinctively Christian intellectual enterprise. Christians, Kuyper said, constitute a world — because they operate by a worldview — of their own, and so need a place where the premises of that worldview can be fathomed and its consequences worked out in a thoroughgoing, consistent fashion. At the same time Kuyper espoused a social philosophy to guide this enterprise. Here operates not human subjectivity varying according to religious conviction but an array of fixed, divinely ordained domains undergirding all human behavior. These "spheres" are to remain mutually autonomous and freely developing, to the flourishing of humanity and the glory of God.

Kuyper put such stock in his university because it provided the linchpin to hold these two concepts together. On the one hand, it would generate a leadership class to fix his movement on the national scene and to produce the scholarship needed to promote the claims of Christianity on the cultural high ground where so much of modern life was governed. On the other hand, these leaders would play on a shared public stage. Their religious claims would need to be translated into policy proposals to advance the common good. Thus "sphere sovereignty" gave the activists in Kuyper's following a template by which to frame their program, while providing the academics with an agenda for research and a charter for creative exploration.

Things start to get complicated, however, when we note how very brief is the allusion to the spheres themselves in Kuyper's speech — little more than one page of the nineteen that the modern English text entails. The sketch is imprecise as well. As to the number of spheres, Kuyper said, "there are in life as many . . . as there are constellations in the sky." He named "a domain of the personal, a domain of nature, of the household, of science, of social and ecclesiastical life," but then mentioned another seven before and yet another three after this list. As for how to picture these domains, they might be "'spheres,' each animated with its own spirit," but then again they might be "cogwheels" in a "great machine . . . spring-driven on their own axles." The image does not matter, Kuyper hurried on, so long as we remember that "the circumference of each has been drawn on a fixed radius from the center of a unique principle." It appears that his evocation of the spheres is not a major part of Kuyper's speech, but only the first word of a social philosophy.

More than anything, "Sphere Sovereignty" reads like the poetic effusions of a bard. The speech accomplishes a great deal of work over a vast terrain in short order by pouring forth a rich sequence of images and allusions, draping them disarmingly over a scaffold that takes some effort to discern. That scrutiny reveals two conclusions: by quantitative measure, "Sphere Sovereignty" is as much a piece of political as of epistemological or social philosophy; by method it is political philosophy told as historical narration. The speech unfolds a heroic saga of world history in which ultimate values are at stake and in whose culminating act the band of believers in his audience are to play a vital role. "Sphere Sovereignty" therefore is a good place to step into a study of Kuyper's political theory. The ideas in this speech need to be compared to the official program he had just elaborated for the party faithful and to the themes he had espoused seven years earlier in "Calvinism and Constitutional Liberties."

Sphere Sovereignty

The cross-pressures in Kuyper's political thought were manifest in the very circumstances of his address. He was speaking from the chancel of Amsterdam's Nieuwe Kerk, the cathedral of Dutch Protestantism, but on behalf of the humble believers in the land who had seemingly been bypassed by time and power. He was staking their claim to social and cultural power, so his speech needed to be insurrectionary, announcing possible reversals in the current status hierarchy. At the same time it had to build for the long run and thus laid out an ontological order that was both dynamic and stable. Kuyper repeated his old conjunction of divine election with democracy but this time substantiated that formal "principle" via a quick survey not of transatlantic Calvinism, as in "Calvinism and Constitutional Liberties," but of world history, of national history, of the history of the Dutch Reformation and Réveil, all rolled into one. Pervading it all is a passion for freedom, a phobia of tyranny, and the goal of order.

The topic of the day being sovereignty, Kuyper opened on the controlling trope of early-modern political philosophy: that sovereignty be absolute and undivided. Since French Calvinist resistance had been both the occasion and the target of that assertion, Kuyper elevated such sovereignty out of human reach and into God's hands alone, then refracted it back down into separate "spheres" of human operation. These powers are not to be re-gathered into one, Kuyper warned, until Christ returns in majesty at the final judgment. Any human claim to unitary sovereignty was blasphemous on the face of it and bound to wreak woe in practice. And in fact, recited Kuyper the bard, such was the grim thread of world history, from the tyranny of the Caesars to the oppressions of the Hapsburgs, Bourbons, and Stuarts, to the contemporary scene where revolutionary claims of popular sovereignty on one side matched Hegelian elevations of "the State as 'the immanent God'" on the other. The historic antidote to these assaults had been constitutional restrictions on the exercise of power, as in the separation and balance of powers theorized by Montesquieu and ensconced in the United States Constitution. But now Kuyper bypassed constitutional measures entirely. Rather, he postulated discrete, autonomous spheres of human life as if to replicate the separation and balance of powers on the ontological level. Not on paper or in formal offices, then, but in the divinely structured creation and in the evolution of organic societies lay the most promising grounds of resistance to the unitary beast.

For all its theocentric claims about the ontological order, however, much less Kuyper's own expertise as a theologian, "Sphere Sovereignty" proceeds with modest biblical evidence and a minimum of theological elaboration. History carries the argument instead. Yet the narrative Kuyper laid out seems to offer scant promise of success. It is mostly taken up with the march of centralization contested by valiant yet faltering heroes of liberty. The Netherlands' own Sea Beggars and hedge-preachers have pride of place in the saga, but these hardly make a convincing case for the theoretical plausibility or future likelihood of the harmonious constellation of spheres that Kuyper wanted to build. He mustered a stronger precedent in "that glorious life, crowned with nobility" which marked the late-medieval Low Countries, "exhibiting in the ever richer organism of guilds and orders and free communities all the energy and glory that sphere sovereignty implies."

At this juncture two silences are notable. For his Reformed audience Kuyper had to gloss over the Catholic ambience in which this late-medieval social order had flourished. More puzzling, he ignored a significant body of Calvinistic political theory that had arisen to explain and defend just the sort of society he had in mind. If "Calvinism and Constitutional Liberties" was the occasion to treat the giants in the Calvinist resistance tradition, "Sphere Sovereignty" should have been the place to invoke Johannes Althusius (1557-1638), syndic of the city of Emden in the late sixteenth century when that Geneva-of-the-North had served both as a beacon and a place of refuge for the struggling Dutch republic. Althusius combined the roles of scholar, civic leader, and ecclesiastical leader on an order that made him in some historians' estimation the equivalent to John Calvin — and should have made him a model for Kuyper's own aspiration. As political philosophy, Althusius's definitive treatise of Calvinist, antiroyalist thought (*Politica Methodice Digesta,* 1603) set forth a consociational picture of politics intended to refute the French Catholic Jean Bodin's theory of unitary sovereignty. In the process it chartered something very like Kuyper's society of sovereign spheres.

For Althusius, human nature was indelibly associational. Communities, not individuals or orders, were the building blocks of society. So also began Kuyper's social ontology: "Our human life . . . is so structured that the individual exists only in groups, and only in such

133

groups can the whole become manifest." Each human association, Althusius continued, was empowered by its original purpose but was also bound by the inherent limits of that purpose so as not to intrude on others — be it other units in the same or in adjoining domains of human activity. Certain powers were delegated upward to the next level by decision of these smaller units, which units remained the constituent members of those broader bodies. Thus, persons were members of households, whose heads delegated some of their political power to town councilors, who in turn appointed mayors and syndics. For economic purposes, citizens joined guilds; for religious purposes, churches; for recreation, clubs. Successive intermediate levels of association then conveyed authority up the scale to more general gatherings: towns constituted a province, provinces a nation, nations an empire.

Human society was thus a pyramid of associations where power remained as close to the base as possible and where different functions of human life developed freely according to the purposes of that function and not at the call of another. No one at any level in any domain ruled without the consent of the governed; decision-making remained closest to those most competent to make and implement them. Moreover, authorities at every level in every domain were constrained by the laws divine and natural that set norms for that association. Thus, individuals within a consociation — the father in the home, guild A in the town economy, province X in the nation — could be disciplined by their fellows or, if need be, by their superiors, for violating their trust.

A more friendly and auspicious antecedent for sphere sovereignty could hardly be imagined. Why did Kuyper not invoke it? Political theorist Jonathan Chaplin suggests that Althusius had been rendered suspect for Kuyper by the work of Otto von Gierke, a premier contemporary (born 1841) German political philosopher. In a book he published the year before "Sphere Sovereignty," Von Gierke completed his project of harnessing Althusius to the evolution of the German constitutional state which he postulated, even in its new imperial form, to be the stable middle between French libertarianism and Russian autocracy. Althusius was thus made to serve what Kuyper deemed to be a false hope and a grim danger. In the process Von Gierke had also secularized Althusius, treating the process of human association as entirely immanent in its drive and court of appeal. On top of these objections we can infer some psychological discomfort on Kuyper's part as well. Althusius's Emden, after all, was also the home of Johannes à Lasco, the subject of Kuyper's early academic fame — and of his then anti-Calvinian argument. From his research and several site visits Kuyper knew Emden too well to be ignorant of Althusius as the champion of its civic life as à Lasco was of its church order. But Kuyper's resolute turn toward Calvin in the intervening years made it embarrassing to valorize Emden for either domain, especially on the occasion of founding a Calvinist university.

But back to Kuyper's speech. What is political theory, named as social ontology and told as historical narrative, doing in a speech that charters a *university?* The answer lies in "Sphere Sovereignty"'s powerful evocation of a fundamental tenet of republican political philosophy: that virtue is a bulwark of liberty. For Kuyper the antidote to unitary power was not just spheres orbiting in theoretical sovereignty, but a resolute citizenry whose moral strength animates the spheres with vitality enough to resist encroachment. And, Kuyper emphasized, to resist even before that the deterioration *within* a sphere — particularly the exploitation of the weaker by the leaders — that invites the state into the sphere's domain in the first place: more accurately, that mandates the state to undertake its divinely given calling to redress abuses of power and reestablish justice. It is finally self-discipline and self-sacrifice by the people that would preclude and withstand statist intervention.

But such *moral* rigor depends much upon *morale,* Kuyper repeated; if we would fight the sloth and corruption that ultimately lead to oppression, we need hope to live a better way. People need a vision contrary to that offered by the hegemonic threat. In other words, the core of political resistance lay in *culture.* There the university served a crucial role. For Kuyper the Free University was to flesh out a robust worldview over against that of the materialist hegemon that was stalking Europe, a worldview that would make of the faithful Reformed remnant a collective player equal in strength — and perhaps one day superior in allure — to the forces animated by secularistic naturalism. At the same time the scholars at the university would be conducting the advanced research on pressing problems of modern life needed to articulate alternative policies from a Christian point of view. As "Calvinism and Constitutional Liberties" warranted revolution by lesser magistrates, "Sphere Sovereignty" gave a charter for Christian public intellectuals.

Party Program

The audience that heard "Sphere Sovereignty" was part of a larger public that had access to Kuyper's newly published two-volume commentary on the new Antirevolutionary Party agenda. *Ons Program* conforms to the nineteenth-century rule that any such treatise, whether it came from Left, Right, or Center, would be part philosophy, part platform, and part propaganda. Philosophy because, as Kuyper taught, no human construction, especially in so controverted an area as politics, was "objective," but instead proceeded from a choice of first principles. Propaganda, because a political party needed to inspire and energize its followers to sustain sacrificial labors over the long run. And finally a platform, because first principles had to be fleshed out and propaganda anchored in a concrete array of proposals that addressed the salient issues of the day and stipulated what government in the hands of the party would try to do. Kuyper's accomplishments over these 400 pages were also three-fold: first, to show the nation — for that matter, to remind his followers — that theirs was not a single-issue cause limited to the school question; second, to maintain an informed and consistent voice across the gamut of public questions without benefit of any formal political training on the part of the author; and third, to set a formidable standard of systematic commentary that rivals were compelled to match. If the Liberals had been disdainful, the Catholics reluctant, and the Conservatives unable to go to their publics with a fully fledged combination of pledge and rationale, Kuyper's pioneering work forced their hand. Mounting a platform as much as an organization was modern politics.

Innovative as it was, *Ons Program* begins on a strongly traditionalist note. The document's twenty-one articles fall into three distinct clusters, the first of which goes at the perennial Calvinist concern for authority. Like "Sphere Sovereignty," *Ons Program* asserts God's "absolute" rule as the only secure bedrock for human affairs. Given the realities of sin, people need to live under transcendent sway; no kind of immanent grounding — be it the best version of social-contract theory or the worst instance of royal caprice — could ultimately deliver both justice and stability. That philosophical premise provided propaganda points more than programmatic direction; for generations Kuyper's followers would play it as a trump card against their opponents' putative relativism. Merely human footings could only be shifting sand, they repeated; the structures erected upon them would wobble between anarchy and despotism, their theoretical warrants swinging from the arbitrary to the abstract. The clearest case in point was the French Revolution, the object lesson memorialized in their party's very name.

The choice of "Antirevolutionary," however, demonstrated that first principles did not resolve all ambiguities. The more venerable elements in the party wanted to label it Christian Historical instead — the term Groen preferred and a testimony to the influence of Burke, Haller, and Stahl in shaping his convictions. Kuyper's Antirevolutionary label bespoke a consistent ideology partaking of the very abstraction that Burke had faulted in the Revolution itself. *Ons Program* insisted that the two names were not in conflict: the "principles" that he now wrought into programmatic framework, Kuyper assured his readers, were rooted in the witness of the Gospel as it had flowered providentially over the course of Dutch history. Yet a tension between a Groenian tradition, supple and conservative, and a Kuyperian tradition*ism,* by turns dogmatic, opportunistic, and radical, was built into the party's very foundations.

The Antirevolutionaries' opponents, on the other hand, had to wonder how "divine authority" would be implemented in a religiously mixed polity. Kuyper deflected their first objections by removing the most common, and discredited, devices traditionally wielded to that end. *Ons Program* rejected any established church in the Netherlands; in fact, it treasured (even if its readers' forebears had once opposed) the separation of church and state. Neither would there be any religious test for citizenship or office-holding. "Church and state each have their own domain," Kuyper declared, "and should come into mutually mediated conduct only through the persons who stand in relationship to both." That is, the conduit between divine authority and state policy would be "the conscience of the legislator," an extension into the modern age of the core liberty that the Dutch nation had defended from the start. Personal conscience, meaning one's animating convictions as much as moral monitor, was "sovereign in its own sphere," free from all state compulsion.

At the same time, Kuyper insisted that this principle gave no warrant for an "atheistic state," a public square purged of any and all religious expressions. If church and state were properly separate, neither religion and society nor religion and politics should be, or could be.

By any standard it was only just — and by Antirevolutionary standards it was positively healthy — for believers to have their say in public affairs. But what if the party organization that Kuyper had recently devised succeeded as he hoped? If the Antirevolutionaries commanded a parliamentary majority, might they not impose a new religious establishment in function if not in name, running roughshod over the convictions of others? Kuyper's answer from principle had to be No: the state was to protect "equal rights for all" in public affairs. His practical answer lay in the program's last article: the party would enter only provisional coalitions, not organic union, with any other group. "Would" here meant "had to." For all of the first article's assertion that they were the "tonic note" in the chord of the nation, seeking to sound forth the will of God in public life, *Ons Program* recognized that Calvinists were in fact a permanent minority, fated to perpetual co-belligerencies with whoever was most congenial to their position on the issue at hand.

The logic of political participation leads on to *Ons Program*'s second concern, a cluster of six articles on the structure of Dutch government. Kuyper repeated from "Calvinism and Constitutional Liberties" that neither Bible nor history ordered a single type of regime for all peoples, so, absent egregious abuses, a nation's history should guide its choices. Accordingly, the Antirevolutionaries were pledged to constitutional monarchy. At this point Kuyper brushed up against his own ambivalence. On the one hand, he was an heir to the cult of the House of Orange; on the other hand, he liked none of the monarchs who reigned in his lifetime. William I had instituted the blighting church regime of 1816; William II had abdicated too much to Thorbecke and constitutional revision; William III was as weak at statecraft as he was loose in morals; the young Wilhelmina would prove much too uppity, and savvy, for him around his term as prime minister. Kuyper thus might have revealed more than he intended in labeling "the sovereignty of Orange" "a mystery." If the republican ethic memorably evoked in "Sphere Sovereignty" sought to find a virtue in the populace that was missing on the throne, *Ons Program* returned to constitutionalism for refuge. Neither royal persons nor democratic publics could be counted on; only enduring structures were reliable. His followers had inherited no love of the Constitution of 1848, but Kuyper called it an improvement upon the instrument of 1813 and committed his party to play by its rules. That meant governance by a cabinet appointed by and so (putatively) under the temporal sovereignty of the Crown but in fact responsible to the States General as the concerted voice of the people. In these maneuvers one can see Kuyper straining to maintain the mystical union of Orange and Nation while riding the momentum toward popular rule.

That trend sparked three proposals for constitutional revision that both made Kuyper's name and sought to implement his vision of society. The first, eventually victorious, was to steadily lower the property requirement for voting until that "privilege" (the ghost of Groen still spoke) was available to all adult males. The second, which never succeeded, proposed to replace provincial with functional representation in the Upper House of the States General. The anomie and discordant individualism which Kuyper and a hundred other theorists feared in democracy was to be corrected by having people's life-roles represented in the national legislature. Thus the Upper House would have seats for business and labor, universities and the arts, agriculture and industry, cities and regions — all the "spheres" of human endeavor which, sovereign in their own domain, would meet to deliberate on matters of public policy in which they had a stake and expertise. Individuals would thus not register in modern life as specks in the mass but as members of functional communities. Meanwhile, in Kuyper's third proposed amendment, the Lower House would be chosen by proportionate representation, the various parties garnering the share of legislative seats equal to their percentage of the total national vote. These allocations would address a perennial challenge of government in making the Upper House frankly a chamber of interests while designing the Lower House to be the site of the nation, where the frame and course of the whole would be prescribed.

That arrangement ran athwart another article in *Ons Program,* the one that called for decentralizing Dutch government. In contrast to his theoretical spheres, whose putative autonomy was yet to be instantiated, the various provinces, cities, and local councils were holders of long-established rights and constituted the most immediate practical counterweight to any state centralization. It was *these* "spheres," in fact, whose complex sharing of sovereignty had defined the Dutch republic in its Golden Age. Kuyper's invocation of providential history warranted the resurrection of their power, but meanwhile his modern representational schemes would erode their salience in national councils.

The Ordinances of God

This paradox leads us back to *Ons Program*'s initial concern with divine sovereignty and forward toward its third cluster of articles, on national policy. How does the imposing divine "absolute" come down into concrete proposals for human life? Through "divine ordinances," Kuyper declared. It was identifying, celebrating, guarding, and translating those ordinances into action that defined his ultimate purpose in politics. He had given them significant attention already in *De Standaard* in 1873 upon his first move into politics, essays that he included as a special section in the first edition of *Ons Program*. He singled out the ordinances again at a high-water mark of his career, the twenty-fifth-anniversary banquet celebrating the founding of the paper. In the peroration of his after-dinner speech he poetized off an original by Isaac da Costa:

> For me, *one* longing rules my life,
> *One* higher urge drives mind and soul.
> And rather may my life's breath fail me,
> Than I ever lose this holy goal.
> It is that God's holy ordinances,
> In home and church, in state and school,
> In spite of all the world's remonstrances,
> Be set fast again, for the good of all.

Like the Free University as an institution, the concept of divine ordinances performed two crucial functions at once in Kuyper's system. First, it limited (though importantly, did not relativize) the authority of any human being or office. The sinfulness traditionally invoked to warrant absolute power for pope or king as an earthly mirror of divine rule made exactly such concentration of power dangerous, Kuyper repeated. His was a theory of divine *ordinances,* not divinely ordained *persons.* Second, *Ons Program* states at the outset how essential it was to recognize against all relative human foundations that there *are* ordinances, that they are *real,* and that they are *from God.* By them God established the limits but also the purposes and powers of the state — and not of the state alone, but of all the other domains of life too. To recall the crucial point from "Sphere Sovereignty," it was not the image of "spheres" or "cogwheels" that defined these domains but, rather, that "the circumference of each has been drawn on a fixed radius from the center of a unique principle." Definitive principle and set radius together formed the business end of the divine ordinance in each domain, just as the ordinances themselves were the business end of divine sovereignty in human affairs.

In that light, Kuyper continued, it became altogether important to learn *what* these ordinances were, *where* they were to be found, how they were to be *discerned,* and how they *applied* to policy formation. Kuyper was most definite on the middle of these two questions, more variable on the first and last. His dicta as to locating and discerning the ordinances accepted the (putative) standards of the secular opposition. That is, taking divine ordinances seriously makes "incontrovertible the assertion that the laws governing life reveal themselves spontaneously in life" and are to be discovered by action and scientific reflection. "God's creation . . . since its very beginning is fully equipped and endowed with all the powers it needs, carrying within it the seeds of all the developments to which it will attain even in its highest perfection." It followed that "all the givens that govern the political life of the nations were present in human nature at its creation."

To be sure, Kuyper assured his readers, the opposition erred by ignoring how radical a dislocation in the arrangements of political life had been occasioned by the human fall into sin. But even if sin precluded deriving sound political theory from any direct reading of "nature," it would be folly for the Christian, especially the Christian statesman, not to harvest the best insights that can be gleaned from the rich and varied history of human political life. Convinced though they were of human depravity, Kuyper recalled, "the spiritual fathers of Calvinism" held in high esteem "the experience of the states of antiquity, the practical wisdom of their laws, and the deep insight of their statesmen and philosophers." Indeed, all these accomplishments "are cited in support of [the fathers'] own affirmations and consciously related to the ordinances of God."

That the Calvinist fathers were also devotees of Scripture Kuyper did not need to teach his followers; rather, he needed to demarcate its sway on political matters precisely. Citing Calvin himself, Kuyper compared Scripture to corrective lenses that restored clear perception of "the partially obscured revelation of nature. . . . What life itself, distorted and derailed by sin, could no longer reveal, God in his love made known in his Word, also for our political life." The latter was not provided for on the level of details, however, but in "the ground rules, the primary relationships, the principles that govern man's life together and his relationship to the most holy God." The only folly worse than ignoring the record of history would be the one in fact committed by the theonomist wing of the Christian Right in the United States a hundred years after Kuyper cautioned his readers against this very error: any proposal which "simply wishes to duplicate the situation of Israel, taking Holy Scripture as a complete code of Christian law for the state, would . . . be the epitome of absurdity." Indeed, human societies were so variable in character and circumstances so fluctuating that "it is impossible to supply a handbook for Christian political theory that is valid for all nations and all times." Anyone who would practice Christian politics thus faced an entry qualification that Kuyper set out with a revealing comparative emphasis: the "knowledge of God's ordinances must be the result of a *thorough* knowledge of the nations and a *fundamental* knowledge of God's Word."

Kuyper thus marked his own movement off from many other theological conservatives, especially those in the Anglo-American evangelical and Fundamentalist movements. He affirmed creation as firmly as they did but countenanced far more than they an unfolding development — an evolution — of human life and society. He shared their concern for order, but by locating that in divinely set developmental goals, he could affirm human creativity and fundamental change. Thus he took history more seriously than they, and like thinkers toward the liberal end of the theological spectrum gave it genuinely revelatory significance for the will and ways of God. When other theological conservatives thought of evolution, they thought of Darwin and challenges to Scripture. When Kuyper thought of it, he drew off Hegel — a Hegel governed by, rather than displacing, God.

From Divine Ordinances to Human Policy

Yet over all the flux of time and place God's ordinances did run, Kuyper continued. These "eternal principles" were "valid for all nations and in force for all times." They would be the enduring *teloi* of creation, better restored to human sight by the corrective lenses of God's revelation. A truly Christian politics must advocate these principles and might even render them into law for a whole nation. Yet such enactment had to proceed by due process in deliberative assemblies under constitutional constraints, so that, however much appeal to divine ordination served Antirevolutionary morale-building, fifty percent-plus-one of the legislators had to believe from some more general rationale that a proposed measure served the common good. That required a return to Kuyper's four-item list. Having seen *where* the ordinances lay and *how* they were to be discerned, the Antirevolutionaries still needed to *apply* them to the level of concrete policy. For that matter, *what* those ordinances were in the first place needed to be spelled out consistently.

When Kuyper first listed the ordinances in 1873 they numbered five: (1) that a nation is "an organic whole" and "not an aggregate of individuals"; (2) that "justice" must prevail over "the fortuitous success of violence" among (and, one may infer, also within) nations; (3) that "imperialism" is intolerable, being a reflection of "Caesar" instead of "Christ"; (4) that God is to be obeyed against the contrary assertions of any "earthly authority," as is the legitimate power within any sphere over against unwarranted imposition from the outside; and finally (5) that "the struggle for freedom and progress" bears a "sacred" character. The first and last of these ordinances proved to be more philosophical parameters than policy directives — the latter clustered more in the middle items on the list. In foreign policy (#3), for instance, *Ons Program* asserted international law and the concert of nations as counterweights to national sovereignty and as checks on imperialist aggression. For the Dutch judicial system (#2) it mandated expeditious trials, capital punishment for capital offenses, and the impartiality of police and legal procedures with respect to class and station. Together, the two aimed at subordinating violence to law at home and abroad. But since sphere sovereignty (#4) was Kuyper's most distinctive tenet, it received the most extensive elaboration and birthed subsidiary divine ordinances along the way.

We might better say that sphere sovereignty rendered as divinely ordained a theory of organic social development resembling that of the German historical school, which had both influenced Groen prior to his evangelical conversion and become entwined with various currents of Romantic social philosophy across the Continent. In other words, it came to Kuyper down the two strongest lines of his own inheritance. His particular contribution was to demarcate within this ideal of a free and vibrant society the "fixed radius" and divinely en-

dowed "principle" of five particular spheres, along with policy prescription attendant to each.*

Two spheres can be treated quickly with respect to policy. The
church grew out of the principle of grace as the first fruits of a new, redeemed humanity on earth. It was defined by the preaching of the
Word and administration of the sacraments, the purity of which neither state nor any other institution was competent to judge. The
church should thus be entirely free of government subsidy or regulation at the same time that it forswore any "right to establish political
principles that would bind the state." *Education* represented a more
complex affair, even though it had been subject to no little sloganeer-
ing to this point. Its nature was ambiguous in that the school was
properly rooted in the family but responded to a legitimate interest of
the state. In earlier times children received all the formation they
needed within the household, but with the social "progress" Kuyper
prized, some necessary skills now eluded the competence of parents
to teach, just as the evolving economy reduced the requisite proximity
of parents (especially fathers) and children in everyday life. Kuyper's
program thus said that the state might properly demand certain standards of competence among teachers and achievement by pupils, but
it should never lose sight of education as a parental responsibility.
Parents' religious and moral convictions, being inviolable rights of
conscience and guaranteed under the separation of religion from
state purview, had to be fairly represented at all levels of education.
This fairness included financing: public revenue should be allotted to
particular schools in proportion to the number of students they enrolled. Moreover — here Kuyper the propagandist took over — since
the majority of the Dutch population still held (or harbored historic)
religious conviction, the religious school should be treated as the
"norm," and the "neutral" or secular school as a "supplement," in
Dutch public education.

The *family,* though the third sphere considered here, was for
Kuyper first in every sense of the term. It was the first institution to appear in history and seeded all the rest. Its health was the foundation
and surest barometer of a society's wellbeing. It grew from nature,

---

*Two additional spheres, the arts and sciences, would receive greater attention in
subsequent decades as Kuyper's cultural interests revived. They will be treated in
later chapters.

prospered by nurture, and properly taught its members how to balance personal autonomy, mutual dependence, and due responsibility — that is, it was society in miniature. Likewise its authority was the source of, model for, and limit upon the state. Properly functioning, it also exhibited church-like qualities in being crowned with love and becoming a school for morals. It set the first limit on individualism and initiated the delegation of powers central to consociational theory. If school and church each had a discrete article in the program, the family bore upon many. That complicated policy formulation at three points in particular. The state might mandate education, but the family — the "father," Kuyper clarified — defined its terms. The state must promote public health by ensuring pure food and water, among other measures, but it might not violate a family's rights of conscience and make vaccination compulsory. To prevent anomic individualism, the franchise should be extended to all heads of households, not to all adult persons. Normally, that meant voting by husbands/fathers; otherwise, by widows/mothers.

The State

Kuyper showed his greatest ambivalence toward the fourth sphere, the *state*. Divinely ordained and the guarantor against chaos and depredation, it deserved obedience and gratitude. Bearing the power of the sword and sharp tendencies toward expansion, it should provoke fear. He refused to join contemporary opinion in seeing the state as the unitary expression of the will of "the people," the modern instrument of providence into which the church itself should be absorbed, or the power that would hold together all other domains in unity and order. *Ons Program* stipulated that the state was *among* and not *above* the other spheres. Yet "Sphere Sovereignty" acknowledged that it "rises high *above* them" with the mandate to regulate the other spheres' mutual relations and to intrude within each and any of them whenever individual rights were abused or the weak were exploited by the powerful. In terms of ordinance theory, the state arose in response to sin and bore the principle of justice, and so Kuyper most commonly declaimed whenever rival political groups promoted the expansion of state powers. But he also sounded a secondary theme at his 1873 debut, a theme that never went away: it was simply wrong to see "the state . . . as a purely external means of compulsion." The sharp distinction that the German historical school taught between a good healthy society, organically developing on its own power, and a negative disciplinary state Kuyper correlated theologically with a divinely endowed creation vis à vis necessary constraints of sin. But within this understanding there was nothing to say that even without sin, a vibrant society would not have arranged for a central agency to coordinate its emerging complexity — the very function that theorists of the modern expansive state prescribed.

Kuyper was correct to see, however, the ominous connection between such cheerful mandates and the rapidly expanding military sector in the European states of his day. In popular and official rhetoric, all these expansions — of arms, industry, education, technology, and the government that fed the lot — mixed together under anxious boasts about national strength, preparedness, and power. Yet while Kuyper bewailed the increasing militarization of Europe, he also called for a stronger defense in the Netherlands. In particular he wanted to bring the army toward parity with the navy so as to guard the eastern borders of the country and not simply its western urban core. Increased patriotism would be a welcome byproduct of the process. Further, military service was to be promoted equitably across all sectors of society; the commonly granted draft exemptions for Roman Catholics should cease. Likewise, the fiscal burden of government should be equitably shared, but also minimized. Thus *Ons Program* opposed any move toward income taxes as likely to expand state activism. It bore down upon the wealthier by calling for a property-tax regime instead, although it acknowledged that people of lesser means owed their due share. These two equities of sacrifice — military and fiscal — spelled a looming conflict, however. As Kuyper's own statistical calculations in *Ons Program* revealed, the European nations' military preparations were inordinately expensive and at direct loggerheads with budgetary restraint.

Nor was Kuyper a simple state-minimalist in domestic affairs. *Ons Program* called for stricter regulation of prostitution and alcohol abuse so as to promote "public virtue." The budget pressures entailed by such policing would elicit droll comment later on during his prime ministership; the cost of achieving educational equity was much higher and more immediately controversial. These proposals also bring us back to the high plains of theory at two points. First, Kuyper varied on how *society* was to be understood. Sometimes he treated it as a separate, fifth sphere, reflecting a tradition that so labeled the domain of voluntarist action that lay between household, church, and state. At other times Kuyper treated "society" as a collection of all spheres *except* the state. In either case, his fulsome trust in the powers and dynamics he regarded as inherent in the social sphere from creation is remarkable. Nowhere did he so minimize the effects of sin as in his assumptions about the macro level of social development. Sometimes — for instance, in his speech against "Uniformity" — he could spy a fearful momentum that was greater than any particular part, and on many occasions he noted individual persons, policies, agencies, or communities perverting their social potential. But in formal theory Kuyper more often celebrated than worried about the direction of the whole.

Here he shared in his era's cult of "progress." This is not surprising when we remember that it was in the half-century from 1830 to the publication date of *Ons Program* that Europe achieved its greatest technological conquest of nature and its concomitant ascendancy over other world civilizations. Much injustice arose in this new order — much oppression of the poor and the weak, much ambition and swagger among the powerful — along with an alarming erosion of Christianity's hold on the elite. Kuyper recognized this; he never believed that the tide of progress would bring in the kingdom of God. Yet he little doubted, either, that on many fronts things were good, in a manner of speaking, and getting better. Sorting out just how that "good" was to be understood, especially in relationship to the perfection demanded by God and dependent on true faith, would be the subject of Kuyper's most telling theological work in the future.

His insistence on warranting behavioral controls as "public virtue" (or, alternatively, "honor") and not merely as "public morality" bespoke another basic ambiguity. Obviously the Netherlands operated with a principled pluralism in which parties of fundamentally different convictions would compete in the arena of a religiously neutral state. Still, *Ons Program* declared, the Netherlands was "a baptized nation" and should accord Christianity special respect. At the least, the state should remove every legal obstacle from the free proclamation of the gospel. Even more, it ought to express a preferential option for the faith by maintaining those usages that derived from its lingering penumbra: for instance, requiring the oath for legal testimony, prescribing Sunday as a day of rest, restricting cursing and blasphemy in public speech and print. It was not just the social utility of these measures that gave them warrant, Kuyper said, though that function was real and worthy. Rather, the honor of God required it and could not be disregarded with impunity. Perhaps most eyes no longer saw the sacred canopy over the Netherlands, but that did not mean it was no longer there. The eyes of faith saw it still and had a mission to call it to view.

Where platform ended and propaganda began on that claim is impossible to determine; Antirevolutionary philosophy stipulated it as a policy and required it as a morale-booster. In any case, the group's differences with other parties were clear enough. Less clear were differences within the party that would strain its unity in the years ahead, especially on the platform points that we have bypassed for now: colonial policy, democratization, and economic affairs. The most immediate strain, however, would arise from Kuyper's challenge not to the peace of the state but to the peace of the church. Many would see that as the greatest besmirchment of God's honor and the nation's well-being. Kuyper saw it as the salvation of both.

CHAPTER EIGHT

Church Reformer

On the morning of January 6, 1886, Kuyper and some of his closest associates gathered outside the Nieuwe Kerk on Amsterdam's Dam square. Unlike the auspicious occasion some five years before, when they had come to open a university, this time they intended to break into the church council room. Hence the odd combination of distinguished lawyers and carpenters in the group. The legal team included Frederik Rutgers, professor of church law at the Free University and head of the board that controlled Amsterdam's church properties; Alexander F. de Savornin Lohman, his colleague on the law faculty as well as a judge on the provincial bench of North Brabant; and Theo Heemskerk, son of none less than the chair and Minister of Domestic Affairs in the current cabinet and a future prime minister himself. Among the workmen were Klaas Kater, leader of the Calvinist labor union Patrimonium, and Bart Poesiat, an elder on the Amsterdam church council.

Confronting them were some guards that had been commissioned by the regional board of the Dutch Reformed Church for just this eventuality — the reason also that a steel plate reinforced the newly changed lock on the council room door. The guard immediately sent for the police; Rutgers and Lohman trumped them with a police commissioner and lawyers for the church trustees. The confrontation, in classic Dutch manner, devolved into a lengthy exchange of views that avoided the use of force except, eventually, by a carpenter's saw upon a panel in the door. Now in control of the premises, Kuyper's party mounted their own guard of club-carrying Free University students, who maintained a round-the-clock vigil for the rest of the year.

This "panel incident" was probably the single most controversial episode of Kuyper's career; it was certainly the dramatic hinge of his campaign for church reform. The symbolic significance of the contest — seizing, or recovering, possession of an iconic church in the center of the capital — was lost on no one, nor was the irony of Antirevolutionaries using what looked for all the world like revolutionary measures. Leaders loyal to the national church played the game as well, huddling outside the church in the drifting snow two days later in a vain attempt to hold their own meeting on the premises. The only surprising development was that, by the end of this standoff, Kuyper had lost the public-relations advantage to his opponents, just as in the larger campaign he would be for once outmaneuvered. The church conflict would be remembered by the label Kuyper gave it, the *Doleantie,* apropos of true believers "grieving" the usurpation of their mother church by illegitimate forces — but also, their opponents said, bearing grievances with no little self-pity in the courts of law and public opinion.

Kuyper himself took a lot of grief in both those venues and in private too, for unlike his great organizing successes elsewhere, his church reform proved to be the greatest disappointment of his life. Far from renewing the entire Dutch Reformed Church as he had hoped, the Doleantie amounted to a separation of some ten percent of its members, and not even a third of the orthodox. Indeed, nothing so riled traditionalists in the national church or so permanently divided the conservative ranks. In splitting the Nieuwe Kerk door, Kuyper not only split the church but opened fundamental questions about the identity and mission of his own movement, of the Reformed tradition, of the whole nation.

What accounted for this unexpected outcome? For one, the venerability of the church. Kuyper's successes to date had occurred in emerging sectors of modernity — mass journalism, mass politics, and expanding higher education. Many wanted the church to be a refuge from all this tumult, protected from change. Then too, Kuyper's core assumptions hid some fault lines that were now exposed. Yet these are the judgments of hindsight, and it is difficult to imagine Kuyper not finally arriving at one sort of showdown or another on the ecclesiastical front. Personally, the "church question" had figured large in both his *Redclyffe* and Calvinist conversions, as in his conflicts with his father. Professionally, it had been instrumental in launching both his scholarly and pastoral careers. Strategically, if, as Kuyper believed, the issues of life proceeded from the indelibly religious heart, then the church was an institution of unsurpassed importance for the future as well as the past. If, further, the Dutch Reformed Church had become at once deformed, sclerotic, and perverted from its true course, then a battle to reform that church — in fact, to complete what had been only half finished in the Reformation of the sixteenth century — was not only inevitable but commendable. Such an endeavor would fulfill, finally, the frustrated agenda of his Amsterdam pastorate. "Church terrain" naturally served for Kuyper as the point of convergence for personal, professional, religious, and world-historical forces. The stakes could hardly be higher.

The Legal Case

Kuyper spelled out his vision for church reform most completely in his 1883 *Tractate on the Reformation of the Churches,* published deliberately on the 400th anniversary of Luther's birth. The more than 200 pages of the volume, like most of the argumentation it spurred, stuck to matters of church law, yet left a clear outline that was anything but dry. As in his political theory, Kuyper began with the matter of sovereignty, which in the church belonged solely to King Jesus and was his to delegate when and as he pleased. Scripture clearly revealed that he had done so not to princes or bishops, nor to popes or synods, but to the full membership of the church via (plaudits to Luther) the priesthood of all believers. Thus, Kuyper's core principle: the essence of the church was present fully and sufficiently in the local congregation, bound by the Word of God. Any broader bands of affiliation that the congregation wished to make were of a voluntary, federative nature.

The application to the Dutch case was clear. Synods and classes did not constitute the church, of which congregations were then but local chapters; just the opposite. Furthermore, only by being freed of the synodical apparatus of boards and commissions that had been superimposed upon them could the faithful be re-opened to the power of the Holy Spirit flowing from their Lord. The results, Kuyper promised, would be revitalized congregations. Believers would be strengthened, nominal members quickened, unbelievers converted, the whole nation elevated in morality to a higher plane of life.

Key values from Kuyper's political theory — localism, democracy, the spontaneous powers of free society — reappeared here. So did his bête noire of bureaucracy. In polemical extremis, Kuyper went so far as to cast a shadow on the time-honored offices of elder, deacon, and pastor in the local church. Had there not been a fall into sin, he said of these as about the state in his political theory, churches would have developed fine without them. They were necessary in the post-lapsarian situation as negative bulwarks against error, but should be closely monitored lest they encroach upon the laity's initiatives. Far worse were the "artificial creatures of the state" imposed by the 1816 church order; upon them, the administrative apparatus of synodical and classical boards, Kuyper poured out the most persistent hostility of his entire career. His other targets could always get a compliment or gesture of understanding along the way, be they political liberals, "the better sort of socialist," or theological Modernists. But no such expression ever crossed his lips respecting the "synodical appara-tus." He pilloried its form and — unusually — extended his sentence from its offices to its officials: these were self-serving and self-perpetuating, bereft of honor, courage, and candor. They were not "men," in the redolent Victorian sense of the word, but minions, functionaries, pygmies.

Not surprisingly, Kuyper's words aroused quick retorts from the accused. More interesting were the rejoinders that probed at the ten-sions in his axioms. If the local church were preeminent, the Modern-ists might ask, why had Kuyper been prosecuting their congregations for altering sacramental formulas and preaching? Because, he an-swered, such changes did not, *could* not, reflect the real sentiments of the membership, only the deviations of an elite that had been artifi-cially empowered by an aristocratic regime that was now finally on the way out. But what if a congregation — say, a gathering of pampered re-gents at a summer resort — opted for liberal theology? Then it would no longer qualify as truly Dutch Reformed, for it turned out that Kuyper's system did have one synod which remained definitive for any church claiming this particular fellowship. Just as every congrega-tion was bound to the Word of King Jesus, so the Synod of Dort of 1618-19 had established in the Belgic Confession, the Heidelberg Cat-echism, and the Synod's own Canons the interpretation of that Word binding upon all Dutch Reformed congregations present and future. Nor had Dort acted arbitrarily in doing so, church historian Kuyper claimed; it was simply codifying the doctrinal consensus that had emerged to that point in the migration of the Dutch churches out of Roman Catholic error. The sixteenth-century parent set the standard for all its descendants; it remained for the children of the late nineteenth century to both restore and complete the work.

But how did such strictures comport with the nation's historic (and Kuyper's own) defense of personal conscience? Because no one was forced to join the church, Kuyper replied. Rather, the local congregation was constituted of those people who had made a full and free profession of faith in the gospel of King Jesus as understood by the confessional standards of the church. Those persons unable to make such a profession were free — indeed, should be encouraged — to start ethical-religious societies of their own, which were doubtless capable of doing some good. The separation would relieve the national church of the friction and hard feelings attendant upon its current mixed state of conviction. But what of all those infants who had received baptism and could not assent to the confessions at the age of discretion; was the sacrament of no effect for them? Was God unfaithful to the promises made at the font? Why baptize infants at all if the later profession of faith (confirmation) actually sealed church membership? Here Kuyper really was torn between poles in his thought, for he could not repudiate infant baptism and be true to Dort, nor just go through the motions that demoted the sacrament to a custodial gesture. In fact, he would run into strong opposition in his post-Doleantie church for taking so high a view of election as to make baptism a sign of presumed regeneration for the infant in question. His only recourse was to affirm, if in anxious hope, that proper nurture would bring the baptized to a free affirmation of the confessional standards.

Church and Nation

That dispute was for a later date; a different question about baptism and church membership loomed more immediately and went to the heart of Dutch Protestant identity. It came not from the orthodox pietists who would press him in the future, nor from the Modernists with whom he had argued before, but from fellow heirs of the Réveil who shared much of his traditional Reformed understanding of the gospel and prayed that it might once again suffuse the national church. This was the moderate irenical circle descended from Isaac da Costa via Continental mediating theology. Genuinely conservative by temperament, they turned out to be the decisive party in the Doleantie struggle. They were chief among the moderates who held a disproportionate share of the slots on the synodical and classical boards, and so they became Kuyper's chief enemy in the strife. The disagreement between the two remained in part theological, for the moderates affirmed (in the words of the old synodical formulation) "the spirit and leading themes" of the Reformed confessions while Kuyper's followers insisted on the "letter" thereof. From the strict confessionalists' point of view, the moderate stance aided the Modernist theological deviations that were their ultimate target.

But their concern for polity was just as genuine, particularly as it touched on the relationship between church and nation. For Kuyper the church was a free, voluntary body called out of the larger society to be, inter alia, a witness to and leaven in that society. For the moderates, and for a good number of ultra-conservatives, the Dutch Reformed Church was the providentially appointed channel of grace to the Netherlands, the historical form in which the kingdom of God took expression in the country's life. Besides, thousands more of tepid or unreflective or indifferent theological hue across the country at large valued the church as the moral expression of the nation, as a vital moral leaven, or as the guarantor in ethics, sentiment, or ritual of national unity or "tradition." Kuyper himself never lost these sentiments entirely; well after the Doleantie he could talk of the Netherlands as a "baptized nation." The issue from his point of view was that the church did not belong to or for the nation; it belonged to "King Jesus," and only by being faithful to him would it be of any good for anybody else. That meant it was to be as pure, vigorous, and disciplined as possible, even at the cost of broad nominal sway.

Two of Kuyper's assumptions — that the majority of Dutch society remained orthodox at heart while being amenable to radical institutional rearrangements — tripped over the consistency of conservatism; if the majority were the first, they would in all probability not be the second. His attempt to trump traditionalist sentiments threatened his own Groenian heritage. Those who appealed to history as the bearer of providence, he said, underestimated the force of sin in human affairs, which could seep in over the passage of time just as well as explode in revolutionary paroxysms. Their argument amounted to mere Legitimism, Kuyper declared, tarring the moderates with the late, unlamented schemes of Restoration monarchs like William I. When his critics replied that his proposal was revolutionary, Kuyper retorted that that particular dishonor belonged to the General Regulation of 1816; he simply aimed to restore the genuinely historic and organically Dutch system ordained by Dort. If in fact the Dutch Reformed Church had never practiced the federative localism that the *Tractate* espoused, nor for that matter much of the church order that Dort had stipulated, then it was high time, beginning in the Luther-year of 1883, to complete the Reformation that the fathers foresaw but had been unable to see through.

Kuyper could point to current evidence to bolster his promise. When he had come to Amsterdam as a pastor in 1870, the Reformed Church there claimed 130,000 members (half of the city's population) but saw only 6,000 to 8,000 persons in attendance on a given Sunday. By the mid-1880s, average attendance had improved to some 17,500-20,000, a register of orthodoxy's resurgence. Since Kuyper's debut as the first democratically elected dominie, all eleven of the new pastors installed in the city were of orthodox hue, while the Modernists were down to three. Even more strikingly, Kuyper pointed to the fortunes of the Christian Reformed Church descended from the Secession of 1834. In thirty-five years it had grown from nothing to over 100,000 members, and would nearly double those numbers in the 1880s alone. If the church in Amsterdam matched their vitality, Kuyper figured, it would be supporting over 300 clergy, not thirty; would be worshipping in 250 buildings, not have just erected its eleventh, and first since 1671; would be offering the poor comprehensive diaconal care instead of neglect; would be educating city children in seventy-two schools instead of leaving them to the tender mercies of the state. The woeful actualities that prevailed in the national church only proved, he argued, how deadened it was to the urgency of the times, how vitiated of vital force. Just as the Amsterdam church council had rejected his proportionate-parishes plan in 1874, so the national synod the next year had declared that its constitutional mandate for the "supervision of doctrine" bore "no import for church law." Thus, Kuyper concluded, had the church descended from being an instrument of the Spirit into a mere "administrative bond."

The Radical Context

Kuyper's *Tractate* concluded with a plan of action based on a type of ecclesiastical triage. Those churches that still offered a faithful service of Word and sacrament should resist the corruptions wrought "by the yoke of the synodical hierarchy," fit themselves for the struggle to come, and begin to give aid to the other two types of churches. These included, at the worst extreme, congregations with false ministers, tyrannical governance, and no hope of recovery; from such "dead churches" the faithful should flee and all other churches should withdraw fellowship. Healthy churches should supply the needs of those so exiled and lead disciplinary strictures against the usurpers. In between the best and the worst stood a middle category where "false preaching" prevailed but where a faithful remnant still held out in prayer for a better day. In those places the faithful should organize as "doleerende kerken" — churches grieving their old home's loss of integrity. Not limiting themselves to mere "lamenting," however, they should also "plead" with God "that their burden be lifted." The hope would be the mother of the act. The aggrieved (category 3), having formed counter churches on site, should join with healthy congregations (category 1) in their region to form shadow classes. Their vitality and conviction would attract people from dead and dying churches (category 2). These new regional bands could then join together in a proper national federation — a genuine Reformed (Gereformeerde) Church, replacing the bastardized Reformed (Hervormde) regime of 1816. As for the latter, unmasked as illegitimate and ineffective, deprived of function and resources, the boards and commissions would simply disappear. À la Marx, Kuyper anticipated a withering away of the churchly superstructure.

However he cast it, Kuyper was proposing a radical, even revolutionary step. But the times were ripe for bold initiatives. As historian Theo van Tijn has shown, the 1880s were the moment when all three rising movements in Dutch society burst out against what was now an almost literally bankrupt establishment. By 1886, the year the Doleantie began, the depression in Dutch farming was a decade old with another decade to run. Amsterdam was no longer the island of prosperity it had been when its new transport links were first opened. To that shelter and the other western cities a massive influx of people from the countryside had turned, only to be stranded when the tide ran out there too. As one sign of distress, Dutch cities were suffering epidemics for the first time in years, and the winters that began and ended 1886 were particularly severe. The years 1885-87, in short, were among the most troubled since the French occupation.

In this context the Doleantie was the radicalized form of the Calvinist agenda for school- and church-reform that Kuyper had first unveiled in Utrecht in 1869, elaborated into a systematic program a decade later, and now put into direct action. Likewise, the Progressive Liberals, who debuted in the 1870s with an education bill to vanquish ignorance, then turned to franchise reform for freedom, now pushed economic legislation to drive out inequity. Domela Nieuwenhuis and the Socialists, in turn, took their organizing crusade in the early 1880s from the cities into the rural north, starting up chapters across Friesland and Groningen where landownership was particularly plutocratic. They agitated everywhere for everything — for bread, for work, for education, for the vote, for land redistribution — but always with a religious tone, proclaiming the apocalypse of the old order and the imminence of the people's promised land. The three movements had contrary programs and premises, but for now they could harmonize in surprising ways on the local level, not least because they all reviled the powers that had run the country into the ground. They also shared the certainty — or the desperate hope — that, in desperate circumstances, a new solution was both necessary and likely to succeed.

This calm retrospect was not available in the anxieties of the moment. In the Doleantie, violence usually remained rhetorical. Elsewhere, popular demonstrations triggered overreaction from undisciplined police at the behest of nervous authorities. In September 1885, when a socialist organizer was brought up on false charges in The Hague for posting anti-royal placards, street protests exploded into a variety of direct actions that left the nominal organizers of the event running to catch up while police swung away indiscriminately. Most notoriously, in July 1886, at the peak of the Doleantie agitation and in the same Amsterdam neighborhoods where it was drawing its greatest support, a working-class crowd went on a traditional "eel-stripping" spree, in which the poor creatures were caught and flayed by young punks to mass cheers amid general rowdiness. This was anything but a socialist assault upon the regime; it was a type of archaic crowd action venting popular contempt for those in power. The police responded with a riot of their own, killing twenty-six civilians, injuring a hundred, and jailing several hundred more. The next year, by contrast, they

stood by when an Orangist mob roared through Amsterdam in celebration of the king's seventieth birthday, threatening anything "socialist" that came into view along the way. In short, the stated authorities
lost credibility precisely when their moral authority was most needed.
From the establishment's point of view, all sorts of agitators, Kuyper
included, were making trouble at the country's moment of peril.

Kuyper's break was also permitted by passages in his personal
life. He had been relieved of his last sibling responsibility in 1879,
when his youngest sister Jeanette Jacqueline married — and married
well — Jacques Rammelman Elsevier. At the same time the older generation was slipping away: Aunt Geziena of grandfather Abraham's
brush-making shop died in 1878, Jo's widowed mother in 1882, his
own mother the year before. The most significant break came with
the death of his father on December 7, 1882. As the old man had been
phobic of being buried alive, his interment was delayed for eleven
days, giving Kuyper a literal whiff of death as he presided at graveside.
That fact, as well as his father's being deaf and nearly blind in his last
years, struck Kuyper as a metaphor for the state of the church which
Jan Frederik had so dutifully served. In any case, Kuyper was now free
of his physical father, as he had become earlier of his spiritual father,
Groen van Prinsterer, and of the ecclesiastical loyalties neither father
could ever break.

Meanwhile, his own progeny was both complete and starting to
move on. An eighth surviving child, a son, was born in September
1882, and was named for Levinus Wilhelmus Keuchenius, head of the
radical wing in the Antirevolutionary Party. "Willy" would be the last
of the Kuypers' offspring; so also Lohman enjoined in his note of con-
gratulations to Kuyper. Indeed, Jo "deserved some rest" — now a
forty-year-old with cardio-pulmonary problems and a string of biennial pregnancies interrupted only twice since 1864. By now his
eighteen-year-old oldest son Herman was ready to start studies at the
Free University. Soon the second-born, Jan Frederik, left home and
country for dental school at the University of Michigan.

Alarms and Maneuvers

The Doleantie maneuverings themselves began in 1882, on two fronts.
In Amsterdam Kuyper returned to the church council after a six-year ab-

sence, quickly reconstituted the orthodox caucus, and began a series of lectures that became the *Tractate*. Out in the provinces he called attention to the plight of the imminent graduates of the Free University. Since the national church did not recognize their degrees for purposes of the pastoral ministry, they were not likely to get a church unless congregations were willing to defy synodical protocols and issue them a call. Within a year, some twenty places had volunteered. The two initiatives converged in April 1883, when 222 delegates from across the country, all pledged to strict confessional subscription, gathered in Amsterdam to get to know each other and plan further action. Their number included seventy clergy. A shadow church had begun to form, with its general staff in the capital and eager troops in the field.

Crucially, Kuyper's caucus now commanded a majority on the Amsterdam council. It put orthodox men in charge of its standing committees, including Rutgers over the property trustees. It stipulated that all pastors and elders hereafter would have to subscribe to the confessional standards — in the face of a recent synodical ruling that ministerial candidates need only pledge themselves to promoting "the interests of God's kingdom" instead of "the gospel of Christ." The caucus appointed pairs of elders — including Kuyper, Rutgers, and Hovy — to shadow the three remaining Modernist ministers on staff. On their recommendation the council refused to accept the credentials of young people catechized under those pastors' auspices. The pastors' "attestation" that the catechumens were of sound morals was insufficient for membership in the church of Jesus Christ, Kuyper insisted. They needed to confess forthrightly that "the Lord Jesus Christ is our only, all-sufficient savior who has delivered us from sin and awakened us to righteousness." The three pastors appealed successfully to the Provincial Synod; the Amsterdam council appealed in turn to the General Synod. In mid-November 1885 it upheld the lower court and told the council to certify the memberships in six weeks, by January 8, 1886. Never mind that the whole attestation process was going by the boards just a week later; the synodical supervisors wanted to force the issue and seize the initiative.

The council dug in to fight back but cut one risky trench. At its meeting of December 14, 1885, it confirmed Rutgers's legal finding that a local church council might take over "free management" of its properties from the trustees; further, that in case of an irresolvable conflict between two parties in a congregation, the property rightfully belonged to the one standing in confessional continuity with the church's founders. The Rev. G. J. Vos, who was in the minority on the council but stood with the majority of the Amsterdam pastors on this issue, recorded the names of the eighty members who supported the motion. He supplied the list to the synodical authorities and, the next day, convened a meeting of a classical board on which none of Kuyper's party sat; it demanded that the Amsterdam council revoke its decision by the New Year. Before the council had a chance to consider that edict, the board met again, on December 21, to vote the immediate deposition from office of all eighty of the council signatories in case of an unsatisfactory reply. That evening the council did meet, and found itself in a corner. The issue had become property, not doctrine or church order, and the schedule was too tight to coordinate friendly support from around the country. Yet the council could not back down without losing credibility. When they refused to recant, the classical board met in emergency session on December 29 to draw up the letters of deposition, and then again on January 4 to ratify them. Much of this was bad process. To top it off, the board had a regularly scheduled session on January 8 to decide the attestation matter; by convening on the 4th instead, it kept property in the foreground. Kuyper's party could thus plead that its breaking into the Nieuwe Kerk on January 6 simply evened the score of irregularities.

Meanwhile reform agitation had been unfolding in the provinces as well, first of all around Voorthuizen in the Veluwe district of Gelderland. The town pastor, Willem van den Bergh, scion of a notable family in The Hague and married into heirs of the Réveil elite, exemplified the type of bright idealist youth (he had double degrees from Leiden in theology and law) that Kuyper attracted in quantity. In response to Kuyper's plea for pastorates, he had urged the neighboring village of Kootwijk — its pulpit unfilled for eighteen years! — to call J. H. Houtzagers, who would be the first graduate of the Free University. The scenario unfolded roughly the way the *Tractate* had prescribed. Houtzagers received no official licensure; Kootwijk issued him a call anyway; the classis refused to certify it; Van den Bergh and the pastor of nearby church, who happened to be Houtzagers' brother-in-law, convened a sufficient number of pastors and elders to constitute a "spiritual classis" which examined him and authorized the call. The process, Kuyper opined in *De Heraut,* was "irregular, churchly, and valid." Houtzagers' formal installation having been announced for February 7, 1886, classis officials delegated two ministers, two police sergeants, and a couple of deputies to block the service, but they arrived at the church to confront a *fait accompli*. At the instigation of Kuyper's son Herman (who was accompanied to the scene by a score of other Free University students), the service had begun an hour early. The newly installed Houtzagers, with everyone else involved, was duly deposed from his post, but the protest spread elsewhere, especially in Friesland, Zeeland, and South Holland. At some places confrontations with classical authorities approached physical violence, requiring police protection for the clergy officially appointed to fill the "vacant" pulpit of a deposed doleant. The torrent of verbal abuse the protesters leveled at such unfortunates was returned in church magazines and regional newspapers.

Legally, the process did not unfold well for Kuyper's cause. In July 1886 the Provincial Synod of North Holland upheld the deposition of him and seventy-four other Amsterdam council members (five of the original eighty had since demurred). On September 16 the executive committee of the General Synod confirmed that decision — the same day, it turned out, that Domela Nieuwenhuis was sentenced to jail on charges of lèse-majesté. On December 1 the General Synod sealed the process with its formal stamp.

The question of church properties took longer to resolve. Finally, in June 1888, the High Court of the Netherlands found the Doleantie network to be a new and independent fellowship, not the legitimate Dutch Reformed Church in unbroken historical continuity with Dort that its legal brief claimed it to be. Indeed, the actions the plaintiffs took to secure their future made their case difficult to uphold. Kuyper convened a national "church conference" at Amsterdam in January 1887 that essentially inaugurated a new denomination. All delegates had to agree in writing beforehand that "throwing off the yoke of Synodical Hierarchy [w]as a duty for every person who would honor the kingship of Jesus in His Church." They then proceeded to decide how to create new church councils, call pastors, recruit members, and form bonds of ecclesiastical fellowship with each other. Kuyper's young followers emulated his prodigious energy in pushing the movement forward in their localities — hiring meeting halls, distributing publicity, keeping up morale, cementing the committed, and recruiting the interested bystander. The national church's classical and synodical boards sometimes helped the process by preemptively deposing people who attended Doleantie meetings (as with the January 1887 conference, for instance) and by badgering some of the movement's formative steps in the provinces.

But the struggle yielded much less than Kuyper had hoped. By the end of 1887 the Doleantie numbered barely 150 out of the national church's 1,350 congregations. Only one in seven of Amsterdam's church members went with him, only one in three of the orthodox. For all the orthodox clergy who had joined the Amsterdam pastorate of late, only five went with him, all of them young. (The maxim that pensions guaranteed loyalty proved true there and across the country.) It was two theological traditionalists, Vos and A. J. Westhoff, that led the maneuvers against Kuyper at classis. Another, Philip van Ronkel, Kuyper's first prized recruit to the Amsterdam pulpit, belabored him in print as proud and power-hungry. J. W. Felix, president of the Free University board of curators, quit his post over the issue, as did Philip Hoedemaker, Kuyper's colleague on the theology faculty and a longtime collaborator in church and school affairs. Hoedemaker proceeded to carry on a press campaign against Kuyper that was "continuous, hateful, and mean-spirited." A bright spot in all these contentions came from Kappeyne van de Coppello, author of the hated Education Bill but a fierce opponent of dull establishmentarians of every sort. He crafted anonymous legal briefs for the Doleantie court cases; Kuyper sent him a silver cup in return.

Dreams of Flight

Kuyper anticipated much of this grief going in. Any momentous struggle will tear apart the bonds of long, tender associations, he acknowledged. "What pain and what wounds do not strike your heart," he asked, "so thirsting for sympathy, as time after time you must pick up the gauntlet when a thousand times over you would rather press in hearty loyalty the hand that threw it down?"

He made this lament at the verge of his own Rubicon, June 30, 1885. That morning he had met with sympathetic clergy to plan the next steps should the synod reject (as it did) the final appeal to certify Free University graduates for the ministry. Two days later, on July 2, he would be reaffirmed as party chairman at the Antirevolutionary convention against petitions from two national-church loyalists. On July 1 the Free University's fifth annual assembly would convene. Now, on the eve of that assembly he addressed its prayer meeting with what observers counted as one of the supreme rhetorical performances of his career. The speech was entitled "Iron and Clay," the image taken from the base of the great idol of world domination that the prophecy of Daniel saw toppled over by the revolt of the Maccabeans. Kuyper pictured his movement, too, as a small stone from the mountain of the Lord that would bring down the synodical Dagon; yet he knew that empires strike back and that people get crushed in the process. Only the greatest of stakes, only the highest of mandates made such risks worth taking, and Kuyper set those out before the assembly. That they had been barred from meeting in The Hague's capacious Kloosterkerk, the church of his erstwhile friend J. H. Gunning, redoubled the lesson. They gathered instead in the smaller building of the Walloon exile congregation. The audience filled the aisles, hung from the balconies, and strained to listen in from the sidewalks outside.

"Iron and Clay" left aside matters of church law to set out the theological, even ontological warrant for the Doleantie. In creation, Kuyper taught, God made each thing after its own kind, ordaining a diversity that brought order out of chaos. The primordial sin thus amounted to "the creature *breaking* off from each other precisely what God had *united*, and *mixing* precisely what God had *divided*." In his theological columns a few years earlier, Kuyper had leaned equally on both sides of this equation, so as to call all the truly Reformed in the Netherlands to join in a purified fellowship. By the time of "Iron and Clay," however, he emphasized division. The whole saga of salvation history, from Eden to Noah to Abraham to Sinai to the conquest of Canaan to Israel's dual monarchy to Christ and the early church, hinged on the right separation of irreconcilable elements. So at the pivot points in the Christian life — *wet, wonder, wedergeboorte, wederkomst* (law to miracle to regeneration to Christ's return) — did God separate believers from sin to secure their salvation. So also in civil history: progress, liberty, and prosperity stem from virtuous rebellion against tyrannical amalgamation. And so to the point: just as the idol in Daniel's vision crumbled upon its foundation of discordant elements, so the national church was doomed by its mixture of belief and unbelief. Division and separation, painful as they would be, were the divine command of the hour. Was this anticlerical, unpatriotic, even "revolutionary," as the opposition charged? "To divide from Christ, to break with Christ — *that* in the realm of the church is the only conceivable revolution," Kuyper retorted. The synod's interposition of itself in the place of Christ at the head of the Dutch church "thus puts the most serious question before all true and loyal servants of King Jesus, whether division from and breaking with so mutinous an organization is not commanded for them by their oath of fealty to their one lawful King." Such a break may never be casual, Kuyper concluded, but once every other means of reform and appeal had been tried and turned back, then breach was a duty, lest one continue in sin.

God might mandate suffering; still, fantasies of flight were appealing. As the church struggle deepened, that option dawned for Kuyper on the unlikely turf of South Africa. Before 1875 Kuyper, along with many other Netherlanders, had taken a dim view of Afrikaner manners and morals and thought that Britain's annexation of the Transvaal in 1877 might be good, as it surely was irreversible. But the Boers' stunning victory at Majuba in December 1880 lit a patriotic fire across the entire spectrum of Dutch opinion. Kuyper viewed the victory as a direct divine intervention, and thus a call for the Boers to rise above their shabby materialism and start building a godly civilization. He gave his personal energy to the cause, interrupting his church campaign right after publishing the *Tractate* to undertake two diplomatic missions to London in November 1883. A scheduled return trip the next month was prevented when he fell sick from overexertion. Kuyper was among the most energetic organizers of the Netherlands South Africa Union, which aimed to raise funds and sympathies for the Boer cause at home and abroad. He also joined a committee to promote Dutch emigration there.

In these efforts he had to tread a thin ideological line. On the one hand he joined with his old history professor, the classic-Liberal Robert Fruin, to affirm principles that all Netherlanders could support — namely, the right of small nations, like the Boer republics, to exist amid grasping empires like Britain, and the creation of space where Dutch culture and overpopulation could spread. Yet Kuyper also found the Boers suddenly to be the mirror of his own movement, a people that (however unconsciously yet!) were traditional Calvinists at heart, plain and virtuous in manners, bold pioneers of Christian democracy. They needed only to be fully organized around their governing principle — a step the Afrikaner governments could advance by making the Free University the exclusive training site for their rising generation of leaders.

Kuyper's enthusiasm peaked with an electrifying address he delivered in March 1884 to a rally honoring a visiting delegation from the Transvaal. Kuyper the ecumenical Hollander saluted the guests for providing the Netherlands with an example of hope amid its current hard times. Then too, chronic arguments over church and state got so wearisome — "also personally," he confessed — that an occasion for celebrating a common cause was a thrill. But the Calvinist organizer also spoke up: Afrikaner independence was all the more vital because, should the Netherlands ever become "intolerable . . . to the free-born Christian heart . . . then the core of the Christian people shall go across the sea to the Transvaal!"

Alas, both of his chosen intermediaries, Transvaal President Paul Kruger and Professor S. J. DuToit, close though they were to Kuyper theologically, rejected his plan for an exclusive Free University connection. That is, Boer leadership decided for a religiously ecumenical and distinctly Afrikaner ethnic identity instead of a resolutely Calvinist one. This too aroused personal pain: "Oh my dear brother," Kuyper wrote DuToit upon having his university plan rejected, "drop by, give me your hand, and all is forgiven. . . . Heal the wound in my heart. Two nights I haven't been able to sleep because of the grief you have laid on my heart." Later, Kruger got to reverse the charges when Kuyper declined to solicit Dutch support for a university in the Transvaal: "His High Excellency had thought that the children of the Lord should stand together and give each other as much help as possible," Kruger's private secretary wrote Kuyper, "so it is now to His High Excellency's amazement that, when you *can* give His High Excellency aid, you refuse to do so and put the blame on His High Excellency. Thus His High Excellency must say that . . . his brother in Christ has bid him farewell and given him over to the enemy."

Call to Repentance

Kuyper thus turned away from the Transvaal in 1885 just as gold was discovered there, with ominous auguries for the republic's future. Yet his dreams of flight continued. In 1886, at the peak of church hostilities, Kuyper mused about following son Jan Frederik to Michigan; perhaps he could lead a migration there, just as the Seceder pastor Albertus C. van Raalte had forty years before. Kuyper broached the idea to Nicholas Steffens, a professor at the theological seminary that Van Raalte's successors had founded in Holland, Michigan, who was also helping Fred get settled at Ann Arbor. Steffens's response was blunt: "You should drop that idea. At least as far as America is concerned, I can see little good in it. . . . We *are on the road* toward those circumstances which you are now opposing." If the battle had to be joined, better that it happen in the Netherlands, where Reformed consciousness was highly developed. In his own Reformed Church in America, Steffens complained, there was little mind for theology, much less for robust Calvinism, while the larger American scene offered the bleak options of revivalists on the hustings and liberals in control of the seminaries. Steffens repeated his warnings in 1891 as Dutch-American immigration neared its peak. With "our Dutch people . . . going under in the maelstrom, I often think that it would be a good thing if the leaders in the Netherlands tried to turn the course of the stream of emigration" to other shores.

Once flight was foreclosed and the missiles of the enemy were raining down, Kuyper responded with one of the more remarkable gestures of the entire Doleantie: he called his own followers to repentance and humility. Already at the point of no return in June 1885 he reminded his readers in *De Standaard* that they were not "better or braver" than their opponents, simply determined to live consistently by their convictions. In the sermon he preached after his deposition had been confirmed, he granted the same to the other side. Whatever injustices the opposition had inflicted were simply the result of the logic of their principle taking them "much farther than they themselves wanted." That "dynamic is familiar from your own soul's experience [with sin], is it not?" he queried the faithful. And had they not committed the very same sins that they spied in their opponents? Who in the crowd had not been "driven by the deeply sinful pull of one's own passions instead of by the movement of the Holy Spirit"? "How we loved the front-row seats! How eagerly did we not savor the strong drink of presumption and usurped power in our own circles, even among our own children! . . . [E]ach of us individually added to the flood of the arrogant assumption of power" that displaced Jesus from his rightful throne in the church. Accordingly, "the One who sends me urges me to warn you all the more seriously to keep your indignation *holy* and *not to sin* in your wrath. Hence I urge you to refrain from all bitterness against *persons*."

Kuyper also worried as the protest settled in for the long run. At the January 1887 church conference that consolidated the Doleantie, he confessed: "I am fearful of the excitement of superficiality. Fearful of the working of the flesh in the people of the Lord. Fearful that precisely our too elevated rejoicing should show how we still understand almost nothing of this redemption that the Lord has wrought." If God's standard were the goal of the struggle, then obedience to that standard was the only measure of success, the sole source of comfort. The proof of the pudding lay in the test of charity. Echoing the "most serious question" he had posed in "Iron and Clay" a year before, Kuyper now called the faithful to ponder not the necessity of but their ethics in resistance. Each of us must ask, Kuyper counseled, "Have I, I myself, reached the point where, in all sincerity before the Lord, I can pray for those who are persecuting me?"

A year further on, at the Free University's annual meeting of 1887, he moved from personal piety to collective mentality. The demonic powers at work in the age would not have attained their current force

> had not the people of the Lord broken troth with him, even in their own inheritance. I tell you, the guilt of this may not be thrown on certain persons, nor upon the intellectuals, nor upon political leaders or the leaders of public opinion. . . . [That its effect] could become powerful also among us, ladies and gentlemen, owes not to some evil oppression, not to some clever conspiracy — no, the cause of it lies in *us and them,* for the human heart of us *both* is so deeply fallen. Or, to be fair . . . in us *still more* than in them, since we celebrate in such high tones that better Fatherland [of God's kingdom] only to be lured again by the charms of *world-conformity*!

Collectively as individually, the Reformed should return to the counsel of the Psalms: "The heights of self-righteousness shed all the waters of grace," but the "waterspouts of God flood the souls of those who bow down before him."

Church Union

As surely as his own ego was part of the fray, Kuyper worried about its power, especially in church affairs. Let there be no "isten" and "anen" (including "Kuyperiaanen") among us, he urged his readers before the strife. Let us rather adhere to the voice of the Holy Spirit as it comes down to us "*in the great whole of the church*. . . . We are from the depths of our soul fiercely and inexorably opposed to people placing us as a new group next to existing groups" on the ecclesiastical landscape. Personally, he added, it would be better that my name be forgotten for all time than that I become known as the "head of a new school." It was ironic if inevitable, then, that the power of his reputation complicated Kuyper's next move: to merge the Doleantie with the Christian Reformed Church. This was the step commanded by the other, uniting side of God's ordination, "bringing together what belonged together." Kuyper had thought about this prospect already in the 1870s and had developed mutual trust with some younger Christian Reformed leaders in the political wars. From the first broaching of a possible union in 1887, the expectation emerged on both sides that it would and should happen. These were people committed to purity, however, and so vigilant about specifics. Would this be a "union," as the Christian Reformed thought, or (Kuyper's notion) a "reunion" of seceders with the legitimate continuation of the Dutch Reformed Church? Would the new denomination be a church (the Christian Reformed shared the old notion of a unitary church with local chapters) or a federation of churches? Instead of planting new congregations, should not the *doleerenden* join a Christian Reformed body in locales where such existed? And what about clerical education? The Christian Reformed already had a seminary in Kampen, focused on the practical formation of pastors; should it be absorbed into a full-fledged university with aims of front-line scholarship?

Beneath the issues lay important group differences. The Christian Reformed, especially their older leaders, tended to be plain people with ordinary jobs, attuned to inward experience and contemplative, even mystical, practices. The process of independent formation and the modest educational pedigree of many of their clergy gave laity unusual influence in their councils. A fair number in the ranks had Anabaptist backgrounds and remained suspicious of politics, deeming the Christian's social duty to end at keeping one's family in order and leavening the local community as one could. All this stood athwart the activist, crusading spirit of the Kuyperians (for such the *doleerenden* unquestionably were, Kuyper's vows to the contrary notwithstanding). They aspired to be players on the political and cultural scene. They bore the master's stamp in being far more sophisticated at organization and fundraising than the old Seceders and quite more interested in social and economic questions. "Money in Doleantie circles was a definite church matter," writes one of their historians, not just an issue for civil politics. They dispensed on principle with the pew-rental system that the Christian Reformed, like the national church, used to cover costs. On the other hand, contrary to Kuyper's theory, his assemblies tended to be "preacher's churches" with lesser roles for lay leadership.

Kuyper's theology raised problems as well, particularly his supralapsarian concept of divine election which led on to an "objective," relentlessly theocentric picture of spiritual life. Christian Reformed infralapsarianism, particularly the self-scrutiny that attended it, made this the first issue to threaten the new church's unity, until the matter was finally settled by compromise in 1905. Yet for years after that peace, worship on the Kuyperian side of the denomination bore his stamp. It was no more sermon-centered than the Christian Reformed style, but its unyielding focus on the authoritative promises of the Word, as opposed to one's personal appropriation thereof, struck some on the other side as thin in heart — all the more so when special services like weddings, baptisms, and funerals were shorn of any human adornment lest God not be "kept at the center." Kuyper argued that baptism should occur as soon as possible to bring the infant quickly under the protection of the covenant. If the mother, still recovering from childbirth, could not attend the ceremony, that did not preclude the father, the head of the family, from making and receiving the crucial promises.

Personal feelings were to give way not just before divine dicta but to the movement's strong — and strongly egalitarian — communal ethos. Offenses that would bar one from the Lord's Supper went well beyond the sexual infractions that dominated the Christian Reformed code. On the other hand, the Kuyperians gave less attention to the nurture of children than did the Christian Reformed, with their concern for personal spiritual development; in the end, one historian concludes, Kuyper never did recover the "church as mother." Rather, for better or worse, the Doleantie strove for "a church of spiritually mature, sober-living, serious people who, consciously assuming God's promises and in the tradition of the historic Reformed church, sought to make visible in their personal lives and the life of the nation something of the kingdom of God."

These issues and more were discussed during a four-year courtship exemplary of the Dutch Reformed passion to get things right. A few Christian Reformed stalwarts were unyielding. Two leaders left for a sister church in the United States, and others vowed not to go along with the merger. The vast majority on both sides agreed, however, and sealed their union into the Gereformeerde Kerken in Nederland (GKN) at a ceremony held at Amsterdam on June 17, 1892. The Christian Reformed side brought to the mix a small majority of its membership (190,000 vs. the Doleantie's 180,000), a larger majority of its congregations (400 vs. 300), and a strong preponderance of its clergy (305 vs. 120). The new body constituted eight percent of the Dutch population, fourteen percent of its Protestants, but possessed an influence beyond their numbers by virtue of their zeal and discipline.

Kuyper's departure also triggered reforms within the national church. Some Modernists, whether convinced or disgusted by his arguments, left for secular ethical societies; the percentage of the Dutch population declaring themselves to be "unchurched" would multiply ten times over, to fifteen percent, between 1890 and 1930. The orthodox among those who remained were thus more influential and determined to prove Kuyper's predictions wrong.

So far as predictions went, Kuyper uttered one during the harshest polemics of 1886 that could hardly have been more wrong, or more right. At one point an anonymous writer, accusing him of Napoleonic ambitions in church and state, ominously asked, "what does Dr. Kuyper *really* want?" Kuyper snapped back,

> If Dr. Kuyper may reply for himself once, then let all know . . . that everything that is within me longs and pants to be done with ecclesiastical strife and all its soul-destroying bitterness. . . . The study of theology increasingly commands my energy, and if the Lord my God may have ordained another ten years for my lifespan, then it is my most jealous and deep desire that I may publish first my *Encyclopedia,* thereafter my *Dogmatics,* and then conclude my life's labors with a commentary on a book from the *Word.* Higher and further my aspirations *do not go.* Personally, I have left the political stage for good, and oh, how I rejoice with my whole heart that I have escaped parliamentary life.

Of course, he had not left politics "for good," not on the party's Central Committee or, it turned out, in the halls of Parliament. He *was* working on his theology, however, and in the year of the Doleantie he set out on a twelve-year run of publications that would include not just his *Encyclopedia* of theology but a theology of culture, a new stream of cultural commentary, and an attempt to bring these all together as a grand rehabilitation of Calvinism — not in a shrunken church, but on the world stage.

CHAPTER NINE

Theologian of the Church

Much of Kuyper's theology stemmed from his ecclesiology, from "thinking through his church ideal and his striving to realize it." This dictum of Dutch scholarship contradicts the charge that "Kuyperian" theology tends to draw elsewhere: that it sells the institutional church short for the sake of Christian engagement in culture. That is just the first paradox. As we have seen, Kuyper's enduring suspicion of the externalities of the church proceeded from the very same passion that motivated contemporaneous high-church parties' devotion to liturgy, sacraments, and the apostolic succession of bishops. Again, for all his devotion to fixed principles and consistent thinking, "the church" to Kuyper was not a fixed quantity but evolved over the course of history. It evolved in his mind as well. At the same time, virtually all of his key ideas on church and culture were in evidence by the time he moved to Amsterdam in 1870.

We can find a way through this by understanding Kuyper's work as a theologian under the rubric of three C's: it began with the church and ended with culture, and the two were connected by Calvinism. Our path, further, divides into three segments. In his first phase, from graduate school through his Amsterdam pastorate, Kuyper worked out a theory of the church proper, moving from an ideal of inner spirituality to an assertion of "Calvinistic fixed forms." In his middle phase, from 1875 through the Doleantie, he used "Calvinist" much less than "Reformed," emphasized soteriology over ecclesiology, and concentrated on church law instead of ecclesiology proper. In the third phase, from the late 1880s through the late 1890s, "Calvinism" returned in force, and church gave way to culture as the center of his attention.

It is worth pausing to consider how Kuyper's ecclesiological thought stood in the context of the rest of his theology. With all Calvinists he espoused a robust Trinitarianism, a radical theocentricity, and an overriding concern with the redemptive work of Christ. The themes of cosmic renewal and personal salvation that he propounded in *The Work of the Holy Spirit* (chapter five) along with the emphasis on the kingship of Christ that we will see him elaborating late in life (chapter sixteen) can be seen in one regard as the larger purposes which his doctrine of the church served. Then too, arguments over the church served his larger campaign against theological liberalism. Yet ecclesiology had central importance for Kuyper in its own right. It marked the crossroads where his twin passions of divine sovereignty and social formation intersected. Here especially, eternity worked in time, the holy encountered the other, and the mutual renewal of soul and society could go forward under the providence of God.

The Incarnation and the Church Visible

Kuyper's early sermons on the church at Beesd set the baseline for his future development. The church, he said, was (1) a free community of the faithful (2) voluntarily gathered out of loyalty to Christ. (3) Animated by the work of the Spirit in the heart, (4) it performed works of righteousness in the world, (5) thereby sowing the seeds of the kingdom of God, (6) which constituted the essential and distinctive teaching of Jesus. Accordingly, the interior life of the Spirit was the believer's only source of strength, and the deeds springing from it were the real measure of faith. External forms, whether of doctrine, governance, or liturgy, figured at best secondarily in this scheme, at worst as obstacles to spiritual integrity. This sort of sentiment was common on the Dutch religious landscape at the time, from Modernists who anticipated the church withering away in the course of cultural progress, to ultra-Calvinists who had separated themselves from the national church in contempt of its empty show, to the mediating center of Ethical pastors who focused upon the spirit instead of institutional busywork. It comported with the à Lasco enthusiasm with which Kuyper began at Beesd and stretched back across his education to his undergraduate thesis.

Another German he had read in school loomed large behind it all

— the Reformed Romantic theologian Friedrich Schleiermacher, who worked to rehabilitate Christian witness from the ruins of the Enlightenment and the invading armies of the French Revolution. From Schleiermacher Kuyper absorbed the ideal of the church as a free and voluntary community that made à Lasco so attractive. For all of Kuyper's later Calvinist enthusiasms, and for all of Schleiermacher's subsequent usefulness to liberal theologians, the German's presence at the heart of Kuyper's ecclesiology never disappeared. His project going forward was to make Schleiermacher safe for Calvin under the rubric of Reformed orthodoxy.

The first hint of a shift appeared midway through his Beesd pastorate, coincident with his turn to Calvin and perhaps with his worship experiences in London while doing à Lasco research there. His inaugural sermon at Utrecht in November 1867 showed him to have skipped forward from that beginning very rapidly indeed. His text was John 1:14, "The Word became flesh and dwelt among us," and his theme, as we have seen, was the key concept of high-church theologians everywhere, the incarnation. "The Church," proclaimed the new Kuyper, "is thus not just a gathering of Jesus' followers; no, it has become in the full sense of the term the body of Christ, the rich organism wherein not just his spirit but Christ himself lives on." Only when Christ appeared in human form could people apprehend God correctly; only thus could the human race be redeemed; only in Christ's continuing presence as the head of a new humanity could this redemption go forward; and only in the outward, visible church did that continuing presence take hold. A visible church necessarily must cast a clear shape, must have the "fixed forms" of doctrine, liturgy, and polity that marked its bounds and mission — and that would mark Kuyper's initiatives on the Utrecht church council. Theologically, to maintain the integrity of the continually incarnated Christ, and pragmatically, so that the church's life might become vibrant and strong, a radical pruning of the body had emerged as the demand of the hour, Kuyper's inaugural concluded: "all that passes itself off as Christian but does not bear its stamp does not belong to its [the church's] essence, is a foreign element . . . [that] must be cut off, the sooner, the better."

Already here, some two decades before the Doleantie unfolded, its ecclesiological foundations were in evidence. Kuyper's sermon promised that a move from a single "mottled" fellowship to two or more well-defined religious bodies — one of them the church of Christ, the others whatever they pleased — would be honest and fair to all concerned, setting up a "noble competition" between the spirit of the church and the spirit of the world that would tell which had the greater potential to glorify God and elevate the human race. The prospect assumed an explosive, dialectical notion of church history at odds with the conservative sensibilities in his audience and with the evolutionary models favored by the leading German schools of the day. Christ's incarnation demonstrated that "the divine does not come forth from the human but continuously breaks in upon it," so that the subsequent "course of development" of his body "is marked by severe shocks":

> On the one side the form of Jesus' church must remain *fixed*, for only in what is steady and enduring is the eternal character of its godly life mirrored; but at the same time this fixed form must be smashed and broken by the movements of the spirit and agitations from without.

The accelerating logic of modern times was precisely one of those movements: "to the eternal shame of the church it must be confessed" that it is owing to external pressures "and not to the life-strength of the church that the leaven of the Pharisees is again being somewhat driven out and the sacred freedom of conscience is again on the way toward reclaiming her rights." Thus does "the spirit of the age . . . serve the Kingdom of God to cleanse and purify the church."

In Praise of the Institutional Church

Notably, Kuyper's battles at Utrecht concerned baptism, the sacrament of membership, and not the Lord's Supper, the sacrament of nurture. That made his next step, defined in his debut at Amsterdam, as remarkable as the Utrecht inaugural had been over his beginning at Beesd. At first glance in this sermon the incarnation seemed to give way to God's "eternal election" as the "fundamental principle" of the church, a move from more generic high-church to specifically Reformed ecclesiology. But Kuyper did *not* highlight election in the text of this sermon as such, only in the preface to its published version — and that after he had developed the theme with his second sermon at Amsterdam, on "The

Comfort of Eternal Election." This signaled the tack his theology would take in the second phase of his ecclesiological development, ten years down the road. His Amsterdam inaugural itself was absorbed in introducing and elaborating his famous distinction between the church as "organism" and as "institute" — but the role and value of the two were quite different from the meaning he would give them still later, in his third phase. These twists and turns are linked up with a tension evident in Kuyper's chosen title, "Rooted and Grounded," from Ephesians 3:17. The first term connoted God's work in redemption as supernatural and autonomous; the second valorized the institutional church as nowhere else in the rest of Kuyper's work. On top of that, Kuyper the Protestant issued this praise simultaneously, that August of 1870, with the meetings of the First Vatican Council, which set forth the highest claims ever for institutional church authority.

"Rooted and Grounded" opens with Kuyper's favorite organic vocabulary to describe the spontaneous order of creation. Had not sin intervened, creation would have been continuously "perfected" until it realized its ultimate "connection with heavenly life." The radical disruption of sin required God to plant a new seed, to institute a new creation, and that seed first appeared by a radical act of grace "in Christ as a *human* life." Here was the incarnation again, breaking into the fallen world-order. In consequence,

> now a double stream runs through the kingdom of the spirits. A stream of the old life that, whatever waves it makes, will run out into the sands before it reaches the ocean. And then another stream, dropping down from God's holy mountain, that never loses its course even though it seems to mix in with other waters.

Through many twists and turns, the stream of grace continuously "deepens its channel to the ocean." That channel, Kuyper concludes, is the church — the visible church. The church's root in the love of eternal election produces a whole new "organism," which makes up the "heart" of the church. The later Kuyper would expatiate on this theme to no end. Here, after just a few lines more, he turns to six pages of marked praise for the church as "institute."

In fact, "Rooted and Grounded" lauds the *institutional* fabric of earthly life per se by planting it back in creation itself. Even before the fall Eden was cultivated — it was a garden, not a wilderness. Likewise, all that is instinctive and natural in life is raised to a higher plane by human effort. Again, the church is not only rooted in divine election but "just as much grounded" on foundations that are the work of apostolic — that is, human — hands. Pentecost was a miraculous divine interjection into history, but since then the church has developed as a human community in which the Holy Spirit dwells. Thus, not only the organism but "the institute of the church exists as an *establishment* of God," a "God-given means . . . to nourish and broaden the organism." At this point Kuyper explicitly invoked Calvin's image of God the Father ordaining the church as a mother to nurture the elect *to* faith and then to maturity *in* faith. This happens, Kuyper continued, through the altogether institutional means of Word and sacrament. From there the church builds community, blending together the spiritual streams that arise out of each believer's heart into the mighty current "that alone makes progress in the Christian life conceivable." It brings believers together over time, lifting the current generation onto "the shoulders of those who have gone before us" into the church of all ages.

On that basis, the faithful can dwell in a city whose atmosphere and language are those of the Holy Spirit and not of the world. It is the church as institute, Kuyper emphasized, that lures us on to "the higher ground of the new life as a fixed figure in reality," not merely as a personal dream. At the same time it "sets itself between us and the world so as to protect the distinctiveness of our life with the power, unity, and order" that it alone can provide. And so having formed a "life-sphere," the church "forms the person, shapes the home, and gives direction to society." Furthermore, it is "called from the root of its own life to show forth its own science and art, to strive in its confession toward an ever more precise expression of eternal truth and toward a purer worship of the Holy One." In other words, Kuyper's whole future program of Christian cultural engagement lay here in symbiosis with the institutional church. God was still building the Kingdom that Jesus announced, but the church is the "scaffolding" of that construction — dispensable at the end but utterly necessary along the way.

Election and the Church Invisible

Kuyper concluded this first phase of theologizing with *Confidentie* (1873), which included his famous spiritual autobiography by way of expounding upon the marks of the church for which he would eventually campaign in the Doleantie. Entering Parliament soon after, Kuyper plateaued theologically until his return from recuperating in the Alps. The next phase of his thought started up soon thereafter. In spring 1879 he began a fourteen-month series in *De Heraut* defending the doctrine of particular grace against notions of universal salvation. He followed that up with a similar exploration of the doctrine of the covenants, then one on the "practical consequences" of these doctrines, before finishing with a nearly three-year series (September 1883 until July 1886) that became *The Work of the Holy Spirit.* Kuyper's second phase, that is, turned to the order of salvation, inevitably personal salvation first of all. It also reverberated with themes from the work he was simultaneously publishing on law and politics. *Particular Grace* ran in *De Heraut* simultaneously with *Ons Program* in *De Standaard;* the series on the Holy Spirit began the month before the *Tractate* appeared and concluded close to the day that his deposition from the ministry was sealed. Both topics and circumstances, then, cast shadows on the institutional church.

Kuyper announced a threefold agenda for this second phase at the start of *Particular Grace.* He wanted to advance the health of the church, uphold the honor of God, and achieve intellectual consistency in Reformed theology as a system. He realized only the second of these goals fully, but then also unfailingly. Like *The Work of the Holy Spirit, Particular Grace* and *The Covenants* asserted and reasserted God's power, majesty, righteousness, and justice, however much that offended the sensibilities of the age. In particular, he did not shy away from warranting the right of God's "good pleasure" to choose some but not others for salvation. Kuyper meant in general to reprove the outsized self-confidence that had been building with the nineteenth century's technological achievements, and in particular to rebuke the self-centeredness of much current Christian spirituality, whether Evangelical, Ethical, or Modernist. In the process he prefigured something of the "wholly other" concept of God promulgated by twentieth-century crisis theology in its equally severe rejection of human pretensions. The fixation upon divine authority also launched his religious thought from the same starting point as the civil politics he was elaborating in *Ons Program.*

Since divine sovereignty was *the* theological fundamental, Kuyper's rhetoric expanded to thwart any compromise or denial of its truth. To espouse the notion of universal salvation in the face of so much evidence to the contrary, he declared, was not just to defy common sense but to posit human ability to cross divine intentions — in other words, to posit a power greater than God. "We very earnestly resist this notion and do so with all the strength that is in us. This idea infringes upon the Godhead of the Divine Being. It abolishes God's essence in the Divine Being. This may not be tolerated. This doctrine must be opposed." The whole cosmos as well as God's being was at stake, for without "the rule that the Lord God sets as the line of action for all of creation . . . there is no providence" — indeed no world, "but only chaos." If so for the natural, how much more for the moral order: "the higher moral earnestness that must inspire our society" depended inescapably on a twofold recognition of sin's pervasive reality and God's transcendent power. The believer's proper response to that power was to bow before it but then also to rise with it to defend God's glory every day. That in turn required a periodic ascent to the heights of heroic spirituality; Kuyper recurrently visited the "mountaintops" in these series, as he had just done in real life. The heroic template was meant for day-to-day spirituality too. Ordinary Christians pray first for themselves, then for their neighbor, and finally for the adoration of God, he observed; the order should be just the reverse. Evangelicals and Ethicals were merely Christocentric; real Calvinists were Trinitarian, with a special relish for God's secret counsel.

This drew Kuyper directly into the *ordo salutis,* a subject we have already seen him elaborate in *The Work of the Holy Spirit.* For our present purposes it is notable that *Particular Grace* and *The Covenants* drew a new line parallel to his ecclesiology, complicating it and also perhaps blocking his announced goal of fostering the health of the church. For in these series the church hardly seems necessary to the process of salvation. God in electing some had planted them "in embryonic form" in Christ; the mystical union between the believer and Christ was unmediated by any institution or community. "Everyone has his *own* tie with which he is bound unto his Jesus," Kuyper declared; no one gains anything from anyone else's connection. The way election works out is equally individualistic: regeneration is the direct operation of the Holy Spirit in the heart, just as conversion is a person's own work in owning her dawning awareness of salvation. The church enters the process by the preaching of the Word which is "ordinarily" the means by which God's calling becomes effectual. But since that effect can take a long time to arrive, as Kuyper honestly acknowledged, many are left for a shorter or longer time to uncertainty — are left, so far as *Particular Grace* takes it, to the speculative abstractions of decretal theology rather than to biblical evidence or the instrumentalities of the church. No mother here, in short, only the classic conundrums of Calvinism.

The Bridge of the Covenant

Alluding to this problem from time to time in *Particular Grace,* Kuyper addressed it fully in his next series, on the covenants. In fact, he insisted that election and covenant were not separate topics at all, but two sides of the same work of God that always needed to be treated together: "The *Covenant of Grace* is the glorious channel through which the water of life flows to us from the depths of *election.*" What was "glorious" in the picture was not the pristine majesty of God but the persistence of divine love as it advanced its purposes through the murky imponderables of human life. From the peaks of divine sovereignty, everything looks clear and settled, Kuyper said, but from our earthly vantage point it is always mixed. Mountain-climbers as they might be, believers must remember that "we do not sit in God's chair but crawl as lowly creatures at his footstool." This was good news for Reformed people, he continued, for many conundrums in the age-old arguments over theology dissolved in the waters of the covenant. Against the most common complaint, the covenant demonstrates that God in election does not treat people like "sticks and blocks" but embeds grace in time so that, as a "brook," it bears the pure waters of salvation down from the mountaintops "through all the bumps and twists of our earthly life." The covenant treats people as we recognize them in ordinary life, enwrapped in "transitional, mixed, and unconscious circumstances," yet all brought to their destined end in God's good time.

Covenant theology could also redeem the Reformed from the charge of spiritual elitism, Kuyper argued. Divine election neither elevated believers above others nor removed them from human solidarity. It was typically those discounted by the world who were chosen by God, he repeated after Paul, and it was the very solidarity of sin and the democracy of redemption that Scripture was teaching in those passages favored by proponents of universal salvation. The "all" and "whomsoever" God would save meant not every person who had or would ever live. Rather, right athwart the rankings of birth, class, sex, and wealth treasured by the ancient world wherein Scripture was written (not to mention the modern world in which it was read), God chose *whosoever* would genuinely believe from across *all* stations in life to eternal glory. Recalling a prominent theme from "Rooted and Grounded," Kuyper now made covenant the forge of a new community spanning space and time. It established a bond between one generation of believers and those who had come before them, preparing the way, and those who would come later as their spiritual progeny. Within any single generation, the covenant placed people who were already aware of their redemption as a saving witness amid "the broad circle of people who do not know it yet."

But to benefit from covenant teaching, believers would have to take it seriously, and long stretches of Kuyper's presentation betrayed his fear that they did not. When thinking about election, he scolded, Reformed people all too often obsessed about the state of their own souls, betraying the very self-centeredness they faulted in Arminians. Their relentless quest to sort out who was and who was not elect arrogated to themselves a judgment that belonged only to God. The consequences were a passivity that fulfilled critics' prediction about the logic of predestination, an inwardness that contradicted the best lights of their tradition, and an inclination toward despair that constituted Calvinism's unique contribution to the annals of human pride. Tellingly for our purposes here, Kuyper labeled this the "holy despair of the sect." The connectedness wrought by the covenant — to past, to future, to fellows, to task — mandated by contrast a *church,* a body that risked impurity for the sake of God's grander purposes.

The opposite of Kuyper's preferred ecclesiology can therefore be seen in his memorable typology of pious sectarianism, especially as it spied some family resemblances across the Calvinist-Arminian divide. Both election-denying "methodists" and election-adamant "passivists" generate three types of spirituality, Kuyper said: one that is genuinely compassionate; a less likeable sort that registers, respectively, as "meddlesome" or "lackadaisical"; and the truly obnoxious variant — the "manufacturing methodism that *produces* converts" and the ultra-predestinarianism that virtually welcomes the damnation of the unconverted. The covenanted church, instead, holds up the task for which God elected people in the first place: not the salvation of their souls out of the world but a part in carrying on God's majestic, mysterious purpose of redeeming that world. *Geen verbond, geen verband,* Kuyper intoned; no covenant, no connection of believers with life, or with each other.

Still, Kuyper acknowledged that the path of covenant theology encounters any number of intellectual difficulties. For one, he had now defined two channels of grace, the covenant as well as the church, and the relationship between them could be confusing. Further, covenantal doctrine might simply relocate allegations of God's arbitrariness from heaven to earth. If, as Kuyper argued, "the normal means" of entry into the covenant was by family lineage, what chance did one have to be born again if one were not born right the first time? Then there was the perennial charge of intellectual inconsistency in the Reformed teaching both divine predestination and human responsibility. Kuyper brought out the usual answers. Viewed from "God's side," the contradiction is only "apparent"; viewed from "the human side," the cosmos shows a coherence — also a moral coherence — that is a function of law, of "fixed ordinances" according to which things "*must* happen." But these answers were open to the usual objections: that the first begged the question and that the second, by insisting that God could not break the laws he had made, subjected the sovereign to something stronger than himself, violating Kuyper's first principle and arguably laying the groundwork for the very Arminianism and deism that the Reformed were determined to oppose.

Kuyper left the matter on a more humble twofold conclusion. The spiritual life he was outlining in these tracts was as complicated in everyday experience as the political life he was elaborating in *Ons Program.* When we take up election and reprobation from the human side, that is, from the "psychological, anthropological, and ethical viewpoints," Kuyper said near the end of *Particular Grace,* "there is a contradiction" between God's good will and human damnation. "[T]hat we *must* acknowledge. *Not* to do that is either not to know oneself or the power of one's own reasoning" — and in either case does "an injustice to the sacred." Yet, equally insoluble contradictions arise if we opt for free will and universal salvation. Such spiritual mysteries can finally be fathomed only as the sovereign Lord "raises us up to the mountains of his holiness" and impels us to humble submission to the due authority of Scripture. And what does Scripture teach?

That grace is the free gift of God, and sin the full responsibility of man. Those genuinely troubled by the paradox and not simply raising objections out of pride would find their very burden to be the doorway to grace.

The Church Organic

Kuyper's third theological phase came after the Doleantie and showed the full impact of his changing fortunes. If he had lost the battle with the institutional church, he could see rising prospects in his political party and the Free University — that is, on the two principal fronts of Christian cultural engagement. Complicating things conceptually, however, Kuyper included every manifestation of that engagement under the rubric of "the church" — the church "as organism" now strongly valorized over the church as "institute." Yet those terms did not mean what they had in his first phase, nor did they stand alone as the only dialectical pair in his thinking. Idea/appearance, being/form, internal/external, spiritual/material, higher/lower, kernel/husk: these and more had marked Kuyper's writing from the start. They now amassed alongside some older couplets dear to Reformed theology — true church and false, visible and invisible.

Sometimes Kuyper slid the two sets of concepts over each other; more often he interlaced them. The result was not just definitional complexity but a mixing of markedly different thought-worlds. The older set came from the tradition of Reformed scholasticism, while the others were the idiom of nineteenth-century organic thinking rooted in Idealist philosophy and Romantic poetics. This later idiom now became as pervasive in his ecclesiology as in his social thought. Romantic organicism could sustain his purpose of celebrating the disparate, the individual, and the free while simultaneously exalting unity and order because it postulated a fundamental harmony between these sets of values, both in nature and in society. More precisely, drawing off the nature-philosophy of Friedrich Schelling, it could link any number of diverse elements as the "expression" of an "organism" that "developed" from a single "root" by its internal "law" (or "principle") toward its inherent end. The words in quotation marks appear endlessly in Kuyper's work, including his ecclesiology, perhaps making Schelling the instrument by which he could finally

reconcile Schleiermacher and Calvin. In any case, such routine shut-
tling from "essence" to "manifestation" and its marked elevation of
the (free) organic over (artificial) mechanism Kuyper took as axiomatic — and as an agenda.

In this context Kuyper reworked his old concept of the church.
The true church was still the mystical body of Christ, embracing all
those elect by God from all eternity and implanted in Christ. Regenerated by the immediate operation of the Holy Spirit, they constituted
the true and invisible church on earth. Then, over time and according
to personal circumstances, they were brought to awareness of their regenerate status as God's calling upon them became effectual in their
conversion. This group was now the visible church on earth, the
"seed" of the new humanity that God was raising up to populate and
to help effect the redeemed creation that awaited the end of time.
Like humanity as a whole, the church was an organism, manifesting
over time the eternal principle of election as it was deployed through
the channel of the covenant. From its debut at Pentecost, the true
church was spreading around the world until it would one day fit into
every niche of the human race — into every tribe and tongue and culture, as the Revelation of John put it — as God's new humanity.

Notably, Kuyper could go on in this vein for a long time without
mentioning any of the "manifestations" usually taken to be the
church: buildings, clergy, worship services, or administrative offices.
All these were functions of the "church institute," which emerged
later in the process. The church as organism could and did exist, not
only in God's eternal counsel but concretely on earth, without them.
The church as conventionally understood, Kuyper explained, emerges
when a local group of the regenerate gathers together to enrich their
new life by means of fuller fellowship. Recalling his *Tractate,* this local body contains the full essence of the church even without the familiar churchly apparatus. Those appurtenances grow from the gathered cell as one (but only one) manifestation of the church's being
and work. The body elects a board of elders to govern it; the elders call
a pastor to preach the word and administer the sacraments; deacons
are installed to carry out works of mercy; delegates are sent to the
broader assemblies of the sister churches with which the local body
has decided to confederate; and budgets are approved to finance the
lot. All the institutional apparatus, however, exists to serve the work
and well-being of the organism and poses a danger (by the power and

money it accumulates) to subvert that mission and become an end in itself. The institute in Kuyper's ecclesiology thus mirrored the "state" in his political theory just as the church organism did "society," with the same invidious valuations.

Spirit over Form

Kuyper recognized some of the unhappy inferences that could be drawn from this model and sought to forestall them. Yes, the impulse that made regenerate individuals want to congregate in the first place had nothing to do with the order of redemption but ran "according to ordinances endowed in our human race in Creation. . . . [It is from] the organic character of the general human race that the organic character of the church arises." If it was thus "not for a moment anything other than a *human* phenomenon," still the church was under such an "influence of a higher power" that it must "be understood as nothing other than the product of the in-working of a higher grace." Likewise, for all that Scripture tells us about salvation from "God's point of view," from the human point of view the operations of the church institute were essential to the process. It was the sacrament of baptism that "sealed" the child of believers in the covenant, and it was through the preaching of the word that God's act of regeneration dawned upon the spiritual seeker — more precisely, was made and kept "central" in the believer's "consciousness." Thus while the "personal life of the faithful in its germ lies outside [the church's] organization," and while in "the coming to be of conversion the institutional church is only an instrumental aid," still "the central action upon the consciousness always proceeds from the institutional church" in the act of preaching.

Moreover, since the covenant brought into the visible church some children who did not manifest faith as adults and others who professed faith but had not experienced genuine conversion (that is, since the visible church was still not the same as the true invisible church), the exercise of pastoral counsel and the elders' discipline remained essential, institutional though they were. This conscious regulatory concession Kuyper supplemented with an unfortunate choice of example in illustrating his ideal of spontaneous church formation. The Dutch Reformed immigrants who had recently arrived in Colorado and New Mexico, he offered, were already a church even though they had not yet called officers. In reality, this enterprise, though proceeding under the auspices of a professor at Kampen Seminary and a Kuyper associate, amounted to one of the sorriest episodes in the annals of Dutch-American immigration. Utterly unsuited for their high-plains environment, deceived and under-supplied by their sponsors, the group barely survived the winter, and many came to ruin. It was pastors and government officials on the scene, "institutional" officers all, who came to their rescue.

Yet the momentum in Kuyper's theory and current practice all pushed toward the "organic" side. Doubling down on his rhetoric, his theory moved from his earlier institute-organism distinction to an institute-organism "opposition." Put "more precisely," he stated, the single undivided "organism of the church" shows a "twofold manifestation: . . . the one *organic*, the other *institutional*." That is, the church comprised an organic organism and an institutional organism. If this was no arbitrary or "accidental" distinction but a "principial and necessary" one, the domains assigned to either side bespoke his preferences. The "institutional departments" in the academic study of ecclesiology included polity, history, and statistics. The "organic departments" studied the threefold Christianization of "personal life" (Christian biography, piety, and "character"), of "organized life" (home, society, and state), and of "non-organized life" (letters, arts, and science). That is, the "organic organism" included everything the 1890s Kuyper was interested in — what later scholars have labeled Christian cultural engagement but what Kuyper himself called "the Christian metamorphosis of the common phenomena of general human life." This indeed evoked the ultimate purpose of the church's whole existence, the fashioning of a redeemed humanity in a redeemed creation. On that new earth, Kuyper repeated, the church as institute will "fall away and nothing but the [organic] organism will remain." But already now, the energy at the cutting edges of modern life was deployed only "minimally through the sphere of the institutional church." Even within the church, the institute tapped "so little spiritual depth that every service in her circle, every vocation to her office, every energy in the service of the Word and Sacrament, however phenomenally organized and activated, derives her essential power from something that falls *outside* her jurisdiction." The church organic too was sovereign in its own sphere.

In a way, Kuyper's ecclesiology had come full circle. He had entered the ministry devoted to à Lasco's ideal of a church living out of its common inner spirit and not by Calvin's outward forms. He shared the worry of the ultimate German mediating theologian Richard Rothe that the church was becoming more and more marginal to the main forces of modern life, a Sunday-morning fellowship of a pious circle restricted to "religious" matters. Rothe yearned instead for an "organic" church made up of the entire community, infusing all domains of human life with godly passion seven days a week, even as its institutional structure withered away. Fatefully, for Rothe only the State (in the Hegelian sense of the "whole moral community of a nation") qualified for that august role, a conclusion that Kuyper early on came to view with horror. Yet Kuyper's alternative constituted something of a Rothean State-within-the-state, a constantly connected body of believers active everywhere while hedged about by "Calvin's solid church form" of confessional distinctiveness amid a pluralistic society.

The Church Liturgical

It was one thing to theorize about the church with other scholars, another to serve a congregation of ordinary people. Kuyper had left his Amsterdam pulpit in 1874, but he never forgot his campaign for liturgical reform there. Some twenty-five years later he took it up again in *De Heraut*. The series went on hiatus in 1901 when he took over the cabinet but resumed in 1910 and finally appeared in book form the next year as *Our Worship*.

The volume added still another layer to Kuyper's ecclesiology, for worship was institutional church work par excellence, yet Kuyper treated it not begrudgingly but with loving esteem. Some old perennials came back to life. *Our Worship* reproved class distinctions in the church at every turn. It repeatedly cut through the crust of custom to recover traditional sources while updating them in a remarkably progressive spirit. Most interesting, in light of the Doleantie's reputation for spawning a "preacher's church," Kuyper advocated reducing the clergy's role both in the concept and the conduct of worship. Ministers should take the pulpit only for tasks requiring ordination, he said: the sermon, service of confession, sacraments, and congregational prayer. All the rest — hymns, Scripture readings, announcements — should be handled by the elders, not least because the preacher "will retain a more humble and brotherly spirit if he is not always the only axle around which everything turns." On Sundays people ought to know that they were going to an *eeredienst,* not a *preekdienst* — to "worship," not to "sermon."

The foundations of his ecclesiology also served as the starting point in liturgy. The sovereign in worship was God as revealed in Scripture; the human center was "the assembly" of the local congregation; neither was to be displaced by officialdom in the form of "the preacher." The purpose of worship was to enter into corporate communion with God, overcoming the separations wrought by sin. That required that the assembly be properly disposed to encounter the Holy in their inner spirit. All outward, material elements had to be subordinated to that end.

Yet across this familiar grain ran strong assertions of institutional forms. It was the elders, ordained officials, who assumed the pulpit when the preacher sat down. The service must open with the Votum, for only its invocation of "the Name of the Lord" transformed the gathered individuals into a corporate body of Christ and united them with the church of all ages. Kuyper liked a common lectionary for promoting ecumenical purposes; likewise the recitation of the Apostles' Creed, which lifted the local church beyond its parochial identity. He commended kneeling in prayer and lamented how that practice had been hindered by the introduction of fixed pews into Dutch churches at the behest of civic dignitaries who wanted, predictably, the best seats in the house. He urged the use of liturgical prayers and faulted the prevailing cult of spontaneous utterance as too likely to indulge the supplicant's ego and to wander into a thicket of discordant, unedifying bypaths. In short, the Kuyper of Utrecht and Amsterdam made his return, lauding "fixed forms" not only in doctrine but once again in a modestly high-church liturgy.

His rationale for this choice was sometimes pragmatic. Spontaneous prayer made it difficult for the congregation to keep up with the speaker's petitions and make them their own, while it also overtaxed the preacher who was nervous about his impending sermon. Kuyper also conducted some keen historical analysis. "Our churches," he wrote to readers with Doleantie and Seceder roots, were beholden to habits established in eighteenth-century Dutch conventicles on the model of seventeenth-century British Puritans and Presbyterians, who were overreacting to sixteenth-century Anglican ritual. Too much of the liturgical landscape remained defined by oscillation between those two poles — and by their inadvertent mirror-imaging of each other. Thus, said Kuyper, naming names, a revivalist like Ira Sankey warbling biblical parables and a professional Anglican choir chanting Scripture both pushed worship toward a cult of performance that would inevitably end in mere market competition. His main objection was theological, however. The pietist free style fostered a cult of inwardness that made it difficult to connect liturgy to life, that mistook spontaneity for authenticity, and that finally eroded any corporate religious authority. This was the ultimate point. The conventicle, along with all the sectarianism issuing from its principles, did not qualify as a church, nor its gatherings as genuine Christian worship, nor its homilies as the real preaching of the Word.

The paramount exercises of the church institute — preaching and the sacraments — occupy one-third of *Our Worship* and illustrate how Kuyper's formal ecclesiology filtered into regular practice. True to his doctrine of unmediated regeneration, the preacher on Kuyper's model was to regard the assembly as a redeemed people of God and not as sinners in need of salvation. He might — in fact, periodically must — call the saints to the "mini-conversions" of repentance and amendment of life, but the definitive work of justification was not his to effect. The Lord's Day was not the time for revivals, altar calls, or seeker services. The preacher's purpose was to promote sanctification, to undertake the long-term pastoral labor that grew from a close understanding of his flock's spiritual condition, refracting Scripture through the heart of his own reflection and experience onto their specific situation. In other words, although Kuyper for once did not use the term, good preaching was organic.

As to the sacraments, the Lord's Supper had over the years received less of Kuyper's attention than had baptism, and his Amsterdam proposals for weekly Communion did not survive the transit to this point. Four to six celebrations a year should suffice, he thought, lest the observance lose its "exceptionally holy character." Yet Communion lacked for nothing in significance: "The worship service reaches its highest point in the celebration of the Lord's Supper." In contrast to his understanding of baptism, where Kuyper waffled between realism and symbolism, the Lord's Supper he cast in unambig-

189

uous terms. He followed Calvin over Zwingli in forthrightly affirming the real presence of Christ in the ceremony and "oppos[ing] any notion that the Lord's Supper is only symbolic." So devoted was Kuyper to the literal form of Jesus' institution that he urged even large city congregations to make every effort to take the sacrament seated around tables in front of the church, logistical difficulties to the contrary notwithstanding. And he showed an odd ecumenical streak in confiding his personal preference for taking the sacrament amid strangers, where he and they would not be distracted by knowledge of each other's sins and questions of adequate repentance.

The Problem of Baptism

Baptism was more complicated and, not accidentally, it developed into a full-scale controversy in Kuyper's new church. As to its mode of administration he countenanced considerable latitude. The original model of immersion no longer applied, he argued, partly for reasons of climate (northern European rivers being less hospitable than Middle Eastern) but more because of theology. The adult converts of the earliest church needed to be demonstrably washed of their sins, whereas infants baptized under the covenant needed only a "sealing" of its promises in the "sign" of sprinkling on the forehead. Yet Kuyper preferred that the font instead of a mere bowl be kept before the congregation as a reminder of the original practice.

One aspect of the sacrament remained absolute, however, and that was the verbal formulary instituted by the church and bearing real supernatural power. Here too the old Kuyper was the new, having held to the same line without deviation for forty years. His original protest at Utrecht involved this issue, and his second-phase book on *The Covenants* had concluded with a linguistic tour de force on the question of whether a child was properly baptized "in" or "to" the Triune Name. The former was the due Augustinian language of the appointed form, Kuyper demonstrated, while the latter indicated a Pelagian error that naturally made it attractive to Modernists but that also deprived the ceremony of any sacramental power. Now, in late career, Kuyper kept the same insistence. The prescribed form must be followed to the letter to effect its purpose for both parties, the church and the child.

That said, the Kuyper who consulted God's point of view had to wrestle with the very necessity of the ceremony. As we have seen, he urged it be conducted as soon as possible, even if the mother was not sufficiently recovered from childbirth to attend. The father was the covenant representative of the family, the congregation the body to which the child was being added, and the prevalence of infant mortality reason enough for urgency in the matter. Yet he opposed the practice of "emergency baptism" by pious laity, since God did not need a few water drops to indicate a dying child's spiritual status. (If born to at least one believing parent, the infant was presumed to be elect.) "If baptism neither adds to nor subtracts from the salvation of the child, why then should one rush or attach such great value to baptism?" Kuyper frankly asked. "There is no escaping this dilemma. That is why . . . [it] is all the more urgent" to observe the sacrament for the sake of its other audience: "to always enliven the remembrance of baptism among the baptized, to remind them of the comfort they possess in the seal of the covenant, and to direct them continually to the obligation of the new obedience that issues directly from baptism."

By the time he published these words, Kuyper had fought and lost a battle in the GKN over the theological construct behind the dilemma. In the first years after the Union of 1892, Kuyper's followers held the initiative in the new denomination while the Christian Reformed party lost ground. The most obvious issue involved competing claims between Kampen Seminary and the Free University over theological education; next came Kuyper's agenda of cultural engagement vis à vis the old Seceder focus on spiritual nurture and boundary-maintenance. Indeed, on this front an old Christian Reformed lion launched an arrow at the heart of Kuyper's ecclesiology:

> To conceive of the visible or local church, in contrast to the church as organism, as only an institute for the service of the Word, only of practical value, a phenomenon of only passing significance, is to damage its character, lower its destiny, and attack its essence. It becomes just one manifestation of the real church set *next to* and on one line with other manifestations, for instance in the social or scholarly domain, by which either scholarship is deified or the church is made worldly.

In 1896, the date of this grievance, the Kuyperian star was so ascendant in the Reformed sky that the protest did not prevail. His very successes, however, increasingly drew Kuyper out of ecclesiastical affairs, ultimately to the head of national politics, and left an opening for the Christian Reformed party to strike back. Feelings grew so bad that at the Synod of 1902 the denomination seemed ready to break apart. It managed to avoid that by letting both Kampen and the Free University carry on pastoral training and by implicitly endorsing Kuyperian cultural activism while explicitly downgrading the ecclesiology behind it.

The GKN Synod of 1905 had to finally settle the fight by ruling on Kuyper's understanding of election and its theological consequences. First, did God choose the elect before humanity's fall into sin (supralapse) — indeed, before creation — or afterward, as Seceder infralapsarianism held? Second, were the righteous thus understood to be justified from all eternity? Third, were covenant children baptized on the presumption that they were regenerate? Finally, was regeneration accomplished unmediated by any instrument, including the church?

The Synod held with the infralapsarians down the line. More precisely, it declared "infra" to be the preferred, and "supra" a lesser though legitimate, track in the Reformed tradition. As to the timing of election it decreed that teaching and preaching should "adhere as closely as possible" to the language of the confessions, which clearly had an infra understanding. The timing of regeneration was established clearly in neither Scripture nor confession, so that the question of whether "God fulfills his promise either before, in, or after baptism must be addressed with great circumspection." Such language was a study in circumspection itself. As one scholar has concluded, the Seceders and Kuyperians posed two consistent but incompatible systems, the first rooted in time and persons, the second in eternity and decrees. The Synod found for the implications of the former without boring down to the foundations of either, in particular bypassing the "Archimedean point of the Kuyperian system," the teaching of unmediated regeneration. By a most un-Kuyperian inconsistency, the church held together.

Kuyper took the setback without public protest because in 1905 he was battling to survive as prime minister. More generally, he had long since embarked on other initiatives. During the late 1890s, when he was recovering what he deemed to be proper Reformed liturgy, he was laying out on the facing pages of *De Heraut* a dramatic new line in Reformed theology. This was the doctrine of common grace, the "seed" of which he located in some words of Calvin but whose "manifestation" he elaborated much further than any predecessor had ever tried. It was the linchpin to his theology of culture, and the subject to which he turned his attention after long struggles over the church.

CHAPTER TEN

Theologian of Culture

Kuyper is best known in English-speaking circles for his theology of culture. Kuyper, more than most other conservative Protestants before or after him, laid great stress upon creation in its own right and as the starting point of theological reflection. He elevated the "cultural mandate" in Genesis (1:28: "Be fruitful and multiply . . .") as an enduring command for humanity to develop the potential endowed in creation as service to God. He made cultural engagement a strategic priority for his followers in the context of their times. And he deployed that effort along the lines of his two key theological innovations: the doctrine of common grace and the epistemology of worldview.

This program as a whole and in each of its parts has spawned abundant commentary, positive and negative. The biographer's role in adding to the mix is neither to elaborate nor to evaluate but to contextualize this dimension of Kuyper's work amid his other initiatives and the dynamics of his day. That is, the *when* of this particular project has something to say about its *what*. The timing is clear enough. Although Kuyper sounded these themes from the very start of his career and reverted to them periodically, he brought them into sharp focus in the decade 1887-98 — the decade just after the Doleantie had gone awry and just when the road to the political promised land opened up. This was the decade of democratization, when the Dutch political system doubled and then re-doubled the size of the electorate. It was the decade when the nation rose from the economic depths to start making real progress on the domestic front. Not coincidentally, it saw Kuyper at his most progressive, certainly at his shortest patience with conservatives in church and state. On the global stage, the same decade saw an explosion of Western imperialism and the harbingers of a cultural revolution that would usher in a new form of Modernism. Common grace, worldview epistemology, and the call to Christian cultural engagement reflected each and every aspect of this scene.

Cultural Activism

Early in his career Kuyper had to assert a public role for Christianity against religious moderates and secular skeptics. His ongoing argument with the Ethical theologians chafed at their limiting faith to existential questions and traditional "spiritual" domains. His inaugural at Utrecht reminded the establishmentarians there that the Reformed tradition did not just warrant national-church prerogatives but made claims on "all fields of life," "every domain." His opening address at the Free University not only defended the sovereignty of various spheres but insisted upon an active Christian part in all of them. The most memorable words of that speech, perhaps of his entire career, were a challenge to the "thinking class" of the nation, which regarded the faith as either erroneous, private, or of narrowly moral relevance. On the contrary, he thundered: "there is not a square inch in the whole domain of our human existence over which Christ, who is Sovereign over *all,* does not cry: 'Mine!'" Kuyper thus grounded Christian cultural activism in the most venerable of Calvinist precepts.

Kuyper leaned heavily upon that fulcrum after the Doleantie. Now he faced not the cultured despisers of religion but pious skeptics of culture: third-generation heirs of the Réveil, with its focus on evangelism and serial charities; Christian Reformed allies, tenacious for the purity of their church; and his own ecclesiastical followers, embittered by the way the powers of church and state had thwarted ecclesiastical reform. To these and others like them Kuyper outlined a new strategy in the memorable address "A Twofold Fatherland," delivered at the Free University convention in June 1887. With the wounds of the church struggle still raw, he admitted that it was tempting to give up on the nation, "our fatherland here below," and he indulged his audience with the myth of a seventeenth-century golden age when pure Reformed religion "defined the direction of [our] public life."

Yet he reminded them that God remained the Sovereign Lord over all history, including the present place and time. If it was manifestly so that "*secularization* is the stamp" of the age, then the Lord must have also provided the means for believers to sound the claims of faith in that context.

To discern those means Kuyper directed his audience's attention to the secularists' road to power: their command of government, public opinion, the arts and science. The faithful were called to work in those same venues, Kuyper reasoned, even — no, especially — from their place on the margin. The temporizers they had just left behind in the national church were fated to remain priests endlessly trying to atone for the mix of purity and impurity with which their cult of unity diluted the gospel. The Calvinist remnant was called to be prophets instead, nurtured in their own networks but stepping forth boldly into public life to call "prince and people back to the Law and the Testimony." This was Kuyper's church-organic living as "a colony of the heavenly fatherland." If that remained always the object of their highest allegiance, believers were still to plant here below deep roots for a long engagement in public life. They were to be patient with small beginnings, searching with the eye of hope for tokens of "a better dawn." Kuyper did not have to add, that summer of 1887, that a bright dawn indeed was at hand for the Calvinist political cause in the expanded franchise currently being negotiated in the capital. Christian cultural engagement was a strategic offensive for a promising future.

Those prospects looked even brighter nine years later when Kuyper addressed the 1896 synod of the GKN at Middelburg, the city of his youth. True, that assembly would deal with formal protests against his teaching from the Christian Reformed side of the denomination, but in assigning him the keynote address the synod had forecast the outcome of the debate. Kuyper took full advantage. As we shall see in the next chapter, another expansion of the franchise was imminent in national politics, and Lohman's Réveil conservatism had just been purged from the Antirevolutionary Party and the Free University. With his own health restored after those combats, Kuyper went after the conservatives in his new church with a bracing vision of the Calvinist future.

It was a weak faith, he began, a trimming of the sovereignty of God, that was at work in the sectarian mentality which accepted a "reduced lot," wrote off the larger world, and hoped only to bequeath to the future safe "little churches" with their "spiritual prattlings" and balm for the soul. The brethren should recall, he noted, that piety and orthodoxy had never been stronger than in the age of the Reformation, when Calvinism had been full of verve and commanded respect. The good news for his followers, Kuyper then said in a startling reversal, was that the golden age had not been so golden. The devoutly Reformed had made up no larger a portion of the Dutch nation then than they did now; they had faced just as strong a foe, wrestled with conflicts and inadequacies as in the present. But the fathers knew that "conflict quickens faith," and that faith led them to accept the high calling to be *an instrument of the Lord in the struggle of the ages.*" True heirs of their Calvinism, Kuyper concluded, would remember that God's sovereignty extends over the whole world and not just the house of the pious; that Christ offers not only the breath of consolation but the Word of Wisdom structured by creation into all things; that personal salvation is less an end in itself than a means to God's larger purpose of renewing the cosmos. "Brothers," he concluded, "*I believe in the future,* I believe in it with all my heart. . . . As Reformed people we have not just in the Netherlands alone but on the great world scene still a future, still a calling, still a holy task entrusted to us."

These two addresses, representing the start and the apex of Kuyper's most confident decade, also unveiled his key ideas for carrying the new project forward. In his synodical address of 1896 he sketched the outline of worldview thinking by which Calvinism could become a player on the intellectual frontiers of the age. Protestantism as a whole had become a spent force in the Netherlands, he mourned, surrendering the cultural initiative to Catholicism on the one hand and pantheism on the other. Now Calvinism should enter the lists by articulating from its definite "standpoint" and ruling "principle" a consistent "Christian worldview in the tongue of our own time." And if that encounter boded conflict, in "Twofold Fatherland" Kuyper pointed to a different frontier, the heavenly kingdom toward which the earthly pilgrimage walked under the canopy of common grace.

Common Grace

Kuyper's work on common grace bore obvious connections with his rising political career. He unfolded the concept in his theology column in *De Heraut* over a six-year period — from September 1895, soon after he had reentered Parliament, until July 1901, when he was forming the cabinet. In fact, he foreshadowed the project already during his first term in Parliament, in 1874, when he dilated on "the natural knowledge of God" that was available to all human beings. The reason is plain enough. Faith-based politics requires some common ground with people of fundamentally different convictions — at least to establish mutual intelligibility and respect for the rules of the game, and at most to build coalitions on issues of common interest.

Still, common grace is first of all a theological concept that addresses a real problem in the Reformed tradition. Kuyper noted this at the very outset in invoking John Calvin's treatment of the "virtue of the heathen" in his *Institutes* (II/3/3). Calvin wondered, as should we, said Kuyper, how it was that "the unbelievers who dwell in our midst often outdo many a child of Christ in their quiet, serious devotion to duty." Historically, "Anabaptists" (more accurately, the pietists and conventiclers in his audience) resolved the conundrum by denying any real virtue outside the true church — a move, he observed, whose dishonesty did little credit to the ethics of those who made it. "Arminians," on the other hand, trimmed the Reformed teaching of human depravity, divine sovereignty, or both. The doctrine of common grace thus salvaged Reformed orthodoxy by seeing the virtues of the unregenerate as fruits of the sovereign grace of God. This was not saving grace, Kuyper emphasized; that went only to the elect by the operations of "particular grace." Yet it was real grace nonetheless, the unmerited favor of God, shed upon all people regardless of their spiritual destiny. Indeed, upon more than all people, for it extended through the whole cosmos, just like the reign of God and the work of the Holy Spirit. It touched the body as well as the soul, peoples as well as persons, things "secular" as well as "sacred." In brief, common grace addressed an old problem in Reformed theology with a classic Reformed answer while warranting Kuyper's new Calvinistic initiative.

Common grace had two goals, Kuyper said; better, it represented two temporal means of reaching the one perennial goal of magnifying the glory of God. First, God by means of common grace intervened immediately after the human fall into sin to delay the death that was the sure consequence of disobedience. Kuyper pointed this out already in *Particular Grace,* the favorite text of those who deny any other sort: "if no curtain of protection had been placed between God and the human race against [God's] fiercely burning wrath, everyone would go alive, directly, and without a moment's delay to hell." At other places he opined that life on earth would have gone on but as a living hell, a chaos of such disorder, destruction, and distrust as to render impossible any productive economy, any formation of culture, any civil society. Common grace thus exercised a "bridling," "tempering" effect that "restrained" or "blocked" the natural outworking of sin. Yet, as Kuyper read early Genesis, these operations were of diminishing effect until God intervened dramatically again in the days of Noah. The twofold covenant laid out after the flood (Genesis 9) amounted to a serious upgrade of common grace. It instituted regularity in nature, as signified by the rainbow, and order in society by the power of the sword. Not accidentally, Kuyper continued, Genesis next records the rapid emergence of culture — of agriculture, manufacturing, city life, music and the arts, and everything else that marks human flourishing. While much of this went awry under renewed human rebellion, he acknowledged, it still set the context in which an elect people could be called and gathered over time. Without common grace, particular grace would not have had a chance.

But there was more. It would be the old pious smugness, Kuyper warned, to see the human race existing only to bring forth the elect. Thereupon he launched forth on the second leg of common grace and into his era's confident interpretations of history. He began by returning to the cultural mandate. God endowed the human race with abilities on purpose, and common grace was the means by which that intention was not thwarted by the fall. All the powers latent in creation and human nature could and must still unfold, more slowly and erratically than they would have absent sin but no less progressively. This was an invitation to celebrate the century's achievements in science and technology, and Kuyper did not pass it up. Nor did he demur at joining the chorus prophesying even greater glories to come in the twentieth century (bitterly ironic as those predictions seem today). The growing mastery of science over nature included such feats as his country's recent conquest of time and space via the railroad and telegraph, and it promised further reductions in the high rates of child mortality that troubled his soul.

Kuyper saluted more than material gains, however. The "higher" levels of thinking, the "nobler" sentiments of family life, the civil tongue of bourgeois discourse, the salience of appeals to equity and

199

justice, the rising prospects of international peace via treaties and arbitration — all these were undeniable improvements over the superstition that had benighted so much life in the past: the brutal tone of pre-modern family relations, the raw exploitation of early industrialism, the unapologetic hauteur of aristocratic regimes. While hypocrisy pervaded much of the contemporary scene, it was a salute that vice paid to real virtues; and while cruelty and injustice still marred any number of social relations, surely no one would wish to return to the harshness of an earlier day. That the official norms of the age afforded leverage for continued improvement was a blessing from the Lord that everyone, including the saints, should appreciate.

In this commentary Kuyper had his eye on "the West," that is, the nations of central and western Europe along with the Anglo domains of North America, where industrial and bourgeois progress had made its greatest strides — and whence ventures of conquest were bringing the course of Western imperialism toward its apogee at just this moment. Kuyper mapped the course of common grace along the same track. Granting that every race and tribe had a culture, in many cases, as in the "backwaters" of Asia and Africa, these had turned in on themselves, becoming "isolated." Only along one track — the grand arc that arose in the Fertile Crescent and Egypt, ran across the Mediterranean to Greece and Rome, crossed the Alps into northwestern Europe, and now spanned the Atlantic to America — had human civilization made *cumulative* progress. Precisely here, in the terms of common grace, creational potential had been most realized to date, and here it would come to its climax. It was Western Europeans and their American cousins, Kuyper elaborated, who best nurtured the fruits of common grace, from technology to human tenderness. It was they who had subdued "lower" passions beneath "higher" ideals, and it was their destiny to have mastery over all the globe, as was now unfolding before his readers' eyes.

This reading of history owed more to Hegel than to Scripture, and Kuyper did not hesitate to link it into the racial hierarchies of the day. Without ever explaining the anomaly of his allegiance to the African Augustine over the pale Brit Pelagius, in *Common Grace* Kuyper bluntly set the white race over the yellow and yellow over black, with red doomed to extinction in the wilds of North America. It was in his commentary on common grace and art that he deployed some of the most offensive rhetoric in his entire corpus.

Beauty does not enrich the *entire* earth. On the contrary, the beautiful, the common, and the hideous today exist next to each other. A lion is beautiful, a calf is common, a rat is hideous. . . . [T]he same is true of people. The Arab appeals to you by beauty of appearance, we Dutch look very common, and the Hottentot fills you with loathing.

At the same time, common grace theology itself, separated from this historical trope, could warrant as sweet a chorus of cultural diversity as postmoderns might wish to sing — or that Romantic social thinking in the line of Herder, Kuyper's own trajectory, originally sounded. In a striking invocation of the social implications of the Trinity, and in another echo of his old critique of uniformity, Kuyper asserted that the image of God, though surely borne by individuals, comes to fullest manifestation in the human race as a whole. The implications were democratic. "If it has pleased God to mirror the richness of his image in the social multiplicity and fullness of our human race," then in "the whole life of the world, the life of Kaffirs in Africa, of Mongols in China and Japan, and of the Indians south of the Himalayas," as well as in the ancient cultures of "Egyptians and Greeks, in Babylon and Rome," and so also in life "today among the peoples of whatever continent," there was nothing "that was or is not necessary" to the fulfillment of the potential that God had endowed in creation to the ultimate display of the richness of his glory.

Common Grace and Particular Grace

This level of generality, however inspiring to Kuyper's readers, glanced over some concrete questions. If they lowered their sights from civilizations to persons, could Calvinists see acts of real goodness in their non-Christian neighbors, read words of real truth in a pagan classic, appreciate real beauty in the work of, say, French Impressionists? Logically, Kuyper had to say yes. If cultural complexes are more, they are never less than the sum of their parts, and if the whole has genuine merit, so must some of the parts. Kuyper cited specific individuals as examples, typically at the level of genius. "The names of Socrates, Plato, and Aristotle have constantly been honored by Christian thinkers," while among the moderns it was an "undeniable fact that . . . Kant and Darwin shone [as] stars of the first magnitude, geniuses of the highest degree, who uttered the most profound thoughts even though they were not confessing Christians." The same could apply to people without fame. The natural science of the day, although conducted "almost exclusively" by anonymous ranks "who are strangers to the fear of the Lord," had "produced a treasure of knowledge that we as Christians admire and gratefully use."

Typically, however, though nothing in his theory required it, Kuyper tended to deal with individual persons in the context of particular grace. Common grace he associated with structures and collectivities — with the formal institutions of government and culture, for instance, rather than with statesmen or artists themselves. He especially emphasized in this regard the potent if informal sinews of custom, habit, tradition, and public opinion. This reflected his Burkean past but also the communal emphases of his political and social theory, the elevation of the organic church in his ecclesiology, even his derogation of soul salvation to the level of means rather than end in his soteriology. In all his theorizing, that is, Kuyper tended to be more concerned with the connections between people, with "the life-relationships of the human race," than with the persons themselves.

Of these relationships, that between common and particular grace became one of his more pressing questions. Unlike some of his acolytes, Kuyper always treated the two in combination, as two "distinguished but not divided" operations of the same God, aimed at the self-same goal of re-creating the whole world until it finally reflected the glory of the divine image. If the organism of the church, made up of those elected under particular grace, would one day fill that world as its new humanity, then common grace permitted the spoiled creation to stay in being while that development went forward. At the same time it produced significant achievements — whether at believers' or unbelievers' hands — that would all be assumed into the new order, purged and refined. Those achievements, in fact, would do much to lift the re-creation quite beyond the Edenic original.

To sort out the complications in the meantime, Kuyper devised a four-part typology that can be best visualized on a spectrum. At the two ends lay the two graces pure and simple. In lands not (yet) evangelized, common grace operated alone, with no small record of accomplishment but no hopeful goal in sight either. In the institutional church, purely reformed, particular grace operated safe from the corruptions of the world. In the two middle segments the two graces overlapped with complex results. Kuyper gave these segments most of his attention from here on out.

The middle domains registered the fact, in Kuyper's opinion, that particular grace strengthened and best realized the possibilities of common grace. Not that believers were more gifted than unbelievers at science, art, technical skill, or political acumen; the opposite was the rule. Rather, those endowed with the insights of the gospel knew the ultimate purposes and norms for these gifts. At the same time their life together in families, churches, and voluntary associations manifested a winsome model, a noble spirit, that their neighbors wanted to enjoy. Thus Christianity, starting out everywhere as the conviction of a doughty minority, could not help but change society for the better as its witness drew more people into its ranks and so shed its influence into its local setting. Where the process had worked longest — i.e., in Europe — the effects were most profound. It was the intensifying effect of particular grace in the workings of common grace, Kuyper claimed, that accounted in no small part for the West's achievement of global supremacy.

Furthermore, the fruits of secular progress could be claimed for Christianity even though many people in these leading nations, particularly in their leading sectors, were no longer believers; their accomplishments were the long-term residue of a once-dominant public faith. This was the first mixed category, then, "the life of non-confessors in a Christian country." In this loose sense of the term, Kuyper said, "Christian" indicated "nothing about the spiritual state of the inhabitants of such a country but only [bore] witness to the fact that public opinion, the general mindset, the ruling ideas, the moral norms, the laws and customs there clearly betoken the influence of the Christian faith." As fruits of that influence he listed the abolition of slavery, the elevation of women's status, "the maintenance of public virtue, respect for the Sabbath, compassion for the poor, consistent regard for the ideal over the material, and — even in manners — the elevation of all that is human from its sunken state to a higher standpoint."

The increasing level of generality on this list shows Kuyper approximating the notions of Christian *kultur* that the belligerent nations in World War I would put forth to legitimate their destruction of each other — and inevitably of the concept itself. Even without that destruction, Kuyper's near equation of Christian and bourgeois in this context evinced little of the critical rigor he was simultaneously developing in his worldview epistemology. Perhaps he was trying one last time to recover the Netherlands as a "Christian nation," now as a nation with a collective Christian memory to which an explicitly Christian political activism could appeal.

In any case, Christian action more tightly defined was the mark of the fourth segment on the spectrum, the second mixed category, "the life of Christ-confessors outside of the church institute." Here was Kuyper's cherished church-organic, the body of believers' work and witness in everyday life, especially on the cutting edges of modern development. Strengthened as these endeavors were by particular grace, they could work in society only because of the points of contact established there by common grace.

In this domain Kuyper used "Christian" in a stricter sense. He borrowed three images from Jesus' Sermon on the Mount (Matthew 5–7) to refract its meanings. The briefest treatment went to the image of "salt of the earth," by which believers' engagement with the ambient culture worked only to preserve it. "The light of the world" he invoked more fulsomely:

> Though the lamp of the Christian religion burns within the walls only of that institute [the church], its light shines out through its windows to areas far beyond, illumining all the sectors and associations that appear across the wide range of human life and activity: justice, law, the home and family, business, vocation, public opinion and literature, art and science, and so much more.

Yet light established only an "external contact." Leaven, by contrast, wrought an "internal kinship," and it was as "a leaven [that] has permeated the three measures of meal" that Kuyper wanted the people of particular grace to participate in the world preserved by common grace, effecting thereby the "Christian metamorphosis" that was at once the ultimate goal and the first fruits of God's eternal design.

Worldview

The interface that common grace gave Christians with people of other convictions was evident not only in Kuyper the politician but in Kuyper the intellectual. He was remarkably attuned to the cultural currents of his time, and at no instance more than in elaborating his second theological innovation, the epistemology of worldview. "Worldview" as an understanding of collective consciousness had its roots in Immanuel Kant's later work and had steadily grown with the German Romantic and Idealist movements stemming from it. By the 1890s, however, an acute sense of crisis in European high culture drove more thinkers than ever to entertain the concept as a solution to two components in that crisis: the question of cultural authority and the question of cultural coherence. As those issues were perpetually atop Kuyper's intellectual agenda, "worldview" offered him a way to put Calvinism at the cutting edge of cultural discourse while simultaneously showing his followers that they had as legitimate a voice in that conversation as their self-proclaimed superiors.

The question of cultural authority arose from doubts about the hard-nosed scientific enterprise that had been staking the strongest recent claim to that authority. The ruthless nation-building and industrialization that marked politics and economy since the 1860s had as their academic partner a "positive" science that warranted the naturalism of its philosophical premises by the amplitude of its technological rewards. On this model, unbiased observers looked directly upon a nature devoid of non-material qualities to capture reality as it actually was. This capture came by discovering the laws that controlled phenomena in a given domain, explaining what had seemed mysterious, revealing order behind what had seemed chaos, and promising ever further grasp of nature's ways. Grasp also meant control; "science" would harvest nature to yield greater bounty, health, and well-being for its human masters. If the process seemed to lack heart, as some critics contended, its enthusiasts pronounced it to be unstoppable, like the "progress" it yielded. The individual or nation that did not want to "get ahead" was foolish.

Yet by the end of the century the fools had become the wise, or at least had achieved critical mass. Some of positivism's critics came from the outside, like philosophical Idealists and the religiously orthodox who argued that a world lacking in spiritual qualities necessarily lacked ethics and purpose. Young leaders in the emerging social sciences and humanities worried (some of them, like William James and Max Weber, nearly worried themselves to death) that a sheer naturalistic study of humanity would erode human dignity and freedom. On this view "progress" looked very much like a prison. The most telling criticism came from within the natural sciences themselves, and first from the "hardest" sciences of all, mathematics and physics. Upon observation it turned out that the behavior of gases had to be understood in terms of statistical probability, not as a definitive picture; and upon reflection it turned out that a mathematical point was a hypothetical and not a "real" entity. The preeminent physicist Ernst Mach complained that the emerging paradigm of atomic theory, which was about to revolutionize physics with (literally) earth-shaking consequences, was not science at all but philosophical speculation. Mach soon had to conclude, with fellow "critical positivists," that science was a human improvisation which did not gaze upon the "real world" as conventionally understood and consequently did not yield true certainty. Ordinary science continued apace despite these questions, and ordinary people still looked to it as a font of plenty. But in philosophical circles and among public intellectuals, the door was now open to reassertions of the creative power of the human observer (the "subject") after a half-century of subordination to the material observed (the "object"). The door was likewise open to reassertions of the spiritual over against the material, intuition over strict empiricism, the vital and dynamic over deadening controls.

In proposing his worldview construct Kuyper entered this traffic and pursued a longstanding dream. His turn to forthright Calvinism came in response to the specter of scientific naturalism that was then (in the mid-1860s) in the booster phase of its ascent. His first publication defended the democratization of the church as a means of defending Christian orthodoxy and invoked worldview tropes in the process. One's position on the question at hand, Kuyper said in 1867, was not susceptible to objective settlement; it all depended on "which corner" one came from, "the Judeo-Christian, incarnational, ethical world- and life-view" or its "heathen, humanistic, aesthetic" opposite. More fulsomely, he inaugurated the Free University in 1880 with epistemological as well as historical and social-theoretical arguments. Recalling the century's contests between empiricists and Idealists, monists and atomists, subjectivists and objectivists, Kuyper emphasized how much first principles directed research programs, how incommensurate were different sets of presuppositions, and how actively they played in all disciplines, not just in theology or philosophy. "What natural scientist operates without a hypothesis?" he asked fifteen years before Mach. "Does not everyone who practices science as a *man* and not as a *measuring stick* view things through a subjective lens and always fill in the unseen part of the circle according to subjective opinion?"

These earlier gestures Kuyper now built into a full system, weaving his epistemology through the massive scholarship of his three-volume *Encyclopedia of Sacred Theology* (1893-94), distilling it in the *Lectures on Calvinism* that he delivered at Princeton in 1898, and purveying it in popular form to his Dutch readers in the final installments of his series on common grace at the turn of the century. Some Anglo-American writers, including Peter Heslam and David Naugle after him, ascribe considerable influence to Scots Presbyterian theologian James Orr in inspiring Kuyper's move to worldview as an organizing motif, though the evidence points as much to a convergence between the two as to any causal relationship. Orr and Kuyper's common steeping in nineteenth-century Germanic thinking is more to the point, as is the coincident appearance of their work with other monuments of the worldview approach. Orr's key text, *The Christian View of God and the World,* came out in 1893, as did the first volume of Kuyper's *Encyclopedia,* two years before Mach published his *Popular Scientific Lectures,* and just as Wilhelm Dilthey began the treatises that would culminate with his full typology of worldviews, the apex of the method.

Worldview epistemology fit any number of Kuyper's desiderata. He welcomed its recognition that everyone, group or individual, operated out of a cognitive framework that was itself not established by reason or science. Contrary to decades of derision from the positivists, it gave people of faith just as good a warrant to stake their claims, and equal potential for realizing those claims, as anyone else. It is "[n]ot as if the knowledge of others rests on intellectual certainty and ours only on faith," Kuyper declared in opening the Free University. "For all knowledge proceeds from faith of whatever kind. You lean on God, you proceed from your own ego, or you hold fast to your ideal. The person who does not believe does not exist."

Worldview also promised coherence in a rapidly expanding universe of knowledge, rendering an ordered whole out of what otherwise would remain a jumble of data. Kuyper was particularly emphatic on this point. Unlike some practitioners of the method, he traced every worldview back to a single "fixed starting point," a leading "principle," by whose guidance the everyday world was explored, by whose logic a meaningful world was constructed.

Further, as the term implies, a worldview embraces the whole world, the same claim Kuyper was now making for Calvinism among his followers. Worldview thus established a mandate for critical Christian comprehensiveness. Believers had to extend the logic of their faith to sites they had heretofore ignored, had to test anew every theory and practice to see if it was of God, had to reconceptualize every place they had taken for granted or had visited on other terms. If common grace could baptize whole cultures as "Christian," worldview analysis delved beneath the surface of every project to ferret out its animating faith.

Worldview was also inherently democratic: that is, it assumed a pluralistic situation, was designed for popular reception, and sought to inspire action. As to pluralism, it was to normalize perennial disagreements among schools that Dilthey entitled his definitive essay on the matter "Der Streit der Weltanschauungen," the *conflict* of the worldview*s*. Some of Kuyper's latter-day progeny have aptly noted that, whereas "philosophy" at the time made claims to universal truth, "worldview" connoted the particular vision of one group or another. Also, philosophy restricted its domain to elite competency, while worldviews aimed to perform philosophy's functions — to provide answers to life's fundamental questions — for a wide range of people. Finally, worldview sought to furnish a feedback loop between convictions and experience, each clarifying the other so as to propel action. We can add that "the wide range of people" in question were often newly literate and newly urban under conditions of industrialism, thus living amid an unfamiliar welter of opinion and circumstance. Worldview was first conceptualized this way by Friedrich Engels; it perfectly fit Kuyper's project.

The Self, the Spiritual, and Science[*]

Still, worldview had some unsettling implications for Calvinists who, after all, were committed to the absolute truth of Scripture and the

---

[*]In all these discussions Kuyper used *wetenschap* (like the German *wissenschaft*) which translates literally as "science" but means in English "advanced study" or "higher learning," including that of the humanities and social sciences. All references to "science" in this chapter carry this meaning unless otherwise indicated.

universal sovereignty of God. Were these claims now true just for Calvinists, and was it the Calvinists' convictions that made them so? Kuyper built in counterweights at key points in his structure to block such implications. These become clear if we trace his theological recapitulation of human development. In the beginning God made everything fit and good. More precisely, Kuyper said, the whole creation was — and remains — the expression of God's thinking: a logos, an organic whole, a fabric of laws. This divine "archetype" was then matched by the "ectype" of the human mind. Reality and observer, object and subject, were tailor-made for each other. Some critics within Kuyper's tradition have noted the residue of scholastic elements in this model, but Kuyper's Romanticism was also at work again. Ontologically, German nineteenth-century *Naturphilosophie,* which he much preferred to its materialist-mechanist rivals, regarded physical realities as the manifestation of inherent Ideas; Kuyper needed only to posit God as the Thinker of these Ideas. Epistemologically, he characterized knowledge in Eden as immediate intuition. Genesis 2:19-20 served as his paradigm: Adam spontaneously apprehended the "essence" of each animal, Kuyper claimed, and so named it perfectly. The same rapport marked Adam's communion with God.

But we live after Eden, Kuyper went on, after the epistemological as well as ontological catastrophe spelled by the fall into sin. Where we once might have intuited truth quickly, we now stumble about through false starts and forgetfulness, by tedious observation and fatiguing effort, to fathom our world. "To Adam, science was an immediate possession; for us it is bread we can eat only in the sweat of our minds, after hard and strenuous labor." As to fathoming God, Kuyper granted that Ludwig Feuerbach was half right; left to our own devices, we each do fashion God in our own image. Not for nothing had Calvin called the human mind an idol-factory. Yet, however broken, Kuyper repeated, God's original order persists. These two competing lines built some potent tensions into Kuyper's system.* There was from the

---

*A similar bi-valence characterized Kuyper's model of the academic disciplines. He designed the Free University along a very traditional plan of the five faculties. Theology studied God, or transcendent spiritual reality; the natural sciences studied immanent, extra-human physical reality. The three other faculties took up the range of human life in between: Medicine for the body, Letters (philology/literature, history, and philosophy) for the soul, and Law for society. On the other hand his design for Theology per se was innovative, arranged not by the five traditional *loci* but by the

start, Kuyper repeated, an organic unity in creation, an organic wholeness in the human mind, and an organic fit between the first and the
second. These now lie in fragments, each and all. We are still called to
think God's thoughts after him, yet our operational system lacks capacity, runs erratically, and moves across a broken plane. Still,
glimpses of the original harmony are more than evident in our fallen
state, and the popularizers of science that his readers could hear
trumpeting the triumphs of progress on every side as the nineteenth
century neared its close Kuyper took to be heralding what God's endowment had made possible.

To settle these ambiguities Kuyper focused in on the human
mind, and joined the era's "return to the subject" in the process. To
begin with, he noted that some of the mind's original integrity could
still be seen in the enterprise of research and scholarship. Just as the
image of God is best borne by the human race as a whole, so, Kuyper
said, the "great temple" of knowledge had been raised stone by stone
by a wide variety of people over the centuries. Each age and agent contributed a piece, even as later generations refashioned or relocated
them by the lights of their time. Yet none of this labor followed "an
elaborate blueprint" drawn up at the start by human hand: "The entire temple was built *without* human plan and *without* human agreement . . . [yet it emerged] with a definite form and style that lets you
guess how the completed building will look." This could only happen
because the laborers were all responding to the plan and works of
God. To this extent, in philosophical terms Kuyper was a Realist.

But the unity of the human race, broken by sin, was broken again
by redemption, whereby God implants a new people upon the earth.
This familiar trope Kuyper in the 1890s started calling *palingenesis* —
a new beginning, a starting over — to remind pious readers that being
"born again" entailed renewal for the whole creation and not just individuals. But if *palingenesis* creates a new people, it necessarily creates a new collective mind. And if there were two peoples in the world,
two minds, concluded Kuyper in one of his most famous declarations,
then there had to be two sciences — two integrated, reflective, tested,
evolving bodies of knowledge. This comported well enough with the
canons of worldview thinking. But whereas some of its practitioners

---

four different sites where the supernatural had broken into human life: Scripture,
ecclesiology, dogmatics, and church offices.

hoped for eventual conciliation among the disparate visions thus wrought, hardliners like Friedrich Engels did not. He wanted not compromise but confrontation, clear bifurcations that prompted action. Kuyper was in this company. The thought-worlds built by Christians and by others were not complementary or on the road to consensus, he declared. Christians saw the world as fallen into sin and therefore as "abnormal" (i.e., being in contradiction to or off the mark set by its proper norms); others regarded the world as naturally evolved from its original state and thus as "normal" (in tune with or steaming under its own power toward what it should be). Neither side's organizing axioms were provable by a commonly shared reason or set of data; both ran on faith, and athwart each other. The much-bruited war between science and religion was therefore perfectly misnamed, Kuyper declared. War there was, but it was war between two faith-based sciences.

The Holistic Character of Truth

It is important not to exaggerate the discord Kuyper saw here. First, as he was simultaneously writing in *Common Grace,* in the scholarly race believers were not necessarily brighter, harder-working, or more accomplished than others; more likely the opposite. Second, not all scholarly contests stemmed from differences in core convictions. Some manifested antagonistic mixtures of personal disposition, experience, and social location; others reflected the dialectic between rival schools inherent in collective reflection. Either way, "friction, fermentation, and conflict" were as much a part of scholarship as of life itself. Third, in their scholarly pursuits people of contrary orientations could hold much in common. Thus Kuyper allowed that *palingenesis* did not affect logic or raw observation, or the routine tasks of measurement and calculation that characterize the "lower" sciences. The "lower-higher" metaphor was just one way Kuyper mapped this landscape. Another was to picture knowledge as a tree from whose trunk grew diverging branches: the more they developed, the farther apart they spread. A third take recalled his image of the temple of knowledge. People of different interpretive frames could use — could even join in fashioning — some of the same stones or joists but would put them in different places and to different purposes in their finished structures, thus in a real sense altering the components themselves. In any case, Kuyper averred, while emphasizing differences "we are equally emphatic in our confession, which we do not make in spite of ourselves but with gladness, that in almost every department there is some task that is common to all."

Yet to Kuyper these were secondary issues. The creation and collation of data, the sorting and interpreting of bits and pieces, this experiment and that paled in significance to the ultimate task of pulling everything together into a meaningful whole under a unified theory. This vision mirrored the pattern he followed in *Common Grace:* as structures figured there, so overall design did here. Gestalt loomed large; individual pieces or persons fell in the frame. Grand forces clashing on the battlefield of ideas were the stuff of his intellectual history — at the cost of the nuances important to any war on "uniformity." Doubtless, Kuyper's passion for order and control was at work again, but equally important was his original assumption about the nature of being and thinking. Kuyper's model was radically relational; it was the connections between things, between people, between subject and object, and between all of these and God that were — literally — of the essence.

Furthermore (to invoke the electromagnetic theory of the day), pervading all creation, both in its original perfection and in its fallen state, was a divine teleological charge, the *purpose* planted in everything by God which gave the whole and every part its destiny and dignity. The question of coherence that haunted cultural analysts at the end of the nineteenth century was also a question of meaning, and Kuyper took it straight on. "Our mind constantly and inescapably asks these three great and mighty questions," he repeated: "whence? how? whither?" Since on his understanding "how" meant "why," his mantra can be translated as "whence, why, and whither," and so places him in striking company. Virtually as Kuyper was penning these words, Paul Gauguin was finishing one of his epochal paintings, "Where Do We Come From? What Are We? Where Are We Going?" (1897). Twenty years later Henri Bergson, precursor of twentieth-century phenomenology, called philosophers back to the "questions of vital interest": "Whence do we come? What are we doing here? Whither are we bound?"

If knowledge is a magnetic field organized by answers to such leading questions, then Kuyper's conclusion was accurate enough:

Christianity and the evolutionary pantheism that he took to be the main alternative on offer were not just incommensurate but positively hostile worldviews, and remain so a century later. But already in his age the question arose whether knowledge really was such a bloc, and what costs are entailed by regarding it as such. Here Kuyper's contrast with William James is particularly revealing. Only four years younger than Kuyper, like him having Calvinist forebears and a vexed relationship with his father, James too passed through deep philosophical anxiety in his twenties before experiencing a virtual conversion. In his, James decided to assert free will as the first act of free will. He went on through a career in experimental psychology to become a pioneer of American pragmatic philosophy. Both men struggled long with the heritage of German Idealism (incidentally, taking respite from their labors at the same water-cures in Germany), and both reserved their greatest contempt for the deterministic monism of Herbert Spencer. Kuyper disliked it because it was a system without God; James, because it was a system. Kuyper craved certainty under a gracious Lord; James welcomed uncertainty so as to make room for human freedom. Kuyper recognized a plurality of worldviews; James, a pluralistic universe.

Blurred Boundaries

As James's quarrel with Spencer attests, thinkers who started from secular premises could come to radically different conclusions. So could Christians. Kuyper himself traced distinct Lutheran, Reformed, and Roman Catholic lines of thought well beyond theology per se. Furthermore, in a silence that boded ill for the future, he did not discuss possible variations within the Calvinist camp. As an empirical statement, then, Kuyper's insistence that the world of knowledge split into just two "sciences" was wrong. But as an assessment of prevailing *currents* it was plausible, and as a rallying cry to his followers it was compelling.

Yet his own momentum pushed against so neatly tied-down a system. It would not do for a critic of Spencerian monism to build what James called a "bloc universe" of his own. Kuyper shared much of James's — and the era's — yearning for energy, openness, and free exploration, as we will see. He took part as well in the campaign led by

Dilthey and Weber to establish a method particular to the "human sciences" over against the materialist reductionism of the natural sciences. Riding the neo-Kantian wave in contemporary philosophy, this project, like Kuyper's, looked for a middle ground between the extremes of Idealism and empiricism that had fought so inconclusively over the previous century. It gave a separate (too separate, Kuyper would complain) place to "values" vis à vis "facts," and affirmed the power of the first both to bring forth and to shape one's understanding of the second. Unlike Kuyper, Dilthey and Weber were reluctant to prescribe any single value-system as normative for all, resorting instead to description of the "ideal types" or "elective affinities" that might explain human behavior. In this sense Kuyper's "normal-abnormal" antinomy belongs in the same gallery as the "once-born" and "twice-born" souls by which James sought to sort out *The Varieties of Religious Experience* (1902); Ferdinand Tönnies's tracking of Western society from *gemeinschaft* to *gesellschaft* (1887); the triad of "naturalism," "objective idealism," and "the idealism of freedom" that composed Dilthey's final typology of worldviews; and the spectrum of correlations between world-orientations and world religions that Weber began to explore in *The Protestant Ethic and Spirit of Capitalism* (1905).

As to his core question, Kuyper's original horror at the implications of philosophical naturalism found him thirty years later, at the end of his epistemological analysis, squarely in the camp of the "subject." To repeat his stunning one-sentence summary of the course of nineteenth-century thought: "Whoever neglects to maintain the autonomy of the spiritual over against the material in his point of departure will eventually come to the idolization of matter by way of the adoration of man." For that reason, "we insist so urgently that the subjective point of departure again be honored" in culture and the academy. Whatever the original match between archetype and ectype, Kuyper concluded that the human mind's operations show it to be "something entirely different from a mirror. . . . [T]he image cast on our consciousness is hardly the one thing" that makes up knowledge, for even without the fall into sin, the mind in exploring the cosmos from its far reaches to its minute particulars would function as a formative, constructing power. How much more so, under the infusions of grace, did the spirit within shape understanding of the world without. If Kuyper was a Realist, he was a most Critical Realist, like any number of eminent thinkers of his day from all different points of view.

The Betrothed, Autumn 1862. Left: a photograph of Kuyper as a newly minted doctor of theology on the eve of his twenty-fifth birthday. His calm look belies his uncertain career prospects and the imminent religious crisis that would be triggered by a novel given him by fiancée Johanna Schaay (right). The daughter of a Rotterdam stockbroker, Jo was subject to Bram's educational campaign to turn her from a child of trade into a proper professional lady.

The Kuyper Family, 1886. Kuyper, Jo, and their eight children sit for a family photo amidst the Doleantie and with twenty-year-old Jan Frederik (seated, right) about to depart for dental school in the USA. The daughters in the front row include (l. to r.) Henriëtte (b. 1870), Catharina (b. 1876), and Johanna (b. 1875). The sons in the back row include (l. to r.) Guillaume (b. 1878), Herman (b. 1864), "Willy" (b. 1882), and Abraham, Jr. (b. 1872).

Mentor and Adversary. Left: A bust of Kuyper's great mentor, Guillaume Groen van Prinsterer. The refined and elite Groen had fought moderate-liberal educational policies in 1857; twenty years later Kuyper battled the more radical proposal of Joannes Kappeyne van de Coppello (right). The ensuing "school struggle" proved to be the making of Kuyper's name and political party.

Two Modes of Rebirth. Left: Kuyper at the time of his encounter with evangelical holiness religion at Brighton, England, in the summer of 1875. This peak experience was soon followed by a deep plunge into physical and mental malaise. Kuyper repaired to the Alps for a long recuperation; the studio pose as mountain climber (right) suggests the spirit as well as the means of his recovery.

Beginning the Free University. An impression of Kuyper delivering his oration on "Sphere Sovereignty" in the august pulpit of the New Church, off Dam Square in Amsterdam. The Free University inaugurated by the speech was housed more modestly at Keizersgracht 162, in the city's canal-ring district.

Helping Hands. Kuyper's two principal collaborators in the founding of the Free University: Willem Hovy (left), Amsterdam brewer and leading financier of the institution; and Alexander F. de Savornin Lohman, a North Brabant jurist and founding professor of the university's law faculty.

F. DOMELA NIEUWENHUIS
(omstreeks 1886).

Two "Radicals" of 1886. Kuyper, a former Reformed pastor, led the party that "liberated" the New Church in Amsterdam via break-in, removing a panel from its council-room door (left). Ferdinand Domela Nieuwenhuis, a former Lutheran pastor and the country's foremost socialist agitator, was jailed in 1886 for insurrectionary behavior. Kuyper's Doleantie promised a better society by a return to the true faith; Domela Nieuwenhuis (right) envisioned a redeemed future by means of popular revolution. Their contrary ideas masked a common spirit detected — and denounced — by polite society.

Opening van het Sociaal Congres op Gereformeerden grondslag.

„Mannen-broeders, vrouwen-zusters! Wij hebben ons Christelijk Kabinet gehad, en nu hebben wij ons Christelijk sociaal congres. De Heere heeft groote dingen aan ons gedaan, en dies zijn wij verblijd. Als ik den blik laat weiden over deze talrijke vergadering, en vooral als ik de tevreden gezichten zie der mannen van Patrimonium, een jaar geleden nog zoo grimmig, dan vouw ik de handen en sluit de oogen, en ik roep den Heere-Heere aan, om Hem te danken, dat Hij op zoo wonderbaarlijke wijze onze wegen leidt en ons telkens de middelen in de hand geeft, om ons groot te maken te midden van de kleinheid diergenen, die den Heere niet zoeken..."

Glory and Grief in the Early 1890s.
Above: a caricature of Kuyper delivering his oration on "Christianity and the Social Question" at the Christian Social Congress in November 1891. The provocative nature of the speech is evident from the varied responses on the faces in the crowd and Kuyper's less-than-dignified posture at the podium. Left: a photo of Kuyper's youngest son, Willy, who died the next summer at age nine.

A BRAHAM de GEWELDIGE

HAHN

"Abraham de Geweldige." This powerful caricature of Kuyper became one of his most famous images. *"Geweldige"* connotes tremendous, mighty, or imposing — the way royalty are designated "The Great" or "The Terrible." The drawing was made in 1904 by Albert Hahn, one of the Netherlands' ablest cartoonists in an age renowned for them. The son of a traditional craftsman, Hahn became an ardent socialist and began drawing for socialist newspapers and magazines early in the twentieth century. Kuyper was a favorite target, although this drawing also conveys respect.

Honored and Reviled. Two lasting, polar-opposite images of Kuyper, vividly depicted in Hahn cartoons. The first (left), originally entitled "In the Name of Christ," dates from the railroad strike in 1903. Hahn satirically quotes from Kuyper's 1891 speech on Christianity and the social crisis: "So you tame animals, so you suppress savages, but that's not how you rule a people." The second (below), captioned "How (Bilderdijk) was paid homage at the Amsterdam Concertgebouw," marked Kuyper's return to public life after his self-imposed exile upon the fall of his cabinet in 1905. It perfectly captures the master's popular appeal among the party faithful.

DE BILDERDIJK-HERDENKING.

Hoe (Bilderdijk) in het Concertgebouw te Amsterdam gehuldigd werd.

"At a Solitary Post." Another 1904 Hahn cartoon catches a dimension of Kuyper's self-conception that was apparent to opponents and neutral observers, if not always to supporters. The figure evokes the Old Testament image of the Watcher on the Walls of Zion, maintaining vigil for Jerusalem through the dark and lonely night. Kuyper often cast world affairs as hovering on the edge of a precipice, with truth and right in peril, needing to be closely monitored by someone steadfast of vision and courage.

Kuyper as Prime Minister. Kuyper's critics thought that he did not wear the symbols of office well, not having been born to "the better people."

The Heirs, Part I. Herman Bavinck (right) succeeded Kuyper as professor of theology at the Free University and as party chairman for the 1905 elections. Half a generation younger than Kuyper, and more congenial in tone and temperament, Bavinck esteemed Kuyper as a visionary and organizational genius, but finally rebelled over Kuyper's refusal to hand on leadership to men of fresher vision and energy. Theodor Heemskerk (below) was the leading politician of the younger cohort. Son of a traditional Conservative political leader, he helped Kuyper at some critical career passages, only to earn his wrath by assuming the prime ministership in 1908 when Kuyper thought it should be his.

Mr. Th. HEEMSKERK.

The Heirs, Part II. Among Kuyper's possible successors, Alexander W. F. Idenburg (left) showed the highest combination of loyalty and ability. He was a successful colonial administrator in Surinam and the East Indies, besides being the aging Kuyper's closest confidant and friend. His long years at tropical posts, however, left him unable to assume high-pressure political activity once he returned home. The succession accordingly fell to Hendrik Colijn (right), who rose through the officer corps in the Dutch army in the East Indies into oil concessions there and banking in London. The personal fortune thus acquired financed Colijn's political career. He served an unprecedented five terms as prime minister between the two world wars.

"Around the Old-World Sea." A photograph taken in Athens on Kuyper's long trip around the Mediterranean Sea, 1905-6. He was sixty-eight years old at the time.

Children of an Aging Father. Top row: Catharina Maria Eunice Kuyper (left) proved the most difficult of his three daughters for Kuyper to handle, while Jan Hendrik Frederik Kuyper (right) proved a grief in choosing Theosophy over Christianity in the East Indies. Above: Kuyper is accompanied by sons Herman Huber Kuyper (left) and Abraham Kuyper Jr. (right) on one of his annual mountaineering expeditions.

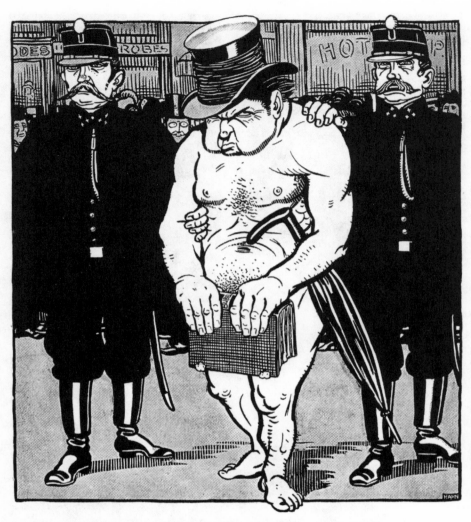

"A New Role." Albert Hahn relished the chance to caricature Kuyper's embarrassing encounter with the Brussels police. Although observers did complain about his (unintentionally) conducting his nude exercise regimen in public view, Kuyper was not hauled off to the police station as the cartoon suggests. Hahn does, however, capture Kuyper's chagrin over the situation.

Nearing the End. In his last decade, Kuyper oscillated between two roles. Above, the elderly chieftain is honored in April 1912 on the fortieth anniversary of the founding of *De Standaard*. The 75-year-old Kuyper (center on the dais) was still the editor in charge of the paper, making his voice heard throughout the land. He also observed a strict private regimen, including long daily walks around The Hague; below, with daughter Johanna.

Funeral for a Man between the Times. Above, Kuyper's coffin is carried out of his house to the horse-drawn hearse that will take him to the cemetery. Below, the long cortege passes down a street crowded with mourners, and with The Hague's electric trams. The traditional format and the icons of the modern world provided a fitting close to Kuyper's life and work.

CHAPTER ELEVEN

Christian Democrat

Of all the vows Kuyper made in the depths of the church struggle, his foreswearing of politics seemed the least plausible. And so it was. His *Encyclopedia* did appear in full, his *Dogmatics* in the form of lecture notes by his students, but his commentary on Paul's epistle to the Romans never was forthcoming. Practicing politics, not writing political theology, increasingly commanded Kuyper's future. Even when out of office, he never left off editorializing, organizing, and maneuvering in party councils, and those labors eventually landed him back in the parliamentary chair that once, "rejoic[ing] with my whole heart," he had "escaped from for good."

His reengagement began in 1887, right after the Doleantie, with the revision of the Netherlands' Constitution and the government's initial responses to the worsening Dutch economy. It climaxed in 1897 with old friends lost, his party split, and another close encounter with psychosomatic collapse. In between, it proceeded by some of Kuyper's most far-sighted and creative work: in political philosophy, a linking of the old antirevolutionary critique to the emerging industrial economy in defense of workers' rights; in program, a leftward tack that turned the Antirevolutionary Party into a thoroughgoing Christian Democratic organization, purged of the old elite who had tried to keep it safe for conservatism. When these "aristocrats" saw Kuyper in this decade, they saw red — in both senses.

The Mackay Cabinet

By 1887 Dutch politics had reached an impasse that stemmed back a dozen years, to the time of Kuyper's first term in Parliament. The religious parties had enough seats to insist on changes to educational policy, while the Liberals were hopelessly divided between traditional and progressive wings over the question of franchise extension. The relentless agitation on both issues in press and Parliament, not to mention the boiling economic crisis, effectively killed the classic Liberal dream of a politics of reason — of liberal Reason, that is, whereby public affairs would be directed by men of broad vision and secular education, chosen by select peers and steering the state by the laws of nature. By the mid-1880s traditional Liberals were arguing against franchise extension from raw partisan calculation, not from principle, while religious conservatives stood on principle for educational equity but against democracy. The stalemate left Parliament crippled amid the turbulence of 1886, when a compromise education bill was vetoed by the Upper House, still under Liberal control, while the Eel Riot and all the social unrest it manifested elicited from the Lower House only obtuse legalism.

It was the need to settle the royal succession (unsettled by the recent death of William III's sole surviving son and the aging monarch's own imminent demise) that provided the occasion for a constitutional revision that broke this deadlock. The result was a classic Dutch study in ambivalence. On educational matters the 1848 charter was not amended at all, once the Liberals pledged to stop reading it as exclusively secularist. As to suffrage, the new measures, while explicitly rejecting universal suffrage, enfranchised any adult male who showed "signs of capability and prosperity." In practice the electorate was expanded from 12 to 27 percent of the adult male population. The electoral map was also overhauled. The larger old districts with two delegates elected on alternating four-year intervals were split up into twice as many units with one representative each, the whole lot to be elected every four years. Whatever the re-framers' intentions, the new system was a clear step toward democracy and dramatic shifts in government. It was a table set to Kuyper's tastes.

He responded with an upgraded dose of familiar prescriptions. If secular and religious elites deemed the unschooled unqualified to vote, Kuyper moved to educate them. *De Standaard* inaugurated a question-and-answer column in which subscribers could have the fine points of politics applied to their particular situations. This education included campaign techniques that could have been borrowed from an American political boss, or from Kuyper's reorganization of diaconal services during his Amsterdam pastorate. The whole country was divided up into sections, districts, and wards. For each locality a list of likely Antirevolutionary voters was compiled, and each of these was leafleted by young volunteers recruited by ward leaders who were themselves part of a hierarchy of supervisors going all the way up to party central, which supplied the propaganda materials. Advice on how to visit potential voters recalled Kuyper's own practices of pastoral calling: "Proceed quietly, calmly, and with assurance. Don't use big words. . . . Go house to house, man to man, and keep records so that you know what's been taken care of." On the new expanded landscape of Dutch politics, one historian concludes, "there was no party that worked its electorate as systematically as the ARP."

With the rank and file in tow, Kuyper made sure things were also coordinated at the top. The ARP delegates' convention approved a fourteen-point action plan that translated the party's general program into concrete legislative goals. Measures were debated by the delegates in open session, an education in itself as well as a progressive step in Dutch political practice. Going into a campaign with a specific platform was equally novel.

Most startling of all was the transcendence of an ancient religious hostility. Kuyper helped arrange a meeting between Calvinist and Catholic leaders that forged a plan of comity whereby each side would support the other's candidate in the run-off phase of the general elections. After three hundred years of fulminating against the pope and for a Protestant Netherlands, Kuyper's Calvinists now joined Roman Catholics to restore a Christian Netherlands. If both secular and religious opponents assailed the result as a "monster alliance" between Dort and Rome, this particular child of Frankenstein would sit in most Dutch cabinets throughout the twentieth century.

It had its first chance immediately. The newly expanded electorate of 1888 returned a 53-47 religious majority to the Lower House, and under the leadership of Baron Aeneas Mackay the first confessional cabinet was installed, to trumpet fanfares across the religious press. Within a year the education question was addressed with a bill that provided state subsidies for teachers' salaries at religious schools.

The social question came next. Responding to the findings of an 1887 parliamentary inquest into labor conditions, the Lower House passed legislation that barred any kind of paid employment for children under age twelve, instituted protective measures for women and for children aged twelve to sixteen, and set the standard work day at eleven hours. These were significant measures. The Labor Act was the Netherlands' first since the Child Labor bill of 1874, and the Education Act addressed the coalition's oldest grievance.

But increasingly Kuyper grew restless. Some of the party's MPs, he complained, supported the Liberal notion that this was the final, not the first, step on the education front. The deeper problem, from his point of view, was structural. While the Antirevolutionaries were demonstrating their capacity to rule, refuting an old canard of the opposition, that very capacity came from the predominance in the cabinet of parliamentary veterans who had long resisted Kuyper's ideological intensity and his command of party organization. In fact, by Kuyper's measure there was only one true-blue Antirevolutionary in the cabinet, Levinus W. C. Keuchenius at Colonial Affairs. Tellingly, it was around Keuchenius that the cabinet's first crisis occurred, and because of the very qualities that Kuyper championed in him.

The Liberal majority in the Upper House rejected the Colonial Affairs budget for 1890 as a rebuke to the minister's ideological outspokenness and otherwise "ungentlemanly" behavior. Kuyper took the occasion to speak out publicly for his friend, and for party discipline. It was a matter of honor for the entire cabinet to stand by each of its members, he insisted, so it should either disband the Upper House or resign. When neither step ensued but Keuchenius was dropped instead, Kuyper took it as a mark of the old half-heartedness now ruining the party's moment of opportunity. This government would not, could not, establish a lasting standard for Antirevolutionaries the way that Thorbecke had for the Liberals, he mourned, because it lacked the combination of character and consistency that Thorbecke had brought to the table. Let it fall then when it must, and let the party learn better for the next round.

In fact, it fell the following year over the question of military service, an issue that divided the coalition as much as education united it. Kuyper's program had called for an end to the purchasing of exemptions from conscription so as to make the burden of military service fall more equitably across class lines. The move would upgrade the quality of the army above its current caliber of paupers and proletariats, thus reduce the hauteur of the officer corps, and instill a national spirit more consistently across the land. Roman Catholics tended to buy exemptions more often than did Protestants, both out of fear of the moral squalor of the barracks and to protect prospective priests from the delays and dangers of military life. When the military service bill of 1891 failed to claim a majority, the Mackay cabinet fell. Kuyper electrified the ensuing party delegates' convention with one of his great keynote addresses, "Maranatha," which cast the upcoming campaign in apocalyptic light. But instead of galvanizing a purer Antirevolutionary regime, the election turned the Dutch government over to Liberal cabinets for the next ten years.

The Colonial Question

It was appropriate that Kuyper's disillusionment hinged on Keuchenius's fall, for colonial matters called up hard passages from the nation's past and hard questions for the party's future. By 1890 the shift from the old state-controlled cultivation system to free markets in the East Indies was twenty years old and had run into all manner of problems. First of all, the move had sparked huge increases in state spending and oppression in the form of the war to "pacify" Aceh. Then too, the flood of entrepreneurs into the area had created a commercial bubble that threatened to burst in the mid-1880s and take down Dutch capital markets with it. The consequent shift to big-bank cartelization had the predictable result of inducing crony capitalism which, in the Billiton Affair of 1882, reached into the royal house. Most of all, the new policy had not brought the native peoples to the Liberals' promised land but simply relocated their oppression from state exactions to free-market exploitation. Neither their culture nor their social system was prepared to deal with untrammeled capitalism, which included an extensive opium trade and the unregulated importation of coolies from China on top of persisting native slave labor.

In this context the Antirevolutionaries' "Ethical Policy" won new attention. As detailed in Kuyper's 1878 program, the approach substituted soft power for hard, development for exploitation, paternalism for neglect. It emphasized cultural over economic factors and hauled the Netherlands before the court of divine justice to atone for (critics would say, to rationalize) its colonial depredations. The East Indies confronted the Dutch with a debt of honor, Kuyper began, a debt that entailed stern obligations but also opened up a worthy destiny. All colonial policy was henceforth to be calibrated to native interests instead of those of the Dutch economy. First off, the government should abolish the slave and opium trades, whatever the cost to public or private purses. It should promote the Indies' financial and, eventually, political independence. Hence it needed to cultivate a native civil service and native education. (In 1874, Kuyper pointed out, there were but forty-four native children in school out of a population of 20 million.)

It would be worse than neglect, however, for these future leaders to be acculturated to the crass materialism of trade or the philosophical materialism of the schools. To truly rise from "backwardness" to "maturity" (a construct Kuyper shared with most Western opinion of his day, conservative or progressive), the native peoples needed Christianity. While ensuring equal rights toward individuals of all faiths, Dutch administrators should give informal support to Christianity, as befit a nation of that heritage. They should remove any barriers to the propagation of the gospel, remove as well their support of Muslim chaplains and proselytizing, and give equal funding to Christian as well as public schools. To use later idioms, this qualified as either cultural imperialism or the indigenization of the gospel. In politics and education no less than religion, Indonesians must assimilate Western offerings to their own cultural patterns.

Of course, not a little of the homeland's disputes echoed through this program, but for Kuyper the imbroglio at Colonial Affairs involved the personal as much as the political. Keuchenius's combination of genuine expertise, ideological passion, and outsider status resonated with Kuyper all the way down. Born (1822) at Batavia (now Jakarta) to Dutch administrators there, Keuchenius quickly rose to high office himself, only to start publishing critiques of Dutch colonial conduct that registered back home like Multatuli* on a Calvinist slant. Upon returning to the Netherlands and standing for Parlia-

---

*Multatuli was the pen-name of Eduard Douwes Dekker (1820-87), a longtime official in the Dutch East Indies whose novel *Max Havelaar* (1860) exposed the depredations of the colonial system there. It caused something of the same sensation in the Netherlands as did the near-contemporaneous *Uncle Tom's Cabin* in the United States. Dekker was notorious in orthodox Reformed circles for his radical opinions in religion, although some shared his critique of Dutch abuses in the colonies.

ment, Keuchenius reaffirmed this reputation by joining the Liberal opposition in 1866 in accusing the Conservative Minister for Colonial Affairs of corruption. The fierce floor fight that ensued built into a major constitutional crisis when King William insisted on royal prerogative to choose his own cabinet ministers. Keuchenius questioned the integrity and intelligence of the king in return (not least because his majesty was also scheming at the time to sell Luxembourg to the French); the Lower House upheld Keuchenius's case and their own prerogative. The affair sealed Keuchenius and the Conservatives in lasting antipathy.

It was thus a sign of Groen van Prinsterer's alienation from the Conservative party and its antirevolutionary poseurs that, in the campaign of 1871, Keuchenius was one of only three candidates to receive his endorsement. It was of lasting significance for Kuyper that he was one of the other two. The affinity between them only grew over time, so that Kuyper named his last-born son for Keuchenius, who served as godfather at the baptism. In family-systems theory Keuchenius provided Kuyper with a worthy substitute for his late brother Herman — a new brother who drew deeper on the faith the more he defended Indonesians' interests, rather than losing his faith, as Herman had at war in Aceh. From a political point of view, Keuchenius's fall in 1890 showed how marginal Kuyper was to the party's parliamentary caucus, ruled as it was by the third member of Groen's 1871 troika, Savornin Lohman. With *this* brother Kuyper had worked most closely to date; from here out they came into increasing conflict in a party civil war that would climax in 1894, one year after Keuchenius's death.

Confronting Economic Crisis

Before that, however, Kuyper was taken up with the Netherlands' continuing economic woes, a preoccupation that magnified intra-party tensions but also launched one of the most significant turns in the Antirevolutionary movement. In a concentrated span of writing and organizing that climaxed at a Christian Social Congress in November 1891, Kuyper led his followers to a forthright confrontation with the emerging industrial future. Economics had never been the strong suit of the Antirevolutionary cause, whose leaders, coming mostly from theology and law, tended to submerge economic questions beneath political-philosophical generalizations. The rank-and-file were habituated to assurances from the pulpit that employer benevolence and employee obedience were all that Christian ethics needed, or was permitted, to mention on the matter.

By the late 1880s these nostrums were manifestly inadequate. That decade saw not just a relative but an absolute downturn in the Dutch economy after an era of easy expansion. The agricultural sector was in the middle of what turned out to be a twenty-year depression, drowning under a flood of imported American and Ukrainian grain. The infant industrial sector stumbled over this first hurdle and could not keep full employment for its own workers, much less absorb the mass of idled people from the countryside. While strikes and labor violence never swept the Netherlands as they did nearby in Belgium and the mining regions of France, local shutdowns in the provinces and the Eel Riot in the capital augured to fearful eyes what might yet be. In short, at home as in the colonies, the 1880s exposed the limits of the free-market economy and invited alternative proposals.

For Kuyper the problem was not external; it threatened his movement from within. The issue came to a head in Patrimonium, a Christian labor organization that included employers alongside workers. Among the former was Kuyper's major funder, Amsterdam brewer Willem Hovy. Since its founding in 1876 it had been content with a program of class cooperation and moral uplift, but by 1891, when it had grown to be the largest union in the country, its worker side was chafing under the pains of the depression and their leaders' inability, or reluctance, to do anything about them. It scored the inadequacies of the Mackay cabinet's new Labor Act. It protested the weak voice that laborers had in ARP councils — no surprise since they still lacked the right to vote. Still, "the lordly gentlemen we help elect" should pay attention, declared Patrimonium President — and Hovy employee — Klaas Kater at the union's 1890 convention. "They must not think they can rely on us forever as their hewers of wood and drawers of water" during campaign season and then forget about us at The Hague. Nor was it truly antirevolutionary to think that "plutocrats and aristocrats know the needs of our back alleys" or have any desire to alleviate them. It was time for greater worker representation in party and in Parliament — time, therefore, for universal suffrage. Were such steps not forthcoming, Kater warned, it might be time "to break with the ARP and form our own party!" Even stronger tones emanated from the

Frisian countryside, in the nation's northwest. Patrimonium leaders there complained that most farms were owned by absentee landlords who cared nothing of their hirelings' lack of food and shelter, even as the rural slump deepened and a series of fierce winters brought starving children to death's door. "Our Frisian Ireland" needed not just universal suffrage but the nationalization and redistribution of land, cried the plaintiffs. Some clergy among them invoked the writings of the American progressive Henry George and an Old Testament model of "Mosaic socialism."

Faced with an exodus from the ARP and fearing the lure of the new Dutch socialist movement, which was especially strong in Friesland, Kuyper called for a Christian Social Congress to be held coincident with the Patrimonium convention the next November. Modeled on similar meetings recently convened by Belgian Catholics and German Protestants, the Congress was to bring together Dutch Protestants of all ranks for a thorough discussion of the "social question" and a set of biblical answers thereunto. Then in May 1891 the bar was set higher with the publication of Pope Leo XIII's encyclical "Rerum Novarum," which launched a century of Catholic social thought.

Thus Protestant honor, harmony within his movement, the road to social stability, and the alleviation of crying need all hung in the balance in Kuyper's mind as the Congress approached. He responded with one of his most scintillating addresses, "Christianity and the Social Question." It assimilated antirevolutionary political philosophy to the social-democratic agenda, laid out a stark challenge to conservatives within his movement, and brought the audience of a thousand that heard it to their feet in tumultuous applause.

But this was not mere opportunism on Kuyper's part, for he had shown a persistent concern for labor issues across three decades of public life. He had chafed at the local count's suzerainty in Beesd, had preached on "Worker and Master according to the Ordinances of God" from his Utrecht pulpit, and had commenced a series on the social question just two weeks after *De Standaard*'s founding. Before that he had published, with his own introduction, a Dutch translation of a pamphlet on "Christianity and Labor" written by Wilhelm von Ketteler, bishop of Mainz and father of the Catholic social gospel. He had aroused ire in Parliament by his disquisitions on the Child Labor Act of 1874, which he opposed as being piecemeal and, as it indeed turned out, ineffectual. Most recently he had addressed the Dutch social situation and the Labor Act of 1889 in a *Standaard* series that was subsequently reissued as *Manual Labor* (1889). Kuyper's concern was not only persistent but consistent, and "Christianity and the Social Question" brought together the themes of these various occasions in grand symphonic chords.

For economic conservatives (that is, neoliberals) and American evangelicals, who assume an automatic affinity between their respective positions, Kuyper's deliverances will be bewildering at best, outrageous at worst. With intense and often heated rhetoric "Christianity and the Social Question" denounced laissez-faire capitalism as inimical to human well-being, material or spiritual; as out of tune with Scripture and contrary to the will of God; as the very spawn of "Revolution." The "Revolution" Kuyper named here was the French, but he could just as well have used "Industrial," for the principles behind and the attitudes stemming from both constituted the deeper revolution in consciousness that Antirevolutionary thinking had always faulted most. Wherein did this revolution lie for economics? In replacing the spirit of "Christian compassion" with "the egoism of a passionate struggle for possessions," Kuyper said. In the abrogation of the claims of community for the sake of the sovereign individual. In the commodification of labor, which denied the image of God and the rightful claims of a brother. In the idolization of the supposedly free market, which deprived the weak of their necessary protections, licensed the strong in their manipulations, and proclaimed the consequences to be the inevitable workings of natural law. In the advertising that inculcated a covetous consumerism as the norm of human happiness. The French Revolution, but as Kuyper repeated throughout his work, also the "utilitarian," the "laissez-faire," and the "Manchester" schools, which were the philosophical apologists for industrial capitalism,

> made the possession of money the highest good, and then, in the struggle for money . . . set every man against every other. . . . As soon as that evil demon was unchained at the turn of the [nineteenth] century, no consideration was shrewd enough, no strategy crafty enough, no deception outrageous enough among those who, through superiority of knowledge, position, and capital, took money — and ever more money — from the socially weaker.

And since "it cannot be said often enough," as Kuyper intoned in "Sphere Sovereignty," that "money creates power," the new bourgeoisie soon took command of the state, overriding its divine mandate to protect the weak and turning it into an engine of their own interests.

That natural law, however, made Kuyper doubt progressive proposals to correct economic abuses by legislation or regulatory reforms. With an eye toward the "laissez faire" Liberals' massive public investments to promote commercial enterprise in the recent past, and the crony capitalism of the current Dutch Indies scene, Kuyper declared: "The stronger, almost without exception, have always known how to bend every custom and magisterial ordinance so that the profit is theirs and the loss belongs to the weaker." Of course, specific reforms might be legitimate. In *Manual Labor* Kuyper countenanced changes in inheritance laws to protect the poor, a break with the Netherlands' historic free-trade policy to protect domestic producers, and tough border controls to protect domestic labor. But besides being prone to elite cooptation, such gestures amounted, Kuyper jibed, to calling upon the physician when an architect was really needed. That is, "[w]e must courageously and openly acknowledge that the Social Democrats are right" to insist that the evils and inequities of the current Dutch situation stemmed from "the *entire structure* of our social system." Socialists were wrong in the blueprint they drew up, he hastened to add, but even there, not so much for the design of the interior as for neglecting to lay the foundations of the house in God's eternal ordinances. Kuyper repeated that these broad principles were laid out along "clearly visible lines" in Scripture and creation, and then repeated it again, as if sheer insistence would obscure the conflict within his own movement over how those ordinances applied to current conditions.

Calvinists' Economics

Since the conversation about Calvinism and economics would be dominated in the twentieth century by the seminal work that Max Weber published just a decade after Kuyper's remarks — that is, by a consideration of how the Protestant ethic fit the spirit of capitalism — it is important to note what Kuyper deemed Calvinism's controlling principles to be. First and foremost, he asserted a preferential option for the poor. Jesus, "just as his prophets before him and his apostles after him, invariably took sides *against* those who were powerful and living in luxury, and *for* the poor and oppressed." Granted that the poor are no better than the rich, Christ and Scripture always reproved their sins more gently than those of the wealthy. So did Kuyper's Utrecht sermon of 1869 with regard to "worker and master." Second, the merit of any economic system, both as to its theory and practice, had be measured by the respect it exercised for human beings as bearers of the image of God and by the basic security it provided for human existence. Reducing laborers to a factor of production violated their dignity and the divinely mandated use of their God-given creative powers, which properly make work an opportunity and a blessing. Third, solidarity was both the biblical ideal for human society and the pragmatic grounds for its true flourishing. God created human beings to live relationally with each other and the natural order under the canopy of transcendent norms. Practically, this obviated any system that proceeded from or to the individual person as isolated or sovereign. It obviated as well any proposal that looked to the triumph or eradication of a particular group or class, or that maximized (whether as means, end, or predictable consequence) the separation or perpetual antagonism of peoples. Kuyper's economics, like his politics, was first to last a communal theory with a communal ethic. In particular, it assigned property rights not a primary but a derivative standing that brought them "hobbling up at the rear of the unavoidably righteous demand" for a genuine social life. And to that end it assumed that people, together, could both understand and competently modify market operations.

But Kuyper was also sensitive to the realities of power and did not expect them to melt away, whether under free markets, socialist controls, or Christian love. Rather, in economics as in politics he proposed to divide and balance powers for the best approximation of justice that might be attained on earth. Thus "Christianity and the Social Question" rehearsed in 1891 what he had proposed in Parliament in 1874 and repeated again in *Manual Labor* in 1889. First, a complete law code for labor needed to be drawn up, similar to commercial, criminal, and civil codes, so that its rights and obligations were embedded within the formal legal system. Second, the educational system should be diversified to provide the trade skills needed to make the future Dutch labor force internationally competitive, rather than forcing all children through standardized book learning. Third, labor should be empowered through collective organization so that it might register its due weight in the struggles and negotiations of economic life. This would reduce not only the oppression but also the demoralization of workers as they found solidarity with their fellows. A concentric array of labor councils, extending from local grassroots out across the entire nation, would more likely be responsive to workers' interests and expertise than would state regulators. These councils would then meet with their employer counterparts to settle terms, conditions, and grievances. The state's role in the process would be to supervise binding arbitration in case of impasses. Finally, returning full circle to the grievances that had prompted the Congress in the first place, economic empowerment required a political basis. Democratizing the franchise would ensure as nothing else that workers' needs would be heard in the halls of legislation. It would also cement their solidarity with the rest of the nation.

Still, Kuyper could not leave off — or even begin — without invoking the "moral" considerations that stood "above" such practical arrangements. Economics too was shaped by collective consciousness: "Because we are conscious beings, almost everything depends on the standard of values which our consciousness constructs," and Kuyper put Christian patience high on the list. This might seem to point back from architect to physician — to Marx's pious physician, in fact, dispensing the opiate of eternal consolation to the masses — but Kuyper typically spoke this way to wealthy agnostics, warning about the price of their derision of religion. Put positively, only proper consciousness would replace materialism and egotism with compassion and equity as the land's prevailing norms. Since the state was incompetent and the market uninterested in generating such values, their cultivation belonged to the agencies of public opinion — church, school, and press. Yet ethos depended on more than ethics. Workers' morality was closely tied to their morale, which in turn was grounded in a sense of their own life chances. Here Kuyper's prescription was definitively petit bourgeois: the channeling of sexual desire within marriage and family relations, the availability of reliable, dignified work, and minimal dependence on welfare subsidies. Each of these pieces would feed upon the others to form energetic, disciplined citizens who did their own part while contributing to a public interest that surmounted their own.

Kuyper's economics thus resonated with his political theory and with some perennial notes of Calvinist social thinking. He was again more concerned with whole integrated systems than with individual parts. He showed a typical Calvinist ambivalence toward wealth — it was more a proving ground for than any proof of salvation. Greed now joined aggression as the worst expression of collective depravity, and a balance of powers was again arrayed to control them. Kuyper's distinctive contribution to this tradition was the constellation of vigorous localism, praise of diversity, and principled pluralism that he asserted in the face of industrial consolidation and labeled "sphere sovereignty." In his own movement his speech, like Leo's encyclical, launched a tradition of social critique that was purposefully Christian, critical of the political economy of Left and Right, and aimed at keeping intellectuals engaged with their blue-collar brethren. As for the latter, Patrimonium took new confidence from the Congress to develop into a mature body of Christian labor advocacy, grounded in gospel mandates for an industrial age.

More immediately, however, Patrimonium delegates found the Social Congress disappointing. On the three major questions that came out of study committees for general discussion, only the report on the legitimacy of the strike was forthright: it was approved as a last resort but then sometimes as a duty. The report on labor councils fudged on the issue of employer membership, and the temporizing resolution that was finally adopted hardly described the keystone that these councils formed in Kuyper's economic architecture. As for the most contentious question, the Frisian radicals fumed as the chair of the study committee on land nationalization went to Free University professor and Amsterdam city councilman D. P. D. Fabius, whom they scorned as the "evil genius . . . [of] aristocracy." Their revenge was to so attack the report in breakout discussions as to keep it from even coming to the floor for a vote. Their greater satisfaction would unfold over the next five years, as Kuyper led an insurgency of "the little people" against "the lord millionaires" on the issue of suffrage.

Splitting the Movement

The Liberal cabinet that assumed office in 1891 took up the franchise question immediately, and the radical character of their proposal threw Dutch politics into an uproar. Reported by the Left-Liberal Minister of Domestic Affairs J. P. R. Tak van Poortvliet, the bill would instantly expand the Dutch electorate from 300,000 to 800,000 voters. That would effect, to opposition eyes, precisely the universal suffrage that the 1887 Constitution had proscribed. The once Progressive Liberal Sam van Houten, whose atheism had appalled the religious parties often enough in the past, now joined most of them in opposition — all of the Roman Catholics along with the conservative Antirevolutionaries, led by Lohman, who had held Tak's portfolio at the end of the Mackay cabinet. Kuyper, on the other hand, supported Tak with a volume of journalism and maneuverings in party councils that within three years left the party split and its two old headmen barely on speaking terms. The fault, if such it were, was not Kuyper's alone, though his superior initiative made him the catalyst of the process. The issue was genuinely substantive if never free from the personal. The outcome was an Antirevolutionary Party run by the "new men" who had been initiated in the school struggle, a party fully modern in discipline and ideology — fully modern as well in the contemporary Continental sense of being more dogmatic and sectarian.

Tak's bill was so ambiguous as to invite and finally die of a hundred clarifications. Just how did one measure the "capability and prosperity" that the Constitution required of people to vote? Tak said a permanent address was the answer, but what was permanent, and what was an address? The classic Liberals set the bar high to guarantee an educated and economically independent electorate; Lohman joined them to quell the passionate masses.

Kuyper condemned the Constitutional provision itself as betraying subservience to "God Intellect and God Mammon." Ideologically he had the harder task, since Antirevolutionaries took it as axiomatic that popular sovereignty defied God's and that "democratic" necessitated "excess." Kuyper prepared his answer at two party rallies already during the Mackay regime. "Not the Liberty Tree but the Cross" used the centennial of the French Revolution in 1889 to limn the *godly* democracy that must oppose it. "Maranatha," the keynote address at the delegates' convention during the 1891 campaign, invoked Christ's final judgment upon the works of man to warrant voting rights for all men.

Both of these deliverances leaned heavily on the antirevolutionary theoretical tradition; it was the innovations and emphases between the lines that bore notice. Thus, "Not the Liberty Tree" looked ahead to "Christianity and the Social Question" by tracing the social crisis back to the principles of 1789, but it also looked back to *Ons Program* to take up the enduring dilemma at the heart of the tradition. It contrasted good antirevolutionary democracy with bad-because-godless democracy on the assumption that a common allegiance to divine ordinances would save freedom from the anarchy-tyranny oscillation of the French Revolution. Godly allegiance was not natural, Kuyper reiterated; it required hearts surrendered to the gospel. But if democracy required Christian faith to survive, where was the freedom of conscience — the freedom to believe otherwise or not at all — that it was the historic mission of the Netherlands to uphold before the world? More immediately, how could a Christian politics be effective without being religiously oppressive? Because the common people of the Netherlands were Christian to the core, "Liberty Tree" answered. Democracy, far from being dangerous, was in itself trustworthy — certainly more trustworthy from a Christian point of view than the system of privilege that had delivered the country over to the rule of secular Liberals with pious Conservative dressing on the side.

Still, granting that democracy was safe for Christians, and fairer to boot, was *Christian* democracy fair? "Liberty Tree" did not finally answer that question, but "Maranatha" did. "Without any craftiness or secret intentions" on our part, Kuyper declared before the assembled delegates and so too before the whole nation, "we accept the position of equality before the law along with those who disagree with us." In fact, Antirevolutionaries needed "to appreciate our Conservatives' *historical bent* . . . our Liberals' *love of liberty* . . . the Radicals' *sense of justice* and . . . the nobler Socialists' *compassion* with so much indescribable misery." Once for all, the Antirevolutionaries' pluralism would be a principled pluralism, operating from their own convictions while respecting those of others. This politics would be effected via coalition with the party that most closely shared the Antirevolutionary agenda of the moment. "Maranatha" emphasized that this would be a co-belligerency and not a coalescence, because the allies in place were the very Roman Catholics whom some within his movement still distrusted and whom others had left the party in order to reject. Indeed, over the next century Catholics would contribute the 40 percent rank-and-file support that the Calvinist tenth needed for victory in national elections. But as Kuyper made clear in subsequent newspaper commentary, this was not the only coalition possible. We ally with Rome against all varieties of Liberals, he said, with Left Liberals against Right Liberals, with all Liberals against the Socialists, and with all Liberals and Socialists against the Conservatives.

That flexibility both reflected and served the other, democratic agenda of "Maranatha." For while Conservatives might be honored for their contribution to national life, they were not the Antirevolutionaries' default ally. Gazing out at the assembled delegates, Kuyper made the point very clear: the ARP was not the safe haven some in the audience had taken it to be in migrating from the ruins of their own party. He brought out heavy theoretical artillery to make the point. While we honor all our opponents as people,

> we take exception to and resist . . . their disastrous *principle,* which is detached from Christ and which is the same in all these groups. Together they form a single spiritual family, bred from a single stock. The father of the *Liberal* is called *Conservative,* the offspring of the *Liberal* presents himself as a *Radical,* and the *Socialist* is the legitimate child in the third generation.

Conservatives were no better set than Liberals to resist Socialist claims. "The oppressed are asking the Liberal why, if 'the people are sovereign,' that sovereign people should any longer be trampled en masse by the oligarchs. . . . They are simply applying the principles of the French Revolution . . . with merciless consistency and without any nobler chords." If "Social Democracy laughs at the bandages our Liberals bring out," Conservative hand-wringing was beneath contempt.

To political philosophy Kuyper added an urgent reading of history. "The politics of Europe is undisputedly in search of a new configuration. The oligarchy of financially and intellectually advantaged classes is finished." It was the historic mission of the Antirevolutionary cause to guard this impulse from mob rule and give it a *"Christian-democratic shape"* instead. "This can still be done *now,*" he told the throng. "But if you squander this God-given moment and let it pass unused, you will be to blame for having thrown away the future of your country and you will soon bend under the iron fist which will strike you in your Christian liberty and, unsparingly, also in your wallets and property." Yet Kuyper could not let democracy's potential dangers have the last word. "Even if the *zeitgeist* were *anti*-democratic, *you* should still seek the broadening of popular influence," for "all the Scriptures preach" and all "history and experience teach that the moral power of faith tends to reside much more among the 'little people' who run short every year than among the affluent who annually increase their net worth."

Showdown with the "Double Names"

The conservatives in his audience, whether antirevolutionary by conviction or convenience, did not take this well, nor the Christian Social Congress six months later, which they either ignored or criticized. The franchise debate only grew hotter over the next two years and inevitably bred an intra-party contest between the two leaders. Lohman issued a pamphlet against the Tak bill in 1892 and protested Kuyper's direction in correspondence with him. "I don't like radicalism," he wrote in 1893, adding that he liked "praying radicals even less than non-praying ones." He also faulted Kuyper's combination of roles. To be chair of the Central Committee and to agitate a particular policy as newspaper editor represented a conflict of interest, or at least a skewing of intra-party debate that was hardly "democratic." Years before, Lohman had reminded Kuyper that journalism and parliamentary work were separate (and sovereign!) spheres entailing radically different skills and duties. He had enjoined him to either stop dictating the caucus's work from *De Standaard* or take over: "the party in the House may not be disrupted by someone who judges everything tactically without himself bearing a single responsibility. I offer you my chair. Immediately."

Now Kuyper half accepted that offer. Agreeing that the pro-Tak position in the party must be argued by someone on the floor, Kuyper accepted election to the Lower House again in 1893. There the confrontation with Lohman became direct and daily, and Lohman himself became less tempered in expression. Your rhetoric and maneuvers show you to be a true disciple of Robespierre, he told Kuyper. There could be no greater insult in the Groenian heritage.

The conflict climaxed in the election campaign of 1894, which amounted to a national referendum on franchise extension and still counts as one of the most hotly contested in Dutch history. Inside the ARP it became a battle for the future of the party. A week before the delegates' convention, nine of Lohman's friends in the parliamentary caucus joined him in a public statement declaring the Tak bill to be unacceptable. Kuyper as usual had out-organized them and turned out an unprecedented attendance of a thousand delegates at the convention itself — many of them "new men" who swamped the traditional elite on the floor. The convention forthrightly condemned "conservatism of every stripe" and committed the party to a platform of "final franchise extension."

As the two sides departed to campaign against each other, Kuyper declared exactly what the war was about. It was to deliver the party from the "men with the double names" who had too long dominated its doings. The foe was comprised of men such as Baron B. J. L. de Geer Jutphaas, Squire T. A. J. van Asch van Wijk, Baron J. E. N. Schimmelpenninck van der Oye van Hoevlaken — and also Squire Alexander Frederik de Savornin Lohman. Plain solid burgher names spelled a better future: Bavinck, Heemskerk, Keuchenius — and Kuyper.

Unfortunately for the pro-Takkians, the double-names had enough clout — and the Liberals, along with the ARP, had enough divisions — to send them down to defeat. The Right Liberals formed the next cabinet, and the Antirevolutionaries, with fewer seats than ever, organized two separate caucuses in Parliament, one under Lohman, the other under Kuyper. The division between the two men and the two outlooks was permanent. It lasted even after Sam van Houten steered through a more modest suffrage bill in 1896 — more modest only in comparison to Tak's measure, for it doubled the Dutch electorate overnight to encompass half the adult males in the country. The 1897 elections swelled the number of seats held by the democratized wing of the ARP and inaugurated an era of unity and prosperity in its ranks. The ARP Right cautiously undertook a series of talks with other conservatives; they emerged a decade later as a separate party, the Christian Historical Union.

The Political and the Personal

This passage in Kuyper's life has been interpreted from radically different points of view. Some regard it as the raw opportunism of a demagogue bent on eliminating rivals, using egalitarian rhetoric as needed. From this angle, Kuyper's later turn to the Right is taken to spell what he really thought all along. Others see a principled reading of history at work, matching the need of the hour to a genuine democratic streak in Calvinism that had been too frequently obscured by the tradition's elites, who were the true opportunists in the fray.

No one can deny that the battle gave Kuyper a great opportunity, effected a real change, and exacted a significant toll. Democracy did triumph in the Netherlands in 1896, and if it did not come in the form of the household franchise that Kuyper espoused, the "individualistic" system that actually obtained boosted the religious parties and made their future success much more likely. Likewise, the undisputed leadership he had now sealed in the ARP made an eventual prime-ministership for Kuyper more than plausible.

Also triumphant was the new sort of mass politics that Kuyper had long championed. Its shape can be inferred by comparison to the traditional type that Lohman represented. Hailing as he did from the bench in North Brabant, where consistent Calvinists were in short supply, Lohman viewed himself as a classic tribune of the people. By his command of the law he would protect minority rights (whether Protestants in North Brabant or religiously-grounded education across the nation) while trying to shed the light of the gospel to unbelievers. Substantively, that amounted to keeping restraints upon the sinfulness of the human heart. Methodologically, it entailed empowering expertise and deference. Once elected, Lohman believed, representatives were elevated above the people and were responsible to conscience alone, not to a party platform or to pressures from mass journalists who, he chided Kuyper, tended to scribble about things they did not understand. Indeed, to Lohman parties were but temporary means to more important ends; not just the democratic ideology but the whole apparatus of modern politics was borderline revolutionary. As Dutch historian Jeroen Koch says of him, Lohman was at heart a bridge-builder, not a crusader, and those bridges were designed to link elites across the court system and Parliament to rule on behalf of the whole nation, not just a single party. Much of this system would indeed be realized over the course of the twentieth century in the regulatory apparatus that conservatives scorn as "government bureaucracy" and "activist courts" — and that was despised by Lohman and Kuyper in their own time. Kuyper, on the other hand, insisted that mass politics was the only alternative. If that made charisma the essential requirement for leadership, Kuyper's own example argues that such did not have to come at the cost of expertise.

Yet the personal costs of Kuyper's triumph were high. Lohman had been a trusted friend and savvy partner on *De Standaard,* in the founding of the Free University, in the Doleantie, and in steady correspondence pre-dating Kuyper's collapse in 1876. Lohman's expertise in jurisprudence and parliamentary work was essential to their success in movement-building, just as his cautious temperament saved Kuyper more than once from his own excesses. Nor was Lohman the only friend lost. In 1888 Ferdinand Domela Nieuwenhuis, the one-time Lutheran minister who had converted to utopian radicalism, successfully ran for Parliament with the backing of the Netherlands' fledging socialists, of Frisian radicals of all stripes — and of Kuyper. Domela returned the favor. "I have sometimes thought that at bottom we do not stand so far from each other," he later wrote Kuyper about these years. "There are whole sections of your writings that I can take over, and indeed which I have used in my speeches." Domela's election scandalized Queen Emma and the established parties; Keuchenius was the only MP who would shake his hand. Kuyper's oldest friend, Isaac Hooykaas, wrote him, outraged. How can you call yourself a Christian and a patriot while supporting such a man? Have you lost all principle?

These cuts took their toll. Kuyper's winter grippe was worse than usual in 1893, disrupting his work and sleep. Things got much worse after the bruising campaign of 1894: Kuyper left on his usual summer vacation but nearly died in Brussels on the way home. He had to repair, once again, to the south of France, then to Tunisia, to rest his nerves and repair his lungs. Once again he had to give up journalism, this time for half a year rather than a year and a half, but this time haunted, not helped, by Lohman. The practical cause of his collapse was that, as twenty years before, Kuyper had added parliamentary work to his existing load; in the 1890s that included daily journalism, party management, and a full university teaching schedule. After his 1876 collapse and again in his mid-Doleantie musings, Kuyper had been perceptive enough to identify parliamentary work as especially stressful to him — whether from its daily grind, its face-to-face polemics, the visions of grandeur it inspired, its submergence of high principle in tedium and procedure, or various of these in some combination. Hooykaas had given him a warning list: "I hate politics! It's a curse on society, the downfall of many people's character, the cause of moral blindness, the source of untruth, unrighteousness, and I know not what." Certainly being surrounded by "oligarchs" and their minions in The Hague must have been aggravating to Kuyper, given his mood and the country's plight. Then too, the conflict with Lohman recalled a grievance as old as his university years at Leiden, where the sons of the elite gathered on the law track to inherit rule in the kingdom while poor ministers' boys lived at home and studied theology in hopes of entering a shrinking profession.

His illness did not incline Kuyper toward peace, however. No sooner had he returned home, on New Year's Eve 1894, than he moved to purge Lohman once more, this time from the Free University. Working behind the scenes with his other old collaborator, Frederik Rutgers, and a new ally, Herman Bavinck, both theologians, Kuyper called upon the 1895 annual meeting of the university's supporting association to institute a committee of inquiry into Lohman's teaching. Hovy, the chair of the board of directors, was caught flat-footed. He had hoped that the two would use the occasion to transcend their political feud for the sake of the university, and was aghast to find that Kuyper had plotted very differently. "*May* you proceed in this way, without a single bit of evidence?" wondered the saintly brewer. "Is this not a *sin* before God?" Lohman pointed out that the process bypassed the university's trustees, who were designated by charter to conduct this sort of inquiry. He kept on complaining about due process after the convention predictably supported Kuyper and as the committee of inquiry predictably turned prosecutor. It did not examine Lohman's actual teaching at all; rather, it determined that the principles which could be inferred from Lohman's teaching were not thoroughly or consistently Calvinistic. Lohman was given an honorable discharge; his son Witsius resigned at the same time from his post next to his father on the university's law faculty. Witsius's father-in-law Hovy resigned as chairman of the board, although he maintained his financial support.

While the investigation was still underway, Kuyper and Rutgers formally inquired of Lohman whether he held any grievance against them that might preclude their taking the Lord's Supper. No, nothing actionable, Lohman replied, but don't think that the "brotherly love" required between church members is "the same as friendship." In fact, Kuyper's bond with the one brother-figure he countenanced as an equal had been broken for good. In this regard it is telling that soon after starting up the inquest into Lohman's teaching, Kuyper published a memoir of the recently deceased Keuchenius. *This* brother had been faithful in the cause of Christ, the tract read, had advocated the cause of the "little people" in the Indies, had been true and consistent to Calvinistic principles. What is more, Keuchenius had carried on a long correspondence with Kuyper that, *inter alia,* detailed Lohman's shortcomings on all these points in his parliamentary work; some of that correspondence Kuyper now quoted for public consumption.

This was airing the family linen indeed. Perhaps literal family dynamics helped push Kuyper over the edge. Keuchenius, after all, was supposed to live on in the name of Kuyper's youngest son, but suddenly that had gone catastrophically awry. In June 1892 Jo summoned Kuyper back from vacation in the south of France with an urgent telegram: "Willy most critical. Come immediately." Kuyper did, but as it turned out, he was only in time for the funeral.

While Kuyper's memoir of Keuchenius recalled sentimental exchanges between him and his newly deceased godson, the meditation he published in *De Heraut* after Willy's funeral made more important points. Recalling the statistics on infant and child mortality that had gone into his study of the social question, Kuyper pondered: "*Why* God calls away one-half of the children of men so early, we know not. *What* is the reason that He brings one-half of His elect to blessedness so altogether differently from the other half . . . is a question that forces itself upon us time and again, but which God does not answer." Kuyper tried to answer anyway, first in the voice from the end of Job: "In His doings with these little ones there is such speechless majesty." All the dead children's great potential remained known to God and would be realized in eternity without their having to endure the sufferings of time. Equally, these puzzles showed how insignificant were the grounds of human pride — that is, showed the equal worth of the little people to the high and mighty. "God's work of grace is not dependent upon your intellectual development," Kuyper said to the generic reader, and perhaps especially to himself. "The little field-flower that scarcely unfolded, only to wither again, was as well watered by the dew of heaven as were the cedar and the palm tree which still stand against the storms."

Kuyper's next *Heraut* meditation evoked Keuchenius, albeit anonymously. "When God gives you a brother who understands you, who lives equally deeply as yourself, or also one who suffered as you suffered, and with the experience of his own heart comes to yours, that human comforting can already sooth and bless you." Since three of Keuchenius's ten children had gone to early graves and two more died in young adulthood, he was well qualified to minister to Kuyper at the time of Willy's death. But such comforts really take hold, Kuyper continued, when we see them, too, as works of God's sovereign appointment, "when he who comforts you does not do it for his own sake but lets himself be used of his God to comfort you, to His glory." That is, it took a Calvinist, a true Calvinist, but this one was now dead, and Lohman gone.

CHAPTER TWELVE

Culture Critic

In 1896 Kuyper declared to his fellow Calvinists, "Brothers, *I believe in the future,* I believe in it with all my heart." Three years later he was telling them, "Our nineteenth century is dying away under the hypnosis of the dogma of Evolution." Seven years before that, in 1892, he cast evolutionary science as one part of a broader problem, "the pantheistic mood of our time." To that syndrome he ascribed any number of evils, including the loss of character and conviction, the erosion of legal standards, the weakening of faith, of clarity in thinking, of morality and vision, of energy yet also of repose. It all added up to personal and cultural atrophy: "[I]t seems here that everything is slipping into death, both national and moral. . . . Second-rate imitators have replaced the originals, and at their feet gathers the world-weary crowd whose lack of animation their lusterless eye conveys. . . . One need not be a devotee of bygone days to be saddened by how flat, unexpressive, and impotent we look compared to the striking figures on Rembrandt's canvases."

Kuyper would find his own way to explain how pervasive decline could live alongside a bright future, but *that* he invoked these two extremes and that he alluded to psychology ("hypnosis") and the arts ("Rembrandt") to make his case was standard for the time. Europe in the 1890s showed two faces to the world. One exuded the satisfactions of power and achievement. Between science and empire, the West was coming to unlock more of the world's secrets, and control more of its surface, than ever before, and that kind of progress seemed to have endless prospects. Yet the other face was weary and anxious, self-consciously so. Essayists by the score pondered a *fin de siècle* mood of lassitude and decay that was said to be engulfing young and old, the higher classes and the middle classes, the city, the nation, the individual, the entire civilization. Commentators searched for some link between the malaise and the confidence. They wondered how long any one group could keep winning at the wheel of history. They worried about the paradox of simultaneous over-determinism and uncertainty at the roots of science; they weighed as well science's fruits of material plenty against its price of spiritual erosion. Even more than in the natural sciences, these doubts resounded in the arts, humanities, and social ("human") sciences. Novelists took up the theme directly. Between 1880 and 1900 American writers produced utopian and dystopian tales as never before or since, while in *Dr. Jekyll and Mr. Hyde* (1886) and *Dracula* (1897) Europeans added two enduring types to the literary gallery of split personalities. Fittingly, the century ended on a bold new venture for comprehending these divisions, Sigmund Freud's *The Interpretation of Dreams* (1899), whose "science" tried to fathom the traffic between "ego," "id," and social expectations.

Freud's work, in turn, opened one of the most dramatic episodes in Western intellectual history, the emergence of a new form of Modernism. Its signals were Picasso's painting, Einstein's physics, Schoenberg's music, Joyce's fiction, the poetry of Eliot and Pound. Posing a wholesale challenge to the established cultural order — an order to which Kuyper too had fundamental objections — the birth of the new Modernism so close to the peak of Kuyper's intellectual career invites some final assessment of his place in the culture of his times. Since the arts most boldly signaled the new turn, it makes sense to begin by considering Kuyper's efforts to explain art to his followers.

Kuyper on Art

Kuyper undertook his arts initiative at the same time that he campaigned for democratic politics and re-defined Calvinist scholarship. He launched it with a rectorial address in 1888, devoted one of his Princeton lectures to the topic in 1898, and wrapped up his long series on common grace on the theme in 1901. One of the first non-theological courses he taught at the Free University was on art; the last was on Impressionism. Part of his motive was to prove his thesis that Calvinism embraced "all spheres" of life, the toughest objection to which arose from the arts. Kuyper himself recited — and substantially agreed with — the standard litany of Calvinism's aesthetic under-performance: no monumental architecture, little in the way of sculpture, a music long on Psalm-singing and short on everything else, an aversion to nudity in painting, and a virtual prohibition on the theater. Every other world religion has its distinctive aesthetic, Kuyper said; one instantly recognizes Buddhist art and Islamic art, medieval Catholic or Byzantine style. What was Calvinist art? And where was it, especially (here was his second motive) in an era when art was becoming more available to, and more important for, more people than ever before in history?

Kuyper eventually came around to answering this question, but the material he could adduce as positive evidence for his hopes was so modest that he spent most of his time postulating indirect contributions instead. If Calvinism had not produced much art itself, it had created the freedom for others to do so. In diminishing "the sensory" in worship so as to make it properly "spiritual" again, it liberated artists from ecclesiastical control. The Calvinist elevation of everyday life legitimated the body as well as the soul, saw as much virtue in the ordinary mother as in the Madonna, and brought common things into the artist's purview. No accident, then, that Hals, Vermeer, and above all Rembrandt worked in a "Calvinist" context. That the gentlemen in question were hardly champions of the Canons of Dort led to Kuyper's other claim, that the arts are supremely the domain of common grace. It was "Calvinism outside the circle of Calvinists in the stricter sense that pressed its stamp upon our national life," he told his Dutch audience. Likewise, it was the ancient Greeks, bereft though they were of Christ and Scripture, who set the standards for beauty — standards that were "objective" and universal, deriving as they did from God's being "the Deviser and Creator of beauty." The Lord had turned the human cognitive apparatus on a classical lathe.

Kuyper was too biblical to leave the matter there, however, and so turned back to the signal tenet of Calvinism. Election was not just politically but aesthetically democratic, he said. It disclosed to the artist's eye a fellowship of suffering and glory beyond the subject's standing or wealth. In following the works of God, the eye of election "penetrates the depth of misery and grasps for redemption behind the somber impress of pain." An artist could work on such a basis, and virtually the last words in Kuyper's six-year series on common grace urged his followers to do so. The believer "who can understand human life in its wealth of appearances and its manifold struggles as these are to be understood in the light of God's word, and can transfer these impressions to the world of beauty, has translated the Spirit of his God into that life." For concrete examples Kuyper had to go no farther than the shores of Scheveningen, where Jozef Israels and his fellows in The Hague School had for a quarter century been painting the dignity and fortitude of common people at their daily tasks. This "poetry" of "unvarnished lives . . . [extrapolated] to the wide domain of humanity" fit Kuyper's prescription perfectly, all the more since Israels esteemed the family as highly as did Kuyper. Or he could have invoked the work of the recently deceased Vincent van Gogh, one-time theology student and evangelist to the wretched of the earth who, though losing his formal faith, had caught the anguish and hopes of human life in unexcelled color and motion. Yet Kuyper passed by these and other potential allies, despite certainly knowing of them. He had private correspondence with Israels but made nothing public of his work.

Part of the explanation for this puzzle lies in the very democratic impulse so pronounced in Kuyper during these years. The religious leaders of the day who were encouraging new trends in Dutch art and letters fell on the conservative side of the political spectrum. They could indulge their hobbies, Kuyper objected, because they were comfortable residents of the established order interested in satisfying — and showing off — their fashionable tastes. Consequently, they had no eye for the demoralizing effects that avant-garde productions could have on ordinary people. To transit safely into modern society common folk needed a consolidated system of faith, a consistent Calvinism in culture as much as in politics, not just a personal "spirit of the gospel" to which they could assimilate trendy wares from the cultural marketplace.

This hints at the specific *purpose* Kuyper posited for art, a purpose that led him toward a very traditional aesthetic and a practical deadend. Without comment or question he linked art to "beauty," instantly walling off a large range of potentially Christian, not to mention actual Modernist productions. True beauty, furthermore, was the earthly shadow of heavenly "glory," and it was this glory — epitomized in the majesty and perfection of God — that Kuyper insisted art try to represent. Granted, the artist deals with earthly appearances, but the human imagination at the hands of "genius" could capture the "higher, nobler, richer reality" behind the forms of nature and display it for all to see. This would "add something to human life which it [otherwise] would never have possessed," thus "improving" the material environment and "elevating" the spiritual sense so that people could glimpse more of grace. Art, that is to say, was to be idealistic, didactic, and inspiring, always pointing toward "higher" things. Its ultimate calling, Kuyper summarized, was to give something of a foretaste of heaven here on earth.

In alternative aesthetics Kuyper saw only trouble. The cult of art for art's sake just now at its peak he deemed irresponsible; art might be a separate sphere, but the beautiful could never be isolated from the true or the good. Bohemian Paris, in turn, amounted to an ersatz aristocracy, complete with corruption, petty feuds, and outward show masquerading as inward quality. Worst of all was the market mechanism, the allure of "money" or "fame." Kuyper's prime example was theater, not evil in itself but by the base product it had to offer to make ends meet. To portray the "raw" or the "low," whether on stage, in stone, or on canvas, was to praise the consequences of sin. This raised a particularly troubling specter in an age of dawning democracy, and Kuyper brought out his hoariest polemic against it. The market established the "tyranny of popular sovereignty in the field of art." Against that, Christian artists ought to perform the "priestly service" of holding up a higher standard for emulation. "Our Calvinism thirsts for harmony and calls for balance," he prescribed. He did not recall, just now, how often his own political and theological commentary drew its best insights from exploring the disharmony and unbalances that needed redemption.

One can only conclude that Kuyper was hopelessly logo-centric. The *full* range of human life had to be treated by words on a page, which remained subject to rational controls. Sounds and images pierced right to the soul and so needed stricter limits, particularly in an age of mass culture. When forced to declare what art Calvinism had delivered in its own right, Kuyper typically referred to the Genevan psalms — that is, to canonical texts sung in the context of worship. Beyond that he dilated longest on a writer from the Dutch Golden Age, Jacob Cats (1577-1660), a lawyer, politician, and diplomat who compiled illustrated "emblem books" of rhymed couplets, chiefly on domestic themes. By Kuyper's day this material had long since passed to the status of proverbial lore; a less likely entry into the pulses of modern art is hard to imagine. A far more successful candidate did emerge from his movement, but by a dialectical process of separation. Piet Mondriaan Jr., son of one of Kuyper's early collaborators, took his art instruction from his father, then from The Hague School, before moving on to Paris and New York where he perfected the abstract style that produced some of Modernism's canonical works. He did so under the inspiration of Theosophy, not Calvinism. Yet he aimed, just as Kuyper taught, at penetrating through the forms of nature to exhibit its "objective" and universal meaning, and so its ultimate spiritual truth.

Kuyper as Victorian

To diagnose the *fin de siècle* more comprehensively, Kuyper turned to philosophy. His 1892 rectorial address, "The Blurring of the Boundaries," opened with remarks on Friedrich Nietzsche (incidentally introducing the German to the Dutch public). Usually treated as an avatar of Modernism or postmodernism, Nietzsche struck Kuyper instead as a conclusion, the flaming out of a meteor that had appeared on the European sky a hundred years before: "Not a single element surfaces in Nietzsche," he averred, "that does not stem, by legitimate descent, from the premises of Schelling and Hegel." Kuyper located the connection in "pantheism," the eradication of clear demarcations: first between the divine and human, then between the fixed and flux, theology and ethics, character and personality. Most ominously, transcendent standards of right were melting into the will of the people, or of the powerful. Along the way German Idealism had given rise to its materialist-empiricist opposite in the form of Darwinism: "What else is the Evolution-theory but the application of the pantheistic process to the empirical investigation of the phenomena?" Nietzsche then took the cult of power warranted by Evolution back into the camp of ethical Idealism, where he trumpeted the Superman as the ultimate Subject of a new creation. What the century's cultural custodians had tried to hide, either from guilt or anxiety, Nietzsche exposed to the light of day: the death of God, the displacement of Christ with Antichrist. "Nietzsche's appearance," in sum, was "the necessary consequence of the pantheistic storm that has driven the flow of our century's life."

On some occasions, Kuyper denominated pantheism as one of the two "worldviews" currently bidding for cultural hegemony. (The other was Catholicism.) In "The Blurring of the Boundaries," however, it was nothing so coherent — more of an impulse bursting out here, there, and everywhere. Much of the presentation repeated themes Kuyper had sounded before, whether the illusions of liberal theology in "Modernism, a Fata Morgana," the need for distinct social domains in "Sphere Sovereignty," or his perpetual yen for objective foundations and certainty. "The Blurring of the Boundaries" can also be criticized for committing the very faults that it was criticizing: over-determining outcomes and conjuring up unities where agents on the ground would have seen real distinctions. Kuyper asserted but did not demonstrate that a "genetic connection" between "our pantheists' [cult of] *process*" and "the worship of *Progress*" had turned modern life into an exhausting frenzy. Nor did he elucidate how a lack of enthusiasm and a fervent cult of Nietzsche could both mark the spirit of the age. His insights on evolutionary theory would be more profitably harvested in his next rectorial address, which took up that topic directly (see chapter fourteen). The greatest value of "The Blurring of the Boundaries" turns out to be its very catalogue of anxieties, along with its ambition to get a grasp on a culture that was coming into crisis.

The culture was that of "Victorianism," and Kuyper — born in the very year (1837) that the queen who lent her name to the era ascended her throne — was part of a generation that had come to maturity at its peak. Now they had to deal with its demise. On the American side this cohort included Andrew Carnegie (b. 1835) and J. Pierpont Morgan (1837), the most eminent industrialist and banker of the age; Grover Cleveland (1837), last of the Gilded Age presidents; religious luminaries like Dwight Moody (1837), the reigning champion of revivalism, and Washington Gladden (1836), pioneer of the Social Gospel; and social reformers like Frances Willard and Henry George (both 1839) who led their respective crusades for Prohibition and land reform as solutions to the vicissitudes of industrial society. On the British side, the great Baptist preacher Charles Spurgeon and Catholic historian Lord Acton were born three years before Kuyper; Walter Pater, paragon of aestheticism, and Thomas Hardy, the seer of naturalism, three years after. Kuyper shared birth *and* death dates (1837-1920) with William Dean Howells, the dean of American Victorian letters; very nearly with Henry Adams (1838-1918), the era's most prescient historian; and close enough with Mark Twain (1835-1910) who in the mid-1890s was entering his dark phase with a "pen warmed up in hell." The definitive Impressionist painters were Kuyper's close contemporaries — Edgar Degas (1834-1917), Pierre Renoir (1841-1919), and Claude Monet (1840-1926). So was the pioneer of the next stage, Paul Cézanne (1839-1906). Likewise, the philosophical founders of social democracy: T. H. Green (1836-1882) and Henry Sidgwick (1838-1900) of England, Wilhelm Dilthey (1833-1911) from Germany, and William James (1842-1910) from the United States.

These figures represent a wide spectrum of interests and opinion, but they might agree on the following bald summary of their inheritance. Victorian society had climbed aboard the train of material power drawn by the engine of technological innovation. Its track was said to be laid out by unalterable laws of historical development, and its destination was promised to be a land of unprecedented liberty, plenty, and — consequently — happiness. That the "liberty" in this formula was belied by the irresistibility of its "laws," that the humane end might be lost to the impersonal means driving the development, and that the science that provided command of nature also eclipsed the supernatural, troubled the night thoughts of Victorian high-culture leaders. Much of their effort went into proving that these costs could be avoided or else paid by surrogates, the favored nominees being feminine sentiment and masculine willpower, educated taste and the literary canon. These measures were to be supplemented by self-imposed discipline and a simultaneous (if contradictory) cult of enthusiasm. Under it all ran the sheer faith that, however obscured its foundations, the track of progress was firmly grounded, its course steady and sure. To "man," as Victorian language aptly put it, had fallen the task of making and managing the re-creation of the world. The human value added to this material quest made it moral, ensuring that God, though arguably now only watching from the sidelines, was there nodding in approval.

Kuyper attacked nothing so often or strenuously as this latter conceit; it had animated his conversion and prompted his rhetorical demolition of theological modernism in 1871. But that makes all the more remarkable the degree to which he shared in broader Victorian patterns. Most obviously, the four careers he pursued, the three nervous breakdowns he suffered, the 200-plus items in his bibliography, all testify to a work ethic gone gargantuan out of conviction that, though the world theoretically belonged to God, the project of proving the fact in detail had fallen to him on every front. Admirers and detractors alike paid homage to Kuyper's "titanic energies," the tremendous "force" of his personality and relentless "drive." The quoted words constituted the mantra of the age, and led to the heart of the issue. The tremendous energies that went into and came out of the technological conquest of nature Victorians had to somehow harness without squelching. Every social order needs to come to some ordered dynamism, but the Victorians faced particular urgency on the point and undertook an especially strenuous search for the right balance. It is telling, therefore, that "dynamic order" aptly characterizes Kuyper's objectives in politics and social theory, in reconciling divine "ordinances" with creational "unfolding." The particular sinews with which the Victorians knit everything together into a unity run through all his work as well: the dichotomous hierarchies of historicism and organicism and the inspiration provided by "ideals."

The Victorian Mind

Victorian hierarchies came as ordered pairs: heart next to head, "male" force balanced by "female" nurture, "civilized" over "savage," and always "higher" over "lower." We have seen the civilized-savage duplex in Kuyper's *Common Grace;* the higher-lower idiom pervaded his understanding of culture in general and aesthetics in particular. He so fundamentally assumed the patriarchy of separate gender spheres that he came to its overt defense only in late career, when the Netherlands began moving toward women's suffrage. More broadly, he took the pattern of dichotomous thinking for granted; thus the long train of common grace and special grace, institute and organism, kernel and husk, everlasting principle and temporal application. On the Victorians' "social question," Kuyper's solution was a justice of order more than of liberty or access — chambers of labor counterpoised to those of commerce and consumers. His reform of the States General would pair an upper house of "interests" with the lower house of "the nation." His scheme for pluralism in education prescribed separate systems well organized and duly registered, with no child left outside. Likewise with his notion of worldviews, so insistently consistent and yielding just two live options. In sum, if the heart of the Victorian so-

cial system lay in "structured competitiveness," Kuyper's key innovations were new deployments of his era's norms.

Victorians understood their dynamic order in terms of development. Above all generations before or after them, says historian Norman Cantor, they had "an addiction to history." This was the epoch of
grand narratives of human events and equally grand "natural histories" in the sciences. Herbert Spencer and Charles Darwin epitomized
the latter; Thomas Macaulay and Karl Marx were, respectively, the benign and radical expositors of the former. Kuyper was their Calvinist
counterpart. As his quick-steps through nineteenth-century philosophy or world history attest, he loved the big picture and loved to fill it
with stark oppositions that created compelling drama. That his grand
antinomies came to look simplistic, that the grand march of the
World Problem toward its culmination in the contemporary West
might have passed through more than four or five stations, appeared
to have had multiple directions, might not have been a march at all, or
even a World Problem — these are the observations of a (post-)Mod-
ernist mindset. Kuyper, with his age, lived in the shadow of Hegel. His
deployment of Calvinist political theory as the "Source and Stronghold of our Constitutional Liberties" was a historical argument pure
and simple; his first Stone Lecture was originally stamped not with its
later "worldview" trademark but as "Calvinism in History." It was said
of George Trevelyan (born 1838) that he sought to save British liberalism by historical narrative. Dwight L. Moody (born 1837) hoped to do
the same for evangelical Protestantism by popularizing the scheme of
dispensational premillennialism. Much of Kuyper's success came
from inscribing and re-inscribing his followers into a noble Christian
story to inspire their labors.

Development taken biologically spells organicism. Victorian
leaders loved the concept for proving their system to be inevitable, yet
capable of improvement. Things were as nature made them to be, yet
could — and would — get better, and the changes from one stage to
the next would proceed, assuredly, by careful, balanced "growth."
Kuyper was not so sure about the latter provision, but otherwise followed organic assumptions in all domains. Few concepts recur more
regularly in his writings. "No single piece of our mental world is to be
hermetically sealed off from the rest," began his famous dictum
about "no square inch" in his founding address of the Free University.
No part of our being, either, he might have added. Kuyper's sociology,

ontology, and epistemology were as anti-atomistic as it is possible to be. Faith was manifested in even as it directed practice, was shaped by just as it worked its power upon context. Societies inherited their character from ancestors and passed it on in their progeny. Ideas grew from "root-principle," which they passed along by the iron chain of logic to the far reaches of word and deed. Learning attained its mission not by heaping up data but by establishing connections, particularly those of whence, why, and whither. For politics and society, Kuyper scored "the Revolution" as much for its splintering of historically developed bonds as for the putative atheism of its theory. Beings had dignity, nature order, society stability, and God glory by virtue of the holistic pattern that held them all together.

The philosophical approach that best fit this scheme was Idealism, particularly in the teleological structures that it predicated of reality. Kuyper's habits on this front were so pronounced that it is helpful to recall how dominant they were at the time. Along with grand narrative, his era favored big-system philosophy, upholding purpose amid the century's flux, offering promise amid the pain of the new city or the loss of the old faith. Victorian Idealism was finally a religious faith, says Cantor, a "secularized substitute for Christianity" that held no contradiction to be final, no setback to be permanent, no failure to be irredeemable. These pieties tended to become more vapid as industrialization ground on. They could even translate into their apparent opposites, as when Herbert Spencer reduced moral progress to material improvement and lowered ideals into mere rational controls. But so long as "mind" carried on in human affairs, unshakable law would work in the natural order to bring everything to plentitude in a predetermined way. As we have seen, some of Kuyper's sharpest words cut at such presumption, yet he offered less an alternative to it than a Christian substitute within the same framework. The architecture of teleology, dogged assurance, and holistic truth marks all of his work. The urgent warnings against "monistic" pantheism in "Blurring of the Boundaries" cannot obscure the vast organic unity he was eager to posit in the Mind of God, in the outworking of Christian principle across all domains, in the conflict between faith and error that marched down through time.

Victorians are probably remembered most of all for the earnest tone pervading these mental habits. Conscientious within and didactic without, they labored as if the ethical structure they claimed to be so certain needed all their effort to remain in place. Kuyper fit the mold well, already from his student years when he scrupulously monitored his faithfulness to "the ideal." Short of direct attacks on God, he bristled most at imputations against his own sincerity. He enjoined his readers to "be serious" when an argument brought ethical norms or eternal life into view, and he might finish with a recalcitrant opponent by saying that the latter could "not be serious." The notions of pantheism, he said in "Blurring of the Boundaries," like those of popular sovereignty in politics, might be justifiably entertained among the intelligentsia but became irresponsible when let loose among the lower orders. More generally, a civilization or religion could be measured by how well it upheld a "firm moral tone" and "earnestness of life." On this score we ought to recall that Kuyper was literally a schoolmaster for twenty years at the Free University and figuratively one for his half-century as a journalist, conducting a night school for the common people in the columns of his newspapers. That role offers a fitting conclusion to this profile, for mass journalism belongs on the Victorian shelf of innovations alongside the compendia of knowledge, outlines of history, digests of world-classic literature, and five-foot rows of books — all marks of the era's passion to disseminate knowledge so as to "uplift" the many. An age that lionized Tennyson, Browning, and Longfellow can hardly be faulted for elitism. Many of Kuyper's simplicities, and much of his repetitive prose, can be laid to this account.

Kuyper the Proto-Modern

For all these commonalities, however, Kuyper both distrusted and disliked the Victorian system. He distrusted it because it could not work, and he disliked it because it worked too well. The two objections dominated his first two major cultural addresses. That the Victorian prescription did not work was the burden of his 1871 critique of "Modernism," which pivoted on the argument that Victorian moral self-construction would not hold. "Man" was not up to being the creator and sustainer of the world; moral commands lacking ontological grounds were the dreamy illusions of a summer morning, quickly dispelled when the storms of life arose.

That the system worked too well was the gist of his 1869 protest,

"Uniformity, the Curse of Modern Life." Here the social and personal costs of technological modernization passed in review, with clear anticipations of *fin de siècle* dirges about energies stifled and originality foreclosed. Such premonitions swelled into a chorus in the 1890s when it was becoming evident that the Victorians' two lines of force ran at cross purposes: accommodation to "progress" removed the footings for any resistance to the lowering weight of conformity. Late-Victorian youth were urged to be autonomous — and taught how thoroughly their lives were pre-determined. In the words of Jackson Lears, the best student of the syndrome on the American side, this induced at once feelings of "weightlessness" and "fragmentation." Not the social control of energies but their personal direction now came into question: Energies to what end? Striving to what purpose? The century thus ended not just on a "social question" but with a "psychic crisis."

Kuyper shared fully in this crisis — and in the cult of vitalism that hoped to solve it. Doubtless, his recurrent breakdowns had various sources, but two motifs stand out. First, as H. Stuart Hughes notes of several pioneer Modernists* in his classic *Consciousness and Society,* Kuyper burdened himself with far too much work, and periodically collapsed when the load became too heavy. This was the last generation of great system-builders, their projects often aborted because of the impossibility of fulfilling Victorianism's macrocosmic demands. The careers of James and Weber were disrupted by long stretches of "nervous collapse"; the literary remains of Dilthey and Twain are full of unfinished projects. Kuyper's insistence on doing it all and his complaints at having too little time to get to important projects signal the syndrome. But the spiritual search launched by his collapse in gradu-

---

*The different "Modernisms" in play need to be differentiated to keep the issues clear. The theological Modernism targeted by Kuyper's 1871 address emerged at Victorian high noon and effected just the sort of accommodation of religious claims to scientific demands that the epoch required. The new cultural Modernism that burst forth in the early twentieth century had no use for this procedure or its results. It yearned instead for real spiritual vibrancy, though it found that more often in exotic or hybrid spiritualities than in the return to traditional Christianity that Kuyper espoused. "Modernization" of the sort that Kuyper's speech on "Uniformity" criticized was an economic and technological process that left Kuyper distinctly, if not always consciously, ambivalent: he detested the standardization it wrought but praised the power and relative prosperity that it brought. The new cultural Modernists showed a similar attitude a generation later; as one of their historians puts it, the question of modern technology posed their "central dilemma."

ate school and again during his first term in Parliament also shows a yearning for clarity and firmness over against a culture of "evasive banality" — indeed, a "blurring of all boundaries" — that Lears locates at the root of the era's epidemic neurasthenia. The Victorian combination of thick social controls with eroded moral authority spelled just the prospect of diminished souls confronting voracious external power that Kuyper most feared in church, state, and the self.

A countervailing vitalist spirit suffused Kuyper's work from beginning to end. Like other proto-Modernists, from Nietzsche to James, from Henri Bergson to Georges Sorel, Kuyper wanted to live life intensely and directly, as a genuine moral struggle. Hence his part in the general attack on positivism and mechanistic determinism. Not just early, in "Uniformity," but also late, in a 1908 tract lauding "Our Instinctive Life," Kuyper valorized intuition against rationalization, vital conviction against learned pose, the reasons of the heart against a science that could but weigh and measure. His recreational pursuits showed a like zest. He hiked every mountain range from Norway to Italy; he loved to wander anonymously in the streets of European capitals. He would tour America and the Mediterranean in his sixties, and he insisted as an eighty-year-old, in 1917, on traveling through wartime Germany to take the baths at Dresden. Among the modes of resistance that Lears delineates (the artisan, the monk-mystic, and the aesthete), Kuyper personified the warrior. His rhetoric was pervaded by martial airs and images as he called his followers to battle, first for the glory of the Lord but also for the camaraderie and renewal they would find in the struggle. Notably, Kuyper also retained the deep religious longing and the transcendent framework of meaning that Lears found to be necessary if any mode of protest would avoid co-optation by the very culture it opposed.

Their personal struggles carried the proto-Modernists' famous turn toward the subject past epistemological questions in the sciences to suffuse the arts and humanities. Carl Schorske finds this turn from materialist rationality toward the interior or psychological pervasive at that laboratory of Modernist invention, fin-de-siècle Vienna. In many of the same ways as did Schorske and Hughes's Modernist pioneers, Kuyper found the commitments of the soul to be the very engines of life. The legitimacy, the necessity, even the superiority of religious perspective he vaunted against empiricist hegemony in scholarship, the classic-Liberal imperium in politics, and rationalist high tone in culture. He did so to reverse Christianity's marginalization, but he promised that science and government would be reinvigorated in the bargain. Learning would remain dessicated, Kuyper declared, so long as it pretended to be divorced from the issues that animate the learner, and Dutch politics would have remained a stagnant pool but for the awakening of ordinary people to fight for their convictions.

Just as in Kuyper's career, the new Modernism spelled a political as well as a cultural turn. The Victorian formula of reason and progress supported political control by and the economic interests of the educated, upper bourgeoisie. When economic pressures became too great to ignore and when heretofore disenfranchised populations could no longer be excluded from the political game, old-liberal privilege and its ideology were both in trouble. Viennese cultural Modernism was born at just this crossroads, Schorske demonstrates. The children of rationalist liberals took flight from the turbulent new politics of working-class and multi-ethnic organization into psychology, the arts, and literary careers. Kuyper grew up in a similar nexus, but he pursued the route of activism, not escape. His attack on theological liberalism both supported and took aid from his assault on the high-bourgeois biases of the 1848 Constitution; his esteem for intuition grew with his experience at cultivating morale in a mass movement; and his vision of pluralist worldviews helped to legitimate religious assertiveness in civic life.

The decisive turn came for Amsterdam, as for Vienna, in the 1890s, when populist politics succeeded in extending liberal premises beyond liberalism's traditional clientele to destroy the liberal regime. In Vienna that upsurge took a sharp anti-Semitic edge as its leaders turned "the people" — Catholic Germans — against an ancient religious Other. In the Netherlands, by contrast, Kuyper allied his Calvinist "common folk" *with* their ancestral Catholic enemy against an old class condescension newly draped in a secularist ideology. If his approach bore uncomfortable similarities to that of Karl Lueger, the anti-Semite-by-convenience who became Vienna's first populist mayor, Kuyper resembled even more Theodore Herzl, who in these years was learning to play the new politics on behalf of Jewish ghetto-dwellers within and far beyond Vienna. Both Kuyper and Herzl combined high manners with the common touch. Both loved the grand gesture and knew that popular politics required mythos as well

as rationality. Both dismissed liberal formulas of incremental progress by appealing to a communitarian past and a redeemed future.
And both reserved their greatest hostility not for avowed opponents
but for temporizers and compromisers in their own camp.

Kuyper as Artist

Granting all these similarities, however, something about Kuyper-as-
Modernist does not fit.* Quite a few things, actually, to judge by the
list of traits historian Norman Cantor abstracts from the movement at
its peak in the 1920s. Unlike the new Modernists, Kuyper was not
ahistorical or microcosmic; he was not at home with their fragmentation, randomness, and frank sexuality; did not reject stark polarities
and absolutisms; would not cut the aesthetic free from the moral; was
not inclined toward either elitism or cultural despair; and was not
content with, much less enamored of, uncertainty. The fluidity between fields that early Modernists pursued Kuyper would box back up

---

*The new Modernism discussed here was full born in the sequence of remarkable
innovations that William Everdell unpacks in *The First Moderns*. In 1900 the new
century was inaugurated with the announcement of three invisibilities at the heart
of life: the quantum postulated by Max Planck, the gene by Hugo de Vries, and the
subconscious by Sigmund Freud. The next year Edmund Husserl pioneered phenomenology in his *Logical Investigations;* in 1902 William James recast the psychology of religion in *The Varieties of Religious Experience;* in 1905 Max Weber recast the
sociology of religion in *The Protestant Ethic and the Spirit of Capitalism*. In 1903 time
was broken into sixteen parts per second by the debut of the first mass-released motion picture, *The Great Train Robbery;* in 1905 Einstein made time relative to space in
five papers that began a revolution in physics; in 1907 August Strindberg radically altered time for the theater in *A Dream Play*. In 1906 Picasso began fracturing space in
"The Last Supper" of Modernist art, *Les Demoiselles d'Avignon;* in 1908 Arnold
Schoenberg pioneered atonality in music; in 1909 W. C. Handy moved to Memphis,
where he started composing the blues that laid the foundations for a radically different American popular music. In 1910 James Joyce was at work on the stories that, in
Dubliners and *Portrait of the Artist as a Young Man,* announced a definitive turn in fiction. In 1911 Vassily Kandinsky published *On the Spiritual in Art* at the end of the
road that had begun with the Impressionists and now got rid of the object in painting altogether. All these strands came together in Modernism's *annus mirabilis,*
1913: the Armory Show in New York City, the tempestuous debut of Stravinsky's *Rite
of Spring* in Paris, the publication of the first volume of Proust's *In Search of Lost
Time,* of Franz Kafka's *The Judgment,* and of D. H. Lawrence's *Sons and Lovers.*

in discrete sovereign spheres. The social-ideological pluralism he had in mind was fixed and finite: a few well-defined pillars, not a kaleidoscope in perpetual spin. All in all, Kuyper wanted to liberate his followers not to demolish the Victorian structure but to preserve it and show how much they deserved to preside there. How they were to survive the claustrophobia of its controls he never said; perhaps he thought vitalism was for leaders, not followers.

In that conundrum, however, he fits very well with the proto-Modernists of American politics, the Progressives. They, too, wished not to overthrow the prevailing order but to humanize it. They too spoke much of liberation — by way of proposing a system more supple and enduring. Like Kuyper they were reformers who indulged a rhetoric of extremity, from William Jennings Bryan's "Cross of Gold" speech at the 1896 Democratic convention, to the thunderbolt with which Theodore Roosevelt accepted the Progressive Party's nomination in 1912: "We stand at Armageddon and we battle for the Lord!" In fact, Kuyper provides a neat cross-section of the American progressive trinity, sharing the vitalism of Roosevelt, the moralism of Woodrow Wilson, and the evangelical oratory of Bryan. In his own time, this hound of classic liberalism, this champion of pluralist experiment, admired no one in politics more than the pride of Victorian Britain, William Ewart Gladstone.

Kuyper would fault this analysis in that he never identified himself as Victorian or Modern but always as "Calvinist" or "Reformed." A notable series of articles he wrote in 1908, halfway through the new Modernism's rapid debut, shows how these categories could combine, however. "Our Instinctive Life" was first of all an intra-party polemic directed against a rising class of professionals who wanted to take over ARP affairs. But its publication coincided with that of Henri Bergson's *Creative Evolution* (1907) and Georges Sorel's *Reflections on Violence* (1908). Its theoretical artillery came from Gustav Le Bon's analysis of the psychology of the crowd. Its theoretical question was the very one Max Weber was engaging at the time — the relationship between charismatic and bureaucratic authority. Wherever else he might have affirmed rational order, on this occasion Kuyper sounded his persistent commitment to energy and passion. Just as animals demonstrate a remarkable level of instinctual intelligence, so did human knowledge in Eden, he repeated; the "perfect knowledge" that Paul anticipates in life after death (1 Corinthians 13:12) would be

that of immediate intuition. Kuyper insisted that the same must inspire any popular movement that hoped to stay alive. Modern politics
requires "the means — as the *psychology of the crowd* demands — to
convert sober realism into enthusiasm, cool calculation into holy
passion." In the ARP's case, Kuyper argued, that inspiration came
from the oratory at the party's biennial conventions — particularly
from the keynote address which sent the faithful out onto the campaign trail.

Kuyper's description of that rhetorical moment is in fact a self-
portrait of his performance over the course of a long career. The instincts of the gathered mass need to be tapped by someone with instinctive "talent" for the podium, Kuyper began. Such a speaker
"takes up his position before the gathering, feels the contact between
his spirit and that of his audience, and opens the tap. Almost auto-
matically the words begin to flow, the thoughts leap out, the images
frolic — psychological art in action." It was "art" indeed, for Kuyper
explicitly lodged his analysis of oratory in a discussion of the artistic
process. Instinctive command is especially "true of the *genius.* He
does not plod and pick away at things; he does not split hairs or prime
the pump. . . . By spiritual X-ray vision he sees through doors and walls
and virtually without effort grasps the pearl for which others grope in
vain." The great artist that Calvinism needed in the struggles of the
age turned out to be Kuyper himself, the master of the political imagination, and "Calvinism" turned out to be his greatest work.

It was also something of a new-Modernist gesture. Kuyper took
Calvinism to be neither the fixed fund of propositional truth that the
Reformed scholastics made of it nor the historically continuous development that the nineteenth century prized. He *said* he treated it in
these (mutually uncomfortable) ways, and he sometimes fulfilled that
claim, but overall he took a third way still. His Calvinism was a constructed country like William Faulkner's Yoknapatawpha County: not
built up patiently from historically documentable facts, nor register-
ing all the facts, but composing a rich tapestry of memory and hope
that was true to the deep resonances of the heart. By his age Reformed
scholastic language was so outworn and orthodoxy so marginalized
that neither its original terms nor its current posture fit the demands
of the times. Kuyper had to pick and choose from the Reformed store-
house to make his case, and he did so powerfully by means of symbols
and images. He cultivated a baroque voice to overcome Victorian sen-

timentality; he clung to Victorian order to enter the Modern age; he used the Modernist moment to cultivate a Calvinist stance. Such multiplicity of poses was *the* mark of the emerging age.

By all accounts the most memorable fête for Kuyper the artist occurred on April 1, 1897, when 5,000 people gathered in Amsterdam to celebrate *De Standaard*'s twenty-fifth anniversary. Actually they were there to salute their chief. Theo Heemskerk, son of a former prime minister and a student convert to Calvinism, organized the event; Herman Bavinck, the rising sun of Dutch Reformed theology, gave the keynote address. The entire Dutch press corps, including the socialists, was present and applauded the pioneer of their trade. Congratulatory messages were read from the podium, and ovations repeatedly swelled up from the throng.

If such an event was almost unprecedented, the achievement it celebrated was rare. By now, half a year shy of his sixtieth birthday, Kuyper could look back over a twenty-year span in which he had helped found a political party, a university, and a new denomination, in all of which he now held unrivaled leadership. He could survey as well twenty-five years of daily journalism and weekly pastoral meditations and Bible studies that instructed ordinary people in the things of heaven and earth; massive volumes of theology and political commentary; an impressive series of orations in cultural analysis. On all these fronts he had over the years worked out a grand pincer movement, bringing his political left and theological right arms together to form a consistent Calvinistic whole. The circle was completed in the mid-1890s when his earlier studies of the "Reformed fathers" matured into an encyclopedic vision that offered a modern "life- and world-view," while simultaneously "Calvinism" emerged in the political struggle as a trope fit for democracy. The "Beggars" of his *Standaard* inaugural twenty-five years ago had become "the little people," still "the conscience of the nation" but now liberated from the conservatives and patricians who had held them back and looking forward to pushing the Liberals out of power.

Well could the evening begin, then, with the crowd singing from Psalm 68:

1. Let God arise and by his might
put all his enemies to flight
with shame and consternation. . . .

7. Lord, when you led us on our march
The rain poured down from heaven's arch
And earth shook with the thunder. . . .

9. You brought us to the promised land,
You poured forth bounty from your hand;
A home did we inherit. . . .

20. Our God upholds us in the strife;
to us He grants eternal life
and saves from desolation.

And well could it end with Kuyper, who had sounded his own share of the thunder in the seventh stanza, linking himself simultaneously outward and upward. None of his labors had been for himself but for them, he told the gathering, "because *your* life has been *my* life, with one common breath of soul shared between us." ("Tumultuous applause," the record notes.) And yet not theirs ultimately, but God's alone. "All that I am as I here stand before you" is nothing but "His gift and His work. He who created me, He who predestined me, He who guided me from my youth" all the way to this place where I now hear these tributes to my person and talents — "it has all been His doing." In fact, one might doubt that there was much ego in the process at all: "This 'I,' this personality is not from me but only given to me by God."

A pious enough Calvinism, but not the clearest self-understanding on the part of so titanic a personage. The years ahead would see the person and his program tried and tested anew — by the travails of the new century, by the mixed blessings of success, by opponents without, and not least by some of the new men who were, that night, leading the applause in the room.

PART THREE

Shadows, 1898-1920

CHAPTER THIRTEEN

Kuyper in America

On August 21, 1898, Kuyper boarded the Cunard liner *Lucania* for a six-day voyage to the United States. The immediate occasion of his trip was to deliver the Stone Lectures at Princeton Theological Seminary and to receive an honorary doctorate from Princeton University. Two larger purposes loomed on his horizon, however, and three distinct audiences hovered in the back of his mind. Kuyper believed that on the American scene these elements could all hold together. That they finally did not was due in part to the disparities between them but also to the polarity of his principles.

To his listeners at Princeton, the academic citadel of American Presbyterianism, and to the other well-placed Protestants he would meet traveling around the Northeast, Kuyper brought a word of warning and a call to resistance. The rising tide of theological liberalism and pantheistic philosophy would sweep the American church away, he prophesied, unless its leaders anchored themselves on confessional bedrock, resisting all compromise. To Dutch-American immigrants, who turned out by the thousands to hear him once he reached the Midwest, Kuyper celebrated America as a land offering a noble destiny and urged them to assimilate quickly to its ways. Finally, to voters back home, Kuyper cast the United States as a living advertisement for the Antirevolutionary Party program: a land pious, prosperous, and free because its "keynote" was Calvinist. To put it in his theological terms, American Protestantism was a mixed bag needing a shot of antithesis, while Protestant America was a land awash with common grace.

Merging the two images into one picture would require Kuyper's best artistry. Even so, his audiences exercised their own tastes. His mainline audience mostly dismissed his critique, while certain parts of his Dutch-American audience applauded his principles only to turn them against his assimilationist advice. These responses, but also an up-close look at the U.S., started giving Kuyper second thoughts later in his trip. His dream hardly turned into a nightmare, but the shades he saw hovering over what had been so bright a landscape stood out by their contrast. They also turned out to be portents of much to come in his own future. An honest retrospect during his voyage home might have led Kuyper to appreciate what Sigmund Freud was discovering in Vienna at just this time: dreams can reveal more of our perplexities and hidden desires than we know, and also call to mind our real possibilities.

The Stone Lectures

Kuyper arrived in a country winding up official celebrations of its triumph in what Secretary of State John Hay called its "splendid little war" with Spain. It was also gearing up for the autumn midterm elections. Kuyper would have much to say on both matters, but first it was time for a late summer hiking vacation in the Adirondacks. By late September his translators were entering his final edits on the lectures, while his Princeton hosts began to worry if he would show up in time to deliver them. Appear he did and delivered they were, three a week between Monday, October 10, and Friday, October 21. An audience of three- to four-dozen people attended them in the Seminary's Miller Chapel.

Set against the backdrop of Kuyper's preconceptions, the lectures can be seen as moving back and forth between the pages of hope and fear. Lecture III, on politics, made a massive claim for Calvinism upon the American past, implying substantial foundations for Christian action in the present. Lecture IV, on scholarship, pulled back to the trenches of opposition between the "normalist" and "abnormalist" paradigms of human nature. The next address opened up a broad field for common grace in the ennobling possibilities of art, but then the final lecture, "Calvinism and the Future," brought back the tone of foreboding. There the world-historical drama built toward a climactic battle between Christianity and Paganism just over the near

horizon — only to end with a remarkably modest set of marching orders. Those still loyal to Calvinism in America, Kuyper pleaded,
should stop being ashamed of the fact and put in the work and
thought required to articulate its "application to every department of
life." Patience and quiet, rather than dramatic battle, seemed the order of the day. If they put themselves at God's disposal, Kuyper suggested, the Calvinist remnant in America might serve as an Aeolian
harp ready to sound the divine music whenever the winds of the Spirit
chose to blow across its strings.

Despite their mixed signals, the lectures did set out a revolutionary proposal that would prove to be Kuyper's real contribution to the
American scene. At least it was revolutionary in the context of Princeton. In defending the name of Calvinism over a century-long war with
Unitarians, Arminians, and revisionists of all stripes, Princeton's
great theologians Charles Hodge and Benjamin B. Warfield had concentrated on defending core Reformed doctrines, predestination not
least among them. Hodge had particularly guarded Presbyterian
church order as well. Methodologically, they had joined the Reformed
dogmatics of seventeenth-century Swiss theologian Francis Turretin
with the scientific model of Francis Bacon to define the Reformed
faith as an unchanging deposit of truth, and to define truth as a system built up by induction from "facts" gathered empirically and individually with a minimum of presuppositions.

On that stage Kuyper exploded his grenades. Calvinism was no
mere dogmatic theology, nor only a system of church order, he established in Lecture I; rather, it was a "life system" whose "root principle" branched out into every domain of human life and learning. This
evoked the holistic, New England form of Calvinism whose latter-day
incarnations Princeton had fought bitterly earlier in the century. It
also manifested the Germanic habits of thought that had worried
Hodge in his own studies in that country and that he had sedulously
kept out of Princeton. Now Kuyper brought them home. In Lecture II
he turned God's sovereignty from a theological tenet into the root
principle of the Calvinist system, and mandated that it be extended
into a comprehensive frame of interpretation, a worldview, within
which alone one could understand the data of perception. Kuyper returned to that call on his final evening: "With such a coherent world-
and-life-view, firmly resting on its principle and self-consistent in its
splendid structure, Modernism now confronted Christianity; and

against this deadly danger, Christians could not successfully defend their sanctuary without developing *a world-and-life-view of their own, founded as firmly on the base of their principle, wrought out with the same clearness and glittering in an equally logical consistency.*"

Warfield was present as Kuyper delivered this pronouncement, and though he went away impressed with Kuyper's passion, faith, and energy, he never comprehended the epistemological revolution Kuyper had suggested. Nor did the next several generations of American evangelicals and Fundamentalists who followed in Warfield's train. Those who would take up Kuyper's charge lived in the circle of Dutch Americans whom he would meet on the next leg of his trip. But first, on the Saturday following the lectures, Kuyper received an honorary doctorate in laws at Princeton University — more exactly, at Nassau Hall, named in honor of Kuyper's lionized House of Orange, and before a full panoply of faculty and dignitaries that included ex-President Grover Cleveland. Kuyper's remarks on the occasion were substantially reduced from the drafts he had earlier composed but still managed to link Calvinist theology, political liberty, and Princeton's heritage tightly together. He got personal, too. Twenty years before, he recalled, he had been nominated for the same honorary degree by the doctrinaire liberal Cornelis Opzoomer at the University of Utrecht, only to see Kuyper's opponents, Opzoomer's friends, scotch the idea. The degree Princeton now bestowed on him thus provided "a little revenge on my antagonists, and revenge with honor — why not admit it? — always offers something sweet to the human heart."

Touring Dutch America

Sweeter still would be the ovations in store on the next stops of his tour, the principal Dutch-American settlements in the Midwest. But as he rode the train to West Michigan, the largest of these enclaves, Kuyper knew he was approaching an ecclesiastical thicket. He kept up with their journals in Amsterdam, so he knew that the mid-nineteenth-century immigration had split into two groups. Those affiliated with the Reformed Church in America (RCA) had joined a venerable denomination descended from colonial times and centered in the middle of the East Coast establishment. Those in the Christian Reformed Church (CRC), which had split off in 1857, assumed a more stringently orthodox and isolationist posture. In the Midwest both claimed the Seceder heritage of 1834, but the CRC had attracted more immigrants of late — and thus also veterans of the Doleantie — because of a fractious battle over Freemasonry in the 1880s. The RCA tolerated Freemasons as members, even as church officers, under local-option rules; the CRC issued a blanket prohibition on the grounds that Masonic lodges were essentially the churches of the Enlightenment and Revolution. Kuyper knew as well that the CRC was building separate Christian schools for its children while the RCA endorsed the public schools as functionally a pan-Protestant establishment essential to the Christian character of the nation. The CRC was all drawn from the group Kuyper called the "little people"; the RCA, even in the Midwest, had some men of stature and influence. Hope College President Gerrit Kollen, for instance, supplied him with a letter of introduction to Vice President Garret Hobart in Washington, D.C. In short, the CRC was gravitating toward Kuyper's Dutch example, while the RCA embodied his American dream.

Kuyper handled the situation artfully. He opened on the evening of October 26 at Grand Rapids' largest downtown auditorium under the auspices of a joint CRC-RCA committee. There he dazzled a crowd of 2,000 with a spontaneous oration celebrating America's noble character and great promise. It was their duty, he told the largely immigrant audience, to train their children in English (their own Dutch was so provincial that some had difficulty understanding his standardized version) so that they might be saved for the church and reach for the destiny that God had in store for them. With its recent triumph in the Spanish-American War, the United States had arrived fully upon the world stage; how providential that children of Calvinism were at hand to bring out that "keynote" of the national character. With their help American influence would be a shower of blessing upon the peoples of the earth. Even more, since history proved that dynamism and progress occurred only when peoples blended and mixed, "America is destined in the providence of God to become the most glorious and noble nation the world has ever seen . . . [eclipsing] the renown and splendor of Rome, Greece, and the old races." Appropriately, Kuyper closed the evening by insisting that everyone sing not, as planned, the Dutch national anthem honoring "pure Netherlandic blood" but Luther's "Een Vaste Burcht" (A Mighty Fortress), honoring the God whom all nations should serve.

The scene then shifted to Holland, Michigan, where Kuyper had two days to look around the "Dort of America" under the lead of RCA notables. As in Grand Rapids, he adapted his message to challenge his hosts. One current and one former professor at the local Western Theological Seminary, Henry Dosker and Nicholas Steffens, were longstanding correspondents of his, and had written him disturbing news about the laxity and superficiality of the American theological scene. Steffens had extended that critique to the RCA as well during the Doleantie, when Kuyper toyed with the idea of immigrating to America. Accordingly, Kuyper invoked his audience's primal memory to bolster his proposals. Just as the city's pioneer A. C. van Raalte had put Christian education first, Kuyper recalled, so should his descendants now. Van Raalte's own sons were among those in the audience who squirmed at this suggestion. As for Freemasonry, Kuyper continued, his hosts might be right that the lodge in the United States, with its English pedigree, had a different character and function than on the Continent; "what works on the Amstel doesn't always apply on the Hudson," he allowed. Still, "the Christianization of Freemasonry is an illusion, and . . . the fruit of Freemasonry always turns itself against Christianity." His concluding address recycled his sixth Princeton lecture, "Calvinism and the Future," to a polite reception, although the Holland *Daily Sentinel* judged both the topic and the antithetical approach to be beyond "the logical reasonings . . . of the common people." A farewell banquet lavished him with many courses and many words from local dignitaries anyway. At midnight everyone toasted his sixty-first birthday.

The next morning Kuyper departed for a week's tour of the Dutch-American settlements in Iowa. His two stops were Pella in the southeast, founded by Seceder pastor Hendrik P. Scholte, and Orange City in the northwest, formed by a hiving from Pella a generation later. Since his speeches repeated the themes of his West Michigan presentations, Kuyper had plenty of time to read the papers, talk with the locals, and formulate his thoughts for the series of newspaper articles he would publish in the Netherlands upon his return. While his portrait registered some of the "shadow side" of America, he presented the country sunny-side up — or at least Antirevolutionary side up. America demonstrated what a free people could do if allowed to pursue a free life, Kuyper asserted. It was prosperous, energetic, and enterprising, setting a standard of living for the world to emulate. Its skilled workers were confident and self-reliant, its upper class was modest and generous, and the distance between the two was noticeably smaller than in Europe. Social interchange was polite and free-flowing, unlike the stiff relations typical of England. Churches were plenteous and full, all supported by donations on the voluntary system he advocated for the Netherlands. The American social tone was pure, much purer than France's, for instance. Suasions against alcohol had benefited all levels of society, from the factory to the university. Most of all Kuyper relished the prevailing public respect for religion, high and low, east and west. Politicians here, he said enviously, almost *had* to profess religious conviction — just the opposite of the Netherlands.

Kuyper was aware of the temptation to hypocrisy these circumstances entailed, but he was arguing here in the line of common and not of particular grace. Thus he could attribute America's social well-being to the twin pillars of bourgeois order, favorites of the Antirevolutionary Party as well: "What conserving social force lies in the fact that half of the population lives on its own property, and what moral social power comes from the circumstance that so few women of marriageable age and condition remain unmarried." The farm scene in Illinois and Iowa struck him as especially propitious for the national future, since the vices he did glimpse on his American tour he associated mostly with cities. Here, his timing and the bias of his hosts muted his prophetic powers. The American countryside in 1898 was (much as in the Netherlands) just recovering from a twenty-year depression that had hemorrhaged farm-workers into the cities and fired the political passions of Populism — passions Kuyper might have recognized from his own pronouncements on the social question. Kuyper's Iowa informants were the winners of this winnowing process and seem to have told him nothing of it. Nor did he seek it out on his own.

In any case, he followed the trail of the displaced to Chicago, the second city not only of America but of Dutch America. As to the city, Kuyper was impressed with the monumental architecture left by Chicago's 1893 World's Fair and by its more general rebuilding since the great 1871 fire. As to Dutch Americans, he was amazed when, once again, some 2,000 of them turned out to hear him speak in their Englewood district, on the southwest edge of the city. He gave them his usual assimilationist message in "The Vocation of Hollanders in

America." It being election eve, he also stoked the political fires. The reporters loved his pun to the Dutch-American crowd: let America's famous Hambletonian horse take you to the polls tomorrow, he joked, so you can vote for the party of Hamilton, i.e., Republican. Nor was this a passing concern. He returned so regularly to politics on his tour that, at this its midpoint,* it is worth pausing to analyze how Kuyper arrived at his position and what that indicates about the interpretive lens he turned on the United States in general.

Dutch Principles Meet American Politics

A political flurry two weeks earlier in Grand Rapids was particularly revelatory. There Kuyper had described himself to a reporter from the Grand Rapids *Democrat* as, accurately enough, a "Christian Democrat." "HE IS A DEMOCRAT!" blazed that journal the next day. Not so, thundered the Republicans' *Herald* in reply, producing local businessman and Netherlands Vice-Consul John Steketee to give the reasons why. Kuyper, like the Republican McKinley administration, embraced the gold standard and high tariffs, Steketee lectured; in fact, Kuyper was "a protectionist of the strongest sort. He is against free trade of any kind in any country."

To clear up matters, Kuyper published a letter in both the *Democrat* and the local Dutch-language Republican paper *De Grondwet*. He began with the core principle he had intoned at the dawn of his political career twenty-five years before: a democratic Calvinist in the Netherlands could not vote Democratic in the United States because that party traced its origins to Thomas Jefferson, who in turn had endorsed the principles of the French Revolution. That said, he regretted "that the Republican program [platform] of 1896 did not as openly declare its approval of Hamilton's Calvinistic principles as their opponents did of Jefferson's."

In this contretemps, principles, policies, and party labels flew past each other in a comedy of errors, or at best half-truths. In the first place, Kuyper invoked high philosophy, Steketee cold cash. Even there the Vice Consul got Kuyper wrong. The Antirevolutionaries until

---

*Election day occurred on November 8, the Stone Lectures had started on October 10, and Kuyper would sail back to the Netherlands on December 10.

recently had endorsed free trade and even now, Kuyper clarified, endorsed reciprocal tariffs only. In any case, they would not countenance rates as infamously high as McKinley had pushed them. As to *the* great issue of 1896, Kuyper endorsed bimetallism — basing currency on silver as well as gold — as had the Democratic platform, adding only that it should be internationally regulated. More generally, the Grand Rapids *Democrat* was correct to note Kuyper's Democratic-like commitment to local control as opposed to the Republicans' preference for stronger, more centralized government. With respect to education, the seminal issue of his own party, the Democrats enlisted Roman Catholics and (usually) Missouri Synod Lutherans, who operated the largest Christian school systems in the country, to the grief — and sometimes active hostility — of Republicans, who were committed to a single, nationwide system of public schools. On the great issue of Kuyper's church politics, it was no less than the great Revolutionary himself, Thomas Jefferson, who had made the definitive move in the American disestablishment of religion, drawing his core support from the most evangelical Christian element in the population, the Baptists.

Most Baptists in the North had shifted over to the Republican Party by the time of Kuyper's visit, but the two parties by no means showed the clear Christian-secularist division familiar to him from the Continent. The prosperous, moralistic Protestants of the Northeast and Midwest who guided his tour generally voted Republican, but in the 1896 campaign McKinley was quite overshadowed religiously by his Democratic rival, William Jennings Bryan, a conservative Presbyterian who espoused peace, Prohibition, and economic relief to the struggling in the name and cadences of the Gospel. Nor was this a fluke. In every election from 1884 through 1916 but one (1904), the Democratic presidential candidate — Bryan, Grover Cleveland, and Woodrow Wilson — came from a conservative Presbyterian background. Half the time the Republican they faced was either a free-thinker (James Blaine) or a Unitarian (William Howard Taft, Charles Evans Hughes): that is, an adherent of the Enlightenment rationalism or Modernism that so troubled Kuyper in the Netherlands. In fact, Unitarians had been a core constituency of the Republicans' Whig and Federalist ancestors back to the dawn of the republic.

If all this complicated any religiously-derived voting mandate, it also pointed up the irony of Kuyper's historical sources. It was a Unitarian, Henry Cabot Lodge, who wrote the biography of Alexander Hamilton that Kuyper cited in his reverential treatment of the man. His dependence on George Bancroft's general history of the United States, a standard source at the time, was more appropriate to his purposes in that Bancroft had converted from Unitarianism to evangelical Christianity and took, to put it mildly, a providentialist point of view of his subject. Yet Bancroft stood foursquare in the party of Jefferson, writing the campaign biography of Martin Van Buren and serving as Secretary of the Navy under James K. Polk.

In short, in the United States the war of the spirits had from the start run across, and not along, political party lines. Kuyper's political philosophy simply could not quite register that fact. This accounts as well for his repeated and egregious misreading of Alexander Hamilton. Antithetical principialism dictated that if Jefferson once endorsed the French Revolution, then he endorsed everything in its train; and if Hamilton opposed it, he must have been Christian, even a Calvinist. In fact, as Kuyper learned from Lodge's biography, Hamilton was of mixed Scots and Huguenot stock and had been brought to America under Presbyterian sponsorship. But in choosing a college he had spurned Princeton for New York as the more promising site for his outsized ambitions, and his rise to prominence coincided with a nearly "complete religious indifference" on his part that is all the more striking in light of his marriage to the Dutch Reformed Elizabeth Schuyler. The religious references Kuyper could find in Lodge's biography came from the post-1792 period, when Hamilton was at his most blatantly opportunistic. A more evident piety did emerge in him after 1800, but only with the precipitous decline in Hamilton's prospects. It was cruelly ironic that before he could much cultivate that piety, Hamilton was sent to his eternal reward by Aaron Burr Jr., grandson of a real Calvinist, Jonathan Edwards. In any case, Republican leaders of Kuyper's own day had no such "Calvinistic" Hamilton in mind but the political-economic Hamilton, champion of trade and empire, of central banks and economic growth, and of a commandeering state run by a proud elite. Kuyper's interpretation of American politics was thus pinned to a figure who resembled nothing so much as his own *bêtes noires:* the Amsterdam regent, all ambitious and worldly, and British Foreign Secretary Joseph Chamberlain, imperial and ruthless.

Yet the Republican heritage did have figures who fit Kuyper's cause. Probably the closest was Jonathan Edwards's other notable grandson, Timothy Dwight. President of Yale, organizer of Connecticut's Federalist Party, devoted to public morality on expressly Christian lines, attracting a middling (not Hamilton's elite) following, Dwight's anti-revolutionary cast had a profile remarkably like Kuyper's own — one point excepted. Dwight was implacably opposed to religious disestablishment, and after it came to Connecticut anyway (in 1817), his followers had to veil their religious claims under a Whig Party platform that highlighted economic issues. Another Federalist founder was John Adams, possessed of the same Unitarian bent as Jefferson. Unlike the latter and quite like Kuyper, however, Adams was a descendant of the commons, not of the gentry, and brought to his statecraft a robust suspicion of human depravity. Alas, Adams was a one-term "failure" as president who, in scotching Hamilton's maneuvers toward a coup d'etat in 1798, had started the New Yorker on his downward spiral. Neither point endeared him to the Republicans of Kuyper's day. Alternatively, Kuyper could have looked to Samuel Adams, the firebrand of the New England Revolution, whose biography was on the same shelf as Lodge's *Hamilton* aboard the *Lucania*. Adams resembled Kuyper in his mobilizing genius and his dream that New England be a "Christian Sparta," disciplined, virtuous, sacrificial. But Adams was a revolutionary of 1776, not a nation-builder of 1787, good at popular agitation but not at bearing lasting power. Kuyper needed someone at America's roots who was both; when forced to choose, he went for Hamilton, the power.

He chose similarly on the contemporary scene. Democrats in 1898 were the party of cultural pluralism, ethnic diversity, and local control; Republicans stood for a unitary nation and firm moral tone under WASP control. Churchgoers who voted Democratic were usually religious outsiders — Roman Catholics above all, but also Protestants more concerned with the purity of the church than with its socio-political influence. Republicans attracted the insiders, the Protestant establishment of the Northeast and Midwest. Since it was they who were supervising Kuyper's tour, it is not surprising that he saw the country in their light. But he was also choosing between two sides of his own yearnings — even more, between two eras. In choosing for Republicans and Protestant hegemony, he was opting for the Dutch Protestant world of his parents. He would entitle the first chapter of his America book "Ons Vooruit" (Our Future). He might have more accurately chosen "Our Past."

American Shadows

On the final leg of his journey, back to the East Coast, Kuyper got to see both the Protestant establishment and the American future close up. He also began to voice more misgivings. Leaving Chicago, he first stopped in Cleveland, where he spoke to a gathering of Reformed, Christian Reformed, and Presbyterian laypeople, exchanged compliments with the local press, and mingled with faculty from Western Reserve University. He repeated the exercise at Rochester, New York, this time at its flagship Baptist Seminary and at the Women's College Club, where he discoursed on "Holland and Its People." The two cities were classic sites on the westward band of New England settlement, and the educators and clubwomen he spoke to exemplified its cultural tradition. Little wonder that he admired them, especially the women. To him Rochester women defined American femininity, a type head and shoulders above the Parisian fashion plate, the English bluestocking, and the Dutch stay-at-home. They were widely read and capable of sustained conversation on history, art, literature, and current affairs. They showed by the vigor and autonomy of their organization how women's full potential could flower under the conditions of free association. That these same qualities raised questions of power Kuyper answered by turning a relatively accurate description into a permanent norm. The powerful influence American women exercised in the unofficial sector of culture formation obviated any need — and any desire, he inaccurately prophesied — by the women in question for voting rights in the official sectors of public life.

But Kuyper must have wondered whether it was better to be rightly or wrongly taken. Already in Chicago a reporter had so misunderstood his remarks about Calvinism and liberty as to label him a "Liberal"; now a Rochester newspaper correspondent who understood better editorialized against his pluralistic school model. His Cleveland lecture on Calvinism and politics elicited praise for praising America but little comprehension of his zeal to restore the Puritan spirit. In Cleveland Kuyper also returned to his warnings about the popularity of German philosophy among American youth, a phenomenon he had likely encountered firsthand in giving three lectures at the Presbyterians' McCormick Theological Seminary in Chicago. He determined to confront it again a few weeks later at the Congregationalist seminary in Hartford, only to have his contact there warn him off that topic for the less controversial lecture on politics instead.

In short, the rising generation of Yankee church leaders had little resonance with Kuyper's antithetical strain. It served better at Middle-Atlantic sites. At New Brunswick Theological Seminary, the old center of Dutch Reformed life in the East, he argued for "The Antithesis between Symbolism and Revelation," and repeated the performance in early December at the Presbyterian Historical Society in Philadelphia. The rising appeal of mysticism among Protestants was understandable in light of the cold rationalism of the Enlightenment, he granted, but in the long run it afforded faith no firm abiding place. Faith for Christians still had to be understood as belief, not merely as trust, and had to look above personal experience to written revelation for its ultimate authority.

A more striking alteration in Kuyper's views came on political ground. Already in Grand Rapids he had voiced worries about the imperialist spirit that the recent war had unleashed, and at every stop on his tour he went on record against "expansionism." This came to a head with his visit to the national capital to meet President McKinley. The meeting had been arranged by Cornelis Willem van der Hoogt, long ago a member of Kuyper's congregation in Amsterdam and now Secretary of the Bureau of Immigration for the state of Maryland under Republican Governor Lloyd Lowndes. Kuyper went to the White House with the highest expectations — or at least trailing the noblest rhetoric. In defeating the Spaniards, in upholding the Calvinistic Republicanism of Hamilton, in standing for God's ordinances in politics, Kuyper had told the press in Chicago on election eve, McKinley reminded him of William the Silent.

The actual meeting — on Wednesday morning, November 30 — was brief and disappointing. Kuyper got right to the point, which was to request American support for the Transvaal against growing British threats to its independence. More generally, he weighed in against further American expansion overseas. McKinley's response was not recorded, but Kuyper found it jolting. He first explained it to reporters as a result of the president's evident fatigue. Later he ascribed it to the maneuverings of Secretary of State John Hay and the designs of Western industrialists upon Pacific markets. Ultimately he wrote it off to McKinley's weakness as a statesman: "What a pity that . . . he *follows* and does not *lead*." In fact, McKinley was simply advancing the Republicans' perennial pro-business, pro-British foreign policy established by Hamilton himself.

It was the sharpest check to his America-fantasy that Kuyper ever received. He did not change his fundamental assessment of American character or his advice about Dutch-American assimilation, but he sensed another strain in that character and some ominous prospects in the future. The United States' new international entanglement would dramatically alter the character of its politics, he told his Dutch readers. To Americans themselves he warned: "Your nation is about to begin a career of colonial expansion . . . if your chief motive is simply commerce . . . [it] will inevitably make you unhappy." For both reasons Kuyper henceforth typically endorsed Democratic presidential candidates: Bryan in 1900 and 1908, Wilson in 1912 and 1916.

Kuyper remained congenial on the rest of his tour, but he did not hide his criticisms. After meeting with U.S. Commissioner of Labor Carroll D. Wright and the head of Maryland's Bureau of Industrial and Labor Statistics, he told Baltimore reporters that the United States' lack of an income tax constituted a clear and inequitable burden upon the poor. Even worse was the absence of laws protecting workers. "Wrong, my good friends, wrong. You should compel legislative action and protection. . . . Holland believes in protecting labor, and in that she is way ahead of the great America. Your capitalistic classes have too much power. The liberal spirit in matters relating to the cause of labor should prevail, but you will come to it, you will come to it. America is a great country."

Kuyper took the occasion to explore possible sites for a Dutch immigrant colony in Maryland, in part to help out Van der Hoogt, whose like ventures in Colorado had come to disaster. The exploratory tour entailed a long boat ride around Chesapeake Bay, during which he regaled reporters with stories, observations, and opinions on whatever they wanted to know. Since he himself wanted to know more about American higher education, he paid a call on Daniel Coit Gilman, president of Johns Hopkins University in Baltimore. There Kuyper could indeed catch the future of the American university, for Hopkins had introduced the model of the German research university to the United States, and Gilman exemplified how a genuine American Christian, as he was, came to terms with it: he made faith personal, peripheral to the business of scholarship.

Assessing America

With his trips to Hartford and Washington, Kuyper's tour was complete. There remained only a last plea for the renewal of vibrant Calvinism, delivered, rather incongruously, at the RCA's prestigious Marble Collegiate Church in Manhattan. He also gave an after-dinner speech to the Algemeen Nederlandsch Verbond (ANV), an alliance for the promotion of Dutch culture and contacts abroad. At the request of the Dutch government, Kuyper helped organize a Midwest chapter during his stop in Chicago and had a similar purpose in New York. The audience was different from any other on his tour: neither immigrants, collegians, nor Yankee elites but clubby bluebloods of old Dutch descent. Kuyper's message was dramatically different too. If Dutch immigrants in the Midwest, or at Paterson, New Jersey, where he had stopped in late November, heard the word of assimilation, here the elite heard a call to preservation. There, Dutch and American matched up well because of their common Calvinism; here, Dutch clashed with Anglo-Saxon out of racial antipathy. It was not the Calvinist but the Netherlandic influence on America's formation that needed to be recovered, an influence so considerable, Kuyper opined, that the United States was equally of Dutch warp as of English woof. To this end Kuyper recommended a variant on the strategy of leadership training he had pursued in the Netherlands: chairs in Dutch language, history, and law ought to be instituted in major universities, and the historical memory of Dutch contributions to America assiduously cultivated among the youth.

The next morning, Saturday, December 10, Kuyper boarded the Holland-American liner *Rotterdam* for Boulogne, whence he proceeded to Amsterdam via Paris and London. The journey gave him time to round out his reflections for the series of articles that would run in his papers in the first quarter of the new year. In them the "shadow side" of things American received more consistent attention, if varying explanations. Sometimes Kuyper intimated that shadows were simply the side effect of towering achievements. Other times he attributed them to the inevitable antithesis that was emerging out of a cloudy but generally healthy tincture heretofore held in suspension by common grace. Upon closer inspection, however, America's shades turned out to be precisely the obverse of its brightness, vices that were the predictable price of its virtues.

RCA professors Henry Dosker and Nicholas Steffens had been telling Kuyper this about American religion for years. Free organization meant perpetual splintering, whether over theological issues, as they said, or also along the class lines Kuyper observed. He agreed with them that energy and enthusiasm too often did not prepare the way but instead substituted for careful reflection and sustained growth. Sunday Schools and revivals got youth in the door but in the process created an aversion to catechesis and theological preaching. Religious disestablishment wonderfully cast the question of faith onto the individual's conscience, but the loss of any sense of covenant or kingdom left those individuals uncertain of the larger body to which they belonged, of the social relationships their faith entailed, and of the development of God's larger work over time. As unbelief steadily concerted its intellectual forces and modern development systematized social forces, Kuyper concluded, the American churches would have to overcome these habits to create a coherent force of their own, both in the life of the mind and in their work in the world.

As a political operator Kuyper was most struck by the boss system that had been so flagrantly on display in the November elections. The phenomenon posed a challenge as well back home, since Lohman could add it to his arguments against mass democracy. The American system certainly did bear a "pernicious tendency," Kuyper told his readers. It gathered too much power to one man, bred contempt for law, undermined the authority of the state, and disrupted the efficiency and reliability of the civil service. Yet the Dutch had forestalled these abuses by insulating civil servants and dispersing electoral choices among multiple parties, not just two. A popular party could avoid the American evil by building an internal pyramid of response and responsibility, as had the Antirevolutionaries. Dutch parties might have charismatic leaders, but they were not bosses. America thus served up a monitory lesson on democracy operating on the basis of interest instead of principle.

In his third function, as journalist, Kuyper went away least impressed. American newspapers might be numerous and energetic, but a more partisan and sensationalist crew was not to be found. Granted, he had toured during election season, and most papers were still party organs, but a similar system obtained in the Netherlands, where a sense of honor and public responsibility nonetheless exercised a moderating influence. Indeed, Kuyper had missed the worst of the yellow journalism by which the American press had stoked war fever against Spain. As it was, he thought that American dailies carried too little foreign news and then tilted it toward the lurid and grotesque, much as they did their local stories. The root of this evil, Kuyper said, was money. Non-party papers were utterly dependent on advertising and so had no independence from market demands. Party organs were beggars at another table. In either case, the higher, educative calling that the press ought to have as a sovereign sphere went aglimmering, eclipsed by "the power of the dollar."

In fact, the theme of money ran through every sector of Kuyper's commentary. Campaign financing lay at the root of the boss system; the power of budgets accounted for the sheer busyness of American church life. Kuyper astutely captured the connection between theological liberalism and the millionaire donors who had made seminaries independent of churches and thus marginalized the voice of the common people. What the synodical boards were in the Dutch Reformed Church, "the richer class" threatened to become in American Protestantism, demanding a gospel that endorsed the world in which they prospered. On the secular side, the rise and fall of millionaires gripped the American imagination, generating hero worship on the one hand and sensationalized scandals on the other. The lust for money pervaded all ranks, Kuyper observed, from the unions below to the great trusts above, all perfectly represented in the brutal athletic competitions where men of both classes took their entertainment. All this evinced a religion of mammon and threatened the wholesale materialization of society. The only antidote would be a reinvigoration of the genuine religious spirit, Kuyper concluded, a spirit not just deployed in the common grace of philanthropy, where America excelled, but in the consciousness of a distinctive Christian conviction fully articulated across all spheres of life.

Legacy

However well this picture promoted Kuyper's agenda at home, in the United States it had little immediate effect. The Protestant establishment was used to an easy trade between property, propriety, and piety, and they were not about to complicate it with theological conditions or close philosophical scrutiny. They were just now embarking on a generation of reform crusades that became known as Progressivism, but these efforts minimized confessional content as much as they maximized moral rhetoric. This was commensurate with the Protestant spirit Kuyper had seen up close: all ethos and no logos. In sum, Kuyper registered on the Protestant establishment's horizon as a momentary celebrity — a Renaissance man of prodigious energy and talents, but not a lodestar for the future. With the Knickerbocker set it was even worse; the ANV clubs came to nothing.

In Dutch America Kuyper's name would live on, but not where he expected. Marble Collegiate Church became renowned not for the "new development of Calvinism" he espoused there but for the positive-thinking nostrums of Norman Vincent Peale. Dosker would leave Holland for the Presbyterian seminary in Louisville, and although Steffens came back from Iowa to replace him, his continued grievances with the RCA's flaccid theology went unheeded. The next generation of RCA leaders either did not know Kuyper or did not care for him. They identified with America as fully as Kuyper had urged, but therefore dropped his principial critique and poured their energies into middle-class moral crusades, especially Prohibition and its not-so-hidden underside, anti-Catholicism. By the time of World War I, the passion had grown so fierce that the student newspaper of the RCA's Hope College took Kuyper's German sympathies to be a mark of his willingness "to be numbered among the baby-killers of the central powers" and against the cause of Christ.

On the other hand, Kuyper proved very influential in the younger and less prestigious Christian Reformed Church, first of all among its rising thinkers and activists but also among a fair number of farmers and factory workers. For all of them he gave a bracing education that both explained their alienation from the world and called them to fearlessly plunge into that world, protected by the banner of Christ that they boldly showed forth. In other words, Kuyper's appeal in the United States registered in just the same places and for just the same reasons as it had in the Netherlands. It endured because his listeners took a slower pace of assimilation than he had urged and a more skeptical view of America than he promoted. They followed instead his Netherlandic method of closely testing the spirits to see which were of God, and which were of mere Whiggery. It was they who kept his Stone Lectures in print and who developed its approach of worldview analysis and holistic Christian thinking. When, after two world wars and a long sojourn in a Fundamentalist counterculture, some conservative Protestants sought to engage the American scene constructively again, the Kuyperian tradition supplied crucial resources for doing so. Among American evangelicals, then, his vision would finally have some of the impact he had yearned for decades before. That his heritage divided left, right, and center shows that the volatility of his vision could cross the Atlantic, too.

CHAPTER FOURTEEN

Life and Death at the End of the Nineteenth Century

Kuyper's book of America reflections, published early in 1899, concluded with the same warning that had marked the last press interviews on his trip. Unless soon reversed, he predicted, the United States' new imperial spirit would corrupt its politics and thicken the "new and much darker war clouds [now looming] on the horizon of international life." The cloud that Kuyper took to be the most threatening would indeed break over South Africa before the year was out, but the Fashoda crisis in the Sudan the year before signaled continuing imperial rivalries in North Africa, while America's "pacification" of the Philippines brought "the crude, cruel game" near the shores of Asia. Violence was striking closer to home too, as European heads of state fell in a steady stream of assassinations: the president of France in 1894, the premier of Bulgaria in 1895, the empress of Austria in 1898, the king of Italy (and nearly the crown prince of England) in 1900. President William McKinley joined the list in 1901. Meanwhile, the wages of character assassination came due in France when the espionage conviction of Army Captain Alfred Dreyfus was exposed as an anti-Semitic plot, toppling the conservative regime that had prosecuted him. Kuyper was so appalled by its conduct that he commended radical novelist Emile Zola for leading the exposé.

Against this background, the sense of an ending that had been building in Europe in the 1890s came to a peak. Kuyper entered that conversation with some of his ablest writing. He gave his last great diagnostic of European culture in October 1899 with his rectorial address on "Evolution." He began writing his critique of British imperialism in South Africa two months later. The two pieces both revolve around the themes of conflict and death. But death had gotten personal before that. In 1898 Bismarck and Gladstone, the twin landmarks of European politics since his youth, both passed from the scene. Then, on August 25, 1899, his wife Jo died at fifty-seven years of age.

Dealing with Death

The place where Jo passed away — Meiringen, in Switzerland's Bernese Oberland — was the site of arguably the most sensational death of all in the late nineteenth century. The town was a mecca for tourists — for the Kuypers in 1899 and especially for the English, who visited there in such numbers as to sustain an Anglican church to accommodate them. It was thus an apt setting for the climactic duel in Arthur Conan Doyle's world-famous stories of Sherlock Holmes. A funicular completed in 1898 still takes the visitor from the village outskirts to the peak of Reichenbach Falls, where Holmes and his archenemy, Professor Moriarty, grappled in mortal combat until the two apparently hurtled to their death on the rocks below. As it turned out, popular demand forced Doyle to bring Holmes back to life, though he was even less willing to indulge notions of resurrection from the dead than he was to (as he thought) waste his creative powers on the Holmes brand instead of producing the elevated literature he believed to be his destiny. Doyle penned his Holmesian tales of rational deduction as parables of science triumphing over the delusions of ghosts, mystery, and the supernatural. His hero had escaped death at the falls by a deft martial-arts maneuver, Doyle later explained. After his first wife died in 1906, then two brothers-in-law, two nephews, his own brother, and finally his son Kingsley perished in or soon after World War I, Doyle turned to the occult in hopes of contacting the departed. Spiritualism had a well-established pedigree among erstwhile rationalists who found the mystery of personal loss harder to fathom than advertised.

Of the far less famous death in his own family, Kuyper said little publicly about its cause, alluding only to a flare-up of Jo's chronic lung problems. In fact, she had been depressed and ailing since the death of their youngest son, Willy, six years before. Kuyper was quite more willing than Doyle to take on the meaning of death and discuss it for his readers, however. The liturgy from Jo's funeral is preserved in Kuyper's papers with copious notes in his own hand. The next issue of *De Heraut* ran a meditation on death, one in a series that continued until his sixty-fifth birthday, in 1902. It appeared in book form as *Asleep in Jesus.*

One constant characterized all his reflections. If, as the local Swiss pastor acknowledged in his funeral sermon, it was especially hard to bury a loved one so far from home, it was all the more important to remember the stout Reformed faith that had suffused her life. The text of the occasion was Hosea 14:9: "The ways of the Lord are right, and the just shall walk in them; but transgressors shall fall therein." That God's ways are right does not mean that they are easy, the pastor continued, but they are never crooked. Our stumbling along the way was more likely evidence of the presence of or a punishment for sin, but the straightness of God's ways meant that our sure hope for final peace need never waver. The text at graveside (Psalm 73:23-28) was more personal, highlighting trust amid faltering strength: "Thou wilt guide me with Thy counsel and afterward receive me to glory. Whom have I in heaven but thee? And there is no one on earth I desire beside thee. My flesh and my heart fail, but God is the strength of my heart, and my portion forever." The mourners ended by singing Psalm 125:2, befitting both the Swiss scene and bedrock Reformed conviction: "As the mountains are around Jerusalem, so the Lord is round about his people, from this time forth and forevermore."

In his *Heraut* meditation Kuyper got more personal. "There you stood with a broken heart by the deathbed. There lay your deceased, lifeless, inanimate, for all the world as if she had been *swallowed up* by death. Swallowed up — a hard word. Devoured, as if by a beast of prey. All at once, gone: the look of the eye, the sweet words . . . everything, clean gone." The experience was no less difficult for believers than for anyone else, Kuyper emphasized for his readers. Yet "God's Word, without in any way discounting the harshness of that reality, turns it around for you. Totally." It opens "your soul's eye" to see that, in Jesus' resurrection, the devouring process has been reversed. For the faithful, Kuyper quoted Paul, the moment of death means that "what is mortal is swallowed up by life."

What happens to the departed next Kuyper explored in the rest of the fifty-two meditations that make up *Asleep in Jesus.* Three prevalent notions he debunked right away. First were Spiritualist yearnings à la

Conan Doyle to communicate with deceased family members. Blood family ends at the grave, Kuyper insisted; thereafter the saints become exclusively part of the family of Jesus. Secondly, he rejected the notion of heaven as an aerie of disembodied souls. On the contrary, Kuyper insisted that the body was essential to genuine humanity. The soul's continuing and conscious existence between death and the Last Judgment, when everyone would become endowed with a resurrected body, was anomalous, second-best. Thirdly, the afterlife was no scene of sedentary singing. Indeed, souls in the intermediate state were as busy as ever, "restless[ly] working [but] without ever becoming weary." Death simply transferred the believer to a new stage of service. A seemingly premature death signaled that God needed just the sort of service which the decedent alone could provide. If Kuyper's therefore was an exceedingly Protestant heaven, all action and little beatific vision, it also exhibited all the diversity he loved on earth. Jesus' saying that his Father's house had "many mansions" meant that each dwelling there would have "a peculiar something of its own by which to distinguish itself from the other." Heaven too will be a pluriform society, "the blessed [gathering] together according to their nature, their talents, their gifts."

Still, at the risk of some contradiction, Kuyper ultimately defined the afterlife by its restfulness. In part this meant that believers had arrived in the "fatherland," no longer strangers or pilgrims subject to scorn and resistance. It also meant having achieved pure being and no longer becoming, resolving one's personal dialectic. Above all, it meant gaining full coherence of personality, a steadiness of soul. What Kuyper most looked forward to was getting beyond the power of temptation — not just the forgiveness of sins but release from the anxiety that one *might* sin. On earth life is strife and conflict, Kuyper repeated, and necessarily so, for without struggle there would be no advance. But the process brought a weariness, moral more than physical, and at this point in his life Kuyper was eager to stand, as he put it, as a pillar in God's temple instead of having to wing around in God's service. The tension between the active and restful images of eternity he resolved with a third, aptly organic motif. Rest and growth came together as one bloomed as a leaf on Christ the vine, nurtured by his roots, manifesting divine beauty, free at last from the sin that on earth twines around everything good.

For all his affirmation of the physical, Kuyper's meditations evinced some body-soul tension. The soul remained the core of the self, the persistent personality. It needed body most of all to express itself. With that, the eternal (and not just intermediate) heaven became a house of witness, reminding the saints below that they had a like calling on earth. Kuyper thus concluded his meditations on a note of relentless struggle, now against everything in modern life that corroded belief in the soul, the resurrection, and eternal destiny. The major address he had to give at the Free University in October would be an epic word in that witness, meant to cut through, as its opening line declared, "the hypnosis of the dogma of Evolution" under which "our nineteenth century is dying away." Kuyper labored at the text from September into October as he lingered on in Switzerland near Jo's grave. In such circumstances, "when that mysterious wave of the demoniac of universal misery breaks against your wearied breast, and when in the broken wave your own personal sin rolls in upon you, then no comfort avails, then no help saves," Kuyper reflected. "Then there is but one way out. . . . God Himself as the Fountain of life . . . must take your soul up into Himself."

Evolution as Science

Kuyper delivered "Evolution" on October 20, the nineteenth anniversary of the opening of the university and the last time he would address it in this role. Indeed, it might have been the last time a leading politician in a Western nation could credibly carry off such an effort. Gladstone might have managed it at an earlier day; Woodrow Wilson, soon to become president of Princeton, and Theodore Roosevelt, who, like Kuyper, would become head of government in 1901, might have done it at the time. But precious few subsequent statesmen could match the command that Kuyper showed of the mediating scientific literature on offer (his text cites exactly the authors that historians of science refer to today), not to mention his philosophical sweep and grasp. Nor could most of the conservative Protestants who would challenge Darwinism in the twentieth century. Unlike them, but much more like traditional Calvinists in his own generation, Kuyper did not insist on literalistic readings of the relevant biblical passages, nor quail at the prospect of a very old earth and resort to fantasies about Flood geology. More controversially, then and now, he did not balk at the transmutation of species or at the "spontaneous unfolding of the species in organic life from the cytode or nuclear cell." He was a consistent Calvinist: "We will not force our style upon the Chief Architect of the universe. If He is to be the Architect not in name only but in reality, He will also be supreme in the choice of style." If that style turned out to be evolution over eons of time, the believer would find nothing in Scripture or theology that posed insuperable objections.

In fact, Kuyper found evolutionary doctrine to be commensurate with Christianity on key issues. It taught the unity of the whole creation under law. It taught the descent of the human race from one pair of ancestors, contrary to racist theories that postulated multiple originals. It made original sin plausible by restoring the representative character of Adam and rendered Pelagian innocence and self-determination incredible. It "declare[d] for monotheism over polytheism" and directed the universe to some other end than the entire happiness of humanity. "To this I might add," Kuyper continued, "that the Scriptural charter of Creation eliminates rather than commends the *dramatic* entry of new beings"; Genesis says that "the earth *brought forth*" plants and animals, not that "they were *set down* . . . like pieces on a chessboard."

In addition, Kuyper accorded Darwinian science considerable merit in its own right. At first he sounded Baconian in "exulting" in the "wealth of facts" Darwin's devotees had uncovered, but he quickly moved to the newer philosophy of science in commending the "impetus" the model gave "to even deeper, more methodical research," which disclosed "an entire sequence of phenomena that until then had not received attention or been accounted for." Its support from embryology, paleontology, psychology, and geography could only be counted as considerable, he concluded.

Still, Darwinism strictly taken was probably at its lowest ebb in scientific reputation in the 1890s, and Kuyper was glad to rehearse the principal complaints against it. He passed by Lord Kelvin's argument that the Second Law of Thermodynamics did not permit enough cosmic time for Darwin's form of evolution to have occurred. He mocked the difficulty experimenters had encountered in trying to breed fertile hybrids across species. More seriously, he noted that the geological column contained enough anomalies of "higher" preceding "lower" forms of life to raise doubts about any simple progressive development over time. The fossil record also showed great gaps between stages of evolution, he noted, bespeaking giant leaps forward more than Darwin's gradual process of change. Furthermore, a gradualist model raised questions about the utility in-process of a feature that some species someday might find useful. The ugly sprouts of wings-in-becoming would hardly engender the sex appeal that generations of rising males in an eventual bird species would need for the preferred procreation that Darwin's theory required. These and other problems raised *the* major issue of the time: heredity, or the transmission of inherited — and, to Lamarckian-inclined evolutionists, acquired — characteristics. Under the weight of these objections, historian of science Peter J. Bowler concludes, "the selection theory [i.e., Darwinism proper] had slipped in popularity to such an extent that by 1900 its opponents were convinced that it would never recover."

Many of these scientific problems would be resolved when the new theory of genetics (being developed at just this time by Kuyper's countryman Hugo de Vries) was synthesized with natural selection theory in the 1920s and 1930s and with the postulation of punctuated equilibrium fifty years after that. But these turns would not have satisfied Kuyper any more than did most of the alternatives to strict Darwinism being advanced in his own time, for they all partook of the philosophical postulates that to him constituted the fundamental problem. To some extent Kuyper here joined a whole generation of conservative Protestant critics (and others beside) going back to Princeton theologian Charles Hodge a generation before. "Darwinism is atheism," Hodge concluded, not because it taught radical change over long time, nor even because it postulated natural selection as the mechanism of that change, but because it denied purposeful design in the process. Various evangelical Calvinists in the Anglo-American orbit accommodated Darwinism on this point by locating a God-implanted teleological drive within the evolutionary process itself, a move with which Kuyper was happy enough. But on the Continent, and in England, he saw non- or anti-teleological theories in command, or immanent-design theories that were just as hostile to Christianity and philosophically incoherent besides.

The anti-design voices, such as the German genetics theorist August Weismann, whom Bowler characterizes as "the most dogmatic neo-Darwinist" of the era, Kuyper either bypassed or used to fault the real targets of his speech, the great science popularizers Herbert Spencer and Ernst Haeckel, who ascribed immanent design to material forces. As Kuyper asserted and subsequent historians of science have confirmed, both talked a Darwinian game of random variations accidentally fitting or missing environmental changes, but both were neo-Lamarckian in seeing an inherent *progress* running through — indeed, governing — all these changes. This progress just happened, yet was nonetheless inevitable, their books taught. The human being was but a particular chemical compound, Haeckel insisted, yet was destined for greatness. God could not be the source of being or of the laws that governed its development, Spencer said mildly, because that all dwelled in the domain of the Unknowable. Haeckel was more forthright: no personal god could possibly exist anywhere but in the benighted superstitions of primitive peoples and organized religion. Yet so ardent was his evolutionary vision that Haeckel eventually imputed religious purpose, even divinity of sorts, within the material stream. The Christians' personal God, Kuyper quoted him saying, was a "gaseous vertebrate" that should be more properly understood as "the sum of all atomic powers and oscillations of the ether." Haeckel thus proposed a new cult of Monism that would worship the Evolutionary trinity of the True, the Good, and the Beautiful. "Ladies and Gentlemen," Kuyper appealed to his audience,

> I do not hesitate a moment to brand such reckless play with the holiest things as the most cowardly quasi-religious invention ever put into words. Why not be honest, have the courage of one's conviction, and frankly admit that [such] Evolution is not only atheistic but anti-theistic. . . . Then you would know that you're dealing with *men,* and both sides could prepare for the newly defined condition.

Accordingly, Kuyper concluded, "Evolution is a newly conceived system . . . a newly formed dogma, a newly emerged faith . . . diametrically opposed to the Christian faith." Nor was this merely a projection of his own fears. Haeckel was only the most popular of a phalanx of German voices who for a generation had been pushing "Darwinism" (actually, a variety of evolutionary schemes) as a comprehensive worldview grounded in philosophical materialism and dedicated to supplanting Christianity in the minds of the populace. They did not lack for success. Haeckel's *The Riddle of the Universe at the Close of the Nineteenth Century* was, despite or because of the pretentiousness of its title, the most popular work of German nonfiction prior to World

War I, selling 300,000 copies. Surveys of the German working class at the time discovered that most of those who considered themselves socialists had been converted from their native Christianity not by Marx but by "Darwin" as transmitted by interpreters like Haeckel. His Monist League functioned as a latter-day Masonic order, providing a ritual home for anticlericalism and seeking to solidify the already considerable educational successes that radical science had attained in broader circles.

Critics of Haeckel, Spencer, and other systematizers of Darwinism often criticized them for extrapolating the master's insights beyond biology into realms where they had no scientific warrant. Kuyper joined this chorus, but then interestingly departed from it. Yes, Evolutionaries were arrogant in pretending to sweep all the domains of social science and the human spirit into their tent. Yes, they were "insolent and condescending, lik[ing] to wound pious feelings" in reducing everything to carbon and motion. No, such claims had no demonstrated, perhaps even demonstrable, proof. "Yet," Kuyper argued, "the German evolutionists rather than the English have undoubtedly derived the correct consequences from their principle." Remaining with the strict "facts" of biology sold short the human spirit, which always yearned for larger meanings. It did not even build true science, which "is consumed with passion for the general . . . law that governs the particular case." Logic and psychology alike need system, holistic and consistent explanations of reality from top to bottom. That was what the "dogma of evolution" had provided for the higher forms of unbelief; for that reason it had attracted widespread allegiance; and only by refusing to make "peace for even a moment with this system *as system*" but rather opposing it with the fully articulated consequences of the doctrine of Creation could Christianity have a chance in the war of the spirits.

Once again, for Kuyper, the matter came down to root principle. Behind the rival schools of Evolutionism lay philosophical materialism, the derivation of life from non-life, the triumph of the mechanistic over the organic, the eclipse of the transcendent. In this connection, Kuyper had compliments for the Pantheism and Modernism that he had attacked on earlier occasions, for these at least maintained, even extended, the realm of the spirit, the autonomy of ethics, the dignity of humankind. They both held to "the idea of a guiding purpose" which Darwinians uniformly denied. Implicitly Kuyper was converging as well with contemporary vitalist thinkers such as French philosopher Henri Bergson and American pragmatist William James. Bergson's irrepressible "life force" Kuyper would locate ultimately in divine rather than human activity, and James's authentication of human freedom he would correlate with God's will rather than the forces of probability. But their scorn for Spencer's blank determinism and Haeckel's reductive materialism he shared in full.

If the ultimate issue was philosophical, for Kuyper the pressing issue was ethical. "The emergence of a new faith has usually gone hand in hand with a certain elevation, a certain ennobling of human life," he said. "This time, however, the 'new faith' is closely followed by the shadow of Decadence." In casting life as a struggle in which the weaker necessarily gave way to the stronger as "the only road to higher development," "the Evolution system" was only too fit for the passion, violence, and "usurpation of power" upon which the nineteenth century was ending. For the personal future it warranted the conquest by Nietzsche's superman over all "lower" forms of human life. For the collective future it spelled the power state crushing the rights of smaller nations. That Nietzsche in fact had scorned Darwinism for rooting human excellence in the muck and that Spencer opposed resurgent imperialism as a throwback to a more primitive stage of history Kuyper simply attributed to their inconsistency. He agreed instead with "Darwin's bulldog," T. H. Huxley, that ethics and evolution were set on diverging paths. Whatever beneficence Western societies exhibited "we owe *not* to the ethics of the Evolution-system but precisely to the ethical powers that Evolution excludes," Kuyper insisted. Those powers were rooted, finally, in the principles of the Christian religion, which, while acknowledging full well the corporate dimension of life, still preserved rather than submerged the individual within the species, and which, while grateful for the progress of modern life, still held to the example of "the Christ of God who seeks the lost and has mercy on the weak."

The South African War

All that said, Kuyper's thinking still drafted considerably off evolutionary models. To be sure, the "stronger" might not crush the "weaker," but what about the "higher" over against the "lower"?

Christianity insisted that the cosmos was "precipitate of the spirit" rather than "sublimate of physical atoms," Kuyper said, because it would not countenance that "all higher organized life be pulled down to the spheres of lower inorganic life." Rather, "the lower [must] be subsumed under the higher." Did that apply in sociology as well as cosmology, as systematic consistency would seem to require? South Africa, where war had broken out the week before Kuyper gave his address in Amsterdam, offered a ready place to find out.

South Africa had receded in Kuyper's mind since the mid-1880s, when the Boers and their Dutch supporters decided upon an ecumenical alliance rather than one defined by Calvinist orthodoxy. Its Liberal leadership gave top priority to rapid economic development instead of focusing on language and culture as Kuyper advocated. The economic strategy played right into Britain's hands, he complained, since both were ridden by "the virus of materialism." The disease exploded into a pandemic with discovery of gold in the heart of Transvaal in 1885. Thousands of fortune-seekers poured into the goldfields from around the world, and thousands more were pulled in from the African countryside. From a backwater that the Boers had settled to avoid modernization, the region became a vital spot in the global industrial order, supplying 20 percent of the world's gold. In a parody of the values of that order, Johannesburg burgeoned in little more than a decade from a village to a city of 75,000. One observer said it resembled "Monte Carlo imposed on Sodom and Gomorrah." Little wonder that by the early 1890s Kuyper was recommending the United States over South Africa as an emigrant destination.

But there were limits to his disaffection, and they were breached in early 1896. Working at the behest of the imperial strategist Cecil Rhodes, an adventurer named Leander Jameson led an armed invasion of the Transvaal in hopes of triggering a revolt by the recently arrived "outlanders" against the Boer government. Rhodes in turn was colluding with Joseph Chamberlain, colonial secretary in the new Conservative regime in London. Kuyper cast them as the two arms of a once-again "perfidious Albion." Rhodes was the tentacle of greed and corruption. Having established monopolies in South African diamonds and gold, he won British charter status for his corporation and the prime-ministership of Cape Colony besides. Chamberlain, on the other hand, represented betrayal of principle. Once a follower of Gladstone, he had broken with his leader's proposal for Irish home rule and hitched his ambitions to the star of imperial expansion. Even though the Jameson raid was a fiasco, the Transvaal government recognized the plot in the air and began a dance of negotiation and war preparation to defend its independence. The maneuvers ended with its declaration of war on October 11, 1899.

Kuyper's principal efforts in the Transvaal cause were journalistic, not only to his usual audience in *De Standaard* but to a broad European readership via the distinguished Paris semi-monthly, the *Revue des Deux Mondes.* Its editor, Ferdinand Bruntière, a Catholic sympathetic to Kuyper's work, thought that he could make a good case for the Boers and contacted him to that effect while Kuyper was still mourning in Switzerland. Kuyper did not disappoint. The closest student of the case ranks his "La Crise Sud-Africaine" with essays by South African leader Jan Christiaan Smuts and Dutch journalist Charles Bossevain as the ablest presentations of the Boer cause in the court of general European opinion. The piece was soon translated into Dutch, German, Swedish, and English, the latter by the "Stop the War Committee" in London.

Kuyper's success stemmed in part from his decision not to make military predictions. While he finished the piece in mid-January, at the high tide of Boer triumphs in the field, it appeared in February, when that tide began to quickly recede. More notably, Kuyper rotated from the religious angle he had previously followed to arguments from history, international law, and contemporary social theory. The latter, especially, showed the complications into which his theology could fall.

The core of Kuyper's tract attacked the legal case that Britain had mounted to justify its actions. His argument here was an advocate's, not a judge's, and so mixed a ready command of international law and comparative immigration policy with special pleading. His appeal to history subjected English behavior to a relentless hermeneutic of suspicion, sometimes with good warrant. His most notable innovation was to turn upside down the praise he had given American Protestantism on his tour just the year before; now, at British missionary hands, activism became meddling, and humanitarianism hypocrisy. This held especially for the sort of English evangelicals he had once honored as co-workers in the sainted Réveil. He linked Methodists and the Clapham sect with Deists as sentimentalists suffering Rousseauian delusions about the noble savage. Indeed, "the Boers know too well that they have had no worse enemies than these gentlemen in clerical uniform," Kuyper sniped. Since the gentlemen in question professed deep concern for native peoples, Kuyper scored good points on a quick tour of British colonial depredations as experienced by North American Indians, New Zealand Maoris, and the Zulu right next door. British missionaries cried piteously about native rights; British troops slaughtered those natives by the thousand.

Races and Racism

Thus Kuyper came to the issue of race, with a reverberation a hundred years later that is the opposite of what he intended. The most startling effect is the measure of his silence; in the eighty pages of his text, the native peoples get three paragraphs. The South African war *was* a race war, Kuyper asserted, but the "races" involved were the Dutch and Anglo-Saxon. The "tenacity of the race from the Low Countries" over against their English overlords stemmed from the "absolute incompatibility" between the national characters of the two. The English were activists, quick to organize but much given to show; the Dutch were slow and introspective, but persevering. The Boer branch on the Dutch tree might fall short (how far short, Kuyper was unwilling to admit) on education, political organization, and proper tone, but they had nothing to apologize for vis à vis the average denizen of Britain in terms of piety and morals. Indeed, they feared above all else that an invading British army would spread syphilis as wantonly as it had in India!

The rest of their profile approximated Kuyper's own ideals. The Boers were hunter-pastoralists and pioneers. They were possessed of "natural sagacity," fierce courage, and an "insatiable love of liberty." They practiced decentralized, direct democracy. Rousseau's noble savage lived after all — only in white skin.

For his polite European audience Kuyper gave the Boers' religious character less attention than their republican virtue. He associated that virtue particularly with "Boer women," who were

> free from all desire of luxury . . . [and] almost exclusively devoted to their husbands and children. They are strong and courageous. Without dishonoring their sex they handle the rifle and mount the horse like men. The enthusiasm of their national feeling often surpasses even that of their husbands.

Above all they were fertile, and that spelled the doom of British policy. England might conquer their men, Kuyper predicted, but "will never destroy the fecundity of the Boer woman. In less than a century, from their former numbers of 60,000, the Boers . . . have grown to half a million. In the coming century, they will reach three, four, five millions, and South Africa will be theirs."

But demography cut both ways, and it forced Kuyper finally to deal with the other "race" at hand. "The Blacks are increasing in South Africa to an extent which may well give cause for uneasiness," he observed. "Profound anxiety" would have been more like it. Kuyper averred from his (otherwise unrecorded) "confidential conversations with men-of-color of all conditions" on his America tour that "conquest over the white man remains and always will remain their chimerical ideal." Thus, the utter folly of British policy: "if, sooner or later, the struggle of extermination between Whites and Blacks breaks out afresh in South Africa, all the responsibility for it will fall upon Mr. Chamberlain and his Jingo journalists." But how could race war break out "afresh" if, as Kuyper claimed in refutation of British "sentimentalists," the Boer subjugation of the native peoples had been so mild and easy? Why so fearful a threat from so benighted a stock? In these contradictions Kuyper's views were one with racist thinking everywhere, from the American South to Nazi Germany. More telling was his departure from some of his usual attitudes. His sympathies for the poor and weak went here to the Boers over against the British but not to the native population, which he derogated as perpetually childlike, "an inferior race." In the United States and his native land, Kuyper applauded "commingling of blood" as the fount of social progress and cultural vitality. But in South Africa he praised the Boers' absolute ban on "race" mixture (regarded as "incest"!) as their highest mark of morality and their only hope for the future.

The only explanation for such a reversal was Kuyper's full-blown subscription to contemporary European race theory, to which he added a dollop of biblical imagery. The theory postulated first a stark hierarchy of fixed qualities, with the "Aryan race" on top and the "Negro" at the very bottom. It also interpreted history as a unified evolutionary development. Kuyper had recently repeated this heliotropic mantra in his first lecture at Princeton: "There is but one world-stream, broad and fresh, which from the beginning bore the promise of the future." It followed an ever-westering course from the Middle

East via Western Europe to the American West. Along the way Africa had been left on the margins as a stagnant marsh, supporting "a far lower form of existence." Kuyper's biblical addendum was "the prophetic blessing of Noah," "in entire conformity" to which "the children of Shem and Japheth have been the sole bearers of the development of the race," while "no impulse for any higher life has ever gone forth" from the children of Ham. It was as if, one observer has said, Kuyper rejected social Darwinism for a social version of Mendelian genetics, crossing "a materialistic theory of selection . . . with an idealistic theory of election."

The South African case also illustrated Kuyper's more general theory of peoples and group relations in light of the theology he was concurrently elaborating in *Common Grace*. In the Netherlands, part of the most advanced region of global development, the antithesis between Christians and others was most advanced, demanding that people sort themselves out according to their root religious principles. In the rising land of the United States — i.e., one less developed but also the land of the future — people might still mingle under the prosperity of common grace; yet the Christians among them were called to hone their religious consciousness in anticipation of the wars of principle to come. South Africa represented humanity at a much earlier stage, with tribes locked in a raw phase of mortal combat. The pastoral Boers and aboriginal peoples faced each other bearing racial seeds of "higher" or "lower" potential, the former settling among the latter as "a conquering race" just as the Normans had among the Anglo-Saxons centuries before. Boer vs. Briton, by contrast, amounted to a contest of national character, the more "natural" folk in this case deserving favor over the merely sophisticated. The observer might wonder if Kuyper was not copying the theory of the much-feared Haeckel that "ontogeny recapitulates phylogeny." Certainly he shared with the much-maligned Rousseau — and the soon-to-be controversial Freud — a real ambivalence about civilization and its discontents.

Legacy

In any case, the history at hand in South Africa proved harsh for Kuyper's favorites. In February 1900, the month his essay appeared, the Boers lost a whole army and two city sieges. In mid-March British forces took Bloemfontein, and so symbolically the Orange Free State; in early June, Pretoria and the Transvaal followed. Just as Kuyper had anticipated from the cases of Aceh and the Philippines, however, the Boers resorted to highly mobile and effective guerrilla warfare. Britain responded with a scorched-earth policy that laid waste some 30,000 farms, and an internment strategy that deposited the guerrillas' dependents in concentration camps. Some 28,000 Boer civilians died there, three-quarters of them children; likewise nearly 20,000 of the 115,000 people of color who had also been confined. Kuyper's essay had opened on a note of rhetorical astonishment that the nineteenth century, which had dawned on the "splendid promise of liberty," was passing away "disgraced . . . by a war of aggression." On another view, the twentieth century had dawned on all too prophetic a note.

Kuyper caught the auguries right. He forecast that Britain would pay enormously before the war was through. It ultimately had to field some 450,000 troops, nearly as many as the entire Boer population, at a cost of 22,000 dead and 200 million pounds in expenditures. Such a course, he continued, "would undoubtedly presage the beginning of the end" of the British Empire — and so, most historians agree, it turned out to be. The follies that British officers Lord Horatio Herbert Kitchener, General John French, and Major Douglas Haig committed in South Africa these same officers would repeat twenty-five years later against German lines in France. In South Africa they ran troops directly at Boer entrenchments at the cost of hundreds of casualties per battle; on the Western front the count would run to the hundreds of thousands, decimate the English elite, and thus weaken the head as well as the arms of British imperial power. Even with all that sacrifice, Kuyper predicted, the conquest would avail nothing in South Africa, for British arms and administration galvanized Afrikaner nationalism as nothing else could do. Meanwhile, demography worked much as Kuyper anticipated. Not even ten years after the peace, the Union of South Africa was constituted on a white-supremacist basis, "Boer" consolidating with "Brit" against London's influence abroad and the native majority at home.

If Kuyper might take this as vindication, he could take only mixed pleasure in the state that white South Africans made. He decried the anglophilic language and culture policy upon which the new government set out. He decried as well, and quite contrary to his theory of pluriform development, the Boers' commitment to cultivating a distinct Afrikaner nationalism centered on Afrikaans as a language. The nationalism was derivative and the language but a patois, he opined; they should rather aspire to be truly Dutch, and Calvinist too.

Key leaders in the Reformed churches in South Africa would work their way to Amsterdam to study at the Free University, and they would have considerable impact in shaping Afrikaner thought and identity in the 1920s and 1930s. They magnified the suggestion Kuyper had taken up from S. J. Du Toit that Afrikaners had a holy calling in their land. They savored the biblical warrant that Kuyper gave to the pluriformity of human cultures, giving the Tower of Babel episode normative status for human history and interrelationships. Most crucially, they adapted philosopher H. J. Stoker's addition of the *volk* to the sovereign "spheres" ordained of God. With that, Romantic sociology and European racism received a warrant beyond appeal — and quite beyond what Kuyper had accorded them.

The results were startling: a system of separate organization based on race instead of religious confession, reflecting and magnifying a gross maldistribution of resources, and embodied in an institutional apparatus that was the nightmare of Antirevolutionary thought. The state under South African *apartheid* became the single largest employer of the white population in the nation. Schools begun under parental control were seized and subordinated to uniform curricula dictated from the top down. The volk-church ideal predominated in the largest Afrikaner denomination; indeed, *apartheid* was arguably rooted more in the national theology of Utrecht than in the neo-Calvinism of Amsterdam. In any case, under Stoker's doctrine of "interpenetration," all the separate Kuyperian spheres were infused with volkish spirit — that is to say, served its hegemony. The 1899 text behind this development was not Kuyper's "Evolution" but Houston Stewart Chamberlain's proto-fascist scripture, *The Foundations of the Nineteenth Century.* That the ethics of righteousness Kuyper defended in his tract could be brought captive by other themes in his system to the purposes of Chamberlain's racism revealed the central blindness in Kuyper's eye, and bequeathed the greatest tragedy of his influence.

CHAPTER FIFTEEN

The Peak of Power

Kuyper approached the 1901 elections with high hopes and a touch of anxiety. His hopes were grounded in the disarray on the Liberal side, as he reminded the Antirevolutionary Party convention that April. If "the Christian part of the nation" simply held together rather than rupturing over *its* divisions as it had in 1897, then their natural majority across the country would assert itself at the polls come June. That prospect, naturally, provoked as great a joy in the ranks as fear on the other side.

Deeper down, the prospect posed a real challenge for a group accustomed to being outsiders. Kuyper's keynote address thus kicked off the campaign on three notes at once. One was boilerplate campaign rhetoric: "the very same Calvinistic principles" that "once made our country strong and great" would provide direction into a glorious future. At the same time he reassured the opposition that "on that decisive day in June, however intense the struggle has been, we shall greet our opponents not as *enemies* but as *fellow citizens*." The greatest challenge would be for his followers to prove their ability to govern, "not as a closed-off group, not as a coterie [his epithet for the Liberals], neither as a self-seeking caste," but with the same sensibility that had always marked their personal and family conduct — as "citizens of our country, seeking the best for our fatherland."

Kuyper's prediction was correct. The religious coalition (Kuyper's followers along with a more conservative Protestant mélange led by Lohman and a substantial bloc of Roman Catholics) swept to a 58-42 majority in the Lower House of the States-General, a ten-seat swing away from a Liberal government that was indeed divided and worn out. Kuyper was also correct in noting that victory came from suppressing in-house hostilities toward Catholicism that had cost his coalition dearly in 1897. He was further correct in anticipating that the responsibility of governance entailed a steep learning curve for the coalition. If anything, Kuyper underestimated how steep that curve would be, not least for himself. His convention speech was also, if understandably, less than candid in acknowledging the remarkable run of legislation passed under the previous decade of Liberal rule, a legacy that constricted some of his own room for maneuver. Finally, and characteristically, Kuyper overestimated the power of "principle" to command history. Instead, events — some predictable, some unforeseen — created much of the agenda and the most serious challenges of his term in office. Half of Kuyper's hopes would be frustrated. But the other half would be achieved, and the momentum he began, eventually harnessed by his successors and opponents alike, made Kuyper's term mark a genuine new era in Dutch political history.

The Liberal Legacy

By almost every measure Dutch society in 1901 was in better shape than it had been in 1891, when Kuyper had delivered his speech on the social crisis. Severe flu epidemics still struck every winter in the early 1890s, and Friesland's "starving time" went on for a few more years. But by 1895 the economic depression that had ravaged Dutch agriculture for twenty years was over and a new twenty-year period of strong, steady growth was at hand. Real wages rose thirty percent from 1892 through 1900 while food prices dropped, yielding better nutrition across the board. The Netherlands' population increased thirty percent from 1890 to 1910 as death rates resumed their downward trend and birth rates stayed high. In part this was a function of rising rates of marriage and at a younger average age, pleasant data for Kuyper's social ideals. Equally good news was a sharp decrease in rates of alcohol consumption, which would continue through World War I. Kuyper — and a great many others, from all political persuasions — could also applaud a remarkable spread of Dutch savings banks: between 1880 and 1900 the number of accounts increased sixteen-fold, the value of deposits even more.

To some extent these trends simply made up for the hard times of the 1880s. But they were also the harvest of the country's substantial investments in education via the laws of 1857 and 1878, which were now supplying improved human capital to sustain economic growth. In fact, by the time Kuyper's cabinet took charge, the Dutch economy was undergoing a "radical structural transformation" marked by real industrialization, continued innovation in agriculture, and sharply increased levels of trade. Dutch international commerce rose faster than world averages even in this late summer of globalization prior to World War I. The colonial trade particularly soared, not least with the end of the Aceh War in 1904, doubling its share of the national income between 1890 and 1913. Icons of the new order appeared everywhere, from the founding of Philips Electric in 1891 to the country's first women's suffrage union in 1898 to the First International Peace Conference, which met at The Hague in 1899. Delegates there could see rails being laid for the new electric trams, and the automobile had already debuted there a few years earlier. Both were dwarfed by the explosion of the Netherlands' bicycle culture, which dated from this time.

These developments instilled a mood of confidence as well as an economic cushion that gave Kuyper's government room to innovate. Similar circumstances made this a great progressive moment around the world, not just in Europe and the United States but in South America, Japan, and China. Different countries (and different movements within countries) defined "progress" differently, of course, and arrived at different outcomes. For instance, one month into Kuyper's term Theodore Roosevelt became president of the United States, beginning twenty years of reformist administrations there. By contrast, as Kuyper left office in June 1905, Czar Nicholas II was scrambling to save Russia from further revolution by promising concessions toward representative government. For all their differences, however, progressive movements shared three motifs. All yearned for a fresh form of politics to replace decrepit regimes. All felt liberated from the dead hand of laissez-faire orthodoxy to intervene in the economy — at least to blunt the hardest edges of the new industrial order, at most to move toward real "democracy" in economic as well as political life. And all anticipated that these changes would unleash a new personal vitality that would lead (one more crucial assumption) to a more harmonious society. Kuyper shared every one of these hopes.

The Netherlands' revival was a trend he inherited, however. The turnaround began under three Liberal cabinets in the 1890s, whose policies redesigned the landscape he would inherit. Even though some of this legislation ironically fated these to be their last years of undivided rule, the Liberal record of accomplishment would be hard for anyone to match, much less a theologically trained leader of a new-style politics and an under-experienced party. The first break-through came in the taxation reforms instituted by Minister of Finance Nicolaas Pierson, a former bank executive and economics professor.* Most of the country's public revenue still came from excise taxes on consumption, a highly regressive system that drained cash from the countryside and left the rich virtually untouched. Pierson's bill taxed interest on investment and business profits, the precursor of an eventual income tax. A few years later inheritance taxes were raised, and the burden and arbitrary character of local taxes were reduced. The goal was not full equity, much less income redistribution, but greater efficiency and more revenue. That is, the bill represented fiscal modernization of the classic-liberal sort that, over time, irresistibly approached Pierson's own progressive-liberal ideal.

If tax policy exposed the fault-line at the heart of Liberalism, the rift was exacerbated by Tak van Poortvliet's franchise proposal in 1893. Indeed, for most of the 1890s, divisions within and alliances across parties were more common than solidarity in any group; the Kuyper-Lohman fight was mirrored among Liberals, Socialists, and Roman Catholics. It was left to the hard-bitten utilitarian Sam van Houten to offer the compromise of 1896 that effectively removed the franchise issue from national politics for the next twenty years despite opposition to it, left and right. Catholics along with Lohman's conservative Calvinists liked Van Houten's proposal only a little more than Tak's. Kuyper lampooned it for being a cloth too big to serve as the conservatives' napkin but too small to cover a democratic table. Even so, the Liberals would discover that, with forty percent of the electorate now being working class and with rising incomes steadily qualifying more and more people to vote, the new law doomed their hold on power.

But one last Liberal cabinet, this time led by Pierson himself, fashioned their lasting legacy. They established a national health ser-

---

*Several other Liberal leaders also had formal training in economics, a crucial asset at this juncture and one typical of progressive movements around the world.

vice with inspectors to enforce uniform codes, and set basic housing standards that municipalities had to meet. With Kuyper's support they eliminated the option of purchasing exemptions from the military draft and instituted Chambers of Labor to represent workers' needs. They fixed eleven hours as the maximum workday and moved toward compulsory arbitration in lieu of strikes. There followed another set of bills that Kuyper opposed. By a one-vote margin, after some of the most intense debates in Dutch parliamentary history, the Lower House made elementary education compulsory for all children. Kuyper objected that the lack of enough Christian schools to serve orthodox parents' demands would effectively force their children into secular education. In the courts, juvenile law started moving from punishment to education in dealing with youthful infractions — eroding the moral basis of social order, Kuyper complained.

Finally, a bill was passed requiring industrial workers to carry accident insurance coordinated by a single government bank. Kuyper accepted the compulsory provision but wanted it extended to all workers, and wanted it provided by local cooperatives on an industry- or company-wide basis. His year-long quest to thus incorporate his localist-communal social philosophy was conducted in collaboration with the chief counsel of a leading Dutch railroad firm, who wanted a voluntary and individualistic system for purely financial reasons. The contradiction was no worse than Lohman and the Roman Catholics working with the anticlerical Van Houten in slowing democratization, but it signaled a collusion that the "red Kuyper" would have resisted. For the Liberals' part, the Industrial Accidents bill was the one piece of a comprehensive package of social legislation that they could maneuver through Parliament. Nonetheless, it "began to prepare the foundations for the modern Dutch welfare state," and it required the support of Antirevolutionary MPs to pass. Adding this to the Chambers of Labor, which Kuyper had long endorsed, the Pierson administration launched the state model that Kuyper's Antirevolutionary successors would extend, and that would become full-fledged after World War II. A pattern was set that Kuyper only half liked, but could not in any case undo.

A Rough Beginning

It was against the backdrop of this record, and even more the high expectations of his followers, that Kuyper formed his cabinet in July 1901. He went on retreat to the Hotel Métropole in Brussels to compile a wish list, then spent a month trying to make it come true. It proved to be a more difficult project than he anticipated. For one, Queen Wilhelmina was loathe to appoint him to head the cabinet. She shared the royal family's suspicion that this "agitator" was a republican at heart, and she had not forgotten his absence from her coronation (during his trip to America) or his putative slurs upon her father. She resented the condescension she perceived in his attitude toward her as a youth (she was but twenty years old) and as a woman. Faced with no alternative, she hailed him to the palace to set some bounds on his administration. There would be strict neutrality with respect to the South African War, lest British naval protection of the East Indies be jeopardized. The pacification of Aceh would go forward, as would reform of the army. And there would be no repeating of a previous instance in which he published Her Majesty's confidential remarks in his newspaper.

The next challenge lay in the Antirevolutionaries' lack of a deep bench. As an upstart movement, they had few members with government experience and relatively few with the state-certified university degree required for office. Just as much, Kuyper's personality worked against him. The one previous Antirevolutionary head of cabinet, Aeneas Mackay, turned down his offer of the crucial ministry of Domestic Affairs; so did Lohman. They remembered Kuyper's criticism too well to countenance a close working relationship with him or shared responsibility for his actions.

More disappointing was Theo Heemskerk's decline of the post. Himself son of a prime minister, Kuyper's aide in the panel-incident at the start of the Doleantie, and chair of the great 1897 fête in Kuyper's honor, Heemskerk seemed destined to be Kuyper's eventual successor. Now pressed hard to join the cabinet, Heemskerk kept hedging, pleading devotion to his post on the Amsterdam city council. Kuyper stressed the priority of the national level. When that did not avail, he invoked providence: "There is no one else. So you can see for yourself God's hand in this and *may* not toy with our country's future." Finally, guilt: "It will be your responsibility before God and man when people hear: 'He sacrificed *the whole Christian cause of people and nation* to be an *alderman.'* Wouldn't you regret this the rest of your life, and wouldn't it become a burden on your conscience that you could never remove?" Nothing worked, however, for Heemskerk was hearing an overruling voice. His wife, a Polish émigré of aristocratic connections, wired Heemskerk from her Swiss vacation: "Kuyper is a liar; the best men forsake him, and you want to stoop to that? It would be madness. I will not go to The Hague under such circumstances."

This was more than a personal setback. With Heemskerk unavailable, Kuyper had to give up his plan to split off from Domestic Affairs a new department of Labor that he would lead himself. He had to take over the old department as it was, diffusing his focus. One structural change he did execute was to become permanent chair of the cabinet, a role that had previously rotated from one minister to the other over the course of the term. Future leaders followed this precedent, making Kuyper functionally the Netherlands' first "prime minister."* For now Kuyper towered over his colleagues, with the exception of two Roman Catholics, J. W. Bergansius at War and Johannes Loeff at Justice. Both of these men, Bergansius especially, had ample experience, good working relationships with both Kuyper and the queen, and a technical command in their departments that won everybody's respect. Bergansius finally carried out the modernization of the army that had been stalled (mostly by his fellow Catholics) ever since the Franco-Prussian War. Loeff's presence gave Catholics assurance of equitable enforcement of the laws and laid the groundwork for future social legislation. But another Roman Catholic, J. J. Harte van Tecklenburg, proved a weak hand at Finance, particularly in light of the Liberals' strong record there. Some eminent Catholics warned Kuyper that Harte was "lethargic" and "pedantic." In fact, only in 1904 did he come up with new revenue sources (tariff increases) to finance the cabinet's efforts to promote temperance, child protection, and army reform while simultaneously slashing the lottery and the state income it represented.

Weak figures on the Protestant side included two "men with double names" whose pedigree proved to be greater than their talent. T. A. J. van Asch van Wijck assumed Colonial Affairs with some experience in Surinam but not in the crucial East Indies. His death the next

*The title was not officially used until 1945.

year allowed Kuyper to introduce the younger Alexander W. F. Idenburg to what proved to be a stellar career in the upper echelons of
Dutch government, proof of the democratic potential upon which
Kuyper had wagered his party. Idenburg looked especially strong
compared to the new minister of Foreign Affairs, Robert Melvil, Baron
van Lynden, from the old Utrecht elite. Melvil van Lynden adminis-
tered the Permanent Court of Arbitration newly founded on Carnegie
money at The Hague, but he was respected neither by the Dutch diplomatic corps (never having served abroad himself) nor by the queen.
Paying more attention to the perquisites than to the business of office, he made one error after another until finally being dismissed in
1904. The ARP's thin ranks told here more than anywhere else.

This was particularly unfortunate, since the first piece of unfinished business that Kuyper inherited was the South African War. He
had thundered for the Boer cause in Parliament and *De Standaard*
during the Liberals' last term, being especially critical of then-Foreign
Minister W. H. de Beaufort's reticence on the issue. Beaufort was the
epitome of what Kuyper disliked in Dutch government — a snob, a
classic free-market Liberal, and a derisive opponent of religious politics in general and of Kuyper in particular. It was painful for Kuyper,
then, to have to accede to the official neutralist posture respecting
South Africa. His response was to make this an "active" rather than a
passive neutrality of the Beaufort type. In the two weeks after Christmas 1901, Kuyper undertook a mission to Paris and London to offer
the Dutch as an intermediary in negotiations between Britain and the
Boer republics. The British cabinet, supporting General Kitchener, replied that they would treat only with the Boers' military command, on
the pretext that they were fighting an insurrection, not invading a nation. Kuyper returned home claiming to have made the Netherlands a
player again on the global scene. In fact, just as Melvil van Lynden
worried, the British took his efforts to signal that the Dutch had given
up on a Boer victory.

In domestic affairs, meanwhile, Kuyper had to implement all the
recently passed Liberal laws on accident insurance and compulsory
education. As these were expansive ventures in uncharted territory,
they took up a great deal of energy and revenue. But his own dreams of
social legislation were even larger. Accident insurance should be extended to all (not just industrial) workers, and to their dependents,
too. Old-age pensions were even more urgent. Both of these, however,

depended upon health insurance, which Kuyper proposed to make compulsory for all. Replicating the Antirevolutionaries' venerable slogan about education, he wanted private insurance to be the norm, with a public option as backup. Kuyper thus offered a complex bill that was an organic whole for an organic society, architectonic in scale, thick with technical details, and markedly different from the classic-liberal, progressive-liberal, and socialist options that were typically on offer. As such, the draft ran into opposition from all sides in Parliament, as well as legal objections from royal councilors and the courts. In the end Kuyper decided to defer this agenda to the second term that he anticipated winning in 1905.

The Prime Minister Gives a Political Education

Beyond policy, Kuyper early on faced any number of questions about the character and legitimacy of a religiously-defined coalition running a modern state. Here the professor could play from his strengths; he turned Parliament's question-hour into something of a seminar in applied political philosophy. Separation of church and state? No one had advocated that earlier or more consistently than I, Kuyper replied, citations from *Ons Program* at the ready. But that did not, could not, mean a separation of religion from politics. Beginning with a quotation from Goethe in the original German, Kuyper offered a disquisition deploying Luther, Calvin, Kant, and the German Idealists to the effect that, as religion and politics both involved fundamental convictions, they necessarily bore implications for each other. But that did not mean a lockstep theocracy, Kuyper continued. No religion prescribes a fixed line of civil policy, least of all Dutch Calvinism. Hollanders have always treasured two things, he maintained: "first *religion,* and second *negotiation.* . . . And I not only prefer but positively hope that these two will never depart from our nation, for it would be miserable to surrender either one. Hold both fast, and the land will prosper."

Kuyper had to return to this point whenever a bill seemed to deviate from his platform or the coalition showed internal disagreements. He had to be more concrete and pragmatic in the Chamber than in the lecture hall or editorial office, as indeed he had already been as an opposition leader during the Pierson administration. "Homogeneity in politics cannot mean and never has meant that the members of a political party come to the same conclusion on every point," he pointed out. "There is not a single political party in this country that does not adjust its principles to circumstances and does not find a degree of difference among its members as to the application of principles." See the Liberals on this, the Socialists on that, and our dearly departed Conservatives over there. As to the charge that my reasonable discourse in this House belies what I said in the press or at party rallies? Surely his audience understood: "we all speak high Dutch in the Chamber, low Dutch at the polls."

The particular partners in this coalition puzzled those who still could not fathom a "monster alliance" between Dort and Rome. What the two shared was more important than their theological differences for political purposes, Kuyper explained. All the secular parties, however personally devout some of their members might be, appealed to strictly human capacities for political guidance, while Catholics and Protestants agreed that, human nature being fallen, the aid of divine revelation was necessary in public as well as private matters. But did not such a broad commonality, the opposition wondered, amount to the very "Christianity beyond theological differences" that his party adamantly rejected for the nation's schools? No, just the opposite, Kuyper replied. Faith in politics works by "the formula of a Christianity *beneath* differences in belief." That is, we start from the top with "the powerful work of the church," which effects an alteration in hearts and homes, from which we hope "a precipitate of the life of faith" will seep "down deeply" into public life.

A Socialist MP countered that such a filtered Christianity amounted to a simple extension of the Golden Rule, which was the aim of his party, too. We do all wish to love our neighbors as ourselves, Kuyper agreed, but the religious parties obeyed this rule out of "the *first* and *great* commandment: You shall love the Lord your God with all your mind, with all your strength." Thus, our differences with the Honorable Member are not that, as a Socialist, he is a radical, for we too want to get down to *radix,* the roots of things, Kuyper declared. Nor is it that he is a democrat, for we too have always been democrats — Christian Democrats arrayed alongside Social- and Liberal-Democrats. Rather, the difference lies ultimately in *worldview,* whereupon Kuyper quoted long sections of Marx and his revisionist disciple Eduard Bernstein to conclude that the Social Democrats' agenda inescapably rested on its materialist philosophical foundations, whereas Christian Democrats necessarily put "spiritual" forces first. Why then not imitate Gladstone? asked an exasperated Liberal; he was surely spiritual enough and moral to a fault but never theologized his politics. Because, Kuyper mourned, precisely that lack of attention to first principles left Gladstone's party prone to the imperialist perversions that overtook it once he retired. Gladstone the Christian could not be an imperialist, but his party, not being explicitly Christian, could, and had, to the grave harm of all Europe.

Ethical Hopes, Violent Means

Such repartee eventually gave way to concrete business. In early 1903 a wildcat railroad strike broke out, frightening conservatives with the specter of anarchy and provoking Kuyper to forceful countermeasures. In early 1904 the thirty-year war in Aceh came to an end thanks to a military surge that raised protests back home about brutality to non-combatants. Two core Antirevolutionary promises thus came into question: a harmonious resolution of the social question and an "ethical" colonial policy. Idenburg helped Kuyper meet the latter challenge; Lohman did not serve him as well on the former.

The Antirevolutionary program had been one of the first to demand radical reforms in the already once-reformed East Indies regime, but by the time Kuyper took office the sentiment had become widespread. In 1899 the Liberal journal *De Gids* published a definitive article on the "debt of honor" that the Dutch owed the Indies, while the Socialists regularly recited the depredations wrought there by wide-open capitalism. Kuyper agreed with that charge but thought the previous state-monopoly to have been no better and the Socialists' "materialist" nostrums quite inadequate. Before any reform could be implemented, however, the last rebellious holdouts in Aceh had to be pacified. This was an ongoing policy specified by royal command, and it was agreed to by all parties, including, reluctantly, the head of the Socialist caucus in Parliament. Given his erstwhile antiwar stance, Kuyper counted it as one of those necessary adjustments to reality he had mentioned in question-time. "Pacification" meant eradicating guerrilla resistance in the interior, and it proceeded by a five-month campaign that left nearly 3,000 locals dead, over a third of them women and children. It was a Catholic MP who led the protest on the floor of Parliament. From the other side of the coalition, Idenburg and Lohman defended "our small band of heroes."

Idenburg wrought such redemption out of the situation as he could by mixing official Antirevolutionary prescriptions with the fruits of twenty years' experience in the East Indies. He also had a supple, realistic personality that was — quite better than Kuyper's — suited for deal-making. The "debt of honor" that the Dutch owed the colonies required, first, an interest-free loan of 30 million guilders ($12 million U.S., later raised substantially) for infrastructure improvement. Economic exploitation would be repaid by long-term economic development. But Kuyper had always insisted that the Dutch needed to invest in the moral well-being of the Indonesians as well, accelerating their cultural development along authentic native lines so as to prepare for eventual independence. The paradox of paternalism and indigenization evident here was compounded by Kuyper's insistence that the Christian interest in the colonies be promoted in the face of its majority-Muslim population. Idenburg resolved the issue with a classic Antirevolutionary separation of public and private duties. The Netherlands, "Christian nation" though it was, had no right to proselytize for the faith in the Indies, he repeated, while prudence cautioned against needlessly provoking Muslim resistance. The government could and should, however, give full attention to religious and cultural factors instead of focusing solely on the bottom line, and in that context it was obliged to create an even playing field for Christian witness. Yet that witness would remain exclusively with nongovernmental agencies in such promising endeavors as schools and medical missions.

On top of that, and typical of progressive regimes around the world, the Kuyper cabinet promoted good government for the colonies as a value in its own right. Idenburg insisted on strict and transparent accounting in colonial affairs. He commissioned a systematic investigation into the well-being of the Indonesian lower classes, a longstanding demand of Dutch progressives which turned out to be just as long in the fulfillment; the survey was published in thirty-five volumes between 1904 and 1918. He also ordered an investigation of the coolie-labor system, much to the planters' dismay, and found the results so appalling that he suppressed publication of the data, releasing only the executive summary. He added an Antirevolutionary decentralizing twist in granting greater self-governance to local communities. The cabinet left hanging, however, the question of opening the ranks of colony-wide administration to native applicants.

All in all, Kuyper could count colonial policy as a solid success. It followed his old principles while gaining support from other parties. It focused and accelerated existing momentum into an enduring policy formula.

His response to the railroad strike, by contrast, provoked enormous dissonance, even though most parties agreed that action had to be taken. The event still ranks as the largest civil disturbance in Dutch history. The trouble began with a walkout by Amsterdam dockworkers in January 1903 in protest against dangerous working conditions and the employers' refusal to recognize their union. By month's end the action had spread to the railroads, bringing much of the nation to a halt. In early February the government called out the militia at Amsterdam and a few other critical junctions, only to see the companies accede to the strikers' terms. This quick triumph rekindled an old debate in socialist ranks. The political wing, under the lead of Pieter J. Troelstra, wanted to protect the workers' gains in Parliament. The anarchist side, inspired by Kuyper's one-time co-belligerent Domela Nieuwenhuis, disparaged such reform Marxism in favor of a general strike. Domela, with his messianic streak, envisioned a spontaneous eruption of revolutionary consciousness from the collective soul of the oppressed, to demolish the old order at one stroke. Demonstrations to that end, however uncalculated, should be ventured as signs of the new day.

That prospect, as well as the troubling implications of the strike just past, prompted the cabinet to introduce a package of three bills in late February. The first repeated Kuyper's (and Justice Minister Loeff's) response in the first instance that an independent commission be formed to investigate labor conditions and recommend such reforms as were needed. The second empowered the government to nationalize public utilities like the railroads in future emergencies and provide substitute workers (likely the military) to operate them. The third declared strikes undertaken for political as opposed to economic purposes to be "criminal" and therefore punishable by law. Troelstra denounced the measures as a declaration of "class war"; Kuyper answered that the public interest required protection against any attempted "seizure" of "the ship of state" by a particular faction.

As the debate in the States General ran on into April, the anarchists upped the ante by calling a general strike. But the response was anything but general, for not only the religious unions but the political socialists doubted the wisdom of the action. Troelstra tried to intervene to "de-escalate" the situation, but the strike dissipated on its own. Thousands of workers lost their jobs, and Kuyper's legislation passed handily. But his image underwent a facelift in the process. Kuyper the social reformer disappeared from view, replaced by the moralizing authoritarian.

Kuyper always did have potential for the latter image. Establishing fixed authority was the starting point of both his social theory and political program, and he sounded the theme explicitly in floor debate during the April general strike. The immediate problem at hand, he asserted, involved a small band of dedicated revolutionaries who aimed "to overthrow authority and to put in its place another authority, that of the workers." Back of that lay a meta-ethical issue involving the fundamental character of the country. All societies exist by virtue of a moral bond, Kuyper declared, a commitment to shared rules and concepts. The anarchists' action broke that covenant and so posed a problem not just for Christians but "for anyone who still holds to our national concepts of justice and morality."

But Kuyper took pains to avoid the authoritarian label. He invoked examples far and near to support a premise which historians of different stripes have tended to uphold — that any non-socialist party in any industrialized country would have taken similar action to his, or worse. Kuyper cited some of these "great disasters": the bloody clashes between Carnegie's private army and striking steelworkers near Pittsburgh in 1892, the Pullman strike that was suppressed by the U.S. National Guard in 1894, the riots and repression closer at hand in Germany, France, and Belgium. By such measure, he argued, to merely call up the militia as he had was a modest measure and, as it turned out, a sound preventive. Finally, he reiterated his party's defense of the right to strike over economic grievances; so the cabinet had demonstrated during the textile strike at Enschede the year before and, indeed, during the initial dock strike in Amsterdam.

Off the record, Kuyper could have claimed even more. The minutes of cabinet deliberations and his personal correspondence indicate that he and Loeff shared a policy of investigation and mediation even after the dock strike spread to the railroads. At that juncture, however, Loeff fell ill and Kuyper turned to Lohman for advice. Lohman lived up to his reputation in advocating sharp, repressive action. He underscored the threat to general order that the strike posed and deftly appealed to Kuyper's self-conception. The better elements of the nation were deeply worried by the strike, he wrote Kuyper, and that fear would spread down the ranks with untold consequences unless a strong and decisive leader took action. The relief so wrought would more than atone for any grief from the opposition. Kuyper did not need Lohman or anyone else to invent this line of thought for him, nor was he inclined to modulate a hard line once he had embarked upon it.

As time went on he defended his policy more sharply, particularly in exchanges with Troelstra. The latter was particularly outraged by Kuyper's characterization of the strike as "criminal," and vented his ire every time the issue came up again. Just as regularly Kuyper replied with a long review of events, delivered in didactic tones. When Troelstra, as a good Marxist, declared that "objective history" would in the long run mark the episode as a defeat for "black reaction," Kuyper replied that no such objectivity was possible, especially regarding such hotly contested events: "I think it's better if we let this fantasy rest." Still, he allowed that Troelstra's yearnings evinced some "noble tendencies that are moving him to cleanse himself of the heaviest guilt that can perhaps lie upon a political leader." "What hypocrisy!" Troelstra injected. The chair called him to order, but this particular bit of Kuyper moralizing he never forgot.

Education and Equity

The moderate opposition was happy to let the cabinet fight with the Socialists over the railroad strike, but their turn came next. First, as minister of Domestic Affairs Kuyper controlled many appointments, including mayors, school inspectors, university professors and trustees, and judges. He had long complained about a Liberal monopoly in this domain and set out to right the balance via affirmative action. That is, without lowering quality, he aimed to raise the proportion of Calvinist and Roman Catholic appointees to approximate their share of the Dutch population. He was particularly sensitive that officials fit the local religious landscape of their posting. This angered Liberals in Parliament and the press, for their pattern of privilege was indeed under attack. The newcomers could not be qualified, old Liberals like Beaufort sniffed; they were *new* men, not the *best* men. Kuyper's appointments especially cut against the grain in four provinces, where one-third of his nominees were installed over the objection of the royal commissioner.* For the upper echelons he typically had to draw from the old Réveil aristocracy as the only candidates with the required schooling. This obstacle he hoped to remove by gaining state certification for private university degrees.

This provision, which would redound to the immediate benefit of the Free University, was part of a broad slate of educational reforms that Kuyper offered, but the most controversial part by far. It is important, therefore, to cover the rest of the package lest it be lost in the shouting, especially since these provisions held real significance for the nation's future. First of all, Kuyper pushed for greater equity in the funding of elementary education. Religious schools were still receiving only 44 percent of the public schools' per-student subsidy; that now rose to nearly 50 percent. While full equalization only arrived in 1917, the Christian schools' share of national enrollments climbed 25 percent already from 1905 to 1910, right after Kuyper's term. The bill addressed general quality too, lowering class sizes while raising teacher salaries and pensions. Moreover, on the motion of a Liberal Democrat, the cabinet convened an Integration Commission to systematically study all phases and levels of Dutch education; its product (1910) remains a landmark.

Thirdly, against objections that this measure should wait until the integration study was completed, Kuyper pushed to dramatically improve Dutch technical and vocational education. His bill provided night schools for working adults, upgraded the Polytechnical School at Delft to an Institute with university status, and chartered new schools for commercial, agricultural, and industrial education, open also to women. Cynics called this camouflage for his more divisive university bill, but Dutch arrears in this domain had long been a concern of his, and he had facts and figures from Germany, Belgium, and the United States at hand to show the gap to be widening over time. Such education was also a matter of class equity — and no little part of his answer to class conflict. While Liberal Democrats promoted these

---

*Constitutionally, the provincial commissioner answered to the queen and possessed advisory but not veto power on these posts.

measures, the classic Liberals with their bourgeois bias had always neglected them, as Kuyper had decried already in his 1891 speech on the social crisis. He was therefore happy to claim the interest of the whole nation as well as of his own socially-rising constituency in upgrading education for the next half-century the way Thorbecke had for the previous one.

Still, it was state certification of private university degrees that drew the greatest attention, and rightly so. This bill amounted to the ultimate test of Kuyper's original project and the pluralistic vision behind it. Accordingly, on February 24 and 25, 1904, Kuyper delivered a 25,000-word Gladstonian oration on the structure and calling of the university, on the Netherlands' thin supply of higher education relative to their neighbors', and on the warrant for acknowledging and equitably accommodating religious differences at the level of formal state policy. His tone was conciliatory, appealing to the common good. Would not the whole nation profit if people of "Christian life-conviction do better than heretofore in their endeavors in the scholarly domain"? Would not civility be improved if we grant equal respect across the religious gaps that divide us? He argued from the history of Dutch higher education, including Thorbecke's mandating "free" education in 1848; from his own experience as a university founder; and from the inescapable role of "worldview" in shaping instruction and research.

The last assertion provoked all manner of resistance. The philosophical education Kuyper had given his newspaper readers over the years he now condensed into a few parliamentary sessions, in a sophisticated give-and-take rarely matched in those halls. To a query about what Calvinistic chemistry would look like, he answered with long citations from Kant on the organic interpenetration of all the sciences within a framework of organizing principles. Such a paradigm is necessarily interpretive, he continued; witness the current hegemony across the curriculum exercised by evolutionary biology. Not just the Free University but public universities too operated within the controls of one worldview or another. The mantra that higher education served to purge students of inherited doctrine so as to turn them loose for "free choice" was both psychologically false and (given the fads of student life) behaviorally unlikely. But would not systematic worldviews squelch free investigation? No, Kuyper replied; Hugo de Vries was free to pursue his breakthroughs in genetics (published

313

1901-3) but neither he nor his students ought to be in thrall to the materialist dogmas of Ernst Haeckel (published 1899). As to the integrity and quality of religious education, Kuyper assured the body "from experience" that the Free University was no "drill school" graduating "dressed-up parrots," but had to be twice as good as the competition to earn half the respect. Finally, if they remembered their history they would recognize that every argument against his bill had been raised a quarter-century ago against Christian *lower* education; as those fears had not materialized, perhaps the honorable members could be guided by experience instead of inherited dogma.

The Liberals were not amused at their shibboleth being turned against them, nor convinced by Kuyper's cannonade of arguments. Interestingly, until the railroad strike the Socialists had endorsed equal funding for all elementary schools, not least to quell a possible rupture over religion in the ranks of labor. But Liberal ascendancy had pivoted on the premise of "neutral" public schools raising a "responsible citizenry" by the dictates of "reason," and Kuyper's bill struck at that notion substantively and symbolically. It augured to them a dramatically different, and not improved, country — indeed, a future full of peril. Their defeat on a party-line vote (56-41) in the Lower House thus left them leaning on the bare majority they still held in the Upper House. That body duly vetoed the bill on July 14 (Bastille Day, it was noted), only to be dissolved the next week by the queen's hand but at Kuyper's initiative. This was a constitutional but highly unusual step, and it caused uproar in the opposition press. Predictably, the special elections returned a religious majority to the Upper House, which then approved the bill in September; it became law the following May. That conclusion and the steps Kuyper took to reach it alienated the Liberals as much as his redress of the railroad strike had the Socialists. The next elections were just a month away.

Cultivating the Spirit

Remarkably, at this acme of his public life Kuyper also produced some of his most memorable meditations, a series that ran in *De Heraut* between October 1902 and January 1904 and was collected as the first volume of *To Be Near Unto God*. The intensity of his public role might have had a reflex effect in Kuyper's private life. He had to give up his other familiar outlets, the theological podium at the Free University and eventually his editorial page in *De Standaard*. His personal voice was thus channeled into the Sunday devotional column, making it something of the premier's spiritual journal.

These particular reflections also showed what Christian mysticism can look like with a Reformed slant. The very day that Kuyper won the 1901 elections he sent his publisher the manuscript of *Drie Kleine Vossen*, the "three little foxes" that threatened the vineyard of God's church (Song of Solomon 2:15). These were intellectualism, mysticism, and "practicalism": head, heart, and hand; reason, emotion, and will — each good in itself, Kuyper said, each damaging if exercised in isolation. In *Near Unto God* that balance shifted. The now-former professor gave the head least regard, and the current prime minister treated the hand of practice with marked ambivalence. The mystical heart took the lead.

Kuyper's series built through three parts: thirteen meditations on scriptural images of God (10-22), twenty on the ways that we come to know God (23-42), and fourteen more (43-56) that oscillated between Christ as the crux of all these insights and the revelatory significance of the saint's affliction. Each meditation was an excursion on a biblical text; Kuyper as ever held Scripture high and binding. But each was concerned to translate the Word into experience, the soul's experience. "All religion is *personal* at the core," Kuyper declared; "the powers of the kingdom communicate themselves to you in the inner man." Amid the hubbub of modern life, even a prime minister's life, it was essential to delve down to the internal, to leave material forms for the spiritual plane and there conduct one's business with the Lord. That business might be terrifying, Kuyper warned, for holy Majesty brooks no human imposition, not from the unwashed sinner and especially not from the presumptuous saint. Yet it was business that had to be done if one wished to have any claim on being a Christian — particularly if one wanted to be busy as a Christian in the world. The "highest" appropriation of the divine comes from *"a hidden walk with God himself,"* said Kuyper, and "the influence that goes out from this hidden walk far excels all others at strengthening our heart."

Near Unto God exercises a venerable theme in Reformed spirituality: the absolute chasm dividing God, eternity, and the demands of pure religion from the realm of humanity, time, and our best efforts; the sole sufficiency of Christ's work in bridging that gap; and the earnest, faltering, yet persistent effort of the believer to appropriate that work, to rest in it, glory in it, cry over it, and yearn for its experiential return once he had, inevitably, fallen again from the ideal. Kuyper's readers would have been familiar with the pattern from *Pilgrim's Progress,* and as in that classic, there is in the first volume of *Near Unto God* virtually no place for the institutional church. Nor does the Holy Spirit appear — not even in Kuyper's meditation on the Trinitarian Name![*] Kuyper's searcher is the solitary individual mystically engrafted into the hidden transactions between Father and Son.

On the other hand, Kuyper was less judgmental than Bunyan. *Near Unto God* gives scant attention to the sins of the world, more to the religious futility of earnest ethical striving, and most to the lassitude of the righteous. How very few even among the devout give sufficient attention to God, Kuyper mourned. How very great, accordingly, were the patience of God and the mercies of Christ. One fraught but telling way to God is through experience of His forgiveness, he noted. It was Paul the persecutor who burned with greatest enthusiasm for God's love, just as it was the prostitute anointing Christ's feet who rendered an enduring model of "tender faithfulness."

As in much mystical reflection, Kuyper explicated the spiritual quest through material images from Scripture. Just as the Son is the supreme image of God among the human race, so is the sun in the astronomical domain; both bring warmth, color, and light. In the animal kingdom God is best signified by wings, which provide both protection and transcendence; in the atmospheric world by the wind, high, spontaneous, and free; among human works, by the temple, the wind's opposite — set, stable, and protective. The Christian life properly oscillates between these poles, Kuyper wrote; likewise, between sunrise and sunset and around the four seasons of the year. Finally, Kuyper echoed the old passion of Dutch pietism to "rightly divide the Word" by speaking to the exact state of each reader's heart. Sorrow for sin declines along three distinct stages, he averred. The responses of the nominal and genuine believer to unanswered prayer are "altogether different." The return of the saint is to be clearly distinguished from the conversion of the sinner. Jesus had a reason for turning the Old Testament's three- into a four-fold love of God — with heart, soul, mind, and strength, and in just that order.

---

[*]Both appear in the second volume; see below, p. 323.

At the center of the series stand Kuyper's meditations on the will (29-34) and love (35-42) as a two-fold path to the knowledge of — not just obedience to — God. Signaling a turn from the systematic intellect he had stressed for thirty years, and with an uncanny echo of the educational philosophy that John Dewey was publishing at the same moment, Kuyper insisted that when it came to knowing God, Christians could learn only by *doing.* More practical circumstances were in play as well. Kuyper's meditations on knowing God via the will (that is, action) appeared during June and early July of 1903, as Parliament wrapped up a stormy six months of dealing with the railroad strike. The series on love followed immediately and carried over into September, when the next session of Parliament opened with the queen's Throne-Address (drafted by Kuyper) which, again, labeled the strike "criminal." In other words, Kuyper wrote these particular meditations during, after, and in anticipation of further harsh confrontations with Troelstra on the floor of the Lower House. What did it mean to "love" in these circumstances? It meant everything, Kuyper said; it was proof of the Christian's pudding. "He that loveth not knoweth not God" read the title of his September 6 meditation. Kuyper took it straight to the top: "the world-riddle and the riddle of our soul ever and always comes down to this one thing: Is there grace, forgiveness and perfect reconciliation for me?" The answer was severe: complete forgiveness from God expects pure love from us, "that deepest love which makes you forgive from the heart those that have wronged you. Only he who so loves, knows God." So Kuyper had to forgive Pieter Jelles Troelstra, who had and would utter all sorts of maledictions upon his policy and character. Moreover, this "must be an honest forgiveness, without any reservation. Not one single seed of anger or bitterness must remain in you." How is this "almost incomprehensible, and yet absolutely necessary" love attained? Only by the grace that enables us to see in our erstwhile enemy the image of God still there, just as God saw it in us when working out our redemption. "Thereby alone," Kuyper concluded, "is the Gospel your salvation."

Kuyper admitted that this might sound like "works righteousness" to traditional Calvinistic ears; likewise with the touchy subject of the freedom of the will. Just as the Reformed fathers discussed the will as they understood it in their time, he reminded his readers, so we must develop their thinking in light of our own. The nineteenth century just past had been preeminently an age of the will, exaggerated to a fault by everyone from German philosophers to captains of industry. Yet this emphasis had to be redeemed, not quashed, for the will was a democratic faculty fit for the new twentieth century, as the intellect was not. Religiously speaking, the will is "the urgency of the soul itself," the faculty of "that living soul-knowledge of your God, which itself is eternal life." Willpower was essential for an embattled Christian politician, too. Two days before his harshest exchange with Troelstra (30 June 1903), Kuyper's meditation in *De Heraut* compared the irresolute man who is blown about helplessly by "tide and wind" with "the helmsman" who, directed by the divine Captain on the bridge, holds firm the tiller, also of the ship of state. "Such is the man of character, the man with will-perception and will-power, who does not drift but steers," Kuyper declared. And what is "this continuous process of being ever more nearly transformed after the Image of God" but the will of God entering "ever more deeply into us"?

"What hypocrisy!" Troelstra thundered at Kuyper two days later. What self-righteousness might I have exhibited, Kuyper seems to have wondered to himself, for his next column meditated upon Romans 7:15: "what I would do, that do I not; but what I hate, that I do." "There is something bold, something brutal, in this will-life of our times," he reflected. That something made Paul's stark paradox all the more necessary for the believer to mind: we draw near unto God mostly by our failed attempts to live up to our stellar ideals. The next meditation in the series captured Kuyper in a morning-after mood, in one of his most poignant moments. The reflection was entitled "Not as I Will," quoting Jesus at Gethsemane and casting the Christian life as the way of the cross. In times of overconfidence, Kuyper began, we see ourselves at "the center of things . . . [with God] there to make us happy." It is "our honor" we have in view — or fighting boldly for God's honor, he might have added. Inevitably, we run into grief and conflict and so fall into lethargy or even depression: "you become suddenly aware that this great God pays no attention to you, that He does not measure or direct the course of things according to your desire." The lesson he had learned at the cataracts of Switzerland after his nervous breakdown now returned: "God's reality, His Majesty which utterly overwhelms you" holds a plan of salvation which is not of, by, and for human beings, but of the Lord alone. Only when our soul "abandons the theory of Job's friends and, like Job, receives the answer from God Himself out of the whirlwind" do we learn that "His counsel and plan

are as high as heaven and consequently exceed our comprehension."
It is thus not ours to seek "the verification of His counsel but to enter
into the life of it," be it through joy or sorrow. Therein lies "our honor
and the self-exaltation of our soul."

The sorrow would descend soon enough.

CHAPTER SIXTEEN

The Peoples of God

Kuyper hoped that the elections of 1905 would give him a second term as prime minister and the chance to pass the rest of his agenda. If the Higher Education bill, the crowning touch of his first term, might be dismissed as self-interested, his second term would attend to the social question and so unambiguously serve the nation as a whole. These two accomplishments — an equitable educational system and his proposed framework of labor and welfare law — would fix the architecture of Dutch society "according to the ordinances of the Lord," which had been his goal from the start.

To win re-election, however, Kuyper made a fateful choice of theme. In December 1901, near the start of his first term, he had taken an ecumenical tone: his coalition would stand on a "Christianity *beneath* theological differences," seeking to "preserve the place of Christian values among the people." In December 1904, he struck the opposite note. There have been all kinds of confrontations between and within parties in the past, he said, but these had now all crystallized into "one great contrast . . . between the *Christian* and the *modern* life-conception." Indeed, down the middle of Dutch society ran an "enormous antithesis," so that the forthcoming elections would decide which side would steer the ship of state for the next four years.

Catalyzing confrontation was a standard mode of operation for Kuyper, and the picture of opposite minds warring for the culture had been with him since his second conversion at Beesd. But he had seldom before deployed "antithesis" to such overt political ends. Moreover, the opposition seized the slogan for their own, turning it against Kuyper in a manner that helped turn the elections their way. That outcome, a profound setback for Kuyper personally, prompted him to re-assess once more the direction and future of his cause. A theme that had wound through his thinking from the start now became his central organizing motif: Christ was not only the Savior but the King of his people, calling them apart *from* the world to assert his claims *in* the world. Yet Kuyper also sensed that world to be fundamentally changing in the young twentieth century, and he searched for new categories by which to grasp it. His answers were quickened by a long trip he took around the Mediterranean Sea in the wake of his defeat — a trip through fourteen countries, three world religions, back into the depths of time, and forward into the perils of European diplomacy. The trip was another of Kuyper's recuperative retreats. At the same time it was a pilgrimage on which the premier-in-exile saw anew what it meant to be the people of God.

The Election of 1905

The election of 1905 was unusual in Dutch history for being focused upon a person rather than a program or party loyalty. It was the country's first instance of modern, slogan-driven politics, and in P. J. Troelstra Kuyper had his first thoroughly modernized opponent, someone as adept as he at the means and ends of mobilization. Troelstra's slogan was simple: "Throw him out!" No one had to wonder who that "him" was. Targeting Kuyper personally worked to firm up the Socialists' co-belligerency with all varieties of Liberals, who otherwise had little use for their program. But while "anti-Kuyper" also meant "anticlerical," the Christian side had no such solidarity. A leading MP on the Antirevolutionary Left was threatening to bolt in frustration over the slow pace of social legislation, while two factions on the Right deemed Kuyper too progressive there and too timid on religious and morals legislation. By casting the election as a religious antithesis, Kuyper hoped to consolidate his own ranks.

His other tack was to try to divide the opposition by scaring the Liberals. He brought back his old charge that socialism represented the logical end-point of liberal principles, so that to avoid their horrid fate Liberals should join his side. Troelstra replied in kind. It was a historical fact that liberalism proceeded from Calvinism, he reasoned, so that if Social Democracy was indeed the child of liberalism as Kuyper alleged, then "Minister Kuyper is our grandpa." The honorable member was "entirely correct" in a formal sense, Kuyper replied. "I have always recognized . . . that socialism has a good side," and that had to come from somewhere. "As [Eduard] Bernstein has said, 'Socialists are Calvinists without God.'"

But these themes in political economy resonated less with the electorate than did Kuyper's excursions on religion. The "modern life-conception" opposing the "Christian" in this election he also called "pagan" or "paganistic," and his frantic clarification that he was referring to a worldview and not to persons was lost in the ensuing uproar. However numerous the Netherlands' nominal Christians, they were allergic to being called heathen in any respect. Finally, the Antirevolutionary Party was not well served with Herman Bavinck as its acting chair (a role Kuyper had to surrender as premier). Bavinck had been reluctant to accept the post — in retrospect, with good reason. He was unversed at this trade and too conciliatory in disposition for an election that was going to be highly divisive.

The results were dismaying for Kuyper and his followers. In the run-off round of balloting (June 28), the religious coalition took 53 percent of the popular vote but nonetheless lost ten seats and thus their parliamentary majority. The casualties were almost all among the ARP, which dropped nine seats, from 24 to 15. Five of the losses came in swing districts that the party had carried in the landslide of 1901, but four were traditionally secure seats lost to party in-fighting. Holding those four would have meant a second term, Kuyper mourned. Most painful of all, seven of the seats swung to the Social Democrats. The dependency of the new Liberal cabinet upon these votes doomed it to a foreshortened term, but that was cold comfort to Kuyper. The electorate was growing rapidly (150,000 voters more in 1905 than just four years before), and in the Social Democrats the religious parties now had a genuinely popular rival to deal with. Kuyper had always fought elites; now he had to differentiate among "the people."

He also had to deal with a crushing personal blow. His first instinct was to retreat. In a move that did nothing for his reputation, he did not wait for the new cabinet to be installed in mid-August but, pleading doctor's orders, asked the queen's permission to leave on vacation as usual at the start of the month. Her Majesty, who had made no secret of her hopes that Kuyper be defeated, observed that it was not quite protocol, but acceded. The trip started with a month at Bad

Kissingen in lower Franconia, then continued around the Mediterranean until the following June. It was on this tour that Kuyper wrote most of the devotionals that make up the second volume of *To Be Near Unto God,* and it is in them that we can observe how he processed his painful defeat.

For the whole prior year (most of 1904 into 1905) Kuyper's devotionals had left the track of *Near Unto God* to explore Old Testament history. This was the chronicle of the holy-yet-faithless nation upon which Kuyper would dilate more in the future. The series culminated, tellingly, in three meditations on Job and one on Psalm 2:2-3, where "the kings and rulers of the earth" are seen "taking counsel against the Lord and his anointed." Kuyper wrote these in January 1905, in campaign mode. He finally returned to his previous track in May and June, as the elections neared. His meditation of June 4 evoked the antithesis: "It is faith in Christ that shall one day bring about the division of mankind in eternity, and it is this same faith that already here on earth leads to this result." All other "badges and rules and relationships," however worthy they might be in everyday life, fade into insignificance against the rule of faith, "the ground thesis for all higher human life." Two weeks later, on election eve, Kuyper underscored the solidarity of the saints by treating the church and the operation of the Holy Spirit, which he had barely touched in the first volume. It was a sign of his spiritual maturity, then, that the first meditation published after his defeat at the polls did not take the obvious line signaled by its title — "O God, My God!" — that is, to Psalm 22:1, also Jesus' cry from the cross, but invoked Psalm 43:4 instead: "I will go the altar of God, to God my exceeding joy, and I will praise you with the harp, O God, my God." Biblically knowledgeable as *Heraut* readers were, they would have immediately recalled the opening of that psalm: "Vindicate me, O God, and defend my cause against an ungodly people; from those who are deceitful and unjust deliver me!" But instead of dwelling on vengeance, Kuyper chose to trace the normative course of spiritual development by which the believer came to an ever deeper, all-encompassing relationship with God as her personal God. Among the riches of that personal bond, Kuyper concluded, was the blessed knowledge that God provides "not a general fulfillment for all alike, but for each . . . that particular supply which he needs."

Still, grief and anger were palpable in the meditations he wrote that post-election summer, pieces he eventually decided not to include in *Near Unto God*. The grief came out in the entries of July: on July 9, a reminder to remember the "deeds of the Lord, wonders of old" (Psalm 77:11); on July 23, as his term neared its close, the valedictory of Moses: "Establish thou the work of our hands" (Psalm 90:17). In between, on July 16, he returned to Habakkuk 3:17-18, the same passage he had contemplated at his career crossroads in 1877: "Though the fig tree does not blossom, and no fruit is on the vines; though the produce of the olive fails, and the fields yield no food; though the flock is cut off from the fold, and there is no herd in the stalls, yet I will rejoice in the Lord and exult in the God of my salvation." Next came the anger, in a seven-part series on the Last Judgment — the judgment not of persons but of nations. It is amazing to think of Kuyper, having taken the baths all week at a German spa, sitting down on a Sunday morning to write of Christ separating the sheep from the goats (the ultimate antithesis), delivering the kingdom to God the Father "after he has destroyed every ruler and every authority and power," and finally annihilating "the lawless one," Satan himself, "by the breath of his mouth."

After anger, finally, acceptance. On September 24 he published the meditation that would later lead off the book version of the series and supply the title for the whole: "But for me it is good to be near God; I have made the Lord God my refuge, to tell of all your works." The first three words of this, the last verse of Psalm 73, echo the opening of the psalm — and Kuyper's understanding of his own trial: "But as for me, my feet had almost stumbled, my steps had nearly slipped. For I was envious of the arrogant; I saw the prosperity of the wicked" (vv. 2-3). How Kuyper had been harboring that pain became evident about a month later, in his meditation from rock bottom. Reflecting on Psalm 143:9 ("Deliver me, O Lord, from my enemies, for I hide myself in Thee"), he wrote: "If there ever were such a thing possible as a despair of faith, then hiding with God" would be its definitive act. There was no such thing as despair *in* faith, he quickly added, yet a person of faith could come to utter despair of himself. This might happen "amid circumstances of utmost perplexity and stress," when a "child of God" realizes that "he must unquestionably suffer defeat and therefore has no courage left." Then he "despairs of all help and deliverance from without, despairs of the working of the ordinary powers and gifts which at other times are at his disposal." He runs from the fray and "hides himself with God," for there "the battle is no longer between him and the world, but between this world and God." And only when it has become clear "that God has righted all . . . does he come out from his hiding place again, in order to finish his course." For Kuyper that recovery took a forty-week sojourn around the biblical world.

The Peoples of the World

Given his age, his chronic bronchitis, and the transportation technology of the time, Kuyper's trek was remarkable. Leaving Bad Kissingen, he took a train across Bavaria and the entire Austro-Hungarian Empire to visit the small and recently (1878) independent kingdom of Romania. His hopes of next touring Russia from Kiev to Moscow were crimped by the revolution that was cresting there just as he crossed the border in mid-October, so he limited himself to the Crimea with its dense Jewish settlements and the battlefields of Sevastopol. In late October, near his sixty-eighth birthday, he sailed from Odessa to Istanbul (he insisted on using its old Christian name of Constantinople) for a couple of weeks, then visited early-church sites in Asia Minor before shipping to Beirut. December saw him touring Syria and Palestine by horse cart, the highlights being a twilight sail across the biblical Sea of Galilee, the holy sites of Jerusalem, and finally Christmas day at Bethlehem. January found him at Cairo, Suez, and the pyramids of Giza (his first camel ride), then by river steamer up the Nile to Khartoum. In February it was Greece and Sicily, and in March a return to Tunisia, where he had recuperated after his breakdown in 1894. Just then he got news that his daughter Henriëtte had returned ill from her trip to America, so he hurried back to The Hague to oversee her recovery. He returned by train and steamer across France, Spain, and the western Mediterranean to spend the rest of April in Algeria and Morocco. Fascinated by the Berbers, he insisted on trekking by automobile over mountain roads hardly worth the name to visit their homeland in the Algerian Highlands. Then he crossed back into Europe and took May to see Spain and Portugal. He finally returned home in June, with a quick stop in Paris along the way.

Kuyper read voraciously throughout the trip and gathered statistical and historical information at every stop, not least through conversations with local authorities. His intent to turn this all into a grand book was nearly derailed when the cleaning maid back in The Hague threw out the whole collection, but a quick call to the trash man managed to salvage three quarters of it. If, as one historian has said, the only thing Kuyper liked better than traveling was writing, then his dream job would be to write about traveling. He spent two years (November 1906–October 1908) at it between other duties, producing a two-volume, 1,075-page account of his pilgrimage: *Around the Old-World Sea (Om de Oude Wereldzee).* The publisher gave it deluxe treatment: folio size, quality paper, embossed covers, gilt-edging, illustrations, and a fold-out map. It was a book for the parlor table but also a remarkable course in comparative anthropology that showed how lands and peoples looked to a Calvinist eye shaded by contemporary ethnic theory at a crucial turn in world history.

By all appearances Kuyper enjoyed his trip immensely. It was expansive and exotic after four years of factional infighting in a small country. Moorish architecture and Arab bazaars, prayers at Hagia Sophia and the quiet of Gethsemane, the veiled Jewish women in Tunisia and the unveiled women of Andalusia, the changing tableau of landscape and manners — it was all fresh, beautiful, startling, and moving by turns. Besides, recently rejected at home, Kuyper felt honored abroad. European officialdom made special arrangements for one of their own — the private railroad car, aides to shepherd him from ship to hotel, a private box for the bullfights in Spain (he left after two kills), dinner with ambassadors at Istanbul, and everywhere private audiences with high officials: with the British governor-general of Egypt and the French chief consul of Algeria, with the king and queen of Romania, with Alfonso XIII of Spain just days before he was nearly assassinated, and with the unfortunate Carlos of Portugal (an artist trapped on the throne, Kuyper thought), who would be murdered two years later. The latter were only two of a string of assassinations that had already run for more than a decade and would continue to a climax at Sarajevo in 1914.

Kuyper bumped into other world-shaking events along his way as well. He arrived in Morocco just as the Franco-German conference over the future of that country was concluding at Algericas, a textbook marker on the road from European imperialism to World War I. He read about, and too readily discounted, the agitations of the Young Turks at Istanbul that would force regime-change in 1908. Confined to the Crimea by the revolution of 1905, yet insisting on his evening exercise, he encountered "socialist patrols" as he walked the streets of Odessa. Back at the hotel he could read about the anti-Semitic riots roiling the region; over 300 Jews were killed in Odessa alone as he arrived there.

The upheaval in Russia stemmed directly from the event that Kuyper took to be the crucial turn of the new century — the triumph of Japan over Russia in their war of 1904-5, sealed by the obliteration of the Russian fleet off the coast of Korea in late May. That triumph, he said correctly enough, had triggered euphoria across Europe's Asian colonies and symbolized a dawning challenge to Europe's world hegemony. That was doubtless one topic of all those sessions with high officials, but Kuyper also heard it echoed at Al-Azhar University in Cairo, in his broodings along the Suez Canal, and at the site of the slaughtered Mahdists in the Sudan. He responded with remarkable ambivalence. On the one hand he took European dominance as a given — that is, as a fact of history and as a normative condition. In this vein he could cite the anti-imperialist "Asia for the Asians" slogan as an insult and a threat. At the same time he acknowledged out of hand the depredations that had attended Europe's conquest and maintenance of their empires, and he added a skeptical assessment about recent attempts to extend their bounds. That the General Kitchener who desecrated the graves of the Mahdists at Omdurman in 1898 would two years later start savaging the Boers in South Africa he did not point out in 1908, or need to. He simply concluded, respecting Omdurman, that "technology" won the war "but personal honor . . . lay with the fallen" — that is, with the Muslim jihadists. That a new mahdi had arisen, and that the British, in their usual strategy of dividing colonists to better control them, were encouraging Wahabist Islam in Egypt to counter the lure of the Ottoman sultan, led Kuyper to conclude that the British hold along the Nile was weaker than pretended. Likewise he faulted French endeavors in Algeria. Whatever short-term boost they had given to morale back home and whatever long-term material improvements they brought on site, they represented a significant net drain on French finances and were doomed by demography. Francofication in Algeria no less than Russification in Poland was both an injustice and a fool's errand.

Kuyper's ambivalence is partly explained by the bifocals through which he looked at a world about to change beyond his, or almost any of his contemporaries', ability to imagine. One part of his lens was ground by the racial typing that dominated contemporary educated European and American opinion. This approach was not necessarily racist (in the sense of being prejudicial and hierarchical) but rather the extant language of ethnocultural analysis, as "national character" would be in the 1950s or "culture systems" today. Kuyper casually used racial categories this way — for instance in characterizing Romania as a blending of "the old Dacians" with "the mysticism of the Slavs," inflected by "the French subtlety" of its language family and directed by the "strong German hand" of its king. This approach could quickly turn essentialist, however, as if all Slavs, Turks, or Arabs had a common, inherited, and unchangeable character that dictated their institutions and behaviors.

Racial thinking invited hierarchical rankings as well, and Kuyper indulged these, especially once he left European shores. While on the Continent he cast Slavic, Roman, and Germanic types as different but equal. In Asia and Africa the rating system took over, and the more distant the view, the more egregious his expression. Thus, sub-Saharan Africans (whom Kuyper had never seen in person except in their African American descendants) constituted one uniform bloc at the bottom of the scale. Closer up, he found every group to have its merits, but in the final analysis he rated Arabs above Turks and Berbers above both.

The other — and predominant — half of his lens was ground by religion. Religion, Kuyper declared, "is and shall remain the most powerful factor in the life of the nations." The Muslim world, despite its wide geographic, ethnic, and linguistic varieties — that is, as a realm of many "races" — lived as one in its steadfast devotion to prayer and the Qur'an. The Slavic soul had been fundamentally shaped by Orthodox ritual; it was Christianity alone that had been able to overcome tribalism and make of the Greeks a nation. Above all, Europe had attained supremacy because its "Aryan" ethnicity had been infused with "Semitic" religion. That is, what would be a nightmare to future Nazis was Kuyper's state of (common) grace. He explicitly rejected the eminent racist and proto-fascist anthropology of Joseph Arthur Comte de Gobineau, who condemned "race-mixing" as the road to degeneration. The lands Kuyper found most attractive — Romania, southern Spain, and the United States — were so because of their ethnic mixtures, and the Gobinesque prescription of ethnic nationalism (under which each people would have its own "pure" state) Kuyper saw as a formula for either ruinous ethnic cleansing, the oppression of minorities, or military strife. Prophetically enough, Kuyper said this in and of the Balkans. Above all, Kuyper rejected biological racism as a sub-species of the materialistic worldview that was his eternal enemy. "Race" for him was a cultural category, a matter not of body but of collective soul.

Kuyper's observations were also driven by local interest — both the nuances of the site he was visiting and the lessons they bore for Dutch circumstances. Thus he took heart from Romania as a successful "smaller nation" surrounded by great powers. He characterized the Ottoman policy of segmented, self-regulating religious communities as a type of "sphere sovereignty." He extolled the city of Fez for its "exceptionally beautiful" urban design, its vibrant university quarter, its provisions for public health, its suppression of prostitution, and the operation of its economic life by "the guild system in its best form" — that is, as a model for Amsterdam. The Berbers he approved for their strong communal organization (as opposed to the "clannish" and "nomadic" Arabs) and their longtime resistance to conquest, also from Spain. Their deep, seamless assimilation of Islam into their native culture recalled his hope for Christianity in the East Indies.

Kuyper came not only to praise, however. His seventy-five-page chapter on the Romani (*zigeuners,* "gypsies") constitutes the longest unrelieved screed in his entire corpus. These were the consummate children of Cain, he declared, metalworking nomads gifted at music but full of bad faith, in both senses of the word. Woven of Central Asian animism and Persian dualism, their religious garb changed chameleon-like to provide them cover in any environment. Such deviousness spelled ethical corruption, a lifestyle of vagabondage supported by petty theft and forthright criminality. Illiterate "parasites," pimps and prostitutes, camp-followers to armies and the jackals who scavenged in the ruins of war, they were the living antithesis of bourgeois probity. Nor were they fringe-players doomed to extinction, Kuyper fumed, for here was the historical source and continuing inspiration of the bohemian lifestyle of the anarchist-artist set that prided itself on being the avant-garde. Decadence, laziness, and revolution, all gathered, predictably, in Paris — this was the "social plague that the Gypsies bequeathed to France," and from there to Europe at large.

The Jewish Question

His essay on the Romani was one of four that Kuyper's travelogue devoted to peoples rather than to the countries he visited. The other three treated Jews, Muslims, and the confrontation of Europe and Asia. The latter he took to be the world-historical question of the future. In that clash, he said, Islam would hold the balance of power. "The Jewish question," on the other hand, had to do with the biblical challenge of religious integrity over against the modern political problem of dual identity. The most important questions, in other words, still revolved around the "seed of Abraham," the three monotheisms rooted in the Hebrew Scriptures.

This was not the first time that Kuyper addressed Jewish affairs. In the 1870s, as part of the process of party formation, he had accused Dutch Jewry of being both the captive and stalking horse of the Liberal regime. Referring especially to more recently arrived Ashkenazim as opposed to the long-familiar Sephardim, Kuyper labeled Jews resident aliens who could not finally belong to the Dutch nation. Their worst characters contributed to the money-lust centered on the Amsterdam Bourse, he alleged, while their more talented types had acquired disproportionate influence in law and journalism. This contrast of best and worst recurred from time to time in Kuyper's political columns and again in *Around the Old-World Sea,* but it must also be said that Kuyper never again questioned Dutch Jews' citizenship. Nor did anti-Semitism play even a minor note in his party program or election campaigns, much less the leading theme that it became in the comparable Christian-Social parties of Germany and Austria. In fact, Kuyper faulted by name the leaders of those groups (Adolf Stoecker and Karl Lueger, respectively), while his larger narrative repudiated anti-Semitism in general and the rising tide of pogroms in particular. Theologically, he rejected the blood libel and any special Jewish responsibility for the death of Jesus; that guilt was as universal as the sin for which the death atoned. Concluded Kuyper: "As someone who confesses Christ with my whole heart . . . by my lights Jews remain a nation chosen by God from all the peoples, whereby I confess with the apostle of Tarsus [Paul, in Romans 11:26] that *all of Israel shall someday be saved.*"

The larger Jewish scene Kuyper pondered with a wary eye. His analysis was nuanced in differentiating the thinner, more assimilated Jewish populations of West and Central Europe from Eastern Europe, where the majority of world Jewry lived. Furthermore, the Jewish situation in Romania, while precarious, looked precarious in a different way than in Russia, while in the Ottoman Empire it seemed much more secure. Kuyper explained these differences by history and culture. Whereas Gentiles in Russia and Romania were novices at business, the presence of Greek and Armenian merchants in Turkey and the Levant helped diffuse the Jewish reputation for sharp trading. He noted besides that the abject poverty of most Jews in the Ottoman and Russian empires should put Jewish commercial stereotypes to rest. Even when in his estimate that stereotype was warranted, he assigned responsibility to the host regimes who had barred Jews from everything but trade; their skill in the learned professions, on the other hand, he attributed to their rigorous education in religious texts. Yet, a few pages later he could blame Jews for a clannishness that invited suspicion and violence, while disparaging Talmudic training for cultivating "clever" argumentation at the cost of a broad, well-balanced mind. He again rejected biological notions of race by tying Jewish ethnicity "inseparably . . . [and] at the core" to its religious roots, but could then observe that the Jewish race was everywhere "physically weaker but intellectually stronger" than their neighbors.

His policy proposals were ambivalent too: "For Europe, and especially for the Eastern countries on this continent, the Jewish question remains an almost insoluble problem." The problems on the ground were real enough. Ghettoization had created a Jewish nation within every nation east of the Elbe, a situation that Ottomans could manage but Europeans could not. The rising ethnic definition of nationhood could not abide such duality and sooner or later would turn bloodthirsty, he feared. Yet the traditional practice of requiring religious conversion for legal equality Jews properly rejected, and the loss of real religion that such a step promoted was the type of modernization he feared the most. Still, Kuyper reflected, to award instant civil equality in Eastern Europe would unleash a flood of economic sophisticates upon untutored peasants and a mass of accumulated brainpower on the capitals, the recriminations for which would spark even bloodier rounds of reprisals. Migration out of the area held the best prospect, he thought, but the United States was pressuring Russia to reduce the flow, while the Zionist colonies he visited in Palestine were so sparse and primitive that he thought it unlikely for a mass exodus there to be viable any time soon. The better chance lay in migration to the Russian interior, where Jewish talent could meet economic need to the mutually profitable end of nation-building. Meanwhile, host nations should start reducing occupational and geographical restrictions and redirect laws from race to behavior, punishing credit manipulation as such, for instance, rather than targeting Jews per se. Finally, it was the Christians' duty to protest anti-Semitism in every form, not least because it spelled an attack on the roots and continuing essence of Christianity.

The Prospects of Islam

Thus linking two monotheisms, Kuyper drew in the third in reflecting on the "enigma of Islam." Here his approach was not ambivalent but contrapuntal. On the one hand, Islam was the object of his supreme envy — a faith that, adapting itself to every culture, steeped its adherents in the conviction that the will of God was supreme over everything from the personal to the political, from the deep roots of time into the everlasting future, and under that conviction had spread a common worldview from Gibraltar to the Philippines. This was Kuyper's dream for Calvinism, the Dutch Golden Age times ten. As to particulars, he admired Muslim achievements in architecture — the Alhambra above all, but the Dome of the Rock and the Grand Mosque in Damascus as well — and he rhapsodized about Al-Azhar University in Cairo, where progressive scholarship had once flourished for seven hundred years in organic connection with religion and life. He noted the rise of pan-Islamic consciousness as a kind of liberation theology against colonial rule. It grounded independence in religious unity and ethical purification. If the "fanaticism" this produced worried him as a European, it echoed all his tales of heroic Beggars in the Dutch war for independence.

On the other hand, Kuyper did not understand how so "legalistic" a religion as Islam could thrive. It lacked the "spiritual depth" of the New Testament's transformative struggle of the "old man with the new." Its core teachings added up to a kind of ethical deism, which explained the sympathy it won from Protestant modernists but also inauthenticated any attempt to vary its palette. Sufi mysticism he dismissed as a pantheistic graft of Persian origin, just as Shi'a was a Persian-nationalist "sect." The Dervishes (one can only imagine

Kuyper watching their ceremonial dancing in Istanbul) displayed the "fleshly" indulgence to which mysticism invariably led.

Islam's ethical rigor collapsed more generally in its treatment of women, Kuyper continued. He brought up this theme at Istanbul with a discussion of the harem which, if less prurient than many Western accounts, was no less condemnatory: polygamy was a font of "unrighteousness that breeds further unrighteousness." On his tour Kuyper regularly inquired into girls' education and invariably found Muslims trailing comparable Christian communities. He also kept records on prostitution in every place — whether it was organized into brothels or conducted by freelancers; whether it was run by Arabs or Jews; whether it catered to locals or (far worse) to the "refined sensuality" of Europeans. One of the most remarkable items in his archive is a detailed statistical table compiled by the consular office in Algiers which he cited to disprove the common claim that polygamy reduced sex-trafficking. Nor was the problem simply a matter of policy; there was a religious error involved. The Qur'an's "desecration of marriage and principled opposition to monogamy undermines the very foundation of the moral life and finally kills any concept of shame." The conclusion was one he had already reached in *Common Grace* ten years before: nothing so starkly proved the superiority of Christianity over every other religion as the elevation of women wrought by the gospel.

Kuyper was willing to overlook much, however, for Islam's help on the great "political world-problem" of the future — what the opening chapter of *Old-World Sea* called "The Asiatic Danger." The "danger" lay most obviously in the prospect that Japan's triumph over Russia would inspire anti-colonial fever everywhere, including — Kuyper reminded his Dutch readers — "our archipelago." That the East Indies were in the second circle of proximity to Japan (after Korea, Manchuria, and Taiwan, where the Japanese had already advanced), and that the Dutch relied for naval protection on Britain (which had just concluded an alliance with Japan in 1902), made this a real problem for Dutch policy and explains the ominous tone in Kuyper's prose. The bigger issue lay on the religious plane, however. Both at the start and the conclusion of his two-volume travelogue he reiterated the lesson made regularly along the way, namely, that religion was crucial for understanding peoples and places, and that European leaders were naïve to believe that technical and economic modernization would cause those religions to disappear. On the contrary, Kuyper said, "they" are not destined to become "just like us." Western innovations could and would become thoroughly assimilated for native ends, as the Japanese had just dramatically demonstrated against Russia.

Kuyper's forecast of the twentieth century thus entwined Hegel with Abraham. "Polytheistic" East Asia was rising against "monotheistic" Europe. In between lay "pantheistic" South Asia (naturally tilting East) and the Islamic world. The future thus pivoted on Islam's affiliation, and the Ottomans were the straw in the wind: "What will prove more powerful, their Asiatic origins or their strong monotheistic persuasion?" More broadly it depended on whether Asians, especially the Muslims among them, would feel their colonial humiliation so keenly as to accept Japanese overtures, or whether Europe could reform its ways so as to cement a grand monotheistic alliance. Kuyper pointed to some hopeful signs, especially in German-Ottoman collaborations and in the Aga Khan's attempt to burnish the universal qualities of Islam to mirror European values. The time might be coming when "Islam will be worth gold to us as a monotheistic ally," he mused. But even if the old Cross vs. Crescent antagonism revived, it would be good "if our conscience could testify that, far from having fanned the flame of that fanaticism by arrogant intolerance, we had often dampened it through Christian longsuffering."

Better yet would be to drop the "notion that we have everything to bring and nothing to receive from the East." In fact, Europe's first priority should be to remember and renew its historic debt to Asia. Here Kuyper skated out on what would become very treacherous ice, only to execute a theological arabesque that served his successors well. World history, he concluded at the end of his Mediterranean tour, is the "enduring struggle between the Aryan and Semitic races." First the Semites flourished at Troy and Carthage, followed by "eight centuries . . . of Aryan triumph" at Rome and Constantinople. Then the Semites came sweeping back on the wave of Islam, eventually to be countered by the rise of Aryan Europe. The generation after Kuyper would know what to expect next, only he argued the opposite. It was Semitic excellence in religion, mixed with Aryan "intellect and command of the material" realm, that enabled Europe to "ascend to the peak of human development." In that light, Kuyper warned, it was ominous to see a new form of modernist theology arising that was "at bottom nothing but an attempt of the Aryan spirit to shake the spiritually Semitic element from its shoulders" and replace it with an Indo-Persian pantheism. Particularly repellent was the proposal "to push a Germanic Jesus in place of the Christ [born] of Shem's line of descent."

The New World at Home

Jesus was much on Kuyper's mind as he was composing his travel reflections, for he was simultaneously publishing in *De Heraut* a series of 158 articles on "the kingship of Christ," *Pro Rege*. The series debuted in January 1907, announcing that the master was back on board; it came to a conclusion exactly four years later, when he was seventy-three years old. It was the last major theological work that Kuyper would finish and, by one account, the first that showed him to be "losing his grip on his material, in that his sweeping generalizations are no longer compensated for by the originality of his thought." Indeed, much of the series retraced ground Kuyper had covered before in *Ons Program, Common Grace,* and his *Encyclopaedia of Sacred Theology.* He now surveyed it under a new theme, or better, an old theme developed systematically for a new situation. The world, Kuyper declared — not just on the far shores of the Mediterranean Sea but at home as well — was undergoing fundamental change, and only a compass set to the pole of Christ the King could guide believers through it. *Pro Rege* is thus best read for its diagnosis of the West one decade into the twentieth century, and for the recalibrations it gave to his Calvinist cultural initiatives of twenty years before.

Kuyper's presentation of the problem was startling. Everywhere — among Christians, Jews, and westernized Muslims — he detected a general decline of religious consciousness, the blame for which fell not on the usual suspects of personal faithlessness or the rise of rival worldviews but on the social-structural conditions of modernity. He did not use that terminology, for he was deploying a new simplicity of prose to reach ordinary readers. In one mounting eighty-page stretch, however, he laid out the anatomy of an emerging new world order defined by constant technological innovation, globalization, urbanization, ever-more rapid communication, the increasing sway of finance capital, the commodification of art, and the triumph of fashion. It was a portrait of mass society under the conditions of advanced industrialism.

That system posed a threat to religion for three reasons, Kuyper said. First, technology's triumph over nature had radically reduced the sense of dependence (he explicitly invoked Schleiermacher) that had long brought many people into "the forecourt . . . [of] the temple of religion," with some of them proceeding on to the "holy place" of true repentance. Secondly, the self was dissolving under the explosion of knowledge and social complexity. "The spirit of a person from youth up becomes dispersed and divided over all sorts of things," Kuyper observed. It "goes unformed," and so was losing its own formative power to integrate pieces into a coherent whole. This mantra, echoed by a host of contemporary complaints about over-specialization, Kuyper focused on his particular concern: "Religion demands above all the concentration of the spirit. . . . [It] is a thrusting into the *unity* of all things so as to come to grips in the hiddenness of the soul with the unity of *the One* from Whom it all comes." But "people don't want that anymore," he lamented. "They're scared of it. And they're too strewn about for it. The spirit is always too full, too beset, too overburdened for it." For this situation, thirdly, the hectic pace of modern life was to blame. The "intense over-stimulation of the nervous life," the complex entanglements of one nation with all others, of family members with outsiders, of work with leisure and the self with everyone and everything all the time by virtue of quick communication and rapid transportation — all this, Kuyper said, has been aptly labeled "the forecourt of hell." All in all, he concluded, "the mighty stream of modern life in the world has loosened, pulled up, and overturned all the roots of religion."

What was growing in its place? Kuyper for once seemed at a loss for words, one measure of the novelty of the situation. Always before he had been able to name the threat: philosophical naturalism, Modernism as ersatz Christianity, one political ideology or another. Now the problem was sheer indifference: "far and away, most who depart [the faith of their youth] do *without* Religion right down to their death." He nominated in passing a generic "spirit of the world" as the devil in the brew, but this came at the end of a more convincing survey of the "world metropolises" that served as the nodal points of the new order. Paris was the capital of "luxury," London of "traffic and trade," Berlin of "knowledge and science," and New York of "money," but their people were all alike enthralled to the power of fashion and opinion.

Who started these tides and directed them, no one knew, Kuyper mused, but to him two "lords" stood out in the mix. The first was

Mammon, meaning a thorough absorption in getting and spending within the horizon of the material world. This was often mistaken for, but was actually worse than, the ancient Hebrews' worship of the golden calf, Kuyper argued. That was sacrifice to a false image of God; Mammon worship was the displacement of God entirely, a veneration of the "magical and thus enchanting power" of wealth, a virtual religion all the more potent for not trumpeting itself as such. The second power was Art, a more ambiguous force. Historically the near neighbor of religion, Kuyper said, Art still attracted a spiritual "aristocracy" yearning for "a small mystical oasis" in the "materialistic wilderness." They found it at museums and galleries, sometimes with Buddhist, spiritualist, or theosophical practices on the side. But these searchers would "never set the tone" of public life. It was Art as captured by Mammon that did — commercialized, lowered, prostituted, feeding the mass compulsion for excitement, excess, and the erotic.

Kuyper came close here to the biblical trope of "principalities and powers" that future commentators would use to name the prevailing forces in advanced-capitalist society — among them, precisely the marriage of Art and Mammon that is commercial advertising. In fact, advertising was being transformed as an industry in New York City at just the moment Kuyper had visited there, but in *Pro Rege* he was more anxious about Madison Square (then center of the theater district) than Madison Avenue. He also invoked the terminology of spiritual warfare that would become popular a century later. There exists an unseen world of spirits that interacts with the visible world in ways we do not fathom and have not yet systematically investigated, he said. These spirits are good and evil, angels and demons, servants of God or Satan. As it happened, the revivals underway at the Azusa Street mission in Los Angeles precisely as Kuyper wrote these words marked the beginning of a worldwide popularization of this and other Pentecostal tropes, often with concrete political identifications of just who on the current scene was doing the work of which master. Kuyper refrained from drawing any such associations. The great battle in the air cut down the middle of every human heart, he insisted. No country, no race, no present institution outside the church could be assigned to one side or the other. At the end times such a sorting would become visible, but *Pro Rege* named no names, avoiding even a pencil sketch of how things might unfold from the current scene into the future.

That interpretive modesty compares well to much Pentecostal and Fundamentalist commentary to come, but it did not help much with understanding the world at hand. Instead, Kuyper took spiritual warfare an entirely different way — and capitulated to the new order in the process. All the miracles and healings that Jesus performed, he told his readers, amounted to a foreshadowing of the human subjugation of nature. Jesus' "wonders" (Dutch for miracles) were models of how nature's flaws would be corrected, its terrors vanquished, its powers recaptured from the thrall of Satan. Kuyper declared that the process had reached its crest in his day, with untold wonders still to come in the future. These technological triumphs are the "yet greater things" that Jesus promised his disciples they would perform. On this score, Kuyper reasoned, King Jesus came as the Son of Man, not the Son of God, exemplifying by sheer spiritual power the dominion over creation originally given to the human race in Eden. With its fall into sin, humanity had forfeited those powers to angels good and evil, but gradually it had been taking back control. By Christ's particular grace his followers were able to carve out a protected domain from the devil in the church, while by common grace this species of spiritual power had been increasingly translated (and was by now routinized) into technical mastery over nature. The powers of the two graces had converged in Europe, explaining its global hegemony.

With this line of analysis, the critical potential in Kuyper's earlier diagnosis suddenly evaporated. The disenchantment of the world, the secularization of life: at what other destination could they arrive than the technocratic metropolis of harried consumers he had bewailed — masters of the globe, lords of nature, slaves to fashion, and deaf to the plaints of religion? Yet his account now made this into a leading purpose of gospel and church. Perhaps the slippage was a sign of the aging process; more likely it manifested the difficulty of undoing the assumptions of a lifetime. From time to time *Pro Rege* showed some disquiet at the determinism of its logic, only to conclude that God had ordained things to move ever "forward"; there was no going back. Likewise, Kuyper broached early on some lines of Scripture that were hard on his thesis, particularly Genesis's assignment of technological prowess to the line of Cain and Paul's denigration of the "wisdom of this world." But Kuyper bypassed these objections more often than answering them.

A more serious lapse came in not pursuing his historic strength at tracing the organic connection of things — in this case, between so-cial structures, technological processes, and moral dispositions. His prescriptions could accordingly be naïve: the only antidote to the sys-tem of Mammon was personal evangelism; the Christian's first duty was to avoid sex in the big city. The most glaring error came in his ca-sual location of demonic powers in nature and not in human nature. Since the two arms of Jesus' grace had embraced our continent, Kuyper declared, "as a spiritual power the demonic is no more . . . what it once was in Europe and still remains in many respects in a heathen land." And "so it is in Christian lands that the in-working of Satan still proceeds but as a ruling power has been once for all bro-ken." In the second thirty-years' war that was about to descend on Eu-rope, his prophecy would be sorely contradicted.

People of the King

How should his followers deal with the new order? Kuyper's answer began with his classic appeal for a new consciousness. The organizing principle of that consciousness was to be the same as in his Calvinist offensive of the 1890s — Christ's kingship over all things. The first site for renewal should once again be the church, particularly the Bible-believing church which, honoring Christ as Savior but not as Lord, had receded from public life into quietistic introversion.

It was not a new theme, but it now served as the keynote of an en-tire system. Kuyper introduced it from his fresh memory of observing prayers in Hagia Sophia. A faithful Muslim venerated the Prophet about 10,000 times a year, he computed. To kindle a like devotion among Christians, it was necessary for them to understand their Mas-ter anew. Accordingly, some 300 pages of *Pro Rege*'s first volume laid out the necessary biblical theology for the task, replete with Kuyper's illuminating comparisons, fine distinctions, and holistic reach. The second and third volumes took up the usual spheres of practical appli-cation: person and church; family, state, and society; the sciences and art. The new — and essential — task was, having asserted *that* Christ ruled, to show *how* Christ ruled in each domain under new conditions. It was here that Kuyper's command wobbled. Bright new insights al-ternated with pedestrian repetition. His best addition came in think-ing about how set structures might be animated with new verve. It was the old question about "spirit" and "form" from his Beesd and Utrecht days, now in tandem with the new century's attention to the psychological, and a strategic priority as his movement matured.

Pro Rege's treatment of the personal sphere amounted to multiplying the roles of the believer (confessor, witness, cross-bearer, soldier, and pilgrim of the Lord) while reaffirming stalwart Victorian character. This was Kuyper's antidote to the amorphous, melting self he saw in the world-city. It also set the personality type that would fill Neo-Calvinist ranks long after his death — the serious, disciplined activist with strong inner direction and equally strong esprit de corps. In the spheres of church and family the old concern for boundaries was still pronounced. Christ the King was first of all a political concept, and due authority its first mark. Thus, in the home "man" must clearly rule over "wife" and children, albeit for purposes of the Kingdom and not for himself. In the church, sacraments served first of all as public markers of who was in and who was out. Local council members were now officers in the army of the Lord, the first line of defense against enemies without and within. The new tone *Pro Rege* struck regarding the family was a strident anti-feminism that we will consider in the next chapter. For the church he took advantage of globalization to underscore the international, ecumenical character of the body while reaffirming its proper local anchorage. This combination of local and global allowed one more assault on the concept that fell in between, the national church — "a fiction," "entirely inconceivable" as an authentic body of Christ.

The new spirit *Pro Rege* prescribed for family and church reflected their place as havens of nurture amid the heartless world-city. Kuyper's two chapters on child-rearing showed his holistic sense in good form, perhaps also reflecting the thoughts of an aging father looking back on his own record of mixed success. The theme shone even brighter in his treatment of Christ not just as head but as the functional heart of the church. If we think of our King as "set off in heaven infinitely far away from us, then there is no fellowship, no tender, intimate union with Jesus in the mystical Body on earth," Kuyper said.

> But so Jesus has *not* willed it and so it never *is* from his side. On the contrary, while you still dwell on earth he draws near you, presses into you, dwells within you, comes into your heart, touches your

soul, grips you at the very root of your life, and brings you as a living member into the mystical Body that he suffuses with his Spirit.

On the arts and higher learning *Pro Rege* re-played some old chords, with plenty of volume. The twin peaks of Kuyper's recent travels — one, the mountain of Jesus' transfiguration, the other atop the Acropolis, gazing down at Athens — served to turn classical form into the summit of human beauty, set by God's "fixed ordinance and law." Christ the King entered the picture in two ways. First, he was the inspiration for the individual Christian artist, whom Kuyper again called earnestly to counter the paganism of the world-city. Second (recalling his university lectures on aesthetics), Christ was the realized Sublime of Edmund Burke, the omnipotent breaking into a fallen world, only bearing grace instead of terror. On science Kuyper returned to the capstone of his worldview epistemology, namely, that all data and theories are interpreted within a framework set by our answers to ultimate questions. But since Christ is the sum of all those answers, Kuyper now added, his Kingship over the domain of knowledge must be complete. Kuyper thus revised one conclusion of his previous work on common grace. Since common grace was restricted to "the everyday development of ordinary life," it is "only from the particular grace which is in Christ Jesus" that we come to understand "the richest, greatest, and most interesting" matters. The wisdom about whence, why, and whither ultimately resides in Christ alone. His majesty "lies not alone in that He has revealed and confirmed the highest truth but even more that He Himself is the Truth and the Truth is in Him."

Pro Rege's most significant revisions concerned the relationship between state and society. Kuyper recognized that "society" had burgeoned in power and scale over the last century, and not as benignly as he had idealized in *Ons Program*. There, suspicion always rested on the state; his dissection of the new world order barely mentioned government at all. It was the massive expansion of economic, technological, and social institutions that had forged the new system wherein the sovereignty of God seemed eclipsed. One step in its retrieval, therefore, was to acknowledge a more active role for the state. Since anarchists were now outdoing Antirevolutionaries at hostility to state power, Kuyper rehabilitated the scriptural evidence that warranted government as a necessity for human survival, an aid to human progress, and God's strong arm for restraining evil. Furthermore, Kuyper lamented, experience taught that society was not up to its duty of self-regulation. Compulsory insurance, Sunday closing laws, antitrust regulations, proper bounds on competition — all these the interested parties should have taken care of themselves. Their failure to do so meant that the state was right to intervene without (on this Kuyper did not give up) exceeding its "boundary" of being a negative response to sin. Going forward, government worked best when it codified customs and consensual rules arising out of society, rather than inventing nostrums on its own.

Christians could enter this mix in a second, more creative way, Kuyper continued, by using modernity's new opportunities for free social formation. Here was the "spirit" side to the rules of the state — and also the site to consolidate force in the contest for influence that modernity opened. Church and family, the institutions by which society had historically been shaped, were irretrievably receding in power, Kuyper declared, and the exclusive devotion of too many Christians to those circles needed correction. Their opportunity — no, necessity — lay in voluntary organizations and the shaping of public opinion. "People have called the Press the king of the world," said this editor closing in on his fortieth year in the trade, and gathered round that throne were topical meetings, lectures, discussion clubs, and action groups. To the objection that these too were among the distinctive, and distracting, markers of the new order, Kuyper replied that any fault lay not in the instruments themselves but in the objectives to which they had been put. King Jesus willed that they be directed to his purposes.

In fact, his readers had already been doing a fair job at voluntary organization, Kuyper noted. Their newspapers, schools, labor unions, and political parties had all arisen from an instinct for self-preservation and the command to be faithful witnesses in new times. Once started, this momentum proved irrepressible, so that "in every area of life, distinct Christian societies or organizations have sprung up almost spontaneously, and in great numbers." The examples Kuyper went on to list etched the outlines of a self-enclosing world: social clubs for Calvinist youth, occupational associations for Calvinists in the work force, music and choral societies for Calvinist free time, student associations for Calvinists at university.

Notably, here and here alone, amid *Pro Rege*'s 1,600 pages, Kuyper focused on the antithesis. Recalling the mysterious forces that drove the inhabitants of the world-city, citing as well current studies in social psychology, he took it as given that behind separate individuals operated a group spirit, a collective soul. How then could Christians work safely, effectively, cooperatively, if enveloped in a hostile aura? Better all around — for themselves, for others, for the common good — if each spirit were lodged in its own dwelling, equipping and operating it for others to see and evaluate. Notably, Kuyper did not suggest encouraging others "to join." *Pro Rege* registered Neo-Calvinism's effective abandonment of domestic missions to the remnants of the Réveil.

With that, Kuyper at this penultimate stage of his career signaled a chief feature of his legacy, the system of "pillarization" *(verzuiling)* that would mark Dutch life until the 1960s, with residual effects still today. Out of the new system grew a complete array of associations in which the various religious or ideological groups — Calvinists, Catholics, and Labor, with liberal humanists carried along by default — could live their separate lives from cradle to grave. It was a tolerable, fair, creative, and clannish division of public space. The question remained whether and how King Jesus' claims extended beyond the Christian pillars into the whole temple of modernity.

CHAPTER SEVENTEEN

The Dilemmas of Christian Democracy

Kuyper staged a dramatic return to public life after his Mediterranean tour. The venue was no less than the Amsterdam Concertgebouw, and the performance was another of his classic orations, this time commemorating the 150th anniversary of the birth of the Dutch poet William Bilderdijk. The reception was rapturous. The best Dutch cartoonist of the day, Albert Hahn, satirized it as the triumph of an ancient conqueror in modern guise, the returning hero borne off on the shoulders of the democratic throng. That image held several layers of irony, not the least being that Hahn, a devout socialist, was a great fan of the masses. Yet in this instance, by his standards, they seemed unaccountably misguided. For his part Kuyper had just delivered a substantial scholarly address that ran in print to forty-three pages of text with another thirty-seven of notes — an odd occasion for popular acclaim. Finally, as Hahn's caption quipped ("How *Bilderdijk* was celebrated at the Concertgebouw"), Kuyper's treatment of the poet contained a fair bit of self-projection. What neither Hahn nor his subject knew was that on the Concertgebouw stage that night the last act of Kuyper's career was inaugurated, with a clear preview of the plot to come.

Kuyper gave his audience the Calvinistic and fiercely Orangist Bilderdijk they expected but also turned him into an avatar of his own program. Bilderdijk was an organic thinker, sweeping away the "cobwebs" of dry Enlightenment rationalism. He was a Romantic genius, reviving the national soul from the torpor of French occupation. Bilderdijk had created a "worldview," Kuyper claimed, and its ontology and epistemology resembled his own. Especially apropos was

344

Kuyper's invocation, in his very opening line, of Bilderdijk's chosen symbol, the matador. Here was a ceaseless fighter, striving not against flesh and blood but against demonic forces that threatened the undoing of peoples and nations. That struggle, suffered life-long, made Bilderdijk less than a pleasant character, Kuyper granted. As with Edmund Burke, a hero in one of Kuyper's earliest orations, his years increased in bitter complaint. But all this had to be forgiven, and not only because such was the nature of genius. Rather, Bilderdijk, returning from exile, had "called back our Netherlandic folk from the shadow of death into the sunshine of life." Should a like "day of wrath" ever descend again, Kuyper prayed, may the Netherlands again be rescued by a new Bilderdijk.

That Kuyper's speech announced his own return from exile precisely one hundred years after Bilderdijk's was obvious to friend and foe that night. Its hints about the future are more evident in retrospect. From here on out Kuyper would consistently criticize the modern disease of "individualism," and his own demands, like the poet's, would grow more insistent. Wrangling and insult increasingly attended him. He fell out with "intellectuals," particularly fellow Christian intellectuals. His political challenge was equal to Bilderdijk's but from the opposite direction. Whereas the poet had scorned everything associated with "progress" and popular rule, Kuyper had to wrestle with the dynamics of democracy achieved: with socialists to the Left, with Christian Democrats he had inspired, most of all with the transition from charisma to routine typical of modern mass movements. Those were the external challenges. The personal one was to become reconciled to the inevitable decay of his powers. That reconciliation came very late.

Arguments in the Party

Back in harness, Kuyper faced the consequences of his decision to bolt the country the year before. Three Antirevolutionary MPs had offered him their seats after the 1905 elections so that he could continue in Parliament, but he had demurred. Nor did he resume his post as party chairman until September 1907. That was only three months before Theo Heemskerk (who led the ARP's caucus in his stead) inadvertently set off the collapse of the minority Liberal government with a speech against its defense budget. The queen then asked Heemskerk to form an emergency cabinet from the religious parties. Kuyper objected to this course on several grounds — that Heemskerk had not consulted him as party chairman, that he had cooperated with the Social Democrats in toppling the Liberals, that the new cabinet's minority status would force it into too many compromises. Better to have let the Liberals continue to decay in power so that the religious coalition could score a more resounding success in the next elections, he argued.

That strategy was defensible, but the complaint about aligning with the Left was not, as Kuyper had done the same in the franchise battles of the 1890s. He admitted to a friend that "there is something personally difficult in all this. . . . After the way I was run off like a scoundrel in 1905, I had quietly hoped for a rehabilitation. Instead of that" Heemskerk's moves amounted to "another push down." Kuyper believed that Heemskerk had plotted the Liberals' demise in advance. He was grieved, if hardly surprised, to learn that the queen had rejected out of hand Heemskerk's recommendation that Kuyper form the emergency cabinet, or that Lohman had endorsed her decision. Most of all, he could not separate issues of personality, policy, and power in this episode, or later. The result was an unnecessarily rocky road for his party over the next ten years, and the loss of friends, colleagues, and something of his own reputation in the process.

Contrary to Kuyper's fears, the religious coalition had its best election ever in 1909, sweeping to a 60-40 majority in the Lower House. The Antirevolutionary members of the cabinet now composed a solid collection of talent and vision. Alexander Idenburg, Kuyper's best friend these years, came back from Surinam to be colonial secretary. In 1911 another acolyte, Hendrik Colijn, became minister of defense based on twenty years' experience in the East Indies. Heemskerk, in charge of domestic affairs, hoped to engineer an overhaul of the constitution to resolve the perennial issues of education and the franchise. Aritius S. Talma as secretary of agriculture, trade, and industry would literally give his life to promoting the package of social legislation left over from Kuyper's term. Originally a minister in the national Reformed church, more recently the leader of the labor-left in the ARP, Talma was a more knowledgeable and experienced version of the red Kuyper of the 1890s.

The whole cast Kuyper could have justly claimed as the mature fruit of his inspiration. Instead, back in the Lower House (since 1908), in his editorials, and at the head of the party Central Committee, he raised questions and voiced doubts. First these were quiet and in-house, but by the end of 1911 he was speaking out in Parliament and in 1912 he went national with a hundred-page pamphlet. The tide crested in 1915 with a long series of editorials in *De Standaard* diagnosing what had gone wrong with the Heemskerk regime (it was roundly defeated at the 1913 polls), followed by a battle of pamphlets in which Heemskerk and his friends fought back.

Kuyper's complaints ranged from substance to strategy to tactics and tone. He argued that Heemskerk should have approached constitutional reform one piece at a time rather than trying for a comprehensive deal. He argued just the opposite about Talma's decision to break up Kuyper's old social-welfare package into a series of discrete proposals. He most belabored Jan Hendrik de Waal Malefijt (who took over the colonial desk when Idenburg became governor-general of the East Indies) for not promoting publicly funded Christian education there on the model that the ARP advocated for the Netherlands.

Each of these complaints was contestable. Constitutionally, there would be no settlement on education without a deal on the franchise. Talma had seen Kuyper's package of social law bog down precisely because of its scale and complexity. As for the colonies, Idenburg himself wrote Kuyper that religious education there was a far more complicated matter than it was back home. On the other hand, Kuyper could accurately contend that the five-plus years of the Heemskerk administration produced less than hoped for, certainly less than its large majority augured. Constitutional revision was left for the succeeding administration. Talma's bills were obstructed, pruned, or killed one at a time, not least by opposition from conservative religious quarters. The acts that did get passed received their enabling legislation only in 1919 (disability and old-age insurance) and 1930 (health insurance). Finally, more critics than Kuyper found Heemskerk weak on some points of leadership; he was an uninspiring speaker who preferred conciliation to hard bargaining.

For Kuyper the latter trait betrayed a deficiency of principle. Heemskerk with his "happy Christianity" was too quick to forget the ultimate issues hiding in prosaic legislation, too prone to trim the cause of the Lord for the sake of parliamentary etiquette. Kuyper advocated the opposite tack at the 1909 party convention, when he resurrected unapologetically his theme from the previous campaign.

Christ said he came not to bring peace but the sword, he reminded the delegates, so his disciples were called to "a battle of principles" to see whether "the course of our governmental policies will be set by *the will of man* or *the will of God*." Nor was the antithesis a formula for political failure. On the contrary: "The Antithesis is the cement of the Coalition. Whoever weakens or obscures it at the same time weakens the cooperation of the Christian parties" and thus opens the way — the only way — for the secular parties to triumph. Four years later, in the wake of Heemskerk's defeat, Kuyper concluded that his cabinet had done just that. Compromising on substance only encouraged the opposition to hold out for more while deflating the zeal of the faithful.

The moral of the story seemed to be that an unrelenting focus on first principles was as good for business as it was for the Lord. But was it so? And was the business at hand getting elected or governing? The first is a perennial question for Christians in public life as the second is for any political party. For pioneers of Christian democracy like Kuyper, the two dawned together as a new and perplexing challenge. Having low tolerance for perplexity, Kuyper instinctively moved toward ideological purity.

It was to his credit, then, that on the campaign trail in good years (1909) and bad (1913) he reminded his listeners of the hard realities of the governing process. To get elected at all, he repeated, we must ally with Christian conservatives to our right and Roman Catholics whom many in the audience still regarded as dangerous. If political friends expected some horse-trading in setting legislative priorities, how much more cluttered would the process inevitably become in maneuvers against the opposition?

Kuyper did empathize with the frustration of the zealots in the crowd. He evoked the noble isolation of Groen van Prinsterer and the freedom it permitted for boldly pronouncing high ideals; were it up to me, Kuyper mused, I would spend my last days in an all-out "guerrilla" campaign. Nonetheless, God having ordained different circumstances, he called his followers to the patience and prudence of responsible governance. Nor as an anti-revolutionary party could they proceed by demolishing the house of state and starting over; we "must build upon what Liberalism has bequeathed us, in its rococo style." That made it all the more necessary to set forth ultimate goals clearly, emphatically, repeatedly, lest they be lost in the dim halls of legislation. For Kuyper, aiming high was necessary to keep up morale in the ranks so as to generate the power needed to bargain from strength in Parliament.

From Heemskerk's point of view, the first problem in this formula was that Kuyper did not trust anyone else to conduct that bargaining; thus, what had been "necessary negotiation" in 1902 became "feckless compromise" in 1912. Secondly, one could not simply turn the rhetorical spigot on and off at will. The parties all had overlapping, not discrete, communication webs, and what one overheard from other sides tended either to alienate the peers one had to negotiate with in Parliament or to disappoint the voters who had been conditioned to expect a steady diet of red meat. Heemskerk opted to speak in a single calm voice, counting on the trust of the faithful to remain firm. That precluded (glancing at Kuyper) the cultivation of distrust by party officials. This was the voice of a lawyer used to managing things one step at a time. Others pointed out some harder dilemmas. Said Anne Anema, a new professor at the Free University, the masses "in normal times are conservative, in extraordinary times are revolutionary, but are never moderately progressive. . . . [Yet] such a moderately progressive politics is exactly what our society needs." What then remained for Kuyper, a radical for gradual change, an orator of extremity in the cause of preservation?

The most serious challenge of all was set forth by Kuyper's friend Idenburg while the Heemskerk regime was still in office: "Great principles these days awaken no enthusiasm," just as you complain, he wrote Kuyper. "The fault for that is *not* only that Heemskerk doesn't give great principial orations. . . . It is in my opinion the consequence that today, more than thirty years ago, material questions are calling for a solution. . . . [Such] points naturally have some connection with higher (or deeper) life-principles, but not so directly, not so clearly, not so precisely." Educating one's children in the fear of the Lord was for Christian parents a clear command of Scripture and conscience. But the question of mandatory disability insurance had no such forthright mandate, and thus found Christians on different sides of the issue. Where then the "antithesis"? And how could so technical an issue awaken the "holy enthusiasm" Kuyper longed for, especially when it became the unholy object of self-seeking politics? Kuyper's opponents in the party put the point more bluntly: "The time of first principles, the time of naïve faith in the virtually unlimited power of the idea appears, in this country, to be over." If so, Kuyper was, too.

The Question of Charisma

The contretemps over the Heemskerk cabinet bore ironic resemblances to Kuyper's fight with Lohman twenty years earlier. Once again Kuyper was complaining that party MPs were too clubby and autonomous, and once again he tried to assert control via command of the party apparatus. Yet Kuyper's defeat of the elite back then had opened the way for a generation of "new men" who included the very challengers he now faced. Unquestioned loyalists like Colijn and Idenburg were part of that cohort, as were neutral parties like Talma, but the dissenters represented the cream of the crop no less than they did. Heemskerk and Simon de Vries, an MP during Kuyper's cabinet and a future minister of finance, were not just political leaders but curators of the Free University. Anema was a successor to Lohman on the law faculty; there Herman Bavinck was establishing his own aura and agenda in Kuyper's place on the theology faculty. The university's first economist, Pieter A. Diepenhorst, also served, Kuyper-like, on the Amsterdam city council and as editor-in-chief of a new antirevolutionary newspaper, *De Rotterdammer,* an outlet for those alienated from *De Standaard.* An independent cultural journal, *Ons Tijdschrift,* had emerged too, as the organ of a still younger generation reared in the movement but now chafing at its segmentation and isolation. They particularly faulted Kuyper's aesthetic judgment, believing that new modernist styles warranted at least more serious consideration. These two groups represented the "individualists" that Kuyper now increasingly sniped at for defying party discipline, the "intellectuals" who puzzled the rank and file with political nuance and demoralized them with non-representational art. For these reasons, although they were more progressive than Kuyper and certainly not rich like Lohman, the three professors along with Heemskerk and De Vries became known as the "Five Gentlemen." Kuyper cast himself once more as the man of the people — now *de kleine luyden,* the "little people."

He set out on a reform program of his own. The first phase was physical. Beginning in 1911 he took his summer vacations at the internationally renowned Weissen Hirsch sanatorium of Heinrich Lahmann, outside Dresden. That first summer he was drubbed so mercilessly with physical- and hydro-therapies that he wondered, he later wrote Idenburg, whether a seventy-three-year-old should be trying such a regimen. Yet once back home he found himself feeling better than he had in ten years. His chronic throat and sinus ailments had responded wonderfully to Herr Lahmann's "daily infusions." From similar treatment and/or his new vegetarian diet the constipation "that has bothered me so endlessly now doesn't give me the slightest trouble. My sleep is better, my sciatica is diminished." His heartbeat was once more "normal, regular, and strong." Even his hearing, which had been steadily deteriorating, seemed to have responded positively to the good doctor's ministrations. As it happened, this proved a fleeting hope, as did his visit to the Parisian inventor of a new "hearing-restoration machine." He could still carry on ordinary conversation but, unable to follow live debate in a large hall, Kuyper gave up his seat in the Lower House in 1912. The Upper House served better.

Reinvigorating the party was the next task, and to that end Kuyper at this late date added a new line to his theoretical wares. Next to the revolutionary track of "Calvinism and Constitutional Liberties" and the complex social array of "Sphere Sovereignty," he now championed the organic bond between charismatic leadership and the popular will. He laid out the theory in a *Standaard* series in 1908, just as the Heemskerk administration got underway, and he drew off the contemporary fascination with instinct and social psychology. If his argument clearly aimed to leverage his own position in the party, it also addressed the live question in political and social theory being asked by the likes of Max Weber and Georges Sorel. How could modern social movements escape the paradox that the institutionalization necessary for long-term survival threatened the very inspiration that gave rise to them in the first place? More generally, where was the place for spirit and passion amid the iron routines of modern life? Kuyper had sounded this worry already in his first major address, "Uniformity, the Curse of Modern Life." Now he came back to it forty years later in "Our Instinctive Life."

Kuyper began his account by extolling the instinctive powers of the animal world. This was his fable of the bees — more accurately, of the spiders, for whom he showed a fascination comparable to Jonathan Edwards's two hundred years before. The wisdom of the insects partakes of the wisdom of God, he began. Even more so does the practical intelligence of ordinary people. In marked contrast to the raptures about frontline scholarship proclaimed in "Sphere Sovereignty," Kuyper now characterized knowledge gained by "reflection" to be artificial and fleeting. The "perfect" knowledge Paul foresaw in the next world (1 Corinthians 13:12) would be "spontaneous, immedi-

351

ate, and completed at once" — closer to the wisdom of everyday life than to the book learning of academics. Yet these were now scheming to recast party operations in their mode, Kuyper complained. In fact, the younger generation was proposing to make policy formation more collaborative via discussion clubs, so that the means as well as the ends of party initiatives would be democratic. They also urged that the trained competence of lawyers and social scientists bear more weight in devising legislation than the generalizations of the clergy.

These proposals Kuyper proceeded to scotch. There are three kinds of people in the world, he declared: the large mass of folk who live by practical wisdom, a few genuine scholars whose all-absorbing studies take them to the depths of things, and then the jabbering class of the superficially learned, who were textbook-trained in secondhand knowledge but lacking the virtues of the other two groups. The professionals most likely to escape this hazard, to bring "the instinctive and the reflective life into a higher synthesis," Kuyper ventured, were precisely the clergy, whose hard study for the pulpit alternated with parish rounds that kept them in daily touch with ordinary folk. The derivative "amphibians" now contesting for party leadership knew not the real life of those they invited to the policy table; otherwise they would know how mistaken their suggestions must be. Within their own sphere of intuitional knowledge, Kuyper declared, commoners neither could nor wished to take part in policy formation. When faced with competing proposals, the role of "the non-learned public" was "to use its own instinctive life as touchstone and for the rest to rely on its leaders."

Kuyper granted that some institutionalization was necessary in his movement but worried about the tendency toward "spiritual decline and emotional impoverishment" that came with the process. His favorite solution was the mass meetings he had built into party operations from the start. There the bonds of trust between leaders and followers were not just formally ratified but made heartfelt. There a village delegate realized that he was part of a vibrant, national movement. A written statement of principles became a living conviction; a campaign platform became the staircase to a better tomorrow. Most of all, the keynote address wove together policy, social studies, political theory, and tactical considerations into an inspiring statement that accorded precisely with what the rank and file "instinctively felt in essence." That leadership common people valued far more than a spot on a study committee.

Such drama was also essential to modern politics, Kuyper continued. Over the long years in power or out, a party "must have the means — as the *psychology of the crowd* demands — to convert sober realism into enthusiasm, cool calculation into holy passion. . . . It is by virtue of the power and animation that radiates from [our] national meetings that we have become who we are." Kuyper sealed the point on a biblical note: while the technical expertise offered by his rivals was like the armor of Saul, the intuitive bond connecting the leader with the faithful was the stone of David that fells the giant. One can almost hear the ovation arising from his readers around the nation. Yet Kuyper's quotation of "the psychology of the crowd" indicated some non-biblical sources behind his insights as well. Just as "Calvinism and Constitutional Liberties" had recourse to French resistance theorists, "Our Instinctive Life" appealed to a French authority, Gustav Le Bon, a pioneer in the study of social psychology. Le Bon was most famous for showing how a crowd could become a being in itself with will of its own that swept up those of its individual members. That conclusion aptly served Le Bon's hostility to the French revolutionary tradition, a conviction he shared with Kuyper. He came there from the other side of the antithesis, however: Le Bon was anticlerical, anti-democratic, and a ruthless social Darwinian. His work fit with its leftist counterpart, Georges Sorel's *Reflections on Violence* (1908), and the pioneering analysis of the "oligarchic tendencies in modern group life" (1911) by German sociologist Robert Michels as attempts to explain a perceived malaise afflicting democratic movements at the very peak of the Progressive tide. Whatever their diagnoses, all three turned for a prescription toward a cult of radical charisma which, after World War I, would find a home in fascism. Contrary to accusations by some later critics, there is nothing in Kuyper or his following that indicates he would have ever taken that turn. It is more to the point to see him, at an advanced age, recognizing the urgency of the problem and trying to tap his long experience for a solution.

The Personal Factor

Kuyper's proposal was personally strategic in that, as one scholar notes, the quadrennial convention operated as his private "applause machine," just as the party's Central Committee did little more than rubber-stamp his edicts. That level of power invited a proportionate level of scrutiny, however, and there Kuyper stumbled twice. The second occasion was simply an embarrassment. On September 21, 1911, Reuters reported that Kuyper had been arrested for "pacing back and forth stark naked" before an open window in his room at the Hotel Métropole in Brussels. The Dutch press and at least one German daily picked up the story, and the socialist *Het Volk* rode it into the ground. Kuyper himself hastened to explain: he was following the mandate of Dr. Lahmann to exercise naked every day to respire the whole body, had not realized that his fourth-floor room was visible to the street, and in any case had not (as Reuters reported) been marched to police headquarters under arrest, much less been led there (as caricatured by Albert Hahn) covered with only a strategically held Bible and a top-hat. Rather, the police had notified the hotel manager, who had reported to Kuyper, who had quickly pulled the drapes, while a lawyer handled things at the station. Yet the story stung, for ridicule is the hardest opposition to overcome. Even Kuyper's own followers must have recalled how often he had held up the "naked crazies" among sixteenth-century Anabaptists as proof of their delusions.

Unfortunately, the Brussels episode came atop a more serious scandal that embroiled Kuyper in 1909. In late June of that year, just after the general elections, *Het Volk* ran the accusations of a Haarlem lawyer that Kuyper, while prime minister, had nominated an Amsterdam businessman for an official decoration in exchange for a gift to the ARP's coffers. The deal was then repeated, the story continued, on behalf of the businessman's brother. Moreover, both transactions had been mediated by a young woman, one Mathilde Westmeijer, who, though Roman Catholic by background, was an official agent of the ARP and on the businessman's payroll besides. Kuyper responded to the allegations after an official investigation had been enjoined. He had indeed recommended the brothers for official honors, he said, but in recognition of the usual voluntary service of national significance; there was no connection between decoration and donation. Kuyper fumed as Troelstra demanded that Parliament conduct a formal inquest, and he was only partly mollified when the special committee that was empanelled found him not guilty without declaring him fully innocent. There was no "conclusive evidence" that warranted criminal charges, the investigators determined, nor any "reason to doubt" the testimony provided by the principals as to their motives and conduct. The committee did raise its collective eyebrows at the "zealous interventions" of the comely Ms. Westmeijer, and noted that one of the two brothers had rendered no national service meriting a medal. That nomination having expired with the end of Kuyper's cabinet, however, it remained technically a private affair. Kuyper himself admitted that his simultaneous functions as prime minister and party treasurer were not well advised, and tried to end the matter on a pious note: "Sackcloth does not disgrace its wearer."

Campaign financing would only grow as a problem for democracies in the future, but with the "decoration affair" Kuyper's prospects for a return to high office were finished. "It was a gripping moment," wrote one reporter, that followed the pronouncement Troelstra delivered from his parliamentary desk:

> "You know as well as we on this side of the House, gentlemen of the Right, that the political career of Dr. Kuyper (the speaker said it slowly, and paused a moment) is over." Dead silence reigned in the House for a few moments after these words . . . the death they announced [was] not a glorious fall in battle but the sad demise in a mud-puddle of one of the greatest political figures the Netherlands has ever known.

Things got worse because of Kuyper's combative personality. Always harder on friends than on opponents, he continued to manifest his passion for control. Alexander Idenburg became the keenest observer of the syndrome as he maintained a correspondence with all sides in the party's quarrels from his safe distance in the East Indies. He rendered his judgments in letters to his wife who, having returned to The Hague for health reasons, lived only a few minutes' walk from everyone involved. Having read their private complaints and then their battling pamphlets, Idenburg concluded that there was plenty of blame to go around. Heemskerk and company had not accorded Kuyper the respect due to the party's elder statesman. After all, he had built the party from the ground up and knew something about strategy and operations. He possessed a willpower and breadth of vision that they could well emulate. "No one else but he could have accomplished" what Kuyper did, Idenburg reflected, for the cause had demanded "not only someone of great knowledge and great competence, of extraordinary talent as a thinker and writer and speaker, but also someone with an iron will, with a thick skin, and with a rock-hard head." Moreover, though Idenburg was too charitable to say it, Heemskerk's complaints could whine on at tedious length.

All that said, though, Idenburg found Kuyper sadly wrong on a whole list of matters. He was wrong to go public with internal party affairs: that, too, emboldened the opposition and deflated the faithful. Nor was the party chief any less touchy than Heemskerk on protocol and pride. Both forgot the Lord's cause, which was the main point, Idenburg lamented; for such an end these highly visible, professedly Christian leaders ought to be able to submerge their personal feelings. Kuyper might rightly expect gratitude and respect in party circles as his "*moral* right" but not to dictate "*practical* arrangements." But as Idenburg noted more than once, Kuyper could hardly distinguish between himself, the party, and the Lord's will. Disagreements on policy he immediately took as personal opposition and thus drove off those who were needed to serve as his conscience now and his successors later. Kuyper had "disciples but no colleagues," Idenburg put it, "sheep but no watch-dogs."

If these were "the defects of his virtues," other traits were just defects. "Kuyper is rough and coarse, no gentleman"; his "deficiency in good taste" often made "working with him so difficult." No doubt Kuyper had heard the snobs in The Hague whisper this point often enough, but to Idenburg the trouble was more a matter of personality than of social class: "The great difficulty with Kuyper is that his feelings are developed in such imbalance. Very highly strung (overstrung, I would say) when it comes to himself; under-developed when it comes to others." Finally, Kuyper "knows so little of life as it actually *is* outside his own circle of converted Christians," yet insisted on delivering the last word on everything foreign and domestic in the name of the Lord. The upshot was something "extraordinarily tragic," Idenburg concluded: "that a man who has done so much, and so much good, should toward the end of his life by his character-traits place himself outside the circle of those who have been formed by him, and thereby lose his power and influence."

These being the sentiments of Kuyper's truest friend, those of the Five Gentlemen can easily be imagined. Their alienation was ominous for the party as the question of Kuyper's successor became urgent. Talma had been the one most likely to push through the social program, but he died in 1916, only fifty-two years old, from over-work in the Heemskerk cabinet. Idenburg was burnt out by his pro-longed stay in the East Indies (extended even further by the outbreak of World War I), where every year of service took two years off most lives.

In that vacuum the star of Hendrik Colijn steadily rose. Son of a Christian Reformed polder farmer, Colijn, like Idenburg, was schooled not at the Free University but at a military academy. Unlike Idenburg, for Colijn the defining moment was not a conversion to Kuyper's ethical policy for colonial development but leadership in the Dutch army's suppression of the Aceh insurgency. That completed, Colijn seized the commercial openings that pacification made possible, par-ticularly the matter of oil leases. The ambitions of Shell and Standard Oil were a bane of Idenburg's existence as governor-general, but not for his junior partner. Colijn was "a man of big things," Idenburg wrote Kuyper. "He sees all salvation in great capitalistic enterprises and natu-rally does not say that he disregards how the natives are treated but is too fearful of what he calls ethical busyness."

Once back in the Netherlands, Colijn again moved from public of-fice (minister of war in the Heemskerk cabinet) to commercial reward as director of a major Dutch oil firm, the Bataafsche Petroleum Maatschappij. Idenburg worried about his grasp of Antirevolutionary theory, which "stands opposed to exploitation of the colonies by the motherland but also — and no less — against exploitation by private parties. Colijn, I fear, does not keep the latter fully in view." As for his Calvinism, Colijn's experiences in reducing guerrilla warfare had left him fixated on order, with less regard for matters of justice. Yet he im-pressed Kuyper as a capable executive if somewhat raw in manner, and he steadfastly took Kuyper's side in intra-party quarrels. Even more, he had funds at hand to see the cause through wartime finan-cial exigencies. Still, Kuyper found the source of that wealth dubious. "He is living very close to Mammon," Kuyper wrote Idenburg in 1915. "May the Lord preserve him." By 1919 Colijn would be living in Lon-don, at the heart, if not of Mammon, of the postwar British Empire with its new Middle Eastern "mandates," working for Royal Dutch Shell, which had merged with his old company. Kuyper was left oscil-lating between gratitude and doubt. "Colijn is outstanding," he as-sured Idenburg. "I appreciate him more and more, even though he has still too little eye for spiritual things."

Troubles in the Home

Problems in the party were oddly mirrored in Kuyper's own family. By the time he returned from the Mediterranean in 1906, three of his surviving children were married and all seven seemed to be embarked on their careers. His oldest son and daughter hewed close to the paternal track: Herman was professor of theology at the Free University; Henriëtte was a force in the national Reformed young ladies' society and her father's amanuensis. Two of the middle children had moved a little further away. Johanna was a nurse who served some time abroad in Java and for the Red Cross during the first Balkan War (1912-13). Abraham Jr. was in the first decade of a thirty-year pastorate in Rotterdam, publishing some books and articles on the side. Guillaume, the youngest surviving son, was an officer in the Dutch infantry. The problems lay with the second-born son, Jan Frederik, named after Kuyper's father, and Catharina, born in 1876 during his recuperation abroad.

"Freddy" put maximum distance between himself and his father. After finishing dental studies at the University of Michigan, he settled in the East Indies, where he serviced the Dutch elite, enjoyed the tropical breezes, and followed his philosophical inquiries into the courts of theosophy. Kuyper had been earnestly interrogating Fred over his state of soul from his eighteenth year on: "Meet with the Lord your God every day, dear boy! . . . Delve down into your heart and ask, *what bond ties my heart to Jesus? Lord, is* there such a bond?" Decades later he lamented in one letter to Idenburg after another that such prayers had proven unavailing. "[H]is soul sleeps . . . in Theosophical dreams," Kuyper said of "my poor Frederik." He thinks he has no need of a Redeemer. "The only one of my children. The others are so rich a blessing to me in their faith, but here I stand powerless." From his side, Fred's surviving correspondence shows warm solicitude, especially at election time. In 1905 he offered a prayer of his own for Kuyper: "I would love to see you spend your future years in peace and easier affairs. You have battled your whole life and undergone much strife"; have accomplished enough for "at least three lives; have experienced success almost exclusively in all your ventures; have reached the highest rung on the ladder. Let it go, then, dear Father." A few years later, during the Heemskerk difficulties, he asked, "Why actually do you live in Holland? Foreign terrain is so very much less cramped. I find my countrymen so often small-minded and childish. Why don't you spend the last years of your life in Brussels or Paris?" Nor was Fred incapable of deep feeling. Returning to the Indies via Switzerland in 1912, he dropped Kuyper a postcard: "Today I visited Mother's grave . . . also the room where Mother died. It was truly an emotional day for me. I had a very painful night."

Painful too, he feared, his father would find the letter with which he finally responded to Kuyper's religious queries. "I appreciate it that you . . . asked about the state of my soul. I feel that you as a Christian must be unhappy about it. . . . [Yet] dear father, it is my settled conviction" that the question of why we have come into the world and what might or might not happen to us after death "lies beyond my ken to fathom." It was all he could do to understand man's brief intermediate period on earth and to conduct himself with integrity. That included avoiding "dogmatic certainty and strife" about unknowable things. It entailed a respect for religion in general for its "positive effects on the conduct of life," and appreciation for select features of particular world religions. But "the only reverence that I can feel without shame for a Higher Power is in a clear conscience and the honorable self-knowledge that I grasp nothing, can grasp nothing, have grasped nothing" final as yet here on earth. People will say that I'm an unbeliever, he continued, but don't you think my honest and considered conclusion is better than that of thousands who simply go through the motions because it's the proper thing to do? "I hope from the heart that you will take this real look into my inner life for what it is," Fred concluded. But Kuyper kept to his old hope. He wrote Idenburg, "I keep praying."

He was much more directive with his youngest daughter, Catharina. Cato or "Too" had a hard time finding her vocation, shifting between education and nursing, and adding in the periodic convalescences characteristic of her time and social class. This frustrated Kuyper and even more her oldest sister, Henriëtte. An organizer and aspiring author like her father, the significantly nicknamed "Harry" was not averse to pointing out Too's perceived deficiencies. When Too received one such rebuke by mail while staying with the Idenburgs in the East Indies, she cut off correspondence with her sister. Kuyper asked her hosts to intervene. Too had the same "psychosis" from which "my dear wife suffered so bitterly from her sixteenth year on," Kuyper revealed to Idenburg; she turned every admonition into a complaint, then aired them ceaselessly outside the family.

Kuyper did not note at this point the other relevant resemblance, of Henriëtte to himself, nor the coincidence that his Jo's alleged complaints started with his own campaign to make her over from a teenager into a consort worthy of a dominie. He theologized the problem instead, and at the deepest levels. Running beneath the sisters' spat were "demonic actions," he discerned. Too's traits were precisely those "on which Satan throws himself and which he misuses to bind the soul." I've been warning both sisters on the matter, he assured Idenburg, "and I can happily say that Harry feels herself fully at fault and has thanked me for opening her eyes to this demonic danger." Yet when similarly confronted, Too "did not answer me directly but went to talk about it with your wife. That's what her mother always did too. Always dragging things out of the house."

Idenburg was too kind to ask Kuyper whether, as to talking out of school, the pot was not calling the kettle black. He did tell him that dear Harry was not quite the saint Kuyper took her to be. When Mrs. Idenburg wrote her suggesting that the Golden Rule might well apply to the sisters' spat, "your oldest daughter" replied with "a series of complaints about Too," including dread at her imminent return home. "On the whole," he warned Kuyper, "I got the impression that not love for her sister . . . but pursuit of her rights and interest stands first in [her] heart." He thought the two simply had profound personality differences and would probably benefit by living apart for a while. Kuyper took that to be a last option, something of a surrender to sin, and later reported that all three sisters were living happily together under the paternal roof. Yet Too not-so-mysteriously came down with "heart ailments" while taking nurse's training during World War I, and went to live with the Warfields in Princeton.

Sex and Suffrage

His trials at home mirroring those in the party, it was fitting that the last new policy issue to engage Kuyper's attention was women's suffrage. The broader franchise for which he fought so hard in the 1890s he continued to advocate against the remaining conservatives in the party as the issue returned to the fore. For the radicals in the secular parties, however, "universal" voting rights meant women too, and there Kuyper drew the line.

On the campaign trail in 1913 he reminded the faithful why. The party program from the start had called for an "organic," "household" franchise, not the "mechanistic" individualism that the radicals espoused. Thus women who headed a home — widows with children as well as single women living on their own — might properly vote, be it that those two circumstances were equally lamentable. But on the fundamental point there could be no compromise. Kuyper thundered: the "holy order of God" rested upon the "principial difference between man and woman." To defy that was to assault the family itself. Women's suffrage would bring in its wake widespread birth control and easy divorce. We have heard it urged "that every post in life be opened to women," he lamented to the comrades; "it's even been suggested that the Amazon be revived, and anyone who will not let her have the vote is called a tyrant in his male egotism."

Kuyper's patriarchy was so pronounced that it needs some contextual qualification. For one, virtually all Dutch political parties of the time, the radicals as well as the religious, saw women's role — even in public life — as maternal. For some it was an antidote to the worrisome individualism that they too saw on the rise in the new century. Leading feminists early on pushed the domestic argument for the vote: women being so vital at home, how could the household of the state thrive without their input? Socialists wanted special provisions for women in and outside of the labor force on the premise that women's well-being made for a happy home, and a happy home humanized the worker's life. Without love and beauty, all was drudgery — a sentiment that Kuyper applied to the rich and middling classes as well. Furthermore, Kuyper praised the female leadership he met on his American tour. In contrast to the two options of "fashion-plate" or "household drudge" that Europe offered women, he enthused that American women demonstrated high levels of knowledge, education, organizational acumen, and civic engagement, all without compromising their morals or demanding public office. Kuyper had in mind the wives and daughters of the Protestant professional class who in fact did provide much of the cultural and social-service leadership in cities such as he visited. They would also prove to be the bedrock of the women's suffrage movement as it bloomed there soon after his trip. In short, women's suffrage caught Kuyper, along with many of his contemporaries, on the logic of their espoused virtues.

His solution was also common — the ideology of "separate

spheres," which postulated differences in essence, hence in character, capabilities, and proper roles, between the two sexes. His distinctive contribution was to suffuse the notion with religion and emotion. The softer side of his rhetoric came out in *Women of the Bible,* a collection of eighty *Heraut* meditations published in 1897, and *The Woman's Place of Honor,* a seventy-page *Standaard* series that appeared in the thick of the franchise debates in 1914. In the first, Kuyper graded his subjects by their relative devotion to God as that registered in their (un)willingness to accept their role in service to others. Their place on the pedestal in his 1914 tract stemmed, predictably, from women's tender nature, which made it prudent as well as principled that they avoid the rigors of public life. Homemaking in the fullest sense of that term, with its power over the character-formation of children and the socialization of husbands, was women's natural vocation and a delight to all who had the proper heart. As for public affairs, cultural leadership on the American model was fine. So was a professional career for single women so long as it fit feminine qualities — for instance, education, philanthropy, and female specialties in medicine.

Feminism proper brought out his harsher tones. His argument stands forth most baldly in two chapters Kuyper devoted to the subject in *Pro Rege,* amid his broader treatment of the family as the first sphere in the order of creation. The *Christian* family, in Kuyper's treatment, was distinguished by the redemption wrought upon its myriad interrelationships by God's re-creation of all things in Christ. With respect to household staff, for instance, that entailed master and mistress establishing such an order of "right and equity" that the servants gave thanks for being in a Christian household. With respect to the nurture of children, the burden of proof again fell entirely on the ones in power. The first duty of fathers as head of the household was not to abuse their authority; the second was to provide for the holistic formation of the child. The wise father shared authority with his wife; in fact, she had a "sovereignty" of her own in the "mixed sphere" of the household. These injunctions followed after arguments of a very different temper, however. The goal for the family might be Christ's re-creative work, but the functional norm for gender relations was purely natural, with not a word of Jesus' own teaching or example. Instead, the biblical figures looming behind Kuyper's words on this topic were Samson and Delilah. God ordained males for strength, females for beauty, he said; man sinned as oppressor, woman as seductress. That contest was no contest, however; women won. There was a "magnetic power," an "irresistible magnetic power," in female charms that bent men to her will. So also there was a depth in her depravity quite below his: "The woman who sins sinks much deeper than does the man. She stands for nothing. Unrighteousness seizes her as a life-rule." Not alone but also not least among the male commentators of his time, Kuyper was profoundly anxious about the power of female sexuality.

What might Christ's redemption spell in this context? First, there was the common grace of the family itself, which Kuyper introduced as an institution to channel sexuality. Within the family, secondly, King Jesus had ordained strong lines of authority via the order of creation: God over man, man over woman. Thirdly, Kuyper dealt out a large dose of the muscular Christianity dear to late Victorians. He protested popular art's feminization of Jesus, insisting that Jesus wanted men to be manlier. There being no words in Scripture to that effect, Kuyper appealed instead to the "rich development of the human race," which could go forward only by robust counterbalances between binary opposites. Just here lay the perversity of feminism, he concluded. Feminism was "nothing but an attempt to retard, falsify, and bastardize" a creaturely given, a "fixed ordinance" of God. "The feminist wants to be a *man,* but cannot and never will be," just as the fop, her only equal in shame, was a male who did not want to be a man. So unnatural were a feminist's aspirations that other forces, male forces, must have provoked them. The "chief cause of feminism," Kuyper declared, was that "so many men remain unmarried," courtesy of the fallen women who provided them cheap sexual services. Following close behind were "the scandalous means that men find" to exercise birth control, thwarting women's maternal instinct. The whole feminist agenda thus stemmed from the rising tide of single, childless women who needed careers to fill their lives; none of this would have happened "but that the egotism of man makes it necessary." One wonders what Kuyper's three adult daughters, all unmarried, thought of these words, particularly in light of his having scared off at least one eligible young man "with *views* on Too." Or his three married sons who, making the demographic turn, produced but seven children among them, one less than Kuyper had on his own.

Political Endgame

Whatever their thoughts on feminism, the ARP was divided on women's suffrage. Herman Bavinck, for one, was enthusiastic for broadening gender qualifications (less so than Kuyper on class). In any case the issue went into an omnibus "pacification" process run by the cabinet that succeeded Heemskerk's. Its prime minister, center-liberal Pieter Cort van der Linden, came into office committed to resolving the issues of franchise and education that had dogged Dutch politics for forty years. When World War I broke out, the matter became urgent out of fears that the Netherlands' neutrality abroad would prove fragile without greater solidarity at home. In the bargain, the radical parties gave up their demand for women's suffrage and the Christian parties backed off their demand that religious education be "the rule" in the nation and secular schools a "supplement." The revised constitution in 1917 granted all Dutch schools equal state funding and all adult males the right to vote.

An equally momentous change, proportionate representation, passed with virtually no discussion. Henceforth, the States General would be elected not by districts but according to each party's share of the national vote. This really was the death warrant for the Liberals, who lost twenty-five of their forty seats in the next election. It was an aid to the ARP, which had lost out under the old system both in 1905 and 1913. It rewarded Roman Catholics even more; accustomed to getting one-quarter of the seats but having a third of the population, they held a permanent plurality in Parliament.

The greatest beneficiaries of all were political parties themselves. No longer the Liberals' ideal of an educated man as elector and elected but a disciplined organization of national scope was the key player in Dutch politics. This was Kuyper's original intention, his pioneering construction, and now his final triumph. With that, his party acceded to the inevitable arrival of women's suffrage in 1921. Without condoning it in principle, Kuyper's successors assured women they would not sin in going to the polls. In fact, it was their duty — so that the party did not lose ground to its rivals.

Even before the pacification, the aging warrior offered several initiatives to help ready the party for the new day. He thought that the social question should headline the new agenda, so he proposed another Christian Social Congress to rekindle the devotion of the faithful, as in

1891. The outbreak of war postponed that meeting until 1919, under others' leadership. Likewise, it was commonly complained that the party had not engaged in any significant discussion of its principles since 1901. Kuyper tried to address that with an updated version of *Ons Program,* published in two volumes in 1916 and 1917 as *Antirevolutionaire Staatkunde.* Yet the work was most notable for its pace of production, not its content. As his publisher later recounted it, the then seventy-eight-year-old Kuyper met with him in 1915 to discuss the project. After deciding its purpose and general outline, the two discussed a delivery date. The publisher watched Kuyper pencil out some quick calculations: the number of pages the book would encompass (some 1,400), the length of handwritten text that entailed, the number of words he could write per week, and the bottom line that, *deo volente,* he would have it done by the end of 1916. He did, on New Year's Eve. This story reveals a marvel of discipline. It also betokens, as did the published text, an absence of the fresh thinking needed to meet the dramatically new circumstances spelled by total war abroad, pacification at home, and the rise of the new world order that Kuyper had espied in *Pro Rege.* It was hardly Kuyper's fault; this was properly the job of a generation still younger than his critics'. By the same token, the work could not have its intended effect.

The one reform that did occur came in practical organization, Kuyper's old strong suit. The party's local chapters were strengthened, a new provincial layer of coordination introduced, lines of communication between these and headquarters made more clear and constant, and the first full-time staff hired. The perennial question of whether the chair of the Central Committee or of the parliamentary caucus was to head the party was left hanging. It was thus with old ideas, updated machinery, and the pressing question of succession that the Antirevolutionary Party faced the end of the world as they knew it.

CHAPTER EIGHTEEN

The End of the World

K uyper was not averse to issuing dire warnings about the course of events. Such was his postmortem on the 1913 elections. "Socialism has seized with both hands all the power of intellect and capital to break the resistance that is offered from the Christian side," he wrote Idenburg. "Even the noblest Liberals go off with them." It appeared that "hell has simply broken loose against us."

This prophecy did and did not come true. The Social Democrats did not seize but ran away from power, refusing to join the cabinet. Cort van der Linden proved to be a noble Liberal; Kuyper found him all in all to be a fair and firm hand at the tiller of state. Hell broke out instead the next summer, as the European diplomats' game of Russian roulette finally took one turn too many. The guns of August 1914 interrupted Kuyper's annual cure at Dresden, and it took him four days to fight through the press of German mobilization to get back home. For the next four years he observed the consequences, the greatest tumult in human affairs since Napoleon, he thought. Eventually he changed the comparison to Noah's flood, a wave of total destruction brought on by human folly and an intransigent refusal to repent.

Even before the war broke out Kuyper had begun writing a theological series — his last — on the second coming of Christ. His conceptual prowess faltered there, however, as it did on the war itself, signs not only of the unprecedented times but of Kuyper's slipping powers. The book, the war, and his political career all came to a close in the last months of 1918. Just two years remained for him and his followers to begin sorting out the meaning of what he had accomplished.

The End of the European Order

Kuyper's commentary on World War I ran along four parallel tracks, alternating by the day or the week. Sometimes he followed the course of armies or diplomatic maneuvering much like any hard-nosed journalist, save for some religious comments added at column's end. Sometimes he undertook geopolitical assessments on a world-historical plane, mixing together the familiar categories of race, religion, and competing civilizations. He always upheld the Dutch policy of neutrality, from principle as well as necessity. He regularly offered theological reflection, particularly upon the folly of human pride. But only toward the end did he arrive at the lesson that subsequent generations took away from the war; Europe's "fratricide" had turned into "suicide." He blamed false principles for its outbreak but could never quite fathom its end. Few could.

Neutral though they were in policy, the Dutch were sharply divided in sentiments during the war. Kuyper joined Idenburg and Cort van der Linden on the pro-German side. More accurately, the anti-Entente side. France as ever represented to Kuyper the unholy trinity of Revolution, Napoleon, and Louis XIV. Russia headed the "growing half-Asian Slavic masses" that threatened to engulf the "Germanic peoples," including the Dutch. In siding with them instead of Germany, Britain had committed the gravest folly, Kuyper fumed. Allying with "heathen Japan" was even worse, so that upon Britain fell the "world-historical curse of having set into motion the powers of the Mongol races." Sore memories of the South African War were at work here, along with shame at Dutch dependence on the British fleet for protection of the East Indies. At the same time, this angle allowed Kuyper to see the illegality of Britain's naval blockades, the pretensions of its civic and religious oratory, and its imperial ambitions in the Middle East. In turn, Germany looked better to Kuyper than it had early in his career, when Bismarck posed a menace to Dutch independence and Gladstone incarnated all that was right. Now Germany represented a bulwark against the Slavic and Asiatic hordes. To be sure, Kuyper found Germany's violation of Belgian neutrality "not guiltless," but Belgium had been foolish too, he said. In their place he would have permitted German armies free passage "under protest" on the precedent of Deuteronomy 2 and the edict of Hugo Grotius, the Dutch (Remonstrant!) father of international law. In sum, Kuyper spread war guilt all around, but he gave Britain's and Russia's greater emphasis.

Theologically, he diagnosed one general and one particular problem at work. Broadly speaking, Europe had smashed upon the rocks of human pride. They had mistaken cultural advances for moral improvement, so that their technical progress had only multiplied their powers to destroy. The situation fit one of Kuyper's favorite mottos: the best, corrupted, becomes the worst. The particular error lay in Europe's having founded international affairs not on "the Right as grounded in God's ordinances" but "on Might" and "pure self-interest." That was reason enough for the Dutch to stay out of the fray, but reason also to fear that the war would be long and unparalleled in destructiveness. The combatants all dreamed of total victory as modeled by Napoleon and Bismarck, Kuyper explained to his readers, but modern nations were too resourceful to be readily vanquished. Only a negotiated peace without victory could forestall unprecedented horrors, and that depended on the United States. "America alone can do it," Kuyper wrote in March 1915, two months before the sinking of the *Lusitania* fired Yankee war fever. He still held out hope in early 1917. The newly re-elected Woodrow Wilson had the right idea, Kuyper thought; the question was whether he had the means and the will to implement it. Wilson's gamble instead to make peace by war thus fated the bitterest fight to the finish. Nor was Kuyper much impressed by the peace of Versailles. The winning powers were either cynical or hypocritical in assigning all war guilt to Germany, he judged. The proposed League of Nations might better be called a "league of winners" that would either prove ineffectual by its lack of capacity or a step toward a tyrannical combination of power that augured the coming of antichrist.

This apocalyptic note drew off the theological analysis Kuyper had been unfolding in *De Heraut* since 1911. "End-times" speculation had been a staple in Anglo-American evangelicalism since the 1870s, and the drive to interpret biblical prophecies in light of current events redoubled during the Great War. In that project, the task of locating just who comprised the antichrist and when the "great tribulation" would begin loomed large. By comparison, these had a much more modest place in Kuyper's work, which amplified instead the themes of divine sovereignty over and the renewal of the whole cosmos as the purpose of the eschaton. As the war dragged on Kuyper gave more at-

tention to "the signs of the times," but the clearer sign in these pages
came from the mixed quality of the series as a whole. It ground on for
eight years, finishing only in December 1918, a month after the guns
fell silent, and it required heavy editing before finally being ready for
book release a whole decade later. (It ran to four volumes even with a
hundred of the original articles deleted.) Son Herman, who did the
editing, admitted that *Van de Voleinding* ("On the Consummation")
lacked conceptual unity, as its various themes now clashed with each
other, now spun off on their own. As Kuyper himself noted early on,
part of the problem was that eschatology was the least developed field
in Reformed theology; as well, the dramatic scale and flux of current
events made an interpretive framework hard to fix. But the greatest
challenge might have arisen out of the categories of Kuyper's longer-
standing project. *Van de Voleinding* began in *De Heraut* immediately
after *Pro Rege* had ended — that is, upon Kuyper's problematic twofold assertion that Christ was lord over all and had chosen a people to
bear out that lordship within a semi-closed circle. Apocalypticism offered one way to resolve the tension. Not the leavening work of the
faithful over time but a dramatic supernatural intervention would
make good on the claims of God's universal rule.

The tension also showed up in Kuyper's daily war commentary as
he passed judgment upon the failed dreams of prewar peacemakers.
Ironically, Kuyper had taken part in those efforts, consulting with Andrew Carnegie about the proposed center for world peace that the
steel magnate wanted to build at The Hague. International law, the arbitration of disputes, and educational efforts to enhance both were all
quite congruent with Kuyper's own views, and the enlistment of millions of people around the world in organizations working for disar-
mament, comprehensive treaties, international courts, and a dozen
other measures registered as clearly as anything the fruits of common
grace. But with war breaking out just a year after Carnegie's Peace Palace had been dedicated, Kuyper called it all a delusion. "The misery
that is now sweeping the world shows the bankruptcy of all scientific,
socio-political, and diplomatic striving outside of [commitment to]
the high God," he concluded. The Socialists' International and the
capitalists' market made his list too. Both had promised perpetual
peace, and both had been swept away in the tides of war. When a socialist paper retorted — accurately enough — that the church had
done no better, Kuyper fell back on a technicality. The governments in

the relevant capitals were mostly anti-clerical when war broke out; thus Christians did not start the war, however they may have been overtaken by its spirit.

In fact, World War I represented the explosion of the civilization wherein, Kuyper said, common grace and special grace had converged to create the world's highest standards and achievements. It was a fratricide between lands that *Common Grace* designated as "Christian nations," "baptized peoples"; and the genuinely devout in every one of them had not lagged a bit in baptizing their country's cause as the Lord's. Furthermore, the enthusiasm manifest in every European capital in August 1914 marked the apex of modern nationalism, just as the long perseverance to victory on the part of France, Britain, and the United States revealed the power of mass democracy that Kuyper had spied long ago. The moral and material resources that were harnessed in the war effort Kuyper had attributed to Christian influence, and he had done so not least to inspire his followers to join the cause of Christian democracy. The aftermath of the war left the question of how the cause and his conceptions would survive, especially in light of Kuyper's own decline.

The Faltering Lion

After his remarkable feat of handing in the two volumes of *Antirevolutionaire Staatkunde* exactly on schedule, Kuyper planned to take the first week of 1917 on vacation in Cologne. He took to bed with bronchitis instead. In the eyes of daughters Henriëtte and Johanna, who would track these last years in close detail, the episode broke something in Kuyper for good. He developed a full lung infection and barely avoided a dangerous surgery. By now *De Standaard* had passed from his personal ownership to that of a committee headed by Colijn, a consequence of the drastic decline in paid advertising since the start of the war. Continuing wartime pressures on the Netherlands' vital international trade, along with domestic price controls instituted to offset the sky-high prices Germans were willing to pay for Dutch goods smuggled around the British blockade, made the Dutch war economy no place for amateurs. In addition, Kuyper had suffered financially in the bank failures at the start of the war. He now lived on an annuity, no longer in charge of his financial house. He was all the more adamant, then, to take his annual summer trip to Dresden in July 1917 despite the vicissitudes of wartime Germany, and without Johanna coming along as his nurse.

The trip went well, courtesy of an attentive German consul at The Hague, who also expedited the delivery to Dr. Lahmann's spa of the page-proofs of *Antirevolutionaire Staatkunde*. Kuyper returned home in September pronouncing himself fit as ever, and proved it by giving the plenary address to the ARP convention in November. He conducted his usual watch-night vigil on New Year's Eve and took the next week in Cologne to begin 1918. But from late January into April he suffered an ominously persistent bronchitis. Good news came toward the end of that season, when Too returned from her two-year sojourn in the United States. The bad news came the next month, when the doctors forbade him to deliver the plenary address to the ARP convention — and that in the year when elections would be held for the first time since the beginning of the war. Idenburg read the text for him instead.

Kuyper's speech, "Wat Nu?" (What Now?), clearly bore the marks of a farewell address. Still, while sounding his oldest convictions and in contrast to what was actually to come out of party councils in the years ahead, it showed a keen grasp of emerging realities. With the franchise and education issues finally resolved, he began, the social question remained the great item of unfinished business. Yet rapid changes in Dutch society left some old Antirevolutionary instincts outmoded. We have long tried to keep political and social questions separate, Kuyper wrote, but that is no longer possible. We have upheld the conscientious, enterprising individual as the source of social well-being, but the complexity of modern society makes each interdependent with all. We have championed the minimal state, but so many domains of life — waterways and postal service, transportation and utilities, the housing, education, health, and safety of industrial workers — cannot simply be left to private initiative or nice promises. The party's calling in this situation was to keep these issues from devolving into a raw material scramble between competing interests. It was the "rich development of the wage laborer" as a whole person that would profit the whole nation, and accordingly that must be the Antirevolutionary goal. That demanded real unity in party ranks. Above all, he concluded, it required the full integration between their professed ideals and their operational priorities. As ever, materialism and dualism were Kuyper's *bêtes noires;* a justice defined by transcendent measures his hope; a cross-class alliance his working goal.

Meanwhile, Kuyper's own dependence on others was deepening. Idenburg and his wife accompanied him to Dresden in July 1918, through a nation suffering acute shortages of staples and witnessing the collapse of their armies on the Western front. It was from Dresden a month later that Kuyper signed over to Idenburg the chair of the Central Committee of the ARP. This was a surrender of his original and most vital political post. First called a temporary measure, it became permanent in November after Idenburg joined the cabinet and Colijn succeeded to the chair. The new government itself marked a watershed: the first elected under the universal male suffrage stipulated by the recent grand bargain in Dutch politics, and the first in which the Calvinists served as junior partners to the Roman Catholics, who were now the Netherlands' largest party. Besides being party chair, Colijn was poised to take over editorship of *De Standaard* and began rejecting some of the copy Kuyper submitted. Kuyper was finished as a politician and almost as a journalist; just as a month hence he would be finished as a theologian.

He was already emerging as something of a legend, as demonstrated by a dramatic episode that same November. With the war just ended, some Dutch radicals thought it a good idea to join the revolutionary tide that was spreading across Germany and central Europe in the ruins of empire. The Dutch Left was divided about the wisdom of the venture. After vacillating again, as in 1903, Pieter Troelstra threw in with the rebels, a move that ironically ended his career simultaneously with that of his old rival. Within a week, the insurgency was quashed by a preemptive mustering of reliable troops in The Hague. The Protestant units in that number were Frisians of a Calvinistic cast. On the evening of November 18, with the danger past, they gathered in front of Kuyper's house to serenade the old champion. He greeted them from his upper window with a mini-oration of gratitude and benediction, invoking loyalty to God and Orange. It seemed like the April days of 1853 all over again, with the "red" threat having migrated from Catholic to Communist.

The next month, December 1918, Kuyper completed his series on the end times and took to bed with bronchitis. It lifted only in May, when he could resume his daily walks. Returning from one, he encountered another demonstration outside his house, this time celebrating the enactment of full and equal funding for religious schools, the other half of the grand bargain. "Today is a day of glory," Kuyper told the assembly, and they joined together in singing Psalm 72:11: "All kings will bow down to him, and all nations will serve him." The text was originally a coronation anthem for Israel's king, which the Calvinist faithful took to be fulfilled in Christ. But the triumph being marked just now was the life project of Kuyper. This was his grand hurrah — and, as it happened, his last. His brief remarks that June day in 1919 were the final public speech Kuyper would ever give.

The "lasts" accumulated steadily. It turned out that he had gone to Dresden for the last time; turbulent conditions in Germany kept him in the rural Netherlands for summer vacation in 1919. That October he celebrated his birthday for the last time with the full circle of family and friends, and gave them something of a valedictory address. A few days later he caught a cold on his afternoon walk in a chill wind, forcing Henriëtte to be summoned home from a conference she was attending as a Dutch delegate in Washington, D.C. On December 18 he wrote his last column for *De Standaard,* ending a forty-seven-year career in political journalism. He conducted his usual watch-night observance to bring in the new year and managed to avoid his annual January bronchitis, only to take a fall during his daily walk on February 1. The four-inch gash that left in his forehead proved to be the least of his troubles, for the dizzy spells that caused the fall would be recurrent from then on. While bedridden from that accident he came down with bronchitis again, so that in April, for the first time ever, the ARP convention met without him. Summer vacation had to be even closer by in the Netherlands, but brought unwelcome excitement anyway. On July 21, during his afternoon nap, a fire broke out in his lodgings, forcing Kuyper to clamber down a ladder from the upper storey to safety below. His arms, if not his lungs, were still strong.

In late August the dizzy spells returned, confining Kuyper to his room except for short limping walks down the block. He could no longer muster the concentration to write devotionals for *De Heraut,* the last outlet remaining to him. Not to worry, he said; he had composed enough in advance to tide him over until his strength returned. But he knew better. On September 21 he resigned his honorific seat in Parliament, and three days later checked *Heraut* page-proofs for the last time.

His two careers were entirely over, and the end approached

steadily. Colijn paid a farewell visit on October 16, and family came by for his birthday, his eighty-third, on October 29. Two days later he took to bed, reduced to communicating by nods and smiles. The death-watch began on November 6. Family members filed past one by one for a blessing, and on the morning of November 8 he slipped away into the eternity where he had always said the real battles of life are waged and our lasting abode remains.

Dividing a Legacy

Kuyper's funeral, on November 12, was a notable public event. Hundreds of the faithful lined the route to the cemetery to salute their champion one last time. They watched the symbols of his rich career pass in array: the student body of the Free University walking behind the bier; further on, his colleagues and successors on the faculty, the leaders of his party and his newspaper, cabinet ministers past and present. The first coach in line carried representatives of the royal family, which he had elevated but never liked; the last, members of his household staff, the sort of "little people" whom he had elevated and did like. The speeches at graveside were appropriately many. The rector of the Free University hailed him as the "founder of a renewed Calvinist scholarship." The Gereformeerde Kerken in Nederland, the denomination he had helped create, bade him farewell with "deep pain." Idenburg spoke words of comfort for "the people," Kuyper's rank-and-file, who had lost "more than a father."

The three most telling remarks were those that presaged the disparate lines by which his legacy would be sorted. Theo Heemskerk, once the heir apparent, spoke on behalf of the government to praise Kuyper's efforts at reconciling the various groups and interests in Dutch society. Hendrik Colijn, speaking as chair of the Antirevolutionary Party, hailed instead Kuyper's "indefatigable struggle . . . for the rights of a group subjected to slander and abuse." Son Herman struck the tonic note of Reformed piety in bringing the ceremony to a close: "We his children know that he was redeemed as a poor sinner who by faith had found peace in Christ."

In the years ahead, the chords of faith would echo first and long. Orchestrating them were Henriëtte and Johanna, who had supervised their father's care in his declining years and who published within months of his passing a detailed account of the same. The book exudes the Victorian cult of the good, exemplary death, its 135 pages structured in descending motion parallel to the ascending stages of evangelical new birth: "evening falls," "the night draws nigh," "the last struggle," "the final sickness," "asleep in Jesus." The volume evoked a folk piety of auguries and premonitory dreams while majoring start to finish in Calvinist providentialism: the ailing one had intended so and so, but God, who knew better, had ordained such and such. Little did we know that this was father's last time for x, y, or z; how comforting that the Father Above had tended to it all in advance.

In that light Kuyper's daughters very frankly treated a central tension in his career. The lust for labor and influence, the regimented discipline that made it good, the passion to make his voice heard, the insistence on doing things his way and on his schedule — these so stamped their father's character that they lingered on even as the objects and avenues of that effort were removed one by one. The Calvinist champion was a man of self-will; the man of faith, obsessed with working; the one humbled before God, yearning to be lifted high among men, and succeeding. The paradox was justified, the daughters judged, because their father was always fighting for God's honor and for Holland's good folk: "the Reformed people," "*our* people," for whom he wrote meditations in advance lest, with his death, they be left without a shepherd. Yet the paradox was still unsettling, so their father's last days became a parable of calm and steady surrender. The dying man's last words were arranged according to formula, and yet with utter fidelity to his convictions. Idenburg prompted him: "Shall I tell our people that God is your refuge and your strength?" Kuyper answered in a whisper, but "emphatically": "In . . . all . . . respects."

Henriëtte and Johanna's assertion that the last genre Kuyper gave up, the *Heraut* devotional, was always first in his heart would provoke eye-rolling from the strong, assertive men who have followed Kuyper ever since, but it had its own claim on the truth. Over the years that column was the first, sometimes the only, piece that many read in his papers, and in the years ahead they would be the only complete works of Kuyper to be translated and vended to an American audience. That is to say, the religious Kuyper was the true and genuine article, the product of intense internal struggles and unceasing reflection, informed by deep knowledge of Reformed theology, and setting it all forth in language that ordinary laity could understand.

375

But the counterpoint between Heemskerk and Colijn at graveside was the true and genuine article as well. Kuyper was the creative, far-sighted Christian Democrat who rewove the legacy of an old tradition into a pattern fit for modern times. He applied the principle of freedom of conscience forged in the struggle for Dutch independence to public life in a mass society, encouraging people of all religious outlooks, and none, not to leave their deepest convictions at the door but to bring them into the councils of government, industry, academy, and media for the greater good of the entire society. So far Heemskerk's "reconciler." But Colijn's partisan was equally in the mix. If Heemskerk's Kuyper helped get everybody at the table to work together, Colijn's agitator got one group to the table in the first place. He did so by forging their nebulous instincts into an active and self-conscious commitment, and building an institutional structure to sustain it on a steady track. Architect, agitator, and conciliator usually do not run in the same bloodstream. The wars they might have created in Kuyper's inward parts he usually managed to deflect onto the public scene. There his followers were inspired, as his opponents were made anxious, by his invocation of another myth of the Dutch founding, that the Calvinist tenth were the Lord's righteous remnant; that to them had been assigned a providential role in the destiny of Europe; that both measures justified theirs being the established religion in the land — freedom of conscience to the contrary notwithstanding — to secure public order and the honor of God. This people, Colijn remembered, also from his plow-boy father, had in the reversals of Revolution been turned into the scorned and despised. These Kuyper had restored to the seats of honor at the city gate.

Between Establishment and Insurgency

Not just the mode but the substance of his teaching was of issue in Kuyper's legacy. Here, ironically, Colijn gave comfort to power as Heemskerk, whom Kuyper suspected of that flaw, never had. Serving as Minister of Finance from 1923 to 1925 before taking over as prime minister through 1926, then heading up four more cabinets from 1933 and 1939 in the teeth of the Great Depression, Colijn counted as his proudest achievement keeping the Netherlands on the gold standard — this, after everyone else had left it, with punishing effects on

the Dutch economy. He adopted Kuyper's cast as a bold leader, repeated Kuyper's warnings about the dangers of materialism, stressed
the importance of character in enduring hard times, and cemented
the "pillarization" of Dutch society into complete, self-contained
ideological segments. But the agenda of "What Now?" went a-
glimmering. Colijn represented Neo-Calvinism as an establishment,
enforcing frugality and order, raising the specter of radicals and unbelief to keep the "little people" in line while fixing them to the cross
of gold. He worried about the Indies and its oil, and lived to see those
lost to the Japanese the year after his own country fell to the Nazi invasion. He died in a German internment camp in 1944.

After the invasion, some of the aging leadership in Kuyper's
movement first hoped to accommodate the occupiers so as to preserve their institutions for a better day. Many in the younger generation rejected that strategy, however, and went underground, where
they composed a disproportionate part of the Dutch resistance. Socialists and Anabaptists were there in number as well, while Roman
Catholics and national church people were underrepresented. In
other words, under conditions of persecution Neo-Calvinism proved
to be as good a resistance movement as Kuyper had promised it would
be. As he had once forecast, but as pillarization denied, they had allied with other radicals, however contrary their principles, in face of a
common enemy.

Back in power after their own liberation, however, the Antirevolutionaries resisted demands for independence by their Indonesian
subjects. They demurred as well at the revolution in social policy insti-
gated by a Labor-Catholic ("Red-Roman") coalition that brought in
the Dutch welfare state. The next social revolution, the breaking down
(doorbraak) of Dutch pillarization in the 1960s, marked the end of
Kuyper's foremost social legacy. His party merged with the Roman
Catholics in 1980 and has had a part in more governments than not
up to the present. Over the years it has held the classic position of European Christian Democracy: a center party trying to uphold social
and moral values above and beyond the more strictly economic agendas of left and right.

The contest between vitality and order also characterized
Kuyper's church and university over time. Herman Bavinck embodied
the vitality principle during his twenty years as Kuyper's successor at
the Free University, but his death coming just one year after Kuyper's

left progressives in an exposed position. They soon came under attack. In the bull's-eye was J. C. Geelkerken, a dynamic Amsterdam dominie like Kuyper fifty years before. He was part of a "young Reformed" cohort who sounded Kuyperian-like complaints against a dormant church that, seeking safety first, ignored both the hungers of the age and the treasures of its past. This time the church was Kuyper's own, however, and it attended to boundary maintenance with the insistency that the master himself had ordained. The issue at hand was "creation vs. evolution," on which Geelkerken invoked Kuyper's cultural-contextual theory of biblical inspiration to reconcile Genesis with scientific thinking. No, declared the GKN synod in 1926: "Snakes are snakes, trees are trees, words are words." Geelkerken and his followers were out.

Some twenty years later, the ax fell in turn on the theological Right. Klaas Schilder, a professor at the GKN's Kampen Theological Seminary, spent the interwar era complaining about compromises and complacency that he found traceable to Kuyper's doctrine of common grace. By the 1940s, his ringing denunciations of Nazism made good on his protest. It was not the occupiers, however, but his own church that prosecuted and deposed him, in 1944, on charges of theological insubordination. That turned out to be the last act of its type in the GKN, one so much repented of that more critical departures from the old ways went undisciplined in the wake of the 1960s. The GKN itself merged with the national Reformed church and a smaller Lutheran body into the Protestant Church in the Netherlands in 2004.

Likewise, the Free University in the 1920s fell under the control of a cluster of leaders reared in the Neo-Calvinist movement and committed to the cause of institutional self-perpetuation. Bavinck's successor, Valentin Hepp, turned to apologetics and appeals to natural law (and that during the ascendancy of Karl Barth!) to defend a common Christian culture against the chaos, disbelief, and extremisms that had been bred left and right in the wake of the Great War. That is to say, he aimed for one of Kuyper's ends via un-Kuyperian methods. The dynamic side of the legacy dwelt outside academic theology. The leading pastors in the GKN turned from systematic to biblical theology to make real the claims of a sovereign God in parlous times. Simultaneously, the creative edge of the Free University turned up in the philosophy department in the persons of Herman Dooyeweerd and his brother-in-law, D. H. T. Vollenhoven. Their project was to turn Kuyper's idea of sphere sovereignty into a full-fledged philosophy, consistently and authentically biblical. The "philosophy of the law-idea," as it was denominated, delineated fourteen distinct spheres of existence (economic, biotic, juridical, etc.) in each of which operated a divine norm that was to guide its development aright. For Dooyeweerd God did not set places but ordained "directions"; as Kuyper would appreciate, to the properly attuned religious heart the world was set free to flourish in all its lush variety. The passion for order was not hidden here, however. God's enlivening word was "law," and a heart improperly tuned, defying that law, wrought "curse" more often than "blessing."

Such an agenda prevailed at the Free University until it experienced the full dimensions of democratization in the 1960s, the great decade of expansion of higher education. From 1960 to 1976 the university's enrollment nearly quadrupled at the same time as its governance was expanded to include students as well as faculty. Full state subsidies made possible the addition of two new faculties, one in medicine, the other in the social sciences, the two domains least practiced at traditional Kuyperian notions of scholarship in Christian perspective. Over the same years the Free University's student body shifted from 69 percent of GKN background to only 29 percent. In 1976 fully one third of the students claimed no religious affiliation at all. The university's constitution in 1971 replaced "Calvinistic principles" with "the gospel of Christ" as the measure of its teaching and research. Lohman won the battle of foundations after all, but not with the results he had in mind.

A Man for Many Countries?

Church builder and scholar are the roles least noted by Dutch historians looking back at the orations at Kuyper's funeral, but they were the source of his greatest impact in North America. As noted in Chapter thirteen, it was not in the venerable Reformed Church in America, close to the Protestant establishment of the time, but in the rather raw Christian Reformed Church that his influence flowered. The CRC drew its identity from the church of the same name that had been founded in the Secession of 1834. That is, these immigrants in the

U.S. took their bearings from a previous migration back in the Netherlands out of the custodial church of the nation into a new body that claimed the real legacy of the Reformation. That separate religious identity grafted readily onto the realities of ethnic segmentation in America, so that the CRC — like its German counterpart in Missouri Synod Lutheranism — became notable for a strong and persistent solidarity, articulated religiously in strong confessional orthodoxy.

Over time, CRC members who became interested in entering American public life in a wholehearted yet critical fashion found in Kuyper's formula the perfect rationale: true Calvinism demands public engagement. They have also found in him substantial resources to feed and direct that engagement, indeed to exercise an outsized influence in their adopted land. This has been particularly true in the realms of Christian higher education and philosophical discussion. The 200 member and affiliated institutions of the Coalition of Christian Colleges and Universities typically feature the "integration of faith and learning" as a leading characteristic of their mission and practice, and the salience of a critical Christian worldview as a leading question in their discussions. Both have been taken largely from their iterations at Calvin College, which took them directly from Kuyper. More broadly, as historians Mark Noll and James Turner have argued, Neo-Calvinism is the only resource available besides neo-Thomism to rescue American evangelicalism from cultural irrelevance, to unite the warm heart at which evangelicalism excels with the furnished mind that public engagement requires and the responsible pluralism that modern society demands.

We can add that Kuyper's appeal to transcendent principles and the international stage is also needed to save American evangelicalism from the reflex patriotism it is perennially tempted to substitute for authentic Christianity as its guide in public life. There are "family values" and the flag in Kuyper, to be sure, but much more — a communitarian ethos, a careful attention to the structures of social order and their multiplication in (post-) modernity, a principled respect for peoples of other religions and none, and warrant for due government regulation in the economic sphere. Above all, he taught a critical method for measuring the socio-political agenda that one draws from the gospel, to see if it is of God. At this writing it is clearer than ever that evangelicals need more than ever to differentiate their professed Christian allegiance, and also their supposed social conservatism, from the gods of the market and of militaristic nationalism to which this group is so perpetually beholden. That is, evangelicals as well as other Americans could use a new application of Kuyperian sphere sovereignty and holistic biblical thinking.

Kuyper's legacy for the non-European world may be glimpsed, ironically, in the downside of depillarization that is evident in the storm currently attending Dutch political life. The *doorbraak* of the 1960s arrived on the heels of the welfare state, with the hidden assumption that the good life in a consumer society would adequately satisfy the yearnings for collective purpose and personal identity. If this turns out not to be so — or if the blandishments of that society seem in jeopardy owing to the influx of inconvenient immigrants — then the agenda espoused by Geert Wilders of the Freedom Party makes a sort of sense. That agenda first casts aspersions against Islam as a religion, but also against any organized religious presence in public life — and in consequence against the public funding of religious schools which was one of Kuyper's distinguishing triumphs. Anti-pillarization turned over manifests itself as nativist solidarity, a discomforting echo of the race-nationalism that inspired Dutch collaborators with the Nazis during World War II. One of Kuyper's grandsons, Elisa Willem Kuyper, the second son of the custodial Herman, shared that sentiment. He followed his grandfather's journalistic career but thoroughly defied his model by leaving the faith, leaving his wife for his younger mistress, and eventually dying with the Waffen SS on the Eastern front.

So obvious a black sheep, however exceptional to Kuyper's principal legacy at home, had its parallel magnified a thousand times in the white sheep of Kuyper's acolytes in South Africa. To be sure, people of other persuasions were the foremost architects of apartheid, its chief operating engineers, and the majority in its rank and file. Apartheid's principles violated Kuyper's on any number of grounds, as we have already seen. But Kuyper's theme of religious solidarity segmented in discrete blocs did prove transportable across a racist grid, so that, even if they were not first and most numerous in its ranks, people who called upon Kuyper were always present, enthusiastically, in the Nationalist Party and foremost in giving apartheid a theological warrant. Kuyper's own fondness for Romantic race theory, and his singularly hostile view of sub-Saharan Africans, made the transfer seem easy. Yet the final test of a thinker might be whether her critical method can be used to expose and correct her substantive mistakes — whether, in Kuyper's language, his principles can work through unhappy iterations to reach a better application. In this regard it is intriguing to recall that one of the leading religious voices against apartheid, Allan Boesak, invoked Kuyper's most famous words to condemn apartheid as a heresy. "Not a square inch of human existence," Boesak testified, not even the system of racial hierarchy and exclusion that South African authorities had set beyond religious critique, stands apart from the sovereign claims of Christ.

More positively, Kuyper's theory of sphere sovereignty has been recommended for adaptation by South Korea's burgeoning evangelical Protestant population as a way to promote civil-society institutions there against a heritage of overweening state power and the rising threat posed by multinational business and financial corporations responsible to no one but themselves. The Justice and Development Party of Turkish Prime Minister Recep Tayyip Erdogan demonstrates that a political party with strong Muslim roots and appreciative of the rights and public role of religion can operate successfully under the separation of mosque and state. The success there has entailed overturning rule by a self-perpetuating, secularistic caste (the military), winning fair and free elections, and opening new ventures in economic and diplomatic arenas that redound to the nation's well-being, just as Kuyper proposed for Calvinism in the Netherlands. Beyond politics, the current search by African Christian theologians to explain the phenomenal spread of Christianity on that continent has postulated a complementarity between the new faith and the people's native culture and "primal religion." Such a proposition can find ballast in Kuyper's theology of common grace and especially in his robust endorsement of the created, and creative, value of every culture under the sun. If this is so in Africa, then it might be so anywhere. There is much we can all learn from a person who asked the right questions and gave enduring methods for seeking, and finding, their answers.

Bibliography

Short References: Works by Abraham Kuyper

"Blurring of the Boundaries." *De Verflauwing der Grenzen* (Amsterdam, 1892). English translation (hereafter abbreviated E.T.): "The Blurring of the Boundaries," in Bratt, *Kuyper Centennial Reader*, 363-402.

Calvinisme en Kunst. *Het Calvinisme en de Kunst* (Amsterdam, 1888).

"Calvinism & Constitutional Liberties." *Het Calvinisme, oorsprong en waarborg onzer constitutioneele vrijheden* (Amsterdam, 1874). E.T.: "Calvinism: Source and Stronghold of Our Constitutional Liberties," in Bratt, *Kuyper Centennial Reader*, 279-317.

"Common Grace in Science." *De Gemeene Gratie in Wetenschap en Kunst* (Amsterdam, 1905). E.T.: "Common Grace in Science," in Bratt, *Kuyper Centennial Reader*, 441-60.*

"Confidentially." *Confidentie: Schrijven aan den weled. Heer J. H. van der Linden* (Amsterdam, 1873). E.T.: "Confidentially," in Bratt, *Kuyper Centennial Reader*, 45-61.

"Conservatism and Orthodoxy." *Conservatisme en Orthodoxie,* in *Predicatiën, in de jaren 1867 tot 1873* (Kampen, 1913). E.T. "Conservatism and Orthodoxy," in Bratt, *Kuyper Centennial Reader*, 65-85.

*All of Kuyper's original is now available in a recent English-language translation, *Wisdom and Wonder: Common Grace in Science and Art,* ed. Jordan J. Ballor and Stephen J. Grabill (Grand Rapids, 2011).

"Evolution." *Evolutie* (Amsterdam, 1899). E.T.: "Evolution," in Bratt, *Kuyper Centennial Reader,* 403-40.

"Geworteld en Gegrond." *"Geworteld en Gegrond": De kerk als organisme en instituut . . . 10 Augustus 1870* (Amsterdam, 1870).

Kuyper Archive, HDC-VU. Abraham Kuyper papers, in the Historisch Documentatiecentrum voor het Nederlands Protestantisme (1800 tot heden), Vrije Universiteit Amsterdam.

Lectures on Calvinism. Lectures on Calvinism (Grand Rapids, 1931 [1899]).

"Maranatha." *Maranatha. Rede ter inleiding van de Deputatenvergadering op 12 Mei 1891* (Amsterdam, 1891). E.T.: "Maranatha," in Bratt, *Kuyper Centennial Reader,* 205-28.

"Menschwording Gods." "De Menschwording Gods het Levensbeginsel der Kerk," in *Predicatiën, in de jaren 1867 tot 1873* (Kampen, 1913).

"Modernism." *Het Modernisme, een Fata Morgana op christelijk gebied* (Amsterdam, 1871). E.T.: "Modernism," in Bratt, *Kuyper Centennial Reader,* 87-124.

Near Unto God. Nabij God te zijn (Kampen, 1908). E.T.: *To Be Near Unto God,* trans. John Hendrik de Vries (New York, 1925).

Ons Program. "Ons Program" (Amsterdam, 1879).

OWZ. Om de Oude Wereldzee (Amsterdam, 1907-8).

"Sphere Sovereignty." *Souvereiniteit in Eigen Kring: Rede ter inwijding van de Vrije Universiteit* (Amsterdam, 1880). E.T.: "Sphere Sovereignty," in Bratt, *Kuyper Centennial Reader,* 461-90.

"Two-fold Fatherland." *Tweeërlei Vaderland: Ter Inleiding van de Zevende Jaarvergadering der Vrije Universiteit* (Amsterdam, 1887).

VA. Varia Americana (Amsterdam, 1899).

Short References: Secondary Literature

AGN, 1956. J. A. van Houtte et al., eds. *Algemene geschiedenis der Neder-landen.* Utrecht, 1949-58. Vol. 10, *Het liberaal getij, 1840-1885;* Vol. 11, *Van liberaal naar sociaal getij, 1885-1914.*

AGN, 1978. Dirk Pieter Blok et al., eds. *Algemene geschiedenis der Neder-landen.* Haarlem, 1978. Vols. 12-13, *De nieuwste tijd: Nederland en Belgie, 1840-1914.*

Augustijn, *Kuyper: volksdeel & invloed.* C. Augustijn et al., eds. *Abraham Kuyper: zijn volksdeel, zijn invloed* (Delft, 1987).

Augustijn and Vree, *Kuyper: vast en veranderlijk.* Cornelis Augustijn and Jasper Vree, eds. *Abraham Kuyper: vast en veranderlijk* (Zoetermeer, 1998).

Bakker, *De Doleantie van 1886.* W. Bakker et al., eds. *De Doleantie van 1886 en haar geschiedenis* (Kampen, 1986).

BGK. A. Goslinga, ed. *Briefwisseling van Mr. G. Groen van Prinsterer met Dr. A. Kuyper, 1864-1876* (Kampen, 1937).

BKI. Jan de Bruijn and George Puchinger, eds. *Briefwisseling Kuyper-Idenburg* (Franeker, 1985).

Bratt, *Kuyper Centennial Reader.* James D. Bratt, ed. *Abraham Kuyper: A Centennial Reader* (Grand Rapids, 1998).

Harinck, *ARP.* George Harinck et al., eds. *De Antirevolutionaire Partij, 1829-1980* (Hilversum, 2001).

Janssens, *Opbouw ARP.* Rienk Janssens. *De Opbouw van de Antirevolu-tionaire Partij, 1850-1888* (Hilversum, 2001).

Kalyvas, *Rise of Christian Democracy.* Stathis N. Kalyvas. *The Rise of Chris-tian Democracy in Europe* (Ithaca and London, 1996).

Koch, *Kuyper biografie.* Jeroen Koch. *Abraham Kuyper: een biografie* (Am-sterdam, 2006).

Kossmann, *Low Countries.* Ernst Heinrich Kossmann. *The Low Countries, 1780-1940* (Oxford, 1978).

Kuiper, *Dolerenden & nageslacht*. D. Th. Kuiper et al., eds. *De dolerenden van 1886 en hun nageslacht* (Kampen, 1990).

Kuiper, *De Voormannen*. D. Th. Kuiper. *De Voormannen: een sociale-wetenschappelijke studie over ideologie, konflickt, en kerngroepvorming binnen de Gereformeerde wereld in Nederland tussen 1820 en 1950* (Kampen, 1972).

Kuiper, *Zelfbeeld en Wereldbeeld*. R. Kuiper. *Zelfbeeld en Wereldbeeld: Antirevolutionairen en het buitenland, 1848-1905* (Kampen, 1992).

Kuiper and Schutte, *Kabinet Kuyper*. D. Th. Kuiper and G. J. Schutte, eds. *Het kabinet-Kuyper (1901-1905)* (Zoetermeer, 2001).

Kuyper and Kuyper, *Oude Garde*. H. S. S. Kuyper and J. H. Kuyper. *Herinneringen van de Oude Garde aan . . . Dr. A. Kuyper* (Amsterdam, 1922).

Kuyper and Kuyper, *Levensavond Kuyper*. H. S. S. Kuyper and J. H. Kuyper. *De Levensavond van Dr. A. Kuyper* (Kampen, 1921).

Lugo, *Religion, Pluralism, and Public Life*. Luis E. Lugo, ed. *Religion, Pluralism, and Public Life: Abraham Kuyper's Legacy for the Twenty-First Century* (Grand Rapids, 2000).

Puchinger, *De jonge Kuyper*. George Puchinger. *Abraham Kuyper: De jonge Kuyper (1837-1867)* (Franeker, 1987).

Rasker, *NHK*. A. J. Rasker. *De Nederlandse Hervormde Kerk vanaf 1795: haar geschiedenis en theologie in de negentiende en twintigste eeuw* (Kampen, 1974).

Ridderbos, *Theologische Cultuurbeschouwing*. Simon J. Ridderbos. *De Theologische Cultuurbeschouwing van Abraham Kuyper* (Kampen, 1947).

Rullmann, *Kuyper-Bibliografie*. J. C. Rullmann. *Kuyper-Bibliografie,* Vol. I-III (Kampen, 1923-40).*

*A much improved compendium in English, *Abraham Kuyper: An Annotated Bibliography, 1857-2010*, ed. Tjitze Kuipers (Leiden, 2011), is the new standard work but appeared too late for use in this biography.

Rullmann, *Kuyper Levensschets.* J. C. Rullmann. *Abraham Kuyper: Een Levensschets* (Kampen, 1928).

Stellingwerff, *Kuyper en de VU.* Johannes Stellingwerff. *Dr. Abraham Kuyper en de Vrije Universiteit* (Kampen, 1987).

Van der Kooi and De Bruijn, *Kuyper Reconsidered.* Cornelis van der Kooi and Jan de Bruijn, eds. *Kuyper Reconsidered: Aspects of His Life and Work* (Amsterdam, 1999).

Van Deursen, *Distinctive Character.* Arie Th. van Deursen. *The Distinctive Character of the Free University in Amsterdam: A Commemorative History, 1880-2005* (Grand Rapids, 2008).

Van Koppen, *Kuyper en Zuid-Afrika.* Chris A. J. van Koppen. *De Geuzen van de Negentiende Eeuw: Abraham Kuyper en Zuid-Afrika* (Wormer/Maarssen, 1992).

Van Rooden, *Religieuze regimes.* Peter van Rooden. *Religieuze regimes: over godsdienst en maatschappij in Nederland, 1570-1990* (Amsterdam, 1996).

Vree, *Kuyper in de kiem.* Jasper Vree. *Kuyper in de kiem: de precalvinistische periode van Abraham Kuyper, 1848-1874* (Hilversum, 2006).

Wintle, *ESHN.* Michael Wintle. *An Economic and Social History of the Netherlands, 1800-1920* (Cambridge, 2000).

Wintle, *Pillars of Piety.* Michael Wintle. *Pillars of Piety: Religion in the Netherlands, 1813-1901* (Hull, 1987).

Wolthuis and Vree, *De Vereniging van 1892.* L. J. Wolthuis and J. Vree, eds. *De Vereniging van 1892 en haar geschiedenis* (Kampen, 1992).

Notes

Notes on the Introduction

"Go back to the living root . . . demands of the time to come," *Lectures on Calvinism,* 171; "there is not a square inch," "Sphere Sovereignty," 488.

Notes on Chapter 1

Kuyper's ancestry is helpfully laid out in Kuiper et al., eds., *Dolerenden & nageslacht,* 284-88, and the family tree attached thereunto. Further explication is given in Puchinger, *De jonge Kuyper;* on Samuel Huber, see 27. Rullmann, *Kuyper Levensschets,* passes along much family lore, including the anecdote about the young lad's head (5), for which see also Puchinger, *De jonge Kuyper,* 30-31.

For early modern Dutch history I have relied on the magisterial work of Jonathan Israel, *The Dutch Republic: Its Rise, Greatness, and Fall, 1477-1806* (Oxford, 1995). Other outstanding titles in English include J. L. Price, *The Dutch Republic in the Seventeenth Century* (New York, 1998); Margaret C. Jacob and Wijnand W. Wijnhardt, eds., *The Dutch Republic in the Eighteenth Century: Decline, Enlightenment, and Revolution* (Ithaca, 1992); and Herbert H. Rowen, *The Princes of Orange: The Stadholders in the Dutch Republic* (Cambridge and New York, 1998). Briefer recent surveys include Paul Arblaster, *A History of the Low Countries* (New York, 2006), and J. C. H. Blom and E. Lamberts, eds., *History of the Low Countries* (New York and Oxford, 1999). The "notorious" behavior of Maurice and William II is recorded in Israel, *Dutch Republic,* 461-62, 600; Orangist proto-democratic tones, 1067-77; and its princely side, 1082-85.

Writing on the religious dimensions of the Dutch Revolt is voluminous. I have followed Israel, *Dutch Republic,* 137-68, 361-72; the statistics cited are on 219 and 365. On the Dutch "later Reformation" see Joel R. Beeke, *Assurance of Faith: Calvin, English Puritanism, and the Dutch Second Reformation* (New York,

1991); T. Brienen, *De Nadere Reformatie en het gereformeerd pietisme* ('s Graven-hage, 1989); and F. Ernst Stoeffler, *The Rise of Evangelical Pietism* (Leiden, 1971). The Patriot Revolt is covered succinctly in Israel, *Dutch Republic,* 1098-1112 (quotation, 1084); voluminously in Simon Schama, *Patriots and Liberators: Revolution in the Netherlands, 1780-1813* (New York, 1977). For the Batavian Revolution and its aftermath, I have relied also on Kossmann, *Low Countries,* 82-100; quotation, 97.

For an overview of Dutch history in the first half of the nineteenth century I have followed Kossmann, *Low Countries,* 103-164, 179-95. Wintle supplies valuable information and analysis of his topics in *ESHN.* The standard treatment of Dutch Protestant history in this era is Rasker, *NHK,* but see as well the more nuanced and detailed studies in Gerrit J. Schutte and Jasper Vree, eds., *Om de toekomst van het protestantse Nederland* (Zoetermeer, 1998). A recent survey in English is Karel Blei, *The Netherlands Reformed Church, 1571-2005* (Grand Rapids, 2006). Important supplements are Wintle, *Pillars of Piety;* the topical studies in Van Rooden, *Religieuze regimes;* and the venerable James H. Mackay, *Religious Thought in Holland during the Nineteenth Century* (London and New York, 1911). The characterization of William I comes from Kossmann, *Low Countries,* 115; on the Belgian Revolt, see 124-28, 140-60 (petition statistic, 149). The statistics on the Dutch economy come from Wintle, *ESHN,* 96 and 74; for larger secular trends, see 48-66, 80-83, 137-44, and 225-34; on the Cultivation System, 214-25 (statistic, 221); on the 1850s as a turning point, 83, 95. William I's regime is described in Kossmann, *Low Countries,* 103-8; the reforms under William II, 181-85; the Constitution of 1848, 190-94; Thorbecke's Liberal policies and constituency, 263-75. Wintle summarizes these changes and gives the statistics regarding franchise in *ESHN,* 252-55. On Roman Catholic emancipation and the April Movement, see Kossmann, *Low Countries,* 277-82; and Rasker, *NHK,* 158-62.

The Algemeen Reglement and its permutations are explained in Rasker, *NHK,* 26-29, 153-58; quotation on doctrinal supervision, 29. Rasker also gives a fine summary of the Secession, *NHK,* 55-70; "visible order of a moral society," Van Rooden, *Religieuze regimes,* 78. On the Groningen theology, see Rasker, *NHK,* 45-54, and Mackay, *Religious Thought in Holland,* 47-69. Jasper Vree supplies important correctives to those sources in "Petrus Hofstede de Groot and the Christian Education of the Dutch Nation (1833-1861)," *Nederlands archief voor kerkgeschiedenis* 78 (1998): 70-93. The Réveil is treated in Rasker, *NHK,* 71-99; explored in great detail in M. Elisabeth Kluit, *Het Protestantse reveil in Nederland en daarbuiten 1815-1865* (Amsterdam, 1970); and subjected to close analysis in Kuiper, *De Voormannen,* 57-66. For its internally diverging views on broader European politics, see also Kuiper, *Zelfbeeld en Wereldbeeld,* 31-45, 50-75. Quotation regarding doctrinal supervision in the wake of 1842 comes from Rasker, *NHK,* 156.

Jan Frederik Kuyper's career is summarized in Kuiper, et al., eds., *Dolerenden en nageslacht,* 286. His views get further play in M. den Admirant, "De Vader van Dr. Abraham Kuyper," *De Hoeksteen* 13/4 (September 1984): 127-

31, in Puchinger, *De jonge Kuyper,* 26-30 (quotation, 28), and in Vree, *Kuyper in de kiem,* 11-19. The family lore on Abraham Kuyper's boyhood is collected in Rullmann, *Kuyper Levenschets,* 5-12, and is treated more critically in Puchinger, *De jonge Kuyper,* 30-33. Koch sketches Kuyper's early years in *Kuyper biografie,* 34-39. The memorials to Dutch heroes are catalogued in Tina Keller, *De Abdij-kerk te Middelburg* (Middelburg, 1988), 6, 10, 13. Kuyper's characterization of his father's theology comes from a valedictory he wrote to a long-standing colleague in 1918, quoted in Rullmann, *Kuyper-Bibliografie,* III, 453. Kuyper's gymnasium years are reviewed in W. Bakker, "Kuyper's Afscheid van het Leidse Gymnasium," *Gereformeerd Theologisch Tijdschrift* 81/1 (1981): 1-21, which includes the text of his Ulfilas oration. On Fruin, see Bakker, 3-4; Stellingwerff, *Kuyper en de VU,* 21-23. Kuyper's memory of the April Movement and his participation therein dates from 1912 and is quoted in Puchinger, *De jonge Kuyper,* 25, 34.

Notes on Chapter 2

The indispensable book for this part of Kuyper's life is Puchinger, *De jonge Kuyper.* One need not agree with all its interpretations to profit from its voluminous extracts from and commentary upon the Kuyper-Schaay correspondence from the period of their betrothal. A contrary interpretation of some of the same sources, with telling if sometimes reductive contentions, is Stellingwerff, *Kuyper en de VU,* 21-46. Koch, *Kuyper biografie,* 34-51, strikes a middle course, more briefly.

For descriptions of Leiden University I have relied on W. Otterspeer, *De Wiekslag van hun Geest: De Leidse universiteit in de negentiende eeuw* (Den Haag, 1992), and the essays by H. Oort and P. J. Blok in *Pallas Leidensis,* ed. S. C. van Doesburgh (Leiden, 1925). L. D. Frank, *Geschiedenis van het Leidsche Studentencorps* (Leiden, 1927), gives a close look at student life. The statistics cited come from Otterspeer, *Wiekslag,* 409, 411, 413-14, and 420. On the ministers' job market, ibid., 433-35; see also Van Roorden, *Religieuze regimes,* 179-81. Kuyper's father's salary is given in Johannes Stellingwerff, "De bekering van Kuyper volgens zijn 'Confidentie,'" *Jaarboek voor de Geschiedenis van de Gereformeerde Kerken in Nederland* 3 (1989): 54. Kuyper's relations with his father are evident from the Kuyper-Schaay letters cited in Puchinger, *De jonge Kuyper,* 64-65, 114-15, 132; "old man" quotation, 65. The relationship is cast in a more benign light in Jasper Vree, "'Aandachtig zelfonderzoek . . .': Kuypers zelfportret in de Confidentie," *Documentatieblad voor de Nederlandse kerkgeschiedenis na 1800* 5 (2001): 3-32.

Kuyper's statements about his religious condition in these years are from *Confidentie* (1873), translated as "Confidentially," in Bratt, ed., *Kuyper Centennial Reader,* 46-47. Stellingwerff, *Kuyper en de VU,* 25, gives the correct date of Kuyper's confirmation. H. J. de Jonge, "Kuyper en de Disputaties Geleid door Cobet," *Gereformeerd Theologisch Tijdschrift* 81/1 (1981): 22-35, is the authority on that subject. On Matthias de Vries, see Blok in *Pallas Leidensis,* 106-9 ("beloved," 107); Otterspeer, *Wiekslag,* 236-38 ("language," 236); Puchinger, *De jonge Kuyper,* 91-94.

Details of the Kuyper-Schaay courtship and betrothal are given in Puchinger, *De jonge Kuyper,* 47-55; for Jo's family tree, see 263-65. Kuyper's epistolary crusade respecting her reading and religion is traced on 41-45, 55-63, 67-73, 83-89, 105-15, 128-32, 145-49; "I've always thought," 118; "a Dominie's wife," 129; "never have I so fully," 61; "by the nature of things," 108; "not *books!*," 62; "a matter of such weight," 67; "tell me why," 71; regarding the Canons of Dort, 60; the Virgin Mary, 111; Jo's testy reply, 72. Kuyper's own theological sentiments are quoted ibid.: "you don't believe," 58-59; "most people put," 79; "the rational and religious feeling . . . commanded to become," 59; "I feel that I need," 108; "to me forgiveness," 58; "how do you know," 108; "religion does not consist," 77-78; "is not yet Religion," 146; "but that's a side issue," 148; "feel God in your inmost parts," 146-47.

On rational supernaturalism in the Dutch church, see Rasker, *NHK,* 32-36. Jasper Vree supplies a more positive interpretation in "The Dominating Theology Within the Nederlandse Hervormde Kerk after 1815 in its Relation to the Secession of 1834," in George Harinck and Hans Krabbendam, eds., *Breaches and Bridges: Reformed Subcultures in the Netherlands, Germany, and the United States* (Amsterdam, 2000), 33-47. On the Réveil, Rasker, *NHK,* 71-99; on the Groningen theology, ibid., 45-54 ("Spirit of Christ," 50), and Jasper Vree, "Petrus Hofstede de Groot and the Christian Education of the Dutch Nation (1833-1861)," *Nederlands archief voor kerkgeschiedenis* 78 (1998): 70-93. The post-Romantic climate at Leiden during Kuyper's student years is sketched in Otterspeer, *Wiekslag,* 573-77, and Rasker, *NHK,* 113-14. J. H. Scholten is profiled ibid., 115-22, in Mackay, *Religious Thought in Holland,* 88-107; extra attention to his Leiden context is supplied by K. H. Roessingh, "De Theologische Faculteit," in Does-burgh, ed., *Pallas Leidensis,* 139-52 ("single great . . . life of all life," "fascinating charm," "prophet in the podium," and "free science . . . psychological variety," 141-42), and Otterspeer, *Wiekslag,* 244-48 ("picture of strength" and "character of granite," 244). Scholten's "witness of reason" is quoted in Rasker, *NHK,* 116.

Kuyper's statements about Idealist philosophy are embedded in several places. See "Modernism": "people turned their gaze," 23; "back to the lowest level," 63, endnote 15; "realism threatens us . . . on our way to it," 25; "Blurring of the Boundaries" ("not a single element," 368); "Common Grace in Science" ("whoever neglects," 456); and *Calvinisme en Kunst:* "whatever bloody lashings . . . operations from the subject" (19-20). His reveries about "above all the busts of great men . . . my heart is my world," quoted in Puchinger, *De jonge Kuyper,* 156.

Roy Pascal, *The German Sturm und Drang* (Manchester, England, 1967), is a cogent and comprehensive treatment of that movement, while Isaiah Berlin features two of its members in *Three Critics of the Enlightenment: Vico, Hamann, Herder* (Princeton, 2000). On the operation of realist and Romantic dynamics in the Sturm und Drang, see Pascal, *German Sturm und Drang,* 269-80, 310-13; on the fateful outworking thereof respecting love interests, 63-66, 141-44; for Kuyper's identification of that phenomenon, see "Modernism," 107-8. His allusion to Hamlet comes ibid., 109; "volcanic," 88; "look around," 89. Kuyper's statements about "age of cold Deism," "I would not be classified," "enthusiasm and resilience," and "if I had to choose" are all from "Blurring of the Boundaries," 368-69.

Puchinger, *De jonge Kuyper,* covers the episode of Kuyper's prize-essay, 91-107, 119-24; Stellingwerff casts it in a more skeptical light in *Kuyper en de VU,* 26-30, and "De bekering," 45-51. Jasper Vree, "The Editions of John à Lasco's Works, especially the *Opera Omnia* by Abraham Kuyper, in Their Historical Context," *Nederlands archief voor kerkgeschiedenis* 80/3 (2000): 309-26, treats its longer-term scholarly aftermath as well. On the Scholten-Groningen rivalry, see Puchinger, *De jonge Kuyper,* 98; Vree, "Editions," 310-11. Kuyper narrates the "miraculous" find of books in "Confidentially," 47-51 (quotations, 50); Stellingwerff offers correctives in *Kuyper en de VU,* 26-28, 320-21, and "De bekering," 48-51. Puchinger tracks Kuyper's progress during autumn-winter 1859-60 in *De jonge Kuyper,* 104-6 (quotation, 106). J. Lindeboom, "Het Notulen-Boek der Groninger Theologische Faculteit gedurende de Negentiende Eeuw," *Nederlands archief voor kerkgeschiedenis* 16 (1921): 32, records the "exceptionally flattering praise" Kuyper's essay received. On Kuyper's collapse in early 1861, see Puchinger, *De jonge Kuyper,* 125-27, 134-44. For Kuyper's chiding of Jo, ibid., 127-30; "a girl that can frankly," 130; "turn away . . . *wrath of love*," 129-30; "you will thank me," 128; "Oh, Bram," 87-88.

The details on the conclusion of Kuyper's doctoral process are in Puchinger, *De jonge Kuyper,* 151-52, 156-58, 160-62; the trials of his candidacy for a pulpit, 154-55, 167-74. His continuing à Lasco research is described in Vree, "Editions," 316-18. Kuyper narrates his reaction to *The Heir of Redclyffe* as a radical conversion in "Confidentially," 51-55; "next to the Bible," 51; "I was fascinated" and "recognized his own limitations . . . ambitions and character," 53; "I read how," 54. Puchinger, *De jonge Kuyper,* 176-95, interprets this episode as genuine; Stellingwerff, "De bekering," 51-57, sees more mercenary motives at work. On the context, audience, and significance of the novel, see Amy Cruse, *The Victorians and Their Books* (Boston, 1935), 42-64; Margaret Mare and Alicia C. Percival, *Victorian Best-seller: The World of Charlotte M. Yonge* (London, 1948), especially 121-41; and Elliott Engel, "Heir of the Oxford Movement: Charlotte Mary Yonge's *The Heir of Redclyffe,*" *Etudes Anglaises* 33/2 (1980): 132-41. Kuyper mentions his renewed religious exercises in a letter to Jo Schaay, quoted in Puchinger, *De jonge Kuyper,* 195; his private confessions appear in other letters: "lascivious thoughts," 187; "when I think," "she is a winsome," and "given me Guy," 189-90. Barbara Dennis analyzes the character Guy as a reconditioned Byronic hero in "The Two Voices of Charlotte Yonge," *Durham University Journal* 34/2 (1973): 183, noting his appeal also to the Gothic-revival taste of the era.

On Kuyper's candidacy for and call to Beesd, see Puchinger, *De jonge Kuyper,* 174-76, 195-96 ("a little jewel," 174); and Stellingwerff, *Kuyper en de VU,* 36-43. Kuyper's statement about "moving heaven" to get the post is cited in

Stellingwerff, "De bekering," 52, from the same letter in which Kuyper quotes *Redclyffe* respecting the "want of hateful money" (194 in The World's Classics paperback edition, Oxford University Press, 1997). Jo's advice against hiring an assistant is excerpted in Puchinger, *De jonge Kuyper,* 188, as is his declaration of being "calm and resigned." Puchinger, *De jonge Kuyper,* recounts their wedding and Kuyper's installation, 196-98.

Notes on Chapter 3

The indispensable studies for this phase of Kuyper's life are by Jasper Vree: "Een vingeroefening in kerkreformatie: Beesd, 1863-1867," and "De dominee van wijk 27, wijk 8, en nog veel meer: Amsterdam 1870-1874," both in Vree, *Kuyper in de Kiem.* Much of the Beesd material is condensed in J. Vree, "More Pierson and Mesmer, and Less Pietje Baltus: Kuyper's Ideas on Church, State, Society, and Culture during the First Years of His Ministry (1863-1866)," in Van der Kooi and De Bruijn, eds., *Kuyper Reconsidered,* 299-310. Stellingwerff views the same span through a gimlet eye in *Kuyper en de VU,* 43-75; Puchinger covers the Beesd years more benignly in *De jonge Kuyper,* 205-56. Kuyper's acolyte Rullmann provides considerable interesting detail in *Kuyper Levensschets,* 25-71.

Kuyper's Beesd inaugural, "Een wandel in 't licht de grondslag van alle Gemeenschap in de Kerk van Christus," is available in manuscript in the Kuyper Archive, HDC-VU. That archive contains over half of his Beesd sermons, all inventoried by date of original delivery. Vree describes Kuyper's social ministry and his conflict with the local powers in "Een vingeroefening," 128-32, 135, 142-45, 156-59. For his spiritual labors and initial theological themes, see ibid., 132-37. Van Rooden, *Religieuze regimes,* describes the role of classes in the Dutch Reformed Church at this time, 175. On Kuyper's à Lasco work, see Jasper Vree, "The Editions of John à Lasco's Works, especially the *Opera Omnia* Edition by Abraham Kuyper, in Their Historical Context," *Nederlands archief voor kerk-geschiedenis* 80/3 (2000): 318-26. The observation about Kuyper turning from history-writer to history-maker comes from Puchinger, *De jonge Kuyper,* 222.

Illuminating sermons from Kuyper's first years in Beesd are those of Christmastide and Epiphany (27 December 1863–7 February 1864); see also Easter and Pentecost themes in 28 March, 17 April–8 May, and 22 May 1864. Quotation of the "knowledge of God" comes from his sermon title for 24 April 1864. Rasker discusses the foremost Ethical theologians in *NHK,* 125-52. In English a brief recent treatment is Wintle, *Pillars of Piety,* 43-44, 50-52, 64-65; older and more discursive is Mackay, *Religious Thought in Holland,* 107-30. Kuyper's statements (and all quotations) about his transition from such positions to stricter Calvinism come from "Confidentially."

Kuyper's second (step of) conversion has drawn markedly different interpretations. Rullmann, *Abraham Kuyper,* 25-32, repeats Kuyper's own account in "Confidentially," 55-61, emphasizing the influence of the "malcontents."

Puchinger supports this view with comparative connections back to the *Redclyffe* episode in *De jonge Kuyper*, 206-13. Stellingwerff, *Kuyper en de VU*, 38-46, argues that not "democracy" but a (misguided) "mysticism" drove the change, together with the influence of Herman Kohlbrügge and the psychodynamics of Kuyper's relationship with his wife-become-mother. Vree, "Een vingeroefening," 137-42, draws compelling evidence from sermons and other manuscripts of the time to make Pierson's defection and the question of Modernism central. On Pierson's defection, see Rasker, *NHK*, 120-21. Kuyper registers the impact of Scholten's change regarding the Gospel of John in "Modernism," 115, with additional personal commentary in notes 31 and 52 of the original. Quotation about Jesus' resurrection is from his sermon title for Easter (21 April) 1867.

Kuyper's three sermons responding to Allard Pierson are of 26 November ("Humanism or Christianity"), 3 December, and 17 December ("definite choice") 1865. On the Syllabus of Errors, Vree, "Een vingeroefening," 137-38; on Mesmerism, 139-42, and Vree, "More Pierson and Mesmer," 308-9. Kuyper's changed sensibility is particularly evident in his Lenten sermons of 1866 (11 February–25 March); his sermons on sin, death, and conversion (20 April–7 May, 27 May, 1 July, and 14 August 1866; 20 January, 3 February, and 3 March 1867); "proof of the validity" comes from the title of Kuyper's Easter (21 April) 1867 sermon. "Modernism" was originally delivered at the Odeon theater in Amsterdam on 14 April 1871; Malcolm Bull, "Who Was the First to Make a Pact with the Devil?" *London Review of Books*, 14 May 1992, 22-23, posits the speech's originality in the use of the term. "By a fixed law," 96; "theological dwarves," 93; "rootless" and "caricature," 94; "dealers in varnish and plaster," 90; "bold negations . . . all-killing Conservatism," 119; "Word became flesh," 124; "once dreamed the dream," 121; "poisonous snake . . . I have seen its victims," 121; "as soon as principles," 89. J. Gresham Machen published *Christianity and Liberalism* at New York, 1923. Vree points out Kuyper's anxiety about his brother Herman's loss of faith in "Dominee van wijk," 352.

For Herman Kohlbrügge, see Rasker, *NHK*, 100-112. Kuyper's statements about the "malcontents" appear in "Confidentially," 59, 55, and 58; see 58-59 for his testimony to Pietje Baltus published on 30 March 1914. Vree discusses the circumstances and outcome of the 1867 revision of church polity in "Een vingeroefening," 146-49, 156-59. The full title of Kuyper's brochure was *Wat moeten wij doen, het stemrecht aan onszelven houden of den kerkeraad machtigen?* (Culemborg, 1867); quotations, 6, 8, 13, 18.

The reigning mentality in Utrecht at the time of Kuyper's arrival there is explained in Kossmann, *Low Countries*, 277-82; and Kuiper, *De Voormannen*, 61-77. Frederik Carel Gerretson offers insightful analysis of Kuyper's development at Utrecht in "Dr. Kuyper's Utrechtse Periode (1867-1870)" and "Dr. Kuyper's Utrechtse Tuchtmeester" [1937], in his *Verzamelde Werken*, vol. 3 (Baarn, 1973), 238-67. Kuyper's Utrecht inaugural sermon was "Menschwording Gods," quotation 261. A good trans-Atlantic overview of the high-church phenomenon is Walter H. Conser, Jr., *Church and Confession: Conservative Theologians in Ger-*

many, England, and America, 1815-1866 (Mercer, Ga., 1984). Elliott Engel, "Heir of the Oxford Movement: Charlotte Mary Yonge's *The Heir of Redclyffe*," *Etudes Anglaises* 33/2 (1980): 132-41, is the most detailed treatment of that topic. Kuyper's statements about *Redclyffe* come from "Confidentially," 54-55. Kuyper's correspondence with Jo about the "gift of Guy" is presented in Puchinger, *De jonge Kuyper,* 190, 192; his Beesd farewell sermon, "Een Band voor God ontknoopt," was published in his *Predicatiën, in de jaren 1867 tot 1873* (Kampen, 1913), 233-52; his autobiographical remarks therein come on 241-42. Quotations from "Confidentially" come from 54, 60, 46; he cites *Hamlet* in "Modernism," 108-9. The incidence of Shakespeare and *Hamlet* citations in Kuyper's corpus is demonstrated in Johan Zwaan, *Prosopographia Kuyperiana,* privately held by the author, to whom I am grateful for sharing that resource. Jasper Vree renders the Kuyper father-son relationship in kinder light in "'Aandachtig zelfonderzoek . . .': Kuypers zelfportret in de *Confidentie*," *Documentatieblad voor de Nederlandse kerkgeschiedenis na 1800* 5 (2001): 3-32.

Rasker, *NHK,* 164-66, summarizes the baptismal and visitation controversies at Utrecht; quotations, 166. The "yoke of synodical hierarchy" comes from the title of a brochure Kuyper published (Amsterdam, 1886) at the climax of his church agitation. Kuyper's active connection to civil politics is evident in the solicitation from voter clubs in Giessendam and Gorkum that he stand for Parliament (Kuyper Archive, HDC-VU, 14 May 1869). His farewell sermon at Utrecht was "Conservatism and Orthodoxy." On the virtues and theological errors of conservatism, 69-72; on its strategic misconceptions, 73-77 ("circle of friends," 75); on form-spirit ontology and developmental dynamics, 78-82; on incarnation and resurrection, 79-80; "Christ posits" and "germ of life," 81.

The church-political and financial circumstances of Kuyper's call to Amsterdam are detailed in Stellingwerff, *Kuyper en de VU,* 56-57, and Vree, "De dominee van wijk," 325-28. His first two sermons in Amsterdam are "Geworteld en Gegrond" and "De Troost der Eeuwige Verkiezing," published in *Predicatiën,* 323-51 and 111-29. Willem van der Schee elucidates the latter point in "Kuyper's Archimedes' Point: The Reverend Abraham Kuyper on Election," in Van der Kooi and De Bruijn, *Kuyper Reconsidered,* 102-10. On Christian world-engagement in Kuyper's Beesd rhetoric, see Vree, "Een vingeroefening," 138-39; Utrecht inaugural quotation, "Menschwording," 270; farewell sermon quotations, "Conservatism and Orthodoxy," 82-83. Statistics on the Amsterdam church situation at Kuyper's arrival are from Vree, "De dominee van wijk," 328-29, which also details his parish work, 332-34, 345-46, and 353. His popularity, baptismal, and catechizing practices are recalled in Kuyper and Kuyper, *Oude Garde,* 35-37, and Rullmann, *Kuyper Levensschets,* 54-56. His church-council maneuverings, sometimes with Modernist cooperation, are covered in Vree, "De dominee van wijk," 330-31, 334-37, 347-50; his opposition to Modernists, 338-40, 344; the moderates' counterattack, 336-37, 348; his liturgical proposals, 330-31, 355-56; his parish reorganization proposal, 348-51, 356-57; "men of standing," quoted 337; "undermines the very foundation," 339. The beginnings of Kuyper's journalistic career are treated in Stellingwerff, *Kuyper en de VU,* 54-55, 63, and Vree, "De dominee van wijk," 330, 343-44.

Details on the Kuyper home, including illnesses, are from a letter of Mrs. C. Q. Herklots to Johanna Schaay Kuyper, 26 July 1870, Kuyper Archive, HDC-VU; and in Vree, "De dominee van wijk," 330, 337, 341-43, 349-51, 354, 360-61. On his visit with Pierson, see Vree, "More Pierson and Mesmer," 308-9; on his work habits at Beesd, see Kuyper and Kuyper, *Oude Garde,* 8-9. Kuyper's career deliberations in 1871 are recounted in Vree, "De dominee van wijk," 337-38; letter to Jo quoted, 338; letter from T. Modderman quoted, 337. His transition from pulpit to politics is discussed ibid., 357-59, 361; Hooykaas quotation, 359. Herman's death and his own children's births are recorded in Puchinger, *De jonge Kuyper,* 260-62.

Notes on Chapter 4

Dutch political and economic history in these years is covered well in Kossmann, *Low Countries,* 206-29, 259-309, and the chronologically appropriate sections in the topical chapters of Wintle, *ESHN.* On the Rhine trade, see Wintle, 191; on the Dutch Liberal outlook, Kossmann, 207-10, 260-65. Of the many overviews of European history in this era, Eric J. Hobsbawm, *The Age of Capital, 1848-1875* (New York, 1979 [1975]), is especially illuminating, not least for its global scope and its integration of material developments and ideology; see especially xvii-xxii, 27-47, 266-306. "Never did Europeans," 147; "victorious bourgeois order," xix.

Kuyper's witnessing of Prussian mobilization is recorded in Jasper Vree, "Een vingeroefening in kerkreformatie: Beesd, 1863-1867," in Vree, *Kuyper in de kiem,* 144; and deducible from Stellingwerff, *Kuyper en de VU,* 56-59. On the *kulturkampf,* see Kalyvas, *Rise of Christian Democracy,* 170-79, 203-15. Dutch political turbulence in the late 1860s and early 1870s is summarized in Kossmann, *Low Countries,* 285-89, 295-300, 304-7; on the "school question," 289-94, 300-302. Johan G. Westra, "Confessional Political Parties in the Netherlands, 1813-1946" (unpublished Ph.D. dissertation, University of Michigan, 1972), gives further detail on the Catholic side, including their military mobilization on behalf of the Vatican, 123-28.

The controversies over Dutch public education under the 1848 Constitution are summarized in Rasker, *NHK,* 94-96. Correlations between various Dutch Reformed theological parties and education policy are laid out in Kuiper, *De Voormannen,* 68-77. Kuyper's 1869 keynote address was "Het Beroep op het Volksgeweten" (Amsterdam, 1869); "tonic note," 13; "minority," 10; other quotations, 17-21. The ensuing polemics are summarized in Stellingwerff, *Kuyper en de VU,* 52-54; epithets quoted 53. The Groen-Kuyper correspondence is available with fine critical annotation in *BGK.* Quotations are from the crucial series of 4 April–24 May 1867: "the warm interest . . . quickened and refreshed," 11 April, 9; "fulfilled a wish," 24 May, 9. A political argument between father and son in

Beesd is recalled in Kuyper and Kuyper, *Oude Garde,* 4. Stellingwerff, *Kuyper en de VU,* makes the "spiritual" father-sonship between Groen and Kuyper a central theme of the chapter on their relationship, 47-82; see especially 49-51.

"Uniformity: The Curse of Modern Life" was originally delivered at the Odeon Theater in Amsterdam, 22 April 1869, and published there that year *(Eenvormigheid: De Vloek van het Modern Leven).* English translation is available in Bratt, *Kuyper Centennial Reader,* 19-44. His ideological analysis runs 21-25; his tour of the contemporary scene, 26-36; his applicatory prescriptions, 36-44. "Multiform diversity," "wild forest . . . modern life," "the flourishing of the arts," and "almost totally devoid," 36; "no longer," "the disappearance," and "do not facilitate," 33; "uniformity of Caesarism," 41; "national will . . . struggle for independence," 43; "I know of no other," 39; "not to oppose" and "our unremitting intent," 41; "Anglomania," "oppose with vigor," and "Javanese," 40. Hobsbawn states (*Age of Capital,* 67-68): "There is no doubt that the bourgeois prophets of the mid-nineteenth century looked forward to a single, more or less standardized, world where all governments would acknowledge the truths of [capitalist] political economy and liberalism . . . , a world reshaped in the image of the bourgeoisie, perhaps even one from which, eventually, national differences would disappear."

Kuiper, *De Voormannen,* 57-66, treats the thought of Bilderkijk and his acolytes. For their subsequent internal divergence regarding European politics, see Kuiper, *Zelfbeeld en Wereldbeeld,* 31-45, 50-75. Kuyper records his political reading in *BGK,* 10 September 1869, 46, and 7 March 1873, 218; Groen gave his recommendations on 5 November 1869, 59. Harry Van Dyke has compiled an outstanding critical edition of *Groen van Prinsterer's* <u>Lectures on Unbelief and Revolution</u> (Jordan Station, Ont., 1989), comprising the 1847 text and a learned 300-page presentation of context, commentary, and critical reflection. The development of Groen's argument can be readily traced in Van Dyke's outline and synopsis, 159-70. On social-contract thinking in particular, see Groen's pages 136-41; on republicanism, including the United States', 141, 243-44, 253-54, but also 263; on Von Haller, Van Dyke's pages 118-19; on the late-medieval roots of the problem, Groen's pages 167, 176. John W. Sap, *Paving the Way for Revolution: Calvinism and the Struggle for a Democratic Constitutional State* (Amsterdam, 2001), records Groen's notion of Holland's "absentee" monarchy, 296.

Groen's indebtedness to Savigny is noted in Sap, *Paving the Way,* 297; Van Dyke, *Groen van Prinsterer's* <u>Lectures,</u> 40; and the best biography of Groen, Roel Kuiper, *'Tot een voorbeeld zult gij blijven': Mr. G. Groen van Prinsterer, 1801-1876* (Amsterdam, 2001), 24-25. The key conceptual role of Lamennais is detailed in Van Dyke, *Groen van Prinsterer's* <u>Lectures,</u> 134-36. On Groen and monarchism, see Van Dyke's pages 217-23; on his response to the 1848 Constitution and subsequent political activities, Van Dyke's pages 79-81, and Kuiper, *'Tot een voorbeeld',* 125-41, 157-66, 181-90; on his antislavery work, Dirk Th. Kuiper, "Theory and Practice in Dutch Calvinism on the Racial Issue in the Nineteenth Century," *Calvin Theological Journal* 21/1 (April 1986): 53-59. "Tribune" quotation is from Kuiper, *'Tot een voorbeeld,'* 182.

Kuyper published "Calvinism & Constitutional Liberties" in 1874. Its theological premises are elaborated, 306-11 ("he also knows," 310; "given a free choice," 305; "democratic form," 310). The Huguenot case study runs 299-306; Kuyper shares the assumption of the day that Hubert Languet rather than Du Plessis-Mornay wrote *Vindiciae Contra Tyrannos*. For the English case, see 292-99; for the American, 286-92. "Calvinism was a petrifaction" and "who had unambiguously," 293; "circle of free," 299; "voluntary, not coerced," 294; "separation of church and state," "necessarily" and "Calvinistic principle," 300; "modern liberties," 286; "the people of the Union," 289; "core of the nation," 287; "We are Antirevolutionaries," 298-99; "what has been refused," 313; "Calvinistic liberties," 314; "the moral element," "heroic faith," and "lesser magistrates," 312; "the question is not," 307; "I hope that at least," 317.

Huguenot resistance theory is well laid out in Julian H. Franklin, ed., *Constitutionalism and Resistance in the Sixteenth Century* (New York, 1969). Sap, *Paving the Way,* affirms it as part of a consistent Neo-Calvinist tradition and notes Groen's aversion to it, 294-95; see also Groen's letter to Kuyper of 2 September 1872, in *BGK,* 194-95. The method and mistakes of Kuyper's appropriation of American history are detailed in James D. Bratt, "Abraham Kuyper, American History, and the Tensions of Neo-Calvinism," in George Harinck and Hans Krabbendam, eds., *Sharing the Reformed Tradition: The Dutch-North American Exchange, 1846-1996* (Amsterdam, 1996). On the French Revolution's roots in suppressed religion, see Dale Van Kley, *The Religious Origins of the French Revolution: From Calvin to the Civil Constitution* (New Haven, 1996). On the "culture-forming" activism of Puritanism, see Michael Walzer, *The Revolution of the Saints* (Cambridge, Mass., 1965).

The early development of the Antirevolutionary Party is explored via comparative local studies in Janssens, *Opbouw ARP.* Harinck et al., eds., *ARP,* covers the entire history of the party; essays relevant to this period include Arie van Deursen, "Van antirevolutionaire richting naar antirevolutionaire partij, 1829-1871," and Janssens, "Antirevolutionaire organisatievorming, 1871-1879." Hobsbawn, *Age of Capital,* describes opposition to parties as a common European Liberal position, 269; Fruin's opinion is recorded in Van Deursen, "Richting naar partij," 38. Kuyper was solicited to run for Parliament simultaneously with his Utrecht Union address; see letters from voter clubs in Giessendam and Gorkum in the Kuyper Archive, HDC-VU, 14 May 1869. Kuyper's notes about potential local leaders can be found in his political papers for 1869 in the Kuyper Archive, HDC-VU. His activities in the 1871 election are covered by Van Deursen, "Richting naar partij," 50-52; from Groen's side, by Kuiper, *'Tot een voorbeeld,'* 206-9; "unnecessary and dangerous" quotation, Groen to Kuyper, 10 January 1871, in *BGK,* 114; "unbelievable spike . . . eye on the future," Kuyper to Groen, 22 June 1871, ibid., 146.

The gestation of *De Standaard* can be traced in *BGK:* Groen's cautions to Kuyper, 27 November 1869, 67; false starts and promotions, 6 August 1871, 152; 3 October 1871, 160; 19 December 1871, 171; the title imbroglio, 7 and 8 January 1872, 173-74, and 12 March 1872, 178-79. Kuyper's inaugural article,

"Vrijheid," is available in English translation as "Freedom" in Bratt, *Kuyper Centennial Reader,* 317-22; "there still remain . . . not be smothered," 321-22. Kuyper's speech at the Christian school teachers' convention in Amsterdam, 24 May 1872, entitled "Het Wilhelmus," is summarized with the extract quoted in Rullmann, *Kuyper-Bibliografie,* I, 151-52. The link of early ARP chapters to Christian school locals is given in Janssens, *Opbouw ARP,* 359. The relationship with the ASWV and the 1873 and 1875 elections is covered in Janssens, "AR organisatievorming," 55-66. On P. C. Mondriaan, see 64; on the Anti-Corn Law League as the ASWV's example, 55; on the classic Liberal model it followed, Hobsbawm, *Age of Capital,* 270.

The acceleration of Kuyper's conflict with the Ethicals surrounding 1872 is portrayed variously in Stellingwerff, *Kuyper en de VU,* 65, and Jasper Vree, "De kraaienplaag: een halve eeuw predikantenverenigingen in de Nederlandse samenleving," *Jaarboek voor de geschiedenis van het Nederlands Protestantisme na 1800* 5 (1997): 107-51. Rullmann, *Kuyper-Bibliografie,* I, 162-65, tracks the journalistic fallout. Kuyper's suspicion of Conservatives' integrity was well precedented in Groen; see Kuiper, *'Tot een voorbeeld,'* 165-66. The contretemps over the statues is played out in the Groen-Kuyper exchange of letters of 25-27 February 1874 in *BGK,* 287-91. Groen's words to Kuyper about his health and habits are found ibid., 7 July 1869, 38 ("Don't try too much"), and 27 November 1869, 67 ("I worry about"). Kuyper's complaints about illness and fatigue can be tracked similarly in the seasons indicated; "my throat distemper," 1 April 1873, 221; "unholy atmosphere," 30 January 1874, 276. A housemaid at the time left a vivid picture of the strains caused by the family's move to The Hague, in Kuyper and Kuyper, *Oude Garde,* 46-53.

Notes on Chapter 5

The most important sources for the Brighton episode in Kuyper's life include Hans Krabbendam, "Zielenverbrijzelaars en zondelozen: Reacties in de Nederlandse pers op Moody, Sankey en Pearsall Smith, 1874-1878," *Documentatieblad voor de Nederlandse Kerkgeschiedenis na 1800* 34 (May 1991): 39-55; and E. J. C. Verbeek, "De Brighton Beweging en Nederland," *Polemios* 9/4 (29 January 1954): 21-24. Rullmann, *Kuyper Levensschets,* 80-94, and *Kuyper-Bibliografie,* I, 180-93, give a decorous overview of Kuyper's participation and its aftermath. The political disputes of the period are covered in great detail in Janssens, *Opbouw ARP,* 79-130; and McKendree R. Langley, "Emancipation and Apologetics: The Formation of Abraham Kuyper's Anti-Revolutionary Party in the Netherlands, 1872-1880" (unpublished Ph.D. dissertation, Westminster Theological Seminary, 1995), 169-99.

Kuyper's first letter of 1875 (5 January) to Groen is reprinted in *BGK,* 330. He described Brighton as a "Bethel" encounter with "the holy presence of the living God" in the *Standaard Zondagsblad,* 13 June 1875. Kuyper's columns on educational policy were collected and published in *De Schoolkwestie I-VI* (Amsterdam, 1875); his exchange with Kappeyne is covered in Rullmann, *Kuyper-Bibliografie,* I, 179; his citation of Ira Sankey's hymn is noted in both Rullmann, *Kuyper Levensschets,* 79-80, and Johannes Stellingwerff, *Kuyper en de VU,* 77. Kuyper's reception in the Second Chamber is described in Langley, "Emancipation and Apologetics," 185-90; set against the backdrop of his earlier journalistic combats with the Conservatives, 176-84. See also Rullmann, *Kuyper-Bibliografie,* I, 188-89 (Kuyper's citation of James 5 and "whitewashed sepulcher," quoted 189); and Stellingwerff, *Kuyper en de VU,* 76-77 ("demagogue . . . enthusiast," quoted 76; "serious influence . . . orator," quoted 77). His ecclesiastical frustrations are described in C. H. W. van den Berg, "De ontstaansgeschiedenis van de Doleantie te Amsterdam," in Bakker et al., eds., *De Doleantie van 1886,* 90-91; his spiritual diagnosis and remedy of the situation are summarized in Rullmann, *Kuyper-Bibliografie,* I, 207-8.

Melvin E. Dieter, *The Holiness Revival of the Nineteenth Century,* 2nd ed. (Lanham, Md., and London, 1996), is the most thorough treatment of the subject. Good analytic surveys are available in George M. Marsden, *Fundamentalism and American Culture* (New York, 1980), 72-101; and David Bundy, "Keswick and the Evangelical Spirit of Piety," in *Modern Christian Revivals,* ed. Edith L. Blumhofer and Randall Balmer (Urbana and Chicago, 1993), 118-44. On Robert Pearsall and Hannah Whitall Smith, see Dieter, 132-57, and Bundy, 123-27; but also the reminiscences of their son, Logan Pearsall Smith, *Unforgotten Years* (Boston, 1939), 3-77 ("magnificent salesman," 33), and granddaughter Barbara Strachey, *Remarkable Relations: The Story of the Pearsall Smith Women* (New York, 1982), 19-60. Krabbendam, "Zielenverbrijzelaars," details Smith's Dutch contacts in 1874-75, 47-49.

The proceedings of the Brighton meetings were published in *Record of the Convention for the Promotion of Scriptural Holiness: Brighton, May 29th–June 7th, 1875* (Brighton and London, 1875; reprint New York, 1985). The volume also discloses the organizers' sequential management of mass emotion and records the titles of the hymns sung. Two of Hannah Whitall Smith's "Bible Readings," "'I Can' and 'I Cannot'" (Thursday, 3 June, 157-67) and "The Rest of Faith" (Saturday, 5 June, 246-54), exemplify her substance and style. The text of "Love of Jesus, All Divine" can be found at http://www.ccel.org/a/anonymous/eh1916/htm/h230.html; of "Simply Trusting Every Day" at http://www.opc.org/books/TH/old/Blue682.html, 27 September 2004. Willem Hovy copied out the lyrics of "Jesus Saves Me Now" in his letter to Kuyper, 26 October 1876, Kuyper Archive, HDC-VU. The communion service of Sunday, 6 June, is recorded in *Record of the Convention,* 390. Kuyper's part was witnessed by F. Lion Cachet, *Tien dagen te Brighton* (Utrecht, 1875), as noted in Rullmann, *Kuyper Levensschets,* 80; Kuyper himself alluded to it in a subsequent address paraphrased ibid., 88, the source also of his "my cup overfloweth" testimony, 81. Bundy notes the political dimensions behind Brighton in "Keswick and Piety," 127-28.

Kuyper reported on Brighton in *Standaard Zondagsblad,* 6-13 June, 1875; defended and extrapolated its teachings and proceedings, 11 July–22 August 1875; and under its inspiration ran series on "Sealing," 5 September–31 October 1875, and "Reformed Fasting," 14 November–12 December 1875. The 3 October 1875 issue excerpted Hannah Whitall Smith, *The Christian's Secret to a Happy Life* (195-99 of Chapter 15: "Practical Results," in the 1885 edition). His mission-festival tour is recorded, with a close paraphrase of his speech at the first (at 's Heer-Arendskerke, 23 June 1875) in Rullmann, *Kuyper Levensschets,* 81-91; "I felt something" and "an open acknowledgement," 86, 87; "making all the promises" and "tangible presence" are quoted from his *Standaard Zondagsblad* report on the event, 11 July 1875. Rullmann records Kuyper's complaints of fatigue in *Kuyper Levensschets,* 92. Smith's letter to him (13 September 1875) is in the Kuyper Archive, HDC-VU.

The results of the 1875 elections are detailed, with Kuyper's optimistic interpretation, in Langley, "Emancipation and Apologetics," 228-30. On the recurrence of his rheumatism, see his letters to Groen, 24 and 28 September 1875, in *BGK,* 344-45; "my inmost state," 345. The harsh exchange between Kuyper and Minister of Finance H. J. van der Heim is recounted ibid., 346-47; quotations 347. Rullmann, *Kuyper-Bibliografie,* I, 188, describes his cold-water and compress treatments. Kuyper's series on "A Christian's Vows" began in *Standaard Zondagsblad,* 23 January 1876, breaking off after the 6 February issue. Hovy's letter of 7 January 1876 (Kuyper Archive, HDC-VU) repeated the official explanation that the Holiness leadership gave of Smith's behavior; see, e.g., Dieter, *Holiness Revival,* 154-55. But see Smith, *Unforgotten Years,* 60-65, and Strachey, *Remarkable Relations,* 33-53, for the fuller private history and family documentation regarding Pearsall Smith's practices.

Stellingwerff treats Kuyper's collapse and recuperation briefly in *Kuyper en de VU,* 79-82; Rullmann, in rich if somewhat hagiographic detail in *Kuyper Levensschets,* 94-103. Citations from Kuyper and Groen's correspondence *(BGK):* "the situation with my head," 24 February 1876 (355); "now, with your eye," 29 February 1876 (357); "bow beneath . . . of your children," 8 March 1876 (358). Kuyper's telegram to Jo on 24 October 1876 is found in the Kuyper Archive, HDC-VU. His mountain-climbing experience and "wandering in the great mass" citation are recorded in Rullmann, *Kuyper Levensschets,* 97; see also the photo section in the present volume for a studio-shot of him in mountain-climbing gear. Kuyper's dream of Groen's death is recorded in Rullmann, *Kuyper Levensschets,* 101, and compared to Nietzsche's vision in Stellingwerff, *Kuyper en de VU,* 80-81. Groen's last letter to Kuyper was 8 March 1876, *BGK,* 358. Two letters from Elizabeth M. M. (Betsy) Groen van Prinsterer to Kuyper (18 July and 24 October 1876) are in the Kuyper Archive, HDC-VU, as are the cited letters from Alexander F. de Savornin Lohman (15 October 1876), J. H. Gunning (25 October 1876), Jo Kuyper-Schaay (24 October 1876), Isaac Hooykaas (28 December 1876), and Willem Hovy (26 October 1876). Stellingwerff, *Kuyper en de VU,* 80-82, traces Kuyper's residences and travels in this period; "nerves all in a tumble," quoted 82. J. Kappeyne van de Coppello notified Kuyper of the 1877 parliamentary schedule by a letter of 18 October 1876; P. Huet recommended renewed Holiness work, 13 April 1877; William Cowper Temple sent an invitation to same, 6 July 1877; and Isaac Hooykaas enthused about a parish position, 20 September

1877, all in the Kuyper Archive, HDC-VU. On the call to the Oosthem parish in Friesland and Kuyper's deliberations thereabout, see Rullmann, *Kuyper Levens-schets*, 103.

Kuyper's series on "Perfectionism" ("Volmaakbaarheid") ran in *De Heraut*, 17 March–4 August 1878, and was published in book form under the same title as Part II of *Uit het Woord: Stichtelijke Bijbelstudien*, 1st series, vol. III (Amsterdam, 1879), 61-163. All quotations are taken from the excerpts provided in English translation in Bratt, *Kuyper Centennial Reader*, 143-63: "mixture of truth and untruth . . . driving forces of our age," 162; "push forward . . . mounting doses," 151-52; "spiritual delicatessen . . . in its organizations," 162, 161; "with Rome . . . ends up in the flesh," 155; "Pelagius always lurks . . . for the holy," 152; "of the holiness . . . incredibly low," 147; "by the born-again sinner," 144; "precisely the shallow," 159; "Unconscious Sin," 157; "the rule prevails," 160; "solid, single-minded people . . . sturdy cohesiveness," 145; "quiet seclusion," 162; "not wish to conceal . . . error, sinful!," 161; "our holiest," 151; "whether the nervous . . . such misappraisal," 163. For the pre–Civil War American critique of revivalism see the sources collected in James D. Bratt, ed., *Antirevivalism in Antebellum America* (Piscataway, N.J., 2005). On the context and role of the Keswick Movement in Anglo-American evangelicalism, see Marsden, *Fundamentalism and American Culture*, 77-85, 94-101, 118-19.

Kuyper's theological columns in the first half of the 1870s were collected in *Uit het Woord: Stichtelijke Bijbelstudiën*, 1st series, vols. I-II; see summaries in Rullmann, *Kuyper-Bibliografie*, I, 170-71, 193-96. *The Work of the Holy Spirit* ran in *De Heraut* 2 September 1883–4 July 1886, and was published in book form in Amsterdam, 1888-89. I have cited the English translation by J. H. DeVries (Grand Rapids, 1956 [New York, 1900]): "entire counsel," 205; "work of the Holy Spirit . . . that of grace," 45-46; "in love's hour," 336; "root of life," 467; "the elect . . . converts himself," 349; "as often as he discovers," 296; "gradually wrought," 297; "exquisite delineation . . . the eternal verities," 532-33. The cosmic, corporate, and historical work of the Spirit is covered in Kuyper's Volume I (3-199); the individual-soteriological phase is treated in Volume II-III/1.iv (203-447). On the first phase see also Vincent Edward Bacoute, *The Spirit in Public Theology: Appropriating the Legacy of Abraham Kuyper* (Grand Rapids, 2005). Kuyper's meditation on Psalm 42 was published in *De Heraut*, 19 January 1890. Citations are from the English translation in Bratt, *Kuyper Centennial Reader*, 148-53: "plains and valleys," "God alone is," "sacred silence," 149; "the roar," "revelation . . . his own soul," 150; "deep anxiety," 153, "double the power," 152; "the child of God," 153; "to the plain . . . imprinted on his soul," 151.

Notes on Chapter 6

The most important secondary accounts for this phase of Kuyper's life include Koch, *Kuyper biografie*, 171-238; Janssens, *Opbouw ARP*, 133-252, digested by the same author as "Antirevolutionaire organisatievorming, 1871-1879" and

"Eenheid en verdeeldheid, 1879-1894," in Harinck et al., eds., *ARP,* 53-72, 73-92; Van Deursen, *Distinctive Character,* 1-67; and Stellingwerff, *Kuyper en de VU,* 83-120. Theo van Tijn locates Kuyper's work in the context of its times and parallel movements in "De Doleantie kwam niet alleen," *Documentatieblad voor Nederlandse kerkgeschiedenis van de negentiende eeuw* 10 (January 1986): 41-46; and "De sociale bewegingen van 1876 tot 1887," *AGN 1978* 13: 90-100.

Stellingwerff, *Kuyper en de VU,* recounts Kuyper's vocational decision upon his return to the Netherlands, 84-89; Koch gives more detail on his journalism in *Kuyper biografie,* 175-78. Janssens analyzes the pre-formation of the Antirevolutionary Party in *Opbouw ARP,* 156-62 ("urgent confessional necessity," quoted 157; my italics); Koch, in *Kuyper biografie,* 178-89 ("thunderclap," 189). E. J. Hobsbawm's observation on "organization, ideology, and leadership" comes from *The Age of Capital, 1848-1875* (New York, 1975), 19; on the potential of the lower-middle class, 246-48. His profile of the general European Liberal regime at the time (266-74) is amplified for the Netherlands in Kossmann, *Low Countries,* 206-10, 259-65; Hans Daalder, "The Netherlands: Opposition in a Segmented Society," in Robert Dahl, ed., *Political Oppositions in Western Democracies* (New Haven, 1966), 197-98; Janssens, *Opbouw ARP,* 227-28; and Koch, *Kuyper biografie,* 171-74. *Ons Program* was published in Amsterdam immediately upon the conclusion of its run in the *Standaard* in February 1879. It appeared thereafter in several slightly amended editions until superseded by Kuyper's *Antirevolutionaire staatkunde: met nadere toelichting op "Ons Program,"* 2 vols. (Kampen, 1916-17).

The 1878 Education Bill is analyzed in the context of the Progressive Liberal agenda in Kossmann, *Low Countries,* 297-302; see also Koch, *Kuyper biografie,* 178-81. Janssens gives the most detailed analysis of the petition campaign in *Opbouw ARP,* 146-55, emphasizing its disjuncture with Kuyper's original plans and party design. See also Koch, *Kuyper biografie,* 182-84; on the mutual distaste of Kuyper and the king, 184-85; "Orange has broken," quoted 185. Kappeyne is profiled in Kossmann, *Low Countries,* 300-301, and in Koch, *Kuyper biografie,* 180-81.

The preparatory work for founding the Free University is detailed in Van Deursen, *Distinctive Character,* 6-14; Koch, *Kuyper biografie,* 221-38; and Stellingwerff, *Kuyper en de VU,* 89-113. Jasper Vree explores the broader context in "'Het Réveil' en 'het (neo-) Calvinisme' in hun onderlinge samenhang (1856-1896)," in Augustijn and Vree, eds., *Kuyper: vast en veranderlijk,* 54-85; "care of souls," quoted 72. Jonathan Z. Smith nominates the 1876 Higher Education Law as the beginning of Religious Studies as an academic discipline in *Imagining Religion: From Babylon to Jonestown* (Chicago, 1982), 102-3. Stellingwerff, *Kuyper en de VU,* cites Kuyper regarding "our future preachers," 99; treats the exchange (also its monetary details) with Elisabeth Groen van Prinsterer, 96; and Kuyper's correspondence with Lohman, 100-107 (advising skepticism toward the Ethicals, 106).

Van Deursen, *Distinctive Character,* 11-12, provides details about the endowment and underscores Lohman's hesitation regarding the narrow theological base of the university. Kuyper's tracts against Van Toorenenbergen are *De Leidsche Professoren en de Executeurs der Dordtsche Nalatenschap* and *Revisie der Revisie-Legende,* both published in Amsterdam, 1879; against Bronsveld, *"Strikt genomen": Het recht tot Universiteitsstichting, staatsrechtelijk en historisch getoetst* (Amsterdam, 1880). Koch, *Kuyper biografie,* provides good summaries of these, 226-31; "pastor-factory," quoted 221; "enemies from without," quoted 227. For Van Toorenenbergen's counsel to Elisabeth Groen van Prinsterer, 227; regarding Kuyper's perpetual enmity with Bronsveld, 229. Kalyvas analyzes the broader pattern of tension between church leaders and the Christian-Democratic movement in *Rise of Christian Democracy,* 6, 18-57; "carried important costs," 29; "Protestantism in the Netherlands" (capitalized in the original) is cited in Stellingwerff, *Kuyper en de VU,* 102. Scholten's commendatory letters to Kuyper, dated 28 December 1879 ("historical standpoint . . . Kingdom of God") and 20 September 1880 ("If our paths"), are found in the Kuyper Archive, HDC-VU.

On the founding of the Christian schools union, see Janssens, *Opbouw ARP,* 154; of the ARP, 164-65; of the Free University, Stellingwerff, *Kuyper en de VU,* 109. On the university's funding sources, see Koch, *Kuyper biografie,* 227; Van Deursen, *Distinctive Character,* 11-12; and a register in Kuyper's hand in Kuyper Archive, HDC-VU. On the university's early quarters, see Ad Tervoort and Marijke Völlmar, *Wetenschap en samenleving: groei en ontwikkeling van de VU-familie in beeld* (Amsterdam, 2005), 123-24; for statistics on the student body, 71-72; on the function and importance of the Union, 33-36, and Van Deursen, *Distinctive Character,* 39-44. All subsequent quotations from Kuyper in the text are from "Sphere Sovereignty": "And so our little School," 489; "To possess wisdom" and "Thinking after God . . . through all the ages," 476; "scholarship often stands," 475; "every State power," 472; "the man of Tarsus," 475; "Is this not" and "the least respected," 479; "is not *giving,*" 479-80.

Janssens, *Opbouw ARP,* ably describes Kuyper's development of a saturated political culture among his followers, 166-80; the process of party centralization, 183-208; and factional tendencies in the early 1880s, 239-52. On Mondriaan, see 165, 178-79; for his work as a political cartoonist, see Herbert Henkels, "Piet Mondriaan and the Hague School," in Ronald de Leeuw, John Sillevis, and Charles Dumas, eds., *The Hague School: Dutch Masters of the 19th Century* (London, 1983), 147. The pattern of interlocking directorates in Kuyper's movement is studied in close detail against sophisticated theoretical backdrop in Kuiper, *De Voormannen,* 381-497, with illustrative charts, 591-98. Intermarriages and other family connections are mapped on 620-41. Extensive data and narratives on these patterns are available in Kuiper et al., eds., *Dolerenden en nageslacht,* thoroughly indexed by family names. For the Esser clan, see 200-220; Hovy, [103-5]; Kuyper, [106-7], 284-95; Rutgers, [110-12]; Lohman, [113-15]; Brummelkamp, 205-6. Hovy is briefly profiled in Van Deursen, *Distinctive Character,* 11-13; his life, character, and career are treated thoroughly in R. E. van der Woude, "Willem Hovy (1840-1915): Bewogen christelijk-sociaal ondernemer," in P. E. Werkman en R. E. van der Woude, eds.,

Geloof in eigen zaak: Markante protestantse ondernemers in de negentiende en twintigste eeuw (Hilversum, 2006), 127-61.

Stellingwerff describes Kuyper's Amsterdam home in *Kuyper en de VU,* 161-63; his allure to his rivals' sons and encouragement of non-Calvinist associates for his children, 165. Christian Hunnigher's reminiscences are found in Kuyper and Kuyper, *Oude Garde,* 59-80; "sermons from likeminded ministers" and Sunday routine, 62. One of his principal collaborators in the Doleantie reproved him for his absence from church; see C. H. W. van den Berg, "Kuyper en de kerk," in Augustijn et al., eds., *Kuyper: volksdeel & invloed,* 173 and 250 n. 6. On the family's dinner-time devotions, 26, 63, 65; on Kuyper's domestic style, 63-67, 145-46.

Notes on Chapter 7

Kuyper's inaugural address at the Free University was originally published on the date of its delivery, 20 October 1880. Citations here are from "Sphere Sovereignty," 461-90. The fullest study of sphere sovereignty as a theory is J. D. Dengerink, *Critisch-historisch onderzoek naar de sociologische ontwikkeling van het beginsel der "souvereiniteit in eigen kring" in de 19e en 20e eeuw* (Kampen, 1948). For shorter, English-language analyses, see Bob Goudzwaard, "Christian Social Thought in the Dutch Neo-Calvinist Tradition," in Walter Block and Irving Hexham, eds., *Religion, Economics, and Social Thought* (Vancouver, 1986), and James W. Skillen and Rockne M. McCarthy, eds., *Political Order and the Plural Structure of Society* (Atlanta, 1991).

The quotations relevant to Kuyper's sketch of the "spheres" are all from "Sphere Sovereignty," 467. His statements about divine sovereignty and world-imperial claims thereunto are on 466 ("the State as 'the immanent God'"); about "that glorious life" of the late-medieval Low Countries, 470; "our human life," 467. On Althusius, I have relied on the Introduction by Frederick S. Carney and Preface by Carl J. Friedrich to Carney's translation of Althusius's *Politics* (Boston, 1964); and on James W. Skillen, "The Political Theory of Johannes Althusius," *Philosophia Reformata* 39 (1974): 170-90. On von Gierke, see Antony Black's "Editor's Introduction" to Otto von Gierke, *Community in Historical Perspective: A Translation of Selections from Das Deutsche Genossenschaftsrecht* [1881], trans. Mary Fischer, ed. Antony Black (Cambridge and New York, 1990), xiv-xxx. Von Gierke published *Johannes Althusius und die Entwicklung der naturrechtlichen Staatstheorien* in 1879. Jonathan Chaplin explains Kuyper's aversion to Althusius via von Gierke in a personal communication to the author, 4 November 2003. On the theme of republican virtue, see "Sphere Sovereignty," 469-71.

The first edition of Kuyper's *Ons Program* (Amsterdam, 1879) included the April 1878–February 1879 series in *De Standaard* that formed one continuous commentary on the twenty-one Articles of the official Antirevolutionary Party Program, plus numerous newspaper pieces ("Bijlagen") that he had published on previous occasions. The volume underwent several subsequent editions, but the ARP Program did not change in Kuyper's lifetime and appeared near the start of every edition. Chapter and page citations below refer to the first edition. Kuyper's crucial 1873 newspaper series on "Ordinantiën Gods" appears in *Ons Program,* 116-29. Citations below are from the English translation, "The Ordinances of God," in Skillen and McCarthy, eds., *Political Order and the Plural Structure of Society,* 242-57. McKendree R. Langley, "Emancipation and Apologetics: The Formation of Abraham Kuyper's Anti-Revolutionary Party in the Netherlands, 1872-1880" (unpublished Ph.D. dissertation, Westminster Theological Seminary, 1995), gives helpful detail and analysis of Kuyper's commentary, 113-60.

Issues concerning sovereignty and its ramifications are stated in Articles 1-5 of the ARP Program and treated in *Ons Program* chapters 1-6. Article 1/chapter 1 deals with the party name; conscience being "sovereign in its own sphere" is stated and explicated, 198-202. Article 20/Chapter 21 covers church-state separation; the "conscience of the legislator" is stipulated 103; "each have their own domain" appears in "Ordinances of God," 252. Kuyper argues against the concept and usages of an "atheistic state" in *Ons Program* chapter 5, asserting Calvinism as the "tonic note" of the nation, 28-33; "equal rights for all" was a perennial slogan in his work, occurring, e.g., in "Calvinism and Constitutional Liberties," 315.

Articles 6-11/chapters 7-12 treat the framework of government; the House of Orange is handled already under the section on authority, 74-78; Orange's sovereignty is declared a "mystery" on 77. On constitutionalism and the Constitution of 1848, Article 7/chapter 8; on cabinet and Parliament, Articles 8 and 9/chapters 9 and 10; on franchise extension, 295-97 and 421-24; on electoral reforms, Article 11/chapter 12, especially 415-20, 424-25; on decentralization, Article 10/chapter 11.

Article 3/chapter 3 announces the centrality of divine ordinances; Articles 12-20/chapters 13-21 present the programmatic applications Kuyper saw issuing thence. The existence, reality, and divine origins of these ordinances are stipulated in "Ordinances of God," 244-45 (italics in original). The "circumference of each" comes from "Sphere Sovereignty," 467; "incontrovertible assertion," from "Ordinances of God," 245; "God's creation" and "all the givens," 246; "spiritual fathers" and "are cited," 248-49; "partially obscured" and "ground rules," 250; "simply wishes," 248; "it is impossible," 255; "knowledge of God's ordinances," 251 (my italics); "eternal principles," 255; the 1873 list of five ordinances, 255-56. Kuyper's poetic invocation of the ordinances is recorded in Rullmann, *Kuyper-Bibliografie,* III, 5. Translation is mine, borrowing from a variant of this poem translated by Henrietta Ten Harmsel, in Bratt, *Kuyper Centennial Reader,* 227-28.

Kuyper treats church-state relations in Article 20/chapter 21 of *Ons Program* and educational policy in Article 12/chapter 13; "right to establish" comes from "Ordinances of God," 252. Dengerink summarizes Kuyper's view of the family in *Critisch-Historisch Onderzoek,* 124-27. On the school's relationship to "the father," see *Ons Program,* 477-78. On the state and public health, see Article 15/chapter 16; regarding vaccination, 806-7, 848-57. Kuyper valorizes the state as a "servant of God," 138-46; "rises high" comes from "Sphere Sovereignty," 468; "purely external means" comes from "Ordinances of God," 249. On defense policy, see *Ons Program,* Article 17/chapter 18; on fiscal matters, Article 16/chapter 17; on their intersection, 862-64, 868-72, 924-31. Article 14/chapter 15 covers "public virtue," distinguishing that from "morality," 761. Kuyper's understanding of the specific way in which the Netherlands was a Christian nation is spelled out 146-54 and the policy implications thereof, 189-97, as well as Article 5/chapter 6; "baptized nation" recurs throughout Kuyper's writings, e.g., "Maranatha," in Bratt, *Kuyper Centennial Reader,* 212.

Notes on Chapter 8

The Doleantie and Kuyper's role in it are covered in Rasker, *NHK,* 153-90; Stellingwerff, *Kuyper en de VU,* 121-58; Koch, *Kuyper biografie,* 239-83; and various of the essays in Bakker, *De Doleantie van 1886.* On the "panel incident," see Stellingwerff, *Kuyper en de VU,* 149-52, and Koch, *Kuyper biografie,* 263-65. C. Augustijn characterizes it as Kuyper's "greatest tactical blunder" in "De spiritualiteit van de dolerenden," in Augustijn and Vree, eds., *Kuyper: vast en veranderlijk,* 185.

Kuyper's comprehensive text on church reform was *Tractaat van de reformatie der kerken* (Amsterdam, 1884); I have cited from the Volksuitgave of 1884. He puts the case in briefer compass in *Ijzer en Leem* (Amsterdam, 1885), 18-21. Secondary analyses are supplied in W. Bakker, "De Doleantie in den lande," in Bakker, *De Doleantie van 1886,* 134-38, and C. H. W. van den Berg, "De ontstaansgeschiedenis van de Doleantie in Amsterdam," ibid., 77-78, 84-85, 95-96; see also Rasker, *NHK,* 181-82, and Koch, *Kuyper biografie,* 252-53. Kuyper lays out his case against the 1816 Regulation and its consequences in Chapter III of *Tractaat,* "On the Deformation of the Churches," 83-115; for a terse, popular summary, see "It Shall Not Be so Among You," E. T. of "Alzoo zal het onder u niet zijn," *Uit de diepte I & II* (Amsterdam, 1886), in Bratt, *Kuyper Centennial Reader,* 126-31, 135-36. His fears even about local church offices are recorded in Bakker, "De Doleantie in den lande," 84-85.

Kuyper's assertion of the Dortian-confessional essence of the Dutch Reformed Church is strongest in *Revisie der Revisie-Legende* (Amsterdam, 1879), and summarized well in C. Augustijn, "Kerk en godsdienst 1870-1890," in Bakker, *De Doleantie van 1886,* 71. His hope that formal division would promote better harmony is expressed in the concluding section of *Contra-Memorie inzake het Amsterdamsch Conflict . . .* (Amsterdam, 1886), digested in Rullmann, *Kuyper-Bibliografie* II, 143-46. The impact of Kuyper's position with respect to the church's role in Dutch society has attracted copious commentary. See, most thoroughly, Kuiper, *De Voormannen,* 164-99; more briefly, Rasker, *NHK,* 164, 169-70; Van den Berg, "De ontstaansgeschiedenis van de Doleantie," 77-78, 91-

94; and Bakker, "De Doleantie in den lande," 134-44. Some of Kuyper's crispest statements of the issue come in *Ijzer en Leem*, 25-26; "De Heelen en de Halven," *Standaard*, 17 June 1885; and *Tweeërlei Vaderland*, 22-23, 28-30. On "Legitimism," *Ijzer en Leem*, 24-25. His argument that 1816 and not the Doleantie was "revolutionary" is put briefly ibid., 18-21; most extensively in "Complot en Revolutie," pamphlet of 30 January 1886 collected in *Het Conflict gekomen* (Amsterdam, 1886). See also Bakker, "De Doleantie in den lande," 134-44, and Koch, *Kuyper biografie*, 252-56.

Statistics on church membership and attendance are taken from Augustijn, "Kerk en godsdienst," 44, 48-52, and Van den Berg, "De ontstaansgeschiedenis van de Doleantie," 77-79, 83, 94-95. "Supervision of doctrine," quoted in Koch, *Kuyper biografie*, 248. Kuyper laid out his campaign strategy in *Tractaat*, 196-204; see also Rasker, *NHK*, 181-82. The "yoke of synodical hierarchy" became a mantra in the Doleantie; see, e.g., *Afwerping van het juk der Synodale Hiërarchie* (Amsterdam, 1886). For "dead churches," *Tractaat*, 198; "false preaching," 197; "doleerende kerken," 199. "Lamenting" and "plead" are quoted from the *Tractaat* by Rasker, *NHK*, 181. The radical climate of the times, set by the economic crisis, is well explained in Theo van Tijn, "De Doleantie kwam niet alleen," *Documentatieblad voor de Nederlandse kerkgeschiedenis van de negentiende eeuw* 10 (January 1986): 41-46, and "De sociale bewegingen van 1876 tot 1887," *AGN 1978*, 13: 90-100. Kossmann, *Low Countries*, 310-11, 314-15, gives a briefer summary. On police riots and the Eel Riot, see ibid., 316, and Van Tijn, "De sociale bewegingen," 95, 97-99. For liberal and conservative condemnations of Kuyper as a dangerous radical, see Koch, *Kuyper biografie*, 274-75. Kuyper's memory of burying his father is recorded in Stellingwerff, *Kuyper en de VU*, 125; for that and Lohman's advice to him after Willy's birth see also Koch, *Kuyper biografie*, 240-41.

The process of the Doleantie is recounted succinctly in Rasker, *NHK*, 182-89; in Koch, *Kuyper biografie*, 256-72; and in Stellingwerff, *Kuyper en de VU*, 139-56. Figures on the crisis for VU graduates stand ibid., 123, 141; image of "general staff" and troops in the field comes from Bakker, "De Doleantie in den lande," 113; "the gospel of Christ," Rasker, *NHK*, 182; "the interests of the kingdom" and "the Lord Jesus Christ," quoted ibid., 182, 183. The procedural infighting is followed in greatest detail in Van den Berg, "De ontstaansgeschiedenis van de Doleantie," 96-103. On the Doleantie in the provinces see Bakker, "De Doleantie in den lande"; Rasker, *NHK*, 186-89; and Stellingwerff, *Kuyper en de VU*, 144-49; "spiritual classis," quoted in Koch, *Kuyper biografie*, 260; "irregular, churchly, and valid," quoted in Stellingwerff, *Kuyper en de VU*, 147. Rasker, *NHK*, 185-86, summarizes the legal process; Koch, *Kuyper biografie*, 266-70, gives more detail. On the Church Conference and the further spread of and hostility to the Doleantie see Bakker, "De Doleantie in den lande," 123-32; "throwing off the yoke," quoted 123. The final scale of the Doleantie is registered in Bakker, "De Doleantie in den lande," 127; Van den Berg, "De ontstaansgeschiedenis van de Doleantie," 103; and D. Th. Kuiper, "De Doleantie en de Nederlandse samenleving," in Bakker, *De Doleantie van 1886*, 237, 239. The opposition to Kuyper from former colleagues is described in Augustijn, "Spiritualiteit," 185-86 ("continuous, hateful," 186), and Stellingwerff, *Kuyper en de VU,* 156-58. Koch, *Kuyper biografie,* covers the hostility from some of his longstanding adversaries, 270-79, but also Kappeyne's assistance, 271-72, for which see also Bakker, "De Doleantie in den lande," 139.

Kuyper's address to the fifth annual meeting of the VU society on 30 June 1885 was *Ijzer en Leem;* on this as a pivot point in the process, see Jasper Vree, "'Het Réveil' en 'het (neo-)Calvinisme' in hun onderlinge samenhang (1856-1896)," in Augustijn and Vree, *Kuyper vast en veranderlijk,* 70-72. "What pain," *Ijzer en Leem,* 28; "the creature breaking off," 13; "to divide from Christ," 20. Kuyper's involvement with South African affairs in this period is detailed in Van Koppen, *Kuyper en Zuid-Afrika,* 45-146; English-language summary, 242-46. On his trips to London and overwork, 116-17; regarding the Boers' Calvinistic calling, 61-65, 134-37; on Kuyper's cooperation with Fruin, 83, 87-90, 119, but also 128-31; the cooling of his support, 133-45. Kuyper's address to the Transvaal-delegation rally — for the context of which, ibid., 121-27 — was published as *Plancius-Rede* (Amsterdam, 1884); "also personally," 14-15; "intolerable," 18-19. His letter of 29 March 1884 to S. J. DuToit is quoted in Van Koppen, *Kuyper en Zuid-Afrika,* 130; his letter from Paul Kruger's secretary F. Eloff, 21 May 1891, ibid., 142. Kuyper's exchange with Nicholas M. Steffens is explicated further in James D. Bratt, *Dutch Calvinism in Modern America* (Grand Rapids, 1984), 46, 60; "You should drop that idea," letter of Nicholas M. Steffens to Kuyper, 7 May 1886; "our Dutch people," ibid., 25 January 1891, both in Steffens papers, Calvin College and Seminary Archives, Grand Rapids, Michigan.

Kuyper's key *Standaard* article (17 June 1885) anticipating the Doleantie is "De Heelen en de Halven" ("The Wholes and the Halves"); "better or braver," 1. His post-deposition sermon (11 July 1886) was "It Shall Not be so Among You"; "much farther" and "the One who sends me," 133; "How we loved," 137; "Have I, I myself," 139. His sermon at the Church Conference 11 January 1887, "Een ziel, die zich nederbuigt," was published in *Uit de Diepte* XXXI-XXXII (Amsterdam, 1887), and is digested in Rullmann, *Kuyper-Bibliografie* II, 182-85; "I am fearful," 183; "the heights of self-righteousness," 183; "the waterspouts of God," 184. Kuyper's address to the seventh annual meeting of the VU society was *Tweeërlei Vaderland;* "had not the people," 23-24; "could become so powerful," 24. His warning against creating a new ecclesiastical party was published at the conclusion of his series in *De Heraut* on the "Practical Consequences" of *Particular Grace,* in early 1882. The series was collected as Part I of *De Practijk der Godzaligheid* (Amsterdam, 1886) and is digested in Rullmann, *Kuyper-Bibliografie* II, 172-78; "isten" and "anen" and "in the great whole of the church," quoted 176; "we are from the depths of our soul" and "head of a new school," quoted 177. Kuyper's next series concluded in July 1882, was collected as Part II of *De Practijk der Godzaligheid,* and is summarized in Rullmann, *Kuyper-Bibliografie* II, 178-82; "driven by the deeply sinful pull," quoted 181-82.

The personalities and issues facing the formation of the Gereformeerde Kerken in Nederland are analyzed in various of the essays in Wolthuis and Vree,

Notes

De Vereniging van 1892; a briefer digest is available in Rasker, *NHK,* 189-90; and Koch, *Kuyper biografie,* 279-83. The outstanding analysis of the inner as well as more formal differences between the two sides is Augustijn, "Spiritualiteit"; on pew-rents and "money," 192, 197; "preacher's church," 189; quest for "objective" worship, 193-94; on baptism and communalism, 194-96; weak nurture and loss of "church as mother," 198; "a church of spiritually mature," 195. These traits and the negotiations that sealed the union are further studied in J. van Gelderen, "Op weg naar de Vereniging," in Wolthuis and Vree, *De Vereniging van 1892,* 35-80. Relevant statistics are given in Gerrit J. Schutte, "Een samenleving in verandering en vernieuwing," ibid., 27; Kuiper, "De Doleantie en de Nederlandse samenleving," 237-39; and Van Rooden, *Religieuze regimes,* 162. Kuyper's famous declaration of his future ambitions came in his 13 February 1886 brochure, "De Vredelievenden in de Besturen," collected in *Het Conflict gekomen,* and is excerpted in Rullmann, *Kuyper-Bibliografie* II, 137-38.

Notes on Chapter 9

The classic study of Kuyper's ecclesiology is P. A. van Leeuwen, *Het Kerkbegrip in de Theologie van Abraham Kuyper* (Franeker, 1946). More recent analyses of value include C. H. W. van den Berg, "Kerk en wereld in de theologie en wereldbeschouwing van Abraham Kuyper," in *In Rapport met de Tijd: 100 jaar theologie aan de Vrije Universiteit* (Kampen, 1980), 140-66; by the same author, "Kuyper en de kerk," in Augustijn et al., eds., *Kuyper: volksdeel & invloed,* 146-78; W. Speelman, "De Demokratische Kuyper," *Segmenten* (1978): 157-99 (157-72 on the church); and Jasper Vree, "Organisme en instituut: De ontwikkeling van Kuypers spreken over kerk-zijn (1867-1901)," in Augustijn and Vree, *Kuyper: vast en veranderlijk,* 86-108. A solid overview in English is Henry Zwaanstra, "Abraham Kuyper's Conception of the Church," *Calvin Theological Journal* 9 (November 1974): 149-81. My summary of Kuyper's theological phases follows C. Augustijn, "Kuypers theologie van de samenleving," in Augustijn, *Kuyper: volksdeel & invloed,* 34-60; Vree, "Organisme en instituut," and by the same author, "'Het Réveil' en 'het (neo-) Calvinisme' in hun onderlinge samenhang (1856-1896)," in Augustijn and Vree, *Kuyper: vast en veranderlijk,* 54-85. The dictum about "thinking through his church ideal" comes from Van den Berg, "Kuyper en de Kerk," 155.

The influence of Schleiermacher on Kuyper's ecclesiology was first asserted by Van Leeuwen, *Kerkbegrip,* 98-100, 118-20, and is conclusively demonstrated in Jasper Vree, *Abraham Kuyper's Commentatio (1860): The Young Kuyper about Calvin, À Lasco, and the Church,* Volume I (Leiden, 2005), 2-4, 49-54, 57, 65. Key early sermons on ecclesiology at Beesd are those treating the articles in the Apostles' Creed on the Holy Spirit and the holy catholic church, delivered 31 January and 7 February 1864, respectively; see Kuyper Archive, HDC-VU. His inaugural sermon at Utrecht was "Menschwording Gods": "The Church is thus not just a gathering," 259; "all that passes itself off," 260; "mottled," 266; "noble competition," 265; "the divine does not come forth . . . agitations from with-out," 261; "to the eternal shame" and "the spirit of the age," 263.

Kuyper's inaugural sermon at Amsterdam, "Geworteld en Gegrond," high-lights "eternal election" in its preface 3-4, but the topic received extensive treat-ment only in his next sermon, "De Troost der Eeuwige Verkiezing" (in his *Predicatiën, in de jaren 1867 tot 1873* [Kampen, 1913], 111-29). "Geworteld en Gegrond" describes the church as organism, 5-8, 11-14; as institute, 8-11, 14-19; "perfected" and "connection with heavenly life," 11; "in Christ as a human life" and "so now a double stream runs," 12; "organism" and "heart," 13; "just as much grounded," 8; "the institute of the church exists," 15; Calvin's image of church as mother, cited 16; "that alone makes progress," "the shoulders of those who have gone before," "the higher ground of the new life," "sets itself between us," "life-sphere" and "forms the person," "called from the root," all 17. The "scaffolding" metaphor is unpacked on 18-19. *Confidentie: schrijven aan den weled. Heer J. H. van der Linden* was published in Amsterdam, 1873.

Kuyper's *Dat de Genade Particulier Is* was published as volume I in the sec-ond series of *Uit het Woord* (Amsterdam, 1884) after running in *De Heraut* April 1879–June 1880. I have used the English translation by Marvin Kamps, *Particu-lar Grace* (Grandville, Mich., 2001). *De Leer der Verbonden* (*Uit het Woord* II/II, Amsterdam, 1885) ran in *De Heraut* September 1880–October 1881. Kuyper ex-foliated the "practical consequences" of the doctrine of particular grace in *De Heraut* November 1881–July 1882 and published them as the first two parts of *Practijk der Godzaligheid* (*Uit het Woord* II/III, Amsterdam, 1886). "We very ear-nestly resist," *Particular Grace,* 77; "the rule that the Lord God sets . . . only chaos," 266; "the higher moral earnestness," 58; "in embryonic form," 94; "ev-eryone has his *own* tie," 87. One evocation of the "mountain-tops" comes in *Leer der Verbonden,* 304. Kuyper paints his model of proper Christian prayer in *Par-ticular Grace,* 178-79, elevates Trinitarianism over Christocentrism, 180-81, and discusses preaching amid the uncertainties of election, 232-33.

All discussion and citations of *Leer der Verbonden* come from its fifth sec-tion, "The Delights of the Covenant": "the *Covenant of Grace* is the glorious channel," 319; "we do not sit," 317; "sticks and blocks," 303; "brook" running "through all the bumps," 324-25; "transitional, mixed, and unconscious," 323. An older but helpful delineation of Kuyper's ideas on the covenant is G. Kuypers, "Abraham Kuyper over Genadeverbond en Sacrament," *Gere-formeerd Theologisch Tijdschrift* 47 (1947): 65-77. Kuyper's concept of the demo-cratic dimension of election is illustrated in "De Troost der Eeuwige Ver-kiezing" and in *Particular Grace,* 320-26; "the broad circle of people," *Leer der Verbonden,* 303. Kuyper faults common applications of election in ibid., 312-19, 351-57; "holy despair of the sect," 319. Kuyper's typology of sectarianism runs ibid., 306-11; "methodists" and "passivists," 309; "meddlesome" and "lackadai-sical," 307; "manufacturing methodism," 307; *geen verbond, geen verband,* 311; "the normal means," 335. Kuyper contrasts the views from "God's side" and "the human side" in *Particular Grace,* 225-41 (quotations, 239), and treats the theme of "fixed ordinances" on 266-68 (quotations, 266); "psychological . . . injustice to the sacred," 240; "raises us up," 192. His ultimate resort to scriptural authority comes on 67.

The third phase of Kuyper's ecclesiology is epitomized in his *Encyclopaedie,* 183-345. His Free University lectures were transcribed and published in five volumes by his students as *Dictaten Dogmatiek* (2nd ed., Kampen, 1910). The church was the subject of vol. 4, *Locus de Ecclesia,* based on lectures delivered in 1892 when Kuyper was finishing the *Encyclopaedie.* Van den Berg, "Kerk en Wereld," lists Kuyper's recurrent paired concepts, 142-43, and explores his organic thinking, 142-51. Speelman carries out that analysis at greater length in "Demokratische Kuyper," 157-69, alluding to Schelling, 159. Zwaanstra draws the same link in "Kuyper's Conception," 156, after Van Leeuwen, *Kerkbegrip,* 118-20. Schelling's religious thought is well summarized in English in John E. Wilson, *Introduction to Modern Theology: Trajectories in the German Tradition* (Louisville, 2007), 49-51, 60-69. Van den Berg, "Kerk en Wereld," 147, notes the analogy of organic church to society as institutional church to state. All quotations are from *Encyclopaedie,* vol. III: "according to ordinances," 194; "the organic character of the human race," 190; "not for a moment . . . higher grace," 189; "central" in "consciousness," "personal life of the faithful," "the coming to be of conversion," and "the central action upon the consciousness," 194-96. The institute-organism "opposition," "more precisely," "organism of the church," and "twofold manifestation" appear on 218; not "accidental" but "principial and necessary," 216. The subjects of the "institutional" and "organic departments" are laid out 218-25; "the Christian metamorphosis" and "fall away," 215; "minimally through the sphere" and "so little spiritual depth," 194-95. Kuyper alludes to current Dutch emigration to Colorado, 204; the episode is detailed by Peter de Klerk, "The Ecclesiastical Struggles of the Rilland and Crook Christian Reformed Churches in Colorado in 1893," in De Klerk and Richard R. DeRidder, eds., *Perspectives on the Christian Reformed Church: Studies in Its History, Theology, and Ecumenicity* (Grand Rapids, 1983), 73-98. Richard Rothe's thought is summarized in Wilson, *Introduction to Modern Theology,* 106-11; "whole moral community," 110. See also Claude Welch, *Protestant Thought in the Nineteenth Century: Vol. I, 1799-1870* (New Haven, 1972), 282-91. Kuyper's parallels to and differences with Rothe are explored in Speelman, "Demokratische Kuyper," 160-62.

Kuyper's *Onze Eeredienst* (Kampen, 1911) collected eighty articles on worship that he had written in *De Heraut* 1897-1901 (covering theoretical background and the elements of a typical service) and fifty more he published there in 1910-11 about baptism, the Lord's Supper, and other special occasions. The volume has been translated (with an approximately thirty percent abridgement) as *Our Worship,* ed. Harry Boonstra (Grand Rapids, 2009), from which all references and quotations are cited. Kuyper's democratic theme is evident, e.g., 86-89, 93-97, 145-46; his emphasis on full worship and not just sermon, 17-18; restrictions on the minister's role, 103-4 ("will retain a more humble," 104); and his outline of the essence of worship, 8-19. On the Votum, 107-15; the role of reciting the Creed, 155-58; kneeling in prayer, 141-47; and the merits of liturgical over spontaneous prayer, 29-36, 137-40, 171-73, 207-9. His historical analysis is exemplified on 25-27, 108-10, 128-30, 174-77; his critique of Sankey and the syndrome he inspired, 121-24; on conventicles, see 18, 119-20, 253-55. Kuyper explores preaching, 174-206, and the Lord's Supper, 261-88 ("exceptionally holy character," 277; "the worship service reaches its highest point," 261; "oppos[ing] any notion," 273). On his strong preference for still using a communal table, 268-71; on the virtues of anonymity, 270. He covers the liturgy of baptism, 221-47 ("If baptism neither . . . issues directly from baptism," 247).

The best treatment of controversies in the GKN between the Union and the Synod of 1905 is in Jasper Vree, "Hoe de citadel onstond: De consolidatie der Vereniging, 1892-1905," in Augustijn and Vree, *Kuyper: vast en veranderlijk,* 200-242 ("To conceive of the visible or local church," quoted 214; "adhere as closely as possible," quoted 234; "God fulfills his promise," quoted 235; "Archimedean point," 236). For further background see J. van Gelderen, "Op weg naar de Vereniging," in Wolthuis and Vree, *De Vereniging van 1892,* 35-80.

Notes on Chapter 10

The book version of Kuyper's series on common grace was published in three volumes as *De Gemeene Gratie* (Leiden, 1902-5), with the supplement *De Gemeene Gratie in wetenschap en kunst* in 1905. Citations from *Gemeene Gratie* are given by chapter as much as possible to overcome the different paginations of successive editions; necessary page citations come from the first edition. Key interpretations of the theory are Ridderbos, *Theologische Cultuurbeschouwing;* W. H. Velema, "Abraham Kuyper als theoloog," *In die Skriflig* 23/3 (1989): 56-73, elucidating themes already laid out in Velema's *De leer van de Heilige Geest bij Abraham Kuyper* (The Hague, 1957); S. U. Zuidema, "Common Grace and Christian Action in Abraham Kuyper" [1954], in *Communication and Confrontation* (Kampen, 1972), 52-105; Ridderbos's rejoinder, "De Dialectische Theologie van Abraham Kuyper," *Antirevolutionaire Staatkunde* 29 (1959): 110-29; A. A. van Ruler, *Kuypers idee eener christelijke cultuur* (Nijkerk, 1940); and most recently, Cornelis van der Kooi, "A Theology of Culture: A Critical Appraisal of Kuyper's Doctrine of Common Grace," in *Kuyper Reconsidered,* ed. Van der Kooi and De Bruijn, 95-101; and Richard J. Mouw, *He Shines in All That's Fair: Culture and Common Grace* (Grand Rapids, 2001).

Kuyper's early statements of the broad span of Christian action come in "De Menschwording Gods" ("all fields of life," "every domain," 24-26) and "Sphere Sovereignty" ("there is not a square inch," 488). Augustijn analyzes Kuyper's changed context after 1885 in "Kuypers theologie van de samenleving," in Augustijn, *Kuyper: volksdeel & invloed,* 43-54. "A Twofold Fatherland" was published as *Tweeërlei Vaderland.* Kuyper describes "our fatherland here below," 8-9; "defined the direction" and "*secularization* is the stamp," 35; on the tools of secular hegemony, 34-35; "prince and people," 36; "a colony of the heavenly fatherland," 32; "a better dawn," 36. Kuyper's address at the 1896 Synod of the GKN is contextualized by Jasper Vree in "Hoe de citadel ontstond: De consolidatie der Vereniging, 1892-1905," in Augustijn and Vree, *Kuyper: vast en veranderlijk,* 206-21. The address was published as "De Zegen des Heeren over Onze Kerken" (Amsterdam, 1896); "reduced lot," "little churches," "spiritual prattlings," 15; "conflict quickens faith" and *"an instrument of the Lord,"* 19; "Brothers, *I believe in the future,"* 21; "standpoint" and ruling "principle," 13; "Christian worldview in the tongue of our own time," 22.

For Kuyper's series on the "natural knowledge of God," see Augustijn, "Kuypers theologie van samenleving," 38-42, and Ridderbos, *Theologische Cultuurbeschouwing,* 98-102. Kuyper's citation from Calvin appears in *GG,* I: 6 ("the unbelievers who dwell"). On the "Arminian" (also "Pelagian") error, I: 7, 138; II: 185-86, 190-91,382, 583-88 [ch. 58]; on "Anabaptist" faults, I: 102-4; II: 65-78 [chs. 9-10]. For the role of common grace in the entire cosmos, see Kuyper, *GG,* II: ch.11, and Ridderbos, *Theologische Cultuurbeschouwing,* 69-72; on the twofold goal of common grace, ibid., 88-93. Kuyper describes common grace as "a curtain of protection" in *Particular Grace,* 217, and uses "bridling," "tempering," "restrained," and "blocked" as both complementary and synonymous terms for common grace's functions throughout *Gemeene Gratie;* a good example is I: ch. 30. See also *Lectures on Calvinism,* 123-25. *Gemeene Gratie* I: chs. 3-12 and 39, treat the Noah episode; chs. 13-38 flash back to Eden and the fall up to the flood.

Ridderbos expands on Kuyper's notion of cultural development as a fruit of common grace in *Theologische Cultuurbeschouwing,* 88-93, 106-31. Clear statements in Kuyper include *Gemeene Gratie* II, chs. 81-83; and "Common Grace in Science and Art," 445-46. On his racial hierarchy and heliotropic sense, see Ridderbos, *Theologische Cultuurbeschouwing,* 198-200; *Gemeene Gratie* II, ch. 89; *Lectures on Calvinism,* 32-40; "beauty does not enrich," *Gemeene Gratie in wetenschap en kunst,* 59. Jan Willem Schulte Nordholt puts Kuyper's concept in larger context in *The Myth of the West: America as the Last Empire* (Grand Rapids, 1995 [1992]); see especially 91. Kuyper articulates the image of God being manifested best in the whole human race in *Gemeene Gratie* II, ch. 83; "if it has pleased God," 626; in "the whole life . . . is not necessary," 619. "The names of Socrates, Plato, and Aristotle" and "almost exclusively . . . fear of the Lord," "Common Grace in Science," *Kuyper Centennial Reader,* 448; "undeniable fact," 448-49. On Kuyper's connection of common grace chiefly to corporate forces, see Augustijn, "Kuypers theologie van samenleving," 52-54 ("the life-relationships," 52).

Ridderbos analyzes Kuyper's relation of particular to common grace in *Theologische Cultuurbeschouwing,* 93-97; Kuyper lays it out in *Gemeene Gratie* II, chs. 32 and 91. Kuyper's four-part typology is spelled out at the climax of *Gemeene Gratie* II, chs. 88-90; "the life of non-confessors," 677; "Christian" indicating "nothing about the spiritual state . . . higher standpoint," 662; "the life of Christ-confessors outside of the church institute," "salt of the earth," "external contact," "internal kinship," and "a leaven [that] has permeated," 677; "though the lamp of the Christian religion," 268. For "Christian metamorphosis," see *Encyclopaedie* III, 195-97, 200, 215, 307-8, 343.

Kuyper clearly foreshadowed his mature epistemology in the portion of "Sphere Sovereignty" dedicated to that concern (see Bratt, *Kuyper Centennial Reader,* 480-88). He articulated his position most fully in the context of his broader understanding of theology in *Encyclopedia of Sacred Theology: Its Principles* (New York, 1898); more briefly in *Lectures on Calvinism,* Lecture 4, "Calvinism and Science"; and in "Common Grace in Science," 441-60. These were originally articles that ran in *De Heraut* 6 May–9 June 1901. Important book-length commentaries in English are Peter S. Heslam, *Creating a Christian Worldview: Abraham Kuyper's <u>Lectures on Calvinism</u>* (Grand Rapids, 1998); David Naugle, *Worldview: The History of a Concept* (Grand Rapids, 2002) (on Kuyper, 16-25); and *Stained Glass: Worldviews and Social Science,* ed. Paul A. Marshall et al. (Lanham, Md., 1989). Important essays include Nicholas Wolterstorff, "Abraham Kuyper on Christian Learning," *Educating for Shalom: Essays on Christian Higher Education* (Grand Rapids, 2004), 199-225; Jacob Klapwijk, "Abraham Kuyper over wetenschap en universiteit," in *Kuyper: volksdeel & invloed,* ed. Augustijn et al., 61-94; and "Rationality in the Dutch Neo-Calvinist Tradition," in *Rationality in the Calvinian Tradition,* ed. Hendrik Hart et al. (Lanham, Md., 1983), 93-111; Del Ratzsch, "Abraham Kuyper's Philosophy of Science," in *Facets of Faith and Science,* Vol. II: *The Role of Beliefs in Mathematics and the Natural Sciences, An Augustinian Perspective,* ed. Jitse M. van der Meer (Lanham, Md., 1996), 1-32; Stellingwerff, *Kuyper en de VU,* 253-82 ("Romantiek en Calvinisme: Kuypers Wereldbeschouwing"); J. D. Dengerink, "Kuyper's wetenschapsleer," *Radix* 2 (1976): 87-102; René van Woudenberg, "Abraham Kuyper on Faith and Science," and Gijsbert van den Brink, "Was Kuyper a Reformed Epistemologist?", both in *Kuyper Reconsidered,* ed. Van der Kooi and De Bruijn, 147-57 and 158-65, respectively.

Kuyper would have recognized the terms of engagement in such classic interpretations of the crisis in European high culture at the turn of the century as H. Stuart Hughes, *Consciousness and Society: The Reorientation of European Social Thought, 1890-1930* (New York, 1958), and Gerhard Masur, *Prophets of Yesterday: Studies in European Culture, 1890-1914* (New York, 1961). More recent analyses include J. W. Burrow, *The Crisis of Reason: European Thought, 1848-1914* (New Haven, 2000); William Everdell, *The First Moderns: Profiles in the Origins of Twentieth-Century Thought* (Chicago, 1997); James T. Kloppenberg, *Uncertain Victory: Social Democracy and Progressivism in European and American Thought, 1870-1920* (New York, 1986); and Carl E. Schorske, *Fin-de-Siècle Vienna: Politics and Culture* (New York, 1980). On the development of "worldview" as an idea and method, see Naugle, *Worldview,* 55-107; Masur, *Prophets,* 160-72; and the essays by Albert M. Wolters, "On the Idea of Worldview and Its Relation to Philosophy" (14-25), and Sander Griffioen, "The Worldview Approach to Social Theory: Hazards and Benefits" (81-118), in Marshall et al., eds., *Stained Glass.*

An efficient treatment of the hegemony of "science" in European culture after 1850 is Burrow, *Crisis of Reason,* 31-67; Everdell, *First Moderns,* details the challenges to the regnant model from within the natural sciences, 30-62. On

Mach, see ibid., 15-17, 185-86; and Burrow, *Crisis of Reason,* 61-64. I take Mach's characterization of atomic physics from Ratzsch, "Kuyper's Philosophy of Science," 12. Early glimpses of Kuyper's worldview approach occur in *Wat moeten wij doen* (Culemborg, 1867) — "which corner" and "the cardinal point of difference," 2, 6; and "Sphere Sovereignty," 481-88 — "what natural scientist," 487-88; "not as if," 486. Heslam argues for James Orr's influence on Kuyper in *Creating a Christian Worldview,* 92-96, and Naugle follows, in *Worldview,* 17, detailing Orr's views 6-13. Dilthey's seminal essays on epistemology, psychology, and aesthetics are listed and dated to 1892-94 in the bibliography in H. P. Rickman, ed., *W. Dilthey: Selected Writings* (Cambridge, 1976), 264-65. On Dilthey's understanding of the pluralism and conflict of worldviews, see Naugle, *Worldview,* 82-98. On "worldview" vis à vis "philosophy," see Wolters, "On the Idea of Worldview," 15-19; on its mass appeal, Griffioen, "Approach to Social Theory," 86-87; on Engels and worldview, ibid., 86-87, 97, 99, 106.

Kuyper's notion of a primordial fit between archetype and ectype is laid out at length in *Encyclopedia,* 63-83; more succinctly in "Common Grace in Science," 443-45. For commentary, see Klapwijk, "Kuyper en wetenschap," 71-74, and Ratzsch, "Kuyper's Philosophy of Science," 2-3. On immediate intuition in Adam/Eden, see "Common Grace in Science," 449-51; "to Adam, science," 451. Kuyper sets out his division of the faculties in *Encyclopedia,* 192-210; see also Klapwijk, "Kuyper en wetenschap," 82-85. On his particular divisions within the faculty of theology, ibid., 85-86, and *Encyclopaedia,* III, 210-11. Kuyper delineates the effects of sin on knowledge in *Encyclopedia,* 106-14. On science as an unguided collaborative effort by the whole human race, see ibid., 155-56, and "Common Grace in Science," 445-47; "great temple" and "elaborate blueprint," 446; "the entire temple was built," 447.

Kuyper introduced the language of "palingenesis" in his 1892 rectorial address at the Free University, "The Blurring of the Boundaries," 400. He elaborates the epistemological consequences for research and scholarship in *Encyclopedia,* 150-82; on "normalists" and "abnormalists," see *Lectures on Calvinism,* 132-38; on the roles of "faith" in all personal and collective knowledge-projects, see *Encyclopedia,* 125-46. On non-religious factors that shape the scholarly enterprise, see *Encyclopedia,* 169-70; "friction, ferment, and conflict," 171. On the common ground shared by the two types of science, see *Encyclopedia,* 157-63; lower-higher, 157-58, branching tree, 162, 168, "we are equally emphatic," 161. Valuable commentary upon these issues can be found in the essays by Ratzsch, "Kuyper's Philosophy of Science," 8-20; Wolterstorff, "Kuyper on Christian Learning," 219-25; and Klapwijk, "Kuyper over wetenschap," 65-67, 74-82.

On true knowledge as architectonic, see "Common Grace in Science," 449-50, 454-55; "our mind constantly," 455. My presentation of William James here follows Howard M. Feinstein, *Becoming William James* (Ithaca, 1984). Gauguin's painting is in the Museum of Fine Arts, Boston; Bergson posed his "questions of vital interest" in *L'Energie spirituelle* (Paris, 1919), cited by Masur, *Prophets of Yesterday,* 256. On the contemporary effort to establish the independence of and find a method for the "human sciences," see Burrow, *Crisis of Reason,* 58-

60, 88-89; Masur, *Prophets of Yesterday,* 159-202; Kloppenberg, *Uncertain Victory,* 95-114. For Kuyper's version of the problematic, see *Encyclopedia,* 137-46, and "Common Grace in Science," 451-54, 456-58; "whoever neglects," 456; "something entirely different," 452.

Notes on Chapter 11

The most salient secondary treatments of this phase of Kuyper's life are Koch, *Kuyper biografie,* 325-90; and Stellingwerff, *Kuyper en de VU,* 185-226. Both build their interpretations around the conflict with Lohman, with Stellingwerff strongly and Koch more moderately critical of Kuyper's behavior therein. The ARP and Kuyper's role in its development in this period are closely studied in Janssens, *Opbouw ARP,* 183-296. See also Janssens' summary coverage of the period ("Eenheid en verdeeldheid, 1879-1894") in Harinck, *ARP,* 73-92, along with Roel Kuiper's treatment of the immediately subsequent years, "Uit het dal omhoog, 1894-1905," ibid., 93-107. The Christian Social Congress is analyzed in background, consequences, and international context in the essays collected in Gerrit J. Schutte, ed., *Een Arbeider is zijn loon waardig* (The Hague, 1991).

Kuyper's yearnings for a purely academic future are recorded in Rullmann, *Kuyper-Bibliografie* II, 137; "rejoic[ing] with my whole heart" comes from the same source. The context and provisions of constitutional revision are explained in Kossmann, *Low Countries,* 350-52, and Koch, *Kuyper biografie,* 343, 347-49; much greater detail is available in E. H. Kossmann, "De Groei van de Anti-Revolutionaire Partij," in *AGN 1956,* 11: 16-22. Ratios of electorate to population come from Wintle, *ESHN,* 253. Janssens, *Opbouw ARP,* 282-90, details Kuyper's subsequent moves. "Proceed quietly" and "no party that worked its electorate" are quoted by Kuiper, "Uit het dal omhoog," 106. The course of the Mackay cabinet can be followed in Kossmann, *Low Countries,* 352-57; Koch, *Kuyper biografie,* 325, 349-52; and Stellingwerff, *Kuyper en de VU,* 187-89. See also Janssens, "Eenheid en verdeeldheid," 89-90. For the provisions of the Education Act, see Kossmann, *Low Countries,* 354; of the Labor Act, 355; the crisis over military service, 355-57. Kuyper's disaffection with the Mackay cabinet is traced in Koch, *Kuyper biografie,* 348-50, 355-57; on Kuyper's Thorbecke envy, 348.

On Dutch colonial policy see Kossmann, *Low Countries,* 398-406; Van Koppen, *Kuyper en Zuid-Afrika,* 224-30; and McKendree R. Langley, "Emancipation and Apologetics" (unpublished Ph.D. dissertation, Westminster Theological Seminary, 1995), 138-43; the education statistic is cited at 142. Kuyper spells out the ARP's Ethical Policy in *Ons Program,* Article 18/Chapter 19, anticipated by his parliamentary speeches from 1874-75 summarized in Rullmann, *Kuyper-Bibliografie,* II, 278-84. Keuchenius's career and character are profiled in great detail by the friendly Frederik L. Rutgers, *Levensbericht van Mr. L. W. C. Keuchenius* (Leiden, 1895); his part in the contretemps of 1890 by Koch, *Kuyper biografie,* 353-57; his polemics during the Billiton scandal, 355; his link with Multatuli, 353; his role in the crisis of 1866-68 in Kossmann, *Low Countries,* 284-88.

Developments in the Dutch economy are summarized in Kossmann, *Low Countries,* 412-18, and Wintle, *ESHN,*172-83. The history of Patrimonium is sketched in G. J. Schutte, "Arbeid, die geen brood geeft," in Schutte, *Arbeider is zijn loon waardig,* 23-25; statistic, 24. H. J. Langeveld, "Protestantsche Christenen van Nederland, vereenigt u," in Schutte, *Arbeider is zijn loon waardig,* gives more detail, also as to Patrimonium's part in catalyzing the Christian Social Congress, 103-16. For a winsome account in English, see Harry Van Dyke, "How Abraham Kuyper Became a Christian Democrat," *Calvin Theological Journal* 33 (1998): 420-35. Kater's remarks are all quoted by Van Dyke, 425; "Our Frisian Ireland" and "Mosaic socialism" by Langeveld, "Protestantsche Christenen," 119. The Frisian radicals' role before and during the CSC is detailed ibid., passim; more briefly in Van Dyke, "Abraham Kuyper Christian Democrat," 424, 431-32. The role of Belgian and German examples for the CSC is cited in Langeveld, "Protestantsche Christenen," 112; the atmosphere of Kuyper's speech, 122. Kuyper's long engagement with the social question is detailed in H. E. S. Woldring, "De social kwestie — meer dan een emanci-patiestrijd," in Augustijn, *Kuyper: volksdeel & invloed,* 123-33. His Utrecht sermon, "The Worker and His Master according to the Ordinances of God," was delivered on 11 July 1869 and is found in the Kuyper Archive, HDC-VU. The von Ketteler brochure he republished with an introduction was *Die Arbeiterfrage und das Christenthum* (Mainz, 1864); Dutch translation = *De arbeiderskwestie en de kerk* (Amsterdam, 1871).

Kuyper's address at the CSC was entitled *Het Sociale Vraagstuk en de Christelijke Religie* (Amsterdam, 1891); all quotations from the English translation by James W. Skillen, *The Problem of Poverty* (Grand Rapids, 1991), 44-47. The "Sphere Sovereignty" citation is at 478 in Bratt, *Kuyper Centennial Reader.* Kuyper's *Handenarbeid* (Amsterdam, 1889) is available in English as "Manual Labor," ibid., 231-54. Many of these themes are repeated in "De Christus en de Sociale Nooden" (Amsterdam, [1895]). "The stronger, almost without exception" and "clearly visible lines" come from *Problem of Poverty,* 33, 68; "[w]e must courageously and openly acknowledge" in "Manual Labor," 234-35. Jesus, "just as his prophets before him" stands at 62 in *Problem of Poverty;* the larger point is laid out 35-42 and 60-63. Kuyper's general principles of diagnosis and remedy come in *Problem of Poverty,* 30-34, 50-54, 59-79; "hobbling up at the rear," 91. Kuyper surveys the real but limited role of government in redressing structural problems in "Manual Labor," 240-42, and elaborates on Chambers of Labor there, 242, 246-48, 252-54. His longstanding proposal for a legal code for labor is elaborated in Woldring, "Sociale kwestie," 131-33. On workers and education see "Manual Labor," 250-51, and *Problem of Poverty,* 89; on worker morale and morals, "Manual Labor," 233-34, and *Problem of Poverty,* 68-76; "Because we are conscious beings," 73. The outcomes of the CSC are detailed in Langeveld, "Protestantsche Christenen," 122-41; for more on the inspiration it gave to Dutch Christian labor organization, see L. J. Altena and A. J. P. Homan, "Zoodra de arbeider niet gevoelt dat hij rechten heeft, dan is hij weg," in Schutte, *Arbeider is zijn loon waardig,* 142-80. A Frisian radical's characterization of Fabius as the "evil genius" of "aristocracy" is recorded in Langeveld, "Protestantsche Christenen," 109.

The provisions and controversy over Tak's franchise bill are covered in Kossmann, *Low Countries,* 359-61; Stellingwerff, *Kuyper en de VU,* 191-97; and Koch, *Kuyper biografie,* 349-61, 364-67 (statistic, 365). Kuyper's Deputies Convention addresses are "Niet de Vrijheidsboom maar de Kruis. Toespraak ter opening van de Tiende Deputatenvergadering in het eeuwjaar der Fransche Revolutie" (Amsterdam, 1889), and "Maranatha. Rede ter inleiding van de Deputatenvergadering op 12 Mei 1891" (Amsterdam, 1891), E. T. "Maranatha," in Bratt, *Kuyper Centennial Reader,* 205-28. "Without any craftiness or secret intentions," "the oppressed are asking," and "the politics of Europe," "Maranatha," 220-21; "to appreciate our Conservatives'" and "we take exception," ibid., 213; *"Christian-democratic shape"* and "can still be done *now,*" ibid., 222; "even if the *zeitgeist,*" 223. Kuyper elaborates his policy of coalition with his concluding words of the series published (together with "De Christus en de Sociale Nooden") as *Demokratische Klippen* (Amsterdam, [1895]), 95.

The growing conflict between Kuyper and Lohman is covered in close detail in Koch, *Kuyper biografie,* 367-90, and Stellingwerff, *Kuyper en de VU,* 195-200. "I don't like radicalism" (also Robespierre), "the party in the House," and charges of conflated roles, Koch, *Kuyper biografie,* 369, 344-45, 346-47. On the election campaign of 1894, see Stellingwerff, *Kuyper en de VU,* 194-96; Koch, *Kuyper biografie,* 374-75; and Janssens, "Eenheid en verdeeldheid," 91-92: "one of the fiercest election campaigns in Dutch political history," 91; "conservatism of every stripe" and "final franchise extension," 92. "Men with the double names," Koch, *Kuyper biografie,* 327; "lord millionaires," 327; see also Stellingwerff, *Kuyper en de VU,* 199. On the aftermath of the elections, see Kuiper, "Uit het dal omhoog," 100-102, and Hans van Spanning, "Van vrij-antirevolutionairen naar Christelijke-Historische Unie," in Harinck, *ARP,* 113-22.

Lohman and his approach are intermittently profiled in Koch, *Kuyper biografie,* 326-29, 335-37, 342-47, 357-58, 386-90. On mass journalism, 328; as a bridge-builder, 333. Kossmann efficiently contrasts the differences between Lohman's approach and Kuyper's in *Low Countries,* 494-95. Domela Nieuwenhuis wrote a very perceptive appreciation of Kuyper in a letter to him on his 70th birthday, reprinted in P. Kasteel, *Abraham Kuyper* (Kampen, 1938), 143-44. For the other side see Isaac Hooykaas's letter to Kuyper, 31 March 1888, Kuyper Archive, HDC-VU; "I hate politics!" The queen's reaction to Kuyper's endorsement is mentioned in Jan and Annie Romein, *Erflaters van onze beschaving* (Amsterdam, 1971), 805-6. On Kuyper's illness, see Koch, *Kuyper biografie,* 369, 376-77, and Stellingwerff, *Kuyper en de VU,* 200. The purge of Lohman from the Free University is detailed at wrathful length in Stellingwerff, *Kuyper en de VU,* 200-217, and with less acidic a pen in Koch, *Kuyper biografie,* 378-83. "*May* you proceed this way" comes from a letter of Hovy to Kuyper, 6 February 1895, quoted in Koch, *Kuyper biografie,* 380; the exchange concerning brotherly love and friendship is recorded ibid., 384-86, quotation 385. Kuyper's memoir of Keuchenius is

Notes

Mr. Levinus Wilhelmus Christiaan Keuchenius (Haarlem, 1895). Jo's telegram to Kuyper is found in the Kuyper Archive, HDC-VU.

Kuyper's meditation on Willy's death (see Rullmann, *Kuyper-Bibliografie,* III, 60-63), "As a Flower of the Field," was published in *Heraut,* 14 August 1893, and then in *In de Schaduwe des Doods* (Amsterdam, 1893). I have adapted the English translation, *In the Shadow of Death* [Grand Rapids, 1929], #41, 255-68: "*Why* God calls away," 267; "In His doings," 266; "God's work of grace," 265-66. The quotations apropos of Keuchenius come from "He Bindeth Up Their Wounds," #43, 271-72. The roster of Keuchenius's children is available in Rutgers, *Levensbericht.*

Notes on Chapter 12

Kuyper's "Evolution" was delivered as a rectorial address, 20 October 1899: "Our nineteenth century," 405. The 1892 address is "The Blurring of the Boundaries": "the pantheistic mood," 368; "it seems that everything," 387, 389. The mood of the 1890s has been scrutinized by any number of historians. I have been particularly guided by Carl E. Schorske, *Fin-de-Siècle Vienna: Politics and Culture* (New York, 1980), and T. J. Jackson Lears, *No Place of Grace: Antimodernism and the Transformation of American Culture, 1880-1920* (New York, 1981). These build on the classic studies of Gerhard Masur, *Prophets of Yesterday: Studies in European Culture, 1890-1914* (New York, 1961); H. Stuart Hughes, *Consciousness and Society: The Reorientation of European Social Thought, 1890-1930* (New York, 1958); and Henry F. May, *The End of American Innocence* (New York, 1959). More recent analyses include J. W. Burrow, *The Crisis of Reason: European Thought, 1848-1914* (New Haven, 2000), and William Everdell, *The First Moderns: Profiles in the Origins of Twentieth-Century Thought, 1870-1920* (Chicago, 1997). On dis/utopian literature in the United States, see Frederic Cople Jaher, *Doubters and Dissenters: Cataclysmic Thought in America, 1885-1918* (London, 1964).

Kuyper's three concerted treatments of art are *Calvinisme en Kunst;* "Calvinism and Art," in *Lectures on Calvinism* (Grand Rapids, 1931), 142-70; and the second half of *De Gemeene Gratie in Wetenschap en Kunst* [*GGWK*] (Amsterdam, 1905), 43-87 (originally a series in *De Heraut,* 16 June–14 July 1901). The principal secondary treatment is Peter Heslam, *Creating a Christian Worldview* (Grand Rapids, 1998), 196-223. Kuyper alludes to his early course on aesthetics at the Free University in *Calvinisme en Kunst,* 5; and Stellingwerff refers to his course on Impressionism in *Kuyper en de VU,* 253. Kuyper notes the common link of religion to art in *Calvinisme en Kunst,* 28; Calvinism's problematical past on this front, 8-10, 28-29; and its positive contributions, 20-27; "Calvinism outside the circle of Calvinists," *Calvinisme en Kunst,* 27; "objective" standard and "Deviser and Creator," *GGWK,* 72; "penetrates the depth," *Calvinisme en Kunst,* 23; "who can understand human life," *GGWK,* 86. On the Hague School, see John Sillevis and Anne Tabak, *The Hague School Book* (Zwolle, 2004), and G. H. Marius's classic, *Dutch Painters of the 19th Century,* ed. Geraldine Norman (Woodbridge, UK,

1983 [1908]), 121-208; "unvarnished lives," 135-36. Kuyper's correspondence with Israels is found in the Kuyper Archive, HDC-VU. Kuiper links Kuyper's aesthetics to his politics in *Zelfbeeld en Wereldbeeld,* 188-90.

Kuyper defines his positive aesthetic in *Calvinisme en Kunst,* 10-17, and *GGWK,* 52-57, 64-69: "glory," 56, 57; "imagination" and "genius," ibid., 62, 73, 76-77; "higher, nobler, richer," 64; "add something to human life," 69. His critique of other contemporary standards comes at 73-75; "money" or "fame," 73. Regarding the theater, 79; the "raw" and "low," 79-81; "tyranny of popular sovereignty," 74; "priestly service," 76; on his followers changing their theology, 86-87. Kuyper lays out "Our Calvinism thirsts" in *Calvinisme en Kunst,* 40; lauds Genevan psalmody, *GGWK,* 78; and discusses Cats, *Calvinisme en Kunst,* 31-39. On Piet Mondrian's origins and development, see Herbert Henkels, "Piet Mondriaan and the Hague School," in Ronald de Leeuw et al., eds., *The Hague School: Dutch Masters of the Nineteenth Century* (London, 1983), 147-54. On Nietzsche, "Blurring of the Boundaries," 364-68; "Not a single element," 368; "What else is the Evolution-theory," 375; "Nietzsche's appearance," 367; "genetic connection," 372. On lack of "enthusiasm" and the cult of the Superman, compare ibid., 388 and 366.

Classic studies of Victorianism are Walter E. Houghton, *The Victorian Frame of Mind, 1830-1870* (New Haven, 1957); and May, *The End of American Innocence,* 3-117. See also Daniel Walker Howe, ed., *Victorian America* (Philadelphia, 1976), especially 3-44; and Lears, *No Place of Grace,* 4-58. Concise summary statements are Norman F. Cantor, *The American Century: Varieties of Culture in Modern Times* (New York, 1997), 15-27; and Daniel J. Singal, ed., *Modernist Culture in America* (Belmont, Calif., 1991), 4-13. Masur captures the tensions of dynamic order in the first chapter of *Prophets of Yesterday,* "The Stress of Success," 1-37. Howard Mumford Jones explores them in great detail respecting the United States in *The Age of Energy: Varieties of American Experience, 1865-1915* (New York, 1971), 100-178; Houghton parses them for Britain in *Victorian Frame of Mind,* 1-23, 196-217.

On Victorian hierarchical thinking, see Burrow, *Crisis of Reason,* 68-95; Daniel J. Singal, *The War Within: From Victorian to Modernist Thought in the South, 1919-1945* (Chapel Hill, N.C., 1982), 5-7, 26-28, 136; and Cantor, *American Century,* 20-23; on antithetical dichotomies, see Houghton, *Victorian Frame of Mind,* 171-72; "structured competitiveness," Howe, *Victorian America,* 18. Cantor summarizes Victorian historicism in *American Century,* 15-19; "addiction to history," 16. For the original title of the first in Kuyper's *Lectures on Calvinism,* see Heslam, *Creating a Christian Worldview,* 88. On Victorian organicism, see Cantor, *American Century,* 18-19; Everdell, *First Moderns,* 9-11. On idealism, May, *End of American Innocence,* 9-19; Houghton, *Victorian Frame of Mind,* 29-33, 298-304; Cantor, *American Century,* 24-25 ("secularized substitute," 24). For Victorian earnestness, see Houghton, *Victorian Frame of Mind,* 218-62, and Howe, *Victorian America,* 21-25.

The best treatment of the social psychology behind the Modernist turn is Lears, *No Place of Grace,* 7-58 ("weightlessness" and "fragmentation," 32); as registered among some European intellectuals, Schorske, *Fin-de-Siècle Vienna,*

Notes

3-23, 181-278; and Burrow, *Crisis of Reason,* 59-67, 152-56, 160-69. On technology posing the central dilemma of Modernism, see Cantor, *American Century,* 39-40. Like Kuyper, Lears connects Nietzsche and "the blurring of boundaries" in *No Place of Grace,* 41; "evasive banality," 7. Burrow confirms Kuyper's association of Spencer's thought with "pantheism" (*Crisis of Reason,* 46). Kuyper's *Ons Instinctieve Leven* (Amsterdam, 1908) is available in English translation as "Our Instinctive Life" in Bratt, *Kuyper Centennial Reader,* 255-77. He highlighted his travels and mountaineering in a brief handwritten autobiographical sketch left in his papers (E-12, Kuyper Archive, HDC-VU). For further detail see the account written by his daughters, Kuyper and Kuyper, *Levensavond Kuyper,* 15, 28-30.

The role of politics in the birth of Modernist culture is best demonstrated in Schorske, *Fin-de-Siècle Vienna,* 3-23, 279-321; for close analyses of Lueger and Herzl, see 133-75. Cantor sketches his profile of Modernism in *American Century,* 43-51. For American Progressives as proto-Modernists, see James T. Kloppenberg, *Uncertain Victory: Social Democracy and Progressivism in European and American Thought, 1870-1920* (New York, 1986), 340-94; and Douglas Tallack, *Twentieth-Century America: The Intellectual and Cultural Context* (London, 1991), 147-58. Kuyper celebrates the role of instinct in human life in "Our Instinctive Life," 256-61; "perfect knowledge," 258; "the means," 276; "takes up his position" and "true of the *genius,*" 260. On the role of art in the Modernist self-conception and cultural production, see Art Berman, *Preface to Modernism* (Urbana, 1994), viii-x, 5-9, 23-26. Kuyper's own role as an artist is glimpsed in Jan De Bruijn, "Abraham Kuyper as a Romantic," and John Bolt, "Abraham Kuyper as Poet: Another Look at Kuyper's Critique of the Enlightenment," both in Van der Kooi and De Bruijn, *Kuyper Reconsidered,* 30-41 and 42-52, respectively. Bolt gives more extensive treatment to this theme in *A Free Church, A Holy Nation: Abraham Kuyper's American Public Theology* (Grand Rapids, 2001), 44-79.

Details on the *Standaard*'s 25th anniversary fête are given in Roel Kuiper, "Uit het dal omhoog, 1894-1905," in Harinck, *ARP,* 102-4. The event is more skeptically interpreted in Stellingwerff, *Kuyper en de VU,* 218-21. Kuyper's speech is published in the proceedings of the event: *Gedenkboek: opgedragen door het feestcomite aan Prof. Dr. A. Kuyper bij zijn vijf en twintigjarig jubileum als hoofdredacteur van "De Standaard": 1872-1 April-1897* (Amsterdam, 1897), 59-82; quotations 60-61, 67. The versification of Psalm 68 comes from *Psalter Hymnal* (Grand Rapids, 1987), stanzas 1, 3, and 6, corresponding to vv. 1, 7-9, and 20 in the biblical text. Jasper Vree traces the ebb and flow of "Calvinism" as a trope across Kuyper's career and its culmination in the 1890s as a holistic system in "'Het Réveil' en 'het (neo-) Calvinisme' in hun onderlinge samenhang (1856-1896)," in Augustijn and Vree, *Kuyper: vast en veranderlijk,* especially 73-78.

Notes on Chapter 13

The fundamental sources for Kuyper's American trip are the collection by that name in the Kuyper Archive, HDC-VU, and his reflections published first in his newspapers, then in book form as *Varia Americana* [*VA*]. Both but especially the first are well worked in the best secondary account, C. A. Admiraal, "De Amerikaanse reis van Abraham Kuyper" (hereafter "AR") in C. A. Admiraal et al., *Historicus in het spanningsveld van theorie en praktijk* (Leiden, 1985), 111-64. A more extensive analysis along the lines laid out in this chapter is James D. Bratt, "Abraham Kuyper, American History, and the Tensions of Neo-Calvinism," in George Harinck and Hans Krabbendam, eds., *Sharing the Reformed Tradition: The Dutch-North American Exchange, 1846-1996* (Amsterdam, 1996), 97-114. *VA* has been republished in an annotated edition along with correspondence from Kuyper to family members in *Mijn reis was geboden: Abraham Kuyper's Amerikaanse touree,* ed. George Harinck (Hilversum, 2009).

Mark Noll, *The Princeton Theology, 1812-1921: Scripture, Science, and Theological Method from Archibald Alexander to Benjamin Breckinridge Warfield* (Grand Rapids, 2001), and Theodore Dwight Bozeman, *Protestants in an Age of Science: The Baconian Ideal and Antebellum American Religious Thought* (Chapel Hill, N.C., 1977), explain the mentality of the Princeton theology. The quotations from "Calvinism and the Future" are found on 194 and 189-90 in *Lectures on Calvinism.* Kuyper's acceptance speech with its "revenge" statement is in the Kuyper Archive, HDC-VU.

On RCA-CRC history and context at this point, see James D. Bratt, *Dutch Calvinism in Modern America: A History of a Conservative Subculture* (Grand Rapids, 1984), 37-79. Admiraal covers the West Michigan episode in "AR," 121-25. Local press coverage included the Grand Rapids *Democrat,* 27 and 29 October 1898; the Grand Rapids *Herald,* 29 October 1898 ("America is destined"); and the Holland *Daily Sentinel* ("what works . . . of the common people") and Holland *City News,* both 28 October 1898. The Dosker and Steffens correspondence is found in the Kuyper Archive, HDC-VU, and at Heritage Hall, Calvin College, Grand Rapids, Michigan. Quotations respecting Freemasonry come from *VA,* 81-82, 126; see further, 55-122, for his comprehensive report on Dutch America to a Netherlands audience. On the Iowa trip see Admiraal, "AR," 125. Kuyper's positive portrait of American life comes in *VA,* 1-22, 123-30, 136-50; "What conserving social force," 19.

The Chicago leg of Kuyper's tour is covered in Admiraal, "AR," 125-28; "Hambletonian" quotation is from the Chicago *Tribune,* 6 November 1898. The war of words in Grand Rapids can be followed in the *Democrat,* 27 October 1898; the *Herald,* 28 October 1898; and (Kuyper's reply) the *Democrat,* 29 October 1898 and *De Grondwet,* November 1898. The interweavings between religious outlook and political behavior in the United States have been well traced by Robert Kelley, *The Cultural Pattern in American Politics* (New York, 1979); Richard J. Carwardine, *Evangelicals and Politics in Antebellum America* (New Haven, 1993); Daniel Walker Howe, *The Political Culture of the American Whigs* (Chicago, 1979); and Paul Kleppner, *The Third Electoral System, 1853-1892* (Chapel Hill, N.C., 1979). The varying American intersections between Christianity and the Enlightenment are brilliantly analyzed in Henry F. May, *The Enlightenment in America* (New York, 1976). Lodge's *Alexander Hamilton* was published in Boston, 1892. On Bancroft see Robert Canary, *George Bancroft* (New York, 1974).

The best treatment of religion in Hamilton remains Douglass Adair and Marvin Harvey, "Was Alexander Hamilton a Christian Statesman?" *William and Mary Quarterly* 12 (April 1955): 308-29, quotation 314. This is confirmed in broader context by such standard biographies as Broadus Mitchell, *Alexander Hamilton* (New York, 1976), and James T. Flexner, *The Young Hamilton* (Boston, 1978). On the status of Hamilton's reputation at Kuyper's time, see Stephen F. Knott, *Alexander Hamilton and the Persistence of Myth* (Lawrence, Kans., 2002). Dwight's standing both in conservative Federalism and American radicalism is captured in Robert H. Abzug, *Cosmos Crumbling: American Reform and the Religious Imagination* (New York, 1994), 30-45. On Samuel Adams see Pauline Maier, *The Old Revolutionaries: Political Lives in the Age of Samuel Adams* (New York, 1980), 3-50.

Admiraal covers the Cleveland and Rochester visits in "AR," 128-30; Kuyper spoke of the Rochester women in *VA,* 38-43. The doubtful Rochester reporter wrote in the *Post Express,* 19 November 1898; the mistaken Chicagoan in the *Tribune,* 5 November 1898 (both clipped in Kuyper Archive, HDC-VU). Admiraal summarizes Kuyper's Yankee-belt lectures in "AR," 125, 128-30, 141; the New Brunswick and Philadelphia lectures, 138-40. Kuyper published *The Antithesis between Symbolism and Revelation* at Amsterdam, 1899. On Van der Hoogt, see Admiraal, "Amerikaanse reis," 130-31; but also his role in Dutch immigration fiascos in Colorado as recounted in Peter De Klerk, "The Ecclesiastical Struggles of the Rilland and Crook Christian Reformed Churches in Colorado in 1893," in De Klerk and Richard De Ridder, eds., *Perspectives on the Christian Reformed Church* (Grand Rapids, 1983), 73-98.

Kuyper's early rhetoric about McKinley is quoted in Admiraal, "AR," 127, 132; their meeting and its aftermath are described on 132-35; quotation, *VA,* 189. He predicts the consequences of expansion in *VA,* 189, and in the Chicago *Daily Inter Ocean,* 11 November 1898, quoted in Admiraal, "AR," 128. His subsequent presidential endorsements are recorded in Van Koppen, *Kuyper en Zuid-Afrika,* 170-73, 286. For the Maryland tour, see Admiraal, "AR," 132, 135-38; quotation, 138. On Gilman, see George M. Marsden, *The Soul of the American University: From Protestant Establishment to Established Nonbelief* (New York, 1994), 140-59. The ANV meetings are described in Admiraal, "AR," 127-28, 142-43; Kuyper's Collegiate lecture, 142; the return trip, 143.

Letters priming Kuyper regarding American religion came from Henry Dosker, 3 January 1893, 13 March 1896, and 15 April 1898; and from Nicholas Steffens, 7 May 1886, 4 January 1888, 27 October 1888, 12 February 1890, 30 December 1892, and 9 November 1897, all at the Kuyper Archive, HDC-VU. Kuyper's own report to his Dutch audience came in *VA,* 123-67. He treated "The Boss System" in a separate chapter therein, 168-84 (quotation, 173), and covered the press, 23-28. "The Power of the Dollar" titles a separate article, 49-54; the issue of seminary endowments comes up 151-56; "richer class," 153.

Developments in Dutch America from Kuyper's trip to 1918 are covered in

Bratt, *Dutch Calvinism,* 37-92. Quotation from the Hope College *Anchor* comes from an undated 1917 clipping in the Henry Beets Papers, Heritage Hall, Calvin College. Kuyper's North American legacy is detailed in James D. Bratt, "De erfenis van Kuyper in Noord Amerika," in Augustijn, *Kuyper: volksdeel & invloed.* This is also available in English in broader frame as "American Culture and Society: A Century of Dutch-American Assessments," in Rob Kroes and Henk-Otto Neuschäfer, eds., *The Dutch in North America: Their Immigration and Cultural Continuity* (Amsterdam, 1991). The recent Kuyperian impact in American evangelicalism is summarized in Mark A. Noll, *The Scandal of the Evangelical Mind* (Grand Rapids, 1994), 215-39, and James C. Turner, "Something to Be Reckoned With," *Commonweal* 126/1 (15 January 1999): 11ff. Examples of current Kuyperian voices from the Right are Charles Colson and Nancy Pearcey, *How Now Shall We Live?* (Wheaton, Ill., 1999), and Bolt, *Free Church, Holy Nation;* from the Left, Nicholas Wolterstorff, *Until Justice and Peace Embrace* (Grand Rapids, 1983), and Hendrik Hart and Kai Nielsen, *Search for Community in a Withering Tradition: Conversations between a Marxian Atheist and a Calvinian Christian* (Lanham, Md., 1990); in the Center, Richard J. Mouw, *He Shines in All That's Fair: Culture and Common Grace* (Grand Rapids, 2001), and *Abraham Kuyper: A Short and Personal Introduction* (Grand Rapids, 2011); George M. Marsden, *The Outrageous Idea of Christian Scholarship* (New York, 1997); and James W. Skillen, *Recharging the American Experiment: Principled Pluralism for Genuine Civic Community* (Grand Rapids, 1994).

Notes on Chapter 14

Kuyper's warning about American imperialism is from *VA,* 191. A full English translation of *Evolutie* (Amsterdam, 1899) is available in the *Calvin Theological Journal* 31/1 (April 1996): 11-50. It is also reproduced with a few minor excisions in Bratt, *Kuyper Centennial Reader,* 403-40, from which all quotations are taken. Kuyper's statement respecting the American war in the Philippines is on 408; his praise of Zola is cited from *De Standaard,* 28 February 1898, in Van Koppen, *Kuyper en Zuid-Afrika,* 284.

The faux death of Sherlock Holmes occurred in "The Final Problem" (set in 1891 and first published in 1893, collected in *The Memoirs of Sherlock Holmes,* 1894); his return is recounted in "The Adventure of the Empty House," collected in *The Return of Sherlock Holmes* (1905). For his defense of the occult, see Arthur Conan Doyle, *The History of Spiritualism,* 2 vols. (New York, 1926). On Johanna Kuyper-Schaay's death, see Koch, *Kuyper biografie,* 435-37, and Stellingwerff, *Kuyper en de VU,* 279. Materials apropos of her funeral are in the Kuyper Archive, HDC-VU. Kuyper's *Heraut* meditation appeared on 3 September 1899 and is included in *In Jezus Ontslapen: Meditatiën* (Amsterdam, 1902; English translation, *Asleep in Jesus: Meditations* [Grand Rapids, 1929]). A fresh translation is included in Bratt, *Kuyper Centennial Reader,* 408-15: "There you stood," 409; "the Word of God . . . swallowed up by life," 411. Kuyper's Pauline quotation comes from 2 Corinthians 5:4. Quotations from *Asleep in Jesus* are on 48; Kuyper's three images of eternity are laid out in meditations #7, 24, and 37, and his call to witness in #52; "mysterious wave of the demoniac," 331; "hypnosis of the dogma of Evolution," is from "Evolution," 405.

The history of evolutionary thinking in its various schools at the time is well analyzed in Peter J. Bowler's series of books: *Evolution: The History of an Idea*, rev. ed. (Berkeley and Los Angeles, 1989); *The Eclipse of Darwinism: Anti-Darwinian Evolution Theories in the Decades around 1900* (Baltimore, 1983); and *The Non-Darwinian Revolution: Reinterpreting a Historical Myth* (Baltimore, 1988). Some important Anglo-American Protestant contributions are studied in David N. Livingstone, *Darwin's Forgotten Defenders: The Encounter between Evangelical Theology and Evolutionary Thought* (Grand Rapids, 1987). Kuyper's statements about "spontaneous unfolding" and "the Chief Architect" are in "Evolution," 436; regarding Christianity's consonances with evolution, 438; regarding scientific method, 416 and 422. Bowler's assessment of Darwinism's unpopularity is in *Evolution,* 246; his characterization of Weismann, 248. Hodge's statement concluded his *What Is Darwinism?* (New York, 1874); on which, see further Livingstone, *Darwin's Forgotten Defenders,* 101-5. Bowler's books above treat Haeckel and Spencer in comparative context, as does Mike Hawkins, *Social Darwinism in European and American Thought, 1860-1945* (Cambridge, 1997), 82-103 and 132-45. Alfred Kelly, *The Descent of Darwin: The Popularization of Darwinism in Germany, 1860-1914* (Chapel Hill, N.C., 1981), covers Haeckel in greatest detail; his purposes and popularity are elaborated on 22-28, 91-94, and 136-41. Kuyper's statements about Haeckel ("gaseous vertebrate . . . newly defined condition") are in "Evolution," 435-36; "Evolution is a newly conceived system," 439; "insolent and condescending . . . consequences from their principle," 435; "consumed with passion," 418; "dogma of evolution . . . system *as system,*" 439; on Modernism and Pantheism, 413-16 ("idea of a guiding purpose," 416); "the emergence of a new faith . . . Decadence," 407; "the only road . . . usurpation of power," 410; "we owe *not,*" 435; "the Christ of God," 439. With respect to ethics and evolution for Nietzsche and Huxley, see Bowler, *Non-Darwinian Revolution,* 162, 186; for Spencer, Hawkins, *Social Darwinism,* 204. Kuyper's concern over "the precipitate of the spirit . . . under the higher" comes in "Evolution," 431.

For the history of South Africa I have relied on Leonard Thompson's title by that name (rev. ed., New Haven, 1995), and Frank Welsh, *South Africa: A Narrative History* (New York, 1999). Peter Warwick, ed., *The South African War: The Anglo-Boer War, 1899-1902* (Harlow, Essex, 1980), features essays on all aspects of that conflict; see also Bill Nasson, *The South African War, 1899-1902* (London, 1999). The contemporary description of Johannesburg as "Monte Carlo" is quoted in Tabitha Jackson, *The Boer War* (London, 1999), 14. Van Koppen, *Kuyper en Zuid-Afrika,* traces Kuyper's works and words on the episode in great detail; the "virus" quotation is on 134, the context and assessment of Kuyper's essay, 179.

Kuyper's essay is available in a shortened version as "The South African Crisis," in Bratt, *Kuyper Centennial Reader,* 323-60. For his critique of British military and missionary imperialism, 336-39; "the Boers know too well," 339.

For the national characters of Briton and Boer, see 327-32; "tenacity of the race," 327; "absolute incompatibility," 328; "natural sagacity . . . love of liberty," 331; "Boer women . . . of their husbands," 332. On African and Boer fecundity, see 339-40 ("The blacks are increasing," 339) and 359 ("will never destroy"); on Blacks' putative race revenge and Chamberlain's folly, 340 ("confidential conversations . . . Jingo journalists"); on "incest" with "an inferior race," 339; on Kuyper's race hierarchy and the heliotropic myth, *Lectures on Calvinism,* 32-35. The assessment of Kuyper's "selection-election" hybrid is by Dirk Th. Kuiper, "Theory and Practice in Dutch Calvinism on the Racial Issue in the Nineteenth Century," *Calvin Theological Journal* 21/1 (April 1986): 73. Kuyper's analogy of Boers with Normans as "a conquering race" is in "South African Crisis," 330; "splendid promise . . . war of aggression," 325.

Thompson discusses the aftermath of the war in *History of South Africa,* 143-53, and important ingredients of the new regime in *The Political Mythology of Apartheid* (New Haven, 1985). Kuyper's skepticism toward Afrikaner nationalism and the new regime is detailed in Van Koppen, *Kuyper en Zuid-Afrika,* 135-37 and 201-8. The role of Calvinism in general and Kuyperian neo-Calvinism in particular in the emergence of the apartheid system has been subject to spirited discussion. T. Dunbar Moodie, *The Rise of Afrikanerdom* (Berkeley, 1975), asserts a strong intellectual if not numerical presence, but also the Utrecht influence. André du Toit, "No Chosen People: The Myth of the Calvinist Origins of Afrikaner Nationalism and Racial Ideology," *American Historical Review* 88/4 (October 1983): 920-52; and "Puritans in Africa? The Paradigm Examined," *Comparative Studies in Society and History* 27/2 (1985): 209-40, contends that his subjects were not too Calvinistic but not Calvinistic enough. P. J. Strauss, "Abraham Kuyper, Apartheid and Reformed Churches in South Africa in Their Support of Apartheid," *Reformed Ecumenical Council Theological Forum* 23/1 (March 1995): 4-27, provides the closest theological-ecclesiastical analysis. My assessments are guided particularly by the materials on 17-23; Kuiper, "Theory and Practice of Dutch Calvinism," 76-78; and H. Russel Botman, "Is Blood Thicker Than Justice? The Legacy of Abraham Kuyper for South Africa," in Lugo, *Religion, Pluralism, and Public Life,* 342-61.

Notes on Chapter 15

The essential book on this topic is Kuiper and Schutte, *Kabinet Kuyper.* See also Koch, *Kuyper biografie,* 439-90. Kossmann, *Low Countries,* provides accessible background information and analysis, 398-438, 473-80, 488-502, 508-16. Kuyper's keynote address to the 1901 ARP Delegates' Convention was "Volharden bij het Ideal" (Amsterdam, 1901); "the Christian part of the nation," 5; "the very same Calvinistic principles," 9; "on that decisive day," 12; "not as a closed-off group," 9.

Details of the Dutch recovery are available in Kossmann, *Low Countries,* 413-18; Th. van Tijn, "Het algemeen karakter van het tijdvak, 1895-1914," in

AGN 1978, 13: 306-13; and Wintle, *ESHN,* passim. On the lingering hunger and epidemics in the early 1890s see P. Hoekstra, "De laatste tien liberale jaren in het Noorden," *AGN 1956,* 63. Wintle, *ESHN,* supplies data on wages, 232; food prices, 56; birth and death rates, 226-27; alcohol consumption, 63; and savings banks, 208. For rates of and average age at marriage, see Van Tijn, "Het algemeen karakter," 309-10. Rates of and yield from educational spending are given in Wintle, *ESHN,* 268. Kossmann, *Low Countries,* describes the dimensions of Dutch industrialization, international commerce, and colonial trade, 414-18; "radical structural transformation," 416. On the icons of the new order, see Hoekstra, "De laatste tien liberale jaren," 60-62. The international character of "progressivism" in this era is well depicted by Thomas Bender, *A Nation Among Nations: America's Place in World History* (New York, 2006), 246-95; on the key role played by "new" economists in the movement, 263-67, and in the Dutch Liberal party, J. T. Minderaa, "De politieke partijen," *AGN 1978,* 13: 448.

The character and initiatives of the three Liberal cabinets of 1891-1901 are covered in Kossmann, *Low Countries,* 357-61; Hoekstra, "De laatste tien liberale jaren," 66-82; and Minderaa, "De politieke partijen," 441-48. Kuyper's characterization of the franchise compromise of 1896 is quoted in Hoekstra, "De laatste tien liberale jaren," 76, which also gives the working class percentage of the expanded electorate. Kuyper's role in the debate over the Industrial Accidents bill of 1901 is covered in close detail in J. Mannoury, "Enkele legislatieve aspecten van het groot-amendement-Kuyper op de Ongevallenwet 1901," in P. A. J. M. Steenkamp and G. M. J. Veldkamp, eds., *Sociale Politiek, Opnieuw Bedacht* (Deventer, 1972), 108-25. "Began to prepare," Wintle, *ESHN,* 277.

The formation of Kuyper's cabinet is covered in greatest detail by Jan De Bruijn, *'Kuyper ist ein Luegner': De kabinetsformatie van 1901* (Amsterdam, 2001), an expansion of his essay in Kuiper and Schutte, *Kabinet Kuyper.* Koch gives a briefer treatment in *Kuyper biografie,* 448-58. On Kuyper's retreat to Brussels, De Bruijn, *Kuyper Luegner,* 36-39; on the queen's attitude toward and meeting with him, ibid., 21-30, 40-42; Koch, *Kuyper biografie,* 448-50. On Kuyper's negotiations with Mackay, Lohman, and Heemskerk, see De Bruijn, *Kuyper Luegner,* 31-32, 43-44, 50-52, 68-74; "There is no one else" and "It will be your responsibility," quoted ibid., 70; "Kuyper is a liar," 71. Kuyper's becoming permanent chair of the cabinet is discussed in Alis Koekkoek, "Leider in eminenten zin," in Kuiper and Schutte, *Kabinet Kuyper,* 101-2, 112-13. The three Roman Catholic ministers are profiled in Gerhard Beekelaar, "De Katholieke minister in het cabinet," ibid., 115-38; "lethargic" and "pedantic," quoted 133. On Melvil van Lynden, see Roel Kuiper, "De valse grondtoon," ibid., 147-49, 152-55; on Van Asch van Wijck and Idenburg, see Janny de Jong, "Ethiek, voogdij, en militaire acties," ibid., 162-70. De Bruijn also discusses Melvil van Lynden and Van Asch van Wijck in *Kuyper Luegner,* 58-63, 91-92.

Kuyper's initiative respecting the South African War is detailed in Kuiper, "De valse grondtoon," 139-47; a representative speech is in Kuyper, *Parlementaire Redevoeringen,* vol. 2 (hereafter *PR2*), 57-60. On Beaufort, see Koch, *Kuyper biografie,* 172-74, 447-49, 475-76. Kuyper's agenda regarding the social question, and the obstacles it encountered, are laid out in Loes van der Valk, "De overheid helpe den arbeid aan recht," in Kuiper and Schutte, *Kabinet Kuyper,* 208-12, 219-29. His theoretical discussions about religion and politics can be read in *PR2,* 46-51, 61-79, 210-20. On religion and politics vis à vis church and state, ibid., 46-51, 62-63; "first *religion,* and second *negotiation,*" 51; "homogeneity in politics," 214; "we all speak high Dutch," 61; the fundamental difference between the secular and religious parties, 61-63; "Christianity *beneath* differences," 77; "*first* and *great* commandment," 79; on being radical, 74; on varieties of Democrats, 76; on Bernstein and Marx, 74-75; "worldview" and "spiritual" forces," 90; regarding Gladstone, 63.

The Kuyper cabinet's colonial policy is examined in detail in De Jong, "Ethiek, voogdij," 157-83; for broader context see Kossmann, *Low Countries,* 398-412; *De Gids* article cited 403. On final "pacification," De Jong, "Ethiek, voogdij," 170-72; "our small band," quoted 172. On Idenburg, Kossmann, *Low Countries,* 405-6, 409; De Jong, "Ethiek, voogdij," 162-70; for his economic policy, 167-69; religion and cultural policy, 164-65; good government emphasis, 173; study of Indonesian lower classes, 169; of coolie labor, 170-71; decentralization, 174-77.

The definitive study of the railroad strike is A. J. C. Rüter, *De Spoorwegstakingen van 1903* (Leiden, 1935). Kossmann, *Low Countries,* 497-98, gives an accessible summary in English; Koch, *Kuyper biografie,* 468-74, examines Kuyper's role closely, as does Van der Valk more summarily in "De overheid helpe," 216-18. On the socialists' divide, see Minderaa, "De politieke partijen," 456-61; on Troelstra's role, ibid., 456, 459-61, and Van der Valk, "De overheid helpe," 218 ("de-escalate"). Kuyper's contribution to the debates in Parliament is recorded in *PR2,* 334-77 (sessions of 25 February–4 April 1903); 404-26 (30 June–1 July 1903); and 441-51 (22 September 1903). Kuyper defends using the designation "criminal," 335, 373-76, and 441-51, and rejects the "class war" characterization, 411. For "seizure" and "ship of state," 335; "to overthrow authority," 376; on the moral bond of society and "for everyone," 372. He references the "great disasters" at Chicago and Pittsburgh at 341 and 543-44; for strikes nearer by, 344. On his support for the right to strike, ibid., 354-55, and Van der Valk, "De overheid helpe," 216. Kuyper and Loeff's differences from Lohman's hard line are summarized ibid., 217-18, and explored in more detail in Koch, *Kuyper biografie,* 469-70; see also Minderaa, "De politieke partijen," 453. On Kuyper's particularly intense debate with Troelstra and other socialists and its long-term effect on his reputation, see Koch, *Kuyper biografie,* 470-74. The exchange following Troelstra's invocation of "objective history" is recorded in *PR2,* 409-10 (session of 30 June 1903).

On Kuyper's appointments policy see Ineke Secker, "Op de voordracht van onzen Minister van Binnenlanden Zaken," in Kuiper and Schutte, *Kabinet Kuyper,* 236-69; and Koch, *Kuyper biografie,* 474-77. Statistics from Kuiper and Schutte, "Het ministerie eener nieuwe toekomst?," in *Kabinet Kuyper,* 310-11. Beaufort's class disdain is recorded in Koch, *Kuyper biografie,* 447-48, 475-76. The content and controversy over Kuyper's education initiatives are covered in ibid., 477-80, and Pieter Boekholt, "Voor de vrijmaking van het onderwijs," in Kuiper and Schutte, *Kabinet Kuyper,* 184-207. Data on the funding of and reforms in lower education are given ibid., 192, 194; on the "Integration Commission," 196-98; on technical and occupation education, 198-204. Kuyper's own addresses on this matter are recorded in *Parlementaire Redevoeringen,* vol. 3 (hereafter *PR3*), 88-115. See Kuiper and Schutte, "Het ministerie eener nieuwe toekomst?," 308, regarding the national significance of this legislation and its appeal to Kuyper's own constituency. Kuyper's oration introducing his Higher Education bill is recorded in *PR3,* 1-53; "Christian life-conviction," 53. He discussed the role of worldview in the architecture of knowledge in the session of 3 March 1904, 53-83. On Kant, 58, 64-65, 69-70; the hegemony of evolutionary biology, 58-59; on purging students and "free choice," 71-72; on De Vries and Haeckel, 65-66; "drill school" and "dressed-up parrots," 75; on the repetition of arguments, 83. Boekholt, "Voor de vrijmaking," notes the Social Democrats' support of education equity, 193.

Nabij God te zijn (Kampen, 1908) was published in two volumes; the English translation *To Be Near Unto God* (New York, 1925), by John Hendrik de Vries, combined these into one. Citations below are from the paperback reprint (Grand Rapids, 1979). The bulk of the original Volume I (#5-56) appeared in *De Heraut* 19 October 1902–13 December 1903, followed by #59-63 (20 December 1903–24 January 1904) near the start of Volume II. Almost all the rest of Volume II ran originally in *De Heraut* from September 1905 through July 1906, that is, after Kuyper's defeat for re-election, and so will be treated in the next chapter. The Foreword of *Drie Kleine Vossen* (Kampen, 1901) is dated 27 June 1901.

On the "spiritual's" superiority over and necessary segmentation from the "material," see *Near Unto God,* meditations #4, 12, 20, and 26; "All religion is *personal* to the core," 140; "the powers of the kingdom," 142; *"a hidden walk with God,"* 140. On the great gap between things human and divine, see #4, 19, 24, 49, and 60. Kuyper's meditation on the Trinitarian Name is #47; on the norm of the solitary soul, #11, 45, and 54; against the substitution of ethics for religion, #13, 37; on the lassitude of the righteous, #27; on the knowledge of God from the depths of sin, #50; on Paul's enthusiasm, 309; "tender faithfulness," 306. Kuyper treats divine images in the sun in #14; wings, #15; wind and temple, #16. His typology of responses to the promptings of conscience appears in #51; to unanswered prayer, #9 ("altogether different," 68); and his reflections on Jesus' interpretation of Deuteronomy 6:5 run from #38-41.

John Dewey set out the basics of his learning theory in "My Pedagogic Creed" (1897), *The School and Society* (1900), and *The Child and Curriculum* (1902). "He that loveth not knoweth not God" is the title of *Near Unto God* meditation #42; "the world-riddle" and "that deepest love," 258; "thereby alone," 261. Kuyper's injunctions that this "must be an honest forgiveness" and is "almost incomprehensible" come from #30 (14 June 1903), quotation 189. His reflections on the contemporary cult of the will and the proper Christian parallel thereunto come in #29 and 30; on the need to develop beyond the Reformed fathers on this issue, in #31; "the urgency of the soul itself," 197. Kuyper's meditation for 28 June 1903 was #32, "Who Worketh in You to Will:" "that living soul-knowledge," 199; "tide and wind," "the helmsman," and "such is the man of character," 201; "this continuous process," 204. His meditation on Romans 7:15 is #33, "What I Would That Do I Not:" "there is something bold," 208. "Not as I Will" is #34: "the center of things" and "our honor," 214; "you become suddenly aware," "God's reality, His Majesty," and "abandons the theory," 215-16; "His counsel and plan," "verify," "entering into the life," and "our honor and the self-exaltation," 216.

Notes on Chapter 16

The most thorough analysis of the 1905 election is George Harinck, "Als een schelm weggejaagd?," in Kuiper and Schutte, *Kabinet Kuyper,* 270-301. See also Harinck, "De Antirevolutionaire Partij 1905-1918," in Harinck, *ARP,* 123-29. Koch covers the election in *Kuyper biografie,* 480-90. The most thorough study of the varied career of the concept of antithesis in Kuyperian circles is by C. Augustijn, "Kuyper en de antithese," in Augustijn and Vree, *Kuyper: vast en veranderlijk:* "Christianity *beneath* theological differences," quoted 168; "preserve the place of Christian values among the people," quoted 169. Kuyper hypothesized the "one great contrast . . . between the *Christian* and the *modern* life-conception" as an "enormous antithesis" in *Parlementaire Redevoeringen,* vol. 4 (hereafter *PR4*), 50, 53.

On the campaign strategies of both sides, see Harinck, "Als een schelm," 275-80; on internal divisions within Kuyper's coalition, 282-87; on his opposition's earlier use of antithetical idioms, 292; "Throw him out!", quoted by Koch, *Kuyper biografie,* 480. On Kuyper's linkage of liberalism to socialism, see *PR4,* 51, and Augustijn, "Kuyper en de antithese," 178, also quoting Troelstra, "Minister Kuyper is our grandpa." See also Kuyper's earlier discourse in Parliament, *PR2,* 553-58; "Formally . . . correct," 553; "I have always recognized," 554-55; "As Bernstein has said," 556. Regarding "pagan" and "paganistic," see Augustijn, "Kuyper en de antithese," 178-81, and Kuyper, *PR4,* 79-80; on Bavinck as party chair, Harinck, "Als een schelm," 271-73, 280. Harinck, "Als een schelm," analyzes the election polling data, 293-95; the increase in the electorate is cited in Koch, *Kuyper biografie,* 480. On the queen's anti-Kuyper tilt and his early departure, ibid., 480, 486.

The only meditations included in *Near Unto God* that originally appeared in *De Heraut* between February 1904 and January 1905 are #64-68, the middle three of which came from Kuyper's series on Old Testament history. Three entries originally from February 1905 are included (#69-70 and 73), four from April–May 1905 (#74-77), and four from election-season issues, 4 June–2 July 1905 (#71-72, 78-79). The regular series resumed on 24 September 1905 with what became #1 in the combined volume, then followed rather consistently from #80 on with the exception of the originals from 8 and 15 October 1905, which became #57-58. "It is faith," "badges and rules," and "the ground thesis" all come from #72 (4 June 1905), 439-40; "O God, My God!" and "not a general fulfillment" are from #79 (2 July 1905), 481ff., 486. The three apocalyptic texts are 1 Corinthians 15:24 [13 August], Matthew 13:49 [20 August], and 2 Thessalonians 2:8 [3 September], respectively. The meditation "from rock bottom" is #58 (15 October 1905), quotations 359-60.

Kuyper's "twin passions" being "traveling and writing" is the observation of Koch, *Kuyper biografie,* 523. The two volumes of *Om de Oude Wereldzee* have Forewords dated 15 September 1907 and 28 October 1908, respectively. Kuyper's essays on each land or people can be readily followed from their tables of contents. Volume I begins with "The Asiatic Danger," then proceeds from Romania through "The Holy Land," treating "The Gypsies" and "The Jewish Problem" along the way. Volume II begins with "The Enigma of Islam" and then runs the sequence from Egypt through Portugal. Kuyper's travel schedule can be deciphered from various references throughout but is conveniently summarized in Koch, *Kuyper biografie,* 493-96. Regarding the Sea of Galilee and the reflections it prompted, I: 433-41; Jerusalem, I: 505-31; Bethlehem, I: 531-39. On his side trip back to The Hague, see Koch, *Kuyper biografie,* 496; on the Berbers, II: 341-50; on the near-loss of his documentation, see Rullmann, *Kuyper-Bibliografie,* III: 322. For the "courtesies" he received en route, see *OWZ,* I: 56, 65-66, 371-72, 401-3, II: 438-40. His impressions of the Young Turks come at I: 368 and II: vi-viii; of the 1905 revolution in Russia, I: 109-11 ("socialist patrols," 111), 128-30, 145-47. Details on pogroms in and around Odessa are given in Niall Ferguson, *The War of the World: Twentieth-Century Conflict and the Descent of the West* (New York, 2006), 67-68.

Kuyper's chapter on "The Asiatic Danger" in *OWZ* begins with the reverberations of Japan's victory over Russia (I: 2-6), which he also ponders at I: 10 and 37-40; "Asia for the Asians" recurs several times after I: 5. On the measures and consequences of European imperialism, see I: 6-7, 11-12, 34-35, 40-41, II: 420-22. On Britain's maneuvers in the Sudan, including the Mahdist movement and Omdurman, II: 147-65 ("technology," 164). On Britain's encouragement of Wahabism (and similarly of Muslim-Hindu rivalry in India), I: 34-35. On French imperialism in North Africa, II: 337-41, 350-57, 381.

Kuyper's use of racial categories is pervasive. His balanced esteem for the Slavic, Roman, and Germanic blocs in Europe is manifest in *Pro Rege, of het Koningschap van Christus,* II: 197-99, and III: 336-38. This was the book version of a theological series he published in *De Heraut* 1907-1910; the passages cited would have first appeared in late 1908 and mid-1910, respectively. Quotations regarding Romania, *OWZ,* I: 52-53, 73; his preference for Arabs over Turks, I: 28-29, II: 25, II: 461-62; of Berbers over Arabs, II: 343-50, II: 405. Religion "is and shall remain," I: 318; on Orthodoxy and the Slavic soul, I: 115, 125-28, 143-45; respecting the Greeks, II: 187-88; on Europe as the synthesis of Aryan and Semitic, II: 504-7; against Gobineau, I: 46-54, 116-17. On Romania as a successful "smaller nation," I: 43, 99. Kuyper uses "sphere sovereignty" in the Ottoman context explicitly at I: 328, but describes it in practice also at I: 247 and 316-17 with respect to Jewish communal autonomy, at I: 404-10 respecting present-day

Lebanon, and at I: 541 respecting Jerusalem. On Fez, II: 386-95; "exceptionally beautiful," 387; "guild system," 392; on the Berbers, II: 343-50, 399-401, 405-8. His chapter on the Romani comes at I: 164-238; "parasites," 235; their bohemian-anarchist legacy, 217-220; "social plague," 218.

Kuyper's early writing on Dutch Jewry ran in *De Standaard* and was published as a brochure, *Liberalisten en Joden* (Amsterdam, 1878). Ivo Schöffer discusses this tract in "Abraham Kuyper and the Jews," J. Michman and T. Levie, eds., *Dutch Jewish History I* (Jerusalem, 1984), 237-60; Jacob van Nes considers it comparatively with other statements, including the essay in *OWZ*, in "Iets over Dr. Kuyper en de Joden," *De Macedoniër Zendings Tijdschrift* 42 (1938): 109-16, 131-48. Regarding Stoecker, Schöffer, "Kuyper and the Jews," 251; regarding Lueger, Kuyper, *OWZ*, I: 269. Kuyper rejects the blood libel and particular Jewish guilt for Jesus' death at I: 284-85; "As someone who confesses," I: 318-19. On Jewish fortunes in Romania, I: 300-308; in the Russian Empire, I: 308-16; under the Ottomans, I: 316-17; on Jewish poverty, I: 311; proclivity toward trade and intellectual professions, I: 286-89, 294-97; "inseparably," I: 262; "physically weaker," I: 290. "For Europe," I: 317; on the dilemmas respecting Jewish options, I: 320-24; on Christian opposition to anti-Semitism, I: 323-24.

Kuyper treats Islam systematically in "The Enigma of Islam," II: 1-51, but also at I: 16-42 and 334-62. As a mirror of ideal Calvinism, see I: 29-31, II: 3-7, 23; on architecture, I: 348-50, 424-26, 511-12, and especially II: 456-70. On Al-Azhar, II: 24-28; on pan-Islamic consciousness, I: 40-41, II: 42-43, 129; "fanaticism," I: 335. His critique of Muslim theology is summarized at II: 7-11; "legalistic" and "spiritual depth," 8; "old man with the new," 9. See also I: 334-35. On the affection Islam won from liberal Protestants, I: 25; on Sufism, Shi'a, and the Dervishes as deviations, II: 10-11, 33-34; on Sufism as "pantheistic," II: 10; Shi'a as a "sect," II: 33-34; the Dervishes' rituals, I: 355-56; "fleshly" indulgence, II: 11. Kuyper's condemnation of Islam's treatment of women is recurrent; see, e.g., I: 356-62; "unrighteousness that breeds," 359. On moral corruption in Cairo, II: 68; on prostitution in Tunis, II: 283-84; in Algiers, II: 327-31; "refined sensuality" and "desecration of marriage," II: 330. On women's status as the measure of Christian superiority, I: 26-27.

Kuyper's apprehension of Asia rising at the expense of the West was shared by many European leaders at the time. For confirmation of the Japanese victory's inspiration of anti-colonialism across Asia, see Sukru Hanioglu, *Preparation for a Revolution: The Young Turks 1902-1908* (Oxford, 2001), which confirms as well Kuyper's concerns (I: 37-40) about a possible Japanese-Islamic alliance, including his seemingly outré warning that some Muslims were proposing to offer the caliphate to the Japanese emperor. Journalist Abdullah Cevdet ventured precisely that in the Cairo paper *Ictihad;* my thanks to Douglas Howard for this reference. Kuyper designates "The Asiatic Danger" as the "political world-problem" at I: 3; "our archipelago" occurs numerous times, e.g., I: 41-42. On the importance of the religious factor, I: 10-28. Kuyper articulates the monotheist-polytheist opposition there, at I: 39-41, and in many allusions elsewhere. "What will prove," I: 18; on Germany's "eastern policy," I: 18, 375; on Aga Khan, I: 35-

36; "when Islam will be worth gold" and "if our conscience," I: 23; the "notion that we have everything to bring," I: 31. His most concise statement of the Aryan-Semitic dialectic in world history is II: 504-9; "enduring struggle" and "eight centuries," 506; "intellect and command . . . from its shoulders," 507; "push a Germanic Jesus," 509.

Kuyper's series on the kingship of Christ was published in book form as the three volumes of *Pro Rege*. C. Augustijn made the "losing his grip" observation in "Kuypers theologie van de samenleving," in Augustijn, *Kuyper: volksdeel & invloed*, 52 n. 114. Kuyper's description of the modern world order runs in *Pro Rege*, I: 30-112. On technology, 39-48; the diffusion of the self, 59-70; the intensity of modern life, 48-58; on Schleiermacher, 42; "the forecourt . . . [of] the temple," 43; "The spirit of a person," 63; "Religion demands above all . . . overburdened for it," 69; "intense over-stimulation of the nervous life" and "the forecourt of hell," 55; "the mighty stream of modern life," 58.

Kuyper analyzed the phenomenon of "world metropolises" in *Pro Rege* I: 71-81, citing particular cities and their signal qualities, 75; "far and away," 82; "spirit of the world," 81. He elaborates on Mammon and Art, I: 92-112; on Art's capture by Mammon, 106-7; "magical and enchanting," 98; "aristocracy . . . set the tone," 104-5. His analysis of spiritual warfare unfolds in I: 195-226; his discussion of miracles and their fulfillment in European science and technology runs I: 123-84, 226-47, 436-47, 468-78. His observations about the "line of Cain" occur in I: 184-95; "The Wisdom of the World" is the chapter title of I: 226-37. Personal evangelism as antidote to Mammon comes at I: 102; the sensual being the icon of the Art-Mammon connection runs through I: 105-12; "as a spiritual power . . . once for all broken," I: 478.

Kuyper reiterates the need for a new consciousness in the church in *Pro Rege* I: v-viii, 21-30, 203-5, 287-97, 339-49, 360-70; on Muslim prayers and resolute theism, I: 1-8. His biblical-theological treatment runs I: 277-559; his treatment of the personal sphere, *Pro Rege*, II: 1-118; of the church, II: 119-346; of the family, II: 347-541. On male headship under Christ, II: 379-401; on sacraments as markers and council members as wardens, II: 202-13, 256-77; on the international character of the church and opposition to national-church notions, II: 191-203, 245-61; "fiction," 203; "entirely inconceivable," 255. On child rearing, II: 509-30; on Christ as the heart of the church, II: 180-91; "set off in heaven," II: 189. He treats the kingship of Christ over art in *Pro Rege*, III: 470-580. On classical form, III: 505-12; "fixed ordinance and law," 507; on the Transfiguration, 512-22, 546-53, and *OWZ*, I: 461-71; on the Acropolis, *OWZ*, II: 220-24; on the Christian artist's calling, *Pro Rege*, III: 542-43; on the Sublime, 558-68. Kuyper's discussion of Christ's kingship and science runs III: 354-469, with his new emphasis evident on 449-69; "the everyday . . . richest, greatest, and most interesting," 463; "lies not alone," 464.

Kuyper treats society and state in *Pro Rege* III: 1-226 and 227-353, respectively. He summarizes the growth of society's power, 1-11, 45-64, and elaborates his higher regard for the state, 239-49. On voluntary organization, 85-95 and 184-94; on public opinion, 194-205; on the urgency of Christian labors in these domains, 1-11, 94, 144, 201-4, 218-26; on antithesis and separate organization, 184-225; "People have called," 202; "in every area of life," 192.

Notes on Chapter 17

This phase of Kuyper's life is treated with somewhat different emphasis than mine in Koch, *Kuyper biografie*, 525-71. For the national scene, see Kossmann, *Low Countries*, 493-516, 545-60, and Henk Te Velde, "Van Grondwet tot Grondwet," in Remieg Aerts et al., *Land van kleine gebaren: een politieke geschiedenis van Nederland, 1780-1990* (Nijmegen, 1999), 161-75. Kuyper's Concertgebouw oration was published as *Bilderdijk in zijne nationale beteekenis* (Amsterdam, 1906). Hahn's cartoon is reproduced in *Kuyper in caricatuur*, Nieuwe herziene uitgave (Baarn, 1920), 49. Kuyper cites the matador image in *Bilderdijk*, 5; treats his nature as a genius, 8-12; his putative Christian-idealist aesthetic, 12, 31; his opposition to the Enlightenment, 13-15, 17 ("cobwebs," 15); his organic thinking, 14, 17, 34-35, 40, 45; his epistemology, 15-16 ("worldview," 16), 28, 42; his militancy, 19-20; its consequent miseries and effects on his demeanor, 20-23 (similarity to Burke, 23, 67-68); his revitalization of the national tongue and soul, 24-25, 31-34, 44-46 ("called our nation back," 46); and his relevance for a future "day of wrath," 46.

Developments in the ARP are thoroughly treated in George Harinck, "De Antirevolutionaire Partij, 1905-1918," in Harinck, *ARP*, 123-55. See also Koch, *Kuyper biografie*, 535-49 (Kuyper's decline of a parliamentary seat in 1905, 526), and Kuiper, *De Voormannen*, 245-50. The Heemskerk government is treated in great detail in Dirk Th. Kuiper and Gerrit J. Schutte, eds., *Het kabinet-Heemskerk (1908-1913)* (Zoetermeer, 2010). Kuyper's disquiet with the Heemskerk cabinet first became public in *Afgeperst* (Kampen, 1912), a brochure criticizing colonial policy, and comprehensively in *Starrentritsen* (Kampen, 1915), 47-90, summarized, 85-90. Heemskerk's retort was *Een word over de genummerde driestarren van Dr. Kuyper* (Rotterdam, 1915); the response of the Five Gentlemen was A. Anema et al., *Leider en Leiding in de Anti-Revolutionaire Partij* (Amsterdam, 1915). On cabinet formation, Koch, *Kuyper biografie*, 525-27; Kuyper, *Starrentritsen*, 47-55; "there's something personally difficult," Kuyper letter to A. W. F. Idenburg, 22 March 1908, in *BKI*, 164. For Kuyper's complaints about Heemskerk's bypassing him and the Central Committee, *Starrentritsen*, 81-83; regarding constitutional revision, 62-65; excessive compromise with the Liberals, 59-61, 65-66; and personal disrespect, Kuyper letter to Idenburg, *BKI*, 451-52. The nature and fate of Talma's proposed social legislation are summarized in Kossmann, *Low Countries*, 499-500, and Th. Van Tijn, "De algemeen karakter van het tijdvaak 1895-1914," in *AGN 1978*, 13: 312. Kuyper's assessment thereof appears in *Starrentritsen*, 58-59, and in letters to Idenburg in *BKI*, 236-37, 392-93. For Idenburg's cautions to Kuyper about the educational situation in the East Indies, ibid., 260-61; for his assessment of Heemskerk's weaknesses (and strengths) as a leader, see his letter to Kuyper in ibid., 428-30; "happy Christianity" quoted in Koch, *Kuyper biografie,* 538. Kuyper wrote a post-mortem on the 1913 elections in letters to Idenburg, *BKI,* 379-81, 391-94.

Kuyper's 1909 keynote address was *Wij Calvinisten* (Kampen, 1909); "a battle of principles . . . *will of God,"* 16; "Antithesis is the cement of the Coalition," 18; on the antithesis more generally, 15-18. His 1913 stump speeches were *De Meiboom in de kap* and *Heilige Orde* (both Kampen, 1913), preceded by *Uit het diensthuis uitgeleid* (Kampen, 1912). On the coalition strategy, *Diensthuis,* 25-27 ("must build upon," 20); *Wij Calvinisten,* 8-12; *Meiboom,* 18-20 ("guerrilla," 19). On reassertion of distinctive principles, *Diensthuis,* 23-24; *Wij Calvinisten,* 12-18; *Meiboom,* 14-17. Heemskerk's attitude to Kuyper is evident in *Een word over driestarren* and letters to Idenburg, *BKI,* 430-34. The letter in which Idenburg conveyed his sense of affairs to Kuyper is in ibid., 247-48 ("Great principles . . . not so precisely"). On the younger insurgency against Kuyper, see Kuiper, *De Voormannen,* 245-50; "in normal times are conservative," quoted 310; "the time of first principles," quoted in Koch, *Kuyper biografie,* 545. Kuyper's critique of the rising law faculty at the Free University appeared in *Starrentritsen,* 69-76; against "individualism," ibid., 68-70, 74; *Diensthuis,* 21-23; *De Wortel in de dorre aarde* (Kampen, 1916), 13-15.

Kuyper described his new physical regimen in a letter to Idenburg, *BKI,* 256-58 (quotations, 256-57). *Ons Instinctieve Leven* (Amsterdam, 1908) is available in English translation as "Our Instinctive Life," in Bratt, *Kuyper Centennial Reader,* 255-77. On animal and human instinct, 256-59; "reflection," 270; "perfect," "spontaneous, immediate, and completed at once," 258. On the Five Gentlemen's proposals, see Anema et al., *Leider en Leiding;* Kuiper, *De Voormannen,* 248-49, 345-46. Kuyper alluded to such proposals satirically in "Our Instinctive Life," 270-71. Kuyper's typology comes ibid., 268-69; "amphibians" and "the instinctive and the reflective life," 268; "boundaries" and "the non-learned public," 267; "spiritual decline and emotional impoverishment," 268; "instinctively felt in essence," 267; "must have the means," 276-77; Saul and David, 277; citation of Le Bon's *La psychologie de foule* (1895; E. T., *The Crowd: A Study of the Popular Mind*), 264-65. Robert Michels's key book is *Zur Soziologie des Parteiwesens in der modernen Demokratie. Untersuchungen über die oligarchischen Tendenzen des Gruppenlebens* (1911).

For the Brussels episode, see Ewoud Sanders, "De Bijbel voor het kruis," *NRC Handelsblad,* 21 December 1987, 12. The "decoration-affair" is concisely summarized in *BKI,* 196, 199, 209-10 (quotations). Jan De Bruijn treats the episode exhaustively in *Het boetekleed ontsiert de man niet: Abraham Kuyper en de Lintjesaffaire (1909-1910)* (Amsterdam, 2005). For Troelstra's role, see Piet Hagan, *Politicus uit hartstocht: biografie van Pieter Jelles Troelstra* (Amsterdam, 2010), 499-504; "It was a gripping moment," 503-4. Idenburg's observations of Kuyper's personality recur throughout *BKI,* in letters directly to Kuyper, occasionally to Colijn or Heemskerk, most often to his wife, Maria Elizabeth Idenburg-Duetz. The matter climaxes in long exchanges all around concerning Kuyper's *Starrentritsen* in 1915; see *BKI,* 550-73. Idenburg's critique of Heemskerk and associates is exemplified in letters to his wife, ibid., 554-55, 556, and

557 ("No one else . . . rock-hard head"). Heemskerk's style of argument is evident in his letter to Idenburg, 430-33. Idenburg's critique of Kuyper grew over autumn 1915. On the mistake of going public with internal grievances, Idenburg to Kuyper, ibid., 550; regarding taking opposition as personal, Idenburg to his wife, ibid., 491; "*moral* right . . . *practical* arrangements," 569; "disciples but no colleagues," "Kuyper is rough and coarse," "extraordinarily tragic . . . power and influence," 567; "the defects of his virtues," 557; "deficiency in good taste," 556; "the great difficulty," 568; "knows so little of life," 62. On Colijn, see footnote to letter of 7 November 1909, *BKI*, 195; and Koch, *Kuyper biografie*, 561-62. Idenburg recurrently complained to Kuyper about Western oil firms; see, e.g., *BKI*, 228, 250, 382-84, and 515. His characterization of Colijn as "a man of big things," ibid., 371; "stands opposed to exploitation," 288. On Kuyper's views of Colijn, see Koch, *Kuyper biografie*, 561-62; and *BKI*, 276, 402. "He is living," 499; cf. 393; "I appreciate him," 366.

Data on Kuyper's children and their careers are available in Kuiper et al., eds., *Doleren den & nageslacht*, 288-95. Kuyper discussed Jan Frederik's situation in letters to Idenburg in *BKI*, 237 ("My poor Frederik"), 276 ("I keep praying"), 285, 296, and 323 ("His soul sleeps"). His early letter to Frederik urging spiritual reflection is dated 10 February 1884 (Kuyper Archive, HDC-VU). Frederik's surviving letters to him are in the Kuyper Archive, HDC-VU; inter alia: 3 January 1905 ("I would love to see"), 1 October 1907, 13 February 1908, 7 September 1909, 13 October 1910 ("Why actually do you live"), 10 October 1911 (his long confessional statement), 31 May 1912 ("Today I visited"), 24 September 1913, and 27 March 1914. The feud between Kuyper's daughters and his analysis of it can be traced in the correspondence in *BKI*. See especially Kuyper's letters to Idenburg, 205, 226, 277, 294-95 (all quotations), and 338 (separation as a last resort); and Idenburg's replies, 226-27, 281 (incompatible personalities), 302-3, 329 (skepticism toward Henriëtte), and 344 (quotations). Too's "heart ailments" are reported ibid., 505.

The questions surrounding franchise extension are summarized in Kossmann, *Low Countries*, 551, 555-57; and are discussed in greater detail in Harinck, "Antirevolutionaire Partij," 131-35, 152-54; Koch, *Kuyper biografie*, 555-58; and Te Velde, "Grondwet tot Grondwet," 161-65, 171-75. Kuyper's campaign rhetoric against women's suffrage occurs in *Heilige Orde*, 18-22; "organic" and "household," 19; against individualism, 18, 22; all other quotations, 20; birth control and divorce, 20-21. Te Velde describes the Dutch consensus on maternal norms for women in "Grondwet tot Grondwet," 161-65; by socialists, 164; by feminists, 165. Kuyper's praise for female cultural leadership in upstate New York occurs in *Varia Americana*, 39-41. His *Vrouwen uit de Heilige Schrift* (Amsterdam, [1897]) and *De Eerepositie der Vrouw* (Kampen, 1914) straddle his sharp critique of feminism in *Pro Rege* II: 401-22, amidst his discussion of normative family life (347-541). On the Christian family, 347-68; on household staff, 444-55; "right and equity," 452. Regarding children, 422-44, 509-30; "sovereignty" and "mixed sphere," 441. On feminism, 401-22; "magnetic power" and "almost irresistible magnetic power," 405-6; "the woman who sins," *Pro Rege* III: 142. On contemporary male sexual anxieties, see Bram Dijkstra, *Idols of Perversity: Fantasies of Feminine Evil in Fin-de-Siècle Culture* (New York, 1986). Kuyper grounds the family in sexuality at *Pro Rege* II: 378; on authority and Christian masculinity, 379-412; "rich treasury of the human race," 411; "nothing but an attempt," 413; "fixed ordinance," 420-22; "the feminist wants to be a *man*," 416. Regarding fops, 402, 409; the "chief cause of feminism," "the scandalous means," and "but that the egotism," see 410. Kuyper queried Idenburg about the mining engineer J. H. Verloop's "views on [the 36-year-old] Too" in a letter of 6 May 1913, *BKI*, 366. Bavinck's support of women's suffrage is recorded in R. H. Bremmer, *Herman Bavinck en zijn tijdgenooten* (Kampen, 1966), 240-41. The circumstances and consequences of the Dutch political "pacification" process are detailed in Harinck, "De Antirevolutionaire Partij," 150-54; for briefer treatments, see Kossmann, *Low Countries,* 555-57, and Koch, *Kuyper biografie,* 555-58. On the Second Christian Social Congress, see Harinck, "De Antirevolutionaire Partij," 147-48; ARP reorganization, 150-52. Rullmann, *Kuyper-Bibliografie,* III: 435, recounts the conversation between Kuyper and his publisher J. H. Kok about *Antirevolutionaire Staatkunde,* 2 vols. (Kampen, 1916-17).

Notes on Chapter 18

Kuyper's response to World War I can be traced in *De Standaard,* particularly his Saturday columns; the correspondence in *BKI* is also revealing. A close secondary study is J. P. Feddema, "Houding van Dr. A. Kuyper ten Aanzien van de Eerste Wereldoorlog," *Anti-Revolutionaire Staatkunde* 32 (1962): 156-72, 195-210; Van Koppen, *Kuyper en Zuid-Afrika,* provides broader context, 213-22, 232-36. "Socialism has seized with both hands," Kuyper letter to Idenburg in *BKI,* 380. Kuyper praised Cort van der Linden to Idenburg in February 1915, ibid., 498. Kuyper's circumstances and those of his children at the outbreak of war are detailed ibid., 467-70; "fratricide" and "suicide," Van Koppen, *Kuyper en Zuid-Afrika,* 216. For Kuyper's assessment of France, see Feddema, "Houding Kuyper," 162; on Russia, ibid., 170-71, and Van Koppen, *Kuyper en Zuid-Afrika,* 214, 233; "growing half-Asian Slavic masses," 233. On Britain, Feddema, "Houding Kuyper," 163-65; Van Koppen, *Kuyper en Zuid-Afrika,* 235-36; and *BKI,* 467. Regarding South Africa, Van Koppen, *Kuyper en Zuid-Afrika,* passim, summarized 236; and Feddema, "Houding Kuyper," 164-66. On Japan, ibid., 169; Van Koppen, *Kuyper en Zuid-Afrika,* 215; "heathen Japan" and the "world-historical curse," Kuyper, *Standaard,* 9 January 1915. Kuyper and Idenburg often exchanged worries about Japan, especially with respect to the East Indies; see, e.g., *BKI,* 467, 478-79, 523, 541. Kuyper's changing attitudes toward Germany are detailed in Feddema, "Houding Kuyper," 195-208, and Van Koppen, *Kuyper en Zuid-Afrika,* 234-36; "not guiltless," Kuyper, *Standaard,* 8 August 1914. On the question of free passage, Feddema, "Houding Kuyper," 156-61; "under protest," 161.

Kuyper's diagnosis of human pride was his very first statement on the war after the beginning of hostilities: *Standaard,* 4 August 1914. For his warning about the price of total victory, *Standaard,* 23 January 1915; "the Right as grounded," Kuyper, *Standaard,* 1 August 1914. On the United States' (prospective) role, see Van Koppen, *Kuyper en Zuid-Afrika,* 214-15, and Kuyper, *Standaard,* 8 March ("America alone can do it") and 24 March 1915. On the peace of Versailles, Van Koppen, *Kuyper en Zuid-Afrika,* 220-21; "league of winners," 221; prospect of Antichrist, 220.

Information on the production of *Van de Voleinding,* 4 vols. (Kampen, 1928-31), is available in Rullmann, *Kuyper-Bibliografie,* III: 463-65; H. H. Kuyper's assessment, 463. On contemporary eschatology in Anglo-American evangelical circles, see George M. Marsden, *Fundamentalism and American Culture* (New York, 1980), 48-66; and Ernest Sandeen, *The Roots of Fundamentalism: British and American Millenarianism, 1800-1930* (Chicago, 1970). The records of Kuyper's consultation with Carnegie and his foundation are in the Kuyper Archive, HDC/VU. Kuyper assessed the failure of various peace projects in his retrospective on 1914 in *Standaard,* 2 January ("The misery that is now sweeping") and 23 January 1915. His response to the socialist retort is in *Standaard,* 13 April 1915.

Henriëtte and Johanna Kuyper give a very detailed narrative of Kuyper's last years in *Levensavond Kuyper.* For the events of 1917 see 14-32; the trip to Dresden, 29-30; the help of the German consul, 15. The character of the Dutch wartime economy is delineated in Kossmann, *Low Countries,* 549-54. Koch details Colijn's role on the *Standaard* in *Kuyper biografie,* 562, 564; see also *BKI* regarding the *Standaard* and Kuyper's financial difficulties, 467-70, 499. The personal events of 1918 are covered in Kuyper and Kuyper, *Levensavond Kuyper,* 32-40; on Too's return, 34; the trip to Dresden, 35. Kuyper's address to the 2 May 1918 ARP convention is *Wat Nu?* (Kampen, 1918); the full text is provided in W. F. De Gaay Fortman, ed., *Architectonische critiek: Fragmenten uit de sociaal-politieke geschriften van Dr. A. Kuyper* (Amsterdam, 1956), 161-71; "rich personality development," 166. Regarding the ARP Central Committee chair, see Koch, *Kuyper biografie,* 562, and Harinck, *ARP,* 150-55. The abortive November 1918 radical rising in the Netherlands is summarized in Kossmann, *Low Countries,* 557-60; regarding Kuyper's place in it, see Koch, *Kuyper biografie,* 562-63, and Kuyper and Kuyper, *Levensavond Kuyper,* 37-40. Kuyper's 1919 is closely covered in ibid., 40-60; the celebration of the school-funding bill, 41-42; "today is a day of glory," 41; Henriëtte's trip to and from Washington, 45, 50-52.

The events of 1920 are given the most attention in ibid., 63-121; on Kuyper's fall, 64-67; on escaping the fire while on vacation, 75-79; regarding *De Heraut,* 80-81, 99; his resignation, 93; Colijn's visit, 103-5. Kuyper's funeral is described in Koch, *Kuyper biografie,* 570-71; source of all quotations. Quotations exemplifying Henriëtte and Johanna's thematic treatment of Kuyper's death are the chapter titles in *Levensavond Kuyper.* On premonitions, see, e.g., 64; on providentialism and the series of final events, 13, 91, 94, 99, 105; on Kuyper's work ethic and character, 19-21, 59, 63, 88; on the process of self-surrender, 19, 42-43, 57-58, 70-71, 82; on his last words, 112.

Developments in his movement after Kuyper's death are traced in the various essays in J. De Bruijn, ed., *Een land nog niet in kaart gebracht: Aspecten van het protestants-christelijk leven in Nederland in de jaren 1880-1940* (Amsterdam, 1978). The character of Colijn's policies and administrations is taken from Kossmann, *Low Countries*, 603-6, 658-59, 667. For a different assessment, see Herman J. Langeveld, *Hendrikus Colijn 1869-1944*, 2 vols. (Amsterdam, 1998-2004). The Dutch experience in World War II is exhaustively treated in L. de Jong and Jan Bank, *Het Koninkrijk der Nederlanden in de Tweede Wereldoorlog*, 14 vols. ('s-Gravenhage, 1969-).

Good studies on recent developments in Dutch society and culture are James Kennedy, *Nieuw Babylon in aanbouw: Nederland in de jaren zestig* (Meppel, 1995); and *Stad op een berg: de publieke rol van protestantse kerken* (Zoetermeer, 2009). Developments in the GKN and Free University are briefly surveyed in English in James D. Bratt, "Kuyper and Dutch Theological Education," in D. G. Hart and R. Albert Mohler, eds., *Theological Education in the Evangelical Tradition* (Grand Rapids, 1996); see 244-50 for the interwar era and 250-54 for the 1960s and thereafter; "snakes are snakes," quoted 247.

More thorough Dutch accounts of the GKN are H. C. Eindedijk, *De Gereformeerde Kerken in Nederland: Deel 1, 1892-1936* (Kampen, 1990); Gerard Dekker, *De Stille Revolutie: De ontwikkeling van de Gereformeerde Kerken in Nederland tussen 1950 en 1990* (Kampen, 1992); M. E. Brinkman et al., eds., *100 Jaar Theologie: Aspecten van een eeuw theologie in de Gereformeerde Kerken in Nederland (1892-1992)* (Kampen, 1992); and Jan Veenhof, "Hondred jaar theologie aan de Vrije Universiteit," in *Wetenschap en Rekenschap, 1880-1980: Een eeuw wetenschapsbeofening en wetenschapsbeschouwing aan de Vrije Universiteit* (Kampen, 1980). The post-Kuyper history of the Free University is recounted from different perspectives in Johannes Stellingwerff, *De Vrije Universiteit na Kuyper . . . 1905 tot 1955* (Kampen, 1987); and Arie Th. van Deursen, *The Distinctive Character of the Free University in Amsterdam, 1880-2005: A Commemorative History* (Grand Rapids, 2008). The literature on Dooyeweerd and Vollenhoven is voluminous; a convenient English introduction from the source is Herman Dooyeweerd, *Roots of Western Culture: Pagan, Secular, and Christian Options* (Toronto, 1979). Statistics on post-1960 changes at the university come from Bratt, "Kuyper and Dutch Theological Education," 251.

Kuyper's American legacy is surveyed throughout James D. Bratt, *Dutch Calvinism in Modern America: A History of a Conservative Subculture* (Grand Rapids, 1984), which also covers CRC and RCA history 1890-1980 in detail. A Dutch language summary is "De erfenis van Kuyper in Noord-Amerika," in Augustijn, *Kuyper: volksdeel & invloed,* 203-28. See also James D. Bratt, "The Christian Reformed Church in German Mirrors," *Calvin Theological Journal* 42/1 (April 2007): 9-32. For the Kuyperian impact in broader American evangelicalism, see Mark A. Noll, *The Scandal of the Evangelical Mind* (Grand Rapids, 1994), 216-17, 234-37; James C. Turner, "Something to Be Reckoned With," *Commonweal* 126/1 (15 January 1999): 11-13; and John Bolt, "From Princeton to Wheaton: The Course of

Neo-Calvinism in North America," *Calvin Theological Journal* 42/1 (April 2007): 65-89.

Details on Elisa Willem Kuyper are available in Kuiper, *Dolerenden en nageslacht,* 292. Literature on Kuyper's South African legacy is cited in the notes to chapter 14 above. On Kuyper's applicability for African Christianity in general, see B. J. van der Walt, "Christian Religion and Society: The Heritage of Abraham Kuyper for (South) Africa," in Van der Kooi and De Bruijn, *Kuyper Reconsidered,* 228-37. Allan Boesak's invocation of Kuyper in court is recounted by Nicholas Wolterstorff in "Boesak's Witness," *Third Way* 9/5 (May 1986): 17. Boesak's relevant work includes *Black and Reformed: Apartheid, Liberation, and the Calvinist Tradition* (Maryknoll, N.Y., 1984), citation of Kuyper, 91; and *The Tenderness of Conscience: African Renaissance and the Spirituality of Politics* (Glasgow, 2008), citation of Kuyper, 213-14. For the South Korean case, see Bong Ho Son, "Relevance of Sphere Sovereignty to Korean Society," in Van der Kooi and De Bruijn, *Kuyper Reconsidered,*179-89.

Index

442